THE GOSPEL OF JESUS CHRIST

VOLUME ONE

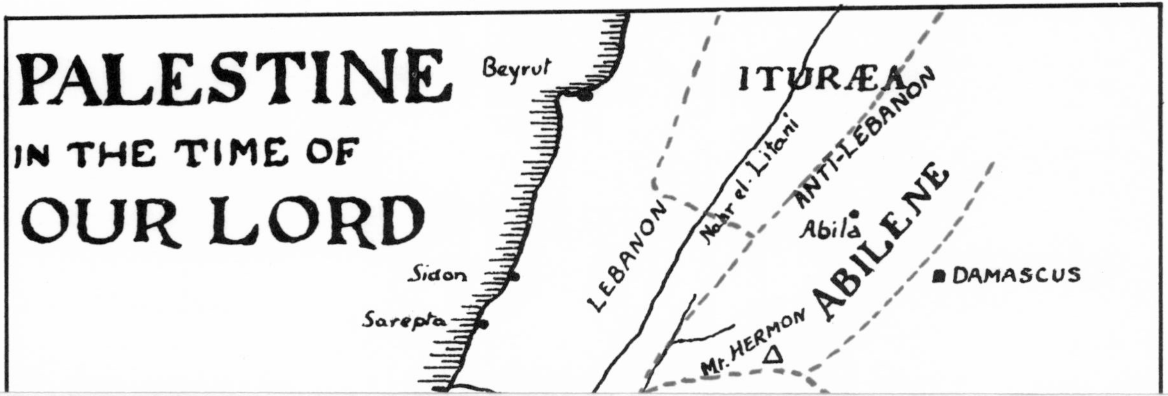
PALESTINE
IN THE TIME OF
OUR LORD
Beyrut
Sidon
Sarepta
LEBANON
Nahr el. Litani
ITURÆA
ANTI-LEBANON
Abila
ABILENE
Mt. HERMON
DAMASCUS

THE GOSPEL OF JESUS CHRIST

By

PÈRE M.-J. LAGRANGE, O. P.

Translated by

MEMBERS OF THE ENGLISH DOMINICAN PROVINCE

Volume I

THE NEWMAN PRESS
WESTMINSTER, MARYLAND
1958

Third Printing, 1951
Fourth Printing, 1954
Fifth Printing, 1958

NIHIL OBSTAT:
ERNESTUS MESSENGER, PH.D.,
Censor deputatus.

IMPRIMATUR:
LEONELLUS CAN. EVANS,
Vic. Gen.

WESTMONASTERII,
die 23a Martii 1938.

Printed in the United States of America
by
A. Hoen & Company
Baltimore, Md.

CONTENTS

		PAGE
	FOREWORD	ix
	AUTHOR'S PREFACE	xi
	Prologue of the Gospel	1
CHAPTER		
I.	THE GOSPEL OF THE DIVINE AND HUMAN ORIGINS OF JESUS	7
	The good tidings	7
	Annunciation of the Forerunner's birth	11
	The Annunciation to Mary	15
	Mary's Visit to Elizabeth	21
	Birth of the Precursor. He withdraws to the desert	25
	Joseph takes upon himself the legal paternity of Jesus	28
	The Genealogy of Jesus	31
	Jesus is born at Bethlehem	33
	The legal observances	39
	The adoration of the Magi and flight into Egypt	41
	The return to Nazareth	48
	Jesus in His Father's House	50
	Jesus at Nazareth	53
II.	JOHN THE BAPTIST AND JESUS	56
	The time of Salvation	56
	The Mission and Preaching of John the Baptist	58
	At His baptism Jesus is proclaimed to be the Son of God	74
	Jesus is tempted	77
	The witness of John the Baptist. The calling of the first disciples	83
	Jesus returns to Galilee	89
	The marriage-feast at Cana	91
	Jesus at Capharnaum	94
	Jesus drives the traders out of the Temple	95
	Discussion with Nicodemus	98
	The Baptist's last witness to Jesus	105
III.	THE MINISTRY IN GALILEE	108
	1. JESUS DEPARTS FROM JUDÆA AND PREACHES IN GALILEE	108
	John is thrown into prison ; Jesus begins His ministry	108
	The woman of Samaria	109

CHAPTER | | PAGE
III. The healing of the royal official's son 118
The beginning of Christ's public ministry 119
The teaching in the synagogues 120
Preaching at Nazareth 123
Jesus at Capharnaum 124
The curing of a possessed man 129
The healing of Peter's wife's mother and other sick . 129
The preaching spreads 130
The call of Simon along with Andrew, James, and John 131
The healing of a leper 132

II. Five Conflicts with the Pharisees 134
First conflict : the cure of the paralytic . . . 135
The call of Levi. The Pharisees are scandalized . 138
A question about fasting 139
The plucking of the ears of corn on the Sabbath day . 142
The man with a withered hand healed on the Sabbath day 145
The first plan to destroy Jesus 147

III. The Beginning of the Gospel Teaching . . 147
The choosing of the twelve Apostles 147
The Sermon on the Mount 149
Conclusion 159

IV. Various Opinions about the Work of Jesus . . 161
The Centurion of Capharnaum 161
The resurrection of the widow's son at Naim . . 163
The mission of the Baptist and the mission of the Son of Man 163
The pardon of the sinful woman 168
The true kindred of Jesus 172

V. The Parables of the Kingdom of God 175
Nature and purpose of teaching by parables . . 175
The parable of the sower 182
The parable of the seed that multiplies and ripens by itself in the course of time 184
The parable of the cockle in the cornfield . . 186
The parable of the grain of mustard seed . . . 187
The parable of the leaven 189
The parables of the treasure, the pearl, and the fishing-net. Conclusion 190
The light will go on increasing 191

CHAPTER PAGE

III. vi. MIRACLES. ENCOUNTER WITH TROUBLESOME DISPOSITIONS 192
The calming of the tempest 192
The cure of a possessed man on the other side of the lake 193
The daughter of Jairus and the woman with an issue of blood 197
Jesus is driven out of Nazareth by violence . . . 201

vii. THE MISSION OF THE APOSTLES AND THE ALARM OF HEROD ANTIPAS 205
The mission of the twelve Apostles 205
The death of John the Baptist 209
Herod Antipas and the Baptist's death . . . 212

viii. EVENTS PRECEDING THE INSTITUTION OF THE EUCHARIST . 218
The first multiplication of loaves 218
Jesus walks on the waters across to the land of Gennesareth 222
The bread of life; some leave Him 224

IV. FORMATION OF THE DISCIPLES AND MINISTRY, CHIEFLY OUTSIDE GALILEE 236
i. PENTECOST AT JERUSALEM 238
The pool of Bezatha at Jerusalem. Jesus heals a sick man 238

ii. THE FORMATION OF THE DISCIPLES 243
Pharisaic traditions and the true service of God . . 243
Jesus grants the prayer of a Gentile woman . . . 248
The healing of a deaf man with an impediment in his speech 249
The second multiplication of loaves 251
Jesus refuses to give a sign from heaven 252
Jesus teaches His disciples 253
The blind man of Bethsaida 255
Peter's confession and Christ's promise 257
The first prediction of the Passion and Resurrection . 263
He who desires to be saved must follow Jesus . . 264
The speedy coming of the kingdom of God . . . 267
The Transfiguration 268
Elias has come in the person of John the Baptist . 271
The cure of an epileptic boy possessed by the devil . 273
The second prediction of the Passion and Resurrection 276
He that is greatest must become the least of all . 277
Forbearance is to be shown towards those who use the name of Jesus 278
Charity towards the disciples of Jesus. The danger of scandal 280

CHAPTER PAGE

IV. Salt 283
Fraternal unity and the power of absolution . . 284
The pardoned debtor who becomes a pitiless creditor . 286
Jesus pays the Temple dues though there is no obligation on His part 288
Jesus leaves the cities of the lake-side 290

III. At the Feast of Tabernacles 291
The refusal of Jesus to manifest Himself at Jerusalem . 293
Jesus goes up to Jerusalem 294
First conversations and impressions during the feast . 295
Teaching on the last day of the feast disagreement even among the Pharisees 298
The woman taken in adultery 300
The light gives testimony of itself, and that testimony is confirmed by the Father 303
The danger of refusing to acknowledge God's envoy . . 305
In Jesus is the salvation announced to Abraham . 306
The man born blind 311
Jesus the door of the sheepfold and the Good Shepherd 316

FOREWORD

A FEW words of explanation are called for by way of introduction to this translation of Père Lagrange's *Evangile de Jésus Christ.* The author has long looked forward to its appearance. A number of years ago he expressed to the late Fr. Luke Walker, O.P., his beloved disciple and friend, the desire that he should undertake the work of presenting the book to the English people in their own language. He willingly accepted the task, but his health and duties did not permit of his carrying out the work alone : a regrettable fact, for no one was more capable than he of interpreting the mind of his former master. But under his direction the work of translation was finished for the most part. Many reasons, however, conspired to delay publication, perhaps the chief among them being Fr. Walker's scrupulous desire for perfection. At his lamented death in 1936 he handed on the work to me who had collaborated with him, expressing the hope that it might one day appear in print. His hope is now realized, and may the result be such as he would not have found altogether disappointing !

In the difficult task of revision and correction I have been greatly indebted to the kind co-operation of my venerable colleague, Fr. Maurice Watson, O.P., and I here wish gratefully to acknowledge his help. But I feel obliged to say that I must assume full responsibility for the translation, at least in so far as its faults and deficiencies are concerned. Mine has been the last word in determining how the thoughts of the author shall be expressed in English.

I cannot conclude without saying how vividly this labour has renewed in my mind the memory of those three happy and fruitful years it was my good fortune to spend at the feet of Père Lagrange in his Biblical school at Jerusalem.

REGINALD GINNS, O.P.

HAWKESYARD,
January 23, 1938.

AUTHOR'S PREFACE

THERE are admirable lives of Our Lord Jesus Christ already in existence. Why, then, should yet another book be written on the same subject? The author of the present work quite frankly admits that this question was continually before his mind as he wrote. He felt obliged to consult the works that had already appeared: but he had to give up doing this systematically lest he should be discouraged by seeing the things he wished to say already said, and so well said. But, after all, is not the gospel unfathomable, and can too much be ever written about Our Lord Jesus Christ provided that it be of use if only to a few souls? Nevertheless, I have given up all idea of presenting a Life of Jesus of the usual kind, preferring to leave the gospels more opportunity of speaking for themselves. They are inadequate as historical documents for writing a history of Jesus in the way in which a modern author would write the history of Cæsar Augustus or Cardinal de Richelieu; but such is their value as a reflection of Jesus' life and teaching, such their sincerity and beauty, that in the presence of their inspired words one despairs of any other attempt to reproduce the life of Christ. The gospels themselves are the only life of Jesus Christ that can be written. Nothing remains for us but to understand them as well as we can.

None have penetrated more deeply into the spirit of the gospels than those who have made them the subject of devout meditation. The Life of Jesus Christ by Ludolph the Carthusian, formerly a son of St. Dominic, is a model of this kind. But not everybody has received his gift.

Many in our days, upset by the numerous attacks on the gospels, have begun to wonder what their evidence is worth. To find that out we must study each one separately; and in my scrupulous care not to explain one by the other I have gone so far as never to ask while studying them separately, whether they would be found finally to agree with one another as to the main lines of a Life of Jesus. St. Matthew, St. Mark, St. Luke, and St. John, each of them has his own genius, his own special sources of information, his own purpose and method ; to get at their secret we must question each one of them separately. But when this task had been performed to the best of my ability—every man can only play his own instrument, as my old novice-master used to tell us—the question still remained whether in the end these four gospels were in harmony or in conflict with one another. This question, of course, has been asked for a long time, ever since Tatian in the second century concluded practically as to their agreement by composing the harmony in which he blended the text of the four gospels into a single narrative. This conclusion was premature and too strong, and it gave rise to a predominating desire to look for harmonization with the consequent danger of overlooking, even in our own days, certain appreciable differences.

On the other hand, the independent critics went in just the opposite direction, dividing, tearing in pieces, reducing the gospels to atoms. To-day we see that the final result of all their efforts has been to leave us the gospels reduced to dust, a dust composed of traditions that are either at variance with one another or dependent one upon another ; and this dust of traditions is far less fortunate than Democritus's atoms, since it never succeeds in forming a living whole. Analysis, of course, is legitimate ; it is a delicate operation and sometimes it may have a merely negative result, as in the case where it ends by recognizing no probability in any recorded event unless it be completely proved. That seems to be the opinion of the radical critics, the one of which we hear most. There are some critics, indeed, who after an examination of tradition have come to the conclusion that Jesus never lived. But that was too much for the more acute school of critics, who saw that Christianity could never have blazed up in the manner it did without something to set it alight. But they failed to see that it was their duty honestly to examine whether or not tradition, however much they supposed it to be fragmentary in origin or at variance with itself in regard to the order of events and many of its details, was at any rate capable of being reduced to vital unity.

On this point we may make appeal to that admirable

principle of Heraclitus of Ephesus, surnamed the Obscure Philosopher: TACIT AGREEMENT IS OF GREATER VALUE THAN EXPLICIT AGREEMENT. What precisely did he mean? The philosopher was accustomed to express his thought with such extreme brevity, but that brevity conceals ideas of a most profound character. Without any doubt he intends to say that the hidden harmony of the universe, which Universal Reason produces in the midst of the apparent disorder of the world, is of greater power and beauty than such manifest harmony as each man thinks he can perceive for himself in the external things of the world. But if this be true of the external world, how much more true is it in the sphere of ideas! Two manuscripts have no more than the value of one, if one of them is merely a copy of the other. Two authors serve only as a single witness if one follows the other slavishly. But two manuscripts that sometimes differ imply two different sources, and their agreement then becomes significant. Every author who has his own sources of information and disposes it according to his own peculiar method is a witness who has a claim to be heard; and if two witnesses, after apparently contradicting one another in their way of relating an event, are found finally to be in substantial agreement, then that agreement is more impressive than if they had first come to an arrangement as to what they should both say.

Two completely open-minded scholars have gone to the root of this question in the following words: 'Agreement that is really decisive is not, as one might suppose, a complete resemblance between two accounts; it is the meeting of two different accounts that resemble one another only at a few points. The natural tendency is to think that the more complete is the agreement, the more decisive it is: but on the contrary we must adopt the paradoxical rule that agreement is the more certain when it is confined to a small number of points. It is these points of agreement in differing statements that provide us with scientifically established historical facts.'[1] Only one reservation is required here: agreement has an importance if a later author, after making enquiries, adheres to the account given by an earlier author. But the chief point of importance here is this: that minor divergences between the witnesses ought not to

[1] *Introduction aux Études Historiques*, Langlois et Seignobos; 8th ed., Paris, 1905, pp. 172 ff.

be alleged against the truth of an event, if those divergences can be brought into accordance by making allowance for different points of view. There is only one reason why the critics will not attempt such a work of synthesis ; they are too much occupied with the work of destruction and look on it as a foregone conclusion that the ruin they thus wantonly cause is beyond repair.

Possibly Catholic scholars have felt the dogma of inspiration as an embarrassment in this matter ; the decisions of ecclesiastical authority do not allow of the admission of real divergences, even though they be but of a secondary character, between the sacred writers. But the same does not hold true when it is merely a question of the order of events. Indeed it would be impossible to write a Life of Jesus that could stand up against the objections of the critics if we were obliged to consider the connecting together of various teachings of Our Lord into one great sermon, or the repeated use of the formula 'after that,' as formal declarations that such was the real sequence of events. The same would be equally true if the different place in the gospel assigned to certain events by different evangelists, or the slight variations in the narrative of parables or happenings, obliged us to duplicate the words and events narrated by the gospels. But St. Augustine, positive as he was in his conviction regarding the inerrancy of the sacred writers, has himself laid down the principle that one writer may have assigned to an earlier time things that another has given later, and it is with the help of this criterion that he was able to compose his work on the harmony of the gospels. He went further in proposing the principles of rational harmonization by admitting not only that one writer may have omitted what another has set down, but also that he may have written the same thing in a different way ; thus the reader arrives at a true understanding of the fact narrated by comparing the different styles of narration. He lays down these principles in an admirable passage that is rich in its brevity : '*Non enim discrepant rebus, si alius aliquid dicit quod alius tacet, aut alio modo dicit ; magis autem conlata invicem juvant, ut legentis intellectus regatur.*'[1] We must follow the example of this great master of theology and give even wider application to his method.

But there remains another difficulty. If, according to us,

[1] Letter CXCIX, 25.

the evangelists have changed the order of events and arranged the discourses without troubling about chronological sequence, are we not left with chaos? Even though we may not be aware of their divergences, we seem left continually under the suspicion that they have little regard for chronological order. It appears to be a case of: 'Guess if you can, and choose if you dare.' This is precisely the difficulty which has up to the present kept us from complying with many kind and pressing invitations to write a Life of Jesus in chronological order.

But we have presumed to make some sort of choice in publishing our Synopsis of the Gospels, which appeared first in Greek and later, with the co-operation of the Rev. Père Ceslaus Lavergne, O.P., in French.[1] It was meant to show that St. Luke's order and chiefly St. John's chronology ought to serve as the basis of a Life of Jesus, inasmuch as such a life can be written at all. Since we claimed no more than to present the Gospel in that manner, our present work is little more than a rapid commentary on the Synopsis along with a few historical observations, following the more or less certain, more or less probable, or the merely conjectural order of events. If it be read in company with the Synopsis it will be found more intelligible, and its imperfections can thus be corrected in the light furnished by the gospel text.

I have, however, striven to make it intelligible to those who have only this book at hand without much time to devote to its study, to those also, I should like to be able to say, who are engrossed in manual labour. For that reason the book will no doubt appear to such as are familiar with the difficulties of the subject to be insufficiently based on plausible arguments. They may think, and even say openly, that I have skipped the difficulties. And indeed I make no pretence of having solved all the difficulties; but I have dealt with such as I was aware of and considered serious in my commentaries on the separate gospels. It would be very unreasonable to expect all my readers to study those commentaries under the pretext that the present work is based on them. But it did seem to me allowable that,

[1] The notes in the French Synopsis are Fr. Lavergne's. The Synopsis has appeared in English under the title of *A Catholic Harmony of the Four Gospels* with introduction and notes by Mgr. John Barton, D.D., S.S.Lic.; Burns, Oates & Washbourne, London.

for the sake of those who have entreated me to spare them even the very appearance of erudition, I might furnish an explanation of the gospels such as was within their grasp, based upon grounds that I had elsewhere tried to show were solid.[1]

When agreement between documents is obtained without any forcing of the texts, we find an additional proof that those texts represent an objective reality. In cases where the different gospels provide us with their own special information regarding some event common to them all, I have sometimes included it in the narrative if it fits easily into the story. But as a general rule it seemed more obviously indicated to borrow from each evangelist the passages in which he appeared to have excelled the others. When St. Matthew, St. Mark, and St. Luke all relate the same event, I have generally followed St. Mark because he seems to have preserved best the original style of the Petrine catechesis. The same is true of St. Matthew, as compared with St. Luke, regarding the narration of Our Lord's discourses. While St. John, the friend of Jesus, is the one who has best penetrated the inmost thoughts of his Master. As for St. Luke, we have already observed that he excels as an historian.

With this general indication of my method I shall be dispensed from multiplying references. The texts of the gospels are sometimes analysed or paraphrased, at other times and more often quoted word for word. The figures in brackets after the headings refer to the numbers of the various sections of the Synopsis. In view of the special character of this work, the notes are chiefly intended to emphasize the relation between the different evangelists.

In writing this work I have constantly sought the help of our Blessed Lady, and I now entreat her to bless it. I should have liked it to be faultless from the point of view of information and criticism. It contains so little in the way of pious considerations that I hardly dare to say that its purpose is to make Our Lord Jesus Christ better known and loved. But on the other hand, may we not say that the

[1] I continually refer the reader to my Commentaries, especially for biographical information and for everything connected with sources. From time to time I refer to the splendid work of Strack and Billerbeck, *Kommentar zum neuen Testament aus Talmud und Midrasch*, of which three volumes have already appeared and which was not at my disposal previously.

god-like calm of the evangelists is the best expression of the soul's wonder when brought face to face with the mystery of Redemption? Love comes afterwards when we meditate on the sacred text which is our light, our strength, and our life. It is to this text that we must always come back.

MARIE-JOSEPH LAGRANGE, O.P.

JERUSALEM,
May, 1928.

THE GOSPEL OF JESUS CHRIST

Prologue of the Gospel (2).

Luke i, 1–4.[1]

BOTH the gospels of St. Matthew and St. Mark open without any prologue ; and the prologue which we find at the beginning of St. John's gospel is not an author's preface. It is a theological statement which presents to us the doctrine concerning the Son of God from a special point of view : we shall not deal with it, therefore, until we reach the end of this book. There remains the short preface of St. Luke's gospel ; it is very enlightening, but we cannot help wishing that it were more explicit.

A custom had grown up among the Greeks of dedicating literary works to some distinguished personage, a custom followed by Jewish writers. Luke addresses his little book to Theophilus, a certain Christian distinguished by the title of 'Excellent,' but otherwise unknown to us. A few years later Josephus, as a Jew writing on things Jewish for Roman readers, thought it advisable to insist at some length on his impartiality. But Luke, following the example of Polybius, thought that his impartiality might be taken for granted, and considered it enough to point out that his aim was to show for his noble friend's benefit the solid truth of what he had been taught. He thus confesses that his purpose is (to use the current term) apologetic, just as St. John states quite frankly in his own case : 'But these (miracles) are written that you may believe that Jesus is the Christ, the Son of God.'[2]

Now only too often apologists have a bad name. They

[1] We must refer the reader to the introductions of our Commentaries on the Gospels for the proofs of our statements here and elsewhere in this book.

[2] John xx, 31.

are accused of being like certain lawyers, not over-nice in their choice of an argument so long as it gets home: of being ready, for instance, to use even bad arguments on people of little discernment likely to be convinced by them. But Luke aspires to be an historian worthy of the name and to convince men who are well able to judge. And, moreover, the very nobility of the cause which it is a writer's ambition to serve puts upon him the obligation of making use only of such facts as are beyond dispute. This means that he must have recourse to none but unimpeachable witnesses. And this, indeed, is what Luke professes to do. Ever since he was first associated with the preaching of the gospel, he had made it his business to get at the facts. This was all the more easy for him, inasmuch as he was, owing to his apostolic work, in constant touch with the very people who had been eyewitnesses from the beginning—with the Apostles, that is, and the first disciples. Now these Apostles and disciples preached first of all among the Jews who had just condemned Jesus on false testimony; their own witness, they claimed, was true. Could they, then, have put forward anything untrue without being at once contradicted by fiercely hostile opponents? People sitting round the fireside at night are content to listen even to the most fanciful of stories if only they are interesting; such things blend with their mood and while away a pleasant hour. But the disciples of Jesus were hardy enough to carry on a work which the leaders of the nation had condemned as subversive of the religion of their fathers. There was one temptation to which the disciples might have seemed in danger of succumbing, from a desire to make their message more acceptable: the temptation, namely, to modify certain features, to portray Jesus as submissive to the Law, deferential to the rabbis, respectful towards the priests. But, far from yielding to it, they gave a faithful account of the very words and deeds for which He had been condemned, and thereby showed themselves absolutely trustworthy. It was precisely this fidelity to the facts which caused their testimony to be instantly punished with imprisonment. Luke had been present more than once when this same testimony had been received with furious outbursts of hatred, though the facts no one had dared to deny. So he was sure of the truth of the story he was about to tell once more. For he was not the first to tell it:

those facts, which had proved for so many men the source of a new life, had been related by many before him. He mentions no names, however. Tradition gives those of St. Matthew and St. Mark ; scholars conjecture others. How do these writers stand to one another ? How are we to make up for St. Luke's silence about them ?

The fact is that, however soon writing may have been used in the service of the Christian Faith, it must have been preceded by the oral teaching which it recorded and preserved at least in part : for in a new doctrine there are often a certain number of points which it may seem advisable to transmit only by word of mouth, at any rate in the beginning. Moreover, if a doctrine is to win men, they must be told something of the personality and doings of the one who gave it to the world. Now it was a first principle with the Jews that any doctrine, if it was to be accepted, must be put forward as from God and be confirmed by miracles : unless it were merely an exhortation to keep the Law. The oral teaching, or catechesis as we call it, comprised therefore a general view of Jesus' preaching and an account of the deeds which proved its authority. The first teacher of this catechesis was naturally the man who had been most closely associated with the Master's work, His companion on His journeys, the undisputed head of His disciples, Simon Peter. It was he who delivered the first discourse upon these lines—the first gospel, so to say. He had already decided that the two extreme points of the catechesis should be the baptism of John and the ascension of Jesus into heaven, and between these two points he would pick out the most significant incidents and the most characteristic utterances, relating them with all the authority of an eyewitness. With the subject-matter thus defined, the main lines of the gospel had now been fixed.

Among the disciples there was one accustomed to the art of writing, Levi, once a publican or tax-gatherer, now an Apostle under the name of Matthew. He had learned how to pack his thoughts into clear and striking phrases, presenting his arguments with the same decision that he had formerly shown when he presented his claims for custom-dues. He took the facts that Peter had related in so spontaneous a way about Jesus of Nazareth and, in the light of proofs drawn from the Old Testament, showed that Jesus was the expected Messiah, the promulgator of a moral law which was the

Old Law perfected through charity. Something of the charm and vividness found in the original narrative of the various episodes of Jesus' life was thus sacrificed to their value as proofs, but on the other hand one advantage was gained. Matthew wrote in Aramaic, Jesus' mother tongue ; hence in his gospel the words of our Saviour, which the Apostle for the most part gathered into five long composite discourses, not only keep their primitive meaning but also remain in their original language.

It is likely enough that other disciples too had set down in writing various incidents, the memory of which they particularly cherished. Jesus' Passion was a sacred memory common to them all, and it was probably the first event to be narrated and the first to be put in writing.

Meanwhile Peter had gone to Rome, where he set up his see as head of the Church. There he went on with his catecheses, speaking, as always, ardently and naturally, lingering lovingly over the details still fresh in his memory, reproducing vividly the impression these had made on him when first they moved his soul. Was this freshness of impression, was this faithful reflection of the reality to pass away with him ? His hearers begged his disciple, St. Mark, to put into writing these various episodes as related by St. Peter. This he did, but without giving much place to Jesus' sayings, either because St. Peter did not insist so much on this point, or because Matthew's admirable composite discourses had already given what was necessary.

St. Matthew, being specially intent on furnishing the proof of Jesus' messiahship, had paid little heed to the order of the events. St. Mark's order was more probable, and to St. Luke it appeared almost completely satisfactory. He himself had not followed Jesus but was only a disciple of the Apostles, and he could not have found a surer guide than the man entrusted with the catecheses of St. Peter. He therefore took over into his own work nearly all that was contained in the second gospel, generally keeping as well the same sequence of events. Nevertheless he was conscious that, in the matter of order, he had improved on that of his predecessor, having made this more definitely his aim and having gone about to seek information on the point ; does he not undertake ' to write in order ' ? It is to be remembered, however, that with the ancient historians, for whom history was an art, order did not necessarily mean purely chronological order such as is adopted by primitive annalists.

Along with the events Luke chose to give some discourses, and—since he attached great importance to putting everything in its place—he distributed them here and there in their proper setting, thereby running the risk of losing the harmonious unity which St. Matthew gives to the long discourses in his gospel. It is probable that Greek-speaking disciples had, quite early, translated the Aramaic gospel of St. Matthew, or at least some of the discourses in it, being more affected by the eternal principles contained in the utterances of Jesus than by his controversy with the Pharisees. St. Luke may thus have read these discourses, and yet not have known the rest of the gospel ; in any case, Matthew's facts and order and his grouping of the sayings had little influence on him.

In Mark—and in Matthew, if he knew the whole of it—Luke would find proof of a considerable gap. Mark is not unaware of the fact that Jesus had preached in Judæa, but he chooses to restrict himself to Galilee ; according to his narrative, Jesus leaves the lake-side *en route* for Jericho only just before the last week of his life : Luke got to know, perhaps from disciples he met at Cæsarea, perhaps from Joanna, the wife of Chusa, mentioned by him alone and on two different occasions, what had happened during a mission of Jesus in Judæa covering several months. And he has given an account of it, but place, occasion, characters, no longer stand out as they would in an account by St. Peter : though the latter, of course, being Galilean born and bred, was not altogether at home in Judæa, and he may not have been present during the whole of the journey. Hence in this whole section, peculiar to St. Luke and of priceless worth, we do not get the details that characterize the story of the lake-side.

St. Luke's prologue contains no reference to the fourth gospel, written later by John, the son of Zebedee, the disciple whom Jesus loved. He too chose to tell once more the story of the gospel, and sure in his knowledge of the inmost thought of One whose heart had been opened to him, he composed what the ancient Fathers called ' the spiritual gospel.' He was certainly acquainted with the three gospels of Matthew, Mark, and Luke, but his work is not a series of notes upon these, nor is it meant simply to supplement them. He followed his own course, but at the same time avoided repeating what everyone knew, except where the repetition was necessary to the plan of his own work; and then he gives it in his own way and according to his own reminiscences. He made a point of being more precise about times and places; thus it is to him that we owe our knowledge of a number of places existing in Palestine in the time of Jesus; our knowledge, too, that the ministry of Jesus lasted two years and a few months, and that He preached at Jerusalem at each of the great feasts, the Pasch, Pentecost, Tabernacles, and the Dedication.

We have already spoken of the translation of the Aramaic gospel of St. Matthew into Greek. The translator did not keep slavishly to the original, but gave the substance of it; as regards some details, at least, he was probably influenced by the gospel of St. Mark.

The exact date of the gospels is uncertain. St. Mark and the Greek St. Matthew were certainly written before A.D. 70, the date of the destruction of Jerusalem: St. Mark, and the Aramaic St. Matthew at least, probably much before. St. Luke, who made use of St. Mark, wrote his gospel before the Acts of the Apostles, which he had finished by A.D. 67, the year of St. Paul's martyrdom, or perhaps a little earlier.

It is with the aid of these four gospels that we shall follow the course of the life of our Saviour, Jesus Christ, and we shall strive to show the harmony that exists between them, without in any way toning down their individual characteristics.

CHAPTER I

THE GOSPEL OF THE DIVINE AND HUMAN ORIGINS OF JESUS

The good tidings.

GOSPEL means good tidings. In the beginning the good tidings were those announced by Jesus, and by John before Him, in the words : The kingdom of God is at hand. When His disciples understood that these good tidings had become a reality in the person of Jesus, in His death and resurrection for man's salvation, the meaning of the word gospel became more definite : the good tidings signified the doctrine of Jesus, the doctrine taught by Him and about Him, which the Apostles were publishing abroad and calling on Jews first, and then Gentiles, to accept.

Hence St. Paul, who was perhaps the first to use the word, speaks of preaching 'the gospel,' meaning by that the salvation which is in Jesus, in virtue of His Passion, for those who believe in Him. The other Apostles, who had been witnesses of our Saviour's life as He actually lived it, and St. Peter most of all, dwelt on the different details of that life, on His words and His miracles, and on all that was comprised under the gospel. We have already seen that, as planned by St. Peter, it began with the baptism of John and ended with the Resurrection and Ascension. This was also the meaning of the term for Peter's disciple, St. Mark.

To make the gospel begin further back might well seem to them unnecessary. The facts relating to our Saviour's infancy had not become known to the world, nor had the growth of faith in the mind of the disciples been in any way due to those facts. During that period Jesus went by the name of Joseph's son from Nazareth. Seemingly, these facts could be left out of account by one who wished simply to get a good idea of the impression Jesus' words and deeds produced on the Jews, and to carry his thoughts back to those early days so as to experience for himself the effect of those words and deeds. The attempt has even been made to regard these facts of the Infancy not as things which played a part in the genesis of the disciples' faith, but as inferences drawn later on from Christian belief after that belief had been formed by the Saviour's public ministry alone. But the truth is that Christians have never admitted any doubt upon the point; nor is there any doubt, though we do not know precisely when these facts came to the knowledge of the Apostles. Accordingly, when St. Matthew, in order to help converted Jews and to resist the attacks of unbelieving Jews, designed to furnish solid proof that Jesus was really the Messiah, he judged it opportune to go right back to his origin. He proved by a genealogy that He was really a descendant of David; he showed that the manner of His birth, that is to say a supernatural conception such as befitted one who was the Son of God, had been foretold by the Scriptures, which had also foretold His birth at Bethlehem and His life at Nazareth.

Then St. Luke, coming after St. Mark, decided that he would include in his gospel an orderly account of the events of the Infancy. It is only during these last few years that we have come fully to understand how these events really form part of the gospel, nay, are the gospel itself if we take the word in its earlier Christian sense. That is to say, with our fuller knowledge of the world of his time, we realize how very opportune Luke's narrative must have been. The noun 'gospel' (*εὐαγγέλιον*) he never uses; but twice in his story of the Infancy he has the verb 'to evangelize' (to announce the good tidings); and we now know that it was precisely here that the usage of the time made it a peculiarly appropriate word.

A custom had grown up in the East of giving to sovereigns the title of Saviour or God-Saviour, and by that very fact an all-important significance was attached to their birth; for if a sovereign was entitled to be called a god it could only be because of his divine origin, and this divine origin was consecrated and made manifest to all men by means of his birth.[1] Already as early as the year 238 B.C., the birth of King Ptolemy had been described as the day on which all mankind began to receive many benefits. In the case of Antiochus of Commagene (from 69 to about 34 B.C.) his

[1] Cf. *Le prétendu messianisme de Virgile; Revue Biblique*, 1922, pp. 570 ff.

birth and coronation were said to be divine epiphanies or, as we say, manifestations. It was about the same time that Virgil was making known to the world that a ruler was to appear who should restore the golden age, the beginnings of which were to be found in a childhood that was miraculous. Finally, in the year 9 B.C., Paulus Fabius Maximus, the proconsul of Roman Asia, made a proposal to the people of his province that they should count the birthday of Augustus as their New Year's Day. In his proclamation he said : 'It is a question whether we receive more pleasure or more profit from the birthday of the most divine Cæsar, for it is a day that might well be compared to the beginning of everything—if not the beginning of all being, at all events the source of all our benefit. For this day has restored all that was in decay and all that had fallen into misfortune ; and a new appearance has been put upon the entire world, which would have perished but for the birth of Cæsar who is the blessing of all men.' Note that it is precisely the birthday of Cæsar Augustus which gives to the world the beginning of good tidings, or *εὐαγγέλια* (gospels) as the Greek puts it. And when a prince succeeded to the throne, his accession was looked on as a second and further announcement of good tidings : thus, when Nero came to the imperial throne in the year 54, he was proclaimed to the world as the hope of all prosperity and the good genius of the universe.[1]

Is it St. Luke's intention, then, to imitate the official protocol ? Perhaps ; but if he does so it is with a tremendous difference. It was rather his intention to accept the challenge thrown down by these proud monarchs or by their flattering courtiers when he claimed the title of Saviour for a Child born in a crib, a Child who at that time had few to pay Him homage. And events have proved that Luke was in the right, for it is from the birth-day of Jesus that we count this new era, the Christian era, which, by contrast with that unknown time when the world first came into being, is like a new creation. Men have not begun to count time, as the proconsul desired, from the birth-day of Augustus, who did no more than restore a social order that has long since passed away.

The gospel, therefore, in the strictest sense of that word, ought to commence with the supernatural conception of

[1] Inscription of Oxyrhyncus, VII, 1021 : discovered in 1910.

Jesus. It was by His public mission that He proved His dignity as Son of God; but it was at the moment of His Incarnation that the Son of God became the Saviour who dwelt amongst us. Wherefore, St. John, who goes into no detail about the childhood of Jesus, has been careful to point out His divine origin right from the opening of the fourth gospel.

The gospel of the Infancy may not have furnished the Jews who listened to Jesus with any motive for belief; nevertheless it provides for us a marvellous light and is a source of delight for all devout and contemplative souls. The very beauty of that mysterious harmony which exists between God's preparation of His design and its execution is itself a motive of faith. It might be said that the Infancy Narrative teaches nothing more than that Jesus is both Son of God and truly man: but is that nothing? Indeed we might almost say that, in His infancy, He is more truly man than at any time during the remainder of His life: that is why Marcion, who would believe only in a heavenly Christ, held the crib and the swaddling clothes in horror. But we mean that He is more human because He is weaker, a mere Child in His Mother's arms, dependent on her and fed at her breast. He works no miracles, for miracles are meant to serve as confirmations of doctrine, and the time for teaching has not yet arrived. Indeed the supernatural is here altogether concealed except for the angelic apparitions, and these are only necessary for the purpose of making known the good tidings to a little chosen group. Mary has to be informed so that she may give her consent: Joseph has to play his part in God's designs: a few shepherds, who stand for the whole of Israel, have to receive the news that a Saviour is born to them.

Therefore St. Luke, convinced as he is of the supreme importance of these facts, begins at once to appeal to those testimonies which, as he guarantees to Theophilus, are trustworthy. He makes two reserved, but quite clear allusions in the course of his narrative[1] which give the reader to understand that the Mother of Jesus herself is the source from which the disciples learnt the most intimate secrets of those humble beginnings, which St. Luke has not been afraid to link up with the most important events of the time.

[1] Luke ii, 19, 51.

Annunciation of the Forerunner's birth (3).

Luke i, 5–25.

'There was in the days of Herod, the king of Judæa.'

The scene opens in Judæa, that is to say in the territory of the ancient tribe of Juda, one of the twelve sons of the patriarch Jacob or Israel, as he was called by God. This tribe, along with the neighbouring tribe of Benjamin, had received signal honour from God by the fact that He had chosen Jerusalem for the place of His Temple, where He had established His presence in their midst. The remnant of Juda had returned from the Babylonian captivity to found a new people which from that time had remained faithful to the worship of the one true God. Some of the descendants of the other tribes had chosen to cast in their lot with this 'holy seed,' as Isaias calls it,[1] but they had now lost their tribal individuality in helping to form one new nation along with Juda. In the years during which the successors of Alexander the Great had ruled in Palestine, this chosen remnant had proved strong enough to withstand all the seductions of Greek culture. For a time they had been shaken, but they rallied their forces with such effect that even the persecutions of Antiochus Epiphanes had done no more than merely strengthen them in their faith. The descendants of the Machabees then became rulers in Israel: but, as the Machabees were of the Levitical race and were high priests before they were kings, it might be said with truth that the nation had only God as its king. The pomp of royalty, however, along with the political intercourse carried on with the idolatrous sovereigns of other countries, had given a worldly appearance to these Hasmonean princes, as the Machabean dynasty was called.

The most zealous upholders of religious reform were a group of Israelites known as *Hasidim* or Pietists, who afterwards developed into the sect called Pharisees or 'the separated ones.' These held themselves aloof from the new dynasty established by the Machabees on the ground that the genuine sceptre of Israel, preserved by God in order that the glory of David and Solomon might be restored to his people, was to be kept for David's line alone. They looked for a son of David, a king who was to be anointed

[1] Isaias vi, 13.

with the sacred oil, one whom they called in Hebrew the Messiah, foretold by prophets and psalmists as he who should deliver Israel and make her victorious over her enemies.

National hopes were raised to the point of fanaticism when it came to pass that the throne of David was occupied by a dynasty that was not even Jewish in origin. During the reign of Hyrcanus, that very feeble descendant of the Machabees, the real power in the kingdom had been usurped by Antipater, a sort of mayor of the palace for the king ; it was said that he was a descendant of Edom, Israel's ancient brother and enemy. His son Herod, whose name, meaning ' the son of heroes,' was Greek like that of his father, had thrown aside all pretence by completely supplanting his former masters. This man had skilfully curried favour with the Romans during their civil wars preceding the accession of Augustus to the purple, by always showing himself ready to pay homage to the victor, were he but yesterday an enemy. In this way he had eventually won the permanent favour of Augustus after the latter had been left sole master of the Roman world. But while he paid court to his imperial master, Herod was at the same time anxious to keep himself in power through the favour of his own subjects. With this end in view he had rebuilt the Temple of Jerusalem in more splendid fashion.

At that time, more than ever before, was the Temple in the Holy City a religious centre for the whole of Israel ; it possessed its own lawful priesthood, and their sacred rites were well attended by worshippers coming from every quarter of the land, more especially on occasion of the three great religious pilgrimages, namely at the Pasch, at Pentecost, and at the feast of Tabernacles or Tents. Each day sacrifice was duly offered ; the smoke of victims ascended to heaven even on behalf of Cæsar himself. But this mark of respect for the Jewish religion shown by Augustus seemed to cast a shadow over the religious fervour of the people. The future was dark. Herod had had his day : he was worn out and aged. And his sons, though they inherited his tyrannical disposition, had not inherited his genius. To whom would the Jewish kingdom fall ? It was a prize for which the Romans were themselves lying in wait. However, it is just when things seem most hopeless that God shows Himself a Saviour.

People were praying fervently for the salvation of Israel and imploring that the Messiah might come ; especially did they make this prayer at the moment towards evening each day when the daily sacrifice of the lamb was offered. During the offering of that sacrifice one of the priests went into the Holy Place in order to burn incense before the Lord.

We must bear in mind that the Temple was not like a Christian church, that is, a house shared by God and the faithful. It was an immense enclosure divided into courts, the largest of which was open to all, whether Jews or Gentiles. Within were other courts cut off by a barrier beyond which none but Israelites were allowed to go. In the court reserved for the priests stood the Sanctuary, a small building containing the Holy of Holies which was reserved for God alone, preceded by a chamber called the Holy Place, whither the priests entered in order to perform their mysterious offices. While the smoke of the sacrifice was going up from the altar of holocausts outside in the open air, the priests renewed the loaves of proposition, lit up the seven-branched candlestick and offered incense in the Holy Place. When the smoke from the altar of incense was perceived going up towards God the Levites chanted to the accompaniment of musical instruments, while the people in the courts offered up their prayers in union with the priest who was offering the incense. Prayers were said aloud for the good estate of prince and people, and in their hearts those who were the more fervent added an earnest supplication for the redemption of Israel by the Messiah.

The day on which the gospel opens the priest who offered the sacrifice of incense was named Zachary. He had a wife named Elizabeth. Both were very old, and they were childless. It seemed strange that they were deprived of this blessing, seeing that they walked blamelessly before God according to his ' commandments and observances.' Possibly a secret hope still inspired Zachary's prayer while he besought the Lord to have mercy on all the people.

Then an angel appeared to him standing at the right of the altar of incense which occupied the place between the loaves of proposition and the candlestick. The name Gabriel indicates that he had the appearance of a man, since Gabriel means ' the man of God ' ; that is to say, a heavenly being in human form. Zachary was amazed even to the point of distress, a prey to that dread felt by all Israelites at the approach of a superior being who is man only in appearance. The angel, however, bade him 'Fear not!'—a command we are destined to hear often on the lips of Jesus; for now God's message no longer takes the form of a threat: it is good tidings. And Zachary is not merely to be allowed to share knowledge of the secret: he is to play a part in its joyful realization, for his wife is to bear a son whom he shall call John, in Hebrew Johanan, which means 'Jaho (the God of Israel) has shown favour.' So great should this child be that, even before the day of his circumcision, the day on which new-born babes took their place among the people of God, he should be filled with the Holy Ghost while yet in his mother's womb. His birth would therefore be a day of joy. By his abstention from wine and all intoxicating drink John was to show that he was consecrated to the Lord. And when the time came, the Holy Ghost would use him as His instrument, even as He had used the prophets and those heroes of old who had delivered the people. John would go forward in the spirit and power of Elias, the most renowned of those who of old were known as the Sons of the Spirit. Such had been the character of all the former prophets, but John was to be distinguished from all the rest by reason of his special work: he was to prepare for the Lord a perfect people. Nor was his mission to end with him, and although the angel makes no definite promise on this point, for he is not commissioned completely to draw aside the veil of the future, nevertheless we are left to conclude that John is merely the forerunner of another. Zachary must have read the prophecy of Malachias, who had foretold how the Lord should come to His Temple preceded by a messenger: 'Behold I send My messenger, and he shall prepare the way before My face; and presently there shall come to His Temple the Lord whom you seek and the Angel of the covenant whom you desire.'[1] In the belief of the rabbis, this meant that the office of forerunner was to be entrusted to Elias, who was to come down again from heaven whither he had been borne in a fiery chariot. Zachary was given reason to hope that this Elias would be no other than his own son John, who was to be animated with the spirit of Elias. And who was the Angel of the Covenant if not the Messiah?

[1] Malachias iii, 1.

So grand a destiny as that, to be the father of the new Elias, might well make the old priest thrill with joy ; but dare he really believe that he was to have a son now that he was so old?

The angel saw how the mind of Zachary was overshadowed by doubt. 'Whereby shall I know this?' the man asked, and certainly there was no objection to his asking for a sign ; to the question he joined a sad remark which betrayed his distrust : 'For I am an old man, and my wife is advanced in years.' Assuredly, his fault was but slight, and, indeed, the angel did not find in it a reason for taking back God's promise. As, however, it showed that he was somewhat hesitating in welcoming these good tidings, the angel condemned Zachary to remain dumb till the child should be born.

In the meantime, the people outside in the Temple courts were wondering that the priest stayed so long within the sanctuary. And when he came out and tried to explain what had happened, he found that in truth he was powerless to speak. This was quite enough to convince the people that he had seen a heavenly vision, though what it was they could not find out.

After the days of his priestly ministry were ended Zachary went back to his home in the hill-country of Judæa, and as soon as his wife Elizabeth realized that she had conceived a child she kept to the house in order to prevent comments on the part of her neighbours. It was not yet the time for the good tidings to be published abroad : first of all, the news had to be given to Mary.

The Annunciation to Mary (4).

Luke i, 26–38.

The angel Gabriel's appearance in the Temple was one of the last occasions on which God there manifested His favour. Before many years were past that holy place was destined to be filled with doleful sounds of destruction and the crash of burning buildings. But as yet its magnificent aspect bore the stamp of ancient majesty, in the midst of which fell that final oracle from on high announcing the coming of God's last herald.

The scene now changes to Nazareth. There everything

that is to take place is not merely more divine than what we have already witnessed : it is wholly divine, for God Himself appears on the scene. But, at the same time, all takes place in a much simpler fashion than heretofore, for simplicity is the condition that befits the advent of the Incarnate Word to mankind whom He comes to serve.

There is no mention of Nazareth in the Old Testament, nor is it named by Josephus or in the pages of the Talmud. An enchanting description of the village is usually to be found in lives of Christ : and, indeed, it is to-day one of the prettiest places in Palestine, with its trim houses perched on the slopes of a lofty hill which overlooks the church marking the site of the Annunciation. But we should sadly deceive ourselves were we to transpose this pretty picture to the time of Herod. The question of the history of Nazareth, indeed, presents us with a difficult problem, and it is only very recently that information has been forthcoming which permits us to form an exact idea of how the little town has sprung up. As we write, the Franciscan Fathers are in the act of rebuilding the friary which is attached to the sacred site of the Annunciation. When Brother John, the very able director of the work, began to lay the foundations, he thought at first that he would be able to utilize the natural rock, which to all appearances was solid. But, on closer examination, it was found that the rock was hollow underneath, there being a series of artificial caves on three different levels, one above the other. The consequence was that he has had to support his building on pillars of reinforced concrete about thirty feet in depth. He believes that these caves, in which no traces of bones or pottery were discovered, must have served as store-rooms for grain, hidden away in a safe place either in a fortress or in some place easy of defence against an enemy : the grain being thus stored so that the inhabitants of the locality might have food in the event of war.

The sacred site of the Annunciation, lower down the hill than the modern village, must therefore formerly have been the stronghold of ancient Nazareth. We find the same to have happened in the case of the Sion of old Jerusalem : first it was the citadel, then it became the lower town when the hill above was occupied by houses and fortified by the massive constructions of the Temple. We conclude, then, that the ancient village of Nazareth was built upon a slight eminence, hardly worthy to be called a hill, which is almost indistinguishable from the hill which rises above it to the west, though it stands well above the valley that falls away to the east. To the north, this slight eminence extends as far as the spring which goes by the name of the Virgin's Fountain. Such, it seems to us, was the situation of Nazareth at the time of Herod. If so, then we must look for the brow of the hill from which the Nazarenes tried to throw Jesus,[1] not at the top of the hill above the present village, but at a much lower spot, namely, at the point where the citadel of ancient Nazareth was built overlooking the valley towards the east.

In the immediate vicinity of the mediæval basilica built on the site of the Annunciation, Fr. Prosper Viaud, O.S.F.,[2] has discovered caves adapted so as to serve for human dwelling. Of such a kind seems to have been the house of Mary which was converted into the crypt of the church built above it, and such was doubtless the common type of dwelling in ancient Nazareth. As a matter of fact dwellings of this kind can still be found in the streets of the modern village, though one would hardly suspect their existence judging from the more modern frontages which conceal them. It seems certain that Nazareth did not escape from this very humble condition until Christian times, and only then because it attracted attention as the scene of the Annunciation. To-day the modern village is climbing higher up the hill and spreading over the eastern hill also, thus forming a sort of amphitheatre overlooking the plain of Esdraelon, which stretches out into the distance as far as the eye can see.

It was probably, therefore, in a dwelling of the meanest kind that the Angel Gabriel found her to whom he had come to bring a message of far more august a character than that which he had lately delivered within the gold-plated walls of the Temple at Jerusalem. She was called Mary, in Hebrew Mariam, a name at that time fairly common. On account of its similarity of form with *mara* (' master ' or ' lord '), a word of the Aramaic language then used by the Jews of Palestine, the name Mariam was probably interpreted as meaning Lady or Mistress ; it is still the Catholic custom to refer to the Mother of Jesus as

[1] Luke iv, 29.
[2] Cf. his *Nazareth et ses deux églises de l'Annonciation et de Saint-Joseph.*

'Our Lady.' She was a virgin and was betrothed to Joseph, a man belonging to the house or family of David. She too appears to have been of the same lineage, as we are led to understand by St. Luke.[1] But at the same time she was, as we know, a relative of Elizabeth, who, like her husband Zachary, was of the tribe of Levi. It was not uncommon to find marriage taking place between the members of one tribe and those of another : hence it seems that Elizabeth owed her descent to a union contracted at some unknown date in the past between a daughter of the tribe of Juda and a son of the tribe of Levi.

This was the second time within six months that the Angel Gabriel had been charged with a message from God : but the whole character of his interview with Mary shows that the content of the present message was of far greater import than that of the message to Zachary. Zachary had been troubled and afraid at seeing the angel. The angel had delivered his message without first addressing any greeting to Zachary. But, in the case of Mary, the angel seeks her out in her own home[2] and greets her thus : 'Hail,[3] full of grace, the Lord is with thee'—words that ever since have been so often repeated by the faithful. This was as much as to tell her that she enjoyed the favour of the Almighty in the fullest degree possible. It was only then that Mary was troubled, and the sole cause of her trouble was amazement at such a high-sounding title as 'full of grace.' She was not afraid, however, even though the angel bids her fear not, for the object of his coming was to bring her a grace from God of even more remarkable a character than the graces she had already received. She was to bear a Son whom she should call Jesus, in Hebrew Jeshua, which means : 'Jaho (the God of Israel) is a saviour.' This Son was to be great : He should be regarded as the Son of the Most High. He was also to be a Son of David, called by God to sit upon the throne of His father : not, however, merely to reign for a few short years, but for ever, because His reign was to last unto all eternity.

[1] i, 32, 69.

[2] The text says so explicitly, though the tradition of the Orthodox Greek Church, based on the apocryphal gospels, puts the Annunciation at the Virgin's Well.

[3] Whatever word is used by men to greet their fellows in an honourable fashion, the meaning is always the same. The Jews wished peace ; the Greeks joy ; in Latin and French it is health ; we wish each other a *good* day.

Thus was it made known to Mary that she had been chosen by God to be the mother of the Messiah : for, exalted as was the title Son of the Most High, it was not necessary to read into it anything more than an indication of the great honour bestowed on the Messiah by the fact that he was to be the adopted son of God. What seems chiefly to have struck Mary in the words of the angel was the announcement that the Messiah to be born of her was to be a son of David. Ought she to conclude from this that he was to be the son of Joseph her betrothed, who himself belonged to the house of David ? Following the dictates of ordinary human discernment—what we like to call the principles of common sense—we should reply without hesitation : Why not ? Would not that be the natural thing to expect ? But, on the other hand, far back in the days of eternity God had disposed the order of things in a very different fashion ; according to that order, the Son of God was to have no other father than God the Father. As for Mary herself, she was astonished by the angel's words and asked : ' How shall this be, because I know not man ? '

We have to admit that this was a surprising question to ask ; so much, indeed, does it appear out of place that many biblical critics want to strike it out of the text altogether. But it is clear that if we were to do this we should thereby completely lose what St. Luke chiefly intends to convey in this passage : it would be like taking away the diamond and leaving only the setting. An author like Luke, possessing such a delicate touch and skilled in the art of expressing delicate shades of meaning, could never have placed on the lips of this Virgin full of grace anything that savoured of excessive *naïveté*, could never have allowed her to interpose mere commonplace truisms in the midst of such a divine communication. Hence, what Mary wished to say was that she was, as the angel well knew, a virgin and intended to remain so : according to the interpretation of the theologians, she had made a vow of virginity and was determined to keep it. Nevertheless, she was far from presuming to oppose her own will to the will of God which He had just begun to reveal to her. Thus, on her lips ' I know not man,' means ' I desire not to know.' She did not say ' I will never know,' having no desire to thwart the designs of God. Hence, she awaits the outcome of her question.

But if this was the case, object those who cannot rise above the mere commonplace, why had she allowed herself to be betrothed to Joseph? To this we might answer that, owing to the will of her parents she would be left with no choice in the matter; and, more urgent still than the wishes of her parents, there was the tyranny of established custom to be reckoned with: voluntary celibacy was not approved of in a daughter of Israel.[1] Had she ventured to refuse, the consequence would have been endless strife between herself and all her kinsfolk, to whose mind her resistance would have seemed altogether unreasonable. Hence she had been betrothed. But her betrothed was Joseph, and the subsequent train of events gives us good ground for surmising what is the explanation of the fact that she was able to reconcile a vow of virginity with the intention of marrying. It may very well be conjectured that Joseph was of the same mind as herself in the matter, surely not an unreasonable conclusion when we remember that these sentiments were shared by so many of their contemporaries: we mean those Jews who are called the Essenes. Joined thus in marriage with this just man, chaste as herself, Mary might be confident of being left in tranquillity and peace to lead a life wholly devoted to God by two souls capable of understanding and loving one another in God.

The angel, therefore, said nothing to dissuade her from the intention of marrying Joseph, seeing that it was a marriage admirably fitted to further God's plan; he merely gave her to understand that her purpose of virginity was still more suitable to God's designs by telling her that the birth of the Messiah was to be the work of none but God and herself: 'The Holy Spirit shall come upon thee, and the power of the Most High shall overshadow thee: and therefore, the Child to be born shall be holy and shall be called the Son of God.' In these words full light is thrown upon the matter, such light, at least, as shines upon the mind from a mystery surpassing the powers of reason. The Child to be born is to have no father but God. Assuredly, it was not the divine operation in Mary's womb that was to make Him the Son of God, seeing that He was that already by His eternal generation from the Father, and there was to be no other person in the Messiah than the

[1] The natives of Palestine say even to this day: 'Either marriage or the rave.'

person of the Son of God. But it can be said that this divine operation in Mary's womb, by which a human nature came into being without the intervention of any other human instrumentality than that of Mary, was to be the cause of the Child's unparalleled holiness ; and, furthermore, it was the reason why He should be given that title to which He has an eternal right, the title of Son of God.

As theologians admit, the union of the Son of God with a human nature was not incompatible with His being born in the normal way ; but how supremely fitting it was that He should address none but God with the august name of Father ! Nothing serves to throw greater light on the truth of the two natures united in one person. And what greater honour could be bestowed on Mary than this, that she alone with the Father could say : 'My Son Jesus !' In this fashion was consecrated that life of perfect chastity which has borne so much fruit for mankind in the form of spiritual blessings.

It was now left for Mary to give her consent to this mystery. In seeking for information she had not been the victim of doubt, like Zachary. Still, the angel gives her, too, a sign consisting in a miracle of an order very much inferior to that of her virginal conception. God's omnipotence was indicated by the fact that Elizabeth, her kinswoman, had conceived a son in her old age, this being the sixth month of the barren woman's pregnancy. Upon this, Mary bowed her head and surrendered herself to the will of God, thereby granting the consent which God had deigned to ask of her : 'Behold the handmaid of the Lord : be it done unto me according to Thy word.' From that moment the mystery of the Incarnation took place in her womb : the salvation of mankind had begun. On the instant the good tidings were known in heaven, and little by little they were to be spread upon earth.

Mary's Visit to Elizabeth (5).

Luke i, 39–56.

The news of Elizabeth suggested to Mary's mind the idea of paying a visit to her kinswoman. In giving her this news, the angel Gabriel had included nothing of what he had told Zachary about the future career of the child

Elizabeth was to bear. But Mary must have guessed that this twofold intervention on the part of God was concerned with the same object. The strong desire she felt to visit Elizabeth was by no means due to doubt about the truth of the sign given her by the angel, for she believed him with absolute faith ; but she wished to assure her kinswoman of her sympathy, and perhaps to talk with her about the destiny of the two children. Thus enlightened by God and inspired by charity she set out to congratulate Elizabeth and to render what assistance she could to this woman who for so many years had been barren, and who now was trying to keep her secret as long as possible.

Availing herself of the opportunity provided by some company of travellers journeying to Jerusalem, perhaps for the Pasch, Mary set out for the hill-country of Juda. By using the Hebrew name Juda instead of Judæa, St. Luke intimates that the town to which she was going was in the territory belonging to the ancient kingdom of Juda, which touched Jerusalem at its most northerly frontier. He does not mention the name of the town, or rather village ; but a tradition already current in the fifth century points to the village of *Ain-Karim*, an Arabic name signifying 'the plentiful spring,' which has been substituted for the ancient Hebrew name of Karem.[1] The tradition has continued unbroken up to our own day, and the village always keeps the feast of St. John with great solemnity.[2]

Four days' journey from Nazareth would have been sufficient to bring Mary to this village. When she entered the house of her friend, Elizabeth was the first to meet her, and Mary greeted her with a kinswoman's affection, at the same time paying that deference to the aged woman which was becoming on the part of a young maiden. By the charm of her smile she showed Elizabeth that she was already aware of what had happened. Then was accomplished what the angel had foretold to Zachary, namely, that his son should be filled with the Holy Ghost even before his birth : the infant leaped in his mother's womb. This might be taken as a dim presentiment of the approach of Him whose advent among men John was destined to

[1] Josue xv, 59 in the Greek but not in the Hebrew.

[2] The site of the Visitation lies a short distance to the west of the fine spring which gives the village its name. There exist monumental ruins dating from the Middle Ages, and the recent excavations of the Franciscan Fathers have uncovered many important traces of Byzantine construction.

announce. His mother, too, was filled with the Spirit of God so that she was fully enlightened concerning the dignity of the Messiah's Mother. Then she, in her turn, greeted Mary, exclaiming in holy rapture: 'Blessed art thou among women and blessed is the fruit of thy womb! And whence is this to me that the Mother of my Lord should come unto me? For as soon as the voice of thy salutation sounded in my ears, the infant leaped in my womb for joy. Blessed is she that hath believed that those things shall come to pass which were told her from the Lord!' Mary[1] replied in the verses of the hymn we call the *Magnificat*, the words of which are enshrined in the memory of every Christian.

It is not unknown, even in our own days, for uncultured Arab women to give expression to their joy by composing a song on the spur of the moment. Such a thing was witnessed not so long ago at Madaba, on an occasion when the Christian villagers beat off an attack made upon them by the neighbouring Bedouin tribe of the Sehour.[2] The same was customary in ancient Israel, and we find a traditional theme for such songs composed on outstanding occasions like victory in battle, birth, and marriage. Moreover, the very expressions used in these chants were handed down from one prophetess to another; thus Mary is evidently inspired by the canticle of Anna,[3] the mother of Samuel, who, hailing her son's birth as the salvation of Israel, then proceeds to sing of a king's anointing, that is to say of a Messiah. In the eyes of Anna, this was merely a manifestation of God's power as well as of that Divine Wisdom by which the vain thoughts of the proud are brought to nought.

We recognize that Anna's canticle was perfectly suitable to the occasion; but, at the same time, we have to admit that, even from its opening words, it completely transcends the mere circumstance provided by the fact that one who

[1] Harnack, following the example of Loisy, attributes the *Magnificat* to Elizabeth instead of to Mary. According to their interpretation, after Elizabeth has spoken a few words of congratulation to Mary, she goes on to thank God at greater length for what He has done for herself. But it was certainly not Luke's intention thus to give greater prominence to Elizabeth than to Mary. And even if we had not the authority of the manuscripts and the tradition of the Fathers to guide us in the matter, there would still remain the certain fact that Luke puts the *Magnificat* here as a reply to the congratulations of Elizabeth.

[2] Cf. *Science Catholique*, October 15, 1890, p. 679.

[3] 1 Kings ii, 1 ff.

has been barren now becomes a mother. In noble fashion she sings of the God of Israel's victory : the bow of the mighty is broken : Jahweh killeth and maketh alive : He shall judge the ends of the earth. It is due only to that note of triumph, to the messianic expectation which raises the mind and heart of the prophetess to such future heights, that Mary was able to find ideas suitable to her own case in the canticle of Anna. The distinctive mark of the *Magnificat* consists in this : that although the expressions of Anna are not too strong to describe what had been wrought in Mary, yet Mary does not find them strong enough to express the humility of one who desires to magnify the Lord. She acknowledges her low estate in order that His may be all the glory ; but at the same time she confesses that all generations shall call her blessed in her reply to Elizabeth's congratulations. Thus, while Anna's song could have been put into the mouth of a hero, that of Mary is suitable for none but the Mother of Jesus. As God has had regard to her in His kindness, so will He deal with all the lowly who acknowledge their helplessness ; but the mighty and those laden with riches, whose hearts are uplifted with pride, shall be brought low and sent away empty. And while Anna's gaze is already fixed upon God's triumph over the very ends of the earth, Mary concentrates all her praise upon the great work of mercy promised by God to Abraham and to his seed for ever.

Nothing, then, in this canticle of Mary is out of place, not even that part of it in which she pays to the prerogatives of the Lord the honour that is their due. It is not merely a question here of an enthusiastic disciple of Jesus who is writing under the influence of His miracles and His resurrection : what we see in the *Magnificat* is the modest joy of a daughter of David, a child of Abraham, who looks back along the course of the centuries to the promise given by God to the ancient patriarch, and who realizes that it has been fulfilled in herself. Already her maternal brow shines with the promised halo that shall be hers owing to the salutation with which all generations are to greet her in their prayers. That prediction of her blessedness has indeed been fulfilled by all generations who have saluted her as Mother of God.

Mary remained with her cousin about three months, but she departed before the birth of Elizabeth's child. The charitable object for which she had come was now fulfilled and her further presence was no longer fitting.[1] Moreover, being so far from home, she had much more reason than Elizabeth to avoid provoking indiscreet curiosity of others with regard to herself.

Birth of the Precursor. He withdraws to the desert (6).

Luke i, 57–80.

When the time came Elizabeth had a son. The news went round, all the more quickly on account of the way in which she had remained so long hidden at home; for Mary's presence had saved Elizabeth from the need of going out to provide for the wants of the household. There was general rejoicing among her friends and kinsfolk.

On the eighth day they came to circumcise him. That was the day fixed by the law, and the command was so explicit that the rabbis even permitted the slight work involved in the rite of circumcision on the Sabbath. By the fact of circumcision a Jewish child was given admittance to spiritual communion with Israel: it served as a sort of deed of contract between him and God and initiated him into the divine worship. It was likewise the occasion for bestowing on him a name, and this appeared all the more fitting in that the name he received generally expressed praise of God or gratitude for divine benefits, even for such an ordinary event as the birth of a child.

It is rather strange that, on the present occasion, the neighbours who came in to offer advice on the subject proposed to call him Zachary, for people more generally preferred to give a son his grandfather's rather than his father's name so as to avoid all confusion. But they doubtless thought that, as Zachary was so old, the likelihood of such confusion would not be of very long standing. They allowed themselves all the more liberty in the matter because the person chiefly interested in the affair was dumb: hence no one troubled to ask for his opinion. Here, however, Elizabeth interposed: she had her rights in the matter, seeing that she was the mother of the child. Indeed, in the days of the patriarchs of old, had it not been Rachel, Lia, and the other wives of Jacob who had chosen their children's names? Elizabeth flatly asserted that the

[1] Cf. *Naplouse*, by Jaussen, O.P., p. 105.

child's name was to be John. But the busybodies refused to yield : 'None of thy family is called by such a name.' Eventually they decided to consult the father, speaking by the aid of gestures, thus making us think that he was deaf as well as dumb. The priest knew how to write : perhaps he had used this means in order to enlighten Elizabeth. Asking for one of those wooden tablets covered with wax which were written on with the pointed instrument called a style, he wrote simply the words : 'John is his name.' The matter was now settled and there was no more to be said. By this act of faith and obedience Zachary's tongue was loosed and he spoke, blessing God with more feeling than all the rest.

So his silence was broken at last ! What questions he had to answer ! What had made him dumb ? What had he seen in the Temple, and what had the angel foretold of this miraculous child ? Curiosity once satisfied about the past, they began to ask with still greater eagerness about the future, their questionings full of a note of hope : 'What an one, think ye, shall this child be, seeing that the hand of the Lord is so evidently upon him ?'

Zachary gives expression to all their joys and hopes in the song we call the *Benedictus*, the canticle appointed by the Church to be recited daily in the divine office of Lauds, originally destined to be chanted at the moment when the dawn was breaking. The happy man had been told of Mary's hopes. Her presence alone, indeed, had been for him a light, and the birth of John joined with the confidences shared with him by his overjoyed wife had increased that light. Therefore, identifying himself with the spirit which was to animate his son, and imitating the humility with which Elizabeth had put her own good fortune in the background before the higher dignity of Mary, Zachary turns his thoughts first of all to the salvation that has already appeared in the house of David : he knew from the promises made to the prophets of old and from the covenant and the oath sworn by God to Abraham that it was in the house of David where salvation was to begin. In common with all the children of Israel, he trusts that God will grant them deliverance from their enemies who hate them : but now, in his eyes, the granting of such peace only means providing the most favourable conditions for serving God in righteousness and holiness.

Thus he makes Mary's thoughts his own, and it is only after blessing God for the advent of her Son that Zachary at last turns to the little child whom God has given him, the boy who is destined to be the Prophet of the Most High : nay, more than a prophet, for this is he who is to prepare the ways of the Lord. God's paths are the paths of the Messiah : John must go before Him who shall not merely be God's ambassador, but who shall act as God Himself. Here the hopes of national deliverance for Israel disappear before a new light which seems to show that the only real enemy is sin against God. Thus it will be John's office to preach salvation through the remission of sin granted by the merciful heart of God, who shall make a star arise in the heavens to shine upon mankind ; for all men, even in the land of Israel, are seated in great darkness, as though awaiting the dawn of day to set out on their journey. The Messiah will show them the right way, the way of peace in which they shall find salvation.

So the canticle ends as it begins : the Son of David appears in the character of a Divine Being : John is no more than his precursor.

The child grew up while awaiting the day of his manifestation to Israel, and the power of the Spirit took hold of him more and more. It was this power which drove him out into the desert to prepare for his mission. The few words in which St. Luke describes this action of the Holy Spirit upon John do not satisfy those who desire ever to mingle human influence with divine. Some, for instance, imagine that in his youth John was initiated into the doctrines and practices of the Essenes, who lived a life of voluntary exile in community upon the shores of the Dead Sea. They did not break with Judaism, but yet they were somewhat infected with Greek thought. Their doctrines were like a revival of Pythagoreanism. They were very insistent on the superiority of soul over body and of spirit over matter : hence they looked on death as the soul's deliverance and were unwilling to beget children and thus be the occasion of a soul's falling into a body. John is supposed to have been trained in such a mental discipline, and in the asceticism and continual rites of purification practised by the Essenes.[1]

[1] We shall return to this point when we deal with John's baptism, p. 64.

But, as we shall see, the Baptist's whole life was a protest against such an intrusion of pagan philosophy into Judaism; for the spirit that animated him was the spirit of the Law, though his special office as the last of the prophets was the guiding of souls to One greater than himself.

Joseph takes upon himself the legal paternity of Jesus (7).

Matt. i, 18–25.

When Mary, on her return to Nazareth, reached the great plain of Esdraelon and looked up at the little village perched on the hill-side, her thoughts must have turned to Joseph, the man to whom she was betrothed. So far, it seems, she had not taken him into her confidence concerning what had happened, for she was sure that she could rely on his delicate reserve as well as on his trust in her. But, most of all, she put her reliance on God, trusting in Him to arrange everything for the best. It was not possible for her to leave Joseph, for that would have involved exposing herself to the risk of scandalous gossip; besides, she had no right to do so even had she wished: such a thing would not have been allowed by existing Jewish custom. Since the time of Our Lord, marriage has been for us a sacrament which binds two persons together indissolubly from the moment when they enter into the matrimonial contract. Until that moment a man has no rights over his future wife; and even should there have been a formal engagement, the parties retain the right to dissolve it.

But things were far different among the Jews. When a girl was given to a man by her father, she from that moment came under his authority. All that remained to be done in order to bring the marriage to completion was that he should take the girl under his own roof. He might take possession of her as wife in the house of his father-in-law if he wished, provided this was done in an official manner. But if a girl, during the time that elapsed between her betrothal and the completion of the marriage, were to be guilty of sin with another, she was considered as a true adulteress and the Law authorized her future husband to denounce her as such. The penalty laid down by the Law was death.[1] There was no strict obligation upon him of thus denouncing her,

[1] Deuteronomy xxii, 23 ff.

but should he neglect to do so his failure might easily be taken as a proof of disgraceful connivance in her sin.

The day came at last when it was evident to Joseph that his betrothed wife was with child. It would not have been unnatural if he had experienced an instinctive feeling of surprise and indignation : but even if such feelings arose, they had no influence upon him. For, if he refuses to expose Mary to public obloquy, it is by no means from a feeling of leniency to one whom he considers to be guilty : it is, on the contrary, as the gospel declares : 'because he was a just man.' Now no one who is just condemns another before he has received definite proofs of guilt ; in the present case there was no proof at all. It might be objected that all the appearances were against Mary ; but, in spite of appearances, Joseph had definite proof of her virtue and serenity, of the manifest innocence of one who was such a pure creature, and his love of her made him certain that he could not be deceived. Do we not follow his example when we wish to defend one whom we confidently love against widespread rumours that have been stirred up about their character ? We find explanations in things that we know nothing about, even in the most unlikely things. Had Joseph not believed in the possibility of some miraculous explanation of the situation, it is hardly likely that he would have showed himself so docile to the admonition he received in a dream.

In the midst of all his anxiety, it seemed to him that the wisest thing he could do was to restore to Mary her freedom, but in such a way as to prevent the possibility of anyone thinking that she had been guilty of any crime.[1] But before he had reached his final decision an angel of the Lord appeared to him in a dream. By addressing him as son of David, the angel suggests to his mind that the Child in

[1] Let it not be imagined that this is merely a pious explanation which owes its origin to an increasing veneration of the Mother of Jesus. It is St. Jerome's own explanation, and none of the Fathers was so versed in the Scriptures as he. 'How could Joseph be called just,' he asks, 'if he conceals his wife's crime ? The truth is that his silence is a witness of Mary's innocence : for Joseph, knowing her chastity and at the same time astonished at what has taken place, conceals by his silence the mystery which had not been made known to him.' Those critics who are so fond of looking everywhere for stories of virgin birth (*parthenogenesis*, as it is called) ought to be the first to admit that the thought of such a thing would come to the mind of Joseph.

question is no other than the Messiah : Joseph is to appear before the world as His father by accepting Mary as his wife, and so hand on to the Child his rights as a Son of the house of David. Hence the angel says : 'Fear not to take unto thee Mary thy wife'—that is, to add the final legal sanction to the betrothal with Mary—'for that which is conceived in her is the work of the Holy Ghost.'

In these few words the first evangelist, St. Matthew, describes what we have already seen set forth at greater length by St. Luke[1] St. Matthew has his own way of announcing the good tidings which are given this time, not to Mary, but to Joseph who is made guardian of the promises given in the Scriptures : Mary thy wife 'shall bring forth a Son, and thou shalt call His name Jesus'—a suitable name, since it means a saviour, 'for He shall save His people from their sins.' Matthew, like Luke, is conscious of the high dignity of these chosen souls, Mary and Joseph. It will take the Apostles a long time to understand the true mission of the Messiah : but Joseph, like Zachary before him, is informed that the Messiah is the deliverer from sin. Matthew has the custom of confirming his facts by alluding to the prophecies of the Old Testament, and here we find the first example of it. He reminds us of the Emmanuel prophecy in Isaias, where there is a very clear reference to the Infant-God : 'Behold a virgin shall be with child and shall bring forth a Son, and they shall call His name Emmanuel, which, being interpreted, is God-with-us.'

A clear prophecy, we repeat, even though a veiled one, for it is only the historical and chronological circumstances in which the prophecy was uttered that make it veiled. But prophecy is independent of time : it is like an aeroplane which soars above the whole country-side so that all places are seen at once and in the same picture. Once the foretold event has taken place and thrown light on the prediction, then all the past circumstances surrounding the utterance of the prophecy disappear like mist before the rays of the sun ; the mind cannot help being struck by the correspondence between the words of the prophecy and the event, especially as this is of so tremendous a nature that no one would ever have dared even to imagine it. With what a

[1] Not that St. Luke merely amplifies St. Matthew's theme ; he relates the gospel of the Infancy from quite another point of view.

sweet power of conviction do these words of Isaias concerning Emmanuel come to our souls on Christmas night !

'For a child is born to us,
  a son is given to us ;
The sovereignty is upon his shoulder,
  and he shall be given the name of
Wonderful-Counsellor,
  Mighty-God,
Eternal Father,
  Prince of peace ;
For the increase of sovereignty,
  and for peace without end
On the throne of David
  and in his kingdom ;
To establish it and to strengthen it
  in right and in justice
From henceforth and for ever.
  The zeal of Jahweh of Hosts shall accomplish it.'[1]

It may be objected that the name of Jesus does not appear among the other names of the prophecy. But the New Testament is not a mere imitation which depends entirely on the Old. On the contrary it is the New Testament which is the reality : the Old Testament is but the figure of the New.

Waking from his sleep and showing by his trust in Mary that he is worthy of being her confidant, Joseph takes his wife to himself ; and when she has brought forth her Son he gives Him the name of Jesus. Thus did it come to pass that Joseph introduced Jesus to the world as a descendant of David.

The Genealogy of Jesus (20).

Matt. i, 1–17 ; Luke iii, 23–38.

There is no question about Joseph's being a descendant of David. Both St. Luke and St. Matthew are in agreement on this point, nor does it appear that it was ever denied during the lifetime of Our Lord. No one could accept Him as the Messiah without believing that He was a son of David, and this He was through Joseph, whom everyone looked on as His father.

St. Matthew starts his gospel with the book of the genealogy

[1] Isaias ix, 6 ff. (Condamin's translation).

of Jesus ; and since it was in Him that the promise made to Abraham was fulfilled, the evangelist sees fit to carry back the line to that father of the other patriarchs, Isaac and Jacob. In following the list of names given by the Holy Scriptures the name of David was reached in fourteen generations. Between David and Jechonias, who lived at the time of the Babylonian captivity, Matthew again found fourteen generations in the list of kings by omitting the names of Ochozias, Joas, and Amasias ; but as there is no doubt that he was perfectly aware of the existence of these three, it is evident that he had no intention of giving a complete genealogy. He again gives fourteen generations from Salathiel to Joseph, and we have no means of testing whether this list is complete or not ; nor have we any proof that Matthew wishes it to be taken as complete. It is quite possible that he chooses to give fourteen only, because the Hebrew letters making up David's name also represent the Hebrew numerals which, when added together, make a total of fourteen. However, our lack of certainty concerning the number of generations between Jesus and Abraham takes nothing away from the value of the genealogy.

In the days of the early Church the kinsmen of Jesus were still known as the sons of David, a fact which, according to the historian Hegesippus, caused a certain amount of alarm to the emperor Domitian. But on enquiry, he came to the conclusion that there was nothing to fear from them and allowed them to go undisturbed.[1]

We still have to answer the objection, however, that if St. Matthew's genealogy is correct and was accepted by everybody, why did St. Luke think it necessary to draw up another tracing the descent of Jesus from David through Nathan instead of through Solomon ? Some commentators have tried to find an explanation by saying that St. Luke does not give the genealogy of Joseph, but that of Mary ; but this does violence to the fact that the third evangelist, like the first, ends his list with the name of Joseph, though at the same time declaring that Joseph is only the supposed or adoptive father of Jesus. Patristic tradition is equally explicit about Luke's genealogy being that of Joseph.

As a matter of fact, there was no demand for any genealogy but that of Joseph ; nor would anyone at that time make any objection if both genealogies were traced through

[1] Eusebius, *Historia Eccles.*, III, 20, 1–6.

adopted sons instead of natural sons, or if either evangelist forsook the direct line in order to trace descent through a collateral line. In the common estimation that would not make them cease to be true genealogies. It was a question of the inheritance of rights, and rights can be transmitted from brother to brother as well as from father to son. Thus, for example, according to the principles of Semitic descent, Henry IV, king of France, would be counted as the son of his predecessor Henry III (though he was not), merely because his right of succession had been recognized by Henry III ; the main thing was that they were both descendants of St. Louis. It may be for a similar reason that Joseph appears with a different father in each genealogy. Indeed, as early as the beginning of the third century, Julius Africanus explained the divergence by making it due to the Jewish legal institution which prescribed that if a man married his brother's widow and had a son by her, that son would be able to count his mother's former husband as his legal father.[1] Whether this supposition be true or not we are unable to decide, but we are none the worse off for that. What would have interested us more would have been any evidence of Mary's descent, seeing that Jesus received the blood of David into his veins from her alone. But there is no material at hand for the construction of the genealogy of Mary.

As St. Luke realizes, the question of the Davidic descent of Jesus was of importance mainly for Jews. But as He is not only the Jewish Messiah but also the Saviour of the whole world, Luke traces his descent to the ancestors of David ; he goes back even as far as Adam, the father of the human race who came from God, not indeed as his son but as his creature. In this way he sets forth Jesus as a new starting-point in the history of mankind, making the day of Redemption a day which corresponds with the day of Creation.

Jesus is born at Bethlehem (8).

Luke ii, 1–20.

Mary and Joseph were thus inseparably united in the bonds of matrimony. Soon after circumstances arose which led them to take the road leading to Bethlehem, for it was there, as the prophets had foretold,[2] that Jesus was to be

[1] See ch. v, § 241. [2] Cf. p. 44.

born. Actually, the prophets do not precisely say so: they merely declare that the Messiah is to come forth from Bethlehem, the town from which David had sprung. And, as Jesus was the Son of David, it could well be said that He also had sprung from Bethlehem. However, it was customary to interpret the prophecy of Micheas in a stricter sense, and, indeed, the fact that Jesus was born at Bethlehem gives to the words of Micheas a much more striking fulfilment.

The higher critics here make the objection that it is nothing but the desire of seeing this prophecy fulfilled which has led certain people to imagine that Jesus must have been born at Bethlehem. Renan sets down with the utmost audacity, as though there were no question about the matter, that 'Jesus was born at Nazareth.'[1] He treats all that St. Luke writes of the enrolment which gave occasion for Joseph and Mary to go to Bethlehem as though it were a piece of pure imagination.

Those, however, who make claims to scholarship must now admit that the truth of St. Luke's story has been confirmed by information gradually collected from newly-discovered documents. The evangelist tells us that the Emperor Augustus ordered an enrolment or census to be made throughout the whole of the Roman Empire, commonly referred to at that time as 'the inhabited earth.' Even Palestine was included in this order for the registration of persons and property, despite the fact that it was still under the rule of Herod. Hence we find Joseph and Mary making their way to Bethlehem.

Quirinius, or Cyrinus as he is called, who was the imperial legate in Syria, was in some way concerned in this enrolment, though it is not yet clear what precise connection he had with it. We have suggested that Luke ii, 2 ought to be translated as follows: 'This enrolling was previous to that which took place during the time when Quirinius was governor of Syria.' If the words of St. Luke be thus understood, then no difficulty arises from the fact that, as far as we know from other sources, only one census was held by that very important personage; this was in the year A.D. 6–7, on the occasion when Judæa was incorporated in the Roman province of Syria, though it was left under the rule of its own immediate governor who was called the procurator of

[1] He has the effrontery to cite the evangelists as proof of this, taking not the slightest notice of what they say to the contrary.

Judæa. This enrolment, which marked the handing over of Judæa to the domination of idolatrous rulers, was the cause of a terrible religious insurrection: hence it was well remembered. It looks as if Luke, out of a desire to avoid all confusion, draws a distinction between the general enrolment of the whole Empire and this particular enrolment which took place at the incorporation of Judæa in the Empire.

Some, however, prefer to think that, as Quirinius was twice governor of Syria, he held the first census during his first term of office as legate. But it is difficult to determine the date of this census, and still more difficult to identify it with that spoken of by St. Luke.

But, whatever be suggested as the explanation, it ought to be admitted that a mere difficulty of chronology, or rather a lack of certainty concerning one particular point of fact, gives no justification to historians for doubting the truth of the fact, particularly when it is one that has every appearance of likelihood. Now there is no doubt whatever that Augustus had a census made throughout the Empire; and if he was desirous of including the kingdom of Herod in that census, seeing that he was shortly to annex that kingdom to the Empire, we cannot believe that he would refrain from doing so out of any regard for that old and discredited tyrant.

A recently-discovered papyrus roll has furnished us with most exact information concerning the manner in which such a registration of persons and property was carried out in the Roman provinces. Persons were registered by houses, that is to say by families and clans, and for that purpose everyone was ordered to go and be enrolled in the place of his family's origin. Thus, Gaius Vibius Maximus, the prefect of Egypt, gave orders that, with a view to the enrolment by families which he was about to make, all who were for any reason whatsoever absent from their paternal place of origin should return in order to be inscribed according to the usual form.[1] This was in the year A.D. 103. It may well be expected that the same formalities were observed one hundred years earlier, when ancient customs had still less chance of having been replaced by Roman law.

In Egypt, it was only the priests who were called upon to show their ancestral rights drawn up in correct genealogical form. But among Semitic peoples even families of the most

[1] *Papyrus of London*, III, p. 125.

humble rank of society prided themselves on knowledge of their ancestral descent. Even to this day, every Maronite who has emigrated from his home in Syria, whether to Jerusalem or even as far as the United States, knows perfectly well to what clan he belongs and to what village in the Lebanon he would have to return for enrolment should that be required.

Joseph, then, as a descendant of David, had to go to Bethlehem. It is not hard to understand why he took Mary with him : he could scarcely have been willing to leave her at home alone. It is not out of question, indeed, that perhaps they had some idea of staying for a time at Bethlehem, since both of them had been informed that Jesus was He who should restore the throne of David. In this manner, therefore, was a prophecy fulfilled through the instrumentality of an order issued by the master of the Roman Empire, as a consequence of which this humble pair set out for Bethlehem. 'What do ye, ye rulers of the world ?' asks Bossuet. '. . . But God has far different designs, which you carry out, even though they do not enter into your minds.'

Thus, now that we have satisfied the demands of the most meticulous critics, we can give ourselves up in peace to the beautiful story of St. Luke, a story filling us with joy, delighting the hearts of children and of mothers even more.

Joseph and Mary, then, have taken the way which leads from Nazareth to Jerusalem and on to Bethlehem. It was a very long journey for one in Mary's condition, for, unless we accept the stories of the apocryphal gospels, we must needs conclude that she experienced some discomfort. At this time the Romans had not yet constructed their wonderful roads ; still, on such roads as there were, the journey might be made by carriage or, more comfortably still, in a litter. But the humble couple were far too poor to afford such luxurious means of travel. Arrived at Bethlehem they sought for lodging, but without success, in one of those big hostelries known in the East to-day as *khans* where men and beasts settle themselves down side by side as best they can. Great numbers of people must have been brought to Bethlehem to the registration office which had been established there. At last Mary and Joseph found shelter, though it was of the humblest description, in one of the surrounding caves sometimes utilized as dwelling-place for man and stable for beasts. It is possible that they were there for several days while Joseph awaited his turn to be registered; at any rate, there it was that Mary brought forth her first-born Son. When St. Luke uses this expression of the birth of Jesus, he knows quite well that none of the Christians of his time will misunderstand it. On no occasion does he refer to brethren and sisters of Jesus. This first-born Son was an only child as everybody knew. But St. Luke, writing according to a pre-conceived plan, is simply preparing the way for what he has to say later concerning the offering of the first-born in the Temple.

In this stable-dwelling there was, as might be expected, a manger, fashioned after the shape of a boat in the usual manner, made to hold the barley with which beasts of burden were fed; Mary used it as a cradle in which to lay the Infant whom she herself had wrapped in swaddling bands. His birth no more than His conception had in no wise injured her virginal state: He was brought forth in some marvellous fashion such as the dignity of God, as well as that of the divinely chosen Mother, demanded.

The traditional site of the crib, for which we have a long-standing tradition,[1] is a little to the east and below the ancient village which stood at the highest point of the slope covered by the modern Bethlehem. The path descending still further towards the east soon passes the limits of the cultivated fields. Bethlehem, even more than Jerusalem, was built at the edge of the desert. To this day it is the place to which the nomad tribes of the desert resort to buy corn and sell their weaving and cheeses. It is not surprising, therefore, to find that there were shepherds guarding their flocks quite near to the place where Jesus was born. In winter, especially at the end of December, the time at which liturgical tradition has fixed the date of the Nativity, the flocks belonging to the villagers would in all probability be housed in sheds of some sort for the night; but the true shepherds of the desert had no such shelters at their disposal, nor would they need them, for down towards the Dead Sea the temperature is much milder than up at Bethlehem. A group of these nomads—they did not belong to Bethlehem—were that night keeping guard over their flocks, talking with one another, no doubt, to while away the time.

[1] Cf. *Bethléem*, by Vincent and Abel, O.P.

Suddenly an angel appears in their midst while the darkness around them is blotted out by a shining light. Its brilliance frightens them, for it is evidently not a natural light.

Then the angel speaks : 'Fear not !' This angel also has come to bring good tidings, a gospel of great joy, as he calls it. It is evident, then, that the gospel he brings is primarily a message from heaven to earth. It is a revelation made to Israel, and that which is revealed gives cause for great joy. It is this ; that a Saviour has just been born in David's city, and this Saviour is both the Messiah and the Lord to whom all homage is due. Let them go and see for themselves that they are not the victims of illusion ; they shall find a Child in a manger, not left naked and abandoned as they might expect to find a child who had been put in such an odd cradle, but properly clothed in swaddling bands.

Then, as though to indicate that heaven too shared this great joy with men, a multitude of the heavenly host of angels appeared also, singing the praises of the God of Israel, He whose pleasure it was to be called Jahweh of the heavenly hosts ; and now the day had come when He was to be acknowledged as the one God of all the world :

> 'Glory to God in the highest,
> And peace on earth to men of good will.'

Thus do the angels declare that God is glorified when He grants pardon to men of good will, that is to those who show themselves ready to welcome Him who comes to save them and give them peace. Such is the gospel as it was announced to these simple men who, in their desert life, had preserved the ancient type of life lived by Abraham when he came as a nomad from Chaldæa, his tent the only place on earth at the time where the true God was worshipped. While in the cities of Palestine Jews could only avoid the defilement of contact with Gentiles by observing a moral isolation into which there crept a large measure of pride, these shepherds of the desert who lived on little, whose standard of morality was strict and whose solitary life accustomed them to the thought of God's all-pervading presence, proved docile to this voice from heaven. They said one to another : 'Let us go over to Bethlehem and see that which the Lord hath showed us.' Coming in haste, they saw the sign given by God : in their turn they spread the good tidings and went back to their flocks.

But it is in Mary's heart, where all God's plans were gathered into one, that we must seek the most faithful echo of all these words and the deepest understanding of all these events.

The legal observances (9–10).
Luke ii, 21–38.

It was now for the promised Saviour, who had thus been announced to Israel, to come forward as the heir of the promise once made to Abraham and sanctioned by the religious rite of circumcision. Abraham had begun this rite and the Mosaic Law had preserved it. As the mother and the adoptive father of Jesus had received no divine instructions to the contrary, no other course was open to them as pious Israelites but to conform to this law. Therefore the Child was circumcised on the eighth day and received the name of Jesus according to the directions given by the angel to Mary and Joseph.[1]

Mary might well have considered herself dispensed from that other law which prescribed that a recent mother should present herself in the Temple in order to undergo a sort of legal purification ; at the same time she was required to offer a yearling lamb for a holocaust, along with a young pigeon or dove as a sacrifice for sin. Poor women were permitted to substitute a pair of pigeons or doves.[2] The law prescribed, moreover, that all the first-born, whether of man or beast, were the property of the Lord.[3] The price for the redemption of a boy was five sicles. It was not commanded in so many words that he must be presented in the Temple, but no pious mother would wish to omit this opportunity of obtaining for him the blessing of the Most-High. Thus, at any rate, did Mary and Joseph understand this command of the Lord ; for if there was an obligation of consecrating to Him every first-born son, then why not offer to Him this Child sprung from David who was to be acknowledged as the Son of God ?

Their arrival in the Temple courts, though attended with so little ceremony, was nevertheless an event of sublime importance, for then was fulfilled the prophecy of Malachias which foretold how the Lord would enter his Temple for

[1] Luke and Matthew thus complete one another.
[2] Leviticus xii, 6–8. [3] Numbers xviii, 15.

the first time. It was fitting, therefore, that He should be greeted by one of the representatives of the prophets, those men of the Spirit as they are called. It was Simeon who filled this rôle. He is described as a just man, full of the fear of the Lord, with all his thoughts set on the redemption of Israel. The Holy Ghost was upon him, says St. Luke, showing thereby that under the Old Law there was a certain anticipation, in the case of some of the just, of that outpouring of the Spirit which was to be characteristic of the New Covenant. The Spirit had made known to him that he should not see death until he had seen the Messiah of the Lord ; and the Spirit which guided him in all things led him that day into the Temple at the time when the parents of Jesus were there.

It was thought by the more enlightened among the pagans that at the moment of death, when the soul was about to break the chains which bound it to the body, it entered deeper into the knowledge of divine things. That hope was here realized by the grace of the Spirit. Simeon saw further than Zachary whose vision was bounded by the frontiers of Israel. Taking the Child into his arms, this true heir of Isaias salutes Him who is to bring salvation to all peoples ; for, though He is the glory of Israel, He is at the same time the light of the Gentiles. Yet this light was not destined to penetrate all the darkness.

From that moment the first-born Child of Mary was made holy to God, in the full force of that expression of the Mosaic Law. It is the same expression that is used by Jesus on the eve of His Passion when He says : 'I sanctify Myself on their behalf in order that they too may be truly sanctified.'[1] Now the manner of consecrating a person or thing to the holy God was by sacrifice. But the first-born of men could not be immolated like animals : hence Jesus was bought back from God at the price of five sicles on the day of His presentation. Nevertheless, the day of immolation awaits Him in the future, and the aged Simeon had a foreboding of this. He saw it as the final result of that opposition to Jesus which was destined to bring Him to His death, a death, however, that was to be the source of life to so many others. The Child lay sleeping quietly in His Mother's arms after the manner of infants : hence it is into the heart of Mary that Simeon sends an arrow of sorrow by addressing

[1] John xvii, 19.

to her this prediction: 'Behold He is set for the fall and for the rise of many in Israel, to be exposed also to contradiction; and thy own soul a sword shall pierce.' This was the first deep affliction of the Mother, thus the first to be stricken even while she awaits the day when she shall be made a partner in her Son's Passion.

Ever since the days of Mary, the sister of Moses, daughters of Israel had been from time to time endowed with the spirit of prophecy. On this occasion one of these joined herself with Simeon in rendering glory to God. She was a widow named Anna, born of Phanuel, a man of the tribe of Aser, who had reached her eighty-fourth year; her husband had died and left her a widow within seven years of their marriage, and now she spent her time in the Temple worshipping God by her fasts and prayers. To all who looked for the deliverance of Israel she cried out that the Saviour was now born. These oracles which fall from the lips of this aged pair while they stoop over the little Child sound like a voice coming from the Tabernacle of old. Perhaps they both understood that Jesus Himself was the true temple in which it pleased God henceforth to dwell.

The adoration of the Magi and flight into Egypt (11).
Matt. ii, 1–18.

After narrating the consecration of Jesus to the Lord, St. Luke leads the Holy Family to Nazareth whence Mary and Joseph have come. But St. Matthew suggests that it was between the presentation of Jesus in the Temple and the return to Nazareth that certain other events occurred, and no historian would consider himself authorized to pass them by in silence merely because St. Luke has omitted all mention of them. Our chief difficulty, however, is to explain why Joseph, whose home was at Nazareth, took Mary and Jesus back to Bethlehem after the ceremony in the Temple just described. There is no evidence to provide us with a positive solution to this problem. It may be suggested that Joseph was waiting for a favourable opportunity of returning to Nazareth, or perhaps his turn to be enrolled had not yet come. Possibly he had made friends with somebody who had offered him hospitality, or renewed acquaintance with some distant relative with whom the census had brought him into touch. However, even if Mary and Joseph were still obliged to make the cave do duty for a home, they were at any rate not much worse off there than they would have been in the home at Nazareth. Whatever may have been the case, we are left to suppose from St. Matthew's narrative, which habitually omits details in its treatment of the facts, that the Holy Family was still at Bethlehem when the Magi arrived ; and it is impossible to suppose that this visit occurred before the Presentation in the Temple, even if we make allowance for a stay of a few days only in Egypt. After the massacre of the Holy Innocents Joseph could not very well have taken the Child to Jerusalem without exposing Him to the very danger from which he had been ordered to save Him, as St. Matthew explicitly states.

Who were the Magi ? The early Christians, especially in the West, thought they were priests of the Persian religion, and that is what the word properly signified. But it was also used to denote astronomers, or rather astrologers : for, apart from the great school of astronomy at Alexandria, the orientals of the ancient world had no further interest in studying the stars and planets than to discover the destiny of children born under their influence. It was probably on account of the ill-fame of the magi-astrologers that the Christians were more inclined to see Persian priests in the Magi of the gospel. But Persia cannot be said to lie precisely to the east of Palestine, and it is precisely from the east that the Magi are reported to have come. St. Justin in the second century and St. Epiphanius in the fourth, both of whom were natives of Palestine, tell us that the Magi came from the country on the other side of the Dead Sea, which was all included under the general name of Arabia : and the very gifts they bring lead us to the same conclusion. It was the gifts of the Magi which made Tertullian think that they were kings, for the psalmist[1] had foretold that the kings of Arabia and Saba should bring gifts to the Messiah. Popular tradition has endowed them with a splendid retinue of followers, and has even found names for them : Melchior representing the Semitic peoples, Gaspar for the other white races, and Balthasar for the negroes.

But as far as the evidence of the gospel goes, we are merely authorized to picture to ourselves certain men of grave

[1] Psalm lxxi.

demeanour who strive to read the future from the stars, their thoughts full of the expectation of some mighty king for whom the Jews were then looking. At that time Jewish hopes would be well known in Arabia where the Jews were so numerous. Possibly they often spoke of that prophecy of Balaam, himself a native of Arabia since he was a prophet of Moab, who had foretold how a star should arise out of Jacob and a sceptre should spring up from Israel.[1] Ever since the days of that seer, who was a contemporary of Moses, the Israelites had clung tenaciously to these vague hopes concerning the coming of some mighty royal personage, and their hopes were known throughout the ancient world. In the popular mind the rising of a new star was always associated with the coming of a king, the first being merely a portent of the second event. Now the Magi had seen a new star arise in the east, probably a comet. Everybody would take it for certain that it was the presage of some glorious reign that was about to take place[2]; the Magi thought of the future king of the Jews about whom these Jews had narrated such marvels. With the idea that He was already born, they set out for Jerusalem, the holy city of the Jews; and there, making no secret of their intention to pay Him their homage, they asked to be shown the place of His birth, for they knew nothing of the state of affairs in Jerusalem, having no idea especially of the ferocious jealousy of Herod which made him suspect even his own children.

The Magi seem to be under the impression that their question about the place of the new king's birth could be answered by anybody and everybody; but, contrary to their expectations, it is met with astonishment on all sides and stirs up the agitation which is the general accompaniment of unexpected tidings. The news is brought to the ears of Herod by his agents, to the surprise of the aged tyrant, who had never seriously considered the possibility of such a rival for his throne. It had not been his custom to ask advice of the Sanhedrin, for he had restricted its power to the mere administration of justice; but on this occasion he called together those of its members who were learned in the prophecies, such as the priests and the rabbis, and asked to be informed where was the place in which it

[1] Numbers xxiv, 17.
[2] Justin, *History*, XXXVII, 2; Servius on the *Aeneid*, X, 272.

was foretold that the Messiah should be born. It was the figure of the Messiah that was haunting him.

This question of Herod introduced a problem which was still the occasion of much doubt and dispute among the rabbis, but we must pay homage to these masters in Israel for the way in which they managed to answer it on this occasion. It was known by all that the Messiah had to be a son of David, but at the same time it was the belief of many that great mystery would surround His appearance upon the earth. It was said that He would at first remain hidden, then suddenly make a magnificent appearance heralded by the prophet Elias, who was to come back to earth in order to invest Him with messianic dignity by pouring on His head the kingly unction, for Messiah meant the Lord's anointed.[1] As He was to be the Son of David, He would be connected with Bethlehem by the fact of his descent, but it was not so certain that Bethlehem was to be the place of His birth. There was, however, one text in the prophet Micheas which seemed precise enough on the point, and the scribes quoted it to Herod without any hesitation. The Hebrew text runs as follows :

' But thou, Bethlehem of Ephrata,
  Little in rank amidst the clans of Juda,
Out of thee shall come to me (*a prince*)
  Who shall be ruler in Israel
And his going forth (*shall date*) from the time of antiquity,
  From the days that are long passed.
He shall deliver them, therefore, even till the time
  When she that travaileth shall bring forth.'[2]

In citing this text they put their finger on the one prophecy contained in the Bible concerning this subject. St. Matthew's manner of summarizing the quotation is such as to give us to understand that from this time forth Bethlehem shall not be so insignificant as it has been in the past.

Herod was reassured by the reply, for who among the men at Bethlehem of an age to be king could give him cause for suspicion ? Nevertheless he showed sufficient interest to ask the Magi to tell him the exact time at which they had first seen the star, and he found that the hero they sought could be no more than a baby. It must have seemed to him

[1] Cf. *Le Messianisme*, by Lagrange, p. 221 ff.
[2] Micheas v, 2–3 (Van Hoonacker's translation).

to be all very fantastic, and if he had attached the slightest value to these strangers' theories he would certainly have sent a few horsemen on their track, and within an hour or two have learnt all there was to know. But he felt that he could rely on his own well-tried knowledge of the political situation. His sons were at hand, such at least of them as he had not already put to death, looking forward to the time when they should succeed him: Archelaus, Antipas, and Philip. No doubt Augustus felt inclined to incorporate Palestine in the Empire, but if he left a king there at all it would surely be none but a prince of Herod's house. It did not befit a consummate politician like Herod to take this astrological and prophetical business seriously. With an air of good humour which made no pretence at concealing a touch of mocking irony he bids them: 'Go and diligently enquire after the Child, and when you have found Him, bring me word again that I also may come and adore Him.' He could hardly have pictured himself in such a posture as that, and those who knew him may well have thought that the jest would end in bloodshed.

The Magi set off and within two hours they were at Bethlehem. Great was their joy when the star which they had seen in the East now appeared towards the south[1] and came to a standstill over the place where the Child lay. The comet, if comet it was, did duty for a guide, and the terms in which St. Matthew describes its movements indicate that such was the rôle appointed to it by Divine Providence. His narrative leaves us to fill in for ourselves the details of how the Magi went about their search for the Child; for, just as the shepherds, though they had been enlightened by the angels, found it necessary to make enquiries in order to prove the reality of the sign they had received, so we may suppose that the Magi asked where they could find the new-born Child.[2] Having found the mean stable which served the Holy Family for a house, they saw the Child with his mother Mary; then, prostrating

[1] This is exactly what happened at Jerusalem, January 10, 1910, when Halley's comet passed from East to West. Everyone was able to observe how its light dispersed as it passed over to the West where, after a day or two, it began to shine again. Many of the peasants slept out of doors that night, fearing lest they might be crushed to death. This comet passed through the solar system on October 9 in the year 12 B.C.

[2] Those who prefer it may suppose that the star shone after the fashion of a searchlight.

themselves before Him, they offered the gifts which they had brought in their saddle-bags for the little king, gold, frankincense, and the fragrant resin called myrrh. In the course of time these gifts have become symbolic : incense for God, gold for the King, myrrh for Christ's burial. The good-hearted Magi, however, had brought such gifts from their own country as other countries were in the habit of seeking there ; but this spontaneous goodwill was the occasion of these gifts being raised to the level of symbolic offering full of a most impressive meaning.

It was not permitted by God that they should fall victims of their own simplicity ; He commanded them in a dream to return home by another way. And we may very easily suppose that, having come by the normal route through Jericho, they went back by tracks to the south of the Dead Sea. But there was still greater danger for the Child, and it was not yet the hour for Him to begin His sufferings or to show His miraculous power. Therefore an angel of the Lord warned Joseph, during sleep as before, commanding him to hasten into Egypt with the Child and His Mother on the ground that Herod would seek to destroy the Child. Joseph obeyed forthwith.

It was a source of pride for the Christians of Egypt that the Holy Family had visited their land, and various places to-day claim the honour of having given them shelter. A fanciful picture that appeals to modern piety is that of Mary sleeping between the arms of the Sphinx with the Child in her lap, while Joseph sits watching by her side listening to the voices of the desert. But none of the old traditions on this subject is worthy of credence. As a matter of fact Joseph had only to cross the southern frontier of Judæa into Egypt in order to find safety, and he need have done no more than that for St. Matthew to read into this flight and sojourn in Egypt, followed by the return to the Holy Land, a likeness between Jesus the Son of God and Israel the adopted son of God : for Israel too had been brought out of Egypt, as Moses relates at length, and as the prophet Osee recalls by his words : 'Out of Egypt have I called my son.'[1]

In the meantime was Herod still thinking of the Magi ? His attendants reminded him that they had not returned as he bade them, so he made enquiries and found that they

[1] Osee xi, 1.

had gone off regardless of his orders. It looked as though he had been made a fool of by these simpletons of stargazers, and he fell into one of those paroxysms of fury which have made his very name an object of detestation. Augustus used to say that he would rather be Herod's pig than his son,[1] for Herod refused to eat pork while he slew his own offspring. The tyrant had inserted barbarous provisions in his will which were meant to ensure that some tears, at least, should be shed when he died.[2]

Now it is no uncommon thing to find incredulity succeeded by superstitious terror, as seems to have been the case with Herod. Was his throne altogether safe from the possibility of some bold attempt? To secure that end the slaughter of some twenty infants or so would count for little with him. So, the Magi being out of reach, he wrought his vengeance on those who, judging by what he had learnt, might possibly be his rivals for the throne; thus he ordered a massacre of the new-born infants in Bethlehem and its neighbourhood, and, in order to be on the safe side, he slew all the children up to two years of age. This was a thing of small significance for the mind of Herod who, already feeling himself stricken by the hand of death, was preparing to seek relief from his unbearable sufferings by visiting the hot springs at Callirrhoe on the shores of the Dead Sea.[3] But what a sorrow it was for the poor mothers! To the mind of St. Matthew this was like the grief of the whole nation. It recalled to his mind the groans and lamentations that were heard when the people of Ephraim were carried into exile. Ephraim was descended from Rachel through her son Joseph; hence, when the tribe was carried off, it seemed as though it was Rachel herself who was heard lamenting over her children and refusing all consolation because they were no more.[4]

What adds emphasis to St. Matthew's comparison of these two incidents is the fact that Rachel the mother of Ephraim was buried near Bethlehem, according to the voice of tradition. Thus, as she slept in the abode of death among the patriarchs, she might well be thought to feel a mother's pity for the innocent victims of Bethlehem. And the

[1] A play upon the Greek words *hys*, a pig, and *hyios*, a son (cf. Macrobius, *Saturn.*, II, LV, 11).
[2] Josephus, *Antiquities*, XVII, vi, 5.
[3] Ibid.
[4] Jeremias xxxi, 15.

Church in her turn shares Rachel's feelings by the way in which she associates her with the sorrowing mothers through the suppression of the Alleluia and the use of purple vestments on the feast of Holy Innocents. In this way there is a perpetual souvenir of Jeremias' lament.

The return to Nazareth (12–13).

Matt. ii, 19–23 ; Luke ii, 39.

The death of Herod took place, according to the historian Josephus, a few days before the Pasch of the year 4 B.C., which was the year of Rome 750. Dionysius Exiguus, a monk of the sixth century, was in error when he gave the year of Rome 754 as the date of Jesus' birth, for Jesus was certainly born before the death of Herod. But we gather from the date given by St. Luke for the beginning of John the Baptist's preaching that Our Lord could not have been born earlier than the year of Rome 750 : hence His birth must have taken place a few weeks, or at the most, a few months before Herod's death. It follows, therefore, that the sojourn of the Holy Family in Egypt could not have lasted long ; for, as soon as Herod was dead, an angel bade Joseph in a dream to return to the land of Israel.

Herod had at first designated Antipas as his successor : but only a day or two before his death he changed his mind and gave Judæa and Samaria to his other son Archelaus with the title of king, reserving Galilee and Perea for Antipas with the title of tetrarch. This arrangement was approved by Augustus with the one exception that he would not allow Archelaus the title of king, giving him instead that of ethnarch or head of the nation. Archelaus' first task was to quell a civil war, and he behaved so tyrannically that in ten years Augustus removed him from power. In Galilee Antipas ruled with more humanity, and thither Joseph made his way, for the memory of Herod's massacre of the Innocents at Bethlehem kept him from going there. Besides it was from Nazareth of Galilee that Joseph had gone to Bethlehem in the first place, and that in itself provides sufficient motive for his return thither in St. Luke's narrative, which simply follows the chronological thread of events. St. Matthew, however, who is writing for Christians of Jewish origin, bids them to observe how the designs of Providence are fulfilled even in those things which seem to happen according to the normal course of events. By becoming an inhabitant of Nazareth Jesus takes on the name given to the people of that village. It was a place of no account, its inhabitants considered as people of poor intelligence and held in very slight esteem, so that to call anyone a Nazorean,[1] the name by which they were known, was practically an insult. But had not the prophets foretold that the Servant of Jahweh should be disregarded and even despised?

This last feature puts the finishing touch to the special character the Infancy Narrative has in the gospel of St. Matthew, a character very different from that we find in the gospel of St. Luke. Indeed there are so many differences that at first reading it looks as though the stories are about different persons. But a further examination proves that the two writers are in agreement regarding the essential points: such as the supernatural conception of Jesus, Mary's marriage with Joseph, Joseph's adoption of Jesus shown by the fact that he has the Child enrolled as one of the descendants of David, the birth at Bethlehem, and the settling of the Holy Family at Nazareth. Such agreement as this is not to be explained by a dependence of Luke upon Matthew, for had Luke borrowed from his predecessor he would not have departed so far from Matthew's narrative as to have produced the apparent divergence of which we have just spoken; or if he had done so, then he would surely have given reasons for his divergence. But it is evident that each evangelist has followed his own plan in pursuance of his own special purpose; the two narratives are based independently on facts known to both writers.

The only thing that bears the appearance of a real contradiction lies in the fact that Matthew seems to be under the impression that Joseph dwelt at Bethlehem and intended to return there, while St. Luke tells us that Jesus was born at Bethlehem only on account of the special circumstances which led to Joseph's going there. But the explanation of the difficulty lies in this: that St. Luke writes as an historian who is at pains to give a convincing explanation of the facts that he records, and historical research is more and more proving him to have been right. St. Matthew,

[1] For the distinction between Nazorean and Nazarean, cf. *Revue Biblique*, 1927, p. 498 ff.

however, evinces much less care about the incidents of life which make up human existence : he moves about in the higher plane of that which is right and fitting. Thus, for example, regarding the fact that Jesus was born at Bethlehem, he reminds us that it was at Bethlehem that the Messiah had to be born. Again, Jesus was brought up at Nazareth : that was the fact. But one might almost say that St. Matthew seems to indicate that this had to be so because so it was determined by the Scripture. In the eyes of the critics this gives him the appearance of an author who is quite ready to invent a fact in order to vindicate a prophecy. But in the two cases just cited, which we can verify for ourselves, it is clear that his theory is based on fact, and not vice versa. Moreover, these comparisons of prophecy and event do not imply absolute coincidence between one and the other ; an unscrupulous author, if he wished to invent a fact to fit a prophecy, would have contrived to make his argument much more conclusive. The critics cannot have it both ways ; if it be objected that Matthew has been ready to make any fact serve to show the fulfilment of a prophecy, then it cannot be objected at the same time that he has invented the facts.

Jesus in His Father's House (14).

Luke ii, 40–52.

Jesus returned, then, to Nazareth, with Mary and under Joseph's watchful care. St. Luke never loses sight of that two-fold truth concerning Jesus : first, that being the true Son of God, He is therefore God like His Father ; but also that He is at the same time one of the children of men, and therefore He conducts Himself in all things like a child. With delicate art the evangelist here inserts an episode which shows us that as the infancy of Jesus was governed by this double truth, so also was his boyhood.

The Child grew up at Nazareth, and parallel with his physical development there took place a corresponding growth in knowledge, though this latter growth was of a fullness such as was to be found in no one but Him. All the time God was beholding Him with ever greater complacency.[1] This regarded the human side of Jesus. As

[1] Luke ii, 40, 52.

for His human intelligence, we learn from the sound teaching of theology, which alone can guide us here, that from the first moment of His conception there had been granted to Him the highest degree of that clear vision of God which is promised to the saints in heaven. But His human nature, though united to a divine person, nevertheless exercised freely all the actions proper to itself; nor did this gift of the beatific vision hinder His human intellect from exercising that faculty of acquiring knowledge which is customary in those growing up to manhood. St. Luke is careful to state this explicitly, for without it the whole gospel would be unintelligible and would be no more than a continual make-believe.

He has also given us to understand that at the age of twelve Jesus was fully conscious of His divine origin. The evangelists in no way attribute this consciousness to revelation or to a process of gradual growth. It must therefore be attributed to that direct vision of God which Jesus enjoyed from the very beginning of His life, for by that alone could His human intelligence have been enabled to fathom the distinction between Father, Son, and Holy Ghost in the bosom of the ineffable Trinity.

Nazareth was near enough to Jerusalem[1] to enable its people to visit the Holy City on occasion of the great pilgrimages, especially that of the Pasch, though there was no obligation of so doing in the case of women and children. It is possible, therefore, that Jesus never went to Jerusalem for the pilgrimage feasts until He reached His twelfth year, when Mary and Joseph took Him there for the feast of the Pasch. After the octave was over the group of pilgrims who had come up from Galilee took the road that led back to the north. Now a child of twelve, especially if he be an oriental, is well able to take care of himself; the parents of Jesus, therefore, were not at all surprised at His leaving them at the time of their departure from Jerusalem in order to walk with some of their kindred or with other children of His own age.

Generally the whole journey was made in four stages, the first, which was the shortest, lasting only about three hours, so that there was no need for the pilgrims to leave Jerusalem until the afternoon. But when it came to evening[2]

[1] About eighty-five miles by the present road.

[2] Perhaps they were at the village of El-Bireh, north of the ancient Maspha, or even at Maspha itself.

the Child was nowhere to be found in the caravan when His parents sought Him among their kinsfolk and acquaintances. Full of anxiety, as mothers may well imagine, Joseph and Mary returned to Jerusalem to look for Him, but the day came to an end without their being able to find any trace of Him. Indeed it was not until the third day that they caught sight of Him in the Temple. A group of rabbis were gathered in discussion, as was their usual custom, while their disciples pressed round eager to gather up the pearls of sacred wisdom that might fall from their lips. There were children among the audience, and one of these was Jesus who, from time to time, even put questions to the masters. The latter, as was and is still their manner, questioned the Child on His reasons for asking, possibly with the object of finding out whether He deserved an answer. His replies to their questions showed such keen intelligence that all were astonished.

It is a charming scene, but a perfectly natural one, and much more convincing than the picture of himself drawn by the historian Josephus : ‘ When I was a child, and about fourteen years of age, I was commended by all for the love I had to learning ; on which account the high priests and principal men of the city came then frequently to me together in order to know the accurate understanding of points of the Law.’[1] All that is simply absurd ; Luke makes no such claims even for the Son of God.

Nevertheless, many a parent would have felt very flattered at the praise bestowed on Jesus by the rabbis ; a mother might very easily have felt gratified by it. But Mary's thoughts were all of grief and surprise, and in the midst of this learned assembly she claims her rights : ‘ Son, why hast Thou done so to us ? Behold, Thy father and I have sought Thee sorrowing.’ And the Child, whose replies all have admired, now answers something which is beyond the comprehension of these scribes : ‘ How is it that you have sought Me ? Did you not know that I must be with My Father ? ’—that is to say, in My Father's house. The evangelist goes on to say that even His parents did not understand these words.

They must have been intended by Jesus, then, in a very profound sense. Now a particularly pious young Israelite might have referred to the Temple as ‘ the house of the God

[1] *Life of Josephus*, § 2.

of Israel our Father,' and everyone would have understood what he meant. But St. Luke means that Jesus already spoke of God as His Father in a very special sense, speaking as the only Son of God would speak. These words form the prelude of the gospel. But Mary, though she was perfectly aware of His divine origin, could not help wondering why He had so wounded her heart.

As for these rabbis, who had showed themselves so kindly disposed towards the precocious Child, but were afterwards to prove themselves so hardhearted towards the young Master whom they thought to be setting Himself up as their rival, this incident was but a transitory gleam of light. But for Joseph and Mary it was a passing shadow of sorrow that soon faded in the joy they felt at finding the Child; for Jesus returned with them to Nazareth 'and was subject to them.' He was to be theirs for many years to come, during which He was to accomplish that which was for Him the sweetest and noblest part of His mission, namely, the sanctification of Mary and Joseph. At the same time, they also bestowed much upon Him: but that is a mystery which is beyond our powers of penetration.

Jesus at Nazareth.

It was when they were both about thirty years of age that John, the son of Zachary, and Jesus, the Son of Mary, came face to face. How had their minds been formed during all these early years? What were their first impressions? What influences had been brought to bear upon their characters? These are the questions we feel inclined to ask, but the evangelists meet our questions with silence; and this silence provides what is perhaps the chief difficulty in composing a life of Jesus. It may be replied, of course, that as far as Jesus is concerned the things that contributed to his mental and moral formation are of no great importance in his life, seeing that He possessed within Himself the Light and Life which were all-sufficing. Nevertheless, He willed to become a man like the rest of us, and, moreover, those with whom He came into contact during these years were unaware of His divine origin. We should like to know what conclusions they may have come to regarding the manner of His upbringing when they witnessed those actions which He performed among them by virtue of His acquired dispositions of soul.

To seek for information on the point anywhere else but in the gospels is useless, and conjectures are of little avail. There are, however, two details recorded for us by St. Luke from which we can learn at least something. We have seen how John grew up in the desert, and by that we are to understand that his formation was accomplished in almost complete solitude under the watchful care of God. Afterwards he came forth as a hermit, a prophet in the spirit and garb of Elias.

But it was not in solitude that Jesus grew up ; His life was spent in the bosom of His family and in His own village. Regarding these years we have one precious detail. When He went up to Jerusalem He stayed behind at the school of the rabbis whose teaching He delighted to hear. Taking advantage of this fleeting opportunity, He was enabled to come into contact with the most celebrated of the masters. From this we may conclude that He was in the habit of frequenting the schools at Nazareth ; later we shall see that He showed Himself to be very proficient in the interpretation of the Law and Prophets. This is clear from the gospels, and we must not let ourselves be led into error on the point because of those angry outbursts of His adversaries[1] simply due to the fact that He disagreed with them about the interpretation of what He, like they, had learnt ; when we speak of what He had learnt we refer to that acquired knowledge of His spoken of above. The whole manner of His life, apart from its manifest holiness, was very much like the life of other men of His own rank, except that He seemed to be both a master of the Scriptures and a prophet after the style of Elias.

He spoke Aramaic, which was the language in common use, though He could, when occasion demanded, speak Greek and Hebrew. He performed the tasks of a manual labourer, following the trade of a carpenter, and was doubtless sometimes employed in building. But this was not extraordinary, for we find that some of the most celebrated rabbis also followed a similar trade ; indeed they took pride in earning their livelihood by the labour of their hands so as not to be under the necessity of taking payment for the lessons they gave in sacred learning. At Nazareth Jesus lived among agricultural labourers and vine-dressers ; later on, by the lake of Galilee, He mingled with fishermen,

[1] John vii, 15.

and in joining them in their labours He followed the directions of Peter and the other disciples who were used to that kind of work. From these different kinds of labour He borrows customs and images for His parables, where He uses them with inimitable skill.

If it be not presumptuous to go so far in this analysis of the development of His human character, we may say that there was in Him, as there is in many others, something of His Mother's influence. Where do we find the grace, the exquisite delicacy, the kindly tenderness that we find in Him? And these are precisely the characteristics of such as have had their hearts softened by the tenderness of a mother's love, their minds refined by communication with a beloved and revered mother who has taken delight in teaching them how to appreciate the more delicate refinements of human life.

And Joseph, too, while perhaps he taught his adopted Son how to smooth the planks of wood, did he not at the same time show himself to Jesus as the very model of a conscientious workman and a dutiful son of Israel? This is the last we shall hear of Joseph in the pages of the gospel. He is the man of silence, the contemplator of mysteries, and as such he has no part to play in the active ministry of preaching. Indeed he was already dead by the time that the kingdom of God began to be proclaimed by Him whom the villagers of Nazareth then called 'the Son of Mary.'

CHAPTER II

JOHN THE BAPTIST AND JESUS

The time of Salvation.

AFTER the long years of His hidden life at Nazareth Jesus is now to begin His ministry in Israel. It is as though the gospel were beginning all over again, and, indeed, in the words of St. Mark, it is actually 'the beginning of the gospel of Jesus Christ the Son of God.' However, this is in accordance with the ideas of the period, for as we have already said it was the custom to ascribe a double epiphany to the deified monarchs of the ancient world. Their first manifestation to the world was on the day of their birth according to the supposition that they were of divine origin; their accession to the throne was their second manifestation. Now, it was not until the day of His Resurrection that Jesus was to be shown to the world as the King of Glory; it was fitting, therefore, that He should be enthroned by His Father in some fashion at the very beginning of His public life. Such is the significance of the events which took place at His baptism.

Furthermore, His dignity as Son of God made it fitting that He should have a forerunner to prepare the way before Him, and it is in this connection that we take up again the threads of that divine plan which has already brought together the son of Zachary and the Son of Mary. We hear no more of angelic visitations to those divinely chosen souls to whom such divine communications seem customary. Now we hear a mighty voice resounding through all the land of Israel by which the hearts of all are stirred to emotion.

It has already been pointed out that this land of Israel which gave birth to Jesus and John was no longer united under the government of a single ruler. Judæa had been incorporated into the Roman Empire, the heir of all the civilizations of antiquity. Successor of the great empires of the East, Rome had been more successful than they in setting up a stable form of government over the numerous and diverse nations beneath her sway. To those who lived at that time, at least to such as belonged to the governing class, it might have seemed that the summit of perfection had been reached, and that there was nothing more to be done except to let the laboriously established civilization of Rome spread over the rest of the world. For, apart from Athens, whose beauty and art still exercised their spell, there was no city in the world to be compared to the City of the Seven Hills with her Capitol, her Forum, and her Palatine Hill. She no longer relied on force of arms, but on the higher authority of reason. Henceforth the world, or what was then called 'the inhabited earth,' was to be one organic whole, animated like the very Universe itself by one spirit, a power guided by reason ; and no one would dream of refusing allegiance to such an authority.

No one, that is to say, but the Jew. It would have seemed ridiculous to draw a comparison between Athens, Rome, Alexandria—those cities set by the sea as if in order to send forth over the whole world their commands and their ideas—and Jerusalem, a mediocre city seated all alone on the top of the Judæan hills, looking out over the desert instead of over the sea. And yet this little city had her own aristocracy and her own history. Nay, more than that, she was conscious of the fact that in comparison with her, Athens knew nothing of the solution of that great, that unique problem—the question of man's destiny, of the world's origin, and of its relationship with God. As for the fortune of Roman arms, she was not impressed by that ; and for the divine charm of Homer she had naught but contempt. To her mind the statues of Phidias, with their austere grandeur, were as much to be condemned as the voluptuous Aphrodites of Praxiteles ; neither one nor the other had any claim upon the homage of men in whom alone was reflected the faithful image of God. It was her conviction—and she was convinced with the certainty that belongs to divine knowledge, for had not God revealed to her His secrets ?—that all the glory of this world is but a fragile treasure. It was true that evil seemed to reign triumphantly in the world ; but she felt assured, precisely because the triumph of evil means that disorder has reached its full measure, that God would now manifest His kingdom upon earth.

So far, however, no one had begun to speak in the name of God, in order to resume the long interrupted series of reproaches, threats and terrible judgements which the prophets had declared to be hanging over the heads of mankind, nor did anyone proclaim anew those distant hopes for the future which are like sunshine after the storm. It was hard to endure the yoke of the foreigner, but the violated honour of God was an outrage far more unbearable than the insolence of the foreign tax-gatherer. Why was God so long-suffering? For what was He waiting?

In the midst of questionings like these suddenly was heard the voice of John, the son of Zachary, in the desert.

The Mission and Preaching of John the Baptist.

Luke iii, 1–18; Mark i, 1–8; Matt. iii, 1–12.

'Now in the fifteenth year of the government of Tiberius Cæsar, Pontius Pilate being governor of Judea, Herod tetrarch of Galilee, Philip his brother tetrarch of Iturea and the country of Trachonitis, and Lysanias tetrarch of Abilene, under the high priest Annas and (under the high priest) Caiaphas, the word of God was addressed to John the son of Zacharias in the desert.'[1]

It is a remarkable kind of comparison to put Tiberius, the all-powerful emperor, alongside Lysanias an unknown princeling. We shall not understand how the evangelist has come to do this unless we view the situation from the spot whither he has led us, namely, in the desert near the banks of the Jordan. At the place in question the valley is wide and forms a sort of amphitheatre between lofty hills. There is no other place on the surface of the earth which reaches such a depth, it being no less than eleven or twelve hundred feet below sea-level. Away on the northern horizon stands the Old Man's Mountain, *Jebel esh-Sheikh*, as the Arabs call it, or Hermon in the language of the Jews. In winter and in spring its summit glitters with the sun-lit snows. You would think that the world ended there with this mountain of the northern region where, the Semites used to say, was the abode of the gods. To the south lies

[1] Luke iii, 1–2.

the Dead Sea, its banks sprinkled with pitch and sulphur instead of flowers. It is often covered by a light mist which grows heavier towards midday, the remains, one might say, of the cloud which rained down destruction on Sodom and Gomorrha. Unlike other rivers, the Jordan does not form a frontier: it is rather a point of union between the inhabitants of either bank, as it is for the waters which descend from the two opposite lines of hills. Both sides of the river had been given to the Children of Israel at their entrance into the Land of Promise.

It is for this reason that Luke first gives us the name of the master of the Roman world, the official year of whose reign provides a means of dating other events, and then enumerates the small principalities on either side of the Jordan, keeping Jerusalem on the western side as his centre of outlook. There it was that Judæa was situated, David's own kingdom where the Chosen People, after the Captivity, had renewed their religious and national life, with the result that the returned Israelites came to be known as Judæans or, as we say, Jews. But, not only was that land the very home of the national spirit of the Jews; it was also a country over which Rome exercised the strictest surveillance. Indeed, she had determined to keep it under her own particular care, and at this time its administration was in the hands of a Roman official named Pontius Pilate.

To the north lay Galilee which, with Peræa on the farther bank of the Jordan, was ruled by Herod, who enjoyed a sort of independent sovereignty. But the title of king was considered too dignified for him; he was a tetrarch. This means, literally, one who rules the fourth part of a country, although the title had come to be used in cases where there was no such actual division. In the present instance, for example, we find two other tetrarchs only, Philip the ruler of the region next to Herod's on the north-east beyond Jordan, and Lysanias whose little state lay to the north and formed the limit of the land over which Israel had claimed domination.

But along with these temporal princes Luke names the high-priest, reserving for him the place of honour: for it was the high-priest alone who formed the bond of union which bound together all the scattered descendants of Israel. The high-priest was Caiaphas, a man who owed his elevation to the favour of Valerius Gratus a former

Roman Procurator of Judæa. Nevertheless, it was to Annas, the high-priest whom Valerius had deposed, that men still paid the honour due to the successor of Aaron. Even Caiaphas, who was son-in-law of Annas, had no choice but to show him consideration.

There is not one of these political details that is not solidly established on the firm ground of historical evidence. Certain scholars of our own day have cavilled at Luke's mention of Lysanias, but two inscriptions recently discovered in the district of Abil, the ancient Abilene, have proved him to be in the right.[1] And though scholars are not quite agreed about the reckoning of the reign of Tiberius, still it is by no means unreasonable to estimate the fifteenth year of that emperor as beginning on October the first in the year 27 of the Christian era. It was probably within a very short while after this date that John made his appearance when he began to preach in all the district round the Jordan.

'He was dressed in (a garment of) camel-hair with a kilt of skin about his waist, and he fed on locusts and wild honey.'[2]

The toga-clad Roman recognized the disciples of the Greek philosopher by their cloak. Similarly, a Jew upon seeing the garb of John immediately had a vision in his mind of the most fervent of the prophets. In the days of old the messengers of King Ochozias had said to their master: 'A certain man met us . . . a hairy man with a kirtle of skin about his loins.'[3] The king had immediately replied: 'It is Elias the Thesbite.' For centuries had people paid honour to this ascetic garb; but times had changed and many false prophets had brought discredit upon it and upon themselves also. Hence it had come to pass that to dress in garments of hair-cloth was only to invite sarcasm: it was the dress of an impostor. 'It shall come to pass,' says Zacharias, 'that if there shall arise any more a man who utters prophecies, his father and mother who begot him shall say to him: Thou shalt not live, for thou utterest lies in the name of Jahweh. . . . And it shall come to pass in that day that the prophets shall every one of them be ashamed of his own vision when he shall prophesy, and none shall any longer put on the hair-garment so as to

[1] *Revue Biblique*, 1912, p. 533 ff.
[2] Mark i, 6. [3] 4 Kings i, 6–8.

utter lies.'[1] Thus the voice of prophecy was heard no more in the land, and consequently there were no false prophets to contradict it with their lies.

After centuries of silence the voice of a prophet was heard again, and this time in circumstances which rendered it all the more remarkable. It was a time of culture and even elegance of manners. Near to Jericho was a place which Antony had bestowed on Cleopatra because of its delightful balsam trees. There Herod had afterwards built himself a winter palace. At such a time and in such a place, luxury on the one side and wilderness on the other, did John arise clothed like a new Elias and no less daring than Elias in the freedom of his language. Such was the power of his words that the very desert was excited, while rumour of him reached as far as the towns in the higher districts. Was God about to intervene? men asked one another. Everybody had known since the days of Amos that 'the Lord Jahweh does nothing without making known his secret to his servants the prophets. When the lion roars, who would not be afraid? When Jahweh speaks, who would not break forth in prophecy?'[2] And, indeed, John was saying: 'Repent, for the kingdom of heaven is at hand.'[3]

Once upon a time the people had gathered together when this call to repentance burst forth from the lips of a prophet. It was the whole nation that had sinned, either by adoring strange gods or by mingling profane rites in the worship of the most holy God. Then the pillars were broken down that had been set up in honour of Baal, Astarte's groves were burnt, the sanctuary was purified; Jahweh granted pardon and the people was saved. But times had changed. Never until the days of Alexander the Great had the world seen such a strange sight as that of a people who refused to fall down and worship before the gods of the conqueror. But the Machabees had refused and had thrown the gods of Greece into the sewer. In return God had given them freedom from the yoke of the foreigner and had set them as rulers over their brethren. From the day of the rededication of the Temple, ritual worship had been carried on there according to the sacred ordinances, the priests offering up the daily sacrifice and celebrating the solemn rites with

[1] Zacharias xiii, 3–4. [2] Amos iii, 7–8.
[3] Matthew iii, 2.

fitting dignity. The nation had no cause for self-reproach. Why, then, this call to repentance?

Nevertheless there were a few souls who understood, for religion had taken on a much more individual character even if it was not much more spiritual than before. Men had begun to think more of their own personal responsibility in the sight of God; and the religion of Israel possessed this undeniable superiority over all others, that neither prosperity on the one hand nor violence on the other had ever been able to corrupt its moral standards. Furthermore, it was always traditional among the ancient prophets to lay emphasis, not so much on the question of bringing herds of victims to the Temple, as upon the effort to stir up the hearts of the Israelites to sentiments of repentance and filial fear; and even more, perhaps, they had endeavoured to move them to charity towards their neighbour.

> 'Know ye not the fast that I love?
> Saith the Lord Jahweh.
> To share one's bread with the starving,
> To give a home to the poor that are shelterless;
> If any be naked to clothe them,
> Not to shun thy brother.
> Then shall thy light break forth like the dawn. . . .'[1]

Great numbers of the children of Israel were sufficiently awakened in their conscience to perceive the sense of words like these, and such of them as felt guilty saw the consequent need of repentance. Their spiritual leaders were well aware, and were the first to declare, that repentance was the one condition of all others necessary in preparation for the coming of the Messiah, who was to come for the purpose of establishing the kingdom of God. The figure of this son of the prophets of old, austere in external appearance, carrying asceticism so far as to deny himself the very modest luxury of ordinary bread, declaring sadly his forebodings of the future, the signs of which he saw in the present—all these are traits which bring a smile perhaps to the lips of many of our contemporaries, be they indifferent or sceptical; nevertheless they are a natural and spontaneous expression of the very spirit of ancient prophecy in Israel. All the same, it is quite possible that the townspeople took

[1] Isaias lviii, 6–8. Condamin's translation.

John for a madman. He frightened, stirred and dumbfounded them as he lifted up his voice amidst those barren sand-hills or among the tamarisk trees on the banks of the Jordan, where the hurrying waters of the river recalled to their minds a remembrance of old-time miracles. He was making the traditional call to repentance for the last time before God Himself appeared on the scene.

Much, however, as John reminded people of the past, there was nevertheless something new in what he said and did ; he invited them to come and be baptized. In other words, they were to begin the work of repentance with an external sign which he would help them to perform. The sign was immersion in water in such a fashion as to make it appear that John was washing them. To be baptized means to bathe the whole body. Those modern scholars who are so fond of attributing everything to the process of slow and natural development that they make no allowance for the initiative that comes from natural genius, do not know what to think of the origin of this rite of baptism practised by John. It is, of course, beyond question that the ancients were familiar with the idea of ritual purification by water. Water cleanses, takes away stains and bestows on the body a sort of purity ; and moral innocence is naturally compared with bodily purity. Hence washing is the natural symbol of a return to innocence of life. Repentance does for the soul what baptism does for the body. 'Come, then,' said John, 'and be baptized as a sign that you take God and man to witness that you repent of your sins.' Both Jews and Gentiles would naturally understand this in the same fashion. But the Jews would go further, for they were accustomed to the practice of washing utensils, even food, and their bodies with the idea of putting themselves in a state of ceremonial purity. Being a holy nation, they thought it their duty to avoid every sort of defilement, not merely of the grosser kind, but also every contamination of the soul which is caused by contact with profane things. Further than this they do not seem to have gone along the way of symbolism. The proselyte was washed in preparation for his circumcision. But in the official rites of Judaism baptism seems never to have been adopted as an external sign of repentance and a changed life.

However, alongside those who stood for orthodoxy, certain groups had been formed outside the scope of the

Law who attached great importance to a more perfect purity of body and soul. They were called Essenes. The old commentators imagined that, while he was in the wilderness of Judæa, John had followed the teachings and adopted the ideas of this sect.[1] The modern critics ridicule the idea; but they make a still greater mistake in supposing that there was a sect of Baptists before the time of John the Baptist. According to them, in this sect we find the origin of the Mandeans[2] who to-day live on the banks of the Tigris above Basra, spending a great part of their lives in the waters of the river. The sect of Baptists is supposed to have paid the honours of worship to water, being persuaded that it partook of divine nature and therefore possessed the power to restore to the soul its original purity which it had lost through the body's defiling contact. John, it is said, was a disciple of theirs, such an important disciple, too, that he rose to the rank of chief leader and became the reformer, if not the founder, of their religion; and from that religion Christianity is supposed to have borrowed the rite of baptism.

This is nothing more or less than a piece of theorizing which two different witnesses prove to be wrong: the New Testament and Josephus. We shall shortly see what sort of portrait the gospels paint of John: the portrait of an Israelite who is true to the Law of Moses. It is thus that Josephus also describes him, adding that Herod Antipas was wrong in fearing that the movement set afoot by John was of a revolutionary character. As for the baptismal ceremony practised by John, the Jewish historian tells us that the Baptist made no claim that it was in any way efficacious for the forgiveness of sin, but recommended it merely as a symbol of that purification of the soul which is brought about by righteousness.[3] Here is a definite and precise account of the character of John's baptism which agrees with what we shall see of the Baptist's own account.

This baptism, however, though it had no power in itself for the remission of sin, was nevertheless a definite step in the way of repentance, for it was an indication of that interior sorrow which obtains pardon of God. Moreover, it was accompanied by a confession of the sins one had committed, and this again was something new. To acknowledge

[1] See p. 27. [2] Cf. *Revue Biblique*, 1927–28, *La gnose mandéenne*.
[3] *Antiquities*, XVIII, v, 2.

oneself a sinner, not only before God in the secret of one's soul, but also before him who came forward boldly as the divine minister of the repentance which he preached, was good proof of the seriousness of a man's intentions in turning back to God. When a man confesses his failures in the observance of the divine law, it is as though he promises to keep the law for the future ; and there was good ground for the hope that God would show mercy on account of the obedience men showed to His voice spoken through the prophet, when John bade them perform this outward ritual of purification accompanied by a confession and detestation of their sins. God calls sinners only to bring them back to Him and pardon their offences.

But what of the sacrifices for sin which were commanded to be offered in the Temple ? Were they of no more use ? We know that the purpose of these sacrifices prescribed for particular cases was to atone for crime and to restore the balance of offended justice. John gave no instructions concerning the offering of such sacrifices, or if he did so we have no record of them ; but neither did he condemn such practices. The carrying out of ceremonies and prescriptions was one thing ; quite other was the turning of the heart to God in order to beseech Him to set up his reign upon earth. The kingdom of heaven preached by the Baptist was nothing else but the kingdom or reign of God. Kingdom of heaven, an expression peculiar to St. Matthew, is what a pious Israelite would say, for his piety forbade him to make too frequent a use of the name of God, even of that divine name which is common to all nations. As for the divine name which was proper to the God of Israel, the Lord Jahweh, that the Jew was strictly forbidden to pronounce at all. In Latin we used the expression *regnum caelorum*, because the Hebrew word for heaven is in the plural. This Jewish usage of substituting the name of heaven for the name of God finds its parallel in our own custom of saying : 'Good heavens,' or 'Heaven's will be done.'

It is more difficult, however, to seize the meaning of the first term of the expression, kingdom of heaven, or kingdom of God. In English the word kingdom has taken on a concrete sense and is generally used to denote the place or country in which a ruler exercises his authority. But formerly the word kingdom meant the same thing as reign or rule, and denoted the power or authority or kingship of the king. We find the same thing in Greek and Hebrew, each of which have but one word to represent both the act of reigning and the place where rule is exercised. Hence, in the New Testament as in the Old, we have to determine each time the word is used which of these meanings it bears. Sometimes, indeed, such fine shades of meaning are attached to the word that it is wellnigh impossible to translate them into our tongue. There is no doubt, however, about the significance of the word in the preaching of John the Baptist. He announces that God is on the point of inaugurating His reign, and that is precisely what the Jews were waiting for. History recalled to them that there was once a time when they no longer wanted to have God as their king. It was in the days when Samuel unfolded to them the holy will of God, and Israel then had small reason for complaint about God's rule whether in peace or war. But the people had become discontented when they saw all the other nations round about them with kings of their own. It was the same in mediæval times when every petty duchy wanted to be a kingdom. And though God complained that His people no longer wanted Him as their king, still He granted their request.[1]

What they wanted was a king to march at their head and lead them in war. In the time of David their wars had been waged with great success, but afterwards they generally met with defeat and Israel had often been put to shame. Moreover, the king had not only taken the place of God : he had sometimes taken sides against Him, thinking it good politics to pay homage to the seemingly powerful gods of the great empires. David's dynasty disappeared together with the nation's independence : Juda became a vassal of Persia and afterwards was in servitude to the Greeks, first to the Hellenistic kings of Egypt, and then to those of Syria. From these last the Jews were saved by the Machabees whose heroism won for them the royal diadem. The new dynasty of the Machabees, which owed its origin to the enthusiastic revival of Judaism in the second century before Christ, made no alliances with strange gods ; but almost unconsciously the Machabean kings began to take on the demeanour of secular princes and ceased to be so desirous as at first they had been of seeing that the rights of God were

[1] 1 Kings viii, 1–22.

respected. The consequence was that they had to stand aside and give place to a man of doubtful origin, that Herod whose god was the emperor Augustus, for Augustus was in truth the master of Herod's destiny.

But God had not forsaken His people. Many a time He had promised, through the mouth of prophet and psalmist, to set up His own kingdom. The day should come when the house of David was to ascend the throne once again in the person of one of David's descendants whom they called the Messiah or the Anointed of the Lord; he should be a king like David and his successors, but a king whose sole purpose would be to introduce the reign of the Lord over His people. This promise was an object of faith for the chosen few of Israel. In order to measure the height of moral perfection to which the aspirations of Israel had been raised by a long series of revelations and merciful punishments, by the fidelity of pious families and the heroism of their latest martyrs, we have only to set this ideal alongside the ideals conceived by the wisest men among the more civilized races.

Plato, for instance, dreamed of a state so well organized that moral goodness would prevail; he had even the courage to undertake three voyages to Sicily with the idea of bringing this dream about. But he came back beaten and no longer presumed to feel so sure of his dream, which, in truth, was as incoherent as all dreams are. Henceforth no one looked to the philosophers for the moral reformation of the state. It was the business of the state to introduce peace and good order, a thing great enough in itself and quite as much as ought to be expected. God could have done much more; for instance, He might have revealed Himself as the origin of all holiness and justice, the source of just laws, the supreme reason of all moral living. Such was what everybody felt. But to say with the Pythagoreans: 'Imitate and follow God,' and at the same time to go on paying worship to pagan deities, was the last word in mockery if it was not a use of words without any understanding of their meaning.

How much clearer everything was in Israel! God who had created the world was the world's sole lord; He it was whom men had to serve as the true King. But as men were deaf to His voice, it was necessary for Him to show Himself that they might know Him and in order that He might take possession of His kingdom. This is what they prayed Him to do. It was not until after the fall of Jerusalem that the formula of the Eighteen Blessings was drawn up ; but these words of the prayer : 'Reign over us, O Lord, Thou alone,' had been on the lips of every Israelite for more than a hundred years before.[1] Those pious Jews, then, who listened to John the Baptist, were longing for the kingdom of God with all their hearts. The 'Thou alone,' however, was not altogether sincere on the lips of most of them, for every good Israelite lived in the hope of reigning with God over the nations whom He was to chastise and bring into subjection. They were ready to grant that it is God who reigns and that He alone has the right to reign. But, then, He needs ministers, for He is so far away in His unapproachable glory. At present, it was solely due to the fact that Israel had accepted His domination and had made it known that God could be said to reign in the world, even in the modest degree in which He did reign. It would be the same, and more so, when the day came in which those who now wrongfully ruled over Israel would be brought to their knees. Such were Jewish ideas on the subject ; the Baptist was well aware of it and he could not endure it.

When a crowd of people gathers together it will generally be found that the elements of which it is composed are animated by very different sentiments ; it is the ideas of the leaders which count for most, though as a general rule the leaders are by no means the best of the crowd in all respects. When there is a question of some course of action which demands self-sacrifice, generosity, enthusiasm, and courage, we do not find that they are the most spontaneous, the most sincere or the most disinterested. According to the gospel narrative it is to the leaders of the people that John the Baptist first addresses himself ; to the Pharisees, in other words. Gradually the gospels introduce these Pharisees along with the Sadducees into the place which they occupy in the narrative. At their very first entrance on the scene they are saluted with insult, we might almost say.

'Race of vipers ! Who hath taught you to flee from the wrath that is to come ? Bring forth, then, fruits worthy of repentance, and do not look as if you were saying within

[1] Cf. *Le Messianisme*, by M. J. Lagrange, p. 153.

yourselves : We have Abraham for our father ! For I tell you that God is able to raise up children to Abraham from these very stones.'[1]

His annoyance springs from his desire to save them. The viper is an animal whose presence is unsuspected, but which stings and kills. It is pity for its victims which rouses animosity against the serpent. Now the Pharisees were looked on by the common people, whom they despised, as the authorized interpreters of the law of God. The people had no suspicion at all that they were wrong in so thinking, and were therefore at the mercy of the venom which was contained in the teaching of the Pharisees. This venom, which John denounced, was their arrogance in putting themselves forward as indispensable instruments of God. ' We are the sons of Abraham,' they said, ' and to Abraham God gave the promises which were made for our benefit. The omnipotence of God is therefore bound up with us.' Such a claim is intolerable to a religious man who has sounded the depths of his own poverty and sinfulness in the sight of the Infinite. Abraham, for instance, had put his faith in the promises of God, but in his humility he had cast himself down with face to the earth.[2] But the Pharisees thought themselves indispensable, and such foolish pride called down the chastisements of God upon their heads. Fully persuaded that God could not allow them to perish for fear that He should be left without true worshippers upon the earth, they were about to commence a desperate struggle for supremacy in which they were doomed to perish. Either John had a foreboding of this or it had been revealed to him by God. ' Already the axe is laid to the root of the trees, and every tree which does not bring forth good fruit shall be cut down and cast into the fire.'[3] It was high time then to repent, and the first step in the path of repentance is self-humiliation by which a man puts himself into his proper place before the infinite power of God. From these stones lying about the rocky hill-sides God could easily raise up genuine sons of Abraham, not indeed sons by carnal generation, but sons in so far as they imitated the faith of Abraham, a faith that was both humble and trusting.

One might have been tempted to believe while listening to this violent onslaught that John, hypnotized by the

[1] Matthew iii, 7–9. [2] Genesis xvii, 3. [3] Matthew iii, 10.

threatened judgements of God, absorbed in his mission as the last of the prophets and carried out of himself by the excesses of his fasts and vigils, was going to ask the bystanders to join him in some extraordinary course of action. There was the well-known case of Judas the Galilean who 'would have none but God as his lord and master,'[1] and he had drawn many of the Jews after him into revolt. There were others who either were not ready to run the risk of incurring cruel measures of repression or else preferred to leave matters to God alone, and were content with recommending a three days' fast. Such was the advice of Taxo who said to his seven sons, after the fast, 'we will go into a cave and die.'[2] Perhaps John was about to invite them to embrace a life of extraordinary asceticism and bodily penance.

Such were the questions which must have occurred to the minds of the listeners who had confessed their sins and were prepared to begin a life pleasing to God. But this man, whom Renan has compared to an Indian *fakir*,[3] replied to such questions with the discretion of a wise spiritual director. One had to beware, on the one hand, of trying to anticipate the hour determined by God, which was folly; and on the other, of sitting down to wait for it with a feeling of discouragement. The only thing to be done was to persevere in the practice of charity and justice. The first and most urgent duty was that of charity. 'If anyone has two coats, let him share with him who has none, and he that has food to eat let him do likewise.'[4] In his own personal asceticism he goes without coat at all, and his food is the food that comes by chance. What he demands is not for himself but for his brethren, in the true spirit of the prophets.[5]

But there were certain professions that seemed to be unavoidably exposed to the danger of sin. The publicans, for instance, came forward: 'Master, what ought we to do?' Public opinion would have been quick to give an unequivocal answer: 'Give up your thieving trade!' It was indeed a fact that the publican's temptation to theft was a strong and permanent one. The State was accustomed

[1] Josephus, *Antiquities*, XVIII, i, 6.
[2] *Assumption of Moses*. Cf. *Revue Biblique*, 1905, p. 483.
[3] *Vie de Jésus*, p. 99. He talks also of the *gurus* of the Brahmins and of the *munis* of India (p. 102). Either he is making fun or else he has been taken in by the facile classifications of shallow scholarship.
[4] Luke iii, 11. [5] Isaias lviii, 7.

to farm out to individuals the collection of certain indirect taxes, such as the customs. The great contractors, farmers-general of the revenue as they were called under the old French regime, in their turn employed subordinates whose business it was to collect the tax. These, whether as a return for their labour or else as a means of robbing both the public and their employers, often demanded the payment of sums in excess of the fixed tax. In the case where these collectors were of Jewish birth, they were exposed to the additional sin of defilement through contact with non-Jews. Even the country-folk, whom the Pharisees despised for their ignorance of the Law, were considered to be not so contemptible as the tax-gatherers.

It is true that princes and rulers made some effort to prevent glaring abuses of the existing system by setting up a public tariff, such as we see, for example, in the tariff inscription not long ago discovered at Palmyra dating from A.D. 137. With the help of precautions of this kind, tradesmen were as well protected then against abuse as they are in our own days when taxes are paid directly into the public treasury. But after all, not everybody knew how to read, and it is doubtful whether the system of taxation in Palestine was as well organized in gospel times as it was later. Fraud was easy while supervision was powerless to remedy the evil. It was rare that one found a good publican, and the whole class of them was considered to be a disgrace to Israel. Not to a single one of them, however, did John say: 'Follow me,' for it was not his mission to make disciples in that fashion. He merely said to them: 'Demand nothing in excess of that which has been fixed for you.'

After the publicans come a group who are generally considered to have been soldiers. But although soldiers can easily be accused of violence, robbery and pillage, they are not generally guilty of false witness such as St. Luke attributes to these men who appear before John. Hence they are not so much soldiers in our sense of the word as police agents employed to compel people, by force of arms if necessary, to pay their taxes; or else they were used as an armed guard, either in the government service or in the service of the publicans themselves. There is no doubt that they were Jews, for foreigners would not have been called to repentance by John, nor would they have desired to know whether it was necessary for them to give striking proofs of their repentance, as did the persons in question. To them John said : 'Molest no man ; denounce nobody falsely, and be content with your pay.'[1]

In the days of old, Moses, before whose angry countenance the people trembled with fear, could show himself the meekest of men when it was his own personal reputation and not the honour of God which was at stake.[2] It was the same with John the Baptist. Terrible as were his threats, he was kindness itself to those who were well-disposed ; and the honour that he felt did not belong to him he could refuse with meekness.

They came to him from all the Jordan valley, both those who inhabited the villas of Jericho and the dwellers in tents at the foot of the mountains of Moab. They came to him from all Judæa, from Jerusalem even, where all this excitement was bound to give rise to the portentous question : Is not John the Messiah ? His remarkable austerity could not but strike the imagination, causing people to wonder whether he was in truth no more than Zachary's son. Had he not appeared with suddenness, coming from the wilderness like one sent by God ? Perhaps he had come down from above. It was true that he worked no miracles ; but it was not miracles that were expected from the Messiah so much as the deliverance of the nation from the yoke of the foreigner. As his mighty voice shook the people from their state of listlessness, they could not help wondering whether he was about to give them the signal for combat and for victory. Such were the conjectures that were formed and then cast aside in the minds of the people, and finally drawn up in the form of a questionnaire by the official religious teachers.

The crowd had first of all asked the question about John's baptism : Was not that the way the Messiah would begin His mission ? Was not John himself the Messiah ? He was quick to undeceive them ; but in the same voice he proclaimed that the coming of the kingdom of God signified that the Messiah was near at hand : 'There cometh after me One that is mightier than I, and I am not worthy

[1] Luke iii, 14. Cf. Jaussen, *Naplouse*, p. 324 ff., for an account of the manner in which the police lent their help to the extortions of the tax-gatherers in Palestine under the Turkish regime.

[2] Numbers xii, 3.

to stoop before His feet to undo the thong of His sandals. I have baptized you in water ; but He shall baptize you in the Holy Spirit.'[1] St. Matthew and St. Luke say : ' In the Holy Spirit and by fire.' The mention of fire simply provides imagery, for we cannot suppose that there is a baptism which is more perfect than that in the Holy Spirit. In other words, baptism in the Holy Spirit is compared to baptism by fire. Water cleanses, but it has not the power to take away every kind of stain. On the other hand, that which passes through fire is either burnt up or else is like gold, which comes forth from the furnace perfectly purified. Baptism in the Holy Spirit, therefore, is a more perfect kind of baptism, a cleansing which penetrates to the very depths of the soul ; for the soul, purified by repentance, is like something created anew by the Holy Spirit.[2]

Quickly changing his metaphors, after the fashion of the true oriental, John next uses the work of the thresher as an image of the work of purification. It is taken for granted that in the kingdom of the Messiah none but the just shall reign with him. But how are the just to be separated from the rest ? In the same way as the reaper cleanses his threshing-floor. He takes up in his large wooden shovel the mingled grains and chaff which have been trodden out by the cattle on the threshing-floor. This he shakes about in such a fashion that the heavy grains remain while the light chaff is carried away by the wind. The scattered chaff is then swept up and burnt, while the good grain is gathered into the barn. But the fire that burns the chaff is no longer a purifying fire, and it is a fire that will never be extinguished. This brings us to a complete change of scene, the image of fire, rather than any logical connection of thought, providing the link with what has gone before. Still, there is the idea of succession of time in the progress of the thought : if we are not purified by the fire of the Holy Spirit, then we must become fuel for a fire like unto that which burns up the chaff. Moreover, it is He who baptizes in the Holy Spirit that shall also later on separate the good from the bad ; to attribute the latter work to the Messiah without the former would be to destroy the whole chain of ideas. It is the Messiah who is in question all the time. The scene closes with him, after having opened with a picture of that period of unspecified duration which may be described as the

[1] Mark i, 7–8. [2] Psalm l [Heb., li], 12–13.

messianic time when the Spirit of God shall be given to men.

At His baptism Jesus is proclaimed to be the Son of God (19).
Luke iii, 21–22 ; Mark i, 9–11 ; Matt. iii, 13–17.

'Now it came to pass in those days that Jesus came from Nazareth of Galilee and was baptized by John in the Jordan.'[1]

The Christian conscience realizes the importance of this event, which, however, would have been hardly noticed but for John's foreboding concerning the character of Jesus : a foreboding which was turned into supernatural certitude by means of a manifestation from heaven.

Jesus came from Nazareth ; rumour had then reached as far as Galilee. Son of Mary, the widow of Joseph, He naturally passed for Joseph's son. To be sure no one had ever seen anything in His behaviour which seemed to require of Him the duty of repentance. Men knew Him as a good Israelite, brought up by His parents in the fear of God and respect for religious observances, His piety continually enlivened by pilgrimages to the Holy City. He had, therefore, no sins to confess. But it was the case then, as it is now ; it is not those whose consciences are the most heavily laden who are the first to come to confession. The holier people were, the more anxious they showed themselves to take a share in that general attitude of repentance which would hasten the day of salvation. At all events, such was the reputation for piety enjoyed by Jesus, such the modesty of His demeanour and His manifest sincerity, that John, warned by an interior voice or possibly by some emotion which recalled memories of his childhood, said to Him : 'It is I who ought to be baptized by Thee, and comest Thou to me ?'[2]

Still John does not cast himself at the feet of Jesus, as we might have expected after the things we have just heard him say ; and when Jesus replied : 'Suffer it now, for thus it becometh us to fulfil all justice,' he gave way and performed upon Him his office as Baptist. How his hand would have trembled had he been sure that he was baptizing the Messiah ! But as yet he did not possess this certainty that had been promised him : 'He on whom thou shalt see the Spirit coming down and remaining, He it is that shall baptize

[1] Mark i, 9. [2] Matthew iii, 14 ff.

in the Holy Ghost.'[1] This divine signal was not given to him until he had showed himself obedient to the request made by Jesus. Then, says St. Mark,[2] 'at that moment when He came up out of the water, Jesus saw the heavens torn open and the Spirit coming down upon Him like a dove; and there was a voice from heaven: Thou art My beloved Son. In Thee I am well pleased.'

For those who saw nothing of these things the baptism of Jesus was a very simple affair; it was a manifestation of good will on the part of Jesus, a mark of His respect for John, showing Jesus to be an Israelite who was eager to go beyond the demands of the Law when a prophet of God pointed out a way of pleasing Him. To seek baptism was in no way a thing that was expected of the Messiah. But one wonders whether there were some who were privileged to see the dove and hear the voice; and the evangelists suggest as much without positively affirming it. For instance, the Holy Ghost appeared under an external form; but, on the other hand, there was nothing particularly supernatural about the appearance of a dove, and only those could perceive its significance to whom God had given the grace of so doing. Certainly John was one of these, for this sign was meant for him. He had announced that one greater than he would baptize in the Holy Ghost; and the coming of the Spirit which remained on Jesus after His baptism was the sign exactly appropriate to this. The dove recalled the mysterious way in which the spirit of God had hovered over the primeval waters as though to make them fruitful.[3]

John understood that baptism in the Holy Spirit was instituted from henceforth; he knew that Jesus was the Elect or Son of God, the Messiah.[4] But even though the revelation was made to John, it remains true that these events at the baptism were meant primarily for Jesus Himself. It is to Him that the dove flies; to Him the voice is addressed, according to the accounts of St. Mark and St. Luke. St. Matthew has written: '*This* is My Son,' instead of 'Thou art My Son'; but this slight change,[5] even if it establishes the fact that the voice was addressed to others besides Jesus, by no means proves that it was heard by all.

[1] John i, 33. [2] Mark i, 10 ff. [3] Genesis i, 2. [4] John i, 32 ff.
[5] It is not certain that St. Matthew's reading is authentic, for certain ancient authorities give the other reading in the first gospel also.

Many modern critics belonging to the Liberal Protestant school have drawn a remarkable conclusion from this heavenly manifestation to Jesus. According to them, this was the occasion when He received for the first time consciousness of His messianic dignity, or, as they put it, when He first felt that He was much more the Son of God than other men. Clearly the text says no such thing. If we want to understand what it does say, we must compare it with those other texts which bring the Spirit of God on the scene. There we learn that it is the office of the Spirit of God to set in motion and to excite the will or the intelligence of certain men, in order to lead them on to heroic action for the salvation of the people.[1] It is the same in the present case. Jesus comes to baptism like other men, for He certainly possessed human nature like them. But now the time had come when He had to set about a mission which was so difficult that it demanded heroism even to the limits of self-sacrifice. It is to give Him the signal to begin that the Spirit comes down from heaven. And as He has taken upon Himself the lowly attitude of one being baptized, a thing more likely to hinder the beginning of His messianic mission than to draw attention to it, the voice of His Father comes to bear witness of the Father's pleasure and to affirm that He is always with His Son, His well-beloved Son. Jesus thus receives the signal for His mission, while the bystanders behold Him invested with the rights which He receives from His Father.

This first public action of Jesus gives us reason for saying that He has not come to destroy the Law and the Prophets, but to bring them to perfection.[2] He receives from the last of the prophets a baptism which is no more than a symbol ; but by His death it will become full of the grace of the Holy Ghost. John's baptism called the Jews to repentance ; the baptism of Jesus will be offered to all nations as the means by which, through their faith, they may receive initiation into the divine life of His resurrection. It will be given in the name of the Father, of the Son and of the Holy Ghost[3] ; of the Father who at the baptism of Jesus named Him His beloved Son, and of the Holy Ghost who flew to Him with love. The historian who strives to convey some appreciation of an historical event, by carefully reconstructing it according

[1] Judges iii, 10 ; vi, 34 ; xi, 29 ; xiii, 25.
[2] Matthew v, 16 ff.
[3] Matthew xxviii, 19.

to the manner in which it would have been understood when it took place, cannot neglect the light that is thrown on certain events by their consequences ; these consequences are undeniable proofs of the significance of the events and of their importance.

Even an unbeliever cannot fail to see that the baptism of Jesus was a very important event. As for the Church, she celebrates the feast of the Baptism on the octave day of the Epiphany, for it was in truth the second public manifestation of Jesus, the first having taken place at the epiphany of His birth, when He was manifested to the wise men from the east. As we have already said, this was after the fashion of that time, when it was the custom of kings to boast of their divine origin. To-day we can understand all this better than ever before.

As for the faithful, to them the wonderful designs of God have always appeared manifest in this incident of the baptism of Jesus. There is nothing surprising for them in the fact that the voice of the Father which sounds throughout eternity was heard by His incarnate Son on the banks of the Jordan ; or that the Holy Spirit, who is the eternal Love uniting Father and Son, should appear on the scene as a link between heaven and earth.

Jesus is tempted (21).

Luke iv, 1–13 ; Mark i, 12–13 ; Matt. iv, 1–11.

The temptation of Jesus is not a part of His public ministry. The scene took place between Him and Satan alone : there were no witnesses. Thus it could have had no influence at all on the opinion people formed of the person, character, and mission of Him who came to preach the kingdom of God. In the mind of the first three evangelists, however, especially of St. Matthew and St. Luke, the event throws a certain light over the whole of the ministry, and there is no doubt that this is precisely the reason why Jesus told His disciples of the incident. We must examine it, therefore, in order the better to understand the way in which the task of establishing the kingdom of God appeared to the minds of the first disciples.

In this temptation, which Jesus overcomes, pious minds see a proof of the way in which Jesus stoops to our level, as well as an evidence of the reality of His human nature like to our own. He becomes an example and an encouragement for us. The thought is as profitable as it is true, and is presented to us by the Epistle to the Hebrews: 'It is because He Himself hath suffered and been tried that He is able to succour them that are tried.' . . . 'For we have not a high-priest who cannot have compassion on our infirmities; in order to be like unto us He hath been tried in every way, yet without sin.'[1]

There is no doubt that Jesus gave Himself to be our model and humbled Himself to our level in thus allowing Satan to tempt Him in His human nature. But at the same time, one fact emerging from this conflict is this: that He won victory after a very remarkable fight. Satan had seen Him preparing to establish the kingdom of God, and he was afraid lest this might mean the end of his own reign. But he did not think it impossible to turn Jesus aside from His task; or at any rate he did his best to draw Him aside into those paths which would only lead to the strengthening of the satanic empire over mankind. These are strange ideas to the mind of the modern world. Yet it is a fact that, even after so many centuries of Christianity, evil exercises a tremendous influence in the world, according at least to those who call evil all that is contrary to the will of God. The ancient Persians, and their successors the Manicheans, had such a strong realization of the spread of evil through the world that they conceived the idea of two almost equal powers, the God of Good and the God of Evil, the world being the stake for which they struggled with one another. First one power gained the victory and then the other; so it would go on until the end, in the far-distant future, when Good should finally triumph completely.

Are we to suppose that the Jews shared in this belief, which is so patently irreconcilable with even the most elementary notions of God considered as the Infinite Good, sole Creator, only Lord, sole possessor of Being which is shared by others only in a participated and diminished form? Yet there are those to-day who maintain that the Jews had adopted this dualism of the Persians, making God to be the Sovereign Master of heaven, Satan the king of the earth. But the fact is that the Jews, taught by the revelation

[1] Hebrews ii, 18 and iv, 15, according to Crampon's translation.

which had been committed to their care, had a true idea of God as the sole Master of the whole world. At the same time, however, they believed in the existence of a world of spirits, some of whom were good, others were bad angels or demons of whom Satan was the master. He was the tempter-in-chief, the one who had seduced Eve and thus brought about the fall of Adam. Having gained this first victory, he had never ceased thenceforth from his efforts to draw men from God and lead them into evil. The measure of the dominion which he exercised in the world was the success he obtained by his efforts. Wherever men worshipped false gods, there Satan ruled supreme.

It is not the place here to prove the truth of this belief, which is common to Christians also. To deny the influence of evil spirits, especially in the sphere of idol worship, would put one under the necessity of finding some explanation of the actual degradation of the people of ancient times with respect to all that concerned religion. How else can we explain the tyranny of those Carthaginian deities, whose existence none could prove, yet who demanded that children should be burnt alive? What other reasonable explanation is there of the fact that the Greeks, even during the golden age of Pericles, paid divine honours to gods who were no better than scoundrels, whom their worshippers sometimes went so far as to make the subject of comic plays?

Though these different kinds of religious worship were not all of such a cruel or shameful character, and were indeed sometimes full of a human charm that is beyond compare, yet in the eyes of the Israelites they were all to be condemned, for the tyrant Satan was responsible for them all. Satan prowled around this little kingdom of God, the land of Israel; he even entered it and fought violently for its possession. But it was there that the announcement had been made that God should reign over the whole world. First, however, there was to come one who was to be the means of establishing this reign, a Messiah, a Son of God, an Elect of God, or called by some such name. Jesus appeared to be the one destined to fulfil that rôle, and Satan thought it high time to interfere.

Is there not something of symbolic significance, containing a secret of great importance for us, in this temptation of Jesus which is presented like the prologue of a play in two voices? The scene is laid in the mysterious atmosphere of the desert with Satan as one of the principal characters. From what happens there we may gather what will be the issue of that earthly drama which is played among men; it foreshadows the way in which the enemy of mankind will be defeated by the work of salvation. In a similar way, though the comparison necessarily falls short, Euripides sometimes introduces into the prologues of his plays some divinity whose part it is to explain beforehand the incidents of the tragedy and to point the moral.

Jesus, then, according to the synoptic presentation of the gospel story, is led by the Spirit into the desert immediately after His baptism and before commencing His ministry. Note that it is the Spirit which drives Him on to action; according to St. Matthew, 'Jesus was led by the Spirit into the desert in order to be tempted by the devil.'[1] That remark leaves us in no doubt about the outcome, for it cannot but be that the Spirit will obtain the victory. But there is no hint that it is the intention of the evangelists to hold the devil up to ridicule; at the same time, neither do they set him up as God's rival. His temptations are formidable, but man's will is beyond the reach of his power. We know that as long as the will refuses its complicity the devil remains completely powerless over us. But he does his best to attract and to draw us on to the slope where we slip before we fall. He knows quite well that if Jesus be really the Son of God no temptation can take hold of Him or move Him in the slightest degree. But suppose that Jesus falsely believes Himself to be the Son of God: then is He not already the victim of pride? Let Him be drawn out by a clever question and He will surely reply with an answer that will at once show what sort of power He has with God.

The matter for temptation is at hand. The temptations described for us are only the last of a series of diabolical attacks, and Jesus, like a hardy athlete, had entered the contest fasting. After forty days without food He was hungry. It was then that the tempter said to Him: 'If Thou be the Son of God, command that these stones be made bread.' Too passionate a desire to satisfy a need that was in itself quite lawful, or the resorting to a supernatural power for His own personal advantage, or eagerness to defend Himself in the face of unreasonable provocation:

[1] Matthew iv, 1.

in such ways did the tempter seek to persuade Jesus to display His miraculous power and so inaugurate the kingdom of God merely to get the better of the eternal adversary. But such motives were imperfect : hence Jesus replies : ‘ It is written that not by bread alone doth man live.’

The reply is enigmatic, as the texts of Scripture quoted by the rabbis often are : their application is at first sight obscure. St. Matthew throws a little light on the enigma by continuing the quotation : ‘ but (he lives) by every word that proceedeth from the mouth of God.’ Man must not obtain his food by any and every means : he must first conform himself to that order of things by which the divine will is manifested. Jesus, therefore, gives a blunt refusal. He declines to act unreasonably by making His divinely given power subservient to His own particular advantage, whether it be for the satisfaction of His appetite or for vainglory.

Jesus quotes the Scriptures. But what does that matter ? The devil knows Scripture too, and quotes it in order to see if he cannot force Jesus to show His hand. He leads Him up to the pinnacle of the Temple and, as it were, invites the crowd assembled in the courts to see a thrilling sight : a man throwing himself down from that dizzy height into the Kedron valley below. ‘ If Thou be the Son of God,’ says the devil, ‘ cast Thyself down. For it is written : He shall give His angels charge over Thee, and in their hands shall they bear Thee up lest Thou dash Thy foot against a stone.’ A declaration of God’s tender care for His children, the Children of Israel. How much greater, then, will be His solicitude for the one who is His most beloved Son ! True : but all the same, kind as God is to those who abandon themselves to His guidance, He can show Himself exceedingly harsh to those who rashly demand that He shall exert Himself to prove that He is on their side. Scripture can be quoted for that also : ‘ Thou shalt not tempt the Lord thy God.’

This reply of Jesus was admirably to the point. Yet, after all, how clever the rabbis were at this play of texts ! The devil had twice challenged Jesus to give some sign of His power, and Jesus had replied with a certain air of timidity. Perhaps His caution was nothing more than a proof that He possessed no extraordinary powers. However, since He was afraid to risk anything of the nature of a prodigy in order to prove that He was endowed with the power of the kingdom of God, perhaps He might be willing to accept for Himself sovereignty over all the kingdoms of the world. How limited is Satan's psychological insight! He has no power of reading the heart, nor can he force it to give up its secrets, so long as it hides itself beneath the protection of God's word. But he is so blinded by self-confidence that he makes this proposal to Jesus: 'Prostrate Thyself before me, and I will give Thee all this wealth and glory.' Is Satan not the lord of the kingdoms of the world if he can thus make them appear as if by magic? For the third time Jesus brings His opponent to the ground: 'Begone, Satan! For it is written: The Lord thy God shalt thou adore, and Him only shalt thou serve.' Jesus has not come on earth to reign Himself, but to work that God may reign and so bring Satan's reign to an end.

Then the devil departs, but only, as St. Luke adds, 'till the appointed time'; that is to say, until the day when permission will be granted him to seek the death of his vanquisher by stirring up all the powers of the land against Him. Till that moment comes Jesus has a clear field for His work of preaching the kingdom of God. And now, as a sign that the victory just won was gained in the superhuman sphere, 'angels came and ministered unto Him': those angels who were not allowed to render Him this service during the course of His ministry.

We naturally desire to know what was the place where this fast of forty days took place, and on what mountain the great battle was won. The mountain has since received the name of *Jebel Quarantal*, the Arabic rendering for 'the mountain of the forty days'; and the hermits of the fifth century chose an excellent situation for it on the edge of the hills which towards the west shut in the plain of Jericho like a wall. These hermits kept a perpetual fast during the time they spent in the caves which honeycomb the hill, the solitary summit of which looks down into the valley where gardens form an oasis of green among the desert sands. Over to the east lies the plain of Moab, a vast stretch of country leading towards Babylon, that mistress of ancient empires which imagination pictures to itself at the further end of the plain. In the opposite direction, behind us to the west, lies the city of Rome, which had at this time assumed the sceptre of the world. Thus, in a certain sense it is true to say that all the kingdoms of the earth could be seen from this mountain, as St. Luke says 'in a moment of time.'

One might say that the whole of this episode of the temptation is enveloped in a sort of cloud, so that the precise details are not clearly visible ; but its reality is none the less visible. And it can also be said that the truths most profitable to the mind and the heart are not always those which are most patient of minute analysis.

The witness of John the Baptist. The calling of the first disciples (22–24).

John i, 19–42.

According to the order of the synoptic narrative it is now time for Jesus to begin His ministry : hence the synoptists lead Him back to Galilee. St. John, however, has further information concerning the sojourn of Jesus in the neighbourhood of the Jordan. Ancient commentators were so much perplexed by this divergence that difficulties were raised against the value of John's narrative. Whatever may be said in answer to these objections, they serve at any rate to show that the faithful in those early days were very much on their guard against insertion among the Scriptures of writings that were not fully authorized. In this case, however, the authority of the beloved disciple was held to be sufficient to guarantee the truth of his gospel : moreover, the difficulties raised are such as to be patient of easy solution.

Had Jesus so wished, He might have chosen His first disciples from among those who had not come under the influence of John the Baptist. But we have it on the authority of the writer of the fourth gospel, who prefers to hide himself behind a sort of anonymity, that some of John's own disciples were influenced by the witness he gave to Jesus : a thing that might have been expected. Further, it is but natural that men coming from Galilee should have established contact with Jesus of Galilee, especially while they were under the influence of that religious fervour which had led them to take so solemn a step as submitting to John's baptism. There, away from home, it was only natural that they should attach themselves to Him as a preliminary stage before that complete surrender to His call which was later to take place on the shores of lake Tiberias. It may be said, then, that the author of the fourth gospel has in an admirable manner put the finishing touches to what we may call the period of preparation, consisting in the transition from the Law to the Gospel. The Baptist's witness to Jesus is his method of proclaiming the good news, and there is nothing to be surprised at if his own certitude about Jesus was sufficient to win over his own disciples.

We remain, therefore, in the neighbourhood where John was baptizing. Now Jesus, we are told, was baptized in the Jordan. But we are not to look for anything of a sacred character or for any special quality in the water of that river. Indeed, during the winter season, so sodden does the rain render the chalky soil through which the river flows that access to it is hardly possible; and even were one to reach the river bank at such a time, it would be difficult to enter or leave the water without slipping and getting covered with mud. It was for this very prosaic reason, if for no other, that John readily chose some other place for his baptisms, some stream, perhaps, that followed a more or less artificial channel. One of these places was at Bethany beyond the Jordan, possibly just below the present ruined village called *Khirbet et-Tawil.* It was here that the Baptist was found by the priests and levites, some of them belonging to the pharisaical party, who had been sent to him by the religious authorities at Jerusalem.

It is commonly held that the Sanhedrin enters on the scene here, and that this intervention is the result of an official meeting of that council. But it is to be remembered that we are dealing with Judaism and not with the Christian Church. In the Church, of course, the rights and prerogatives of the hierarchy are absolute. Had the religious organization of Judaism been of the same character, then certainly we should have reason for surprise at the fact that John had presumed to preach without permission. But the people of Israel did not constitute a Church, and their men of God had never considered themselves subject to the authority of the priesthood. If there was question of distinguishing false prophets from true, there was only one means according to the teaching of the Law,[1] and

[1] Deuteronomy xviii, 22.

that was to see whether or not their predictions came true. If they turned out to be false prophets, then it was for the authorities to punish them, and the Mishna[1] teaches that the competent authority for passing judgement on false prophets was the Sanhedrin. But even granting that, at the time of which we are speaking, the Sanhedrin was admitted to be the supreme tribunal in this matter, it would still remain true that its office was merely to pass judgement on the accusations brought to its notice. It is a far cry from that to the notion that the Sanhedrin was a sort of watch committee whose duty it was to keep an eye on the various movements that stirred the minds of the people. On the contrary, it was a complicated organization consisting of members drawn first from the high priests, secondly from those who were recognized as rabbis, and thirdly from the group of the aristocracy, and its authority could be invoked only on occasion of some well-defined complaint. In the present case, the fourth gospel suggests that we have to do with a small group of ringleaders who have taken upon themselves the business of seeing that the authority of their own party is preserved. Indeed, it is the first move of that group whom this gospel simply names the Jews, so called because, as religious leaders of the people, they were its representatives ; and to them belongs the responsibility for the hostility with which the populace regarded its Saviour.

John, they held, was disturbing the accepted customs of piety and good religious order by his new ceremony of baptism, by these manifestations of repentance, and by the precision with which he foretold the coming of the Messiah. Moreover, he showed but scant respect for the Pharisees and had even abused them. What would become of priestly privilege and the reputation of the masters in Israel if every person of no consequence were to be allowed to raise such a commotion, even though it were over such a matter as repentance ? John, however, was a person of some consequence seeing that he was a son of Zachary the priest. It was thought necessary, therefore, to interrogate him in such a way as to avoid the appearance of making any accusation. They simply demanded : 'Who art thou ?' But, considering the state of excitement that prevailed, it was evident that this question was merely the cloak for

[1] Cf. Sanhedrin i, 5.

another, namely : 'Dost thou make claim to put thyself forward as the Messiah ?' With that frankness of his which was at times somewhat rough, John made the direct reply : 'I am not the Messiah.' Then was he the one whose business it was to prepare the way for the Messiah by bringing about a revival of religious and moral life in Israel in preparation for the reign of justice? In a word, was he the prophet Elias come back to earth? Elias, as the Scripture taught, had been caught up to heaven in a fiery chariot,[1] and it was expected that he would one day return in order to manifest the Messiah and anoint him. Trypho the Jew, when St. Justin disputed with him during the following century, was still looking for Elias to return and perform that mission. Now, as a matter of fact, it was true that John had been charged with the duty of fulfilling that mission of Elias ; but all the same he declares plainly that he is not Elias in person.

Then was he perhaps the Prophet? Unless they came to the conclusion that John had received no mission from God at all, the Jews could hardly refuse to regard him as a prophet ; for they were accustomed to receive God's commands at the mouth of men inspired by the Spirit of God, and these men had so often preached the duty of turning back to God, or, in other words, of doing penance. But here the questioners speak of 'the' prophet, that is the great prophet for whom they had waited so long, who was to be charged with a most high mission, a prophet like Moses,[2] the Elect of God above all others, perhaps destined to be anointed as the Messiah Himself. 'No,' replies John, for such a person as that seemed far beyond his measure.

Surely a man like John, they argued, the son of a priest who had fulfilled his sacred functions with honour, a man, too, who showed such boldness in stirring up people's minds, ought to be aware of what he was or, at least, of what he claimed to be. The priests and levites sent by the Jews apologize for their insistence and plead their duty of rendering an account of their mission to those who have commissioned them.

But the answer was staring them in the face : John was a preacher of repentance, and he told them so in words borrowed from Isaias : 'I am the voice of one crying in the wilderness : Make straight the way of the Lord.' He was

[1] 4 Kings ii, 11. [2] Cf. Deuteronomy xviii, 15.

a voice, therefore, announcing that the Lord was about to come along the way now that it was made passable. The ways of the Lord are his own, it is true : but He is pleased to make use of man in order to make ready His way.

Some of the envoys who were Pharisees then took up the enquiry on their own account. They admitted that all good Israelites had the right to preach repentance if they liked : but if John was not the Christ, nor Elias, nor the Prophet, then by what authority had he introduced this totally new rite of baptism in connexion with repentance, calling all men to be baptized ? Beneath this question there was concealed an evil design, but John does not refuse to reply. This time, however, his reply takes the form of an act of homage to Him whose forerunner he is : ' As for me, I baptize with water, and merely by way of preparation. But there is one greater than I, and He will do greater works.' It is surprising that the curiosity of the Pharisees rests content with this answer, for they could not have been satisfied. But perhaps they did not wish to confuse the issue by concerning themselves with this unknown personage, who might, after all, be no more than a creation of John's over-excited imagination. It was John himself about whom information was required, and he appeared to be taking shelter behind someone else. He would say nothing more, and they would have to be satisfied with what they had got.

When John spoke those solemn words about the mysterious one who was already among them, whom men could see and to whom they were able to speak, it appears that he already realized the significance of what had taken place at the baptism of Jesus. He declined to point Him out more plainly to the agents of the Jews ; but on the following day, when he happened to be with his own followers or else in the company of certain persons whom he could trust, he saw Jesus coming towards him and the great secret escaped his lips : ' Behold the Lamb of God, who taketh away the sin of the world.' It was as though he said that *there* was the innocent holiness which was come to cleanse the world from sin. The words he went on to speak serve as a commentary on the scene at the baptism which took place between himself, Jesus, and the Spirit of God. There are some who maintain that the fourth gospel omits all mention of the baptism of Jesus, because its author considered that the event had been sufficiently described by the earlier evangelists. But there is a very clear allusion to it in these words of the Baptist : 'I saw the Spirit coming down like a dove from heaven and remaining upon Him.' It was by this sign that John was enabled to recognize who Jesus was ; and the real relation between the sign and the thing signified shows that the meaning is that Jesus is to baptize with the Holy Ghost.

John had been surnamed the Baptist because he was considered as the baptizer *par excellence*. Yet the chief thing that he sees in the person of the Messiah is that the Messiah possesses a pre-eminence even in the matter of baptizing ; for He is to baptize in a better way than John, since He will take away the sins whose wickedness John condemns.

The next day after that (it was of importance to give the count of these days, and the evangelist here gives us a hint that he is in a position to do so), two of John's disciples are struck by hearing him call out again : 'Behold the Lamb of God,' and their hearts are stirred at seeing the loving reverence with which he looks at Jesus. They follow Him. But He had not asked them to do so, and when He turns round to say : 'What seek you ?' they answer with a certain embarrassment : 'Rabbi (or Master) ! Where dwellest Thou ?' The good fellows knew no more flattering mode of address than to call a man by the name of Rabbi ; for it was beyond their conception that anyone could be great in the sight of God were he not at the same time a doctor in Israel, a master in the knowledge of the Scriptures. Jesus replied : 'Come and see.' They went, therefore, to see the place where He dwelt—we are told that the time was about ten hours after sunrise—and they learnt that Jesus was indeed the Messiah. One of these two was Andrew, the brother of Simon, and we can only infer that the other was none but the narrator of this scene which remained in his mind as the most precious memory of his youth. Andrew then goes to look for his brother, and when Simon appears the Master, fixing His eyes upon him, changes his name to Peter. It is not until later[1] that we are told the reason for this change of name, but we understand even now that this mark of affectionate care is a sign that Jesus takes possession of Peter as of one who is already His own.

[1] Matthew xvi, 17 ff.

Jesus returns to Galilee (25).

John i, 43–51.

Simon and Andrew lived by the shores of the Lake of Galilee, and that unnamed disciple, whom we believe to be John the son of Zebedee, was a fellow-countryman of theirs. After Jesus had thus attached them to Himself it was only natural that He should join them on their way back to Galilee. The shortest way home from the banks of the Jordan for those who dwelt by Lake Tiberias was to follow the river, passing through Archelais and Scythopolis,[1] as far as the southernmost point of the lake. From there to Bethsaida, a fishing village at the north end of the lake by the mouth of the Jordan, it was a few hours' journey by boat. There it was, doubtless, that Jesus met Philip who, like Simon and Andrew, belonged to Bethsaida. Philip is called by Jesus, and he obeys the call with such enthusiastic conviction that he starts his apostolic work immediately by calling upon Nathanael to acknowledge Jesus of Nazareth, the son of Joseph, as the Messiah. The expression ' son of Joseph ' comes naturally to his lips, for he, like everyone else, knows nothing of the divine origin of Jesus. And such a designation is not without interest, for it serves to show that we are getting near the little country where Jesus was brought up and where everybody knows everybody else. Nathanael also was of that district, coming from Cana,[2] which was not far from Nazareth. Cana is almost certainly the modern village of *Kefr Kenna*, about five miles from Nazareth ; we have this on the authority of an ancient tradition reported by St. Jerome. Certainly the village is of great antiquity, for an Aramaic inscription has been discovered there in its original position.

But neighbours are not always the most charitable of people : the people of Thebes, for instance, owed their reputation for clumsiness chiefly to their neighbours at Athens. Thus Nathanael's answer to Philip is the objection : ' Can anything good come from Nazareth ? '[3] Eventually,

[1] Nothing is left of Archelais but ruins ; Scythopolis is the modern Beisan, which was the biblical Beth-shan. It has become famous on account of recent excavations there which have revealed some Egyptian *stelæ* and, chief of all, the temple of Astarte. (Cf. 1 Kings xxxi, 10.)

[2] John xxi, 2.

[3] Cf. John i, 46.

however, he yields to his friend's entreaties; whereupon he learns that Jesus has the power of reading the secrets of the heart, though He shows no resentment at Nathanael's scepticism, as He indicates by the words: 'Behold an Israelite indeed, in whom there is no guile.' But Nathanael's misgivings are not yet banished, for it is easy to pay compliments. 'Whence knowest Thou me?' he asks. Jesus replies: 'Before that Philip called thee, when thou wast under the fig tree, I saw thee.' We might feel tempted to ask what he was doing under the fig tree. But it was surely nothing reprehensible since Jesus calls him a good Israelite. Was he dreaming of the redemption of Israel? At any rate, amazed by this power which Jesus showed of seeing what was hidden, Nathanael cries out: 'Rabbi! Thou art the Son of God: Thou art the King of Israel.' He meant to say that Jesus was the Messiah: but this time, instead of being too hesitant he goes too fast, as Jesus gives him to understand. Turning to His first friends who are standing by, Jesus says: 'Amen, amen, I say to you: you shall see the angels of God ascending and descending upon the Son of Man.'

Everyone in Israel knew how at Bethel Jacob had seen a vision of a ladder reaching up to heaven with angels going up and down,[1] a pledge to the traveller that God would be with him: 'Neither will I leave thee till I shall have accomplished all that I have said.' Jesus declared that God's promise to the patriarch would be fulfilled in His own case also; and the truth of this would be so manifest that the sight of what Jesus was to accomplish would convince His disciples of the divinity of His mission. This conviction would not be a mere short-lived belief produced by surprise at what He was to do: it would be a conviction based on the evidence of His supernatural works.

This conversation, then, was of great significance, and we can understand why it is that the evangelist has made it the starting point of a period of three days, at the end of which we find ourselves at Cana, the home of Nathanael.[2]

[1] Cf. Genesis xxviii, 10–17.

[2] John makes no mention of Bartholomew, always associated with Philip in the synoptic gospels. But it is most probable that he is the same as Nathanael and bore both names. Indeed the commentator Ichodad, who flourished in the middle of the ninth century, takes this for certain.

The marriage-feast at Cana (26).

John ii, 1–11.

The narrative leads us to think that Nathanael conducted his friends to his native village of Cana for a wedding-feast in which he had some concern. Among those friends Jesus was doubtless also included since we find that His Mother had been invited. There is no authority, however, for supposing that Nathanael himself was the bridegroom, still less for concluding that it was John the son of Zebedee, the author of the gospel. These are only unprofitable conjectures, and modern historians of the life of Christ take scarcely any notice of them. It seems to be suggested by the evangelist that Mary had come from Nazareth to Cana, having been invited beforehand, and was there met by her Son. As He had been detained on his way home with His disciples He could not be invited until it was heard that He had returned.

St. John relates very few miracles, only seven in all ; but he has been careful to give a very special prominence to the first of them. The presence of Jesus at a wedding-feast is of itself very significant. More than once in the history of the Church has the false zeal of heretics striven to banish marriage from the Christian life ; such heretics took the name of Cathari or 'the pure.' But orthodox Christians found no difficulty in taxing them with heresy, seeing that Christ had given divine approval to the lawful union of husband and wife by His presence at Cana. And there are many others in our own day, far more numerous than the heretics of old, who want to abolish what they style the antiquated institution of marriage ; they too are faced with the example of the wise and zealous prophet, Jesus of Nazareth. He chose to take part in the rejoicings of a wedding-feast because, in God's name, it consecrates that common life embarked upon by two individuals who love one another, a common life in which they take upon themselves the obligation that devolves on parents of bringing up well the children given them by God. Marriage is an occasion for rejoicing among people of all races and times. In Israel,[1] as in all other places, the principal festivity was

[1] Judges xiv, 10.

a feast at which the two families, formerly not acquainted with one another, sat down together. The Hebrew name for the feast is the same as that for a drinking-party (but without the connotation generally attached to that expression), for wine serves as a bond of friendship when used in moderation to rejoice the heart of man. Galilee was a land of vineyards almost as much as Judæa.

At the wedding-feast of Cana the wine ran short, though the hosts must have saved it up in preparation for a long time before. This may have been due to the fact that more guests arrived than had been expected. Seated at the table near her Son, Mary was foremost in noticing the embarrassment, and sure that He shared her feeling, she turned to Him in her pity and said simply : ' They have no wine.' It was a request of extreme gentleness, and could hardly be called a suggestion, much less the expression of a wish. Hence there seemed nothing to call for a direct refusal in case Jesus did not agree. Nevertheless He does refuse to accede to this touching suggestion, and replies : ' Woman, what is that to thee and to Me ? My hour is not yet come.'[1] Which of us would address his mother as ' Woman ! ' ? But the word in Hebrew usage, and even when translated into Greek, is expressive of honour : far from having the air of unbecoming familiarity, it has rather the character of solemnity. Thus we find Eliezer addressing the mother of Rebecca.[2] And the reply as a whole has to be interpreted by Semitic usage, for this expression : ' What is that to thee and to me ? ' is of frequent use among the Semites and has a clearly defined meaning.[3] Were we to consider the Greek alone we should be inclined to translate the words as meaning : ' What is there between thee and me ? '[4] Not only would that be very harsh, but, if we consider the relations between a son and his mother or the circumstances of this situation, where there is no occasion for a family quarrel, such a translation would be absolutely meaningless. Moreover, even to this day the Palestinian Arabs constantly use the word *malesh*, meaning ' What to thee ? ', when they wish to say something equivalent to our ' Don't worry ! ', or the more colloquial ' Never mind ! '

[1] John ii, 4.

[2] Cf. Josephus, *Antiquities*, I, xvi, 3 ; and Dion Cassius, LI, 12, etc.

[3] It is gradually being admitted that an Aramaic source lies behind our fourth gospel, especially with regard to the sayings it contains.

[4] As Fillion has done.

All that Jesus says, therefore, to His Mother is that there is no occasion for either of them to intervene in the matter ; to do so would cause a sensation, and the time has not yet arrived for Him to draw attention to Himself. It was not His intention to appear on the scene until the Baptist had finished his mission, as we shall see later on. But, strange as it may seem, Mary, probably reading His looks rather than His words, understands that because of her request His first intention is to be somewhat modified. Expecting something out of the ordinary, she says to the waiters : 'Whatsoever He shall say to you, do ye.'

Six great vessels of stone stood there, just like many that have been discovered near to springs or wells in Palestine, of the sort that could easily serve when the Jews were performing their ritual ablutions. At a word from Jesus these vessels were filled up with water, and the water became wine. Such was the circumspection with which the miracle was performed that the steward, whom his duties kept in the room where the guests were drinking, was at first unaware of what had taken place. But concealment was impossible and the disciples learnt of it. Thus was the glory of Jesus made manifest ; His true glory was still invisible, but it shone through these deeds of divine origin. Thereafter the disciples believe in Him, not now merely as a Teacher of doctrine but as One in whom is deposited the power of God. It is the miracle which has just taken place that decides them : Jesus has power over the elements. But they must be still more amazed by His goodness. This Son, who has the power of determining the hour of his own destiny, does not disdain to anticipate that hour out of reverence for His Mother. Doubtless some might think that it was a waste of divine power to use it thus for so trifling a cause. But surely men have no ground for complaint if God, in His condescension, is so kind as to grant them a favour even for the satisfaction of their material needs. John's former disciples, at any rate, find in this incident a higher lesson than that, seeing in the miracle a figure of that great transformation which was to be brought about by the Messiah. In the water changed into the wine of healing and strengthening could they not see a figure of John's baptism transformed into baptism by the Spirit ?

Jesus at Capharnaum (27).

John ii, 12.

The only incident recorded by the evangelist between the wedding-feast at Cana and the Pasch at Jerusalem is a visit by Jesus to Capharnaum. It is likely enough, however, that during this time He had gone back to Nazareth, especially as it is only in passing that He calls at Capharnaum with His Mother, His brethren, and His disciples. As for these brethren of Jesus, it has been the constant belief of Christian tradition that they were not the children of Mary, who remained always a virgin. Later on we shall find them mentioned again in connection with Nazareth. Here the evangelist has no intention of suggesting that they put themselves at the head of Jesus' disciples ; on the contrary, we find later how little belief they have in Him.[1] But for the moment as He has not yet declared Himself to be the Messiah, their old relations with Him remain unaltered. The circumstances of the narrative indicate that the group is on a journey rather than definitely settled in a fixed place : and, indeed, Capharnaum was a natural place of call for Galileans on their way to Jerusalem, for few were desirous of going by way of Samaria. Perhaps, too, we might conclude from St. John's very brief notice of the visit that Peter, Andrew, and Philip, who came from Bethsaida, had arranged to meet the rest at Capharnaum.

We must allow of a certain lapse of time between the baptism of Jesus and the Pasch, for it is hardly likely that He would have returned to Galilee merely for a few days ; nor can we suppose that the fishermen of Bethsaida had already forsaken their nets so as to be permanently with Jesus. The evangelist passes from one incident to another like a giant who marches along by stepping from one hill-top to another. It is left for us to fill in the silences where necessary if we wish to form such a complete narrative of the events as is postulated by the bird's-eye view left us by the evangelist.

[1] John vii, 5.

Jesus drives the traders out of the Temple (28–29).

John ii, 13–22 ; Luke xix, 45–46 ; Mark xi, 15–17 ; Matthew xxi, 12–13.

St. John tells us that Jesus *went down* to Capharnaum, and he goes on to say with equal accuracy that He *went up* to Jerusalem. The Pasch was near at hand, and it was the duty of every Israelite to appear before the Lord to offer vows and sacrifices in the Temple where God had His chosen dwelling-place. From every quarter of the Holy Land went groups of people, driving before them flocks of sheep destined to provide the paschal lamb. Some even drove bulls and heifers intended for more costly sacrifices ; for many Jews also came to Jerusalem from the great cities of the Roman world, such as Antioch and Alexandria, Cyrene and Rome itself, some of whom were very rich and desired to offer numbers of cattle in public sacrifice for Cæsar's preservation, hoping by this means to ingratiate themselves with him. It was necessary, therefore, to have ready a large number of cattle, great and small, for sale to these strangers who bought what they required on the spot, applying to the money-changers for the necessary currency ; from these also they obtained the Jewish half-shekel which the Law ordered to be paid by all as the sacred tax.

All this trafficking was carried on within the Temple. We, who are accustomed to look upon our churches as God's own house, where we are admitted to intimacy with Him, find it difficult to tolerate traders even at the doors of the church. But we are to observe, however, that the actual Holy Place or sanctuary (ναός) of the God of Israel was strictly reserved to God Himself and the few priests who went in from time to time to fulfil their duties. But the name of Temple (ἱερόν, sacred place) was extended to include also the courts which surrounded the Holy Place, these courts in their turn being encircled by an enormous wall. The whole composed what was called 'the house of God.' It was in these courts that were crowded together the herds of oxen and flocks of sheep, along with the sellers of doves and the money-changers, seated at little tables like writing-desks on which lay glittering heaps of gold and silver coin. Moslems who have made the pilgrimage to Mecca and have seen the tremendous *haram* or enclosure with the famous black stone housed in its centre would be more at home than we in such a scene as that just described. The Moslem, clamouring for a lower price when being shamefully exploited by the sellers of the sacrificial sheep at Mecca, furnishes us with a picture to the life of the Jewish contemporaries of Jesus. How could anyone pray in such an uproar? How could he offer to the Lord with a contented mind the gifts which had been bought with such haggling? Nor were the imperfections of the faithful made up for by the priests, who alone were licensed to slay the victim, when the priests also calculated how much profit each victim would bring to them.

Jesus cannot tolerate such profanation. With no other authority than that conferred upon Him by His title of Son, He determines that the house of His Father shall no longer be a market. Arming Himself with a whip made of cords hastily gathered together in His hand, He drives them all out—and they are so quick to take flight that He reaches only the laggards of the crowd that runs before Him—overturning the tables left there by the money-changers with their heaps of small coinage.

So quickly did He go about it that His disciples, amazed to begin with, never thought of helping Him. When they came to think of it afterwards, perhaps very long afterwards, they saw the meaning of His zeal and bethought themselves of what the Scriptures said concerning zeal for the house of God: 'The zeal of Thy house hath eaten Me up.'[1] These words of the psalmist were very applicable to Jesus, who, like Elias before Him,[2] was consumed with zeal, and like Elias He had a foreboding that this zeal would cost Him dear. In fact the Jews—it was those influential and suspicious Jews whom we have already seen interfering with the Baptist—demand of Jesus some sign of His authority in thus upsetting the established order. He replies: 'Destroy this temple and in three days I will raise it up.' As we shall soon see, He was already working miracles, but He does not now quote these as His authority. He remains true to the biblical tradition[3] according to which the sign put forward by God or by His prophet is some future event which must be believed now. This type of

[1] Psalm lxviii [Heb. lxix], 10. [2] 3 Kings xix, 10.
[3] Exodus iii, 12; Isaias vii, 10 ff.; xxxvii, 30.

sign still leaves room for faith and trust in God : God who has time on His side, and in whose hands lies the future.

But we have to confess that this reply of Jesus was obscure ; even the disciples failed to understand it at the time and, indeed, did not see its meaning until the resurrection of Jesus had provided them with the key. The Master, however, was fully entitled to give an enigmatic answer to these Jewish rabbis who laid such claims to subtlety : or, rather, He had already settled that His resurrection was to be the principal sign of His authority and mission. Understanding would come in due time. And the enigmatic form of His answer preserved for us by the evangelist guarantees the fact that later events were not responsible for putting this prophecy on the lips of Jesus; that is to say neither were the facts of the fulfilment copied from the prophecy, nor was the prophecy made up afterwards when the death and resurrection of Jesus had already taken place. The scene took place in the Temple, and the comparison is borrowed from the Temple : 'Destroy this temple, and in three days I will raise it up.' But He was speaking of the temple that was His body, says the evangelist, who perceived this fact only long afterwards.

The Jews, however, look for no mystery in the reply and are only too quick to see absurdity in it : 'Six and forty years was this Temple in building, and wilt Thou raise it up in three days ? ' Further discussion, they thought, was useless. Ordinary sensible people had grown accustomed to the wild follies of the Zealots : was it possible that Jesus belonged to that desperate band ? So the leaders of the people leave their enquiries for the time being, but with the determination to keep Jesus under observation.

When the Jews spoke of the six-and-forty years spent in building the Temple they had in mind the building operations set on foot by Herod the Great in the eighteenth year of his reign,[1] and still incomplete. The workmen were not discharged until the procuratorship of Albinus[2] in A.D. 63. This detail of the gospel narrative, set down apparently without design, provides a very useful means of dating the present event. Herod's eighteenth year corresponds with the year 20–19 B.C. ; forty-six years from that date brings us to the year A.D. 27–28. That would be the fifteenth year of Tiberius, the date given by the gospel for the beginning

[1] Josephus, *Antiquities*, XV, xi, 1. [2] Ibid., XX, ix, 7.

of John the Baptist's preaching.[1] And if his preaching began at the commencement of the fifteenth year of Tiberius, that is to say in October or November, therefore, seeing that Jesus was baptized in January according to liturgical tradition, the Pasch of which the evangelist here speaks must be that of the year A.D. 28.

The three synoptists have put the expulsion of the traders from the Temple during the Pasch which immediately preceded the Passion ; and this seems to be demanded by their plan for they mention but that one Pasch. The fourth gospel, however, goes into greater detail. Still, the main thing is what Jesus did rather than when He did it, and its significance remains whatever be the date of its occurrence. The Son of God in the house of His Father breaks out into a spontaneous burst of zeal, because He cannot endure to see the holiness of the place so profaned. But the Temple is His own house also. True, He had been there before but that was at the beginning of His career. His coming there was the coming of God ; as Malachias, the last of the prophets, proclaims : 'Behold I am about to send My messenger, and he shall clear the way before Me ; and immediately the Lord shall come to His Temple, the Lord for whom you long and the angel of the covenant whom you desire. Behold He cometh, and who shall endure the day of His coming, and who shall be able to stand before Him ?'[2] First was to come the forerunner and after Him the angel of the covenant, the Messiah, who is the Lord Himself.

Discussion with Nicodemus (30).[3]

John ii, 23–iii, 15.

Many believed in the name of Jesus because of the miracles He worked during His sojourn at Jerusalem. But

[1] Cf. Lagrange, Comm. on St. Luke iii, 1.

[2] Malachias iii, 1–2 ; translation of Van Hoonacker.

[3] It looks very much as though this scene is out of place and as if it ought to come during the last Pasch of Jesus. We read in v. 23 that Jesus works many miracles, while further on (iv, 54) John speaks of his *second* miracle. Again, the teaching about the way in which the Son of Man is to be lifted up appears again during the last Pasch (xii, 31 ff.). Further, ancient gospel harmonies such as the Diatessaron of Tatian and that of the Codex Fuldensis place the discussion after Christ's last entry into Jerusalem. But the evangelist has quite deliberately placed it thus early (cf. vii, 50) : he means it to provide an explanation of that baptism with the Spirit which shows the pre-eminence of Jesus over John the Baptist.

the Scribes, who were the teachers of the Law, were less ready than the humbler folk to surrender themselves to Him. Faith is easier where there is docility of mind, and that it is not so easy to find in those whose business it is to teach others. Nevertheless, some of them felt disquieted, wondering whether they were not resisting a voice from heaven. At any rate, they felt bound to make enquiries: they did not wish to give a rash assent to His teaching, but at the same time they were unwilling to condemn Him unheard. But the step was a delicate one, for the religious leaders of the people had been ill-disposed towards Jesus since He had been guilty of what they considered an act of foolish zeal. To take this man seriously would only be to compromise one's self; hence Nicodemus, one of these Jewish rabbis, came to Jesus by night.

He was evidently a man of good will, but, as is often the case with those who are considered to be very intelligent, he finds it difficult to make up his mind through the very habit of weighing the pros and cons and of considering all the probabilities of the case. He was lacking in the natural impulse of simple souls towards the mysteries which satisfy the cravings of the human heart. Most of all is he afraid of being taken in by grand words for which he cannot find a reasonable meaning. There is hence a brusque tone about the conversation. But it is impossible for us here to comment on it word by word; it lasted part of the night, though only its general theme has been preserved for us. But that theme shines luminous in the darkness.

It was Jesus' method to discuss subjects of deep import with the Jerusalem rabbis, while in Galilee He adapted His teaching to the simple capacity of the country folk. Thus He opens before the gaze of Nicodemus a view which reaches right up into heaven, but He shows him only the things which have a relation with man's salvation. The first step necessary for entrance into the kingdom of God is to be born again or to be born from on high: the Greek word used by St. John will stand either meaning. There was much for Nicodemus to be surprised at here, for the Old Testament said nothing about this. It is true that the idea is to be found in the writings of Philo, the Alexandrine Jew who was living at this time, but it is hardly likely that the philosophical speculations of the Alexandrine Jews had reached as far as Judæa. Philo was desirous of attracting the attention of educated Gentiles to the Law of Moses. He spoke of a rebirth that was to come, by which he meant that the soul left the body at death in order to be born again ; that is to say, it became a being endowed with simplicity, no longer joined with a body ; and the soul in that state required no mother, having a Father only, and that Father was its Creator.[1] But Philo had no notion of the new birth spoken of by Jesus, who meant such a transformation of our very inward being, even while the soul was still united with the body, that it could aptly be called a new life altogether. The cause of this rebirth was the Holy Ghost ; the waters of baptism were the means to it. John the Baptist had pointed to such a baptism as the special work of the Messiah. When this point was reached it was time for Nicodemus to begin at least to understand, for had not the prophets spoken of the days when the Spirit of God should be poured out in order to change men's hearts and make them docile and pure ? 'O God !' the psalmist had cried, 'create in me a clean heart and renew a right spirit within me. Cast me not away from Thy face and take not Thy Holy Spirit from me.'[2]

The transformation brought about by this rebirth, though deep within us and spiritual in character, is none the less real. The spirit is like the wind, invisible but none the less active. We find Socrates, the first of the Greek philosophers to insist expressly on the real existence of spiritual beings, employing a similar comparison : 'The winds themselves are not seen, though we see the effects which they produce and we feel them when they blow.'[3] So it is with spiritual things like the soul whose reality can be grasped by the mind alone. Jesus, however, was referring to a supernatural effect produced by the Holy Ghost in the souls of men, such as cannot be perceived by natural reason alone. But as the Spirit is quite free to do what He wills He can make Himself felt when it so pleases Him, even though we do not clearly know whence He comes and whither He goes : that is, we do not clearly understand what He has in view. So it is in the case of men quickened by Him, born of the Spirit : we see the working of the Spirit in them though we do not see Him. Since the action of the Spirit

[1] *Quæst. in Exod.*, II, 46 ; cf. *De Vita Moysis*, II, 288.
[2] Psalm l [Heb. li], 12 ff. ; cf. Ezechiel xi, 19 ; xxxvi, 26 ff.
[3] Xenophon, *Memorabilia*, IV, iii, 14.

is supernatural it follows that none can rightly teach us about it but He who is familiar with heavenly things. Jesus declares that He Himself is the revealer : He knows these secrets for He has come down from heaven. But He reveals only such heavenly secrets as are connected with the things of earth ; that is to say, He teaches what things a man must believe if he wishes to be saved.

If baptism is to merit the name of rebirth it must be preceded by a sort of death. To be reborn in a mystical fashion a man must really die, though not by a death that consists in the separation of body and soul. The new life of the Christian, which he will live while continuing his existence on this earth, is to be the beginning of a life that is divine preceded by a mystical death, a death brought about by union through faith with the death of Christ. St. Paul was to explain this more fully in the time to come ; all that Jesus does at present is to give Nicodemus a glimpse of the fate that awaited the Son of Man, who is no other than Jesus Himself, the Revealer. He must be lifted up. This might be thought to signify His return to heaven whence He has come ; but no : He is to be lifted up like the brazen serpent in the desert, fastened to a stake : ' Whoever being struck (by a serpent) shall look upon it, he shall live,'[1] provided, however, that he puts his trust in God who has willed to heal him by this sign. So, when the Son of Man is lifted up in that manner—by this was meant the Crucifixion—eternal life shall be to them that believe in Him.

These different stages of the supernatural life, hitherto unknown to men, were thus revealed to Nicodemus : birth by means of baptism and the Holy Ghost, along with belief in Him who has come down from heaven, these things lead men to life with God. But this was only to sow the first seed in the mind of one who was Himself a teacher. Nicodemus was a master in Israel, and it was his business to try to fathom these words and to ask for further enlightenment if he did not fully understand. He held his peace : perhaps dawn was now breaking and he did not wish to be seen by others. Everything, however, points to the conclusion that on this night light began to dawn upon him.

The evangelist evidently sees in this discussion with Nicodemus a welding of the New Testament on to the Old by means of the doctrine of the Spirit. Was it not while

[1] Numbers xxi, 8.

speaking to Nicodemus of the Spirit that Jesus had said to him: 'Art thou a master in Israel, and knowest not these things?' Jesus was conscious of borrowing from no other source than the Scriptures. Was it not from Israel, through the revelation given to John the Baptist, that had come knowledge about the Spirit bestowed at baptism? Based, then, on these foundations, the mystery of spiritual birth and spiritual life was revealed by the authority of the Son of Man, from that time forward the Author of our faith.

But there are many critics of the gospel who declare as a certainty that the doctrine of baptismal rebirth or regeneration has been borrowed from the pagan mystery religions. It is a mere commonplace among scholars of the science of comparative religions that the rite of initiation into these mysteries was held to be a regeneration, a birth into a new and divine life. No one, however, ventures to pretend that this was the meaning of initiation into the ancient Greek mysteries, for they had so little connection with any question of moral betterment that Socrates refused to be initiated precisely on that account. And it is hardly likely that the comparison of initiation to moral reformation originated in the mystery religions of the East. The principal of these were the mysteries of Cybele and of Attis, and they were of so vile a character that for a long time the authorities were reluctant to countenance them in Rome.

These scholars ought to take account of the unquestionable fact that, in theory at least, the morality of the ancient philosophers was of a higher order than that of the pagan religious sanctuaries: and if any notion of a better life attached to initiation this was due to the influence of philosophy. Instead of borrowing from the mystery religions Seneca led the way for them when he described the change wrought in himself due to a sudden strong resolution.[1] And though he calls it a transfiguration or transformation, there is nothing to be surprised at in his use of this word considering how much talk there was at the time about the process of metamorphosis; the word transfiguration in his

[1] Seneca, *Epist. IV*: '*Intellego, Lucili, non emendari me tantum sed transfigurari*. I feel myself not merely changed but transformed.' What was changed was his resolve; he understands what a lot there is for him to do: *nec hoc promitto jam aut spero, nihil in me superesse quod mutandum sit*. He would like to explain this sudden change to Lucilius: *tam subitam mutationem*, but he cannot. All this is merely the reflections of a philosopher and has nothing to do with the mysteries.

mouth has nothing of the sublime meaning attached to it since the Transfiguration of Christ. About the beginning of the Roman Empire those mystery rites, by which it was intended that certain privileged persons should be brought into union with the deities whose business it was thenceforward to take care of their welfare, were also given the signification of moral renovation ; but again this was due to the influence of the philosophers. These rites represented the initiated person joining the society of the goddesses after death ; thus initiation had come to be looked on as a sort of rebirth following upon death. But no mention of this has been discovered, in spite of the most persistent research, in any writing earlier than that of Apuleius, dating from about A.D. 150 ;[1] and there, in a work that shocks even those who make no claim to moral fastidiousness, we find only a meagre resemblance between its doctrine of regeneration and the mystical reality of rebirth which is represented by the New Testament in so clear and definite a manner. In fact the only intention of the pagan author has been to give an air of charm to his grossness by clothing it in the deceptive garb of a false mysticism.

Far from the expression ' born anew ' or ' reborn ' being reserved to denote the state of a person after initiation, we find that Apuleius first uses it of the occasion when his hero, having been changed by metamorphosis into an ass, is by the favour of Isis changed back into human form.[2] He speaks of him as now ' in some sort born anew ' although he has not yet received the rite of initiation : he is merely betrothed, as it were, to the service of the sanctuary—a new metaphor which Apuleius considers as appropriate as the former one. When at last he is initiated he is again ' in some sort born anew,' and it is here that the author explains the comparison.[3] At the moment when the mysteries are revealed to the one being initiated he is considered to be standing at the gates of death : he s dead by a sort of fiction, and it is for this reason that it is safe to entrust him with the secret, for the dead speak no more. But at the same time, and by a similar fiction, he is considered to be

[1] Metamorphoses, XI, 6. The people cry : ' *Hunc omnipotentis hodie deæ numen augustum reformavit ad homines* (has restored him to his human form) : *felix hercules et ter beatus qui vitæ scilicet præcedentis innocentia fideque meruerit tam præclarum de cœlo patrocinium, ut renatus quodam modo statim sacrorum obsequio desponderetur.*'

[2] Ibid., XI, 16. [3] Metamorphoses, XI, 21.

saved from death by the mercy of the goddess. Nevertheless this salvation or restoration to health is of an uncertain nature, says Apuleius; it lasts but a moment, and hence the initiated one must run the race of salvation all over again. In all this we see the manner in which this African writer, fifty years later than St. John's gospel, fumbles about until at last he finds suitable words to express his meaning: the man who again receives his human form after having been changed into an ass is, as it were, born again, and so is the man who is considered to be dead as a preliminary to initiation. Moreover, Apuleius is speaking only of the mysteries of Isis; there is no sign of the use of this expression at so early a date in the other mystery rites.

It is also to be particularly observed that in St. John the comparison denoted by the expression 'born again,' an expression which is so clearly defined and reappears more than once in the pages of the New Testament,[1] is a comparison between two different forms of life, the life of this world and that spiritual life which is divine. To those who are of the faith it is evident that the latter form of life is necessarily more perfect than the other; but of this there is no sign in the mystery religions. No promise is there made that the one who is initiated will receive a new share of divine being; the mysteries merely consecrate him to the tutelary deities. Not even by way of metaphor does Apuleius say that initiation turns this hero Lucius into the goddess's son: Lucius is, and remains, the son of the priest who accepts him as partner in the service of the goddess, the mistress of them both.

In conclusion, then, we may say that a doctrine like that of the gospel, so definite and so rich, with such well-defined origins and such immense fruits, cannot be explained by making it dependent on a number of vague symbolic rites, unconnected with one another and unproductive of any fruit in the form of spiritual life. That is the essential thing, the life of the spirit, and it was a thing unknown to the mystery religions: the teaching and the death of Jesus have revealed it. There is matter for nothing but mere literary curiosity in the similarity of metaphorical expressions found in writings which owe their origin to such different principles as the religion of Christ and the mystery religions.

[1] Titus iii, 5; 1 Peter i, 3; 1 John iii.

The Baptist's last witness to Jesus (32).

John iii, 22–30.

St. John, the only one of the evangelists to tell us what Jesus did before officially commencing His ministry of preaching, now says that He came into the land of Juda along with His first disciples. As a matter of fact He was already in Judæa, since He was at Jerusalem, its capital; but now we find Him going to some unnamed place in that country. As He baptized in that place it must have been somewhere in the Jordan valley, not far from the spot given by the evangelist as the scene of the first baptisms; otherwise St. John would surely have told us that it was a different place. But it was John who had gone to another place, as the gospel expressly states: 'he was baptizing at Ennon, near Salim.' Ennon or Ainon, according to an ancient tradition, preserved for us by Eusebius who was bishop of Cæsarea in Palestine at the beginning of the fourth century, was about eight miles south of Scythopolis, the modern Beisan. In that neighbourhood are still to be seen a number of pools, natural or artificial, particularly near *ed-Deir*, where the ruins of a Byzantine church doubtless mark the site of Ennon.[1] Ainon, in the Aramaic tongue spoken by Jesus, signifies 'fountains.' A place now called *Tell-Sarem*, about four miles to the north, evidently represents the name of Salem. We have here a sign of the care shown by the evangelist to establish his facts.

John and Jesus could not have been very far apart,[2] for we are told that John's disciples took offence when they heard what the disciples of Jesus were doing. With singular simplicity the evangelist first of all says that Jesus was baptizing, and then proceeds to correct it by saying that it was not He but His disciples who did the baptizing.[3] He clearly relies on the intelligence of the reader to seize his meaning which, after all, is plain enough; in other words, Jesus merely by His presence allowed or authorized others to baptize, although He Himself did not administer baptism. This is enough to suggest to a reader of intelligence

[1] Cf. *Revue Biblique*, 1895, pp. 506 ff., and 1913, p. 223.

[2] It is surprising to find M. Fouard supposing that Jesus is now in Idumæa. He relies for that on Mark iii, 8.

[3] Cf. iii, 22 and iv, 2.

that the baptism which Jesus was to give, that is baptism with the Holy Ghost, has not yet been inaugurated. Baptism with the Spirit clearly supposes the gift of the Spirit, and the Spirit had not yet been bestowed;[1] nor could baptism mean initiation into a new life before the Christian had been united to Christ's death on the cross.

It is not difficult to gather what the author of the fourth gospel wishes to convey by means of these allusions which, though not very explicit, are still perfectly coherent. If Jesus had already instituted His baptism in the Spirit then there would have been no occasion for John to go on administering his own type of baptism. Yet in fact John was not to lay down the mission he had received until the Messiah gave him the sign to do so; he showed no dissatisfaction, however, when he saw some of his disciples turning towards Jesus. As for Jesus Himself, at present He left His own disciples free to gather together such new recruits as showed themselves disposed to learn His teaching and willing to become disciples themselves when He should call them to follow Him. Such must have been the character of this transitional stage of the gospel history. The author of the fourth gospel is often accused of substituting a Divine Word of transcendent character in place of the altogether human Jesus depicted for us by the synoptists: yet it is he who has preserved for us this picture of Jesus following a course of action which, though it can hardly be called tentative because it is so consistent, yet conveys at least an atmosphere of caution. At any rate, there is nothing of brilliant display about it.

But in spite of the way in which Jesus refrained from beginning more completely his own mission, in spite of the humble docility with which the Baptist awaited the sign for his own to cease, a clash arose owing to certain remarks made by one of the Jews on the subject of purification, remarks which the disciples of John could not tolerate. We cannot be sure whether the question was about the ceremony of baptism or about the reason of those ceremonial purifications to which the Jews thought themselves obliged. This Jew made a show of zeal and claimed to speak on behalf of Jesus, though in truth he had not understood what was the spirit of Jesus. But at any rate John's disciples hold Jesus responsible, seeing in Him one who has put

[1] John vii, 39.

Himself up as a rival of their master and has been guilty of the fault of drawing to Himself more followers than John. It seemed to them ungrateful on His part to draw followers from the very man who had borne witness to Him. It is the very loyalty of John's disciples which leads them astray. But if John, being only the forerunner of the Messiah, had borne witness to Him, was that not a sign that he was ready to confine himself to the part that had been committed to him by God? They do not recognize their master's true greatness. That zealous soul, with his austere but loving heart, could not rest content with a mere melancholy resignation at having to give way before Jesus. His own decline makes him thrill with joy, for after all is he not the friend of the Bridegroom? Now that he has heard the voice of the Bridegroom his soul overflows with gladness.

Painted as it were with one stroke of the brush, but a stroke inspired with divine love, there is here presented to us the picture of the Divine Bridegroom joined to a mysterious bride in a marriage that outstrips description. In the past God had testified to His love for Israel, likening His covenant with her to a betrothal that should be followed by an everlasting union. But the virgin daughter of Juda, chosen out of thousands, had proved herself unfaithful; the tender-hearted prophet Osee had felt in his heart and even in his flesh the sorrow of the Heavenly Bridegroom who had been betrayed by her. God had repudiated the guilty woman. What, then, is the meaning of this new marriage bond? Is it now the human race that the Messiah seeks to wed? John the Baptist does not say, and perhaps he does not know; all he knows is that the Bridegroom is here and that he is the friend of the Bridegroom. All attention, therefore, must be fixed on the Bridegroom, and John joyfully withdraws into the background.

CHAPTER III

THE MINISTRY IN GALILEE

I. JESUS DEPARTS FROM JUDÆA AND PREACHES IN GALILEE

John is thrown into prison ; Jesus begins His ministry (35).

Luke iv, 14 ; Mark i, 14 ; Matthew iv, 12 ; John iv, 1–3.

WE do not know whether, even after these words of John, his disciples were able to understand what was in their master's mind. If some of them did understand, then they showed it by following Jesus, at least after John's death ; but we cannot help admiring those of his disciples who remained faithful to him while he was in prison. Some of them seem not to have been affected by the preaching of the gospel—perhaps they had already quitted Palestine—and it was only later at Ephesus that they received the baptism of the Holy Spirit.[1]

John had very soon been cast into prison by Herod Antipas, the tetrarch of Galilee, and it was from his prison cell that he sent forth that cry of great tenderness with which he set the seal upon his mission. But we shall return to this later when we come to speak of his martyrdom. The Pharisees, who as a body felt little sympathy with John's preaching, were relieved to think that his troublesome outbursts of fervour were finished with ; but they very soon found out that now Jesus was becoming the centre of increasing excitement. Hence from their point of view things were no better : indeed, judging by the scene which had recently taken place in the Temple, things seemed to be worse. Jesus now returned to Galilee along with a few disciples who had come with Him on pilgrimage to Jerusalem ; He had no desire to throw Himself in the way of the Pharisees and their plots. Moreover, now that John was removed, the time had come for Him to begin preaching the kingdom of God on His own account in the land of Galilee.

[1] Acts xix, 1–7.

The woman of Samaria (36).

John iv, 4–42.

If He was to avoid irritating the Pharisees, Jesus could not return home by way of Jerusalem. He might have followed the same route as once before and reached the shores of the lake of Galilee by going back along the Jordan. However, some reason unknown to us led Him to join the road from Jerusalem to Nazareth at a place not far from the present town of Nablus.[1] The Paschal feast was now over, hence the Samaritans were no longer on the look-out for Jewish pilgrims whom they were in the habit of molesting; moreover, Jesus and His companions would come up from the Jordan either by way of Aqrabeh or else along the Wady Farah, and so reach the hostile city from the east. No one expected Jews to come from that direction. In order to see the meaning of certain incidents that took place during this stay of Jesus among the Samaritans it is necessary for us to call to mind the history of their quarrel with the Jews of Jerusalem.

The kingdom of Israel, which became the enemy of the kingdom of Juda after the schism of the tribes, chose Samaria for its capital. King Omri showed great genius in choosing for the site of this city an isolated hill, never built on before, which provided a very strong position.[2] The city was rebuilt by Herod after the Roman style and renamed Sebaste (in Latin Augusta) in honour of Augustus, and it goes by the name of Sebastiyeh to this day. But although the name of the city was changed, the country still went by the name of the Land of the Samaritans. The nationalist and orthodox Jews of Jerusalem manifested a profound contempt for these Samaritans whom they did not consider as true Israelites; and, indeed, they were descended for the most part from non-Israelite colonists settled there by the Assyrian conquerors of the country, chiefly by Esarhaddon. These colonists had brought their own gods with them. Still they had been influenced in some degree by the

[1] Almost completely destroyed by the earthquake of July 11, 1927. For an account of this city see *Revue Biblique*, 1923, pp. 120 ff., and P. Jaussen's *Naplouse*.

[2] The recent excavations have verified this.

Israelite element that had remained in the country. First of all, it was a universal law in the ancient world that a man had to pay homage to the god of the land in which he dwelt, and further, as is often the case, the new-comers had begun to take pride in a strong attachment to their new home and to the customs of the country.[1] Hence after the return of the Jews from captivity in Babylon the Samaritans had expressed a desire to contribute towards the rebuilding of the Temple; the returned exiles had refused their offer. But as they worshipped the same God as the Jews, even though they showed themselves hostile to the religious authorities at Jerusalem, these Samaritans could not be regarded merely as Gentiles; they were considered as schismatics. An example of the lengths to which such religious hatred as this can go is shown to us in the case of those orthodox Greeks who, before the fall of Constantinople, chose Mohammedanism rather than submit to the Papacy.

The enmity between the Samaritans and Jerusalem came to a head when the priest Manasses, whom the hierarchy at Jerusalem had expelled from the Temple, took refuge in Samaria and set up there a rival altar.[2] In opposition to Mount Sion he established the sanctuary on Mount Garizim. This hill, rising alongside Mount Ebal, looks towards the south over a narrow, well-watered and very fertile valley, through which runs the direct road between Galilee and Judæa. In this valley, which was protected on the east by the ancient city of Sichem, the Samaritan sect had established its centre, especially as Samaria had been destroyed by the Jewish prince Hyrcanus in 128 B.C. It was later rebuilt by Herod as a pagan city. In that locality religion could be linked up with the very ancient stories of the time of the Judges, when Abimelech, king of Sichem, was the chief prince of Israel: with the stories of the patriarchs, too, for Jacob had given his son Joseph a piece of land near Sichem.[3] From the top of Mount Garizim can be seen a wide view: the modern town of Nablus, the site of the altar on Mount Ebal where Josue promulgated the Law,[4] the ruins of Sichem down in the plain, the village of Askar, the

[1] For an account of the Samaritans during the Persian period see the Assouan papyri, edited by Sachau.

[2] Cf. Josephus, *Antiquities*, XI, viii, 2.

[3] Genesis xxxiii, 19 and xlviii, 22.

[4] Cf. *Revue Biblique*, 1926, pp. 98 ff.

tomb of Joseph and Jacob's well,[1] the plain of Mahneh, and the mountains that shut off Jerusalem to the south.

In choosing this route, therefore, for His journey to Nazareth from that part of the Jordan valley which lay within the bounds of Judæa, Jesus had to pass through Samaria. The road that comes up by Aqrabeh emerges from the hills at the south of a rich plain covered by fields of waving corn in the spring-time, and crosses it diagonally as far as Jacob's well. From there the travellers could see the ruins of Sichem a short distance to the north. The ancient city had for a long time been in a state of ruin, and about the time of the Seleucids its site had been moved to the valley that lies between Ebal and Garizim. During the reign of Vespasian it had taken the new name of Flavia Neapolis in honour of the emperor, and thus has become the modern Nablus. But recent excavations have shown that the old site of Sichem[2] was still occupied during the period of the Roman domination of Palestine, though the ancient city at that time went by the name of Sichora, for it can be taken as certain that the Sychar of the gospel is the more recent Aramaic form of the ancient name of Sichem.

As the travellers approached the little town of Sychar they came across a well at the roadside. Jesus was tired and sat down on the edge of the well to rest His weary limbs after the climb from the valley, while His disciples went to the town to find food. This detail is preserved for us by the writer who speaks of Jesus as the Word, the Son of the Father, who is God like His Father; but the same writer knows that Jesus has taken upon Himself all that capacity for suffering which is the common lot of humanity. He is tired out and thirsty.

About midday a woman comes to draw water. There is nothing strange in that if she dwelt at Sychar, the ancient

[1] Renan, *Vie de Jésus*, Appendix, p. 493: 'The topography of vv. 3–6 is very satisfactory. Only a Jew of Palestine who had often entered the vale of Sichem that way could have written it.'

[2] I have expressed the contrary opinion in my commentary on the Gospel of St. John, but the excavations of Sellin and Welter at Sichem in 1927 have proved that I was wrong, and have solved all the difficulties that I raised in the commentary. As the Samaritan woman lived quite near to the well she would come there for water. The name Sychar, later changed to Askar, was transferred to a hamlet about half a mile east of the ruins of Sichem after that site had been completely abandoned. There is a well at Askar near which people built their houses.

Sichem, which was about two hundred yards away and had no water of its own. As this Samaritan woman lowers her pitcher into the well Jesus begs her to give Him a drink. No one would refuse such a small service as that, and the woman does not think of saying no. But she wants to show that she recognizes the speaker as a Jew and that she is going to do Him a favour. How comes it that He, a Jew, is so different from His proud and contemptuous countrymen that He deigns to ask for water from a Samaritan woman ?

Jesus is not pleased at the somewhat jesting, yet aggressive, tone in which the woman speaks. She thinks Him but a narrow-minded Jew ; yet there was He, able in His greatness and generosity to bestow on her living water. Did she but realize who it was with whom she had to do *she* would be the one to beg.

The woman is provoked to reply. Where was He to get living (i.e. running) water, seeing that He had not even a vessel with which to draw water from this deep well ? Was He able to make water spring up from the ground and thus show Himself to be mightier than Jacob, ' our father Jacob ' as she says with emphasis, who had to dig this well in order to provide his children and flocks with water ?

But what would be the use of a miracle like that, and what purpose would be served by such ordinary living (i.e. running) water ? Jesus is speaking of a different sort of water and of a far more amazing miracle, though it is a miracle that lies hidden in men's souls. He who drinks of *His* water shall thirst no more, for he will have the spring within himself, a spring that begins to flow during this life and goes on flowing still in that eternal life to which the power of this water shall lead him.

The woman then replies : ' Lord, give me this water, that I may thirst no more, nor come hither to draw.' She seems docile in her acquiescence ; but she is far from being artless, and, moreover, she has not understood the lesson. We catch a smile, almost a sneer, on her lips. Come, then, she seems to say : let us see this great prodigy ! But here Jesus strikes the decisive blow : ' Go, call thy husband, and come hither.'

Still critical, the Samaritan woman pretends that she finds a flaw in that penetrating power by which Jesus appears to claim knowledge of the secrets of eternal life.

'I have no husband,' she says. 'That is true,' replies this mysterious personage, 'for thou hast had five husbands, and he whom thou now hast is not thy husband.'

Here we must interrupt this terse conversation. There are some listeners who have drawn very near to Jacob's well—we mean the modern critics. They too claim the right to tell this Samaritan woman the truth about herself. They strip her of her human character as a woman, vivid as that character is, and turn her into a mental fiction, a mere symbol of her country which had formerly worshipped five different deities, brought thither from Mesopotamia along with the colonists whom the king of Assyria had transported into Samaria. As a matter of fact the Bible does speak[1] of five nations, but it mentions seven gods. But precise details are nothing to the allegorists. As early as the thirteenth century a commentator had drawn a comparison between five false gods and the five husbands of the Samaritan woman: at that period it was the fashion to draw allegorical meanings from the words of Scripture. Nevertheless, the above-mentioned commentator did not call into question the woman's reality; instead of taking her for an inconstant wife of doubtful morals he only brought against her the very unlikely accusation of practising the idolatry of her ancestors. The modern critics have still less respect than this ancient commentator for the literal sense of Scripture, but they are no happier in their interpretation. They would have us believe that the Samaritan woman here stands for the Samaritan nation which Jesus addresses as follows: 'You Samaritans were formerly idolators and now you are schismatics.' However, they turn her into a woman again so that she may go and speak to her compatriots, who, as John shows us, were of better dispositions than the Jews and more docile towards Jesus. No, the writer certainly intends to depict a woman of flesh and blood, cunning and shrewd of mind, but at the same time full of sensibility and honesty once her heart has been convinced; and her conviction does not proceed from arguments drawn from ancient history but from the fact that the secrets of her life have been laid bare. It is not ancient history but her own history that touches her heart.

So she had really had five husbands, which, to say the

[1] 4 Kings xvii, 30 ff.

least, was not very creditable. One or other of the five may have died it is true. But five! She must then have been divorced several times. And for what reasons? It is hardly likely that the fault was on the side of all the discontented husbands. At any rate that was not the verdict of public opinion; so eventually, unable to find another match, she had consented to take a partner without the security of marriage.

Every Jew who had been to school would know by heart the story of the ancient idolatry of the Samaritans, but how was it possible for a mere stranger to be aware of this woman's disreputable history? The woman therefore gives in: 'Lord, I see that Thou art a prophet.' But she soon leaves such dangerous ground; she feels safer on the religious topic. And, it may be, now that she is convinced of this prophet's supernatural insight she wishes sincerely to ask His opinion on the religious question, a thing less irksome to her than the private admonition she fears He may give her. The poor woman points with trembling hand to the neighbouring mountain, saying that the patriarchs and all the fathers of old had worshipped there: Jacob who had dug this well, Joseph who had received this field as his inheritance, even Abraham himself, according to the local tradition of the Samaritans which had been inserted in the Scriptures by an adroit alteration of the text.[1] But the Jews, she says, maintain that Jerusalem is the place where God is to be worshipped. A choice had to be made between the two, for a nation can have only one centre of worship. But both Samaritans and Jews had the same ancestors, and they both made the same claim. Which of them was right? The question was one for a prophet.

Jesus does not evade it. In the past the Jews had right on their side, for the letter of the Law unquestionably supported their claim; and they had also the promises regarding the future. But now, what mattered one mountain or the other? Was the Father to have no worshippers but in one tiny country? Then came the words: 'The hour cometh, and now is, when the true adorers shall adore the Father in spirit and in truth'; and that will be neither on this mountain nor at Jerusalem only, but wherever a faithful

[1] By reading Moreh instead of Moriah for the place of Isaac's sacrifice (Genesis xxii, 2), understanding Moreh of the mountain which overshadowed Sichem.

heart, recognizing God as a spirit, adores Him in a spirit of sincere abandonment to the truth that it recognizes and possesses. Greece had already seen its national religious rites attacked by the philosophers ; but the philosophers had not provided any substitute : on the contrary, more often than not they themselves had followed the general fashion and practised the worship of false gods. Among the Jews it was the true God who was worshipped ; but as God was the Creator of all mankind and not merely of the Jews, then He ought to be worshipped by all men and in all places. Not that Jesus wishes to put an end to all external worship, a thing which is so well adapted to the needs of human nature. But to adore means to render a worship of homage and praise, and the essential thing is that such adoration, wheresoever and by whomsoever it is paid, should proceed from an inward disposition of the soul, so that the adorer may become one with God who is a spirit. The hour that was coming was the time when the worship of God should be such a spiritual worship, and the Christian faithful have always adored God in that fashion. Thus, when He announced the coming of that hour, Jesus, who was more than a prophet, yet uttered a prophecy that has clearly been fulfilled all over the world.

The Samaritan woman thought she was conceding a great deal when she gave Jesus the title of prophet. She is pleased at His reply, though it is still a little beyond her. However, she no longer shows any desire to be contentious ; she even volunteers the profession that, like her compatriots, she looks for the Messiah. He will explain everything when He comes. To this Jesus says simply, but no doubt in a tone that forces conviction on the soul of the listener : 'I am He : I who speak to thee.' The woman is startled even to bewilderment ; she puts down her pitcher and goes off to the town. The haste with which she goes is a guarantee of her belief ; but a still stronger proof of her faith lies in her proclaiming what tells so much against all her past life : 'Come and see a man who has told me all the things that I have done.' And since she, a weak woman, very weak indeed, does not dare to impose her own conviction on others, based as it is on such a personal motive, she merely suggests it by asking the question : 'Would He not be the Christ ?'

The Samaritan woman's pleasant chatter is certainly less moving than the silent tears of the woman who was a sinner or Mary Magdalen's cry at the empty tomb ; but what animation, what ingenuity, what art we see in her ! And her heart is true, despite her past disorders which, no doubt, she had not hesitated to justify in the eyes of others, even though she could not deceive herself. When Jesus, at His final reply, speaks with authority, she lets fall the shield of national pride and disdain behind which she has sheltered. Her first act of contrition is to confess her sin, the second is to act as an apostle to others, and in doing that she repeats her confession. Here we have a wonderful and unparalleled demonstration of the power of Jesus. She was a woman well accustomed to disputes, but though one might suggest that she had more than met her match in Jesus, yet we prefer to leave it unsaid, for the words of Jesus rise far above her horizon. They do not speak the same language, for her mental vision is bounded by the things that have formed the common subject of gossip with her neighbours, while He lives in contemplation of the merciful plans of God. From the thought of drawing water she goes on to the idea of Jacob and his well, then to the patriarchs and to the mountain whose summit they see before them, passing capriciously from one subject to another in such sort that her talk leads nowhere ; while all the time He is gently guiding her thoughts to the desire of grace, to the life of the soul and adoration of the Father. There is no trace in His manner of Socratic irony : He does not employ that pretence of ignorance which has for its object to lead one's adversary to show off his knowledge, and inevitably causes him to reveal how little he really knows. He makes no claim to knowledge of divine things as He does with the rabbi Nicodemus ; but it is plain, nevertheless, that He possesses it, and His kindness of heart leads Him to share it with this sinful woman, for whose salvation He manifests such great condescension. How like Him, the Teacher and Saviour of mankind !

Meanwhile the disciples had returned. The attitude towards women in the land of Israel at that time was similar to what it is in Palestine to-day, where a woman is respected in such a way as to make her almost unapproachable. A traveller would not even ask her the way. Hence in the days of Our Lord it was not customary for a man to hold a long conversation with a woman whom he might meet ; the disciples, however, have too much respect for their

Master to show their surprise by questions. When the woman has gone they urge Him to eat of the food they have brought out of the town ; but He, whose thirst had provided Him with an occasion of raising the thoughts of the Samaritan woman to the desire of God's gift, refuses to eat before teaching His disciples. To do the will of God who had sent Him, that is His true food ; and to show that this work is at hand He uses the example of the harvest now ripening all around them, the dazzling brightness of the midday sun making it appear to their eyes as though it were white. So long as the corn is not ripe we can give an excuse for not troubling about it by quoting the proverb: 'Yet four months, and then the harvest cometh.'[1] We leave it alone, then, for the earth is doing the work for us and preparing a rich crop. But we must know what to do when the moment comes. And sometimes it is not the sower who reaps ; but what does that matter ? If it be God's work, then both sower and reaper will share the same joy. In the case of the work of which He now speaks, it is God's servants of old time who had sowed, but it is now time for the disciples to begin their work. To the mind of Jesus, they have already been sent out. Into what field ? He does not yet say, but later on He will tell them that their field is the world.[2]

An abundant harvest, however, was already before their eyes, for some of the Samaritans of Sichem-Sychar who had been won over by the woman's firm belief hurried towards the well and invited Jesus to stay among them. He stayed two days, and they received His teaching with such docility that they were able to say : 'We ourselves have heard Him, and we know that He is indeed the Saviour of the world.'

The grandeur of this title is astounding, though on their lips it has not the special character that we now give it. Unlike the Jews, this hybrid nation of Samaritans was accustomed to bestow the name of Saviour on any sovereign, howsoever he ruled, whether well or ill. With greater reason, then, could they call the Roman emperor the Saviour

[1] This is Origen's interpretation, though the general interpretation is that the words refer to what the disciples have said, namely, that it would be four months yet before the harvest was ripe in the valley of Sichem. This would mean that the incident occurred about the end of January. But the phrase 'Do you not say ?' rather indicates that Jesus is using a proverb. Moreover, He compares the spiritual harvest to an existing reality, for He goes on to say : 'See, the fields are already turning white.' Hence it must have been summer.

[2] John xvii, 18.

of the world. But if that was so, could they hope for less from the Messiah than they hoped for from the emperor?

St. John is not the only one to speak of the good dispositions of the Samaritans. The first documents of Christian teaching which were chiefly intended for converted Jews, the gospels, namely, of St. Matthew[1] and St. Mark, say nothing of Christ's teaching among the Samaritans; but St. Luke, who was writing for Gentiles, deals much more kindly with this people.[2] After the Resurrection these first seeds sown among them by Jesus were developed by the preaching of the Apostles.[3]

The healing of the royal official's son (37).

John iv, 43-54.

When Jesus left the Samaritans and returned to Galilee He called at Cana as He had done on the former occasion, though for what reason we do not know. Soon after His arrival He was told that an official had come belonging to the court of Herod Antipas. The man was therefore a Jew. From Capharnaum, where the duties of his post caused him to dwell, he had climbed the hill which leads from the lake to the plain of Galilee. The man was in great trouble of soul because his son was in danger of death, and he begged Jesus to go down and heal him. His faith was quite sincere but by no means perfect, for he never dreamed that the Master could work a miracle from such a distance.[4] Jesus calls his attention to this point; but was that the time for argument, when any moment might be too late? The officer therefore replies with agonized impatience: 'Lord, come down before that my son die.' Jesus answers this cry of affliction by granting the father's prayer more promptly than he could have dared to hope. 'Go thy way. Thy son liveth.' The father believed and went his way. Thus briefly does the evangelist tell the story.

Since the man believed, he could hardly show great haste to verify the miracle; besides, he would have to allow his animals and followers some rest. And the sacred text itself

[1] Out of consideration for Jewish prejudices Jesus forbade His disciples even to go among the Samaritans when He first sent them out to preach. (Matt. x, 5.)

[2] Luke x, 33; xvii, 11, 16. [3] Acts viii, 25. [4] About eighteen miles.

declares that it was not until the morrow that he met his servants coming to tell him the good news. The fever had abated the day before at the seventh hour, that is at about one o'clock in the afternoon. It was precisely the time when Jesus had spoken, and the man's faith, now more firm than ever, spreads through all his household.

Thus is it made manifest that the supernatural power of Jesus did not depend on His touch, or on any treatment, formula of words or exercise of influence on the sick person's mind or nerves. It was, then, superior to anything that misguided men might seek from the practice of magic. Magic, as everyone knew, was powerless to heal or to destroy unless the magician had at his disposal either a hair, or a nail or at the very least a thread from a garment worn by the person on whom he wished to exercise his magic. But with Jesus we are in another sphere altogether ; it is the sphere not of the material but of the spiritual world.

The beginning of Christ's public ministry (38).

Luke iv, 14–15 ; Mark i, 14–15 ; Matthew iv, 17 ; John iv, 45.

Every movement started among men, whether it be religious or secular, is a matter of gradual development. Even very great men need to prepare themselves for the carrying out of their mission. In a group, one member will gradually attain to a position of predominance by giving proofs of his power of leadership.

Now Jesus possessed a divine authority which was subject to no such conditions. Nevertheless, it was part of His divine plan to observe the ordinary rules which govern human nature, at least in so far as was necessary for the accomplishment of the supernatural purpose He had in view. And the fact that St. John records (and he is the only one to do so) that there was a period during which Jesus made what may be called a series of experiments, is a sure proof of his fidelity to historical facts. Before delivering His grand attack, Jesus makes, as it were, a number of minor attacks on the enemy in order to train His men and give them confidence.

At first He seems to obey the call of the Baptist, but it is only that He may receive the homage of John ; and this act of homage truly stands for a ceremony of investiture in which an institution that has become out of date yields to the new order of things. Then He appears at Jerusalem acting as an intrepid avenger of God's rights, while He leaves to His disciples the task of conferring a rite of baptism which later on Jesus will transform into Christian baptism. When passing through Samaria He calls His disciples to action, and to those Samaritans who manifest good will He grants the first fruits of His redeeming apostolate.

Finally He returns to His own country. The voice of the Baptist is now silent ; no more is he heard preaching the kingdom of God. It is now time for Jesus to inaugurate that kingdom by proclaiming that it has begun. What Jesus does, says St. Luke, He does by the power of the Spirit ; He teaches in the synagogues and His fame spreads through all the surrounding country.

The teaching in the synagogues.

Jesus begins to preach the kingdom of God by teaching in the synagogues. This fact has been somewhat overshadowed by the pleasing picture we preserve of Jesus speaking His parables from a boat to the crowd gathered on the shore, perhaps also by the false idea left in people's minds by Renan's Galilæan idyll. Yet the four gospels are quite definite and unanimous on the point : Jesus often spoke in the synagogues. It is merely another example of the way in which He followed the accepted customs of His time and of the manner in which He turned old religious institutions to account while putting a new spirit into them.

The synagogue, which we think of chiefly as a place of prayer, was in fact primarily intended as a school for religious teaching. There could be no question of performing worship there in the strict sense of the word, since the only place for that was the Temple at Jerusalem. In the days before the exile the children of Israel were only too prone to break that rule, using the nearest sacred hill to offer sacrifice, and that not always to Israel's God but sometimes to Baal or Astarte. After the authority of the Law had been firmly established owing to the work of Nehemias and Esdras, public worship was no longer celebrated except in the Temple. The three annual pilgrimages to the Temple, however, even on the supposition that people were able to make them, were not sufficient to satisfy the ever-growing religious sentiments of the nation. Still less did they satisfy those Jews who had migrated in large numbers to foreign lands. As sacrificial worship was forbidden them by the Law, except under the condition laid down, the consequence was that this Law became the sole bond of union between one Israelite and another, between the Israelite and his God. It became necessary, therefore, to learn it and to teach it, and the rabbis spent their lives at this task. But ordinary folk were under the necessity of earning their daily bread. Still, the week provided one day of rest, the Sabbath, a day on which it was the custom to meet together. It is natural for us to think at once that the meeting was for the purpose of prayer in common. Community prayer was practised in Israel: there was the liturgical chant which accompanied the offering of sacrifice. But was it considered lawful to separate this chant, which was merely accessory, from the great act of sacrifice, to sing psalms apart from the worship of the Temple? Without doubt it was. Yet the fact remains that to the mind of the religious leaders of the nation, now no longer the priests but those who were learned in the Law, it seemed that the instruction of the people was of more importance than anything else. Hence they took advantage of these sabbath meetings at which the people were gathered in one building in order to comment on the Law and to exhort them to practise it so as to reform their behaviour in accordance with the commands of God. One form of this commentary went by the name of the *Halakah* or The Way, and might best be compared to sermons on the Decalogue. The books of the prophets were also taken in their turn, for exhortation should follow teaching; moreover, the most effective argument by which Israel might be persuaded to return to God was the easily verified fact that punishment was predicted for those who refused. The whole history of Israel in the past, with its alternation of apostasy and repentance, provided an inexhaustible stock of soul-stirring examples. This kind of teaching was called the *Haggadah* or Story and may be compared to sermons on the lives of the Saints.

The meeting at which this teaching took place was named *keneseth* in Hebrew, but those who spoke Greek called it a synagogue (συναγωγή).[1] Soon the word came to be used for the *place* where the meeting was held, as has also happened in the case of ἐκκλησία (*ecclesia*, church), another Greek word for meeting or assembly.

It was impossible for an organized body such as that to continue without a head, hence a ruler or president of the synagogue was appointed, assisted by a sort of sacristan. But as there was no religious hierarchy outside Jerusalem no one had the exclusive right to the office of teaching in the synagogue. There were doubtless a number of people more capable than others and more readily listened to; but the ruler could, as he liked, invite any Israelite to address the synagogue, though he might be only a passing stranger, provided always that he were of blameless life and that he were known to be sufficiently versed in the inspired writings.

The institution was so well adapted to the requirements of the condition in which the Israelites found themselves that it spread everywhere. In the time of Jesus the Jews claimed to regard it as an institution which owed its origin to Moses. Ever since the time of Christ it has remained as the bond by which the Jews all over the world have been kept closely united; and the reading of the Law, along with the recital of traditional prayers and sermons on the Law and Prophets, have succeeded in keeping alive among them that fervent religious conviction which serves as the foundation of a morality that is both lofty and steadfast. And of that morality their strong national sentiment is at once the source and the result. Racial feeling draws them together, and that feeling is strengthened all the more by their common ancestral faith. That is what the institution of the synagogue does for Judaism as a whole; the local synagogue played a similar part for every little town. It was the centre of Jewish patriotism in every place throughout the world where the Jews of the Dispersion were scattered; much more so was it the centre of patriotism on the sacred soil of the Holy Land.

We can understand then that when Jesus returned to Galilee with the intention of preaching the kingdom of God, which was now not merely at hand but actually inaugurated in His own person, He would naturally desire

[1] In Egypt called *proseuche* (προσευχή), as we learn from documents of the time of Ptolemy III (257–221 B.C.).

to offer His fellow-citizens of Nazareth in their Sabbath meetings at the synagogue the first-fruits of the word of salvation.

Preaching at Nazareth (39).

Luke iv, 16–22.[1]

Jesus, then, went to the synagogue 'according to His custom,' says St. Luke. It is beyond doubt that He had always shown Himself assiduous in the performance of His religious duties, and His piety was known to all. It was also known that He could read, for on occasion He would quote the sacred text for the enlightenment of His relations and acquaintances. Therefore when He offered to read in the synagogue no hesitation was shown in handing to Him the sacred scroll of the Holy Scriptures which then, as to-day, was the chief treasure of each synagogue. He received it from the minister of the synagogue and unrolled it reverently, stopping as by chance at this passage of the prophet Isaias :[2]

'The Spirit of the Lord is upon me,
because He hath anointed me to announce the good news to
the poor ;
He hath sent me to proclaim deliverance to captives
and sight to the blind,
to send the oppressed away free,
to proclaim the Lord's year of grace.'[3]

This passage is quoted by St. Luke from the Greek version of the Scriptures. Jesus must have read it in Hebrew and then translated into the Aramaic dialect which was used in Galilee. It was a proclamation of good news : God was about to intervene : a sort of jubilee was about to begin.

[1] We follow the order of events as given by St. Luke since it bears the marks of probability. But when he makes the rejection of Jesus by the Nazareans follow immediately on their approval of Him, his order does not seem so probable. But Mark and Matthew also join together in one account the story of Jesus' success and rejection at Nazareth, although their account comes at a later period of the gospel story. In our opinion the two episodes belong to two different times, and Luke himself, when he refers to the miracles worked at Capharnaum (iv, 23), gives reason to think that the rejection of Jesus must have taken place later.

[2] Isaias lxi, 1 ff.

[3] To limit Jesus' preaching merely to one year is as much as to say that the time of salvation was restricted to one year, though the common belief was that the period of salvation was to be very long, perhaps without end. It is a year, at any rate, that is not yet ended.

Isaias was thinking not so much of the return of the captives from Babylon as of the happiness promised for messianic days. He borrows his metaphors from the sufferings endured by the people during his own time: poverty, captivity, blindness, especially moral blindness, oppression by conquerors or by hard-hearted masters. Jesus went on to explain how this scripture was now fulfilled, gently leaving His hearers to conclude that the messenger who brought them news of this grace was no other than Himself. He seemed so worthy of such an office that 'all paid homage to Him and wondered at the words of grace that proceeded from His mouth.'

Even if this fine show of enthusiasm had not been destined very soon to disappear and to give place to a brutal feeling of enmity, nevertheless Jesus had no desire that it should be thought He depended on the attachment of His relatives and fellow-townsmen. And as Nazareth, situated far from the great high-roads, was hardly a suitable place for preaching a doctrine that was intended to penetrate far and wide, Jesus left the home of His childhood and went to settle at Capharnaum; though, seeing that He spent all His time wandering about in pursuit of souls in order that He might lead them back to God, one can hardly speak of His settling anywhere. He went down from Nazareth, then, towards the lake of Galilee.

Jesus at Capharnaum (40–41).

Luke iv, 31 ff.; Mark i, 21–22; Matthew iv, 13–16; vii, 28 ff.

When we look down at the lake from the surrounding heights and catch sight of a little basin of blue water set in the midst of a ring of barren hills with not a white sail on its surface, beholding in its waters the picture of no pleasant villages but, at times, the reflection of the snows of Hermon which stands out far to the north, there comes to the mind the image of those lakes of the high Alps, rarely visited and almost unknown, which God seems to have placed among the inaccessible and dazzling peaks merely to serve as a mirror of the sky. But when we begin to descend towards the lake the basin seems to grow bigger, the shores to recede, and we see signs of life : flocks and herds approach the water to drink, clumps of trees mark the site of Capharnaum and Bethsaida, Tiberias comes into view with its surrounding wall of black stones. There is still an aspect of desolation, but it is a desolation that is bathed in light, made cheerful by a riot of colour, and transfigured by sacred memories.

In the days of Jesus the precipitous eastern shore was more thickly populated than it is to-day, and the tiny sea constantly furrowed by boats carrying busy travellers from one landing-place to another. The plain of Genesareth, made fertile by abundant springs and a tropical sun, provided a rich soil for cultivation. Capharnaum, situated on the high-road from Jerusalem to Damascus and serving as the frontier post of the Holy Land, was a centre of attraction both for Jews and foreigners. Doubtless the shore of the lake was well wooded all round, though it is very rarely to-day that the traveller finds a tree under which to shelter from the heat of the sun. Still, there is always a certain freshness of air to be found down by the shore, and there the fisherman coming off his boat and the husbandman leaving his plough would mingle with the shopkeepers and people of the town when their own day's work was done, tasting the enjoyment of the very pleasure of living during the delightful hours of the evening. Of a strong and vigorous physique, the dwellers by the lake did not find the great heat oppressive, tempered as it always is by the breeze that comes down from the mountains in the north-west.

The Galilæans were unlike the Samaritans, for they had been won back to their ancestral faith by the Machabees and remained sincere in their attachment to Judaism, even though it was a Judaism which lacked those casuistic subtleties which were the pride of Jerusalem. Yet the Galilæans were destined to follow the example of their brethren of Jerusalem in the days to come, when, after the fall of Jerusalem, the celebrated rabbinical schools were established at Tiberias. In the time of Jesus, however, their faith was of a simple character, though none the less fervent on that account. Like their fellow-Jews, they were looking for the kingdom of God, and they even found grounds for hoping that it would commence in their own land. Had not Isaias so foretold ?

'Land of Zabulon, and land of Nephthali on the way of the sea, Galilee of the Gentiles ![1] The people that sat in darkness have seen a great light, and on them that sat in the region and shadow of death a light is risen.'[2]

The Galilæans were very proud of the light of the Law and were therefore very restless under the yoke of the Herods, conscious all the time that behind the Herods were the Romans. Whenever a leader came forward they were always ready to strike a blow for freedom. Only lately they had put their hopes in such a leader, Judas the Galilæan, but they had been disappointed ; nevertheless, in the secrecy of their hearts they cherished hopes of a better leader than he had proved to be.[3]

As soon as Jesus began to teach in the synagogue at Capharnaum this simple and straightforward people immediately perceived that He followed a method to which they were unaccustomed ; in the words of St. Mark,[4] they were astonished that He did not teach like the Scribes : He taught with authority. These Scribes were the teachers of the people, and the very signification of their name, which means writer or copyist, provides a good indication that all their authority to teach proceeded from the Law, with which it was taken for granted that they must be very familiar seeing that they had copied it so often. A few words of explanation are here necessary in order to show what is meant by St. Mark's comment.

The Christian, no less than the Jew, venerates Holy Scripture and regards it as inspired by God ; nor does he admit that anyone, not even the Sovereign Pontiff himself, has the right to contradict its teaching. But for us Scripture is not everything ; its teaching is completed by Tradition handed down from the time of the Apostles, and this Tradition is of equal authority with Scripture. The rule of faith, however, is not the interpretation of Scripture given by this or that doctor of the Church : it is a definite formula which the Church recognizes as correctly representing the truths or dogmas revealed by God. This formula contains

[1] In Hebrew, literally, 'the district of the nations' (*gelil ha-goyim*) ; in other words, peopled with foreigners. From *gelil* we get Galilee.

[2] Isaias ix, 1-2 (Heb. viii, 23-ix, 1), quoted in Matthew iv, 15 ff. This passage of Isaias forms part of the Book of Emmanuel which is specially messianic.

[3] Cf. Lagrange, *Messianisme chez les Juifs*, p. 19.

[4] Mark i, 22.

truths of faith which we are bound to accept, along with moral truths intended for the government of our conduct. But within this sphere of truth, whatever be its extent, are contained only those unchangeable dogmas which are co-eternal with God Himself. There are, however, a multitude of human actions which are conditioned by the different circumstances of time and place in which men live, and the laws regulating such actions are therefore subject to change. Thus the discipline by which the Church rules her members always takes into account the progressive development of human society and of its manners. In this sphere the Catholic Church, under the guidance of her chief Pastor, is endowed with full authority to make such changes as are profitable in view of man's eternal destiny: as for the things which concern the temporal good of mankind, they are left to the civil power to arrange according to the dictates of right reason.

Now in Israel,[1] as is still the case in purely Mohammedan forms of society, everything was arranged according to the religious law, not even excluding those things which we are accustomed to regard as outside the sphere of religion. The religious law of Israel was the Law given to Moses on Sinai: it was looked on as an inviolable unity which had never been and must never be altered. On this account the Scribes, who were the doctors of the Law, were driven to exercise tremendous ingenuity in order to draw from the sacred text the conclusions which, in view of changed circumstances, were suggested, nay demanded, by reason. By this exercise of mental gymnastics they performed prodigies of clever subtlety and over-refinement. So long, however, as their interpretations were adapted to circumstances people accepted them, closing their eyes to the fact that they had been extracted from the text by such weak and artificial methods of exegesis. It was laid down as a principle that all these commands were issued under the authority of the Law alone and of Moses its author, to whom God had revealed it. But when it became only too obvious that there was lack of agreement between the letter of the Law and its interpretation the Scribes had recourse to the explanation that both the one and the other came down from Sinai: the letter in an open manner, the interpretation by means of the secret channel of unbroken tradition

[1] Except in Turkey since the reform established by Mustapha Kemal.

through Josue, the patriarchs, the prophets, the men of the Great Synagogue. Innovations therefore, when they became prevalent, were credited with no less authority than that of traditional truths just come to light.[1]

Far different was the method of Jesus whose mission it was to reveal the truth on His own authority, a power not shared by the Church, for she teaches that revelation finished with the death of the last of the Apostles. It is her office to guard the revelation deposited in her care, a treasure created by Jesus and entrusted to her. He spoke in God's name, with His own authority: but that authority was divine.

Here we place our finger on the underlying cause of the hostility shown to Jesus by the doctors of the Law. He did not attack the Law: nay, He observed it with great exactitude. But He preached a doctrine that was purely religious in character, raised far above the merely accidental circumstances of political and social life, too lofty to be affected by any changes in human knowledge. The Scribes, on the other hand, had striven to make the whole discipline of life, even of knowledge, accommodate itself to their legal traditions. Their system was the framework of the whole life of the nation. Such a system would command respect as long as the Scribes had the upper hand; but once religion came to be looked on as the only thing that mattered, people would naturally think that they had the right to arrange as they pleased that part of their life which was outside the immediate scope of religion. It seemed even possible to the Scribes that the followers of this new religion might be so bold as to consider the old system completely obsolete and hence reject the authority of the doctors of the Law; while the Law itself, once the human legislation contained in it was abandoned, would be in danger of losing all its ascendancy. That was as much as to say that the very existence of the nation would be endangered; that religious unity, upon which was founded the political unity of the nation, would disappear along with the power of the Scribes.

We do not mean to suggest that the good folk of Nazareth were able to foresee all these consequences: St. Paul, indeed, was the first to bring them out. But there must have been some of the rabbis who had forebodings of them. The feeling caused by Jesus' manner of teaching in the minds

[1] Cf. *Messianisme* . . ., pp. 137–147.

of simple folk was merely one of amazement along with a touch of admiration. At all events, thought they, He must be a prophet since He spoke so well and so persuasively, not at all after the manner of the Scribes ; moreover, He spoke with more authority than they.

The curing of a possessed man (42).

Luke iv, 33–37 ; Mark i, 23–28.

There were others who were astonished, and disagreeably so : we mean the evil spirits whose power was now threatened. The long struggle which Satan would have liked to avoid by overthrowing his enemy at one blow, as he had tried to do in the desert, was now to begin.

In the synagogue at Capharnaum there was a man possessed by an unclean spirit. It is possible that the demon had not yet made his presence known ; but now, exasperated by the presence of Jesus, more particularly by His voice, he speaks up in the name of the whole company of demons : ' Why hast Thou come here ? Thou art come to destroy us ! I know who Thou art, the Holy One of God.' Jesus rebuked him and drove him out, the unclean spirit uttering a loud cry as he went out and causing his victim to writhe convulsively. If the people have been astonished by Jesus' teaching they are now stupefied with amazement. The miracle, at any rate, proved to them that the authority assumed by Him was by no means usurped. The deliverance of this poor man, then, came opportunely : it set a divine seal upon Jesus' teaching and showed immediately that the power He enjoyed was to be used for the good of mankind. By this deliverance of one who had been the victim of diabolical power, and by the confession of defeat on the part of the demons, the kingdom of God was already commencing.

The healing of Peter's wife's mother and other sick (43–44).

Luke iv, 38–41 ; Mark i, 29–34 ; iii, 11–12 ; Matthew viii, 14–17.

Upon leaving the synagogue Jesus went to the house of Simon and Andrew. They were natives of Bethsaida, but they too had come to live at Capharnaum, doubtless to be nearer Jesus. James and John had also come ; they have not yet been mentioned, but John was probably Andrew's companion down by the Jordan. These, then, form the group of the first disciples.[1]

Peter's wife's mother was ill with fever. Jesus comes to her, having been begged to do so by His companions who discreetly let it be seen that they hope He will condescend to heal her. He takes her by the hand and raises her from the bed—probably no more than a few mats spread upon the ground. The woman is straightway cured and is well enough to wait at table during the frugal meal that follows.

In that one day at Capharnaum the whole gospel is contained. People hear of the healing of Simon's wife's mother following on the casting out of the devil. At first their enthusiasm is kept within bounds because the Sabbath forbade all disturbances that might have the appearance of work. But when sunset brought the celebration of the sacred rest to an end they immediately brought the sick and the possessed to Jesus : all the little city was crowded round the door. In the midst of the clamour loud above all was heard the voice of the evil spirits, conscious of a secret power which compelled them to fall down and cry : 'Thou art the Son of God !' Jesus drives them out and puts them to silence ; He also heals those who are suffering from various diseases. Thus His first contact with the people betrays His sympathy ; in His kindness of heart He has compassion on their ills which He bountifully relieves.

The preaching spreads (45).

Luke iv, 42–44 ; Mark i, 35–39 ; Matthew iv, 23.

At last they return to Simon's house, where Jesus agrees to take His rest. But as His first desire is to teach His disciples what is the interior principle from which all apostolic work must proceed, He rises very early in the morning without disturbing the rest and goes out to a deserted place to pray. When Simon discovers this he is uneasy and goes after Him along with the others ; having found Him, he points out that everybody is anxious to see Him. But

[1] Such seems to us to be the order of the events. The final call of the disciples had not yet taken place.

Capharnaum has been favoured enough: the word must now be carried elsewhere. Jesus was heard preaching in all the synagogues of Galilee,[1] one after the other.

The call of Simon along with Andrew, James, and John (46).

Luke v, 1–11; Mark i, 16–20; Matthew iv, 18–22.

Not until now, according to the order of St. Luke's narrative, does Jesus make known to Simon how fully He intends to associate him, and others also, with the work of His mission. But there is nothing surprising in this delay. He had first to show them in what the work consisted, and on that account He wished to give them, while they were in His company, an actual example of His programme of work.

Up to this time it had been the custom of the first disciples to leave their Master alone to His work, so that now they were engaged in cleaning their nets while He was preaching at the lake-side. Their two boats had just returned from fishing, having brought in nothing but seaweed or the rubbish that floats on the water. Jesus interrupts their work and, going on board Simon's boat, asks him to pull out a little. Seated thus in the boat it would be easier for Him to be heard by the crowd, and they would have no occasion to press around Him. Afterwards He says to Simon: 'Launch out into the deep and let down your nets for a draught.' It was not a question of letting down the net at random, but of lowering a very long triple net slowly into the water as the boat advanced. When they had gone far enough the fishermen had to row back to their starting point, while they splashed the water with the oars so as to frighten the fish into the meshes of the net.[2] This was what Simon, along with his brother Andrew as we may suppose, had been doing all night: but without result. It cost him something to begin it all over again, yet he replied: 'Master . . . at Thy word I will let down the nets.' He does so, and this time the catch is so big that the nets burst. James and John who were in the other boat had not joined

[1] In the text of St. Luke we read Judæa. If the reading is correct it is doubtless meant in a very wide sense so as to include Galilee.

[2] Cf. Biever in *Conférences de St. Etienne*, 1910–1911, pp. 305 ff.

in the fishing; they were hailed to bring their boat, and both boats came to land laden with fish. Peter had already witnessed many miracles, but this one frightens him. Doubtless he has already realized that Jesus intends to take him along with Him, for now he hesitates, even draws back, pleading his unworthiness: 'Depart from me, for I am a sinful man, O Lord.' The others also trembled with a religious fear. Jesus says to Simon: 'Fear not! From henceforth thou shalt catch men.' The call and the promise are first addressed to him alone; but the others were fishermen too, so they are also called to catch men. Bringing their boats ashore, they left all and followed Him.

The modern mind shies at miracles more readily than did men of old: it finds them a difficulty. Yet the modern mind has an additional motive for belief in the present case; it has had the advantage of witnessing the fulfilment of the prophecy spoken by Jesus. Simon has indeed been a fisher of men, and his successors still continue to direct that work by the command of Christ; they call other men to their help, but it is they alone who have chief charge of the whole work of the apostolate, who determine its boundaries and choose apostles for that mission of peace which frequently gains its victories by means of the blood of its martyrs, a mission which must be continued until the gospel has penetrated to the ends of the earth. When we read of this miraculous draught of fishes, surely no one will expect us to close our ears to that command of Christ which has been obeyed during all these centuries: 'Launch out into the deep. *Duc in altum.*' On the contrary, it is an astounding fact that the successors of Peter have continued to launch out always further, and that fact is more wonderful than the miraculous draught of fishes.

The healing of a leper (47).

Luke v, 12–16; Mark i, 40–45; Matthew viii, 1–4.

In a place that the evangelists do not name—St. Mark says that it was in a house—a leper came to Jesus. Throwing himself at His feet, he besought Him: 'If Thou wilt, Thou canst heal me.'

Leprosy is still found in Palestine, especially in Jerusalem. It is always an object of horror, but the Christian charity of certain devoted women who look after the lepers is great enough to overcome their loathing for the disease. In the time of Jesus, however, the chief preoccupation was to isolate the leper from the rest of the community. It is difficult to define precisely the disease that was then called leprosy: the term was wide enough in meaning to include several different kinds of skin disease. It included in any case tuberculous leprosy which causes swelling of the joints, and sometimes finger-bones and other parts fall off completely. This disease, to-day common in Palestine, is not described in the Bible. There were leprosies which were thought to be curable: the priests alone had the right to pronounce on the cure, for a man was rendered ritually unclean by the disease, which was regarded as a punishment from God. But true leprosy is incurable, and the only hope of being cleansed from it was by looking for special intervention on the part of God.[1] Fear of contagion, repugnance inspired by the disease, the legal uncleanness which tainted the victim, all these reasons had given rise to legislation which banished the leper from contact with his fellow-men. He was compelled to don a funereal garb by which he might easily be recognized, and even commanded to denounce himself to the passer-by with the cry: 'Unclean! Unclean!'[2]

We can understand, then, what was the audacity of this leper who entered an inhabited place, even a house, in order to come near Jesus. He had broken the Law. But he was to be pitied, and moreover his faith was perfect. The Master's first feeling is one of compassion. The leper has appealed to His will: yes, He does will it. A cleansing is asked of Him: He grants it. Furthermore, He adds a gesture which no leper would have dared to look for: He touches the unclean man, and that gesture has become instinctive for heroic souls. Jesus has the right to touch the leper, inasmuch as the leprosy vanishes at His touch.

After thus giving way to His kindness of heart, Jesus comes to the question of the leper's position before the Law. With a certain show of severity,[3] He represents to him that he must be gone on the instant for fear of astonishing and scandalizing those who saw him enter. He is cured, but his legal position is not yet secure. The miracle does

[1] 4 Kings v, 7. [2] Leviticus xiii, 45.
[3] For the meaning of ἐμβριμάομαι see *Commentary on St. John*, p. 304.

not dispense him from the obligation of having his cure verified by the priests. From them he must receive a certificate which he can show to everybody as a sort of testimonial that he has recovered his rights in society. Besides, he must offer the sacrifice prescribed by Moses for the case.[1] Until all is in order he must say nothing to anyone, for once re-admitted to the company of his fellow-men he would no longer take the trouble to fulfil his duty.

That, it seems, is just what happened. Doubtless it was a bad case of leprosy which had gone so far that all hope of improvement had been given up. There was a great sensation, therefore, when the man published the news of his instantaneous cure. In the case of fever the cure is gradual as the fever falls ; recovery from other diseases depends to some extent on the condition of the patient ; but skin diseases are plainly visible and their obstinacy is well known. The miracle, therefore, was plain for everyone to see ; yet Jesus had commanded secrecy. He knew, of course, that His miracles did not remain hidden and that they were exciting the hopes of the populace, but He was determined not to let loose any disturbance about a Messiah. He therefore avoided entering the towns in broad daylight. But this did not endanger His ministry, for now the crowd followed Him into the desert.

II. FIVE CONFLICTS WITH THE PHARISEES

All this could not fail to disturb the Pharisees. The priests at Jerusalem were taken up with their duties, some of them chiefly occupied with secular affairs, and hence there was no immediate show of dissatisfaction on their part at the growing movement in Galilee. There, as everywhere else where Jews gathered, was to be found a group of doctors of the Law. They all held together, following the lead of the great rabbinical schools of Jerusalem, united by their inclination for the study of Scripture, their religious zeal, and their passion for domination. This Galilæan group sent word of what was happening to the rabbis at Jerusalem, who had been already put on their guard by what Jesus had done down by the Jordan and by the expulsion of the traders from the Temple. They knew

[1] Leviticus xiv, 2–32.

that the over-zealous preacher had gone away from Judæa, but now they learnt that He was carrying on His campaign somewhere else, and more vigorously than ever. He was working miracles, He was attracting the populace, He was recruiting disciples and was beginning to take them about in His company. This was a thing which they could not tolerate ; they must learn for themselves who and what this new teacher might be.

They had reason for suspecting Him, but provided that He agreed to serve their party what was to prevent their profiting by His reputation ? They must see for themselves. Members of the Judæan group were sent to join the scribes of Galilee with whom they now continually mixed, keeping Jesus in sight in order to spy out opportunities for putting Him to the test. With no provocation on His part, but merely as a result of circumstances, especially of the miracles which the people obtained from His goodness, five different conflicts occurred between Him and the Pharisees. They are placed by St. Mark and St. Luke consecutively, probably a logical rather than a real order.[1] The end of all this was to be settled hostility towards Jesus, and we must not forget this hostility and the motives which determined it when we later read the severe judgment which Jesus pronounced upon these men, who, inasmuch as they were the adversaries of His mission, were also the enemies of the people's salvation.

First conflict : the cure of the paralytic (48).

Luke v, 17–26 ; Mark ii, 1–12 ; Matthew ix, 2–8.

Capharnaum, where there was an important synagogue and where Jesus now generally lived, clearly provided the Pharisees with the most favourable opportunity for watching Him. When the people learnt that He had quietly returned thither and was in a house, they crowded around, the Pharisees and Scribes well to the fore, in such great numbers that the door was blocked. Jesus began to speak to the people, and we may take it that there was no room for objection in His teaching since no reproof was offered. The calm, however, was disturbed by an extraordinary

[1] Matthew, who is usually more systematic than the other evangelists, has divided the five conflicts into two groups.

scene. Little by little the roof was seen to open, bits of earth and lime falling in the process on those who were sitting below. Finally the opening was large enough to allow room for a pallet to be let down by ropes: on the pallet lay a paralytic. The four men who had brought him had mounted to the flat roof by an outside stair, and there, digging a hole in the roof, they had pulled out the mass of plaster rubble resting on twisted reeds and the wooden beams which formed the ceiling. The beams were loosely fixed, and by removing one of them a sufficiently large opening had been made. This was doing a sort of violence to Jesus, but they felt assured beforehand that their violence was forgiven and regarded favourably. The paralytic was let down to the ground and lay there without a word; the boldness of what had been done was quite enough to manifest his desire and his faith. Jesus said to him: 'My son, thy sins are forgiven thee.' We can well believe that the man was asking for this also in his inmost heart, since he was begging the favour of such a cure as God does not usually grant to those who take no pains to please Him. Therefore when Jesus said this, the paralytic's hopes were merely deferred, not disappointed. No one spoke; but the Pharisees, as if by common consent, merely through the instinct of their common beliefs, were inwardly moved by the same feeling of astonished indignation: 'How does this man speak thus? He blasphemeth! Who can forgive sins but God alone?' But it is also God alone who can read thoughts, and Jesus shows that He knows them. To give a yet clearer sign of His power He says: 'Which is easier, to say to this paralytic: Thy sins are forgiven thee or to say: Arise, take up thy bed and walk? But that you may know that the Son of Man hath power to forgive sins on earth (He saith to the paralytic), I say to thee: Arise, take up thy bed, and return to thy house.'[1]

The man at once arises and carries his pallet away, while the bystanders bless God with rapturous admiration; the thought of connecting blasphemy with one who holds such extraordinary power does not enter their minds. Such forgiveness of sins was unheard of, but it is overshadowed by the miracle that was apparent to all eyes; for it is evident that the man's friends would not have had recourse to such a stratagem as letting him down through the roof

[1] Mark ii, 9–11.

had not his condition been considered as hopeless. Hence what chiefly impresses the crowd is the astounding nature of the miracle. No doubt there may have been some among the Pharisees also who shook their heads and said : 'We have never seen the like.' But the novelty seemed to augur ill to their minds, firmly fixed as they were in the principle that God alone could forgive sins. In their opinion not even the Messiah could do such a thing without encroaching on the divine rights. By what right, then, did Jesus act? He had spoken as 'Son of Man.' Obviously He had not meant to suggest that every son of man had the right to do the like.[1] That is ridiculous. What, then, did Jesus mean by the expression 'Son of Man,' and why did He apply it to Himself?

This is a problem still debated among scholars. How would the Pharisees have solved it? The more erudite among them may have called to mind the celestial being of Daniel's vision, 'like unto a son of man coming upon the clouds of heaven.'[2] But what was there in common between this apparition and Jesus of Nazareth? It could not, they thought, have been an apparition of the Messiah since it came from heaven, and was not the Messiah to be born of David like a true son of man? Now the reconciliation of this apparent opposition was exactly the problem the Pharisees should have set themselves to solve : there was no answer to it in their books. The problem was to be solved in the person of Jesus Himself, but He judged it prudent first to prepare men's minds to understand its solution. He was guilty of no ambiguity in choosing an expression which drew special attention to the human nature assumed by Him in its full reality ; on the day of His appearance before the Sanhedrin He was to declare that this was the identical expression chosen by Daniel to indicate the Messiah's heavenly origin. But the name of Messiah was not so suitable for this purpose as the expression 'Son of Man,' seeing that the mere mention of it stirred up hopes of national freedom not unmixed with the less worthy desires of political domination, slaughter, and pillage. It was a word with which to turn people's heads. Jesus could not renounce this royal title, however ; but He had first to empty it of its worldly meaning, purify it, spiritualize it, and at the same time extend its embrace to the whole human

[1] The opinion of Wellhausen. [2] Daniel vii, 13.

race. The Son of Man was the title chosen by Him in order to lead the Jews to the notion of that universal salvation which had been proclaimed by the Scriptures.

The call of Levi. The Pharisees are scandalized (49).

Luke v, 27–32 ; xv, 1–2 ; Mark ii, 13–17 ; Matthew ix, 9–13 ; xii, 7.

The occupation of publican was looked on with such contempt that Jesus seriously compromised Himself in the eyes of the Pharisees when He invited a man who followed that occupation to become His disciple ; nay, a publican who was actually at the moment engaged in his duties. The first Christians were well aware that Jesus had called a publican to follow Him, and they accepted the fact reverently. But out of respect for the Apostles they preferred not to name too openly the man to whom that mercy had been shown. It is thought that this is the reason why St. Mark and St. Luke have called him Levi, a name that does not appear in the list of the Twelve. It was left for the grateful humility of the first evangelist—and it comes very near to being a sign manual—to give the name Matthew to Levi in this place and to call him a publican in the official list of the Apostles. That the same man bore two names is likely enough, for it was quite a common custom. We see, then, how difficult it is, even for Christians, to realize that to be called by Jesus confers the noblest of all titles.

Jesus, therefore, as He passed along the lake-side, saw Levi the son of Alphæus engaged in his occupation as a publican : He said to him : 'Follow Me.' The man rose and followed Him. He follows Jesus and obeys Him joyfully. He asks the Master to a meal in his house and there is nothing to be surprised at if he invites a few of his former fellow-publicans, perhaps those whose honesty was beyond reproach.[1] But there were 'sinners' present too. Some

[1] The chief Roman publicans only accepted the post of farming the taxes in order to plunder the countries subject to Rome ; but there is no doubt that there were minor officials among the tax-gatherers who were honest. A conscientious Jewish tax collector in the service of Herod had every right to the respect of his fellow-countrymen ; but the whole class of publicans was considered disgraced, and the Pharisees were more reluctant to forgive Jews than others who followed that occupation.

of these were doubtless sinners in the sight of God : others, even if they kept the moral law, did not trouble themselves about Pharisaic precautions for avoiding legal uncleanness. The mere act of eating with foreigners was held in horror by the Pharisees, and it was done in this none too scrupulous society in which not only is Jesus consenting to mix, but with which He is not even afraid to let His disciples come into contact.

The Pharisees would have thought themselves defiled merely by going into the dining-room. They therefore wait for the disciples as they come out and, not daring to address the Master for fear they might put Him on His guard, they ask without even naming Him : 'How is it that He eats with publicans and sinners ?' The disciples had not even thought about it : a sad state of mind to be in ! But Jesus answers for them : 'They that are well have no need of a physician, but they that are sick.' The Pharisees knew that well enough, and they regarded themselves as both teachers and physicians of the common people, whose ignorance they considered must necessarily leave them sunk in sin. But the medicine of the Pharisees was chiefly preventive, for they took good care to avoid the sick for fear of contracting contagion ; they gave imposing prescriptions from a distance, and the first thing in the prescription was that it was of absolute importance to consult *them.* Jesus, however, does not fear contact with these poor people ; He goes out of His way to seek it. Righteous men, like the Pharisees, stand in no need of Him. He does not remind them that they are closing the way to God against themselves by their contemptuous pride ; He only says : 'I came not to call the just, but sinners.' A truly divine utterance ! 'I came not. . . .' Where, then, was He formerly ? Did He not belong to the earth, He who had just called Himself Son of Man ?

A question about fasting (50).

Luke v, 33–39 ; Mark ii, 18–22 ; Matthew ix, 14–17.

A little while after there was a fast day for the Pharisees and John's disciples. Fasting for the Greeks meant hardly more than mere abstention from food. But in the Jewish fast, going without food had the character of a symbol ;

it was a mode of humbling and belittling oneself, of appeasing the divine wrath or submitting to its consequences. Thus, with the Jews fasting was essentially a rite of repentance and mourning. The Law prescribed it on one day only, the Day of Atonement, and then it was binding on all. But fasts were also kept in memory of great national calamities, like the capture of Jerusalem by the Chaldeans on the ninth day of the month Ab.[1] The Pharisees unquestionably kept other fasts apart from those of simple devotion, which John's disciples joined them in observing, following in that the example of the great ascetic, their master. But ordinary people occupied in hard work did not lay this additional burden upon themselves, and Jesus had not imposed it upon His disciples.

It might be thought that no one could object to that; nevertheless the Pharisees, as well as John's disciples, complained. St. Luke names the former, St. Matthew the latter, St. Mark mentions no names. The probability is that adverse comments were made here and there, and although those who voiced them were without doubt animated by Pharisaism, yet it may be taken for granted they would pretend not to be actuated by party spirit. The complaints are started by onlookers, or rather by spies. This time they address their enquiries to Jesus, as usual in a roundabout way, asking Him for what reason His disciples do not follow the example of pious people, seeing that He must have chosen these disciples in order to lead them along a more perfect way than that followed by the generality of people. He replies with a comparison, and the point of the comparison concerns His own person. The friends of the bridegroom, those gay companions of his former life who in the picturesque language of the Semites are called 'the sons of the nuptial couch,' whose business it was to see to the wedding feast and by their talk and songs to make things go with a swing, can *they* be expected to put on a sad demeanour while the feast is still in progress? The bridegroom is being taken from them, and when he enters on his new life, then they can show their regrets, but not so long as he is still with them. Jesus Himself is the bridegroom; the day will come when He will be taken away from His friends, and on that day they will fast.

Jesus foresaw, then, that He would be separated from His

[1] About July 14.

disciples. Would there be time before that for Him to reign along with them? But was there any question of reigning? His prediction was guarded, yet it left an impression of sadness: Jesus taken from His own, and His own left to sorrow! To us its meaning is plain, fulfilled as it is in the fast we celebrate on the anniversary of Christ's death and during the days preceding that mournful commemoration.

This reply of Jesus vindicated His disciples: the joy of His presence took from them every reason for showing signs of sadness in such a case as this, where the sole motive was the example set by the Pharisees, an example followed so submissively by the disciples of John the Baptist. Yet He wished to teach a deeper truth. His disciples were not with Him simply to be His companions: by His teaching He breathed a new spirit into them. That spirit was not in contradiction with what is essential in the Law, as later on Jesus will say openly. But at present there was no question of any command of the Law: it was a question of new practices added to the Law by the Pharisees, perhaps with the intention of preserving it more safely against the assaults of time. A bad system indeed! For when a garment is worn out we do not sew a new piece on to it, for a slight movement will pull the new piece away and bring with it some of the old material round it: thus the rent is made bigger still. Or when wine-skins are worn thin through being jolted about on the ass's back, is that the time to put new wine into them? It will only ferment and burst the skins. These disciples of His, therefore, since they have been imbued with a new spirit, should not be required to take part in observances inspired by the spirit of the Old Law. That would be a piece of patch-work which would only end by showing up more clearly than ever the decay of the legal institutions, such at least as they were in the Pharisaic interpretation. Fasting is not condemned; it is even foreseen for the future when, after the renewal of man's religious sense, it will be practised with a new intention: 'New wine in new skins!'

Doubtless this lesson is profound rather than clearly to be seen on the surface. But Jesus, with the foreknowledge of what was to come, relied on the future to elucidate His words. Now we can fathom their meaning. The ill-natured people who had questioned Him suspected danger to the Law in the future ; they gained little by their question. After all, since the fasting in question was not of obligation the disciples were not at fault. But it is clear that the answer given by Jesus had a tone that was none too sympathetic to Pharisaic observances. The hostility of the Pharisees went on growing, and they were exasperated by finding no motive for it out of which they could concoct some vital case against Jesus. But the Sabbath was to provide them with the opportunity they sought.

The plucking of the ears of corn on the Sabbath day (51).

Luke vi, 1–5 ; Mark ii, 23–28 ; Matthew xii, 1–8.

Jesus was walking through the corn with His disciples, and they, either because they were hungry or else mechanically and absent-mindedly, plucked the ears and began to taste the ripe but still tender grain. It was therefore only just before the harvest. If the conversation with the Samaritan woman took place when the barley was whitening, and if the grain eaten by the disciples was wheat, which is much more pleasant to the taste, we may suppose that an interval of about two or three weeks separated the two incidents. It is true, of course, that down by the shores of the lake the harvest is ripe earlier than in the plain of Nablus ; but it is possible that the present incident occurred on the plain above the lake, called the plain of Hattin. If so, then the time would have been about the beginning of June.

To pluck a few ears of corn or a few figs from the trees as one passed was a common practice ; no one objected to that. But the incident with which we are dealing took place on the Sabbath day. As the Sabbath was the day of rest it was only permitted to take short walks, but it was the general custom to go out on the Sabbath. In our own day at Jerusalem you will find all the Jews out of doors on the Sabbath strolling slowly within the prescribed Sabbath day limits, called the *erubin*.[1] Jesus had evidently not transgressed these limits for He is not found fault with on that

[1] The Sabbath limit was 2000 cubits from the place where a man lived. But sometimes one finds several Jewish houses connected up with wires, and by this device they are reckoned as one so that the Sabbath limit may be extended.

account; but to rub the grains out of the ears of corn, was not that to perform prohibited work?

The question makes us smile, but to the Jews it was a serious matter. Harvesting on the Sabbath day was expressly forbidden by the Law,[1] and Pharisaic casuistry had included under harvesting every action, however trifling, that could be said to be like harvesting.[2] All this can be found in the rabbinical books,[3] where we also learn that it was forbidden to pick fruit, or even to climb a tree, lest one should shake off the fruit even unintentionally. Nay more, as the Sabbath was the law of creation and hence binding on all nature it was forbidden to eat an egg that had been laid or fruit fallen from a tree on the Sabbath day. The reproach uttered by the Pharisees, then, has all the marks of probability. They addressed it to the Master without even giving the name of disciples to those at whom it was aimed,[4] thus insinuating the impression that their question is not motived by ill-will. Surely, they say, the disciples are doing what is forbidden. They wish it to be thought that they are charitably inclined to conclude that there must be some excuse for what the disciples are doing but would like to know what that excuse is.

Jesus replies to the question by quoting an example from the Scriptures, the example of what the young King David did during his time of trial, David the chosen one of God. In that case there was no question of Sabbath observance, but the matter at stake was a legal point just as explicitly determined by the Law as was the Sabbath rest. Only the priests were authorized to eat the loaves of proposition,[5] the bread, that is to say, which had been exposed in the presence of God upon the altar in the sanctuary. To satisfy his own hunger and the needs of his companions David had obtained permission from the high priest to receive the sacred loaves which had just been replaced by fresh loaves.[6]

[1] Exodus xxxiv, 21.

[2] Cf. Strack and Billerbeck, *Einleitung in Talmud und Midrash*, I, p. 617.

[3] Cf. *Mishnah*, *Shabbath*, VII, 2, which gives a list of thirty-nine kinds of forbidden work.

[4] According to Mark ii, 24.

[5] Leviticus xxiv, 5 ff.

[6] 1 Kings xxi, 2 ff., where the text names Achimelech as the priest; but his son Abiathar, who succeeded him, was present (1 Kings xxii, 20). St. Mark says: 'under Abiathar the high priest,' for Abiathar's name appears so frequently in the biblical history of that time as to link his name with that of David.

Was that a violation of the Law? Was it not rather the fact that the high priest wisely interpreted the Law in order to meet a case of necessity? True, the disciples had not David's excuse: but at the same time their neglect of the Law was much more slight. The essential thing was this: where there is question of a positive command which does not involve any eternal principle, one must go back to the original purpose of the Law. This was the case in the question of the Sabbath: when God bound the Israelites to rest on that day His purpose was to secure their benefit, not to tie them down by an absolute command which took no account of circumstances or of the relative importance of various actions. In a word, as Jesus boldly expressed it: 'The Sabbath was made for man, not man for the Sabbath.'

This statement, which goes right to the root of the matter, is recorded by St. Mark, and there is no reason to doubt its authenticity. To it he adds a declaration which depends for its understanding on St. Matthew's text: 'so that the Son of Man is lord even of the Sabbath.' What has been said above of the authenticity of the principle enunciated by Jesus concerning the Sabbath can be repeated also of this conclusion which He draws. Indeed, it bears all the signs of probability when we observe how He refuses to meet the craft of the Pharisees with craft. They have tried to make Him affirm that He sets up a new standard of Sabbath observance, but He declines the honour. No: on the contrary his chief concern is to make clear what is His mission in such a way as not to draw attention to its messianic aspect. In His former encounters with them He has claimed the power to forgive sins in His character of a physician who has come to cure the victims of that malady. He has proclaimed the beginning of a new order of things, an order that is dependent on His own person: now He declares that He is master, even of the Sabbath.[1] Pursuing His usual method of argument, that drawing of principles from particular cases which even the simplest of people can understand, He reminds His hearers that the priests in the Temple appear to break the Sabbath by the tasks they perform, yet no one blames them for that. But there is now in the midst of them one who is greater than the Temple, namely the Son of Man. He who forgives sins is also

[1] Matthew xii, 5 ff.

master of the Sabbath, master in the sense that He is the judge of what is lawful for His disciples. He is master too in a more absolute sense, as the future will make clear. There is here no threat to the principle of the Law, for the Sabbath rest will always be for man's advantage : it gives him leisure and makes it easier for him to draw nigh to God. Nevertheless, the power of the Son of Man which He has transmitted to His Church was used when a day for the Sabbath was chosen on which, instead of commemorating the rest taken by God after the creation of the world, a rest which symbolizes the divine conservation of the world, we commemorate the resurrection of Christ.

The man with a withered hand healed on the Sabbath day (52).

Luke vi, 6–10 ; xiv, 3b ; Mark iii, 1–5 ; Matthew xii, 9–13.

The question of the Sabbath, always a burning one, was now raised. In our own days Jerusalem has witnessed the sight of a Jewish High Commissioner, once a minister of the British Government, walking nearly two miles in full-dress uniform on the king's birthday so as not to cause his chauffeur to break the Sabbath. And a certain Jewish author[1] who has written to prove that the Mosaic Law is not unchangeable would have similar scruples on this same fundamental point.

It was on this vital matter that the conflict with the Pharisees was to end in mortal combat. The incident put before us here by the first three evangelists provides a typical case, in which a merciless legalism strives in vain with the compassionate heart of Jesus, the eternal source of Christian charity.

Jesus was again in the synagogue, and amongst those present was a man with a withered hand. The Pharisees by now knew Jesus well enough to suspect that He would want to heal Him. But would He dare to do it on the Sabbath day? If He did, then He would provide them with a splendid opportunity for accusing Him of a thing that He had done openly in the synagogue, without respect either for the place or for the scandalized crowd of faithful.

On this occasion no more than on the previous one does

[1] Harold Wiener, *The Law of Change in the Bible.*

Jesus shirk the issue, though now the danger is more pressing. He even makes an open declaration of the principle which is involved in the case of this poor man. Bidding him to come forward into the midst of the assembly, He puts the question : 'Is it not better to do good rather than evil on the Sabbath day, to save a life rather than commit a murder ? ' We should think that the rabbis might have answered yes without compromising themselves : a general solution of that kind did not stand in the way of dispute about cases in particular. Yet they were silent, for they had made up their minds to grant nothing that might compromise them even unconsciously. It may have been pride which made them refuse to argue with this tiro in the art of disputation : they certainly showed hardness of heart by their silence, for the disabled man was there before their eyes, his withered hand pleading with them, yet they will not say a word to authorize Jesus to heal it. There are modern scholars who say that they were right : rabbinical jurisprudence permitted work on the Sabbath when there was danger of death, but not otherwise. In the present case there was no question of urgency.

It was evident, however, that Jesus meant to go on further. He had put forward the suggestion that what rendered an action lawful on the Sabbath day was its moral value, even though in performing it there was danger of breaking one of those regulations with which the rabbinic lawyers, with their narrow-minded reasoning, had overburdened the Law : as, for instance, that it was unlawful to pour water over a sprained limb on the Sabbath, or to draw the blood from a wound. The enemies of Jesus persuaded themselves that all they had to do was to let Him go on and work His own ruin : it was certainly a splendid opportunity. But, conscious of the hardness of their hearts, Jesus looked upon them with sadness, even with a holy passion of anger. This is the only occasion where anger is attributed to Him, and here it is recorded by St. Mark alone,[1] so little did it seem compatible with His goodness of heart. And, indeed, His anger remained without effect, and only His goodness was revealed ; for at the command of Jesus the man stretched out his hand and drew it back full of life and movement.

[1] Mark iii, 5.

The first plan to destroy Jesus (53).

Luke vi, 11 ; Mark iii, 6 ; Matthew xii, 14.

This was the last straw : from now onwards the Pharisees were determined. For a long time they had been defied, but now they had a case against Him, and a good one as it seemed to them, nor was there any lack of witnesses. As they were in the territory of Herod Antipas it was deemed advisable to come to an understanding with some of the influential people of his petty court. They met in secret and discussed ways and means of bringing about the downfall of the innovator, though as yet no definite plan was formed.

III. THE BEGINNING OF THE GOSPEL TEACHING

The choosing of the twelve Apostles (54).

Luke vi, 12–16 ; Mark iii, 13–19 ; Matthew x, 1–4.

We come now to a decisive moment in the ministry of Jesus. At first He had preached repentance because the kingdom of God was at hand ; and as the evangelists have preserved for us only one feature of that early preaching we are led to think that it was all in the style of the prophets of old, especially Isaias, dwelling specially, as in the sermon at Nazareth, on the mercy shown by God in thus intervening in human affairs. But we find Him already, at that early hour, gathering disciples about Him, among them Levi the publican, since known as Matthew. Nathanael was in all probability the disciple we know as Bartholomew. Others also—how many we know not—were in the habit of spending more or less frequent periods in his company. The Pharisees had been led by their very instinct to meet Him with opposition, but the questions by which they sought to trap Him had provided the Master with an opportunity for revealing that His teaching was based on new principles very different from theirs. He had let it be seen that His work would still be carried on after He was gone.[1] He had therefore to train these followers of His and bestow on them an authority derived from His own : they must be the first

[1] Mark ii, 20.

hearers of His teaching and also His witnesses. He decided that they should number twelve, which was the number of the tribes of Israel: for just as the patriarchs born of Jacob were the glorious ancestors of the whole nation and the pride of each separate tribe, a bond also which bound them together in one family, so the twelve Apostles were to be the forefathers of the new Israel that Jesus had come to found.

Before taking this step, which was already decided on as part of His work, Jesus betook Himself to prayer. He went up the mountain and passed the night in earnest supplication. As man, it was His duty to pray; but He also set us an example, and here teaches His Church to make special prayers to beg God for faithful pastors.

Seven of the twelve had already been admitted to a privileged intimacy with Him; as for the rest, we do not know when they first felt drawn towards Him. They were Thomas, James the son of Alphæus (so called to distinguish him from the son of Zebedee), Simon surnamed *qanana*, Aramaic for zealous but not necessarily 'the zealot,' though there is only one word for both meanings in Greek. We use the term Zealots to denote a Jewish sect inspired with a fierce zeal for the independence of Israel, maintaining that none should be obeyed but God. The ideal was a praiseworthy one, but in practice it was only too often spoilt by excesses of the worst kind. But as Simon's surname is retained in the list of the Apostles we ought to understand it in its more general sense of fervent zeal for God. With Simon is generally associated a Judas whom we call Jude in order to distinguish him from the traitor. With the same object Luke calls him the son of James, while Mark and Matthew mention him only by his surname Thaddæus, 'big-chested.' The last is Judas Iscariot, a word which means the man of Kerioth, a small town in the south of Judæa. The fact that the traitor is placed among the twelve is enough of itself to prove that this number was determined by Jesus. Unless this had been notorious no one would have dared to introduce Judas into the group of the Master's intimate friends.

Simon, though he had not been the first to come to Jesus, is always mentioned first with his surname Peter. This alone shows the specially important position he occupied amongst the disciples. Andrew, his brother, is not always put in the second place. To James and John, who will more than once be associated with Peter in the Master's special favour, Jesus gave the name of Boanerges, Sons of Thunder, because of their impetuous ardour.

The Sermon on the Mount (55–75).

Matthew v–vii ; Luke vi, 17–49.

The Twelve had been chosen in order to be leaders ; but they were not leaders yet. They were, however, the first to be initiated into the doctrine of the kingdom of God. Jesus was now to make a plain declaration, though He had already given certain clear glimpses of what was His attitude to the revealed Law, and of what was that higher perfection to which He was calling those willing to follow Him. As was befitting, this declaration was made with a certain solemnity, though there is nothing of ostentation about it. All who read the gospel with the simplicity of those who wrote it are struck by this trait in the character of Jesus : He had so little liking for pomp and display that it would be shocking to mention the word theatrical in connection with His actions even if only to dismiss it. Nevertheless, His Sermon on the Mount has been compared with the promulgation of the Old Law on Sinai. But where are the lightnings and thunders, the holy fear that seized the Israelites, the command not to approach the smoking mountain ? As once before Jesus had a boat for a pulpit, so now He sits on the ground surrounded by the multitude. He is on a mountain simply because He has gone up there to pray and to choose His disciples, and the crowd has followed Him. For the sake of convenience He comes down a little way from the mountain-top to a plain where everyone can sit in comfort.[1] The plateau of *Qurn-Hattin*, which is overlooked by hills but at the same time high up and far from Capharnaum, fulfils the conditions quite well. Others have proposed *Um Barakât* (the Mother of Blessings), overlooking Tabga.

The commotion aroused by Jesus had become so wide-

[1] There is no difficulty in harmonizing Matthew, who speaks of a mountain, and Luke, who speaks of a plain, for Luke too has placed the call of the disciples upon a mountain : he is merely showing that Jesus has descended to a flat place on the mountain side.

spread that it was no longer confined to Galilee. People came even from the south of Jerusalem, that is to say from Idumæa, which had not long ago been conquered by the Hasmonean kings and was still smouldering with hostility towards Judaism. Inhabitants of Tyre and Sidon also, to the extreme north of the Promised Land, came begging to be healed. When Jesus saw this multitude waiting upon Him He opened His mouth and spoke.

His discourse has been recorded by St. Matthew and St. Luke in somewhat different ways. We should be led to conclude that they were giving two different discourses, were not the resemblances so close, especially if it were possible to suppose that Jesus had on two different occasions pronounced an opening discourse. It is preferable to admit that Luke, since he was writing for Gentiles, confined himself to what concerned the new way of perfection which consists in the law of charity ; Matthew, however, faithfully preserved that which gave to the discourse its historical character, namely the contrast between the new doctrine and the old, and the bond which made them one ; the bond is the bond of charity, but it is a charity which goes further than what is demanded by the Law, though at the same time it grows out of the old revelation like the fruit fulfilling the promise of the flower. We must therefore go to St. Matthew's text in order to appreciate the primitive character of the sermon : there we seem to hear the words, the tone, the very accent of Jesus when we read it for ourselves. Here we cannot attempt more than a modest analysis of the discourse.

The sermon opens with a sort of introduction which we call the beatitudes ; Luke adds a complementary counterpart by showing the unhappiness that comes from the dispositions contrary to the beatitudes. But the contrast thus created actually adds nothing that is essential.

The main part of the sermon is made up of two points : what relation has the teaching of Jesus to the Law and the Prophets, and how is His spirit different from the spirit of the hypocritical Pharisees ? Secondly, what ought to be the attitude and practice of His disciples ? Then in a brief exhortation the hearers are called upon to put His teaching into practice.

The introduction alone contains a complete doctrine, treasured by mystics of every age. St. Augustine and St.

Thomas Aquinas have treated of it in its broad outlines, while Pascal has dealt with it in a way to please the modern mind. It is the doctrine that truth cannot bear fruit in the soul—nay, it cannot even be understood—unless the will, what we call the heart, is first rightly disposed towards God. If the heart is barren of feeling towards God the intelligence remains blind. Therefore, to begin with, instead of those ordinary inclinations which a man feels for the good things of this world, he must substitute the contrary desires which are based upon appreciation of the real value of things, whether they are the deceitful pleasures of the senses or the things which are of real worth. In this way there must be brought about a reversal of values, and a conviction that happiness will in the end be the lot of those who seem to lack those false pleasures that men seek so eagerly.

In St. Luke the contrast between poverty and riches, laughter and tears, is set down in so striking a manner that a superficial reader might easily consider the matter as one entirely concerning temporal prosperity, and think that Jesus, like a good revolutionary, had promised to the poor their revenge upon the rich who looked down upon them ; and further, that this revenge was not long to be delayed. But this would be a mistaken idea. For in what way does this desire, this vindictive desire of others' goods which can be appeased by depriving the wealthy in a spirit of vengeance, resemble the call to renunciation that echoes through the whole Gospel of Jesus Christ? Indeed St. Luke, like St. Matthew, has from the very first line shown us from what point of view we are to read what he has written. There will, indeed, be a transformation, but it will be in the kingdom of God : and here we are to understand the kingdom of God in eternity. Far from stirring up His disciples to seize those temporal possessions of which they now suffer such a lack, He goes on to promise them humiliation and ill-treatment for His name's sake, reminding them that their reward will be in Heaven. We have to admit, therefore, that these abrupt and violently contrasted sentences of St. Luke, conceived as they are in a style to suit the intelligence of Semites, needed to be toned down to suit other readers ; hence the amplifications in the Greek of St. Matthew, where we are reminded in every sentence of the true spiritual sense of the sayings. Matthew does not simply say 'the poor,' but 'the poor in spirit,' which means those who feel their own powerlessness to satisfy their longing for the kingdom of God. The thirsty are athirst 'for righteousness.' The merciful, the clean of heart, the peacemakers, are already on the way to the kingdom of God; we must therefore understand 'the meek' and 'they that mourn' in the same sphere of religious and moral life. Similarly, to inherit the earth will not mean increasing one's earthly domain, but entering Heaven as a child of God. The only reward the disciples are to look for in this world is to suffer persecution as did the prophets in the early history of Israel.

This glance into the past, with its implication that the disciples of Jesus are the successors of the prophets, furnishes a neat introduction for the first point of the sermon. What is the position of Jesus in regard to the Old Law?[1] This is one of the greatest problems of the New Testament and one that the Apostles themselves had to solve in several matters, for the Master had only laid down a general principle and given a few applications of it. According to some, indeed, St. Paul is not in agreement with Jesus about the principle. The Master asserts, they say, that the Law will not pass away: the Apostle regards it as abrogated. And it is not enough to reply that Jesus meant that He was bringing the Law to its full perfection. When we find Christians doing away with the rite of circumcision, the very symbol of the covenant between God and His chosen people, what becomes of Christ's declaration that 'not one jot or tittle of the Law shall pass away'?

Jot (*iota*) is the Greek name for *iod*, the smallest letter of the Hebrew alphabet; a tittle represents one of those tiny orthographical marks by means of which certain similar letters of the Hebrew alphabet are distinguished one from another. Does this mean, then, that Jesus accepted the claim of the rabbis that the written text of the Law, even down to the very letters, was to remain unaltered right to the end of the world? So scrupulous were the rabbis in the work of safeguarding this material integrity of the sacred writings that they took the most minute precautions, even

[1] There will be found in our Commentary on St. Matthew the reasons for regarding as additions to the primitive discourse certain passages, which, moreover, are not found in St. Luke's sermon, namely, Matthew v, 13–16, 18, 25–26; vi, 7–15 (the Pater), 19–34; vii, 7–11, 22–23. Matthew has, however, established a close connection between verses 17 and 18 of chapter v, and has shown the full meaning of the perpetuity of the Law, both by the position of his treatment of that idea and by the words with which he ends verse 18.

to the extent of counting all the letters of the Scriptures, in order to make sure that each new copy contained them all.

It was not by a scrupulous zeal of such a kind, however, that Jesus was inspired. But did He at least intend to say that every single one of the commands of the Law should be retained for all time? If so, then He was contradicted by St. Paul, and St. Matthew has even made Him contradict Himself in what follows the above declaration. The opinion of the rabbis on this point also, the question, namely, of the everlasting character of the Mosaic ordinances, was entirely puerile and impossible. According to their view, the Law was made up of a list of commandments, some positive, others negative in character, the number of these commands being so fixed that they could be neither added to nor diminished. Such a law as that is impossible of observance over a very long period, and the Mosaic Law itself was modified as time went on; nay, even Moses himself, during the journey of the Israelites through the desert, had amplified certain of the laws which he had formerly promulgated as binding for ever.[1]

We must understand the expression 'for ever' in this connexion as meaning stable and permanent, as opposed to laws of a merely temporary character. To think otherwise would be to subscribe to that rabbinic mentality which is irreconcilable with the ordinary exigences of human life. But Jesus was far from doing that. Taking divine revelation as a whole, comprising both the Law and the Prophets, He asserted His right, not indeed to change it but 'to fulfil' it: that is to say, to bring it to its perfection.[2] His meaning here is beyond all doubt, and therefore ought to serve as a basis for the right understanding of that other saying of His which is so difficult: 'Amen I say unto you: till heaven and earth pass, not one jot or tittle of the Law shall pass till all has been fulfilled.'[3] There could have been no object in the making of this twofold declaration other than to show that the Law, unchangeable in substance because it has man's perfection for its aim, was to continue its application during the period which was just beginning. Do not let us understand Jesus as saying that the purpose of His coming is to *accomplish* the Law and the Prophets, or that the Law and the Prophets are to remain in their

[1] Cf. Numbers ix, 6 ff. with Exodus xii, 14 ff.
[2] Matthew v, 17. [3] Matthew v, 18.

entirety until everything they contain has been *accomplished.*[1] To understand Him thus would be to regard His mission as an end in itself. It was indeed an end, but it was also a beginning. We have to bear in mind that the Law and the Prophets are religious and moral truth. Now how is a *truth* fulfilled? Surely by the fact that, while remaining unchangeable in substance, it becomes ever clearer to the minds of men, revealing more and more its content of ideas, manifesting an ever greater fruitfulness in its effects.

Truth in God is the source of an inexhaustible activity, and when that truth is revealed to men it is impossible that it should remain as a mere dead letter. Truth does not change—it is error that changes and so perishes—yet truth in order to come to its perfection undergoes a real development, such a development as is essential in everything that serves the purposes of human life. Not one jot or tittle, then, of the essential elements of the ancient revelation shall perish.

The words in which Jesus makes this declaration contain a parable. Just as a Jewish scribe watches with anxious care lest he should leave out a single jot or tittle which he considers essential to the correct reading of the Scriptures, so God also keeps careful watch of each seed of truth which He has sown in His revelation. An essential development was given to that revelation by Christ, a development such as was destined never to be repeated. What we have said of the original revelation we must say also of the truth thus amplified by Christ: it will stand for ever until it too shall have attained that complete development to which it is destined by God. A real progress will mark its development, whether that progress is a consequence of revelations granted to private individuals or of the contemplation and practice of truths already revealed; and in all this it is the Holy Spirit who is always the guide.[2] To deny that Christ had in mind what was to come to pass after the end of His earthly mission would be equivalent to making Him say that the world was to end with Him.[3]

[1] To 'accomplish' does not mean to bring to perfection but to carry out.

[2] John xvi, 12 ff. provides us with the key to this difficult passage in St. Matthew: 'The Spirit of truth will lead you to the complete truth.'

[3] Read the fine analysis of Newman's thought in M. Jacques Chevalier's conference at Oxford (*Les Lettres*, July, 1927): 'Identity of form can only be an identity of death. Identity of life supposes continual change, the very continuity of which is sufficient to ensure unity and identity. . . . In the notion of time is contained the idea of continual change, but the very purpose of that change is in order that things may remain the same. . . .'

Having laid down the principle, Jesus begins to draw certain conclusions by way of application. The Law forbade homicide: Jesus will not have us even to become angry. Not only must we pardon those who have offended us, we must be the first to seek reconciliation even when all the fault has been on the other side. Again, the Law condemned adultery: we must understand that as a condemnation of every impure desire. The Law permitted a man to repudiate his wife, though in so doing it merely tolerated for the time being a thing that was in itself undesirable: what the Law in reality demands is that perfect union between husband and wife which death alone has the power to dissolve.[1] The Law forbade perjury, but a true disciple of Jesus will avoid all oaths and will content himself with a simple 'yes' or 'no.' The Law prescribed retaliation for injuries: 'An eye for an eye, a tooth for a tooth.' Jesus does not condemn this in so many words. Formerly, in those states of society possessing no public authority strong enough to repress crime, people freely took the work of vengeance into their own hands: and in such circumstances it was found necessary to keep things within bounds by determining that the satisfaction required by the avenger must be measured by the damage done by the offender. Christ's ideal, however, was that we ought not to resist evil in those cases, at least, where the injury is done to one's own person. In heroic words He recommends to us a patience that is beyond the ordinary powers of human nature: 'If anyone strike thee on the right cheek, turn to him the left also.' It is evident that there is in this no question of a command: Jesus puts the matter on so high a plane in order to win from us at least a little kindness towards others: 'If anyone compel thee to go one mile, go with him other two.'

In the teaching put forward by the Law, the Prophets and the Psalms, insistence had been laid upon the love of one's neighbour. But who was this neighbour? This is a question which will come again later.[2] Surely the neighbour belonged to a special privileged category: and there was another category, that of one's enemies. Every good Israelite, like certain of the psalmists, thought it right to

[1] The question was proposed in a solemn fashion by the Pharisees and we shall return to it (on Mark x, 11 ff. and Matt. xix, 9). Cf. ch. iv. § 214.
[2] Cf. ch. iv, §§ 157–8.

hate and curse his enemies, for were they not also the enemies of God? Hence the Law did not forbid hatred, provided one had a just motive for the hatred: so at least thought the Pharisees. Jesus, expressing His thought in a Semitic language—and Semitic language is barren of expressions for fine shades of meaning, using the same form in order to express what is of precept and what is merely tolerated—sums up in these words the current opinion of the time concerning the traditional teaching of the Law on this subject: 'Thou shalt love thy neighbour and hate thy enemy.'[1]

But Jesus shows a better understanding of the all-embracing power of the precept of charity. Charity, as everybody knows, makes a man forget injuries; but He shows how it goes further still. It extends even to our enemies. There are no more limits to it than there are limits to the loving-kindness of the heavenly Father who makes His sun to rise upon the good and upon the bad. Are we to love only our friends? Why, the very publicans do as much. The disciple of Jesus must aim higher than that: his model is no less than God: 'Be ye perfect as your heavenly Father is perfect.' Thus Jesus gradually passes from an express command of the Law to this maxim with which He concludes, in which one might say was represented the whole spirit of the Law. He contrasts the perfection that He has come to teach with the Law and its insufficiency, and with the distorted interpretations of the Law.

He next proceeds to speak of certain practices which, though quite good in themselves, are really pleasing to God only if performed solely for His sake. How could it be possibly pleasing to Him when a man gives alms, or prays, or fasts merely to show off his piety before his neighbours? Doubtless there will always be found everywhere some who act thus, but Jesus has in mind a distinct class of hypocrites. He refrains from mentioning the Pharisees more explicitly, but no one could mistake His meaning. The Jerusalem Talmud speaks of one class of Pharisees who

[1] Matthew v, 43. The first part of this sentence is found written in the Law (Lev. xix, 18), but not the second. Moreover, Jesus does not cite the exact words of the Law. Thus it is clear that it is His intention to oppose His own revelation to the false interpretation of the old revelation. His own revelation is based on what is expressly commanded in the Law, and He makes the formal precept of the Law concerning charity cover all the situations in which, according to the ancient dispensation, it was considered legitimate to hate certain enemies.

wear their good deeds on their backs so that they may get praised for them.[1] This is a well-known characteristic of the whole sect. The religious aristocracy of Israel were convinced that God's honour was in their keeping; and hence, the Jews by their good or bad deeds caused God to be honoured or despised in the eyes of the Gentiles. This sense of responsibility was a strong inducement to avoid evil, but at the same time to conceal evil from notice if they had committed any. In this they justified themselves on the ground that the glory of God was safeguarded by thus keeping up their own reputation for goodness. But their party spirit went to even greater lengths. The sole source of Pharisaic authority was their reputation for learning and religious zeal; but in reality they were working for the honour of their own sect, even when they distinguished themselves from the common run of the people by their devotion for the Law and their good works. When they gave alms they contrived that others should know it; they prayed in the corners of the streets where, while able to pray undisturbed, they could still be seen; they fasted often, and ordinary devout people went into raptures over their emaciated appearance and ascetic features. Thus they received the reward they coveted, the esteem of men.

But, in order to please our Father in heaven, we must seek Him in secret: Jesus lets fall from His lips words that are touched with a delicate humour and not without a touch of exaggeration: 'Therefore, when thou dost an alms-deed, sound not a trumpet. . . . Let not thy left hand know what thy right hand doth';[2] and again: 'But thou, when thou prayest, enter into thy chamber and having shut the door, pray to thy Father who is in secret'; and finally: 'When thou fastest, anoint thy head and wash thy face.' In this way He taught us to perform what we do for God's sake alone, and, what is more, to take care that our good deeds shall not be known. It should be enough for us that God is pleased, and if we love Him truly we shall not desire our good deeds to be seen by others.

Then there is the wonderful truth that man's love for

[1] Cf. Commentary on Mark xii, 40.

[2] Matthew vi, 2. The rabbis well knew how unpleasant it was to see a man making a show of almsgiving, and from Proverbs xxi, 14: 'A secret present quencheth anger' (in him to whom it is given) they concluded that alms must be given in secret. This apparently similar example shows clearly the difference between them and Jesus in spirit and method of teaching.

God flows out towards his neighbour also. In charity towards our neighbour consists the whole of the Law, and we can make sure of observing that Law perfectly by following a very simple rule: 'All things whatsoever you would that men should do to you do you also to them; for this is the Law and the Prophets.'[1] But, it is to be noted, it is the Law and Prophets understood according to the new spirit which brings them to their perfection. Hillel, who had been the leader of the Pharisees before the time in which Jesus lived, had said something of the same kind but at the same time very different: 'That which you do not like don't do to anybody else; this is the whole of the Law, and all the rest is only the explanation of it.'[2] And such indeed is the standard of justice. But while charity too respects the boundaries which mark off our neighbours' rights, it is not content with merely abstaining from doing wrong to others. See how intensely everyone loves himself, with what far-sightedness and skill he pursues his own interests! What a noble ideal it would be to use the same ardour in the service of our neighbour! It was in this that St. Augustine placed the golden rule. But of course that golden rule cannot be observed until the love of God has driven out self-love and so made way for the love of our neighbour. Thus, for prayer we seek solitude; but if our neighbour should enter on the scene, charity will make us leave our solitude and become active. Such is the substance of the New Law. The Old Law consisted entirely of exhortations to good works; and under the New Law too there must be no falling off in good works now that they are to be inspired by a pure love of God and our neighbour. Not a word did Jesus utter in His preaching such as would lead anyone to believe that the knowledge of His doctrine is a kind of charm which of itself ensures eternal life. Nothing would be further from the truth. Whoever has listened to His words, even if he has believed them, will be rejected by Him unless he has put those words into practice. The doctrine of Jesus is not like one of the pagan mysteries: it is offered to all indiscriminately, and is not like knowledge communicated to a privileged few which brings special benefit to the hearers of it. In a word, there is nothing savouring of a passive pseudo-mysticism in the doctrine of Jesus. It is a call to action, but our action is to take the

[1] Matthew vii, 12.

[2] Talmud, *Chabbat*, 31a.

shape of doing our heavenly Father's will: 'Not everyone that saith to Me, Lord, Lord, shall enter into the kingdom of heaven; but he that doth the will of My Father.'[1]

Ever since that saying was uttered Christian philosophers have pondered over the question of moral conduct and the conditions requisite for Christian perfection. Their teaching more and more reduces itself to this: that the whole of perfection consists in uniting ourselves with the will of God by fulfilling it to the best of our ability, or at least by resigning ourselves to it. But all that was made plain by Jesus in one word.

Conclusion.

This opening sermon of Jesus, which bears the character of a kind of programme and has in view a new order of things, is clearly meant for a period during which things were to be better, but a period nevertheless situated in the same conditions as those of the existing world. For had Jesus merely intended to put Himself forward as the Prophet of a kingdom of God which was to be set up in a world completely transformed by innocence and happiness, and built upon the ruins of the present wicked world condemned by God to destruction, then the whole Sermon on the Mount would be unintelligible: nay, it would be a standing example of absurdity. But, on the contrary, He declares that His disciples will have need of all their endeavours in order to preserve their goodness; they will have to live constantly in the face of bad example against which they must be ever on their guard. The new era that is now beginning is to be a time of conflict; the time will be long, and nothing is said to determine how long it will be. The followers of Christ are to go on living under the same conditions of the world as obtained formerly, for the old Law will still apply, but they must live under the guidance of a new principle.

By its very definition a law is composed of a number of precepts the observance of which must be within the power of all who are subjects of the law. It is of the nature of a law to command, not to offer advice; though all are free, if they wish, to undertake things that imply greater perfection than what the law prescribes. Had the Law of Moses

[1] Matthew vii, 21.

been nothing more than a mere body of precepts intended to govern a man's conduct in the performance of his positive duties, social and even religious, it might have been argued that the coming of Jesus abrogated that law, since He wished men to act from a motive that is higher than mere obligation, the motive, that is to say, of charity ; and it is of the nature of charity that it is capable of always greater perfection. Far from laying down rules demanding the minimum of good conduct, He gives counsels of perfection that are bounded by no limits. The paradoxical form in which some of His directions are expressed is clearly intended to show that in this way of the counsels charity can always surpass itself. Truly we can join with St. Paul in saying that we are no longer under the Law, but under the regime of grace.[1]

Yet the Law itself had given some glimpse of this truth in those burning exhortations to love God which we find in Deuteronomy. It was through the medium of this fundamental principle concerning the love of God, and through all the moral consequences flowing from this principle, that the Law had to remain in force for ever. Jesus taught very simply, not by any process of reasoning, but in a concrete fashion by the use of examples, what St. Paul was later to bring out more clearly in his dialectical manner. The Master's teaching is none the less of a very practical character, suited to all times and conditions, for human nature is the same in all ages. It is clear that He has no intention of proposing a visionary golden age to take the place of living under obedience to the Law ; He merely sums up the Law in the one precept of charity, but a charity that is better understood and better practised, and practised all the better for the reason that it will still have difficulties to overcome. The whole of His teaching aims at giving us a higher ideal of righteousness, so that everyone, now that God begins again to reign in the world, may reach the kingdom of God that is above, where alone is to be found perfect happiness in union with God.

[1] Romans vi, 15.

IV. VARIOUS OPINIONS ABOUT THE WORK OF JESUS

The Centurion of Capharnaum (76).

Luke vii, 1–10 ; Matthew viii, 5–10, 13.[1]

After the Sermon on the Mount Jesus went back to Capharnaum. Here St. Luke, without any show of introducing His reader to an historical situation with which he would be unfamiliar, writing as a man writes when he knows that his reader will understand, makes allusion to an interesting feature of the social and religious condition of Galilee. At Capharnaum there was a centurion, that is an officer of subordinate rank supposed to have a hundred men under his command. Though he was a pagan he nevertheless could have been in the service of Herod Antipas, if that tetrarch was as rich as his father, Herod the Great, and hence able to hire mercenary soldiers.[2] We read in the Old Testament how of old the kings of Juda had captains of a hundred men.[3] But whenever St. Luke speaks of a centurion he always uses the word of Roman officers. The centurion was to the Roman legion what the mainspring is to a watch. Centurions were employed likewise in the auxiliary cohorts of the army. Perhaps the Romans had established a small post of soldiers on the frontier of the territories governed by Antipas and Philip, and if they did so no one was in a position to object to it.

This centurion, then, was probably in the Roman service; he seems evidently to have been trained in the principles of Roman discipline. But, like many pagans of that day, he felt a strong attraction for the Jewish religion. Contemporary philosophers, even those who held the doctrines of pantheism or practised idolatry, preferred to speak of the *one* God. They could not but see that the Jews were more logical in worshipping no other god but Him. This man had not followed up that line of reasoning so far as to profess Judaism, but at any rate he seems to have been on excellent terms with the Jews. Hence he asks them to carry his request to Jesus. He had a servant who was sick unto death, and this servant was very dear to him. Not all the people of the ancient world, particularly in the East, were

[1] Along with Fillion we follow Luke's narrative as it is more detailed.
[2] Cf. Josephus, *Ant.* XVII, viii, 3.
[3] 4 Kings, xi, 9, 15.

insensible to the instincts of human nature to the degree which is implied in the cruel treatment of slaves by the Roman Law. Indeed, there often existed a real affection between a master and a good slave. Encouraged by what he had heard about the extraordinary powers of Jesus, the centurion begged Him to come and heal his servant. The Jews to whom he entrusted his request were sure that Jesus, Himself a good Israelite, would not refuse the favour to this man who, though a foreigner, had been so kind to the Jews as to build the local synagogue, and in that synagogue Jesus Himself had often prayed and heard or explained the Law.[1] They make known to Him their request and in reply Jesus follows them. But already a scruple had entered the good centurion's mind. Doubtless the Jews had often come into his house without fearing to contaminate themselves, for they always took care to purify themselves afterwards. But could he expect the same of a man like Jesus, if indeed He was a man? For perhaps the centurion thought He was one of these demi-gods that people spoke of. If he had not dared to approach in person to present his request to Jesus how then could he invite such a being, one powerful enough to work miracles, to cross the threshold of his house? And so he sends his friends to tell Him: 'Lord, trouble not Thyself, for I am not worthy that Thou shouldest enter under my roof. . . . But say one word so that my servant may be healed.' He is well aware of the wonderful effect of the spoken word, he knows the power of a word of command. An order goes out from our lips and, as it were, travels out into the distance in order to accomplish its object. How often has he not experienced the same thing in dealing with the men under him! 'Go!' he had said, or 'Come!', and the thing would be done.

Jesus showed admiration for him, not altogether without that air of surprise which is characteristic of every feeling of admiration; for, as we have said, Jesus in everything followed the normal conditions of human nature. Then He declared: 'I say unto you, I have not found so great faith, not even in Israel.' At that same moment the centurion had the joy of seeing his servant healed. The Church has

[1] At Tell-Hum, ancient Capharnaum, the ruins of a synagogue have been discovered, and even the ruins prove what a splendid building it must have been. But they are the ruins of a synagogue which could not have been built before the end of the second century A.D. Still, it may easily have been built on the site of the former synagogue.

done him the honour of putting his words on the lips of those who are about to receive the Eucharistic Body of Him who comes for the healing of the soul.

The resurrection of the widow's son at Naim (77).

Luke vii, 11–17.

But Jesus showed still greater power ; by His word He recalled a soul from that mysterious abode where disembodied spirits dwell. The touching scene of this event is described by St. Luke in words of delicate pathos : a young man stricken down by death being carried to the grave on a stretcher, the only son of a widowed mother : the crowd moved by emotion : our Lord stirred to pity, venturing to say to the mother : 'Weep not !' Then He touches the open coffin, commands the young man to arise, and restores him to his mother. Whereupon the people cry : 'A great prophet hath been raised up amongst us ; God hath visited His people.' Not merely did they wonder at that sovereign power : they are constrained to love that goodness also. The memory of this incident is still recalled by the name *Nein* which belongs to a tiny village lying to the south-east of Nazareth (*en-Nasira* as it is called) and almost opposite Thabor.

The mission of the Baptist and the mission of the Son of Man (78,79).

Luke vii, 18–35 ; xvi, 16 ; Matthew xi, 2–19.

If God had visited His people, it meant that the Messiah had come. Hence there began to be discussion about this great question. More especially must it have been the subject of passionate discussion among John's disciples, for their master from the first had warned them of the approach of Him who was to come, and had pointed out Jesus to them as the one who was destined to take away the sins of the world. And now John was in prison. Josephus tells us that the place of his imprisonment was Machærus on the mountains overlooking the Dead Sea from the east, and consequently a long way from Galilee. There his disciples were allowed to see and talk with him, and they reported to him the different stages of Jesus' activity, narrating how He was proclaiming the kingdom of God as John himself had done, and also driving out devils and healing the sick. Such activity was extraordinary, but it by no means proved that He was the Messiah. It was the common opinion of the rabbis that the prophets of old had worked miracles ; Elias and Eliseus, indeed, had even raised the dead. The mission of the Messiah was held to be something altogether different. John's disciples, therefore, did not believe that Jesus was the Messiah. But John had already expressed his mind on the subject ; was he to go back on his word, to have doubts about the vision he had seen at Jesus' baptism, and to contradict himself by doubting about Jesus ? It is not possible that St. Matthew and St. Luke thought so when they related John's plan of sending two of his disciples to ask Jesus : ' Art Thou He that cometh, or look we for another ? ' ' He that cometh ' are the very words John had used[1] to designate Him who was to baptize in the Holy Ghost and cleanse the threshing-floor of the chaff. St. Matthew does not forget this ; on the contrary, we may say that he here reminds us of it. That very fact throws light on what was the Baptist's own state of mind, which was surely this : why did the Mighty One whom he had announced delay to fulfil in a most glorious manner the rôle allotted to Him ? Would not people naturally conclude that they must look for another ? He does not entertain any doubts about the mission of Jesus, but all the same the time seems long while he lies in prison at Machærus. Moreover, he thinks of his disciples whose doubts have not yet been dispelled.

The reply of Jesus can hardly be understood as a mere affirmation of what John already knew, and what his disciples also knew since it was they who had told him about it. Before we can understand its true significance we must first have an idea of what is the force of an argument drawn from Scripture. It was commonly thought, as we have already said, that the working of miracles was not a sufficient proof of the Messiah. Yet it is to be noticed that miracles are given as such a proof by Isaias,[2] and everyone would easily recognize his words even though Jesus does not name the prophet :

[1] Matthew iii, 11. [2] Isaias xxix, 18 ff. and lxi, 1.

In that day the deaf shall hear the words of the book ;
Without shadow and without darkness the eyes of the blind
shall see.
The humble shall rejoice in Jahweh,
And the poorest shall exult in the Holy One of Israel.[1]

What was here taught by the Scripture was this : that the significance of miracles was not to be limited to the external act of healing. People were cured if they had sufficient faith to demand it, and their faith was increased by the miracle. Their ears hear the word, their eyes perceive the truth. The sum of it all is that ' the poor receive the good news of salvation.'[2]

So the time has begun in which good reigns in the world. John, as well as Peter, was dreaming of a Messiah who was to appear in triumph. But he must leave Jesus to work in His own way, seeing that he has recognized Him as one who is doing the work of the Holy Spirit.

When Jesus concludes with the words : ' Blessed is he that shall not be scandalized in Me,' He is not condemning His friend the Baptist ; on the contrary, He is about to pay him honour. His intention is to warn us against that ever-present temptation to ask from God striking signs and wonders through our failure to realize that His ways are the ways of patience and gentleness.

John's disciples did not regard this reply as unsatisfactory and unworthy of being taken back to their master. But did they understand it ? When they had gone, Jesus made known how John's mission and His own had been joined together by God ; He declared what was the divine purpose in which the old covenant was made subordinate to the kingdom of God. He showed also how lacking in understanding were the doctors of the Law who had failed to recognize John and now were failing to recognize the Son of Man. By associating Himself with John, He proves conclusively that He did not consider him to be wavering in the testimony which, as the forerunner of the Messiah, it was his duty to render.[3]

[1] Isaias xxix, 18 (Condamin's translation).
[2] Isaias lxi, 1, a saying which Jesus applies to Himself at Nazareth.
[3] We have explained this incident in the way that seems to us most consonant with the text. But another well-authorized opinion considers that John was fully enlightened concerning Jesus and only sent his disciples to Him in their own interest.

Jesus asks the crowd whether they went out into the desert to see a reed shaken by the wind. But who would go to such trouble merely to see the thickets of reeds growing on the banks of the Jordan or by the springs, waving with every breath of wind? The thought of John was still present to their minds, so they must have understood well enough that Jesus was making a contrast between him on the one hand, as the very type of unshaken constancy, and a bending reed on the other. Perhaps they went out to the desert to look for a man clothed in all the refinements of luxury! But they knew well enough how poor and rough was his garb. From the man beneath that garb, just like what Elias of old had worn, they looked to hear the words of a prophet; and John was indeed a prophet, charged to announce God's coming. It was in God's name that Malachias had written:

> 'Behold I shall send My messenger, and he shall clear the way before Me.'[1]

Further on the prophet identifies the messenger with Elias: 'Immediately after the coming of the forerunner, the Lord will make His entry into His palace or His temple; that is, He will come to abide in the midst of His people, thus satisfying their impatient longing for Him.'[2] Jesus knows that this prediction is now fulfilled; He fulfils it in His own person. The Elias who was to come before the Lord is in reality John the Baptist.

The messenger of the Lord is, then, more than a prophet, greater than all the prophets, the greatest of all the sons of women. No one, of course, would presume to compare John with Him whom he has come to announce, seeing that all the glory of John springs from his office as the herald of Christ. Moreover, the Baptist had been destined by God to serve as the last stage in the dispensation of the Law and the Prophets. After him was to begin the kingdom of God. Already, says Jesus, men are taking that kingdom by storm, the violent are laying hold of it: that is to say, there are some who are ready to sacrifice everything in order to gain the kingdom of God. So far is this kingdom superior to the covenant made on Sinai, so truly is it the goal foreseen by the prophets, that the least in the kingdom of God

[1] Malachias iii, 1, after Van Hoonacker's translation.
[2] Cf. Van Hoonacker's commentary *in loco*.

is greater than John. Jesus is not speaking here of rank in heaven—He refused to allot places there[1]—but of the surpassing dignity of each member of the new dispensation. Here the principle is laid down ; it was left for St. Paul to explain how baptism, received with faith in the redeeming death of Christ, ranks higher than the ancient rite of circumcision which preceded baptism.

We can excuse those who listened to the Master and failed to understand this mystery ; but there was no excuse for the scornful attitude adopted by the spiritual leaders of Israel, who arrogated to themselves the right to sit in judgement on all things and to condemn whatever did not meet their approval. John the Baptist had come in ascetic garb. That was all very well on the surface, they argued ; but, after all, it might only be a cloak for some trickery of the devil. The Son of Man ate and drank like other men ; whereupon these critics judged that nothing could be expected from a person like Him, a glutton, a wine-bibber, a friend of publicans and sinners. What could be done to satisfy such hyper-critics ? They were like a set of disagreeable children who find fault with their companions whatever game they propose. In such a case the complaint of the latter is quite justifiable : 'We have piped for you and you have not danced ; we have mourned and you have not beaten your breasts.' Thus these disdainful Jews stood apart, holding aloof from the religious enthusiasm which God was enkindling amongst the people. Happily there were others who showed themselves more docile. These are the children of Wisdom who understand her ways ; the homage they pay her justifies her in the face of her calumniators.

In this lesson taught by Jesus on occasion of the question put by John's messengers He accepts unreservedly the dispensation of the old covenant, but at the same time He places it in complete subordination to the new dispensation. There is no break of continuity, nothing of the old is abandoned, but He shows in the strongest terms possible how the new order is superior to the old. The whole of St. Paul's thesis is there. The doctrine of Marcion, who rejected the Old Testament and thus censured Wisdom anew though in another fashion, is condemned before it is uttered. There is no passage in the Scriptures from which

[1] Matthew xx, 20 ff.

it emerges more clearly how truly St. Paul was only what he professed himself to be, a disciple of the Lord. At the same time we perceive how different from our Lord's is the quality of St. Paul's genius. The latter uses the argumentative method, proving his thesis from Scripture and reason. But in the words of his Master there is no trace of reflection or argumentative effort. Jesus sees the divine plan already in realization. There is no tormenting of the mind in order to find suitable words to express new ideas : all is simple and homely in character, with examples and comparisons such as everybody could understand. The very letter of the Old Testament which He here cites serves to reveal more clearly that the work which God was to come to do is being done by Jesus.

If we reject the authenticity of these words, then there seems no good reason why we should attribute authenticity to anything He says. And if He really spoke in this fashion, what are we to think of Him ? But great as He reveals Himself to be, there is not a word of His to give ground for any idle expectation of a kingdom of God that will come down from heaven complete and perfect. No, the kingdom of God has already begun, and in order to enter it some are using a sort of violence ; others reject it with indifference, for, having disregarded the Baptist's message, they now stop their ears against the Gospel. They fail to understand God's plan, for they judge everything according to their own ideas, and always find some pretext for refusing to accept His will.

The pardon of the sinful woman (80).

Luke vii, 36–50.

The case of this sinner, the woman whose forgiveness is related by St. Luke, is an instance of that holy violence done to the kingdom of God in the person of Him who was contemptuously named ' the friend of sinners.' Here, more than anywhere, do we feel that we ought simply to read and shed tears instead of making comments.

There were evidently some of the Pharisees who had not adopted the policy of reserve towards Jesus, unlike those who never addressed Him except in order to embarrass Him with their questions. It seems at least that Simon, who invited the Master to his table, felt some natural sympathy with Him, though he did not on that account cease to watch Him. The scene took place somewhere in Galilee. Jesus was reclining like the others on a low couch, with knees doubled and feet naturally turned outwards away from the table. A woman comes in, a sinner, and known as such to the people of that little town. In her hands she bears an alabaster vase full of perfumed oil ; her purpose is to anoint the feet of Jesus. Having placed herself behind at His feet, so that she is not visible to Him, she stoops to pour the oil and bursts into tears, and her tears flow over His feet. She had not foreseen this outburst of emotion and, hurriedly loosening her hair, she wipes the feet of Jesus and kisses them before anointing them with the oil.

Jesus did not interrupt her. It was evident, then, to all that her touch was not abhorrent to Him ; He did not make a reproving gesture like a virtuous person who feels himself placed in a false position. And yet, thought Simon, He must know who she is, if not by repute at least by His gift of prophecy if He really is a prophet. He was indeed a prophet, and He showed it by reading his host's thoughts. Then He propounds to him a parable : there were two debtors who could not pay. The creditor forgave them what they owed, one a hundred *denarii*, the other fifty. Which of the two would love his benefactor most ? A pessimist would have taken this opportunity for declaring to what depths human perversity can go : the more benefits men receive the more hatred they show. Simon, a little surprised at being asked to solve so easy a problem, replies nevertheless with Pharisaic gravity and good sense : 'I suppose he to whom he forgave most.'

The Master gently points out that this sinner is in a similar case by comparison with a good man like Simon. The Pharisee, free from reproach in his own eyes regarding his attitude towards Jesus, has omitted to show Him any of those services which were paid to those held in honour. His conduct has been correct, barely so, and cold. But this sinner. . . . With what kindness Jesus speaks of her repentant love ! Luke has said that she kissed His feet ; *He* says : 'Since I came in, she hath not ceased to kiss My feet,' so touched was He by her repentance and love. What conclusion will He draw ? The most logical inference from the parable would be : 'She hath shown much love because much hath been forgiven her.' But the Master does not bind Himself down to an exact parallel between the parable and the reality with which the parable makes a comparison. The parable is meant merely to put the listener on the right path to the truth. The sinner is there awaiting forgiveness, and God forgives only those who love Him. No soul can remain in a state of indifference towards God ; it either loves or hates. Sin is an obstacle to love : where love appears sin is blotted out. Yielding to the prompting of His heart, Jesus utters the words from which all the theology of forgiveness springs : 'Her many sins are forgiven her because she hath loved much.' The parable at the same time strikes at people like Simon on the other hand : there is not much to be forgiven in their case, but they have very little love.

Does it mean, then, that we cannot have a great love for God unless we have first offended Him ? God forbid ! The manifest intention of the divine Physician is to give hope to sinners ; four centuries later St. Augustine's tears fell when he thought of the woman who was a sinner. Jesus also wished to give a warning to those who think themselves dispensed from the obligation of loving God on the ground of their being so good that there is nothing in their conduct which calls for forgiveness on His part.

But all that has been said concerns offences against God and that love for God which blots out our sins ; yet this sinner has shown love only for Jesus. How simply He takes God's place, counting as addressed to God those protestations of repentance which she has just made at His feet !

Curiosity concerning the historical facts here asserts itself and brings us down from the heights in order to ask the name of the woman. This is a celebrated problem. The independent biblical critics of our own day maintain that this anointing of Jesus by the sinful woman is merely another version of the anointing which took place at Bethany.[1] This was also the opinion of Clement of Alexandria, due probably to a confusion of memory,[2] and several others among the Fathers seem to be of the same mind. In that case this woman could have been no other than Mary, the sister of Martha and Lazarus. But the two

[1] In Mark, Luke, and John. Cf. No. 228 of the Synopsis.

[2] Cf. *Revue Biblique*, 1912, pp. 504–532 : *Jésus a-t-il été oint plusieurs fois, et par plusieurs femmes ?*

anointings are different in place, for one was in Galilee, the other near Jerusalem ; in time, because one took place at the beginning of the ministry, the other eight days before the Passion ; and they differ especially in spirit, one ending in forgiveness, the other being a foreboding of burial. It is true that a Simon appears on each occasion, but the name was a common one.

The common opinion among Catholic scholars is that the two anointings are distinct. In contrast with the former opinion, they hold that the text of the New Testament provides no ground for identifying the sinful woman of Galilee with Mary of Bethany to whom so much honour is paid.[1] It is of no use appealing to tradition for the identification of the two women, for there is no coherent tradition on the subject.[2] And although it is true that there is one tradition in the Latin Church which identifies them, nevertheless this tradition dates only from the time of St. Gregory the Great ; moreover, the Greek Church has always held the opposite view.

If, then, the sinful woman cannot be Mary of Bethany and Mary of Bethany is identified with Mary Magdalen, it follows that the sinful woman cannot be Mary Magdalen either. But neither is it possible to identify Mary of Bethany with Mary of Magdala, who came from Galilee to follow Jesus. St. John distinguishes them very clearly. As Mary Magdalen was not Mary of Bethany, since she came from Galilee, she might possibly be the sinful woman. This question depends for its solution entirely on St. Luke. Immediately after the scene of the woman's forgiveness he mentions the women cured by Jesus and describes how they showed their gratitude by providing for His needs. One of these women was Mary surnamed Magdalen, that is, native of Magdala, out of whom He had cast seven devils. St. Luke, therefore, introduces her as a figure of whom he has not previously spoken. Diabolic possession by no means implies a sinful life, nor does it exclude it. Strictly speaking, we might suppose that Luke did not want to disclose the sins of Mary Magdalen, who had become a

[1] John xi, 2 should be understood of what the evangelist is about to relate.

[2] Fr. Urban Holzmeister, S.J., thus ends his very careful study of this question : 'From this enquiry there emerges very clearly one single conclusion : to the question whether there is any coherent tradition (in favour of identity) we must certainly not answer in the affirmative.' (*Zeitschrift für katholische Theologie*, edited by the Jesuits of Innsbruck, 1922, p. 584.)

fervent disciple of Christ revered by the early Christians, and hence deliberately refrained from identifying her with the woman that was a sinner. Thus the latter, though she certainly cannot be Mary of Bethany, might be one with Mary Magdalen. But if it be true that Luke wished to hide their identity we certainly cannot gather that fact from his text; the contrary rather would seem true. And if he had other intentions he kept them to himself.

Those who maintain that these three women are one and the same have recourse to psychological arguments in order to support their contention. They profess to recognize in all three the same person, with the same disposition, the same manner of behaviour, and the same ardent love. There is some weight in this argument as regards Mary the sister of Martha in the gospel of St. Luke, and Mary the sister of Martha in the fourth gospel: the woman who listens eagerly to Jesus without bestirring herself to serve Him is very like the woman who stays at home until her sister calls her, while it is Martha who waits on Jesus and runs to meet Him. Has that Mary—without question tremendously loving and very much loved, but at the same time so calm—has she the disposition of Mary of Magdala, so fervent, active, and anxious, dreaming of the impossible, such as St. John reveals her at our Saviour's tomb? Mary of Magdala and the sinner would be more of the same stamp. Perhaps we had better conclude with Bossuet: 'It is more in harmony with the letter of the Gospel to distinguish three persons.'[1] M. Fillion, along with Fr. Knabenbauer, prefers to take this course, which, indeed, can claim the support of 'great scholars like Estius, Tillemont, Calmet, and Mabillon.'

The true kindred of Jesus (81–83).

Luke viii, 1–3; Mark iii, 20–21; Luke viii, 19–21; xi, 28; Mark iii, 31–35; Matthew xiii, 46–50.

By choosing the Twelve Apostles Himself Jesus taught once and for all that spiritual authority in His Church is to be conferred on men specially called. But in their work they find splendid helpers in those devoted women who,

[1] Quoted by Fillion, Vol. II, p. 329.

consecrated to God or else living in the world, take the lesser cares of the Church under their charge. This too was foreshadowed in the public life of our Lord : nay more, the beginnings of it were present in that group of women who also wished to follow Jesus out of gratitude for His goodness to them, and who in their generosity used their possessions to contribute towards his needs, for His preaching no longer left Him opportunity to support Himself with the work of His hands as He had done for so long. St. Luke names some of these women : Mary, distinguished from the other Marys by her surname Magdalen ; Joanna the wife of Chusa, Herod's steward—we might call him minister of finance were it not too pretentious—and last of all Susanna. But he adds that there were many others. Doubtless we should be in error were we to picture all these people following the Master always in procession, so to say. Rather they arranged that some should always be with Him to attend to His needs. Although the Twelve were not always with Him, yet it certainly seems that Peter, James, and John never left Him, at least while He was in Galilee. Thus there was formed around Him the nucleus of a new spiritual family, and He taught that all might belong to this family, encouraging them to come by letting them see that it depended only on themselves. In this could be clearly traced the Church of the future, at least in its outlines.

In these days, so loose are the bonds which formerly bound together the members of one people or tribe, so slender are the ties which attach us to any outside our own immediate family circle—and even there the bond is often of a very weak kind—that it is hard for us to realize the strength of those ties by which people of the ancient world, both of West and East, were bound together to make up that larger family we call the clan. In our own day that primitive constitution of society will be found best preserved in the East. It gives rise to a self-sacrifice that is admirable ; it is also the occasion frequently in the East of serious obstacles to the independence of the priest, for a priest must treat all the members of his flock alike, whether they are of his own clan or not. In Greece and in Italy at the time of Jesus the city was a tiny local fatherland, formed by the grouping together of various clans who lived under the protection of the city's laws ; and such a city thus became the object of men's noblest affections. In Palestine there existed only the clan-family which held itself responsible for the welfare of its members who, though united with all other Israelites by one national bond of fellowship, yet belonged more intimately to the clan-family. Hence it was only natural and in accordance with custom that the kinsfolk of Jesus should show concern about that consuming activity of His which threatened to wear out His strength.

One day in particular the crowd so hemmed in the house where He was with His disciples that He was unable even to take food. 'His own people'—evidently not the disciples, seeing these were in the house with Him, but relations in a wide sense—came from their homes to take charge of Him, for people[1] were saying: 'He is beside Himself.' This step was surely prompted by kindness. They wonder whether Jesus is not going to excess or in danger of being misguided, and their intention is to bring Him back to the family circle and to persuade Him to return to His ordinary occupations. Perhaps, too, they are in fear of being made to shoulder the responsibility for all this disturbance. That Mark has recorded this incident is sufficient of itself to prove his perfect candour and truthfulness.

Where did these relations come from? Some would be from Capharnaum itself; but disquieting rumours may have reached Nazareth, and some of the relations probably came from there. It is at the moment of their arrival at Capharnaum that the Mother and brethren of Jesus appear on the scene, according to the first three evangelists. Not that it was His Mother Mary who was responsible for these proceedings: the initiative came from those at the head of the clan. But the outcome could hardly be a matter of indifference to a mother's heart; her place was there, little as she shared the general anxiety about her Son. Her confidence in Him at the marriage feast of Cana had already showed that she was not likely to let herself be overcome by such fears. The brethren of Jesus are those whom St. Mark calls 'His own,' and consequently relations who were not necessarily brethren in our sense of the word.

Finding it impossible to get through the crowd, the relatives of Jesus send a message asking Him to come out.

[1] I at first translated 'they (the relations) said': but I think we must accept the arguments of Mr. Turner (in the *Journal of Theological Studies*, XXV, pp. 383 ff.), who maintains that the relations came *because they had heard people saying*.

Someone says to Him : 'Thy Mother and Thy brethren are outside seeking Thee.' He answers : 'Who are My Mother and My brethren ?' Then, looking round on those sitting with Him, He says : 'Behold My Mother and My brethren. Whosoever doth the will of God, he is My brother, and My sister, and My mother.'[1] Thus did He inaugurate spiritual relationship, that great family which includes, in the words of St. Luke, all 'those who hear the word of God and do it.'[2]

In this reply, therefore, is contained a fundamental point of His teaching. It manifests the nature of His preaching : a most cordial appeal to men of good will, along with an assurance that if they come to Him they will find a heart full of the most tender human affection. So much is perfectly clear, but other considerations may be drawn out of His words. The sacred duties that are owing to the family are by no means denied : Jesus does not renounce His Mother. What we do see, however, is that He attaches more value to her devotion towards God than to the care she showed for her Son when He was an infant in the cradle. The Church has given us the true meaning of His words in placing Mary at the head of her Son's new spiritual family, far above all the Saints.

V. THE PARABLES OF THE KINGDOM OF GOD

Nature and purpose of teaching by parables (85).

Luke viii, 9–10 ; Mark iv, 10–12 ; Matthew xiii, 10–15.

Just as St. Matthew has set before us in the comparatively long Sermon on the Mount what we have called the programme of Jesus, so also does the same evangelist devote a complete chapter to a series of parables about the kingdom of God. As in the former case, so here too we may conclude that he has probably grouped in one place things spoken in different circumstances ; but St. Mark is at one with him in picturing for us the very homely scene of Jesus preaching by the lakeside about the kingdom of God. Again, St. Matthew agrees with St. Mark and St. Luke concerning the time at which this important teaching began in the ministry of Jesus.

[1] Mark iii, 33 ff. [2] Luke viii, 21.

At the beginning of their gospels the three evangelists state the theme of the Master's teaching to be the coming of the kingdom or reign of God. It was precisely for this that He had been sent.[1] At Nazareth He had announced that in His person was inaugurated the time of grace. He had invited a few Galilæans to join in His work. In their presence He had called a large number of people to the practice of perfection, and had admitted into His family all who heard His words and resolved to put them into practice. That was what He meant by the kingdom or reign of God, and it had been made clear enough to all when, speaking once more about the relation His own work bore to the prophecies spoken before Him, He declared that the least in the kingdom of God ranked higher than the greatest of the prophets. And now the moment had come for a fuller explanation of this kingdom of God in which so many had placed their hopes. He therefore devotes a day to the teaching of parables concerning the kingdom of God.

But there is something here which seems strange to us, namely, that what we gather from this new mode of teaching is less clear than what we have already learnt. If we wish to form a just idea of the perfection that constitutes the kingdom of God it is better to meditate on the Sermon on the Mount than upon the parables which are expressly devoted to that subject. What is the reason of this surprising phenomenon ? Is it possible that, after having taught openly for a time, Jesus decided to clothe His thoughts in a more obscure form ? Did He choose the parable in order to veil His meaning and thus punish a nation which had shown no disposition to follow Him ? This is a celebrated question about which the greatest minds disagree, and before approaching it we must first discuss the literary character of the parable.[2]

As the parables are among the very gems of the Gospel we must not be surprised to find hostile critics denying to Jesus the authorship of some of the most beautiful and significant among them. In order to give their contention some rational basis in fact these critics insist on the essential distinction between parable and allegory. But, they maintain, all the parables that we know for certain to have been

[1] Luke iv, 43.

[2] Cf. *Revue Biblique*, 1909 : La parabole en dehors de l'évangile, p. 198 ff. and p. 342 ff.

uttered by Jesus belong to the class of similes or comparisons and not to that of the allegory.[1] They add—and this is perfectly true—that a parable is clear in its meaning, while an allegory is obscure.

Now it is a fact that the parable and the allegory are two different figures of speech which we must distinguish, as the Greek writers distinguished them with their very precise analysis. Allegory is composed of a series of metaphors. If we say: 'He fought like a lion,' that is a simile; if we say: 'A lion in the battle, he leapt upon his prey,' that is a metaphor, or rather, as it stands, it is a group of two metaphors and consequently the beginning of an allegory. In order to understand an allegory properly we need a key; for instance, we must know here that the lion stands for Alexander the Great and the prey for Darius Codomannus. And if the allegory be prolonged we may be at a loss to know what each metaphor represents: hence this style of writing is not uncommonly obscure.

The allegory is a series of metaphors, each one of the metaphorical terms being representative of some further reality. The parable is nothing more than a comparison between two different situations, and the terms in which the parable is expressed are used to describe some well-known truth or to tell a story; we are not to take them singly and look for some corresponding term in the truth or situation which the parable is meant to elucidate. There was no question among the Greeks that the purpose of the parable was to enlighten. Greece was the land of clear ideas. Thus parable lies at the basis of all Socratic reasoning, for Socrates had the habit of using homely examples in order to throw the light of current ideas upon questions that were obscure. Aristotle, too, spoke of the parable and classified it with his customary accuracy. He gives the following example: Ought magistrates to be chosen by lot? No, for that would be as foolish as to choose a pilot by lot; in either case we require a man competent for the office. Sometimes the simile is continued until it takes the form of a little fable, but that does not change the essential nature of the parable. Thus we have the story of the horse which, in order to have his revenge upon a stag, invites a man to mount his back: the horse may have his revenge, but at the price of his liberty. Beware then, when looking

[1] Cf. Loisy, *Études évangeliques*, p. 37.

for a defender, lest you find a master. Unless the situation chosen in order to solve the obscure question be clear in itself and fit the case, the parable is a failure. But the parables of Jesus are models in this respect; they ought not then to be obscure.

Such is what is strictly required by literary rules; but when it is a question of literary taste these rules are not always obeyed. The rhetoricians, indeed, went so far as to condemn them, and had the good taste to acknowledge the beauty of a mixed style which blended simile or parable with allegory and metaphor.[1] It is evident, then, that the critics are ill-informed when they maintain that the combination of fable and allegory is simply to be classed with the monstrosities of mythology and imagination.[2] Moreover, even when the pure parable is deliberately used as a method of teaching, it may sometimes, owing to the nature of the subject chosen, be incapable by itself of rendering the lesson as clear as the teacher desires.

Generally speaking, the clarity aimed at by the Greeks concerned truths attainable by human reason. As soon as reason has succeeded in proving the existence of God it confesses that it has reached a sphere into which it cannot enter. Even the most courageous and determined of the Greek rationalists, Aristotle, here laid down his arms: 'Unbegotten and incorruptible beings are doubtless of great worth and divine, but they are the things of which we know the least . . . but, without any doubt, as they are of such worth, even a slight acquaintance with them is more pleasing than the knowledge of the things by which we are surrounded, just as it is better to see the smallest part of some object that we love than to have full knowledge of many other beings. Nevertheless, the nearness of the things surrounding us and their natural kinship with us are advantages which compensate us for our lack of knowledge of divine things.'[3] The Jews would by no means have consented to renounce the knowledge of things divine as the condition of obtaining clarity of ideas. To their mind divine revelation was gradually dissipating some of the darkness that will always envelop us here below. The

[1] *Illud vero longe speciosissimum genus orationis, in quo trium permixta est gratia, similitudinis, allegoriæ, translationis.* (Quintilian, Instit. orat., VIII, vi, 48.)

[2] Cf. Jülicher, *Die Gleichnisse Jesu*, I, 107.

[3] *De Partibus Animalium*, I, 5, from Bréhier's translation; cf. his *Histoire de la Philosophie*, I, p. 324.

way in which that teaching was communicated was, and had to be, by analogy with created things : that is to say, God was made known by His works. But this mode is altogether inadequate, as is clear when we consider the infinite abyss that lies between the two terms of the comparison, the Creator and the creature. And this was more particularly the case where the Semites were concerned, for they, unlike the Greeks, did not attach supreme importance to the acquisition of clear and well-defined ideas. Though the Semitic mind turned as if by instinct to those higher regions of being that Aristotle glimpsed but neglected, yet it had not learned how to be exact in thinking of matters less difficult of understanding. It rather preferred a certain deliberate obscurity which challenges the enquirer to a more careful investigation, and which enables the teacher to display a subtle genius in presenting the matter under an enigmatic form, a thing of profit to the disciple who arrives at understanding by dint of reflection or by asking his master for an explanation of the enigma.

The parables of Jesus have none of this subtlety : they draw attention only to their object, not to the literary skill of the preacher ; they have as much clarity as their subject allows of, but sometimes they are mingled with allegories. Have we any right to object if Jesus uses the parable as it was used by His own fellow-countrymen, if He refuses to tie Himself down to a theoretical distinction of literary forms established by the Greeks but which they themselves did not always observe ? If several of the Fathers and ancient commentators have been inclined to see far too many allegories in the parables of Jesus, yet St. Chrysostom clearly perceived their special character, and we must follow his example. When Jesus, however, propounded parables to the Pharisees in order to give them to understand what chastisements they were drawing down upon themselves by their implacable hostility, the simile became an allegory, and an allegory that was clear to everyone : for the terms of the allegory stood for people who were well known, people who were present. Moreover, as Jesus was not infrequently Himself personally concerned, as representative of the kingdom of God, in the lesson which He strove to bring home to His hearers by means of the parables that He propounded, allegory inevitably crept in, even into the parables, on account of His own entry on the scene. But it is not this mixture of allegory with parable that caused the parable to be obscure ; on the contrary, it would rather seem to render the parable more striking by these allusions to a person well known to the hearers.

Why, then, do the evangelists seem to characterize the whole of this parabolic teaching as obscure, and intentionally obscure ? This assertion of theirs is indeed harder to understand than the parables themselves, an enigma that we must proceed to examine. What makes it still more difficult to understand is the fact that this notion of the evangelists is put forward as the exegesis of a passage from Isaias, himself a very difficult author to understand. However, it all becomes clear enough provided that we interpret words spoken in a Semitic language according to the laws governing the spirit of that language. Now it is characteristic of Semitic speech to let its meaning spring out like a flash of light from the clashing together of ideas which are expressed in a very positive and unconditional form, without any toning down, the ideas being set in the most vivid contrast one to the other. In the time of Isaias, as in the time of Jesus, God willed to save His people, as is shown by the fact that He raised up a preacher and charged him to call the people to repentance, bidding him to call them with words that are impassioned, full of tenderness, yet at the same time threatening, so that every means might be used which would obtain the result desired, namely the people's conversion. That this was God's purpose is evident : it follows from the very language He employs, which is clear, urgent, compelling the Israelites to make their choice. That choice, however, is foreseen, and it will drag them to destruction. Go, then, said the Lord to His envoy, with the angry bitterness of love doomed to disappointment : go and speak to them that they may harden their hearts and may not be pardoned !

A strange remark, but one of touching beauty ! Now what happened in the time of Isaias happened also in the time of Jesus. The evangelists could not help seeing it, and they knew quite well that it was not God's fault. We have to try to enter their thoughts and follow their train of ideas. It is true, however, that as regards the parables of the kingdom of God, Jesus abstained, in the interests of the crowd, from making His doctrine perfectly clear. It was a subject that could not be approached directly, so great was the danger of coming into conflict with preconceived and stubbornly-held ideas. The rabbis had kept their teaching about the kingdom of God within moderate bounds owing to their study of the Scriptures, but it needed correction all the same.[1] But the common people, under the influence of more adventurous spirits, often looked on the kingdom of God as a sensational intervention of the Lord through the agency of His Messiah, an intervention that was to bring about the political deliverance of Israel and the chastisement of her enemies.[2] This they awaited with a blind confidence calculated to paralyse every effort to establish the true kingdom of God by the fulfilling of His will. These false ideas, which were strengthened by the many apocalyptic writings of the time, made it easier for them to accept the Sermon on the Mount (when they accepted the kingdom of God without realizing it as such) than to substitute the true notion of what the kingdom of God was to be in place of their own false conception of it. The rabbis, be it said to their honour, never ceased from preaching the necessity of living righteously in order to merit the reward of the world to come, of that world above, which was to follow the resurrection. When Jesus demanded a righteousness more perfect than theirs in order to fulfil the true spirit of the Law, He ran no risk of shocking any men of good will who were longing for something new and better. They would think of it doubtless as some new way of manifesting repentance, some special effort to be made in expectation of the joys of the kingdom of God.

A certain danger of misunderstanding arose from the use of this expression, the kingdom of God. Whether it was through an excessive preoccupation with the words of the expression, or through the concentration of all hopes on the Messiah, people entertained false dreams about the way in which God was to intervene on behalf of Israel. It was on this account that their notion of the kingdom of God needed to be changed. Instead of looking for an invincible leader who was to lead the nation to victory, they had to lay hold of a teaching which was to have effect for all mankind and not merely for the Jewish nation. The beginnings of this teaching were to be unpretentious, its success was to be slow, and yet for its sake men had to be ready to sacrifice all. Was the kingdom of God, then, to be so

[1] Cf. *Le Messianisme*, p. 148 ff. [2] Ibid., p. 116 ff.

insignificant at the start? But Jesus determined to give an answer to general expectations, to utter the fateful word in which the kingdom of God should be shown in the character with which it was endowed in the designs of God, even to lay stress on the sacrifices that were demanded of those who would enter that kingdom. That was the critical moment, when those who heard Him were called upon to give up their grandiose expectations and accept His view of God's kingdom, to set about the work as God would have it to be, no matter how humble and hard it might seem. To prepare their minds for this Jesus employs the parable, thus making them think and giving them occasion for asking questions. Though not presented in all its distinctness, nevertheless the teaching of Jesus was clear enough, and if it appeared obscure to His hearers, that was because their hearts were of no help to their minds: the Sermon on the Mount had not produced in them all its fruit. They were still dreaming of an earthly happiness which they expected to be granted to them without cost to themselves. As yet Jesus does not reveal to them all the renunciations, sufferings, and sacrifices His followers will have to face, but He makes appeal to their good will. They have not the will to understand.

This method of teaching by parables, a method inspired by mercy, adapted to the capacity of uneducated minds and throwing as much light as their state of mind allowed them to perceive, was not at present intended as a punishment. But the time came when that punishment was deserved, and then their disregard of His goodness added another reason to those which drew down justice upon them in place of the mercy He had offered. This is what Jesus already knew beforehand and what the evangelists have recorded. And God, foreseeing all, had therefore said to the Messiah what He had once said to Isaias, full of divine anger because of His slighted love: 'Speak in such a way that they will not understand. Shed so much light that they may be blinded by it.'

The parable of the sower (84, 86).

Luke viii, 4–8, 11–15; Mark iv, 1–9, 13–20; Matthew xiii, 1–9, 18–23.

That day, then, Jesus had resolved to speak to the multitude about the kingdom of God. The subject was a difficult one, and His hearers little disposed to accept a teaching that completely upset their expectations of a glorious happiness which was to come without any trouble on their part. In order to stir up both their minds and their good will He sets before them similitudes in terms which were familiar to them all ; nevertheless, He does not apply these similitudes to the subject of His teaching except in a general way, for He wishes to stimulate their curiosity and enlighten them gradually. The sermon was to be long, and the crowd which He found collected there was of a more mixed character than were those who had followed Him for the Sermon on the Mount. That He might be able to talk in peace, the Master went on board a boat and sat down, while the audience remained on shore facing the lake.

His first parable, that of the sower, was easy to follow for those who lived in the fields of Palestine. The sower casts his seed, and some of the grain falls on the paths which neither wall nor hedge separates from the field. That falls to the share of the birds. Can we not see them snatching at the grain as it comes out of the bag, even before it reaches the ground? In some places, especially on the hill-sides where the tiniest plots of ground are utilized, patches of good land are set among the rocks. The sower avoids the rocks, but without noticing, he throws the seed in places where there is an outcrop of rock covered with a thin layer of soil. The seed shoots up more quickly there, but is soon dried up by the sun. The sower in the parable has not bothered to pull up the thorns, for there is no call for very great industry and labour in a country where the soil is so light and fertile : he will content himself with cutting them down when he mows the wheat or barley. But by that time they will have shed their seed and will have grown up thickly in among the corn so that they choke it. But in the meantime the good ground has received its share of the seed, yielding fruit thirtyfold and at times a hundredfold.[1]

When alone with His disciples, Jesus explains this opening

[1] It would be difficult to find such a yield as a hundredfold even in the most fertile parts of Galilee. This figure, then, of itself suggests to the mind a fruitfulness that is supernatural. However, we see from the Old Testament that it was an expression consecrated by use. But see an article in *Biblica*, 1927, p. 84 ff., by Rev. Fr. Sonnen of the Congregation of the Mission, who speaks of grain yielding 240 or 250 fold on the shores of the lake of Tiberias ! On the other hand, read the article of Rev. Fr. Biever in *Conférences de Saint-Etienne*, 1910–1911, pp. 274–5.

parable of His long discourse. The seed is the word or doctrine which He teaches. We are immediately, therefore, bordering on allegory. We should find some difficulty, however, in explaining all the other terms of the parable in an allegorical fashion. The seed is always the same, always good, no matter where it falls, and so is the word. But when a sudden temptation of Satan stops the word from having its effect even before the mind has considered it, snatching it out of the mind as it were before it has been able to reach the heart, that is something in the moral sphere which corresponds with the grain falling by the wayside where it is eaten up by the birds. So, too, the stony ground is the figure of those changeable dispositions in a hearer of the word who, though enthusiastic at first, easily becomes discouraged. The thorns that choke the corn stand for the desire of riches and for all those worldly preoccupations which absorb our activity and paralyse our good desires. The good ground is good will. When Jesus said to the multitude : 'He that hath ears to hear, let him hear,' He meant to stir up their curiosity and show Himself prepared to give to all this simple explanation which would give them a hold of the kingdom of God, for this kingdom could not establish itself and bear fruit in them unless they lent their co-operation.

The parable of the seed that multiplies and ripens by itself in the course of time (88).

Mark iv, 26–29.

This parable is peculiar to St. Mark. No explanation of it was given, but like all the others its meaning would follow upon careful reflection, and Jesus Himself showed the key. We know to begin with that the situation therein described has its analogy in the kingdom of God ; what happens in the temporal order is guided by the law which governs what happens in the religious sphere. What takes place when a man cultivates the earth ? The sower casts his seed upon good soil and he has only to wait for harvest time. Whatever efforts he makes to hurry things on will all be futile. The seed will develop of itself : it only needs time. Time is a necessary condition of growth, and the result for which the sower hopes is bound to come.

So it is in the kingdom of God. It is patent to all that the kingdom of God is being established by Jesus. The Galilæans, naturally eager and over-excited by their hopes, feel disposed to hasten the object of their desires by turbulent measures. Was it not to be expected that God should establish His kingdom in a violent and dramatic fashion, as was foretold in parabolic manner by the book attributed to the ancient patriarch Henoch? 'I speak concerning the elect, of them do I utter my parable: He shall go forth from His dwelling, the Holy and Great One. The God of the world shall go forth thence upon Sinai, and He shall appear in the midst of His army,'[1] and so on. But no, God's work is not to be accomplished by a divine manifestation attended by an instantaneous effect. It is a long business and it must have time.

This little parable is a perfect model of the true parabolic style. It contains in itself nothing allegorical. If God were the sower, how could He be likened to a man that does nothing? Is it not He who ripens the crop by warming it with His sun and moistening it with His rain? Nor does the sower stand for a hearer of the word, whether of one kind or another, for it is not the hearer who puts the seed into the earth. And is not he also rather invited by Jesus to work for the kingdom of God? We cannot even say that Jesus is the sower, as if He were urging Himself not to be anxious about the success of His work. We must conclude, then, that here we have light thrown on the working of the kingdom of God by means of a certain phase of the law of nature. Let us rest content with this lesson ourselves, a very expedient one when it was first delivered and equally opportune at all times: a lesson of confidence in the hidden power of the kingdom of God. That power cannot fail to produce a rich harvest at the time appointed by God; time is required for every work that involves growth. There must be neither violent interference nor discouragement, though we may not be able to understand why God seems to leave things to go their own way. He is working all the time at the ripening of the seed.

[1] *Book of Henoch*, I, 3-4, after M. l'Abbé Martin's translation.

The parable of the cockle in the cornfield (89, 93).
Matthew xiii, 24–30, 36–43.

The similitude of the cockle shows us another aspect of the kingdom of God. In Mark's parable the sower was bidden to put his trust in the virtue of the seed sowed in the good soil. That of itself was a guarantee of the harvest. But it might seem that there was need for the farmer to interfere at least if the cornfield was being overrun by bad seed, and still more if the harm was due to a neighbour's ill-will, who had gone to the length of scattering cockle over a cornfield that was already sown. Yet to interfere even in such a case was a very delicate operation, and might easily do more harm than good. It was not advisable to risk pulling up the wheat with the cockle. So even in such a case as this a man must put his trust in the Providence of the Father who rules over nature. No one could fall into the error of thinking that the cockle and the wheat would be mingled permanently : the wheat that feeds man and the cockle which causes a sort of intoxication yet does not appease hunger.[1] But once they were gathered in at the harvest it would be easy to separate them.

Such was also to be the law of the kingdom of God. . . . Was evil, then, still to go on being mixed with good even in that kingdom ? Was the kingdom of God not to produce the very flower of virtue which was guaranteed to bear its fruit ? That was the common opinion. In the days of the high priest who was to come, said the Testament of the Twelve Patriarchs as if echoing the prophecies, 'sin will vanish and sinners shall cease to do evil . . . and he will grant to the saints to eat of the tree of life, and the spirit of holiness shall be upon them. And Beliar (Satan) shall be imprisoned by him.'[2]

Alas ! no ; it was not to be thus in the kingdom of God which Jesus was preaching and founding. The parable, considered as a parable, gave quite a clear answer on this decisive point ; but it was susceptible of a more detailed

[1] The Rev. Fr. Paul Couvreur, prior of the Trappist monastery at el-Athroun, relates how a lazy mule was fed on cockle when her owner wished to sell the beast, with the result that she became too frisky !

[2] *Le Messianisme* . . ., p. 74.

allegorical explanation which Jesus imparted to His disciples at their request. He Himself was the sower, and He was scattering His word through the world, full of joy at gathering together disciples who were docile to that word. But the devil was working against Him, and he, too, was gathering followers. Jesus showed how the patience of God was enduring this mingling of good and evil, until the day when the angels should come to lead the good into the kingdom of God, while the wicked are to be cast into the furnace of fire.

Thus the prospect changed from the kingdom of God on earth to God's kingdom in heaven. His hearers, faithful to the teaching of Judaism, were in no doubt about the future destiny of the just and of sinners ; but they made the mistake of applying the conditions of eternity to the things of time. Jesus had not come to preach the advent of another deluge that was to be inevitable and final, but to make men better by leading them to God. That was what the kingdom of God meant. Virtue was to be practised in combating evil, not however with the expectation of suppressing it entirely : that would be to attempt the impossible. It was not the Sower's intention to paralyse effort on our part by declaring that the intrinsic power of the kingdom of God was sufficient of itself. Neither did He prescribe indifference in the face of evil : the struggle against evil implies that we be on our guard against the influence of wicked men. He simply warned His disciples against the unrealizable hope of completely extirpating evil from the world. It is good to have patience even with the evil that lies within ourselves and compels us to cry to the Father.

The parable of the grain of mustard seed (90).

Luke xiii, 18–19 ; Mark iv, 30–32 ; Matthew xiii, 31–32.

Jesus foresaw the likelihood of His hearers, even His disciples, being scandalized, and never tired of forewarning them. The kingdom of God, they thought, must be something great. It was surely to appear with striking magnificence, for had not the Law been given long ago on Sinai with impressive solemnity ? All through history the Law had been defeated in its purpose by the people's bad will. But the kingdom of God, so it was thought, was to be different precisely in this, that it would impose itself with sovereign power, reaching to the very ends of the universe at once. A century before the time of Jesus the Book of Jubilees had declared : 'The Lord shall appear before the eyes of all, and all shall know that I am the God of Israel.'[1] Some even went so far as to invoke the testimony of the Sibylline oracles, so greatly venerated among the Gentiles : 'Then will God send from the sun a king who will make the bane of war to cease throughout the whole earth.'[2] Even the Pharisees, though they used greater restraint than the seers of the Apocalypses in their description of the kingdom of God, were hoping for a restoration that would be complete and immediate through the intervention of God's manifestation of Himself : 'So we hope in Thee, O Iah, our God, that we may see speedily the magnificence of Thy power ; that Thou mayest take away the idols from the earth and utterly destroy the false gods.'[3] Hence in places where the prophets spoke of the coming of God, the Jewish translators frequently substituted *manifestation* of God for *presence* of God ; thus they turned the presence of a hidden God into a splendour that was visible.

But this is not the meaning of Jesus. He has compared the kingdom of God to a grain of wheat : He now goes further and likens it to an even tinier seed, to the almost imperceptible grain of mustard seed.[4] He sweeps away all vain theatrical imagery and leads back His hearers to reflect upon that hidden interior power of the kingdom of God that alone is of importance. But small as are the exterior beginnings of that kingdom, it will yet grow until it shelters the birds of heaven in its branches.[5] It is one and the same thing : that which once was small now becomes great. If we say with M. Loisy that here there is an antithesis between the gospel preaching and the kingdom as it is shown developed in its final manifestation,[6] it will be because we still hold to that false conception of the manifestation of the kingdom which Jesus has set on one side : because we conceive of that development of the kingdom as something dramatic in effect when it is merely a continuous movement, or as a sudden transformation when it is

[1] *Le Messianisme* . . ., p. 148. [2] Ibid., p. 117.
[3] The *Alênu* prayer. Cf. *Le Messianisme*, p. 153 ff.
[4] Cf. article of Rev. Fr. Biever, *Conférences de Saint-Etienne*, 1910–1911, p. 280 ff.
[5] Ezechiel xvii, 23. [6] *L'Evangile et l'Eglise*, 1st Ed., p. 16.

only a normal growth. It is the gospel preaching, still recognizable in that tiny mustard seed, which will itself become a great tree. No doubt there will be a striking contrast between the first beginnings and a later stage of development, for the kingdom will have grown in its outward appearance ; nevertheless it will have grown by the power that is within it and without ceasing to be what it was before. As for the birds of heaven sheltered in its branches, they could easily be recognized as the people who were obedient to the teaching of Jesus. It was in this manner that His first hearers were taught and so preserved from that fatal prejudice which was the great stumbling-block of the Jews. For us this teaching has the significance of a prophecy that has been fulfilled. In the light of history we are witnesses of the humble beginnings and the progress of the kingdom of God, of its advance from synagogue to synagogue, from shore to shore, its passing from hostile Jews to contemptuous pagans. We have merely to open our eyes in order to see it established in the whole world, giving shelter to so many souls who live within it for God, who invites and waits for all nations to practise its righteousness and enjoy its peace.

The parable of the leaven (91).

Luke xiii, 20–21 ; Matthew xiii, 33.

By the growth of the mustard seed into a tree, or rather a bush, was shown the extension of the kingdom of God. There is not much increase in the size of the bread through the addition of leaven, but at any rate the bread tastes different, and all men like it better. In this parable the kingdom of God is likened to a hidden force, just as the leaven is concealed in the dough, but it is a force that is full of activity, like the leaven affecting the whole mass of dough. Without any doubt, also, the kingdom of God, under the form in which it was then expected, ought to be a better kind of kingdom ; the Israelites were already good, but the Gentiles were to be converted. The conception of a spiritual force, however, whether conceived as working within the soul or among men as a group, was absent from the dreams of the Jewish seers. Even the rabbis, who could discourse endlessly on the transformation to be wrought in the kingdom of God upon plants, animals, and men, make no mention of that power of God which, according to St. Paul, is the whole Gospel.[1] Once again, therefore, one of Our Lord's very simple comparisons adumbrates the doctrine of His great apostle and is seen by us to be a prophecy. Astonishing as the spread of the gospel may be, yet such a different doctrine as that of Islam is still spreading before our eyes. Nevertheless, it has never succeeded in imposing itself by force of an inward conviction, and it only prevailed at first by the power of the sword. And think what the surroundings were in which this leaven of Christianity was to be placed for its task of enlightening men's minds, reforming their morals, setting right their social relations, and making their souls divine !

The parables of the treasure, the pearl, and the fishing-net. Conclusion (94–95 ; 92, 96).

Mark iv, 33–34 ; Matthew xiii, 44–50 ; 34–35 ; 51–52.

After giving the main features of the kingdom of God, Jesus urges His hearers to possess themselves of it, even at the sacrifice of everything they have. Was it then within their reach ? Did it depend on them whether they obtained it ? Such was not the idea of those who expected to see it appear suddenly in majesty, transforming the world and its inhabitants, imposing itself on them by the splendour of the Lord God. But He had given them to understand that this kingdom was a doctrine—doubtless the very doctrine He had preached in the Sermon on the Mount—and that this doctrine's destiny hung upon the dispositions with which it was received. It was time, therefore, to call upon them by the use of homely comparisons to set to work in order to gain the benefit of the kingdom, in the way that they would not hesitate to act if they wished merely to gain money. This is the significance of the very clear and urgent parables of the treasure and the pearl. And as they were on the shores of the lake, and so far He had taken almost all His comparisons from farming and housekeeping, He ends with a comparison that brings in fishermen. He had already promised Peter that He would make him a fisher

[1] Romans i, 16. In Strack and Billerbeck's enormous compilation there is no comment on Matthew's verse except technical details about leaven, etc.

of men, and there is an illustration of the kingdom of God in that too. The great net brings in fish, both good and bad. So long as the fishing is not over they are all left alive together. Thus also at the end of time will take place the sorting of good and bad, a sorting that is for ever.

Finally Jesus adds a touch that shows the relation between the doctrine of the Sermon on the Mount and the kingdom of God, which consists of a word which is animated by the power of God. Just as He was come to complete or perfect the Law, so the teachers of the future who have been initiated into that word will be like 'a householder who bringeth forth out of his treasure new things and old.'[1]

The light will go on increasing (87).
Luke viii, 16–18 ; Mark iv, 21–25.

So as not to interrupt the series of parables about the kingdom of God we have made no mention of a very precious remark of Our Lord's concerning their apparent obscurity : that obscurity was only for a time, and it was in the nature of things. The time had not come for giving full light, because it is the necessary condition of all prophecy to seem clear only when it has been fulfilled. The teaching that was being given of the kingdom of God afforded simply an instantaneous view of the new order of things now begun. God has never revealed the future as if He were unrolling a film showing beforehand the events that were going to happen. But that was no reason whatever for growing restive, because even so Jesus was giving a great light, and a light is not meant to be put under a bushel. If there was still some obscurity, clearness would come later. Pay good heed, said Jesus, to what you are hearing. Even by itself it is a most precious gift. For one gift leads on to another if only a man has the desire to profit by what he has received. If he has not that desire even that little light will itself go out.

[1] Matthew xiii, 52.

VI. MIRACLES. ENCOUNTER WITH TROUBLESOME DISPOSITIONS

The calming of the tempest (97).

Luke viii, 22–25 ; Mark iv, 35–41 ; Matthew viii, 23–27.

Jesus had revealed nothing of what He purposed when He said to His disciples : 'Let us go over to the other side of the lake.' According to St. Mark it was the evening of the very day on which He spoke the parable about the kingdom of God. Perhaps He meant to leave the Galilæans time for reflection, or desired to escape their pressing attentions when He came ashore after speaking the parables. Or was it that He now wanted to carry the good word to the other side of the lake ? Foreseen lack of success would not have prevented Him from making the attempt. What is certain is that His departure was unexpected. The disciples obey, taking Jesus just as He is and without advising Him to protect Himself against the cold of the night which was now falling. In providing us with these details, which would have been neglected by an author of style, St. Mark admirably shows us how familiar was the life of that little community of Jesus and the disciples. Jesus, weary no doubt from having preached earnestly for a long time, left the management and work of the boat to His disciples who were more experienced. He sat in the stern, the guest's place,[1] and fell asleep leaning on the cushion that is always to be found there. A great wind sprang up. On the little lake the storms that rush through the north-western gap in the hills are sometimes terrible, and the craft of these fishermen were frail. One false movement would have been enough to upset the boat, which was already filling with water. The rowers, in their anxiety losing their respect a little, wake the sleeper : 'Master, doth it not concern Thee that we perish ?' He rebukes the wind and, as if speaking to a troublesome person, says to the sea : 'Silence ! Be still !' And there came a great calm. Then He said to the disciples : 'Why are you fearful ? Have you not faith yet ?' If their faith had been perfect they would have known that Jesus was watching over them even while He slept. Nevertheless they do instinctively turn to Him for

[1] Cf. Odyssey, XIII, 74 ff.

supernatural aid, for they did not expect Him to save them by taking an oar. When Satan urged Him to satisfy His hunger by a miracle He refused ; but He performs a miracle for His friends, for it will make their future trust in Him all the firmer. They know now that the winds and sea obey Jesus.

The cure of a possessed man on the other side of the lake (98).

Luke viii, 26–39 ; Mark v, 1–20 ; Matthew viii, 28–34.

When the tempest was stilled Jesus and His disciples landed. What happened then is related by all three synoptists. We will follow the most detailed account, that of Mark, which Luke surely had before him when he wrote : Matthew merely gave a brief outline.[1] Hardly had Jesus landed when He was attacked, so to speak, by a wild creature coming out of a tomb which he used for a dwelling-place. People had often tried to bind him with fetters and chains, a thing still done in Palestine before the Great War, when unfortunate lunatics were fastened with iron chains to the church porches. This individual, however, was unusually strong ; he would burst the fetters and break the chains to pieces, and then rush into the mountains overlooking the lake, crying out and wounding himself with stones. Jesus, with His knowledge of the unseen, saw at once that he was possessed by the devil and said : 'Go out of this man, thou unclean spirit.' But the devil cried : 'Why dost Thou interfere, Jesus, Son of the most high God ? I adjure Thee by God, torment me not.' Thus, by an amusing irony it is the devil who in a way exorcizes Jesus in God's name, and yet beseeches Him and salutes Him as Son of the Most High. (This was the name the Gentiles gave the God of the Jews, since His real name was unknown to them, the Jews not considering it lawful to utter it.) Thus he who was exercising such tyrannical sway over his victim felt helpless before Jesus, for all his adjuring Him. We see how unfounded is the charge sometimes brought against the evangelists of being dualists, that is, of believing in the existence of a second (evil) principle on an equality with God. Following the custom of exorcists, Jesus

[1] Matthew mentions two possessed persons, but one of them being probably only the companion of the chief character, he leaves him undescribed.

commands the devil to disclose his name. The devil eludes the question by answering: 'Legion! For we are many,' which must have made the disciples shudder, for a legion numbered six thousand men, a veritable army corps for those days. And yet this devil, or this multitude of devils—Mark still uses the singular, though later he will use the plural—beseech Jesus not to send them out of a country in which they fared so well, for it was mainly inhabited by idolators. Must they give up the tributes they received and be chained in the abyss, where a terrible punishment awaited them? And as there was a great herd of swine feeding there, the devils, thinking perhaps to play a good trick on Jesus by stirring up the inhabitants of the district against Him, beg Him to allow them, if they must let go of their man, to take refuge in the swine. It was poor compensation, but how could one refuse! Jesus was certainly not deceived by their manœuvre, but He disdained to treat them as rigorously as He might have done and gave them leave. The devils do not wait to be told twice. They rush into the swine and the swine—about two thousand of them—hurl themselves into the lake. Not that they took a perilous leap from the brink of a cliff, for there is everywhere a space, sometimes a considerable space, between the mountains and the water's edge; but their onrush carries them on from the high ground without a stop. The swineherds are seized with consternation; they run to tell their story in the city. People hasten to the spot. What has happened? One glance at the bearing of the demoniac tells them: he who hitherto had been more like a wild beast than a human being was seated clothed and in his right mind. Soon the newcomers know all: the sudden appearance of the possessed man, his cure, and, as a result, the mad rush of the swine. They had lost valuable stock, but their land was freed from a maleficent power that attacked even human beings and reduced them to the condition of beasts. How should they act? To attack Jesus for the affair would hardly be wise, seeing that He was endowed with such great power. To render thanks would be equivalent to admitting that He was an envoy of the God of Israel. Until then they had kept on good terms with the evil spirits cheaply enough by means of offerings and sacrifices. They politely ask Jesus to go away.

But there was one, at any rate, who had understood and

was moved, and seeing that Jesus was going away he wanted to follow Him. This was the poor demoniac. Jesus did not rebuff him, but gave him to understand that he would be doing better work for God by staying amongst his own people. He thought well enough of him to judge that, left thus, he would not fail in that work. He would remain as a witness, beyond all cavil, of the divine act that had restored human dignity to a slave of the devil : 'Go back to thy house, to thine own people, and tell them all that the Lord hath done for thee, and that He hath had mercy on thee.' Though not so well known as the Magdalen out of whom Jesus had driven seven devils, and who became 'the apostle of the apostles,' this man, too, was an apostle, and he set to work to publish throughout the Decapolis all that Jesus had done for him.

It was a gift beyond all compare, an outpouring of mercy such as those cannot appreciate who weigh the loss of a herd of swine in the balance against it. In their opinion Jesus had treated the rights of property rather too lightly, supreme Lord though He was. But had the devils waited for His formal permission before doing harm, and would they have abstained from doing further harm? They, at any rate, were reduced to impotence.

Thus the ill-will of the lakeside inhabitants does not allow Him to complete His work and deliver them from slavery to the devils. He charges the cured demoniac to preach the word to them. It is the first step in the conversion of the Gentiles ; for the Decapolis, or 'the ten cities,' though conquered by Alexander Jannæus, had been freed from the Jewish yoke by Pompey. People have disagreed about which were the ten cities making up the Decapolis : but Gerasa and Gadara were of the number, as well as Scythopolis.

Where ought the scene of these events to be placed? The difficulty is a famous one and deserves our attention, chiefly because of the variants in the text of the gospels. Mark speaks of 'the country of the Gerasens.' But Gerasa, a famous city (to-day called Jerash), was situated about thirty miles south-east of the lake. To anyone writing, say, at Rome, the difficulty that this distance presents might not stand out in all its clearness, but even so it is impossible that he could have made the mistake that would have to be supposed. The Greek Matthew surely wrote 'country of the Gadarenes'; but between Gadara, a city admirably situated on a high hill to the south of the lake, and the lake itself was the River Hieromax, and the swine would have been drowned in that. And so Origen definitely concluded that neither of these names was likely, and being assured that there was once upon a time a city named Gergesa on the lakeside, proposed the reading 'country of the Gergesenes or Gergeseneans,' the name of an ancient people formerly driven out by the Israelites;[1] at any rate it was due to his influence that this reading became prevalent in so many old manuscripts of the gospels. But it seems too erudite a conjecture to be relied upon.

It will be observed, however, that these different names for the scene of the incident are not precisely names of a city but rather of a region that might be fairly extensive and have a chief city more or less close to the lake. Despite the variants, the evangelists were surely all thinking of one and the same spot on the eastern shore of the lake, and thanks to persevering research it seems that we can now fix the spot with real probability. The starting point in the situation is the place from which the swine hurled themselves into the lake. Nowhere does a steep descent from the mountain go right down to the water, which is often some considerable distance from the slopes. But at a place called *Moqâ edlô*, where there is situated a sulphurous spring which marks the frontier between the British and French mandates over Palestine and Syria, the shore is hardly more than thirty yards wide and the distance must formerly have been still less. Above this spot the slope is very steep and, moreover, is honeycombed by natural caves which may very well have been used as tombs, though they cannot be stated with certainty to have been used for that purpose.

Granting this, what was the neighbouring city? We might hesitate between two ruins. *Qalaât-el-Hosn*, to the south, appears to answer exactly to the description of the city that Josephus calls Gamala. The ruin stands opposite to Tiberias and is in the shape of a gigantic camel's hump, whence it gets its name. Near by there are numerous tombs hewn out in the rock, and these may well have served as dwellings, for they are even furnished with doors of basalt. But the name does not resemble those found in the gospels,

[1] Genesis xv, 21.

nor was any tradition ever preserved there regarding this matter. On the north side, about a mile and a quarter from *Moqâ edlô*, lies the ruined village of *Kursi*, the Arabic word for throne. But Père Abel has clearly shown[1] that the Greek form of the name, *Chorsia*, was a transcription from the Aramaic and existed before the coming of the Arabs, for we find that St. Sabas visited *Chorsia* in the sixth century and prayed there, doubtless in commemoration of some gospel incident; and later tradition regarded it as the place we are seeking. One confirmation of the tradition can be found in the fact that the walls of a Byzantine city can still be distinguished to the east of the existing village. The Aramaic name of *Chorsia* may have given rise to Mark's 'country of the Gerasens' and Origen's 'Gergesa,' while Matthew preferred a better known name, Gadara, a city very renowned as a centre of Greek culture. In this case the place of the demoniac's deliverance would be *Moqâ edlô*, and the neighbouring city referred to in the gospels would be Kursi, though it is also possible that the man took up his dwelling in the tombs situated further to the south.

The daughter of Jairus and the woman with an issue of blood (99).

Luke viii, 40–56; Mark v, 21–43; Matt. ix, 18–26.

This story of the possessed man was told in detail by St. Mark and St. Luke, though it seemed to end in disappointment. Along with it they relate two miracles which caused no great sensation at the time, the first because the goodness of our Saviour allowed it to be, as it were, stolen secretly from Him; the second because He took steps to prevent the news of it being spread abroad immediately. It is easy to see from these instances in what light the evangelists regarded miracles, and they were imitated in that respect by the early Christians. When they talk of miracles they do not always appeal to general belief in them or to the testimony of a whole crowd of people. To their mind, for a miracle to be worthy of credence it is

[1] See Kursi, in the *Journal of the Palestine Oriental Society*, 1927, pp. 112 ff.

enough that it should have been attested by witnesses chosen by Jesus, the same witnesses who will vouch for His Resurrection. They clearly recognized that this was the Master's plan, and it was one which brought out the principle of authority and hierarchy.[1]

It was impossible, however, for Jesus to escape the curiosity of the crowd: as soon as He landed at Capharnaum or somewhere in the vicinity He was surrounded before He had time even to leave the shore. A man of some importance named Jairus—perhaps the president of the synagogue, or at all events one of its chief members—makes his way through the throng and falls at the Master's feet, beseeching: 'My daughter, only a child, is at the point of death: come, lay Thy hands upon her that she may be safe and live.' Without a word, Jesus follows him, moved by his sorrow and faith. The father in his distress seems to tell Jesus how He ought to work the miracle; but that is merely because he has often seen Him lay His hands on the sick and heal them. The interested crowd grows in number and flocks around the Healer.

In the meantime a woman had resolved to approach Him. She had been afflicted with a loss of blood for twelve years, and had spent all she possessed in consulting doctors; but it was all of no avail; her illness rather grew worse. Her only hope was in a miracle. But her condition rendered her unclean according to the Law,[2] and at the slightest suspicion that she suffered from this complaint people would have driven her away mercilessly, and overwhelmed her with reproaches for having exposed so many of her fellow-Israelites to defilement. Consequently, she could not ask aloud to be cured. Not daring to imitate the audacity of the leper whom Jesus had cured, she has no other resource left than to approach Him who poured forth such divine power around Him and take Him by surprise. She comes up from behind, fearing to be driven away if she makes herself too noticeable, and succeeds in touching the hem of His garment: that is, the tassel of woollen threads which the Jews fastened one to each of the four corners of their cloak. The Law commanded this explicitly,[3] and Jesus observed it exactly. The woman immediately felt that she was healed.

[1] Acts x, 41: 'Not to all the people, but to witnesses preordained by God.'
[2] Leviticus xv, 25. [3] Numbers xv, 38.

Such a miracle, as St. Mark and St. Luke observe, could not have been performed without the knowledge of Him who was responsible for it. A health-giving power had gone forth from Jesus, and He had been conscious of it ; He had therefore consented to it. We need not attribute this knowledge to the divine light that enlightened His human intelligence and enabled Him always to see God face to face ; for in His mission as prophet and worker of miracles also Jesus received special enlightenment touching things belonging to the supernatural order. Nevertheless He very earnestly asks the question : 'Who hath touched My garments ?' He had not seen the woman, and He followed the common rule of human nature in acquiring knowledge from experience by the use of His senses and intelligence. This was one of the conditions of the abasement He took upon Himself in His Incarnation, when along with our human nature He assumed its natural limitations and its capacity for development. Hence St. Mark frankly states that Jesus looked around to see who had touched Him. Nor are the disciples, with Peter at their head, surprised at His questioning them, though they do not disguise the fact that the question seems naïve : 'Thou seest the multitude thronging Thee, and Thou sayest : "Who hath touched Me ?"' Why, everybody.

The woman knew well enough what had happened : she came forward frightened and trembling and confessed to Him the whole truth, which He already knew. Jesus did not wish her to go away with the idea that He could be constrained or taken by surprise, in the way that was looked for by the pagans who practised magical arts. What had won her cure was not that furtive touch, but her faith. Healed of her infirmity, she goes away with her soul at peace. And thus the woman vanishes from the Gospel.

Legend has tried to fill in the silence. The apocryphal Acts of Pilate[1] call her Veronica. Eusebius, the Bishop of Cæsarea during the fourth century, a man of critical mind, echoes a tradition which made her a native of Paneas, to-day Banias, in northern Palestine. According to that tradition, she had even erected on a stone near the door of her house a bronze image of herself kneeling before a man who was stretching out his hand towards her.[2]

[1] *Acta Pilati*, VII. [2] *Hist. Eccl.*, VII, xviii.

This incident had scarcely hindered the group, of which Jesus was the centre, in its advance towards the house of Jairus. While He was still speaking, someone came to tell the ruler of the synagogue: 'It is useless to trouble the Master any further: thy daughter is dead.' Before the man had even time to decide what to do, Jesus, who had heard everything, said to him: 'Fear not: only believe.' A miracle had been promised in response to his faith, and the fulfilment of the promise was dependent on the stability of that faith: whether the child was dead or not would make no difference to what Jesus had decided. None of the crowd, however, are allowed to enter the house except Peter, James, and his brother John, whom Jesus chooses as the witnesses of the greatest of His mysteries. When they arrive, they find a group at the door mourning and crying. Jesus says to them: 'Stop all this noise and weeping: the child is not dead but asleep.' It is true that death is often likened to sleep, particularly when it comes as a release. But in this case they had seen the child die, and they derided Him. If He did not even know that she was dead, what was the good of His coming at all? Would He have been able to cure her even if He had come in time? After such a confession of ignorance, it was impossible to imagine that He had the power to bring the dead back to life.

Thus, in spite of all the miracles He had performed, we see that the popular applause was by no means of a permanent character. The smallest thing that could be made a matter for scepticism diminished their enthusiasm for Him. Without deigning to give them any answer, Jesus sends away all these needless mourners, some of whom were there merely for their own profit. He goes in with the father and mother, followed by his three disciples, touches the young girl's hand and restores her to life.

Both Elias[1] and Eliseus[2] had raised the dead. But what a struggle there had been, against God as it were, in the earnest prayer they had offered, in the stretching of the prophet's body over the corpse, 'mouth upon mouth, eyes upon eyes, hands upon hands,' as if by restoring its warmth they could force the soul to return. For Jesus, a simple gesture and an imperious command had been enough. St. Mark determined to preserve the two words of that

[1] 3 Kings xvii, 19 ff. [2] 4 Kings iv, 33 ff.

command just as Jesus had uttered them in Aramaic: *Talitha kum.* 'Young girl, arise!' And there is another difference also between Jesus and the prophets which shows His goodness rather than His power. The prophets had restored a son to his mother, as Jesus too had done at Naim. But on this occasion, seeing the stupefaction of the girl's parents, He bids them give her something to eat. She had been restored to normal life at the age of twelve.

Having performed the miracle Jesus enjoined secrecy upon the witnesses, and it seems to have been fairly well kept. No doubt the sneerers refused to give way even in the face of evidence, and preferred to admit that they were wrong in the first instance. At all events the evangelists record no enthusiasm and no expressions of gratitude. St. Matthew merely says that the rumour of the incident spread throughout the whole country-side.

Jesus is driven out of Nazareth by violence (100).

Luke iv, 22–30; Mark vi, 1–6; Matt. xiii, 54–58.

Capharnaum, where Jesus now lived, had been the centre of His preaching for a long time. Yet He did not forget His own home, the humble city of Nazareth where He had been brought up from youth to manhood, where He had devoted so many hours to work and prayer, and especially to that work which was His masterpiece, the perfecting of Mary's soul. Joseph, whom He had loved as a father, was dead. But when Jesus revisited Nazareth, it was not for the purpose of seeing His kinsfolk: He went to preach the kingdom of God. If we have been right in dividing St. Luke's narrative here into two different episodes, then it was during Our Lord's second visit to Nazareth that He was driven out with violence. On the first occasion the people of Nazareth, proud of the rising reputation of their fellow-citizen, had merely shown astonishment, but an appreciative astonishment, at His way of preaching. In the narrative of the three synoptists His expulsion followed immediately upon His warm welcome. But so complete a change of front is hardly explicable unless some new circumstance had arisen to embitter the feelings of the people of Nazareth. They might have shown themselves indifferent in His regard, as others were, or even contemptuous on account of His lowly origin ; but that was no reason for trying to throw Him down a precipice, as St. Luke narrates. This sudden fury implies a hatred that had been long growing, and the cause of it is not difficult to find : Jesus had forsaken His own city and Capharnaum was getting the benefit of His miracles. This jealousy of theirs becomes apparent from the way in which He voices what was in their minds : 'Do here also in thine own country all that we have been told has happened in Capharnaum.'[1] We assume, therefore, that some time must have elapsed between the two scenes ; the first visit must have taken place at the time given by Luke ; the second at the time indicated by Mark and Matthew. In that case the whole story goes with a very natural action, advancing from astonishment to distrust, and then to rage, granting the interval of time that the people's change of disposition implies.

Ill-humour appears at the very beginning. By what right does He come teaching ? We know Him too well, they say, to give any credit to what He says. Did He not work as a carpenter here ? 'Is not this the son of Mary, the brother of James and Joses and Jude and Simon ?' He has not thought fit to stop at Nazareth, but are not his sisters here amongst us ? Jesus has not asked them to recognize Him as Messiah, so they do not give a thought to such an absurd imagination as that a workman should think himself called to the throne. But He does set up as a teacher, and they know well enough that a carpenter has not much time for study. People say that He works miracles. If so, why does He work for His living ? Physician, they thought, heal Thyself ! In times past, when a prophet arose he appeared in unaccustomed garb and none knew where he came from, just as Elias the Thesbite had appeared before Achab and Amos of Thecua before the priest at the sanctuary of Bethel. On the other hand Jeremias, whom his neighbours watched grow up in the humble village of Anathoth, had suffered scorn and ill-treatment. No man is great in the eyes of those who have seen him babbling as a child ; at all events he is not the one to lecture those who once cuffed his ears. Jesus knew this very well ; He knew that a prophet has but a poor reception in his own country, amongst his kinsfolk, and in his own home. But since His

[1] Luke iv, 23.

fellow Nazarenes knew it so well also, they must admit the consequence of such a truth, namely, that this is precisely the reason why many are deprived of the graces that a prophet brings to those who believe in him. It is strangers who benefit by these graces, like the widow of Sarephta in the time of Elias and Naaman the Syrian in the time of Eliseus.[1] So they must not be surprised if He does not work the same miracles at Nazareth as He has worked at Capharnaum : faith is normally required as the condition for begging and obtaining a miracle. Ill-will has the unhappy power of hindering the exercise of goodness.

This allusion to Capharnaum and to Gentiles who had been preferred to Israelites threw them into a fury, though they were in the synagogue. What exasperated them was that Jesus had laid bare the evil root of their jealousy. They dragged Him to the top of the hill on which their city was built to throw Him down. But He, without making Himself invisible, merely by the use of His own personal power, passed through their midst and none dared to pursue Him. We have already spoken of the site of this precipice from which they tried to throw Him. Some look for it south of Nazareth where there are several precipices, but they are all too far from the city.

An ancient tradition, which owes its preservation to the piety of past ages and to honour which a little chapel has been built, shows the place where Mary stood anxiously watching this scene. The disciples assisted at it too. For them the whole episode was symbolic of the fate that was to befall their Master. Nazareth typified the nation of Israel in revolt against the prophet sent to them by God. Naaman the Syrian bathing in the Jordan prefigured the call of the Gentiles to baptism. And even if the disciples did not see the parallel at the time, they perceived it after the Resurrection and it encouraged them to turn to the Gentiles with the Gospel.

The unmannerly language of the Nazarenes regarding Jesus has often been made to serve as an argument against Mary's virginity. They may not be sufficiently well-disposed to their fellow-citizen to espouse His cause, but at any rate, it is argued, they know well enough who He is. And if they are low-minded people, so much the better, for on that account they will not be the sort of people to devise

[1] 3 Kings xvii, 9–10 ; 4 Kings v, 1 ff.

metaphysical explanations of how Jesus was conceived in a supernatural fashion, or to invent that rare example of asceticism, a married woman who is at the same time a virgin. And precisely because this objection drawn from the words of the Nazarenes deals with a question of fact and not with any philosophical notions, it creates an obstacle to the Christian faith for many persons of great intelligence who feel an attraction for that faith on account of its lofty character. For after all there is no getting away from a fact, and if Jesus had brothers and sisters whose names were known at Nazareth, on what grounds does the Church pay homage to Mary as a virgin?

But what are the facts?[1] They can be deduced only from the gospel texts, and it is no exaggeration to say that the words spoken at Nazareth, far from disproving the virginity of Mary, throw decisive light on the fact that Jesus had no brothers or sisters born of her. The evangelists have recorded these words with complete simplicity: therefore they did not in any way consider them to be in real contradiction to what they already believed. Luke makes the people of Nazareth say: 'Is not this the son of Joseph?'[2] As these people knew nothing of the mystery on which Luke has written at length, they could not have spoken in any other fashion. Thus they merely bear witness to what was outwardly apparent and about which there was no difference of opinion, for Mary was really married to Joseph. But what about the brothers and sisters? According to the significance of the Greek terms used they are indeed brothers and sisters; but the Semitic terms represented by the Greek can without any question be used of cousins or even more distant relations.

Then there is the question of the proper names, and these indeed are of great help for arriving at a true solution of the problem. It will readily be admitted that if anybody in the primitive Church had any chance of passing as the brother of Jesus it was James, called expressly by St. Paul 'the brother of the Lord.'[3] Now a James heads the list at Nazareth; it is therefore the same James. He is the brother of Joses, and the evangelists know very well who is their mother—a Mary who is certainly not Mary the Mother of Jesus.[4] She was known as 'the mother of James and

[1] See author's *Commentary on St. Mark*, III, 31–35. [2] Luke iv, 22.
[3] Galatians i, 19. [4] Mark xv, 40; Matthew xxvii, 56.

Joses.'[1] It is thus that the Arabs even to this day name a woman when they wish to call her by a name of honour. If these two are not the children of Mary the Mother of Jesus, then by what right can we ascribe to her Jude and Simon who follow in the list of the brethren of Jesus? Moreover, a very ancient tradition with which we may here supplement the gospels regards Simon, under the form Simeon, as a cousin of Our Lord.[2] The sisters, of whom no memory remains, cannot claim any closer relationship with Jesus; besides, brothers and sisters all together make too large a number. The whole group simply designates relations,[3] and it is ridiculous to imagine that there were brothers or sisters who remain unknown, if those whom the people of Nazareth mention as the best known were merely cousins.[4]

VII. THE MISSION OF THE APOSTLES AND THE ALARM OF HEROD ANTIPAS

The mission of the twelve Apostles (101–102).

Luke ix, 1–6; Mark vi, 6–13; Matt. x, 5–16; xi, 1.

Jesus does not stop preaching because He has been cast out of Nazareth by His compatriots. On the contrary He wishes the good news of the kingdom of God and the call to repentance to be more widespread, and He therefore calls the Twelve and sends them out to preach two by two. This first mission serves to foreshadow what will be their apostolate after His nation has handed Him over to the Gentiles. But for the time being it is to His own nation that Jesus is still devoting all His care, for it is this people that He has come to call, the appointed guardian of the promises and of the Scriptures. It is to them, therefore, that He now addresses the word of God by means of His disciples. Hence He bids the Twelve not to take the way of the Gentiles nor to enter the cities of the Samaritans, but to go rather to the lost sheep of the house of Israel.

It is not the object of their mission to draw attention to

[1] Joses (Jose) or Joseph, according as it was pronounced.

[2] Given by Hegesippus, a historian of the second century, quoted by Eusebius, *Hist. Eccl.*, IV, xxii, 4.

[3] 1 Corinthians ix, 5.

[4] As Renan imagines in his paradoxical solution of the difficulty, *Vie de Jésus*, p. 25.

Himself. He does not commission them to recruit partisans for His messianic claims. And He counts so little on their enthusiasm for turning to good account the miracles He Himself has worked that He gives them power to work the same wonders themselves : casting out devils, healing the sick—and St. Matthew even adds raising the dead. The impression He had made, deep as it was, was in danger of fading away. But that did not matter. What did matter was that God's call should resound throughout the whole land of Israel : 'Repentance ! For the Kingdom of God is at hand.' Time was short and it was necessary to act quickly. Yet Jesus does not call on His disciples to use haste. He gives them instructions which take their character from the country and the situation in which they were uttered, but the substance of them is adapted to all times, places, and circumstances. In a word, two things are required for one who would succeed in such a mission as that with which He charges His disciples : disinterestedness and a whole-hearted devotion to the task.

Disinterestedness must be beyond all cavil, carried even to the extent of poverty ; and not a mere show of poverty, but a poverty that is voluntarily chosen.[1] A traveller in Palestine always took with him a few flat cakes of bread for the journey and wrapped a few coins in his head-cloth or in his girdle ; if he rode an ass he would put on two coats as a protection against the cold. But the disciple must take neither bread nor money at all, and no second coat ; he must travel on foot, and he is allowed therefore to provide himself with the poor man's staff to help him along ; for foot-gear let him wear simple sandals, strips of leather attached to the sole of the foot by a strap. This meant having the appearance of a beggar. But even the professional beggar carries a wallet that he has every intention of filling, though he might be begging in the name of religion. We read of a mendicant who begged in the name of Atargatis, a Syrian goddess, and who was able to render thanks to his patroness for his gains. We are interested to learn that he filled his wallet seventy times during each of

[1] Here we follow St. Mark's text because it brings out the ideas in stronger relief than the text of Luke and Matthew. Moreover, it seems to represent better the actual words of Jesus, with its alternation of prohibitions and permissions. In Luke and Matthew the prohibitions are given in a much more unqualified manner. The essential thing underlying it all was to make clear what was to be the poverty of the missionary.

his rounds.[1] The disciples are to have no wallet to fill. Abandonment of themselves to the care of Providence must be their daily rule, or rather the rule of each moment.

Having arrived at some village, the disciple who labours in preaching the kingdom of God must give all his attention to that duty. As to the question of hospitality, that has always been the rule in the East. At the very least there will be a guest-house for the reception of travellers. But a public place of reception like a caravanserai, with its continual bustle of arrival and departure, the travellers preoccupied by their own affairs, the servants not infrequently indulging in behaviour so coarse as not to be free from viciousness—such a place was in no way suitable for treating of the affairs of the soul. The Apostles are therefore to choose a private house : it is hardly believable that no one at all will ask them in. Once invited, they must remain at that house until they go on to another town. Perhaps other people may come to offer an invitation. Acceptance would mean exchange of compliments, waste of time, hurt feelings. They can see everyone by keeping to one house ; for though the Oriental is very jealous of the privacy of the rest of his house, the reception chamber is at any rate thrown open to all-comers. All through the day and the whole evening there will be free entrance for anyone who wishes to talk with these strangers about the expectations that are stirring all hearts in Israel.

It may happen, however, that some town may not be disposed to receive the messengers of good news ; or else, when curiosity is satisfied, may refuse to believe them. If the inhabitants behave in that way it will be equivalent to bearing witness against themselves that they are not of God's people. When a Jew returns home from a visit to a Gentile land—and every Gentile land he regards as unclean—he spares the sacred soil of Palestine all defilement by shaking the Gentile dust from his feet before entering. Thus the disciples also are to ' shake off the dust from their feet for a testimony against ' such froward people.

Here again Jesus struck the highest note of human heroism. His Apostles were to serve as the model for all future generations of Apostles. Some of His admonitions are adapted to the circumstances of the time and are not

[1] Taken from an inscription published in 1897.

to be taken as literally binding for all times and circumstances. But it would be idle to undertake the conquest of souls without first being possessed by a desire for their salvation so absorbing as of itself to exclude all self-seeking. That is what St. Dominic and St. Francis realized so well: the apostolate requires poverty, and poverty is a preparation for the apostolate.

Thus the Apostles set out on their mission of preaching, driving out devils, healing the sick. St. Mark adds that they used anointing with oil on some who were sick and healed them.[1] Doctors in the East always use oil, especially for dressing wounds. As Mark is speaking of the sick, and of apostles, not doctors, the anointing to which he refers was surely in the nature of a rite used for obtaining a cure. Just as Jesus did not baptize, so neither did He use this rite; but His disciples would not have taken it upon themselves to employ it unless He had prescribed it to them. The Church has regarded this practice of the Apostles as a prelude to the sacrament of Extreme Unction,[2] to which St. James alludes more plainly.[3] Rationalists deny the sacred character of this anointing evidently because they are unaware of the firm conviction of the early Christians regarding it; for the exaggerated importance given to the anointing of the sick by the Gnostics and Mandæans[4] shows clearly that, at any rate, they made no mistake about the significance it had in the New Testament passages. It was not, however, the intention of Jesus so to bind up the power of the Apostles with this rite of anointing as to make a clear distinction between theirs and His own sovereign power. Just as the work of baptizing was left to them so also, in thus preparing them for their future ministry as pastors, He was preparing to entrust to their care the grace granted through the sacrament of Extreme Unction to the sick members of the Church which He was founding.

[1] Mark vi, 13.

[2] Council of Trent, Sess. XIV, *Doctrina de sacra extr. unct.*, *Cap.* 1: *Sacramentum . . . apud Marcum quidem insinuatum, per Jacobum autem Apostolum ac Domini fratrem fidelibus commendatum ac promulgatum.*

[3] James v, 14 ff.

[4] Cf. *Revue Biblique*, 1927, p. 509.

The death of John the Baptist (34 ; 103–104).

Luke ix, 7–9 ; iii, 19–20 ; Mark vi, 14–29 ; Matthew xiv, 1–12.

The mission of the Apostles must have occurred during the winter, since it came to an end before the Paschal season.[1]

When the work of sowing the fields was over in Palestine men folded their arms and sat down to wait for the harvest. That was the favourable time for long talks, when everybody was at home. The disciples sent out by Jesus had stirred up the people's hopes on nearly all sides. Consequently rumours began to reach the petty court of Herod Antipas, the tetrarch of Galilee and Peræa. Everybody had his own opinion about Jesus, and in these opinions no one gave much thought to the Messiah, for was not he to manifest himself in a halo of glory ? But as Elias had to precede the Messiah and confer the royal unction upon him, perhaps Jesus was Elias the forerunner come down from heaven whither he had been taken up. According to others, who were not so enamoured of the extraordinary and preferred unquestioned historical tradition, Jesus was simply a prophet like all those whom Israel had heard in the past. Herod called to mind that other man who had recently stirred up popular feeling, namely John the Baptist. But him he had beheaded. There were times when he reminded himself of that brutal deed and wondered who Jesus could be. All around him there were whispers—for people dared not speak it too loudly—that John had risen from the dead : that although he had worked no miracles during his lifetime, now he had come back from the dead with a divine power at his command. And Herod, when remorse assailed his irresolute soul, would himself expect to see his victim rise again before his eyes. It was the recording of these half-formed opinions that led Mark and Matthew to relate the account of John the Baptist's imprisonment and death.

That imprisonment had served as the signal for Jesus to begin His own ministry, and here we learn the reason for John's being cast into prison. It was but one of the many

[1] As we shall see in John vi, 4.

tragedies which had stained the palace and family of Herod the Great with so much blood that even Augustus was nauseated.[1] The doom that lay upon the sons of Atreus was more striking perhaps, but not more bloody, than the plots which formed around that tyrant, with his jealousies, his suspicions, and the feminine intrigues in the midst of which he floundered and from which he freed himself by cutting off heads. Herod Antipas was his son: he had inherited his father's ambition but not his indomitable energy. He had married Herodias, his brother Philip's wife, says St. Mark, a thing stigmatized by the Law as adultery.[2] In those days John was preaching repentance. But if such licentiousness was treated with servile respect how could men presume to hope for God's mercy? John did not hesitate. We do not know whether Herod asked to see him in order to seek his opinion on the matter or whether John approached the tetrarch on his own initiative, acting under the inspiration of that Spirit of righteousness which animated the prophets of old; but at all events he bluntly declared: 'It is not lawful for thee to have thy brother's wife.' To silence him Herod threw him into prison. To have revealed his real reason for this would have been equivalent to publishing what was an unpleasant rebuke. In view of the excitement caused by John's preaching, a very plausible excuse was provided by a pretended fear of some revolutionary movement that would be displeasing to Rome. But obviously the tetrarch wanted to satisfy the hatred of Herodias who was feeling uneasy. She was not satisfied: only death would silence that voice. For John went on speaking. In irons he was not greatly to be feared; but all the same he was calling down the judgements of God, and Antipas, more of a Jew than his father, was troubled by this. Between Herodias and John he was at his wits' end; he literally saw no way out of his perplexity.[3]

Herodias was on the watch for a favourable opportunity. Like all Oriental princes, Antipas was in the habit of keeping his birthday with much festivity. On this occasion everything was as usual, banqueting, much drinking, flute-players and dancing girls, when suddenly a young girl of

[1] See above, p. 47. [2] Leviticus xviii, 16; xx, 21.

[3] ἠπόρει according to the reading in three MSS. The Vulgate exaggerates in saying that Herod *did* many things by John's advice.

the race of Herods and Hasmoneans, the daughter of Herodias by her first husband, was seen coming in dressed as a dancing girl. Such obliging kindness along with the hesitating grace of her movements, which professional habit would have rendered more confident but at the same time would have vulgarized, also her desire to please, touched Herod and unsettled him. The enthusiasm of his courtiers completed his infatuation. Nothing seemed too costly to reward such charms. The traditional phrase : 'Ask me for the half of my kingdom' was only a meaningless exaggeration : but Herod added an oath to it. The child had done what her mother had told her ; the mother therefore had to be consulted. Returning immediately, the girl demanded with an imperious and defiant air : 'I will that forthwith thou give me in a dish the head of John the Baptist.' She would have no delay. There were plenty of dishes on the table. The king had only to keep his word.

The command was a hard one. The tetrarch, sobered now, sees the trick and realizes the danger. He feared John ; but a broken oath seemed more to be dreaded still. The dancing girl, whom all have applauded, will publicly upbraid him for breaking his word ; his courtiers will once again smile at his wavering character which earns him the contempt of Herodias. Around him stand attendants waiting to do his commands. Within a few moments the guard who had acted as executioner brought to the young girl John's head in a dish. As M. Fouard has excellently said : 'The shadow into which the prophet desired to sink[1] cloaked his martyrdom. No witness told how he received the iniquitous command and how peacefully he died.'[2] They could not refuse to allow his disciples to give him the honours of burial ; these came and took his body and laid it in a tomb. The Church would pay great honour to that tomb if she knew where it was and had it in her charge. In the fifth century it was thought to be at Sebaste where a church, now a mosque, perpetuates the Baptist's memory.

The most fervent of John's disciples never claimed that their master had risen from the dead. The rumours of Herod's court died away along with the tyrant's remorse.

[1] Cf. John iii, 30. [2] *La Vie de N.-S. Jésus-Christ*, I, p. 426.

Herod Antipas and the Baptist's death.

In these days, when aberration of critical judgement has gone so far as to deny the existence of Jesus, it is worth remarking how the evangelists, while they have no pretensions to treat of current history, are yet in agreement with what is known of it, particularly from the historian Josephus. The Baptist's death brings Herod Antipas on the scene, and the tetrarch's character enables us to appreciate his relations with Jesus; they were few but significant. The events of his period of government help us to determine the dates of the gospel.

Herod Antipas, warned by the disgrace of his brother Archelaus in which he came near to being involved,[1] adopted the course of action best calculated to maintain his position in his little principality. The chief point was to win the emperor's favour by an attitude of complete submission. In this he showed such assiduity that sometimes the secret information he sent to Rome anticipated the official reports of the Roman generals on their own operations.[2] But it was likewise necessary not to give Rome any excuse for intervention by causing discontent among his own subjects. Antipas took care therefore to humour them in their religious beliefs; whereas his brother Philip, tetrarch of a country that was more than half pagan, permitted images on his coinage, Antipas refused to allow this. He built Tiberias in honour of Tiberius, but at the same time he erected a synagogue there. He was probably punctilious in going to Jerusalem for the feasts. Less of an egoist than his father, he identified himself more than he had done with Judaism, and shared his people's respect for the Mosaic law and religion. He was tetrarch of Galilee and Peræa, and thus his realm was exposed on its eastern frontiers to the incursions of the Nabatæan Arabs, whose kingdom was then at its highest pitch of prosperity under Aretas IV. Shrewd politician that he was, Antipas had

[1] When Judæ was annexed to the Empire in A.D. 6.

[2] This is attested in regard to Vitellius by Josephus (*Ant.* XVIII, iv, 5). We refer the reader once for all to the same place for the history of Antipas. See also Schürer's monograph, *Geschichte des jüdischen Volkes im Zeitalter Jesu Christi*, I, pp. 431–449, and that of Walter Otto in Pauly-Wissowa's Encyclopedia, Supplement, 2nd fascicule, articles Herod (18), Herodias, Herod Antipas (24).

married this king's daughter. In a word, all his actions show him to have been a clever schemer, with more prudence than passion. He was indeed, in the words of Jesus, a fox.[1]

But all his cunning schemes were upset by a fatal infatuation. While on a journey to Rome, Antipas paid a visit to his brother Herod: that is the only name Josephus gives him, but it would be very strange if he had no other name to distinguish him from his brother Herods. This Herod always lived as a private citizen. Perhaps he was a man of very mediocre abilities; at all events he seems to have been without ambition. In all probability he had been betrothed as early as 6 B.C. to Herodias, who was a grand-daughter of his father, Herod the Great, and claimed descent from the Hasmonean line also through her grandmother Mariamne, the wife so beloved by Herod the Great before he put her to death. We do not know when that fatal journey occurred; Otto dates it at the beginning of the reign of Tiberius, about the year A.D. 15, or at the very latest before 26, because in that year Tiberius left Rome never to return; and what was Antipas going to Rome for except to cultivate the favour of Tiberius? It may be, however, that Antipas was received by Tiberius at Capri even after the emperor's departure from Rome, just as in that island Tiberius received Agrippa I, the nephew of Antipas; or Antipas may have contented himself with transacting his business with Sejanus, the emperor's minister, who was not put to death until the year 31: and this is the more likely, seeing that Antipas was later accused of intriguing with Sejanus. All things considered, however, the year 26 would well satisfy for the journey, and even for the marriage with Herodias.

At this time she would be over thirty.[2] Antipas conceived for her a violent passion which blinded him to the consequences. No doubt she shared the same passion, but in her it was united with cold calculation, and she demanded the dismissal of his first wife. Full of ambition, as she later revealed, she was determined to be the wife of an independent prince, and his only wife. It was arranged that the flight and marriage should take place upon the return of Antipas. This was accordingly done, and Josephus

[1] Luke xiii, 32.

[2] She cannot have been born later than 8 B.C. or earlier than 15 B.C. At the betrothal of which we have spoken she would be three or four.

is no less shocked than John the Baptist at this adulterous union, a thing contrary to all the ancestral laws; and it was all the guiltier in that Herodias had a daughter, Salome, by her previous marriage.[1] Here we learn the name of the young dancer mentioned by St. Mark. Josephus does not give her age.[2] She was still young however, as was the custom of the time, when she married her uncle Philip the tetrarch of Ituræa, and it was doubtless shortly before his death, which took place in the year 34, seeing that she gave him no children. In all probability it was a marriage of ambition, for Philip was some thirty years older than she; that is just what might be expected from the daughter of Herodias and the insolent girl who demanded the Baptist's head.

But the Nabatæan wife of Antipas had no intention of enduring such an insult. Informed of what was afoot, she had gone to Machærus and then on to her father under the pretext of an ordinary visit. Aretas conceived a violent hatred for the man who had repudiated his daughter. Hostilities, however, began over a quarrel concerning frontiers. After raids on both sides they came to a pitched battle. Antipas was completely routed and sent word of the affair to Tiberius. Vitellius the legate of Syria received orders to avenge him. But he, having no great love for the tetrarch, did not hurry himself, with the result that the death of Tiberius on March 17, 37, brought matters to a standstill. It is in connection with the defeat of Antipas that Josephus mentions John the Baptist. Amongst the people, he says, some thought it was a punishment from God because Antipas, fearing that the Baptist's preaching might end in sedition, had caused him to be put to death at Machærus.[3] Unfortunately the Jewish historian does not give the date of this important event. The Jews knew that

[1] *Ant.*, XVIII, v, 4: 'They have a daughter Salome: after her birth Herodias, scorning the ancestral laws, married Herod, her husband's brother, born of the same father, her husband from whom she was separated being still alive.' It would be forcing the text to deduce along with Otto that the second marriage took place immediately after Salome's birth.

[2] Assuming that her mother married at eighteen, she could not be more than twenty at this date, A.D. 29, but might be younger.

[3] *Ant.*, XVIII, v, 2: 'Now Herod, who feared lest the great influence John exercised over the people might put it into his power and inclination to raise rebellion (for they seemed to do anything he should advise), thought it best by putting him to death to prevent any mischief he might cause, and not bring himself into difficulties by sparing a man who might make him repent of it when it should be too late.'

the wrath of God hangs over the heads of the wicked for a long time ; so the crime may have preceded the punishment by some years.

Before we compare the reason given by Josephus for John's death with the narrative of the gospels, let us see how Antipas was led to his ruin by his weakness for Herodias. It was a great mortification for her to see Agrippa, her own brother, reduced to unfortunate straits on account of his misconduct. She succeeded therefore in persuading her husband to give him an honourable position.[1] But a quarrel at table upset all. While at dinner under the influence of wine, says Josephus,[2] the two brothers-in-law fell to insulting one another. Agrippa had to go and seek his fortune elsewhere. He found a brilliant opportunity in Caligula's friendship, and when Philip the tetrarch died, that emperor gave the tetrarch's realm with additions to Agrippa along with the title of king. Herodias could not endure that her husband should remain a mere tetrarch while another member of his family wore the royal diadem. By dint of entreaties, for Antipas was no contemptible slave of a frowning woman, she persuaded him to go and ask the young emperor for the same favour. But Agrippa had not forgiven, and a denunciation of Antipas reached Baiae, where Caligula then was, at the same time as the two petitioners, namely, the tetrarch and his wife. Antipas was stripped of his dominions, which were bestowed on Agrippa, and exiled to Gaul[3] whither Herodias, faithful in misfortune, accompanied him.

Clearly this account by Josephus owes nothing to the gospel, but neither do the evangelists depend on the Jewish historian, so different is the view of the Baptist's death in each case. Yet their agreement is beyond question : the marriage of Antipas with his brother's wife, contrary to the Law ; the existence of a daughter of the first marriage of Herodias ; the influence of Herodias over her husband, though he was sometimes refractory ; the tetrarch losing his common sense under the influence of drink ; his regard for the Jewish religion when not carried away by passion ; and finally the death of the Baptist, an intrepid preacher of

[1] That of ἀγορανόμος at Tiberias. *Ant.*, XVIII, vi, 2.

[2] ὑπ' οἴνου. Ibid.

[3] To *Lugdunum*, not Lyons but *Lugdunum Convenarum*, or St. Bertrand-de-Comminges. Cf. *Ant.*, XVIII, vii, 2, with *Bellum*, II, ix, 6.

repentance. There is very little therefore for captious critics to lay hold of: in fact two points only. First, Mark gives the name Philip to the first husband of Herodias. He is accused of having confused him with Philip the tetrarch. Certainly some Christian interpreters of the gospel of St. Mark have fallen into that error,[1] and have interpolated one version of Josephus accordingly; but Mark makes no such mistake, for he says nothing of Philip the tetrarch. Luke mentions him,[2] but his gospel was later than Mark's. The fact is that the plain Herod of Josephus must have had another name also, and may have been called Philip like his brother. The case was not uncommon in the Hellenistic period: Antipas had a brother named Antipater, which is the same name.[3] But this point is of no consequence. What is more serious is the fact that, according to Josephus, Antipas took proceedings against John of his own accord, as a political measure: the verdict of the critics is that the whole story in the gospels about the banquet is a mere fiction. Schürer and Otto, however, who accept the story, find no difficulty in admitting that the two reasons for John's death are perfectly reconcilable, a fact that is fairly obvious. But we should go further still and maintain that without Mark's account the facts cannot be properly understood.

Let us first observe a point made by Otto. For the successors of Herod the Great, Josephus can no longer draw upon histories of particular individuals, like that of Nicholas of Damascus which he had used for the first Herod: he writes with the aid of a universal history and 'in aphorisms.'[4] One of these aphorisms or clichés is the hackneyed attribution of events to 'revolutionary innovations.' If we may believe Josephus, Herod had John taken away to Machærus: and this is very probable. The presence of John in Galilee, even in prison—or rather, especially in prison—was likely to stir up those in his favour. At Machærus, Antipas was at his ease. The fortress had been built by Herod the Great who, in the early days of his reign, had felt the need of a place of refuge for his wives and his treasure till better

[1] This is the case with the Slavonic version of Josephus, on which it would not be safe to rely in order to defend Mark against the Greek of Josephus. Cf. Berendts, *Die Zeugnisse vom Christentum im slavischen 'De Bello Judaico des Josephus,'* in *Texte und Untersuchungen*, N.F. XIV, 4 (1906), p. 7 ff. and 33.

[2] Luke iii, 1. [3] Cf. Otto, loc. cit., p. 159.

[4] *Ganz aphoristisch*, Otto, p. 172.

times came. It was a regular den of brigands. The ruins, still known as *Mekawer*, lie to the east of the Dead Sea almost opposite Hebron; the place stands on about the same level as the plateau further east, but is divided from it by a deep and precipitous valley.[1] Antipas had only to leave John to end his days in some dungeon, for the tetrarch was not cruel by disposition. Indeed, but for the influence of Herodias, would he even have had John imprisoned? Critics who admit the main facts of the life of Our Lord—and there are few who do not—cannot find any explanation of the relations of Antipas with Jesus if they hold that his attitude towards the Baptist is sufficiently described by what we read in Josephus. Would one and the same man really have behaved towards John with such senseless cruelty and merely out of arbitrary precaution, yet have shown such great tolerance in the case of Jesus, a tolerance moreover that was mingled with an amused curiosity and not particularly disagreeable? Josephus knows that the marriage of Antipas met with disapproval. There is nothing surprising, therefore, in the fact that John should have voiced that disapproval. Herodias had obtained the dismissal of her rival, in spite of the risk of serious ensuing difficulties. She could not suffer her marriage to be condemned and even endangered in the name of Jewish traditional law. John's protest was not long in coming, and for that reason it seems to us the marriage took place in the year 26, the nearest date to the year in which, according to St. Luke,[2] the Baptist began his ministry, namely 27, and the nearest also to the defeat of Antipas in the year 36. Herod had incurred the displeasure of Aretas, and he saw threats of war arising on his eastern frontier. Herodias was now in his possession, and he had kept his word that he would have no other wife. He would surely have hesitated to incur the displeasure of his own subjects, in addition to that of Aretas, by dealing harshly with John. But after he had been incensed by John's rebuke to him in person and urged on by his wife, he decided to put this troublesome individual in a secure prison. Herodias saw that this was as much as she could win from him; she therefore had recourse to stratagem, along with the aid of lust and wine. She seized a favourable opportunity, the only one she had, when

[1] Cf. *Une croisière autour de la Mer Morte*, by Abel, O.P., pp. 30–41.
[2] Luke iii, 1.

Herod went to Machærus to organize the defence of the frontier ; for there he thought that the crime she desired could be accomplished almost in secret.

Thus, far from being contradictory, the two accounts of John's death are rather complementary and in a most convincing way. Some vague political excuse provided the simplest explanation of the murder for an historian not fully informed of the facts. But the true motive springs from the character that Josephus himself has drawn of the tetrarch ; a prudent ruler, friendly to everybody, when not led astray by his wife or besotted by wine. We can confidently rank the Baptist's death amongst the deeds of which the circumstances, whether public or hidden, are best known to us.

VIII. EVENTS PRECEDING THE INSTITUTION OF THE EUCHARIST

The first multiplication of loaves (105–106).

Luke ix, 10–17 ; Mark vi, 30–44 ; Matt. xiv, 13–21 ; John vi, 1–15.

The disciples of the martyred prophet came to tell their master's friend of the sad event and of their loving care for his burial. Some of them, especially such as were animated by John's spirit, thereupon followed the example their former companions had set when they followed the Lamb of God, as their master had saluted Jesus. Neither St. Mark nor St. Luke tells us what effect the news of the murder had upon Him. St. Matthew seems to regard it as the reason why He left Galilee ;[1] but as he troubles little about chronology and still less about establishing any causal sequence between the incidents he relates, we cannot conclude that Jesus departed immediately after the murder, or that there was any very precise connection in time between the one event and the other. A certain time must have elapsed between John's death and the growth of those uneasy fears which made Herod see the phantom of his headless victim rise in his imagination when people began to tell him about Jesus. It was not until his return from Machærus, when he began to wonder whether Jesus too was a prophet who would stand in his path, that his suspicions

[1] Matthew xiv, 13.

became dangerous. As a matter of fact Jesus had no intention of assuming the rôle of prophet and avenger of wrong. He was no less ready than John to offer His life in sacrifice, but He knew that this was to be at Jerusalem.[1] Consequently He avoided coming into conflict with Herod, who moreover had already been sufficiently warned about his wickedness. Further, His mission was greater than that of a prophet. Not that it was to have more outward splendour, but that a prophet, chosen to act from time to time as the instrument of the divine will, must be manifested by his austerity of life and burning zeal if he was to be able to rebuke kings. The mission of Jesus was higher and of a more permanent character. As He had come to found a society that was to be open to all men, Jesus ate and drank like everyone else. This does not mean that He forbade asceticism, but He did not make a law of it. Nor did He wish His followers to think themselves obliged to admonish those who were entrusted with an authority that really comes from God : that was no longer the business of private persons moved by a personal inspiration from above, but of lawfully constituted spiritual authority.

Lastly, Jesus had another reason for withdrawing. His Apostles had returned from their mission and they needed rest.[2] In solitude with Him they would recover their vigour. Doubtless they had much to tell Him and still more to learn from Him ; in Galilee, where the people flocked after Him in such numbers, it was impossible for Master and disciples to converse together in peace. Jesus therefore retired with His disciples by boat and took the direction of Bethsaida in order to come to a desert place. At Bethsaida[3] they were in the territory of the tetrarch Philip, who had much improved the city, possibly by rebuilding it altogether further north at the modern *et-Tell*, and had given it the name Julias in honour of that woman of sorry fame, Julia, the daughter of Augustus. The ruins of the former fishing village are probably represented by *el-Araj* near the spot where the Jordan enters the lake. South-east of this place a great plain stretches away to the hills. It might be described as a desert, particularly in comparison with the plain of Genesareth which was amazingly fertile. But like

[1] Luke xiii, 33. [2] Mark vi, 31.

[3] It is merely to harmonize biblical texts more easily, and without any need at all, that some have imagined another Bethsaida west of the Jordan.

the desert of Juda both plain and hills are green in the spring ; so that when the first three evangelists speak of the green grass they are in perfect agreement with St. John, who also speaks of the grass and the approach of the paschal feast, which was the feast of the spring.[1]

As the little band crossed the lake by boat they should have arrived before anyone coming by land. But their intention had been guessed, and the people of the eastern shore were already there, soon joined by those from Capharnaum ; so that when Jesus landed, the boat having perhaps been delayed by the dead calm and oppressive heat of early April which makes rowing so exhausting, He found Himself surrounded by a large crowd. We cannot but admire the simplicity of the evangelists : they are in no way disconcerted by this apparent disappointment. On the contrary they emphasize the fact that Jesus, wanting to be left alone, is besieged by a great multitude. But still more admirable is His kindness : He does not turn elsewhere to seek solitude, but is moved with compassion for these sheep without a shepherd. At once He begins to teach them, and at some length, so that one would think that He was forgetting the hour. The disciples note with anxiety that the day is drawing to a close. It is all very well to talk about the kingdom of God, but after all there are the needs of life to be thought of. It is about time for Jesus to end His sermon. They do not tell Him so plainly, but ask Him to send all these people away in order that they may procure some food for themselves in the neighbouring villages and hamlets. Thereupon He replies to His disciples, whom He leaves to look after the material needs of His little band, by giving them the following command which is intended to put them to the test : 'Give you them to eat.' It was a thing easily said, but, as Philip observed, two hundred pence would not be enough to enable them to do it ;[2] and had they got so much ?

They were good fellows, these friends of Our Lord. Each one wants to put in his word and make himself useful. Andrew, Peter's brother, has seen a young boy with five barley loaves and two fishes : a sensible young hawker who has brought his wares with the certainty of being able to dispose of them at a profit. But Andrew's suggestion is tantamount to an admission that the disciples have no

[1] John vi, 10 and 4. [2] About £7, but worth much more.

supplies of their own. Then Jesus says: 'Make them sit down on the grass that they may eat.' By this time the disciples were used to handling crowds, and they arranged the people in groups so that they presented the appearance of garden beds[1] spread over the flower-studded grass.[2] The number was about five thousand. Then solemnly—for all the evangelists have observed that He prayed—Jesus raised His eyes to heaven, pronounced the blessing, and broke the loaves which He gave to His disciples to be distributed among the people; likewise with the fishes. All ate their fill. Then Jesus commanded that they should gather up what was left over so that nothing might be wasted. Some Jews had the custom of showing still greater carefulness about the scraps, and would gather up even the crumbs that had fallen from the table.

It was plainly Our Lord's intention to give this improvised repast, which might have been taken standing, the character of a proper meal. The guests take their places on the grass, but in a regular order. The master of the house Himself breaks the bread while pronouncing a blessing, according to the proper custom, and the remnants are gathered up as if the meal had taken place in a dining-room. The Pasch was near at hand; at the next Pasch after that Jesus was to distribute His Body to the Apostles under the form of bread. It would be untrue to say that the Sacrament of the Eucharist was instituted that day for the benefit of a whole multitude; but it was already one of the preliminaries of that sacrament, given by the Master for His followers to think about. Hence the prayer He offers up, which the rabbinical writings simply call a blessing, St. John calls a thanksgiving, *eucharist.* It is as a symbol that this scene has its full significance. Amazing as it is in itself, it is still more amazing as a presentiment of the future, and it is in this latter character especially that it appeals to our minds and hearts as an outward sign pointing towards a spiritual reality which is not merely of higher order than the miracle, but belonging to a different order altogether.

It is a fact that Catholics the whole world over receive, under the same form of bread, that which they believe to be

[1] Mark vi, 40, πρασιαί.

[2] In the plain south of Gaza we have picked anemones, periwinkles, and even tulips, and these flowers are just as abundant on the shores of the lake of Galilee.

the one Body of Jesus Christ. Some receive unworthily, some out of a motive of vanity, and still more from routine ; but countless numbers really find therein the food of their souls, along with a more urgent call to serve God and a fresh impulse to love Him better. That this stupendous thing should have been typified by a miraculous multiplication of bread seems reasonable ; that this miracle should have blossomed forth into such fruits of salvation, of itself bestows on the miracle an aspect of probability. The harmony between the type and the reality begets conviction. Moreover, the miracle itself was at once so incomprehensible and so public that it was the cause of tremendous enthusiasm. We learn this from St. John alone, but it is the key to the whole situation. No mention of the word Messiah is made as yet, for Jesus has not manifested Himself as a king. But beyond doubt He must be the great prophet whom men awaited, for no prophet had ever done anything so divine on Israel's behalf. And this prophet would become the Messiah if He were crowned king. He was already king, and it only needed that He should be acknowledged as such in order that He might begin to act as king. They therefore sought to compel Him to assume this new rôle ; but He was not of their mind.

Jesus walks on the waters across to the land of Gennesareth (107–108).

Mark vi, 45–56 ; Matt. xiv, 22–36 ; John vi, 16–21.

After the multiplication of bread we are told immediately by Mark that Jesus made His Apostles board their boat and set out without Him. Why did He send them away alone ? Were they not right in showing reluctance ? We are inclined to think so from what St. John tells us about the dispositions of the crowd. Jesus was still, though in His quiet manner, combatting their false conception of the kingdom of God which made them look for a temporal king, a king who would be like other kings except chiefly for the fact that He would be armed with the power of God. Unless He succeeded in calming this tumult that had arisen among them in consequence of His miracle, revolution would be on the way, their error would only be strengthened, His real mission misunderstood. Crowds are fickle. The danger was foreseen, but if it was instantly averted the storm that had gathered so quickly would as quickly disperse. However it was of great importance that the disciples should be sheltered from the contagious enthusiasm which had seized the crowd. They must go away. But had Jesus gone with them, the most unruly spirits in the crowd would have laid hold of all the available boats and followed. He therefore gave His disciples strict orders to cross to the other shore opposite Bethsaida,[1] that is to a place in the neighbourhood of Capharnaum. He would rejoin them later. Thereupon He went away from them. He did not intend to harangue the crowd and ask them to disperse, for the speeches of an unwilling candidate only have the effect of making his supporters more determined still. The simplest course was to disappear altogether. This would be followed by a certain amount of fruitless excitement on the part of the crowd, but night would soon come and everyone would look for shelter. Jesus therefore went off alone to pray on the hill-side. The disciples, left to themselves, still waited. It was already dusk, but Jesus did not return. At last they decided to start.

It often happens in Palestine during the spring that after a day of *sirocco*, a violent wind rises in the south-west. On this occasion such a wind caught the disciples who were rowing their hardest. The struggle went on a long time and the boat made no progress. It was nearly three o'clock in the morning when from a distance Jesus saw them utterly exhausted. It was from a feeling of compassion, surely, that He went to them, walking on the water. Yet, in order to try them, He made as if to pass them by. From the boat He looked like a phantom, and seeing Him, they were afraid and cried out. Whereupon Jesus said : 'Courage ! It is I. Fear not.' Peter, impressionable as ever, ever quick to come forward and feeling confident of his courage, answered : 'Lord, if it be Thou, bid me come to Thee upon the waters.' At the word : 'Come !' he springs towards his Master. But the wind redoubles its force, and Peter trembles and begins to sink. 'Save me,' he cries out, and Jesus taking his hand brings him back to the boat. The wind drops, and soon they reach the shore which could

[1] This has always been translated 'towards Bethsaida' (Mark vi, 45), and in consequence it has been assumed that there were two towns of that name. But we think that πρός can mean 'opposite,' especially with πέραν.

not have been very far distant.[1] Some of them had already fallen at the feet of Jesus : 'Indeed Thou art the Son of God.'

But, astonished as the disciples were at all these marvels, they were not yet fully enlightened. They had themselves worked miracles in His name ; they had acted as His instruments in the multiplication of the loaves ; they had seen Him walk on the water. He had, then, complete power over nature. But what was all this leading up to, seeing that He would not let the people make Him king ? He demanded of them an obedience for which they could not see the reason ; where then was He leading them ? St. Mark tells us that they were more than ever astonished within themselves. A critical hour was approaching for them.

In the meantime some fishermen had noticed Jesus approaching the western shore of the lake with His disciples. The people were still full of excitement after the event of the previous day ; confidence in His miraculous power had increased. From all sides the sick were brought to Him and He healed them. To judge by St. Matthew's account this may have occurred during that morning ; according to St. Mark, however, the time was much longer, extending over the journey Jesus undertook immediately after the falling away of the Galilæans.[2] In spite of their abandonment of Him, there remained always among the crowd some who were favourable to Jesus ; for He was always willing to heal the sick, and that alone was enough to make them follow Him.

The bread of life ; some leave Him (109–110).

John vi, 22–71.

Meanwhile those who had stayed on the other side of the lake had realized that the disciples had taken the only boat left on the shore, and had gone without their Master. They must have looked for Him on the plain and in the hills ; but He was nowhere to be found. Having spent the

[1] According to John vi, 19, they had already gone twenty-five or thirty furlongs. The lake is more than fifty-four furlongs wide, at its greatest width, but much less at the north.

[2] Mark vi, 53–56.

night—doubtless a disturbed one owing to the storm—as best they could, those who were the keenest to follow Him, especially those from Capharnaum,[1] were under the necessity of crossing over by the bridge at Bethsaida ; and now there was none of that joyous enthusiasm of yesterday which had made them ready for anything. They were therefore very well pleased when they saw several boats come in from Tiberias, and they immediately took advantage of them to cross to the western shore.[2] More inflamed than ever, though somewhat annoyed by the disappearance of Jesus, they did not abandon their design and persisted in seeking Him to find out the explanation. Their first word is the rather abrupt question : 'Rabbi, when camest Thou hither ?'

Here begins one of His instructions that is of the deepest significance. Despite interruptions, contradictions and murmurings, it continues without wavering like a boat tossed about yet carried on by the ceaseless waves. These interruptions, which break the evenness of a conference carried on in dialogue form, have often concealed the unity of its teaching from superficial readers. Others have criticized the lesson as too mystical in character, too remote from the homely and simple style of Jesus as portrayed in the Synoptic Gospels. In reality it is the subject that is mystical and sublime ; but it was suggested by the occasion, and it is treated in such a way as to be understood—so far as that was possible—by an ordinary Jewish audience.

It starts from bread, which Jesus had recently distributed with such liberality, and which serves as the symbol of His teaching. He declares that His mission is to give the bread of life : in other words, that He is the revealer sent by God to lead those who believe in Him to eternal life. And as the dialogue leads to a point where it becomes necessary to admit that the bread which He will give comes down from heaven, Jesus declares that He Himself is this life-giving bread, and that He is invested with the power of restoring the dead to life. But how does He give this life to the world ? Is it by the immolation of His flesh ? If so,

[1] John still speaks of the crowd, for he does not vary his style ; but evidently only the principal moving spirits persisted in following Jesus.

[2] Owing to the winds, boats never remain for the night on the eastern shore. Boats leaving Tiberias at night always come in again that evening. Observation of these facts coincides exactly with what is related by St. John, though it has been asserted that this is merely a lucky accident.

then men cannot have access to that life without partaking of His immolated flesh ; whence the necessity of eating His flesh and drinking His blood, that in Him they may have the life of the spirit which will blossom out into eternal life and the resurrection.

The supernatural logic of this teaching is faultless ; but was it suited to the occasion after barely a year's preaching of the Gospel ? In answer to this we may say to begin with that it grows out of the incident which had impressed the crowd so vividly. It was the multiplication of the loaves that provided the subject, or at any rate the symbol. Jesus gives the true bread, and He is that true bread. But should He not have spoken of the reality corresponding to that symbol straightforwardly and clearly ?

Although St. John has not reproduced the earlier narratives of the Synoptic Gospels, yet he had them in front of him. He joins the Synoptists, however, in relating the multiplication of the loaves, precisely at the point where it was necessary for him to make the crisis that then arose perfectly clear. Let us recall what we have already learnt from the events which have led up to this point. Jesus had first preached repentance in view of the advent of the kingdom of God. He had worked miracles, several of them having been performed in order to demonstrate, besides His power and goodness, the authority He had to forgive sin and to decide how the Sabbath ought to be kept. Next He had shown Himself as a lawgiver with the right to bring the Law of Moses itself to its perfection. On the occasion of the Baptist's message, He had clearly shown how superior was the new order He was founding to the old order of the Law and Prophets. By that time men must have begun to ask themselves whether He was not claiming to be the Messiah establishing the kingdom of God. But of what was that kingdom to consist ? For the conception of the kingdom of God must govern the conception of the Messiah. Jesus therefore sought gently to correct the popular ideals, raising the thoughts of the people above earthly cares and turning their minds to the ideals of righteousness, purity, charity, and forgiveness ; at the same time He gave them a glimpse of how the divine power working among men was to have a long development, nevertheless with a view to that eternal life which is to be in the kingdom of God. And thus He prepared their hearts to understand that the Messiah's mission was concerned only with the human soul and its destinies. But all to no avail. Political designs ; material desires ; longings for revenge ; all that perversity of the natural man which makes him lay hold of God's promise as a powerful instrument for his own use and at the same time as a specious excuse to cloak his base desires ; even in the better sort a zeal gone astray owing to ignorance of the true ways of God : all this confused medley was seething in Israel and was about to boil over. They wanted a king, and they wanted to compel Jesus to become the Messiah of their dreams.

Was it not high time—for His time was limited—that Jesus told them openly what He was, what God had charged Him to do, what was their duty towards Him who alone could save them ? Yes, He was to save them, not from their political enemies, but from sin. He was to give them life, not a life of abundance consisting of corn and wine and oil, but a spiritual life which was the first fruits of eternal life. His departure to the hills had been a critical moment ; there was a danger that they might misunderstand altogether, with the result that his mission in Galilee would end in failure. But it had to come to that when all was said and done. It is not surprising that St. John has related this catastrophe, but it would be surprising if the Synoptists had passed it over in silence. They have not done so, and here again fundamentally there is agreement, though the Synoptists have expressed the matter in a different fashion, under the form of the misunderstanding which followed the exposition of the parables. But this was only the first stage of the rupture, which is completed in the Synoptic Gospels by Christ's farewell to the cities of the lake. In the gospel of St. John the call to the spiritual life is more clearly expressed, the person of Jesus brought out more in relief ; but both he and the Synoptists show that the rupture was complete. We cannot blame the fourth evangelist for having included this incident from the Synoptic Gospels in order to explain the falling away of the Galilæans, which, as we shall have further occasion to note, the first three gospels so plainly imply.

This instruction, then, at Capharnaum after the multiplication of the loaves was of a crucial nature : Jesus explains, as He was bound eventually to do, that His mission is of a spiritual character. Many a passage in the Synoptic

Gospels says the same thing, but here it has that special feature introduced by the symbol of bread on account of the preceding miracle. The symbol leads naturally to the Eucharist. For this reason, and also because of the unity of the subject, it seems necessary to put the concluding part of the discourse, which specially concerns the Eucharist,[1] at the same time and place. With regard, however, to this point in particular, it is by no means easy to see the need for an explanation of the Eucharist just then. Our inclination rather is to see the difficulty of presenting a subject like that to ill-disposed minds without at the same time giving explanations that would seem indispensable. If St. Matthew composed the Sermon on the Mount from sayings spoken by Jesus on various occasions, we see no reason why St. John should not have done a similar thing here if he thought it profitable. But there does seem some advantage to be gained from introducing the doctrine of the Eucharist, distributed under the form of bread and typified by the multiplication of loaves, at the culminating point of a discourse on the Bread of Life ; and we are so carried away by the beauty of this wonderful transition that at first we have no thought for chronology. But if the historian decided that the teaching about the Eucharist ought to be placed shortly before the Last Supper and in a more restricted company of disciples, we should be inclined to say that he was right—without ceasing to admire the Johannine arrangement of the sayings of Jesus.

With these prefatory remarks let us enter the synagogue at Capharnaum whither Jesus has been followed by His unwelcome partisans.[2] Probably it was not the Sabbath day, seeing that the boats had crossed the lake. But a certain solemnity was ensured by the religious atmosphere of the place, though this did not preclude discussion. Instead of answering the question : 'Rabbi, when camest Thou hither ?' Jesus begins the conversation by asking them to examine the real motives for their recent messianic excitement. His multiplication of the loaves had seemed to them a foretaste of the superabundance of good things that they looked for at the hands of the Messiah : crops as high as horsemen, vines flowing with wine like rivers. Let them rather seek the food of the soul, the food that abides unto eternal life. It is He who gives that food, for the Father

[1] John vi, 51–58. [2] John vi, 59, 60.

has set His seal upon Him by confirming the doctrine of Jesus with miracles. The people of Capharnaum have seen enough of these miracles to make them regard Him as a Master, one chosen by God to convey His commands to them. They ask Him : 'What must we do in order to meet God's wishes ?' They can hardly speak of anything but what is to be *done*, of works, that is, and we can hardly blame them for talking like Jews. But obedience to the works commanded in the name of God implies faith, and their faith is too vague. It is fixed upon God, but it must also be fixed, and with complete confidence, on Him whom God has sent. Had they arrived as far as that, these people who had tried to make of Him the instrument of their own passions ?

They begin to understand now that the claim made by Jesus is a very lofty one. A prophet might speak in God's name and recall them to the observance of the Law : but would he demand that absolute submission of mind which seemed to know no limit ? To make such a claim it was not enough to advance a miracle which, after all, was not so great as the one performed by Moses when he gave the people bread from heaven. The barley loaves had not come down from heaven ; they had not even fallen from the sky like the manna. But what did that matter in truth ? The true bread from heaven is He who comes forth from God and is consequently sent by God. Moses has no jurisdiction in that sphere : the Father alone, the Father of Jesus, can give life to the world by bestowing on it that bread. The thought has thus advanced. The Son of Man gave bread, that is, doctrine : now He is life-giving food. In the past the Law had been likened to bread and the tree of life—a natural comparison. But the other comparison is harder to understand. Nevertheless Rabbi Aqiba was one day to interpret 'the sustenance of bread'[1] as meaning the Talmudic doctors, since the Book of Proverbs in the name of Wisdom said : 'Eat of my bread.'[2] Was Jesus, then, the Wisdom of God, and did He hold within His own person a spiritual doctrine profitable to the souls of men ?

Not understanding Him, and so neither venturing to raise objection nor expressing deliberate assent, they say :

[1] Isaias iii, 1.
[2] Proverbs ix, 5.

'Lord, give us this bread, always,'[1] and not once only, as He had done in the case of the miracle worked with ordinary bread. Certainly these people were not hostile to the Master. Though they could not rise to the level of His thought, they gave a last sign of good will. Jesus therefore answers them with great kindness, not by offering them the bread they ask without having any exact idea of what it is, but by an explanation along with an appeal. The bread He speaks of is a spiritual bread which has no need of being given more than once, for its efficacy does not diminish after the fashion of material things. Once a man has tasted it he will never hunger again, for this gift is by its nature imperishable, and as far as God is concerned the gift will never be taken back, for God's gifts are without repentance. But, once again, this bread is Jesus Himself. He has come, and now it is for men to approach Him by faith. He will reject no one, for those who come to Him are brought by the Father who has sent Him from heaven; and the will of the Father is that Jesus should keep them unto eternal life, unto the resurrection on the last day. But, alas! those to whom He speaks, those who have seen Him and see Him now, refuse to believe in Him.[2] In fact, His kind of Messiahship disturbs them. They were willing perhaps to allow that the Messiah should have something to do with the resurrection of the dead, so that those who had died as martyrs in the past might share in the earthly bliss which the Messiah was to inaugurate.[3] But there seemed to be no question of that bliss now. Eternal life, the last day . . . did not that mean doing away with happiness on this earth and depriving them of just revenge for all the ills they had endured? Thus their own expectations are pushed into the background, their part in the triumph of the Messiah is no longer spoken of and is abolished. Disheartened, they go away.

Others appear on the scene, but indirectly, in a way of their own with which the Synoptists have made us familiar. The latter call them Pharisees or Scribes; St. John often describes them as 'the Jews,' meaning by that those who

[1] John vi, 34. It is tempting to take πάντοτε in the sense of the French *toujours*, 'whatever it may be, give it to us all the same.' But Jesus means it in the sense of 'always,' and it does not seem that there is the twofold meaning here.

[2] Verse 36 should probably come after v. 40.

[3] On this very vexed question cf. *Le Messianisme*, pp. 130, 176 ff.

are opposed to Jesus. Instead of questioning Him openly, as the others had done, they talk among themselves with a sort of muttering that gives a sense of hostility ready to break out but coldly restrained. Accustomed as they are to argument, they have perceived the crucial point quite plainly beneath the metaphor of the bread and have followed it through the intricacies of the discourse : Jesus claims to have come down from heaven. That was one of the marks of the Messiah, but it was not true of Jesus the son of Joseph ; they knew His father and mother ; they came, these 'Jews,' from the same neighbourhood as Himself and were not to be imposed on.

In dealing with them the Master adopts a sterner note. He begins by calling them out, as it were, into the open : 'Murmur not among yourselves.' They look on themselves as appointed judges ; the standard of action is what seems good according to the light of their minds. But they are altogether in the wrong. The very reason why they do not show themselves docile to the teaching of Jesus is because they have not received light from God. That light is necessary and it suffices. *They* cannot come to Jesus because they are not drawn by the Father. Not that this excuses them. If men are to be drawn by God they must desire it, whereas these 'Jews' trust in their own knowledge. Other men, those who have accepted the Father's teaching, come to Jesus.

The Jews might ask : 'Does this teaching, then, give the vision of God ?' No ; for no one has seen the Father save Him who is with God, that is the Son, Jesus Himself ; and if the Jews reflected on this they would ask themselves whether a Son who beholds the Father because He is with the Father, is not the Son of God in the strict sense.[1] But Jesus does not pause to speak to them of His sonship. All that He wants to do now is to show that men cannot come to Him except by faith, under the impulse and light that the Father gives. And since He is appealing to faith, He contents Himself with saying again that He is the object of that faith, He the bread come down from heaven ; and whosoever eats of this bread will never die. Those who ate of the manna are dead, for no natural bread, even if miraculous in origin, can preserve a man from temporal

[1] However exalted may seem this vision of the divine life, it does not go beyond what we shall find in St. Matthew (xi, 25–27) and St. Luke (x, 21–22).

death. But He is the spiritual bread which is free from the conditions of change, and which therefore bestows a spiritual life that is endless. Every kind of bread acts according to its nature and the end for which it is designed. Beneath all this there lies the reminder that man has the formidable use of his free will : though he can accept life, he can also refuse it so long as that life which is now offered to him is not yet transformed into eternal life.

This return to the subject of the bread come down from heaven now reveals itself as a transition to a mystery that is more difficult to understand. Jesus had already said that the bread of God gives life to the world.[1] It is of the nature of bread to *sustain* life. He now goes on to insist : 'I am the bread of life, the living bread. . . .' How can bread *give* life ? It is spiritual bread which has that property, since it actually gives spiritual life. Jesus, who was this bread, was to take away sin and give life to the world by His death, which God had destined Him to and laid upon Him, and by the immolation of His flesh. He therefore had the right to declare that His immolated flesh was the life of the world, and in order that His meaning may be clearer still He will soon speak of His blood. It follows then that to feed on the spiritual bread that He Himself was, is to feed on His flesh : He declares this explicitly.

The Jews are so astonished that they resume their murmuring. Some of them, it may be, try to understand the declaration in a figurative sense : the greater number judge it absurd and refuse to consider it. Jesus maintains it with the greatest energy. He goes on to say that this eating and assimilating of His flesh and blood is the necessary means of union with the Father by means of the Son. Just as the Son lives by the Father, so he who is united to the Son will live by Him and have eternal life.[2] After that the Jews no longer debate among themselves. Such clear words defy the most ingenious subtleties of interpretation : 'Unless you eat the flesh of the Son of Man and drink His blood. . . . My flesh is meat indeed, and My blood is drink indeed . . .' They could only let Him go on speaking.

Let us recall the words of Bossuet, which still retain their force against those who even to-day hold to the figurative

[1] John vi, 33.
[2] This might also be understood as meaning that Jesus lives *for* the Father, and that the faithful ought to live *for* Him.

sense :[1] 'All this, you say, is mere mystery and allegory : to eat and drink means to believe ; to eat the flesh and drink the blood means to look on them as separated on the cross and seek life in our Saviour's wounds. If that is so, O my Saviour, why dost Thou not speak simply, and why leave Thy hearers to murmur, to be scandalized and forsake Thee, instead of telling them Thy meaning plainly ? But here, the more they murmur against Him, the more shocked they are at such strange words, the more He stresses them, the more He repeats them, the more He plunges, so to say, into difficulties and mysteries. He had but to say one word to them. He had but to say : "What troubles you ? To eat My flesh means to believe in it ; to drink My blood means to think upon it ; in fact the words simply mean meditating upon My death." That would have ended all doubt ; there would have remained no shadow of a difficulty. Yet He does not speak thus. He leaves His own disciples to succumb to temptation and scandal for lack of saying just one word to them. That is not like Thee, O my Saviour. No, certainly, that is not like Thee. Thou hast not come to distress men with long words that lead to nothing : that would be finding pleasure in proposing paradoxes merely in order to bewilder them.'

The meeting had not been without profit for His persistent enemies. They saw His new-found friends already out of their depth, and they rejoiced to see the innovator caught in His own toils. But there were others who were grieved, the disciples who had been with Him now for some time, who had given themselves wholeheartedly to their Master and so far seemed to appreciate His teaching. Some of them, however, had gradually weakened in their attachment : their devotion was now merely nominal. On that day there was hesitation in the minds of nearly all, and they were even then making up their minds to turn back. Really, they thought, this last discourse of Jesus was offensive in every way. Could anyone even listen to it without protest? In this critical hour Jesus does not forsake them. By proving to them that He reads their thoughts He makes a fresh appeal to their confidence : He asks them to trust to Him for the meaning of His words, which are spirit—that is, past human understanding—and yet are life, with a spiritual life that is necessarily mysterious. He has often repeated

[1] *Meditations sur les évangiles, La Cène,* XXXVe *jour.*

that He has come down from heaven. They are loath to believe it. But suppose they see Him going up to where He was before, will not that convince them? Let them have patience, then. It is the spirit which gives the life of which He has spoken: the flesh, with all that the word implies of change, corruption, and mortality, the flesh of itself would profit nothing. He is just as aware of that as they. But He sees that His words do not reach their hearts. He observes with sorrow that some of them do not believe. Many go away and leave Him.

Yet to-day there are many critics who seize on the words with which Jesus condescends to the difficulties of His disciples, on this distinction between spirit and flesh, and see in it a retractation instead of a help to the deeper understanding of His changeless doctrine. Consequently, they take these words in a sense different from that in which they were understood by the disciples, who were not the less repelled even when Jesus spoke them. Because St. Paul speaks of the opposition between the spirit and the letter,[1] they here take the spirit that vivifies to be a figurative sense, whereas the profitless flesh they understand as the literal sense. But there is not the slightest sign here that Jesus is explaining a parable. The aim of His whole discourse was to replace natural longings by a strong desire for the spiritual and divine life. If the disciples think that the flesh profits anything, they have understood nothing. As for the flesh of Him who has come down from heaven to give life to the world, it partakes of a spiritual nature; it is under this character that they must understand it is given to them. Such is in fact the mystery of the Eucharist. When we have affirmed the reality of the Flesh and Blood in this sacrament, we have to add that the eating takes place in a spiritual manner; the Flesh is of no profit unless it be received in spirit as well as in truth. Jesus does not say that so plainly here; all He gives is a first intimation of it for which He requires faith.

It is easier for us because of the truly prophetic character of the words of the Gospel, declaring the necessity of feeding on the Body and Blood of Jesus so that we may live by His life and by the life of the Father. We see around us great numbers of men, absorbed in the cares of the present life, devoting all their endeavours to obtain from it their happiness, since they do not place their hopes in the happiness of

[1] 2 Corinthians iii, 6.

the life to come; these turn their backs on Jesus. Some there are who long for spiritual benefits and seek them in Jesus Christ their Lord; but the Eucharist repels them. They accept it only as a commemoration of what is past and gone; thus Jesus ceases to be present for them, and is despoiled of the divine attribute of omnipresence, of being always with His followers. He is banished to a moment of history. Soon people lose the habit of seeking Him in heaven; they still like to appeal to His doctrine and His personal character, but His doctrine is only that of a prophet or a wise man, so He Himself can be nothing more than a prophet or a wise man. They ask how could this *man* give us His flesh to eat? To that there is no answer. But that God, who gave life to the world by His Son, should not have wholly withdrawn Him from the world, but should have left Him present in the world in order that the Flesh which saved it should still sustain it, does not that seem worthy of His goodness? Does it not seem consistent with the very plan of the Incarnation? It is, moreover, the only right meaning of Scripture, as is admitted nowadays even by unbelievers who, though they do not acknowledge its authority, are concerned to discover its true meaning.

In this prophetic scene the faithful are represented by the Twelve. To them Jesus turns, saddened by the departure of so many whom He loved, and says: 'And you, will you also go away?' Simon Peter answers for them all: 'Lord, to whom should we go? Thou hast the words of eternal life, and we believe and know that Thou art the Holy One of God.' His mind had been raised to thoughts of the world to come, to which it was the desire of Jesus to lead all these Galilæan disciples. Peter was making an act of faith in Jesus Christ, as one sent by God and sharing in His holiness. Later on he was to be enlightened still more. There was another disciple, Judas, who by his silence seemed to consent to Peter's promise of fidelity; but even already his heart was no longer with his Master. Perhaps he had come to Jesus out of a motive of self-seeking and ambition, and had already been wounded in his greed and pride. Or had some occurrence of which we know nothing changed his sympathy for his Master into aversion? Would that he had gone away with the rest! Jesus intended us to realize that He was not duped. But He endured the presence of the man who was to betray Him.

CHAPTER IV

FORMATION OF THE DISCIPLES AND MINISTRY, CHIEFLY OUTSIDE GALILEE

THE first year's preaching ends in failure, despite the ever-growing enthusiasm of the people ; and it is St. John, the revealer of the Word Incarnate, the evangelist who is accused of transforming the whole gospel in order to glorify the Word, it is St. John who declares to us that failure along with its causes in the plainest terms. But the truths that come most into conflict with our fallen nature are the truths that are most salutary for the soul. Henceforward, at any rate, there was no more room for illusion ; the disciples are forewarned.

From this time Jesus was to devote Himself more fully to the formation of those who are called to carry on His mission ; His own special work is to consist in the surrender of His life. During the days now to come He will plainly foretell both His Passion and His Death, and He will declare what are the hard conditions under which men must work out their salvation. But although He is to suffer and to die, nevertheless the kingdom of God is to be established after His Resurrection, concerning which He now speaks openly. Galilee has refused to understand what kind of Messiah He is ; He now leaves Galilee in order to visit the northern frontiers of Palestine, and afterwards Jerusalem, Judæa, and Peræa. It is not any fear of Herod which decides Him to go away : He knows only too well that He will receive still less consideration at Jerusalem. But it is there principally, face to face with the rabbis, in the very centre of worship and religious teaching, in His Father's temple, that He is to reveal what He is.

We have seen that during this first year He went up to Jerusalem for the Pasch. Did He return thither for Pentecost and the feast of Tabernacles ? It may have been so, but at all events St. John says nothing about it.[1] Either these journeys never occurred, or if they did, nothing happened worthy of note for the progress of the gospel. To the mind of St. John, this first year was sufficiently accounted for by the ministry in Galilee. During the second year, however, he brings Jesus to Jerusalem for the feasts of Pentecost, Tabernacles, and the Dedication; and each of these pilgrimages is made the occasion of some fresh development in the revelation of Christ's divinity.

Surprise is caused by these two different forms of teaching used by Our Lord: one in Galilee, represented by Peter's catechesis as given us by St. Mark; the other chiefly at Jerusalem, shown to us in the recollections of St. John. We are far from saying that St. Peter did not accompany his Master to the Holy City; but he was certainly less at home there than John, who had—we do not know how—connections at Jerusalem even amongst the hierarchy. Perhaps, too, Peter thought that the conversations or, to tell the truth, the disputes into which Jesus was drawn by the hostility of the Pharisees, were of too subtle a quality to serve as matter for his own daily preaching to the people. There is no reason also why we should not see something of St. John's own genius in the manner in which Jesus' teaching at Jerusalem is presented. But in the other gospels too the revelations of this second year are more profound, there is more light thrown on the person of Jesus, on His own sacrifice, and on the sacrifices which He demands on the part of others. We are in a loftier region, in a more rarefied atmosphere. The determination of His enemies becomes more marked, the devotion of the disciples more deliberate though still imperfect, and it is gradually strengthened by closer communion with their Master. He is engaged in founding the Church instead of that earthly kingdom with which He will have nothing to do.

[1] We follow the order given by the tradition of the ancient gospel harmonies which places the events of Chapter VI before those of Chapter V.

I. PENTECOST AT JERUSALEM

The pool of Bezatha at Jerusalem. Jesus heals a sick man (111–113).

John v, 1–47 ; vii, 1.

The Paschal season, already near when Jesus multiplied the loaves, was spent by Him in Galilee. Afterwards He went up to Jerusalem for some feast of the Jews which is not described more fully, but cannot be other than Pentecost since it was followed by the feast of Tabernacles. 'The feast of Weeks,' so called in Hebrew because the people then offered in the Temple the first-fruits of the harvest ripened during the seven weeks after the Pasch, was named Pentecost in Greek, an equivalent name since it means (the feast) 'of the fiftieth day.' By the time of Jesus an historical commemoration had been attached to this feast, namely that of the promulgation of the covenant on Sinai. It therefore provided an occasion for renewing one's zeal for the observance of the Law.

Now it happened that Jesus, as He was either entering or leaving the Temple, went into the porch or colonnade surrounding the pool situated near the city-gate called the Sheep-gate, so named because by that way the sacrificial lambs were brought to the Temple. This pool was in the gorge which of old had served as a protection for the northern wall of the Temple, and it was cut out of the side of a hill which had recently been included within the city-walls. The hill was called by the Aramaic name Bezatha, and the pool naturally bore the same name. It was oblong in shape, surrounded by four colonnades and divided into two equal squares by a fifth colonnade. This arrangement, which we are able to recognize with certainty from the excavations,[1] throws light on the passage in St. John, who thus shows himself to have been perfectly acquainted with the place.[2]

[1] Cf. *Jerusalem* (Vincent et Abel), II, 4, pp. 685 ff. and Pl. 75.

[2] He says that the pool *is* at Jerusalem, and that is quite correct, for there is no reason to doubt that it was still there during the period of Roman domination in Palestine. People still believed in the miraculous efficacy of its water (cf. op. cit., p. 694). A certain healing power was attributed to the water and was probably more active when the fresh water, held back by a sluice, entered the pool and caused the water to bubble. The Jews were no doubt disposed to attribute a supernatural power to the water, and that opinion has crept into the gospel text by means of a gloss, verse 4, which we do not hold to be authentic.

Jesus found there a great number of sick people, blind, lame, and halt, all begging for alms, though they were there in the hope of something better than alms. In fact they hoped for a cure, for the one at all events who should first succeed in throwing himself into the pool after the water was moved.[1] Among the cripples Jesus saw one who was a paralytic, according to the description of ancient tradition. Whatever was his malady, he was incapable of moving at least to this extent that, by the time he had painfully got ready to go down into the pool at the bubbling up of the water, someone else would be there before him. Jesus offers to heal him, and without even requiring from him that act of faith which He saw him prepared to make, said : 'Arise, take up thy bed and walk.' The man, conscious that he was cured, picked up his pallet and went away. Now it was a Sabbath day. This remark is not made by the evangelist out of a mere love for exact detail : it is of weighty importance. Not only had Jesus worked a cure on the Sabbath day without urgent need, but, what was more serious, He had commanded the healed man to carry away his pallet. Now it was considered unlawful even to wear ornaments on one's dress that it might be necessary to fasten or unfasten on the Sabbath.[2]

Such a violation of the customs introduced by their forefathers could not be borne by the Jews, that is to say, by those Pharisees and Scribes attached to strict traditional observance who were the adversaries of Jesus. The man doubtless considered that one who had power to cure him must be a good interpreter of the Law. But who was He? He does not know what to reply to the Jews who question him minutely. So little intention had Jesus of parading His power that He had vanished in the crowd. Later the paralytic finds Him in the Temple, ascertains His name and informs his questioners. At once they remember that Jesus is an old offender[3] of whom they had somewhat lost sight. Seeing their displeasure, He shows Himself quite willing to

[1] Strack and Billerbeck (II, p. 454) quote the Rabbi Tanchuma (*circa* A.D. 380), who speaks of a man cured of the itch by bathing in the lake of Tiberias at the moment when the fountain of Miriam began to gush up to the surface of the water. That was regarded as a miracle, and no doubt they believed that only one person could benefit each time.

[2] To this the rabbis added casuistical subtleties about the gravity or lightness of the fault. Jeremias (xvii, 21 ff.) had indeed forbidden the carrying of burdens, but for purposes of trade (cf. Nehemias xiii, 19 ff.).

[3] Matthew xii, 14, etc.

explain His conduct : ‘ My Father worketh until now, and I also work.’ The origin of the institution of the Sabbath was due to the fact that God rested on the seventh day.[1] Instructed Jews, however, were quite aware that this rest of God was only a figurative expression to mark the stability of the order which God had brought into the world. God is ever working, otherwise everything would crumble into nothing. Like God, Jesus also works, interpreting the Sabbath in the spirit in which it had been instituted. There was nothing blasphemous in His words when understood in this way, not even for the Pharisees. But they interpret His words as meaning that Jesus claims the right to work as the equal of God : and if He were only a man, as they thought Him, that would have been blasphemy. They will later condemn Him to death for that very reason.

But the time had not yet come for making that solemn declaration of His equality with God ; so instead of answering : ‘ It is true : I am equal to God ’—or rather : ‘ Because I am God I am equal to the Father ’—He merely asserts His right as one sent by His Father. His reasoning, however, far from excluding the fact of His divinity, on the contrary takes it for granted, since the one who is sent is the only Son of the Father ; yet He has received in His human nature certain prerogatives which are consequent on the personal union of that nature with the divine nature, and it is on these prerogatives that He now insists. Such is St. Cyril of Alexandria’s interpretation of this discourse, in which Jesus seeks to calm the anger of the Jews by adapting His language to harmonize with that human aspect of His which was due to a nature really human, but a human nature which was at the same time endowed with the highest privileges. Jesus could hardly begin more modestly than by saying, as He does, to those who accuse Him of daring to set Himself up as the rival of the Father : ‘ The Son cannot do anything of Himself but what He seeth the Father doing . . . for the Father loveth the Son and sheweth Him all that He doth . . .’[2]

[1] Genesis ii, 1–3 ; Exodus xx, 11 ; xxxi, 17.

[2] Nevertheless, it has been possible to interpret this phrase in the trinitarian sense, for the divine, uncreated, eternal nature of the Son, identical with the nature of the Father, is yet received from the Father, who is the sole principle of the nature of the Son. *Filius habet potestatem a Patre a quo habet naturam.* (St. Thomas, Ia, Q. 42, a. 6, ad 1.) But taking the discourse altogether, the Son is speaking as exercising the mission of His Incarnation.

The rather long discourse uttered by Jesus on this occasion was free from interruption, which we may take as a sign that His words did not seem too bold to the mind of His Jewish audience. He does not proclaim Himself to be the Messiah ; that title, as understood by the Jews, would be at variance with His mission. He is, if they like to think so, a spiritual Messiah such as He had revealed Himself in Galilee, and the Son of God to whom the Father shows His works because the Father gives Him power to perform these mighty miracles. The chief work He has come to do is that of bestowing life on those who seem to be alive, but who are dead in the sight of God. Let them believe that He is sent by God, let them honour the Son, and they will have eternal life within them. The Son communicates to them the life that He has received from His Father, and He will judge them in the name of the Father. That voice of the Son, which now begets in them spiritual life by means of faith, is the same voice which will be heard once more at the resurrection, whether it be resurrection unto life or resurrection unto death.

Here we recognize again the teaching of the first part of the sermon on the Bread of Life, though now without the symbolism introduced by the multiplication of the loaves. The idea of Jesus as judge adds nothing essential to that teaching, for those who believe are not judged because they have already passed from death to life. The distinctive note of the present discourse is this revelation of the intimate relationship that exists between the Father and the Son, a revelation which prepares the way for the declaration of identity of nature in Father and Son ; a declaration, however, which in no way militates against that relationship of Father to Son and Son to Father which implies that they must be two distinct persons.

In the latter part of this discourse Jesus points out to the Jews the reasons why they ought to believe in the mission that He has received simply under His character as Son. The grounds of such a belief are not capable of being arrived at by a process of reasoning from self-evident principles, for the mission of the Son depends solely on the Father's will. It was a question of fact, and as in every question of fact there was no other course but to examine the testimony of witnesses. There was first the testimony of John the Baptist, of whom Jesus speaks in the past tense ;

John was therefore already dead.[1] After his death the Jews seem to have become more favourably disposed towards him, doubtless because he had died a martyr's death in defence of the Law. But Jesus reminds them how John had borne witness to the truth by pointing to the one who was to come after him.

A mere man's testimony, however, was not in itself sufficient in the present case, though the testimony of this last of the prophets was not without weight in Israel. There was a further testimony which was of a more conclusive character, namely the witness of deeds, that is to say the testimony of miracles by which men might recognize that a person was sent by God. Even at Sinai their ancestors had not seen God Himself nor heard His voice. This very feast of Pentecost which the Jews were now celebrating could not but recall to their minds the memory of Moses, the great mediator between Israel and God, whose testimony was recorded in the Scriptures where it stood for the very testimony of God Himself. Since the Jews are so diligent in searching the Scriptures, it ought to be evident to them that the Scriptures also bear witness to Jesus. But the fact is that only too often the chief motive of their studies was to obtain among one another a reputation for learning, and they were far from being inspired simply by the love of God. Therefore Moses, the greatest of those to whom God had entrusted His word, the very prophet in whom they set their hopes, Moses himself shall be their accuser before God : 'For,' as Jesus adds, 'he wrote of Me.'

The Synoptic Gospels reason in precisely the same way, though in different terms and in a less didactic manner. John's testimony was indeed precious, but after all it was rather Jesus who had given authoritative testimony to John,[2] than John to Jesus. The Father had given testimony to Jesus by means of all those miracles enumerated by the Synoptists which St. John barely mentions, and by those expulsions of the devil concerning which the fourth gospel is completely silent. All four gospels, however, are careful to make that appeal to the testimony of Scripture which Jesus here lays down as a principle, though the Synoptists,

[1] Here we have a very important indication and reason for assigning the Bezatha incident to the Pentecost following John's death. He was beheaded shortly before the Pasch.

[2] Matthew xi, 7–10 ; Luke vii, 24–27.

St. Matthew especially,[1] do so in a much plainer fashion than does St. John. St. Paul could not help seeing how in the person of Jesus were thus linked up together the Old and the New Covenants. The error of Marcion in making the Old and New Testaments opposed one to the other is therefore without a shred of evidence. And at this time, when, to the great scandal of the Jews, so many impostors were publishing absurd claims to divinity based on old pagan fables, Israel ought to have felt herself reassured when she saw how strictly Jesus, God's ambassador, adhered to the words spoken of old by God. It was no new religion that He was putting forward ; He did no more than include Himself in the worship paid to the Father, whose Son He was. What He proposed to the Jews was a development of their faith, parallel with the development that had taken place in their Law. And all this He does with an infinite reverence for His Father from whom He derives all that He has and is, whose will is His law : His Father, the source of life and last end unto which all things are led by the Son.

The only effect produced by all this on these ill-disposed Jews was that they made up their minds to do Jesus to death. He therefore retraces His steps to Galilee.[2]

II. THE FORMATION OF THE DISCIPLES

Pharisaic traditions and the true service of God (114).

Mark vii, 1–23 ; Matt. xv, 1–20.[3]

St. John has just told us that Jesus returned to Galilee. In the gospels of Mark and Matthew we find Him there, watched by Pharisees and Scribes who had come from Jerusalem. The leaders in Israel, seriously upset by the words of this man who assumed the title of Son of God and thought Himself above the law of the Sabbath on that account, have therefore once more delegated some of their adherents to see if they can catch Him in the act of violating established custom. There was no difficulty about that when they were dealing with the disciples of Jesus who, though they were devoted to the Law, were simple-minded

[1] Matthew xxi, 42 ; xxii, 43 and parallels.
[2] John vii, 1.
[3] St. Luke's plan had no need of these questions of rabbinical casuistry, of which no mention is made in his record of the inaugural discourse of Jesus.

men and little versed in the *minutiae* of rabbinical casuistry. Before long they were observed taking food with unwashed or, as was said, *common* hands, which was a serious offence. In later times it was told of Rabbi Aqiba that he had risked death in prison, where he had only enough water to quench his thirst, rather than omit using it to pour over his hands before eating.[1] This rinsing of the hands, which had to be done twice in order that the second rinsing might remove all traces of the first since the water would be contaminated, was done by simply washing the tips of the fingers. But if a Jew had been to the market, where he ran almost certain risk of defilement through contact with Gentiles, this hand-washing had to be done more thoroughly, right up to the elbow, with the aid of about a hundred gallons of spring or rain water—an immense quantity for Palestine.[2] In this place St. Mark adds that the Jews carefully washed cups, pots, and brazen dishes.

What was the origin of such exaggerated scrupulosity about physical cleanliness which they thus accounted as legal purity? It was certainly not found in the Law, and although by clever manipulation almost anything could be squeezed out of the Scripture texts by the rabbis, none of them claimed to be able to deduce this from the texts.[3] They had therefore to be content with the authority of the ancients; in other cases this had been considered sufficient for the determination of right and wrong in religious matters, and for the Scribes the authority of the ancients was as sacred as the Law itself. But there were no grounds for such an attitude. As interpreters of the Law it was the business of the Scribes to interpret it and not to burden it with new observances which distorted the very spirit of the Law. Through all these ceremonies of purification the Pharisees had given a dangerous significance to what was an admirable principle of the Law, namely that Israel must behave as a holy people. That law of holiness bound Israel first of all to legal purity, particularly in the choice of food,[4] and it served as a very necessary barrier of division

[1] Strack and Billerbeck, I, p. 702.

[2] In our commentary on St. Mark we have written of the washing, by sprinkling, of things bought in the market. There is never any question of this, however, in Jewish writings, which seems to show that it was not a common custom.

[3] Reference was made, however, to Leviticus xv, 11.

[4] Leviticus xi, 44 ff.

rom the nations by which Israel was surrounded and whose worship was so impure. But it was a wholly external measure, and ought not to have been allowed to swallow up everything else. Thus the prophets had been sent, Amos at their head, to preach purity of heart, and charity especially, which was dearer to God than all observances. But the Pharisees, instead of making that love of God, which was the first principle of the Law, the animating principle of the ancient regulations also, devoted all their attention to the work of cultivating among the people the sense of their superiority over the Gentiles. That superiority was made to consist in taking care to avoid all contact with Gentiles as well as with everything that was not legally pure.

Jesus resolved to show up by a striking example this deviation from the true spirit of religion which is so characteristic of all Pharisaic tradition. The Law commanded: 'Honour thy father and thy mother; he that curseth his father and his mother let him be put to death.'[1] Although there were doubtless bad sons in Israel in spite of the commandment, yet they were certainly fewer there than elsewhere; but it was in Israel alone that hardness of heart and ingratitude paraded under the mask of reverence for God. The Law contained another precept that nothing once vowed to God might be devoted to any other use.[2] It was argued that a vow concerning some particular and concrete object ought to be considered of greater importance than an obligation that was more general in character, such as the command of the Law that parents are to be honoured. It was observed that there was no commandment that parents should be provided with food, or that children should hand over to them this or that. Therefore, when a son was asked for such a service by his parents, he would, in order to cut short their solicitations, consecrate to the Lord whatever it might be that they required. The consecration was a fictitious one in so far as he did not deprive himself of the use of the object; but at the same time it was irrevocable since it would have been considered sacrilege to give the object to anyone but God.

The discussions of the rabbis prove that this flagrant abuse of religion was practised. Rabbi Eliezer (about A.D. 90), who had a reputation for holding singular opinions, expressed the wish that at least some means might be found

[1] Exodus xx, 12; xxi, 17. [2] Leviticus xxvii, 1–34.

for annulling these wicked vows. But it was thought that there was no way out of the difficulty, because the Law was explicit about the validity of vows, and the strictness of the Law was held to apply even to vows that were immoral in character. Eventually, however, it was granted that a doctor of the Law could dispense from such a vow. Even if the rabbis of Our Lord's day were not responsible for inventing and propagating this subterfuge for escaping from filial obligations (and He does not reproach them with it), at any rate, by declaring a vow valid even if it were contrary to religion and humanity, they prevented a bad son who had made such a vow from rendering assistance to his parents even though he afterwards repented of the vow. This was tantamount to neglecting the commandments of God for the sake of traditions which owed their origin and continuance to men.

Having laid down these principles clearly, Jesus leaves the Pharisees to judge for themselves what was the worth of their scruples concerning legal purity before eating. But He desired to point out the way for the solution of this problem to such of the crowd as were willing to listen to Him. Under the form of an enigma He contrasts what goes into a man with what comes out of him. From the circumstances which brought about this discussion we understand that what goes into a man is food, a thing which has no moral quality in itself; what comes from him is his actions, good or bad. The Law, it is true, contained a whole list of unclean foods, and Jesus abstained from eating them. What He therefore wishes His hearers to understand is this: that food which is clean according to the Law—and there is no question of any other kind—could not stain the soul even if it were touched with unwashed hands. He is not derogating from fidelity to the Law; the rabbis knew that better than anyone. But He denounces their traditions as a distortion of the Law, though the rabbis claimed that these traditions were its safeguard, its protecting hedge, and they were proud of them as a masterpiece of their assiduous study and clever subtlety. Hence they were annoyed and pretended to be scandalized. Even the Apostles were somewhat concerned about the matter. To think of incurring reproof from such masters as the rabbis! Certainly the disciples would never have tried to defend what they had done. But to His followers Jesus says: 'Let them alone;

they are blind guides. Now if a blind man leads a blind man, both of them will fall into the ditch.' A child with good sight can easily lead a blind man ; but if a pair of blind men left to themselves try to face the crowd with each other's assistance, with what caution will they grope their way along ! The Scribes are blind men who think themselves in the light ; they advance to the precipice without any hesitation, leading along with them the mass of the people who obey their authority.

Reassured by this, the disciples—or rather Peter in their name—begin to ask what the parable means as soon as they are alone with Jesus in the house, probably the one He used when staying at Capharnaum. To their ears alone He explains His meaning with a force and a realism that is unusual with Him. St. Mark has preserved the exact wording for us. The heart—and the heart alone is of consequence here—cannot be defiled by what a man eats. In philosophical terminology this would have been expressed thus : since man, considered as man, is reason and will, he cannot be defiled by material food because it can have no contact with the spiritual part of him. And that is precisely what the word ' heart ' means in Hebrew usage, the spiritual principle in man. The functions of the material heart are not in question. By the heart is here meant the faculty of loving God and keeping one's self pure in His sight. Hence what enters into a man has nothing to do with the heart : ' it goeth into his belly and goeth out into the privy.'

Thus was solved a grave question of principle. The Law of Moses had, it is true, consecrated certain customs that were traditional among the Israelites, and when God thus approved them they received the force of divine law. But the prescriptions of the Law of Moses were not to be understood as denying the principles of common sense ; the distinction between clean and unclean foods was not in itself a question of conscience, but only because this distinction had been imposed by positive law. Later on the Apostles came to understand the immense significance of this obvious fact, and St. Mark goes on to say : ' This was a declaration that all foods were clean.' Not that this declaration did away with the positive law on the subject ; it was meant simply to show that this law *was* a positive law or perhaps that it was a merely temporary enactment. The main thing henceforth was that no one should misunderstand what it was that God chiefly asked of man. It was not He who had prescribed those scrupulosities of outward cleanliness that were mistaken for purity of soul. Purity of soul belongs to the heart; similarly it is from the heart that proceed those evil thoughts which are the root of all the vices, such as the sins which do in effect destroy bodily purity, those which defy God like blasphemy, and those which injure our neighbour like theft and murder.

Jesus grants the prayer of a Gentile woman (115).

Mark vii, 24–30; Matthew xv, 21–28.[1]

Capharnaum seems to have been the place where Jesus stayed longest after His return from Jerusalem. He now directs His steps towards the north-west where lies the district of Tyre, which He traverses northward as far as Sidon. But He comes back at once to the lakeside and reaches the domain of Philip, visiting Bethsaida and Cæsarea. The evangelists do not enlighten us about the object of this visit to Sidon. If Jesus had wanted to escape pursuit by the police of Herod Antipas, He would have avoided going into that tetrarch's territory to begin with after His return from Jerusalem. Nor does there seem any intention on His part to preach outside the borders of Israel, for He does not address the Gentiles. His purpose then was probably to avoid arousing Herod's uneasiness, by frequently moving from one place to another and keeping away from the neighbourhood of Tiberias where Herod usually lived. People came to ask for miracles and gathered eagerly to hear Him as He went from place to place; but in that way there was no permanent centre of excitement. By taking His disciples far away from their usual occupations, far too, as much as was possible, from the annoying enquiries of the Pharisees, Jesus gained the advantage of having them more completely under His influence in order to bring them up after His own spirit.

In spite of His desire for solitude, He was recognized as soon as He entered the district of Tyre. A woman threw herself at His feet begging for her daughter to be delivered

[1] The story is omitted by Luke, for some of his Gentile readers might have been offended, wrongly supposing that the dogs were an allegory for them. Matthew has developed Mark's rather abrupt style.

from possession by an unclean spirit. The pagans believed as strongly as the Jews in these seizures of man by a being stronger than himself, and it was the pagans who were responsible for the word 'demon' by which they meant beings much lower than the gods but superior to men, malevolent beings who annoyed men in every way and led them on to evil actions. This pagan woman Mark calls a Syrophenician, for the old Phenicia had become part of the Roman province of Syria. Matthew calls her a Canaanite, the old Israelite name for the inhabitants of Palestine; it is just as if we were to speak of the French as Gauls.

Her request is not granted, for the time of the Gentiles has not yet come: 'Suffer first the children to be filled, for it is not good to take the children's bread and throw it to the dogs.' In a place like this, so near to Israel, everyone would be aware of what the Jews claimed for themselves. This woman would also know what miracles Jesus had worked on their behalf. She had no difficulty, therefore, in understanding the meaning of His reply: it was a refusal. But would Jesus return to this district after He had completed His work among His own people? Very aptly, without any sense of grievance but full of confidence, she returns parable for parable: Is it not the truth that, even before the children have finished eating, the little dogs snatch up the bits which fall from the table? It is faith that Jesus sees in this witty reply coming from the woman's anxious heart—the faith that draws miracles from Him. The miracle she desires is already performed, He tells her, and she departs full of confidence. She found her daughter freed. We may ask, if Jesus allows the Gentiles to snatch this crumb from Him, what will it be when their time has come?

The healing of a deaf man with an impediment in his speech (116).

Mark vii, 31–37; Matthew xv, 29–31.[1]

Continuing his way northward Jesus comes to Sidon, the very ancient capital of the Phenician cities. It was not so rich as Tyre had been in the days of its glory, but it continually regained its prosperity after decline. Its situation

[1] The general purpose of this passage of Matthew is to serve as an introduction to the second multiplication of loaves. Properly speaking, there is no parallel to Mark's narrative here in the other gospels.

in the midst of a ring of well-watered gardens was beyond compare. If Jesus passed through the city, He did not, however, make any stay. Traversing the line of lofty hills to the south of the Lebanon mountain-range, He turned south-east as if with the intention of reaching the lake of Galilee; but avoiding Herod's territory and crossing the upper Jordan, probably at the place known as the Bridge of Jacob's Daughters, He arrived at the Decapolis. Even assuming that He did not stay anywhere, the journey must have taken several days: they were precious days for the disciples.

It was somewhere within this extensive district of the Ten Cities and not very far from the lake[1] that they brought to Jesus a deaf man with an impediment in his speech. They begged Him to lay His hands on the man; they therefore believed in the Master's power, but at the same time were under the impression that this rite of laying on hands had some special efficacy and that Jesus could not do without it. Already once before Jesus had not thought fit to act in the manner suggested to Him,[2] and, as before, when He raised the daughter of Jairus from the dead, so now He does not admit the crowd to see the miracle. He takes the man by himself—this does not exclude the disciples—puts His fingers into the deaf ears, and touches the man's mouth with spittle from His own mouth, then with a sigh He raises His eyes to heaven, saying: '*Ephphata*,' which means, Be thou opened!

We might almost say that this miracle requires greater effort on His part. Yet it was He who had healed the officer's son at a distance. Why then did He now choose to adapt His actions to the character of the malady, to touch the ears and tongue, to use spittle, speech, and command? Was it not He who had only just delivered a possessed child without even giving any order to the evil spirit? Perhaps He wanted to show His disciples that His sacred humanity contained the remedy suited to all our ailments. Whatever the method He employs, the miracle proceeds from His free will; but, as was proved on the occasion of the healing of the woman with an issue of blood, there really existed in Him a power which co-operated with the action of God who is the primary cause of the miracle.

Jesus demanded silence concerning this miracle, but He

[1] Mark viii, 10. [2] Mark v, 23, 41.

did not obtain it. More than ever was His fame spread abroad by the wondering and joyful crowds.

The second multiplication of loaves (117).

Mark viii, 1–10 ; Matt. xv, 32–39.

By this time they had arrived near to the lake of Tiberias. Jesus had gone up a hill and was sitting there. People came and put their sick down before His feet. When He healed them a new outburst of religious fervour arose, for at sight of all these miracles a chorus of praise arose to the glory of the God of Israel.[1] Then there took place one of those incidents which people were beginning to be accustomed to look for from Jesus in His goodness. The whole multitude had been with Him three days, and other sick people were continually being brought ; with the cures the crowd grew in number. Everything was forgotten at sight of this extraordinary spectacle. They had nothing to eat. Jesus, therefore, after having rewarded their faith by miracles, took compassion on them. He would not let them go away fasting, for some of them had come from afar and might have fainted on their way home. It was then the full heat of summer which is very oppressive in that low-lying basin surrounded by mountains.

On this occasion the Apostles had a little store of seven loaves—hardly enough for their own needs—and a few little fishes they had caught. Jesus took the loaves and, giving thanks, He broke them and had them distributed by the disciples. He did likewise with the fishes. Four thousand people were thus fed and seven baskets[2] filled with the fragments left over were taken away.

He dismissed the crowd without any difficulty. The place of the miracle was almost the same as that of the former multiplication of loaves, and must have been near the shore, for Jesus at once went on board a boat with His disciples. He came then, says St. Mark, into the region of Dalmanutha.

[1] Matthew xv, 31. After the incident of the Canaanite woman we do not expect to find numerous cures granted to pagans who thus give glory to the God of Israel, a strange God to the pagans. Here, therefore, the speakers are Jews. In Philip's dominions, especially north of the lake, the Jews were assuredly in the majority.

[2] The baskets used for carrying food were larger than those (called *kufas*) used in agriculture.

St. Matthew says the region of Magedan.[1] Both names are unknown apart from this place, but it seems likely that the region referred to must be on the western shore, for there we are about to meet the Pharisees again.

Jesus refuses to give a sign from heaven (118).

Mark viii, 11–13 ; Matt. xvi, 1–4.[2]

Hardly had Jesus and His disciples landed when they were approached by a number of Pharisees from the neighbouring city who were particularly unfriendly, for they came merely in order to dispute. Doubtless because they were discontented at the turn the conversation took, they broke it off by asking Jesus for a sign from heaven. It seemed a not unreasonable request in so far as the Messiah was expected to give proofs of His divine mission. But had not Jesus continually given such signs by means of His miracles? Although He had not put them forward as proofs—as did the false Messiahs when they promised such marvels as the dividing of the waters of the Jordan, if only the people would first follow them—and although the cures He worked were signs of His goodness of heart as much as of His power, nevertheless that did not detract in any way from the divine value of these signs. The Pharisees, however, want things to be done in the manner that seems good to them. They would prefer some extraordinary phenomenon taking place in the sky. This obstinate adherence to their own opinions draws a sigh from Jesus. These men of His own time, His own brethren, this generation to which He Himself belongs since He is of the same race, seem determined not to yield until they have received the sign they require. It will not be given them. Jesus returns to the other side of the lake whither the Pharisees will not follow Him.

[1] The two evangelists are in agreement on the point that the place where they landed was not precisely a town but a district belonging to a city. Mark's name, Dalmanutha, seems to be more no than a repetition of *εἰς τὰ μέρη* in Syriac. Matthew's Magedan, read by Eusebius as Μαγεδαν, is asserted by that writer to be in the neighbourhood of Gerasa. The reading Magdala in Matthew seems to be a correction of Magedan in favour of some place that is known.

[2] We here follow Mark. Matthew's text is composed of different incidents. Cf. Luke xii, 54–56 and Matthew xii, 38–42, which we shall see later. It is only natural that the Jews should often have demanded a sign.

Jesus teaches His disciples (119).

Mark viii, 14–21 ; Matt. xvi, 5–12.

The departure had been sudden, and as the Pharisees had come to meet Jesus by the shore, the disciples had not thought of going into the city to buy bread. As soon as they were out on the lake they remembered, but then it was too late. They had only one loaf or small cake of bread which had been left in the boat, for they often snatched a light meal while in the boat, eating bread with fish or olives and quenching their thirst with water from the lake.

Jesus was still sad at heart. On the side of the lake from which He had just departed the Pharisees had acquaintances among Herod's courtiers, frivolous individuals who perhaps had been responsible for that haughty demand for a sign asked by the Pharisees when they came to embarrass Jesus. These courtiers had little regard for the things that concern the soul, but they were eager in search of novelties and pleased at the idea of witnessing some striking marvel. The Master is concerned to put His disciples on their guard against the danger of such a mentality, which He likens to leaven. Leaven causes the dough to rise by means of fermentation which, as people already knew, was merely a process of corruption. In a similar way when evil thoughts are put into the heart they unfailingly corrupt its simplicity. Herod's servants, like their master, thought only of worldly pleasure, and they sought to gain his favour just as he courted the favour of Tiberius. The Pharisees, it is true, preached virtue, but they loaded themselves with observances that encumbered the free movement of the heart towards God, even when these observances were inspired by a zeal that was sincere. Full of solicitude for His disciples and wishing to arouse their attention by means of the enigmatic character of His words, Jesus breaks the silence with a cry of : 'Take heed ! Beware of the leaven of the Pharisees and the leaven of Herod !'

But it is *His* thoughts alone that are concentrated on the things of the soul. Intimate as the disciples are with Him, witnesses of His life and hearers of His word, they move as it were in a different atmosphere. The same set of words have one meaning for Him and another for them. They think of the bread that keeps them alive, and it was doubtless only at this moment that they perceived their negligence in omitting to bring a supply. Jesus usually relied on them to attend to the necessary provisions. At once they begin to dispute among themselves, and we can well imagine that it is because they try to shift the responsibility for the oversight on to one another. This causes Jesus to grieve. How is it that they are so dull to perceive spiritual truths? Have they also eyes that they may not see, ears that they may not hear, hearts that are hardened? But they *have* seen, no detail has escaped them, and they have forgotten nothing. For when Jesus asks them how many baskets full of fragments they took away at the first multiplication of loaves, they answer without hesitating : Twelve. And how many baskets on the second occasion? Seven. If they have forgotten nothing, then why have they not understood? Everything that He says and does has a moral significance, a religious meaning ; it is a call to raise up ourselves simply to God instead of allowing ourselves to be absorbed by earthly cares. He by no means promises that He will renew the miraculous multiplication of bread on their behalf in order to make good their negligence. But even if they think only of bread when He speaks to them of a leaven that is of a secret character, that bread should remind them of the great miracles which He has used in order to teach them such lofty truths. They must equally understand in a spiritual sense what He has said about the leaven of which they have to beware. Indeed they did consider the matter in this way, and they understood that their Master wished to warn them against the corruption of the spirit, as we learn from Matthew.[1] Henceforth they are more attentive to the wonders worked before their eyes, and they learn how to interpret them as a sign to be believed in.

Certainly no one can say that St. Mark has tried to shield the Apostles from blame. It has even been maintained that he deliberately shows up their shortcomings ; but that is going a little too far. After all their attitude was quite natural ; and a few lines further on St. Mark comes to St. Peter's confession. This one warning, however severe it may have been, has not completely changed their

[1] It is Matthew alone who draws this conclusion (xvi, 12), which brings the episode to an end in the same way as it had begun.

dispositions. The disciples did not doubt their Master; they had faith in Him and were faithful to Him. But they allowed themselves to be taken up by their daily cares, not being as yet wholly absorbed by zeal for the kingdom of God. Who would venture to blame them? The slowness of their will is due to dullness of understanding. Men of the people as they were, living by the labour of their hands, absorbed until now in daily solicitude concerning the necessities of life, they did not find it easy to lay aside that solicitude. Jesus took them as they were, and gradually accustomed them to imitate Him in raising their minds to higher things. On occasion He rebukes them in the manner and with the energy that we learn from the gospels. He is severe with His friends, as He is severe in reprimanding His enemies. It is no idyll; it is rather a hard school of perfection. But so much the more did they perceive in all this a love that was deep, exacting, yet at the same time tender as a father's.

The blind man of Bethsaida (120).

Mark viii, 22–26.

Thus they were back once more in the neighbourhood of Bethsaida, where the two multiplications of bread had taken place. We know that the evangelists have not told us all that occurred during the ministry of Jesus; still the impression left by the narrative of Mark, which is the most detailed, is that the recent journey across the lake was all to no purpose. There is no reason to take scandal from this; on the contrary it gives us an occasion for recognizing what was one of the essential features of Our Lord's life, one of the laws ruling His Incarnation. He had plainly shown Satan, at the time of the Temptation, that He was determined to adhere to the will of God without seeking any personal advantage by interfering with the laws of nature. Later He gave commands to the powers of nature when circumstances seemed to require His intervention, but most often He allowed Himself to be guided by events, taking them as signs of His Father's will. After having met with this bad reception on the western shore of the lake, He returns to the eastern shore and resuming His journey northward He enters Bethsaida. He was well known there, and there were no Pharisees to come between Him and the multitude.

In the city He was asked to heal a blind man by His touch ; He agrees to do so, but His manner of procedure is more mysterious than ordinarily on these occasions. He had only recently refused in the presence of His disciples to give a heavenly sign ; perhaps it was His intention not to astonish them so soon after by arousing popular enthusiasm in performing publicly a miracle which could have been taken as a messianic sign.[1] He takes the blind man by the hand and leads him out of the town, puts spittle upon his eyes, lays His hands on him, then asks him whether he sees, as if He were doubtful about the efficacy of the treatment. The man answers : 'I see men like trees walking.' Jesus then lays His hands on the man's eyes and he then begins to see everything clearly. He is commanded to go back home without passing through the town. Thus the miracle was concealed from public knowledge ; indeed it was almost hidden from the Apostles under the appearance of slow improvement and the natural action of saliva, which people considered as beneficial in cases of disease of the eyes, provided it was the spittle of a person who was fasting.[2] The miracle was however undeniable, though there was no display about it ; and Mark certainly did not relate it merely in order to explain Peter's confession. Being something done by Jesus, it must, like all else that He did, contain a lesson.

Increasing light is the natural symbol of the mind's advance towards truth. If the blind man only recovered his sight by degrees, was it to be wondered at that the Master's lessons penetrated the minds of His disciples only little by little ? The time would come when they would see plainly, when moreover they would understand the wisdom of that slow preparation. St. Mark, who draws more attention than the other evangelists to the Apostles' slowness of understanding, intended to show by this miracle-parable how Christ's method of teaching was typified by the healing of blindness. His method was harmonious, full of gentle condescension, but at the same time it was effective in gaining its object.

[1] Isaias, xxxv, 5.
[2] Talmud of Jerusalem, *Shabbath*, XIV, 14d.

Peter's confession and Christ's promise (121).

Luke ix, 18–21 ; Mark viii, 27–30 ; Matt. xvi, 13–20.

And now the time had come when Jesus, to fulfil His Father's purpose, had resolved to determine perfectly clearly the relations between Himself and His disciples. They were His followers ; they were devoted to Him ; they loved Him ; they knew Him for a prophet powerful in word and deed, the Son of Man and the Son of God, and these things served to indicate that He was the Messiah, though His manner of action did not seem to be in harmony with the rôle of Messiah. When was He to enter on His real career, and what was that career to be ? What part would *they* play in it ? Jesus had refused to be hailed as Messiah by the multitude, but perhaps He would agree to accept the title from them. In a word, there is a strong temptation to think that, notwithstanding their very intimate and affectionate relations with Him, there was a doubt still weighing on their minds. Jesus therefore is now about to urge them to speak openly to Him, to reveal to Him their thoughts. Once He has got them firmly to agree that He is the Messiah foretold by the Scriptures, He will tell them what God expects of the Messiah, what sort of death is decreed for Him, what glory is reserved for Him. He will tell them also what God also demands from those who resolve to follow the Messiah. It is now that the true nature of Messianism appears ; it is nothing but the spirit of Christianity. As Jesus has to die before entering into His glory, He must now reveal the preparations He has made for the period following His death, arrange the plan that His work is to follow, and make known His purpose of founding a society with Peter at its head. Not everything is disclosed—it never is on this earth—but a wonderful prospect is revealed to our gaze : the human race organized in a way to pursue an altogether new ideal.

Continuing northwards, they came to the neighbourhood of Cæsarea Philippi which was on the extreme borders of the land of Israel, but in territory that was now pagan. It lay near one of the sources of the Jordan consecrated to the god Pan by a temple in his honour ; hence the name Banias by which this lovely spot is still known. The city bore the name Cæsarea after the emperor, whose worship was soon to overshadow the worship of all other deities, and it was called Cæsarea of Philip because that tetrarch, half pagan himself, had built the place in honour of Cæsar Augustus. Here there was no sign of that bitter opposition of the Pharisees which had its centre at Jerusalem but pursued Jesus even into Galilee. Here no crowds thronged the roads after Jesus. The disciples, knowing that He did not preach the kingdom of God to pagans, wondered what was the purpose of this journey into a district which, although thickly populated, left them feeling more lonely than if they were in the desert. In a lonely place[1] on the road,[2] and therefore still a long way from the city, Jesus first prays, as though to recall His disciples to recollection and to emphasize the divine character of the step He was about to take, and then offers His friends the opportunity of unburdening their souls by confiding to Him all that is in their minds. In order to help them He first asks what other people think of Him. They reply that some take Him for John the Baptist, others for Elias, others still mention Jeremias or one of the old prophets. Remarkable conjectures, these! Thus the ministry of Jesus was marked by so many miracles that no one could take Him for a mere ordinary man. With the death of John the Baptist had vanished the spirit of the ancient prophets, and it seemed too much to expect that such wretched days as the ones in which men now lived should produce a new prophet. There was nothing left to hope for but the Messiah. The more learned among the Jews knew that the Messiah was to be preceded by Elias whose office it would be to anoint Him. That Jesus did not put Himself forward as the Messiah all seemed agreed; but was it possible that He was Elias, the Messiah's precursor? According to others the rôle of precursor was to be filled by Jeremias or some other of the ancient prophets, no one knew whom. Others finally held that God's evident purpose in raising up John the Baptist could never be prevented by that prophet's obscure death; John had come back to life, was at work again and would soon declare himself openly.

'But you,' Jesus went on to say, 'whom do you say that I am?' Peter answered: 'Thou art the Messiah.'[3]

[1] Luke ix, 18. [2] Mark viii, 27.
[3] Expressed by all three Synoptists in the same terms.

He had asked them all their opinion, and Peter was answering for them all. But Peter did not take the time to find out what each one thought for himself. Whether it was that he already felt certain, or whether he spoke from his eager and impulsive nature, he asserted without hesitation what was dictated to him by his faith and his love. What Peter believes with all his heart is that Jesus is the promised and awaited Messiah.

St. Mark's narrative stops there, as does that of St. Luke who here follows Mark according to custom. But there is something unfinished about the incident so recorded. How is it that, after Jesus has questioned His disciples about what they and other people think of Him, He does not tell them in His turn who He really is? It is evident that He did not question them in order to learn, but in order to teach. A curt recommendation to say nothing about Him to anyone could just as well be taken for a denial as for an approval of what they say. It may be that St. Mark stopped there because it was not St. Peter's habit to speak of the surpassing honour paid to him in the words with which Christ had congratulated him. St. Matthew, however, preserves for us Peter's answer in a form such as is demanded by the occasion, and it is an answer that is conformable with a more complete confession on the part of Peter. He answered: 'Thou art the Christ, the Son of the living God.' Such an answer suits the circumstances.

Jesus had given an explanation of who He was after the first multiplication of bread. He had not been willing to accept the title of King, for a different title suited Him better, that of Son of God come down from heaven. Almost all were scandalized, but Peter, in the name of the Twelve, had confessed that Jesus was the Holy One of God. St. John alone has related these facts, but they give a perfect explanation of Peter's second confession which was fuller and more exact because he had been inwardly enlightened. The three synoptic gospels had, however, already brought up the question concerning Christ's divinity, whether on account of the forced admissions of the demons[1] or on occasion of the admiration shown by the people at sight of His great prodigies.[2] St. Peter takes up his stand on this important point more definitely than anyone had ever done,

[1] Matthew viii, 29; Mark iii, 11; v, 7; Luke iv, 41; viii, 28.
[2] Matthew xiv, 33.

for he does not merely say like those who saw the stilling of the tempest : 'Thou art indeed a son of God,' but : 'Thou art the Christ, the Son of the living God.' And thus he shows that he has really understood the words of Jesus : 'As My Father who liveth hath sent Me.'[1]

When Jesus declared before His judges that He was the Son of God, the high priest rent his garments. Had He not been really the Son of God, Jesus must Himself have shown a holy indignation at Peter's bold utterance. At all events it was due to Him to make some answer. We possess that answer, and it still resounds in our ears, day by day and age after age. Why should we not declare that it is the fulfilment of prophecy and understand it in the light of prophecy?

Thus hailed as Son of God, Jesus in His turn names the father of the man to whom He speaks and immortalizes the name of Jona. But it was not from his father nor from any relation of flesh and blood that Simon, son of Jona, had learnt the truth that he has just declared ; by his love for Jesus he has been admitted to intimacy with the heavenly Father, and it is He who has revealed the truth to Simon. Jesus therefore, in the name of His Father, confirms what Simon has said of Him. And now He is going to say what He thinks of His disciple. Before the disciple chose Jesus as his Master he was called Simon. Jesus had already made known[2] His intention of calling him *Cephas*, a name taken from the Aramaic word meaning a stone or rock. We do not know whether the word was already in use as a proper name, or whether Jesus created the name for His own purpose. Dwelling upon the meaning of the word He declares : 'And I say to thee, that thou art Peter (*Kepha*), and upon this rock (*kepha*) I will build My Church, and the gates of hell shall not prevail against it.' 'Against it'—that is to say against the Church—a word we cannot utter now without at the same time clothing it with a grandeur that is immense ; but when it was first uttered by Christ it did not convey any idea of the innumerable congregation or gathering of those who were to follow Him. Understood whether in a universal or more restricted sense, the Church is a community of men which Christ compared to a building on a rock : the rock was the man who had uttered the mystery of the divine sonship of Jesus.

[1] John vi, 57, 58.
[2] John i, 42. See above, page 88.

Peter, then, was to be the foundation and the organ of divine truth.

Over against this building we are given a glimpse of another, a citadel defended by towers ; it is thus the symbol of a hostile power. The gates[1] of which Christ speaks are the gates of Hades, as the gospel calls them, a name borrowed from paganism where it was used to denote the abode of the dead, but used by the Jews to refer to a place of torment for the damned. It is therefore the kingdom of Satan that sets itself up against the earthly kingdom of Christ, but it will never be able to triumph over it or shake the foundation on which Christ built it.

We are given to understand, then, that Peter was to be the spiritual head of the kingdom of Christ, its appointed teacher of truth. By the use of a different symbol Jesus goes on to show the universal character of Peter's power. He will give to him, as to the head of His earthly kingdom, the keys that every master of a house during his absence entrusts to his faithful major-domo ; and, since the earthly kingdom is founded merely as a preparation for the heavenly kingdom, whatever measures Peter takes on earth will be ratified in heaven. If he binds on earth, the sentence holds good in heaven ; if he looses, pardon is granted in heaven. Binding and loosing are, as it were, representative of the extreme limits which include all the administrative acts of him who has the keys of that kingdom which is begun on earth and brought to perfection in the presence of God.

Such are Christ's words to Simon Peter. He does not say : 'I give thee this power, to thee and thy successors.' Had He so spoken, He would have needed to explain who and what these successors were to be ; He wished to say nothing that would give an indication of the duration of the kingdom which He was founding. Any historian who weighs the value of words will therefore beware of forcing their meaning, and he will raise no difficulty in admitting the contention of all sects of Protestantism that Christ's promise mentions none but Peter. At the same time he will demand that Protestants first recognize that Jesus was really speaking to Peter, and not merely playing with words ; that He was not indulging in equivocation by summoning Peter and

[1] Formerly we used to refer to Turkey as the Sublime Porte on account of a great gateway, in the form of a pylon, which formed the entrance to the Grand Vizier's office at Constantinople.

saying to him : 'It is rather striking that you are called Peter, for I shall build My Church upon a rock, and I am that rock.' No ; the Church is really built upon Peter in the sense that he is its head. That is the way in which Peter understood it and the other Apostles too, since they respected his authority.

Peter went to Rome and suffered martyrdom there. There his tomb was shown. The Church did not die with him, however, and was it to have no other head ? Someone took Peter's place as shepherd of the Roman flock, and therefore inherited Peter's power over that flock. But what of the Church as a whole, the Church which had such a vivid consciousness (so forcefully insisted on by St. Paul) of being a unity, of being the body of Christ ? Was it to have no foundation ? Christ had appointed Peter as the foundation, and although Peter was dead the building remained ; it had the same enemies, and it still stood firm thanks to the rock on which it was built. Indeed it was Peter who remained all the time, though no longer Peter in person but his office, delegated to the one who had taken his place. Christ's promise could not fail ; the very fact that there have been successors of Peter indicates the object for which that promise was made. It was guarded in its manner of expression, but its full meaning appeared when the realities of the situation in which the Church was placed forced the revelation of all the truth the promise contained.

So true is this that some critics—those of the most independent character—maintain that the Roman Church herself has added to the gospel these lines which have been responsible for her success down the ages. But in answer to this we have only to point out the fact that the Roman Church has not been free from opposition in the exercise of her authority. When Pope Victor imposed his will in the Quartodeciman dispute he was met with resistance from the Bishop of Ephesus. But if this felicitous Petrine text was only of recent origin, what would have been simpler than for the bishop to have pointed this out ?[1] Moreover there is not a passage in the whole of the four gospels which

[1] Had the text been composed in the second century for the benefit of the Roman Church it would certainly have alluded explicitly to Peter's successors. The truth is that it was the existence and history of the Church of Rome which revealed the profound sense of the words. The authentic meaning of the text has been fully stated by the Vatican Council.

is more clearly Aramaic in terms, metaphors, and construction. Some see in this proof of the contention that the Petrine text is to be attributed to the editorship of some Jewish Christian who desired to support Peter's claims among the Palestinian faithful. But if these claims were in fact admitted, would it not be far simpler to say that they were admitted because they were based on an authentic declaration of Christ? The nearer we approach to the source of these claims, the easier it is to explain the facts. After the Resurrection Peter assumed the direction of all. He was already shown in the gospel acting as the chief of the Apostles. He could not have acted thus without the knowledge of Jesus; and if Jesus Himself was the real head, it was for Him to give some explanation of what was meant by St. Peter's place and office. This He did in terms that told the greatness of that place and office in the Church, in terms that laid down the conditions for the future—a future as yet hidden, nevertheless a future in which Christ's word was law. And we see with ever-growing clarity how that word of His still rules, and with a power that is ever more effective.

The first prediction of the Passion and Resurrection (122).

Luke ix, 22; Mark viii, 31–33; Matt. xvi, 21–23.

More than a year had passed—more than half the time allotted to His ministry—before Jesus welcomed and confirmed His Apostles' faith in Him as the Messiah sent by God and as Son of God. The Galilæans would have acclaimed Him as Messiah if only He had put Himself at their head, but they had refused to believe in a spiritual Messiah. The name of Messiah was likely to be misunderstood; therefore Jesus commanded His friends to keep silent about it. We see all the more reason for this when we call to mind that the Apostles were still in ignorance of the humiliations which were to precede their Master's glory. From now on they believed firmly in the glory that was to be His, and that made it all the more necessary to remove any illusions they might still retain concerning the Messiah and earthly triumph. This Jesus proceeds to do immediately. Before a year was out He was to meet His Passion; in speaking of this He ran the risk of making them anticipate that source of scandal, an inevitable source of scandal for them even after He had forewarned them. They acknowledged that their Master was the Son of God ; but at the same time He was Son of Man, and as such was destined for suffering. Would not Israel take up arms to rescue Him from that ? No ; on the contrary He would be rejected by the elders of the nation and by the priests. He was to be put to death. In that case, what about the glory of the Messiah ? He would rise again on the third day.

Such a glorious outcome of his Master's sufferings seems insufficient to the heart of Peter, who is aghast at hearing this clear and unmistakable assertion. He is the more upset inasmuch as his own faith has been expressed with such great assurance. He alone of the disciples—and not without a touch of that presumption which was the defect of his resolute character—takes it upon himself to cheer his Master, even to rebuke Him : 'God forbid, Lord, it shall not be so.'[1] But a moment ago Peter was enlightened by the Father ; now he is no more than the mouthpiece of common human aspirations. But on this, as on the former occasion, the reply of Jesus is quick to come, and it is as strong in reproach as the former reply had been warm in approbation : 'Go behind Me, Satan : thou art a scandal unto Me.' But in spite of that we cannot but congratulate Peter on being so much loved by Christ.

He who desires to be saved must follow Jesus (123).

Luke ix, 23–26 ; Mark viii, 34–38 ; Matt. xvi, 24–27.

Of course Peter could not be for Jesus a cause of stumbling ; it was not in his power to turn Jesus from accepting the sorrowful Passion laid upon Him by His Father. Rather was it Jesus who was to become the stumbling-block and the rock of offence for the two houses of Israel, as Isaias had said.[2] There were always some among the crowd who were won over by His words and His kindness ; but were they ready to follow Him under any conditions ? On this point every doubt was now to be removed, especially for those who were already His disciples. Jesus utters those words which set in such strong contrast life here below and

[1] Matthew xvi, 22.
[2] Isaias viii, 14. See *Le Scandale de Jésus*, by Père Allo, O.P.

life in the next world, words which compel a man to make his choice, to renounce the world and life itself if necessary, even to renounce himself unless he wishes to be rejected by the Son of Man when He comes in His glory. In two or three words He describes the ascent of the soul to the summit of perfection, and that ascent begins from the resolution to be saved which each one must make.

In dealing with this subject a careful writer, striving to set out his ideas in a logical order depending on the end which was desired, would have inverted the order followed by Jesus in this discourse. The desired end is that we may not be rejected by Him who is the arbiter of our salvation. It is salvation alone that matters, and even the whole world is of no account in comparison with the soul's salvation. The soul must therefore be saved, even at the risk of life. To accomplish that we have to follow Him who will decide the soul's destiny. But the order of ideas is different in the words which come from the lips of Jesus. Perhaps it would be better to say that His meaning grows out of the chain of His ideas. It is of Himself He speaks, and of those men of good will who profess themselves ready to follow Him. It is necessary that they renounce all self-seeking and be resolved to bear their cross like men condemned to death. A strange paradox, to ask men to save their souls by first sacrificing their lives in so real a manner as that! To lose one's life means, as we still say, to give up the ghost or the soul; but when a man offers up his life for Jesus and the gospel he saves his immortal soul. So great is the worth of the soul that, if a man were to lose it, there would be nothing he could give in exchange in order to get it back. No, not even the whole world, if he had it at his disposal, would be enough. Then, tearing the veil from the future, Jesus reveals Himself coming as the Son of Man with the holy angels in the glory of His Father. When He so comes, those who have been ashamed of Him and His words, who have allowed themselves to be scandalized on account of His humiliations and failure, He in His turn will deny.[1]

Now they know what Jesus is and what they must be. He is the Messiah; He is even invested with that judicial power which ordinarily the Jews did not grant to the King who was to come, reserving it solely to God. But He is a

[1] Mark and Luke express the matter thus: Matthew in a more general fashion says that Jesus will render to everyone according to his works.

suffering Messiah, and He must be followed along His path of sorrow. What is the exact measure in which His followers will be obliged to exercise renunciation? Jesus does not answer that question. He only lays down the essential condition which consists in the readiness to give up everything for His sake, even life itself, and in the resolve really to follow Him without being ashamed of Him or of His teaching.

Thus the gospel of the kingdom of God becomes the gospel of what must be believed concerning Jesus and of what must be done in regard to Him by those who believe. There is nothing new in this doctrine except Himself. The Jews were already familiar with the distinction He draws between the present world and the world to come; moreover the book of Wisdom had taught them what price, in the shape of suffering, would have to be paid by the despised righteous man in order that he might attain to life with God.[1] Jesus adds only one condition of salvation: that we follow Him. He retracts nothing of what He has said concerning the kingdom of God on earth; nay, He has just been making provision for the continuance of that kingdom. He adds that He is in close touch with it, just as He is in close touch with the kingdom of heaven. At this point it must have been recognized even by the multitude that the ultimate goal of His mission was eternal life. The true purpose of the Messiah was to lead men to that life, and those who did not follow Him would be shut out from eternal life.

He had already taught such a transcendent Messianism after the multiplication of the loaves and during the feast of Pentecost, as we learn from St. John. There He had expressed it in even grander terms, though here in the Synoptists we find something more. In the fourth gospel Jesus had revealed Himself as the one who gives life and who will raise the dead. Men had only to believe in Him in order to receive the life that He was to give and to be admitted as well to that life of glory which was to follow the resurrection of the dead. But there nothing was said of the sorrowful Passion:[2] yet it had to be taken into account. The law imposed upon the Master must in some way be

[1] Wisdom ii.

[2] Unless we are to say that it is referred to in the enigmatic expressions of John iii, 14 and vi, 51 (52); and even then the question remains whether John vi, 51 belongs to the same period as the earlier part of the discourse in ch. vi

applied to the disciples. Here then Jesus appeals to their good will, their courage and their self-denial ; and so strong is that appeal, so encouraging is His promise that we shall be with Him if we follow in His footsteps, that untold numbers of human creatures have embraced that way of suffering. It has even seemed sweet to those who have taken up the cross in imitation of their Saviour and have renounced the pleasures of the world, in full confidence that when He comes in His glory He will not deny *them.*

The speedy coming of the kingdom of God (124).

Luke ix, 27 ; Mark ix, 1 (viii, 39) ; Matt. xvi, 28.

This work of saving souls by leading them to follow Him was to be the normal consequence of His mission which He had begun by establishing the kingdom of God upon earth. That is doubtless the reason why the Synoptists have placed here a notable saying of Jesus which St. Matthew has linked closely with what has just preceded. The sombre prospect of the cross was of a nature to raise doubts about the speedy coming of that kingdom of which Jesus had so often spoken up to the present. So He solemnly declares that it will not be long delayed ; even some of those who listen to Him now will witness it. Thirty years were to pass before St. Paul[1] thought he could say that the word of God had resounded through the whole world, that is to say, as far as the extremities of the world subject to the empire of Rome. Then the kingdom of God was in truth established, fortified with a divine energy, as St. Paul calls the gospel,[2] manifesting itself in word and work.[3] The seed was evidently the seed of a great tree ; the future could be judged by the beginnings.

Jesus was therefore once more exercising His prophetical powers when He saw so near to Him that which He had founded, what St. Mark calls ‘ the kingdom of God come in power,’ and what St. Matthew describes as ‘ the Son of Man coming in His kingdom.’ The two expressions are synonymous, for according to St. Matthew the Son's kingdom upon earth is nothing but the territory over which

[1] Romans x, 18. [2] Romans i, 16.
[3] Romans i, 4 ; xv, 19 ; 1 Corinthians iv, 20.

He has made God to reign,[1] and where His power is continually exercised.[2]

The Transfiguration (125).

Luke ix, 28–36 ; Mark ix, 2–8 ; Matt. xvii, 1–8.

About eight days[3]—six full days according to Mark and Matthew[4]—after Peter's confession there occurred an extraordinary scene, to which there is no parallel in the life of Jesus except the scene of His prayer in the garden of Gethsemani. These two scenes stand in opposition to one another, like strophe and antistrophe. In both cases Jesus takes Peter, James, and John apart in order to pray along with them ; in both the disciples are heavy with sleep ; in both Jesus receives a visit from on high. But the Transfiguration serves as a sure pledge of Christ's future glory, while Gethsemani shows Him to us in the lowest depths of human abasement. Several of the Fathers were of opinion that the same witnesses were chosen for the former as for the latter scene so that the memory of the glory of the Transfiguration might serve as a safeguard against the scandal of the agony in the garden. Peter was chosen because he was the appointed head of the Apostles ; John was the beloved disciple ; and his brother James, who refused to leave him, was to be the first of the Apostles to shed his blood for the gospel.

This is the only occasion on which the Synoptists have been precise in giving us the exact interval of time between two events, and we may clearly gather from this that it was because they saw some connection between them. And indeed the Transfiguration is the confirmation of what Jesus intended to teach when He led Peter to make that confession which He accepted, rectifying it on the all-important point of the Messiah's sufferings—a thing that the Apostles found so difficult to accept—while He maintained their faith in His future glory. But in this new scene there is so much light that we are as it were dazzled by it. Jesus had said to the Jews : 'If you had believed Moses you would believe Me, for he wrote of Me.'[5] Here Moses comes

[1] Matthew xiii, 24 ff.
[2] Matthew xxviii, 20.
[3] Luke ix, 28.
[4] Mark ix, 2 ; Matthew xvii, 1.
[5] John v, 46.

from heaven to bear witness to Him. The Jews knew that Elias would announce the coming of the Messiah, and the Baptist had appeared representing Elias. And now Elias associates himself in person with Moses in paying homage to Jesus with whom they both talk. In this scene all that was most divine in Israel's past does homage to the new prophet and upholds what He has foretold about the scandal of His death. At the same time the glory that Jesus has said is to be His in His Resurrection is already manifested in Him as belonging to Him in His own right. But recently He had accepted the title of Son of God, and now this name is given to Him by a voice that can only be the voice of the Father.

If we consider in one view the whole history of religion, observing the dependence of the new covenant on the ancient revelation from which the new covenant breaks away in order that it may gather unto itself all the nations, noting the continuity of God's plan which leads up to Jesus whom all acknowledge to be greater than all the great men of the past, witnessing the manner in which He is to-day worshipped along with His Father, we cannot help being amazed at the way in which the whole of that miraculous history is sketched with a few strokes of the pen in this story of the Transfiguration. Mere human genius could have written nothing comparable to that, for it knows nothing of the future. Moreover, the incident is related with a simplicity and a realism that make it impossible to suppose that the evangelists intend it to be understood merely as a symbol, or that they themselves have invented the story as a symbol. It is true that the mountain is not named ; but that alone indicates that the incident has not grown out of some divine apparition foretold by the Old Testament, amplified by the evangelists in such a way as to give their story the appearance of historical reality. Had that been the case they would certainly have called the mountain Hermon or Thabor so as to harmonize the story with the Psalm :[1] 'Thabor and Hermon shall rejoice thy name.' It may have been for this reason that tradition has chosen Thabor as the mount of the Transfiguration. Thabor is not so high as Hermon, a mountain which would have required a great effort to climb, and Thabor lies nearer the centre of Jesus' preaching. But it is more probable that the traditional

[1] Psalm lxxxviii (Hebrews lxxxix), 13.

choice of Thabor was due to the memory of ancient tradition concerning the site of this event.[1] The ascent of this mountain requires labour, but we may imagine that the reason why Jesus chose this spot, an isolated peak looking out in every direction over the plain, was in order to invite His disciples to join with Him in prayer. There was a small town on the summit, but that would not prevent their finding solitude up there.

Wearied by the walk—it was still summer—the three chosen disciples slept while Jesus prayed. When they awoke they saw His face transfigured and His garments shining with a whiteness such as no fuller could achieve. Moses and Elias were talking about the death He was to suffer at Jerusalem, the death He was 'to fulfil,' in the words of St. Luke, as a duty laid upon Him. Peter addresses Jesus, and—how characteristic it is of him !—his good will is not altogether free from a certain presumption. He points out that it is a good thing he and his companions are there, for now they can quickly put up three huts made of boughs, one for Jesus, one for Moses, one for Elias. The disciples like faithful servants will sleep out in the open and guard the tents of the guests. So he had not understood that neither Jesus who was at that moment manifesting His glory, nor Moses and Elias who were the heavenly guests of Jesus, had any need of shelter.

The answer to his suggestion comes from on high in the form of a cloud. It was not merely a rain cloud, and the disciples were filled with fear when they saw it come between the sun and themselves, enwrapping Moses and Elias along with Jesus. A voice was heard : 'This is My beloved Son. Hear ye Him,' giving them to understand that it was the voice of the Father, coming out of that same cloud which of old 'covered the Tabernacle of the testimony, which the glory of the Lord filled.'[2] The cloud was then a visible sign of the loving presence of God in the midst of His

[1] Origen cannot be quoted in favour of this tradition for he is silent about Thabor in his commentary on St. Matthew. The *Selecta in Psalmos*, vaguely attributed to him, cannot be his, particularly as regards what is there said concerning Thabor (P.L. XII, c. 1548). Nor does Eusebius choose either Thabor or Hermon, as might have been suggested to him by Psalm lxxxviii, 13. The oldest testimony in favour of Thabor is that of Cyril of Jerusalem (Catech. XII, 16 ; Migne, P.G., XXIII, 744). It ought to be said that since his time the tradition has never varied, and it is represented in our own day by the splendid church built by the Franciscans on the summit of Thabor.

[2] Exodus xl, 32.

people: now it was appearing for the last time, for from henceforth God was to manifest Himself through His Son. And it was certainly Jesus to whom the voice referred, for the disciples, as soon as they looked round after their momentary dazzlement, saw no man but only Jesus.

Elias has come in the person of John the Baptist (126).

Mark ix, 9–13; Matt. xvii, 9–13.[1]

As Jesus came down from the mountain with the three privileged disciples, He charged them to be silent about what they had seen and heard. He had good reason for choosing them alone as witnesses of that glittering transformation He had undergone. A larger group, with less understanding than these three, might the more easily have fallen victims to their own suggestions and have concluded that they were witnessing the beginning of Jesus' time of triumph. Indeed He puts even these three upon their guard against such an error by commanding them not to speak of the incident until the Son of Man shall have risen from the dead. In thus maintaining that He was to rise again He reaffirmed that He had to die. But would His resurrection from the dead give Him a better body than that He now had, which had shown itself capable of being so wonderfully transformed? The chosen witnesses promised to keep silence and kept their word, but they revealed their uneasiness to one another: 'When He shall be risen from the dead.' . . . What did that mean? Afraid to question their Master about a thing which He had so clearly affirmed, and full of the vision which still haunted their eyes, they tried in vain to reconcile this long delayed arrival and speedy departure of Elias with what they had learnt from the Scribes about the office to be fulfilled by that prophet. If only he had stayed in the hut which St. Peter had so obligingly offered to build for him! But now they could no longer count upon Elias, and there was something obscure about it all that Jesus alone could throw light upon. They ask Him: 'Why then do the Scribes say that Elias must come first?' First means before the Messiah, and Elias had appeared after Him.

[1] There was no need for St. Luke to speak of this specially Jewish question to Gentile readers.

They have a further difficulty which Jesus gathers for Himself, namely that Elias was supposed to put everything straight in order to prepare the way for the Messiah.[1] But he has done nothing of the kind and seems inclined to do nothing.

From this we see that the disciples still stood just where they were before, so preoccupied with the teaching of the Scribes concerning a King who was to come in triumph that they are unable to make up their minds to face all the prophecies which deal with the suffering Messiah. It is upon this aspect of the Messiah that Jesus bids them to reflect. If the Scribes are right, 'how is it written of the Son of Man that He must suffer many things and be despised?' The prophecy to which He refers, doubtless that in which Isaias shows how the Servant of God must be rejected and put to death,[2] must be fulfilled; it is the regulating principle of all. The prophecy concerning Elias will similarly be fulfilled, but it must be interpreted in harmony with the prophecies of the Messiah. Such as the Messiah, so must the forerunner be. In fact Elias had already come in the person of John the Baptist, and had fallen victim to his own zeal: 'So also shall the Son of Man suffer from them.'[3]

The true office of Elias as forerunner of the Messiah was in fact explained by the history of the prophet's life; this could be seen not only from his words but also from his fate. One had merely to recall how he had been persecuted through having incurred the hatred of Jezabel[4] in order to see in him a prototype of the Baptist who had fallen a victim to the hatred of Herodias. The exact parallel between the two prophets made John the Baptist a veritable Elias. The mission of Elias was therefore completed, and there was no reason to await his coming any longer.[5]

So natural is this dialogue, so clearly does it show us the anxious questions filling men's minds at that time, and the answer to those questions which Jesus was to provide by following out the sequence of events in that plan which centres in Him, so silent is it about any question of the

[1] See above, p. 14. [2] Isaias liii. [3] Matthew xvii, 12.
[4] 3 Kings xix, 1 ff; xxi, 17–26.
[5] The words of Jesus make no allusion to the return of Elias at the end of the world; nay they seem rather to exclude it since Elias has already come in the person of John the Baptist. This solution is supported by Huby, S.J. in his commentary on St. Mark (p. 204).

miraculous, that even the critics are inclined to admit its genuineness. But it can only be understood through the difficulty found by the disciples in reconciling the glory of Thabor with the prediction of the Passion, the teaching of Jesus with that of the Scribes. It is as though a light from on high had been reflected in the obscurity of their minds which, though so simple, were so encumbered with prejudice.

The cure of an epileptic boy possessed by the devil (127).

Luke ix, 37–43a ; Mark ix, 14–29 ; Matt. xvii, 14–21.

It was not until the following day that Jesus and His three companions rejoined the group of the disciples. His absence had therefore probably lasted three days at least. During the interval the other nine disciples—if all the Twelve had been with Jesus—had been engaged in a matter from which they had not come with credit. A man had approached them leading his son by the hand. The boy was possessed, he said, by a devil who was dumb and who revealed his presence by convulsions during which the boy foamed at the mouth, gnashed his teeth, and became rigid. The unhappy father had heard of Jesus and now was come to beg Him to deliver his son. Not finding Jesus he had appealed to the disciples. A crowd had collected, among them certain of the Scribes, for they were always to be found wherever there were Jews. These wished to have something to say in the affair and were disputing with the disciples about the best way to drive out the devil who was so crafty that he refused to disclose his name. As all the efforts of the disciples had proved unavailing, the Scribes had taken them to task. The onlookers were doubtless saying to one another : ' If only Jesus were here,' when He came up. The people crowd round Him with surprise and joy, and He asks what is the matter.

So far we have merely narrated the course of events from the disciples' point of view, set down by Mark in a striking picture just as it presented itself to those who came down from the mountain. It would be impossible to find a better example of concrete and picturesque expression. So vivid is the writer's view of what happened that the chronological order of events is lost sight of. We seem to arrive along with Jesus, we share the anxiety of the bystanders. To whom, however, does Jesus address the words which seem to be torn from the very depths of His soul? 'O unbelieving generation! How long shall I be with you? How long shall I suffer you?' The father was asking for a miracle, but as it were at random, not with any real confidence in the power of the wonder-worker. The Scribes were wrangling with the disciples, perhaps telling them that their Master would have no better success than they. The crowd was entertained and felt sure that whatever happened it would be a sight worth seeing. What causes the sadness, rather than anger, of Jesus' words is this proof that so much effort had been in vain. He has come from heaven and is like an exile on this earth, but He has come for their good. If they do not understand Him, would it not be better for Him to go away and leave them to their vain thoughts? But no; kindness again prevails. 'Bring him unto me.' The boy is brought and goes into a fit. Convulsed by the spirit, he falls to the ground and rolls about foaming at the mouth. On other occasions the devils had expressed terror in the presence of the Son of God by cries and words; this one is silent. Jesus questions the father. How long has the complaint lasted? And the father, surprised perhaps at hearing such enquiries made after the fashion of a doctor, answers in the same manner: From his infancy; and often he—that is the unseen and dumb spirit who is the cause of the trouble—has thrown the boy into fire or water. 'But if thou canst do anything, take compassion on us and help us.' 'If thou canst,' replies Jesus. Is that all the faith the man can show? More is needed to obtain a miracle. Then the poor father cries out: 'I do believe! Help Thou my unbelief.' This humble desire does duty for everything; Jesus asks for nothing more from him. As a fresh gathering of people causes the risk of some disturbance, He commands the dumb and deaf spirit to come out. The devil utters a cry of rage, the fit reaches its paroxysm, and the child collapses rigid as one dead. Then Jesus takes him up and the child stands. Luke, who was a physician, notes that He cured the boy, as though to distinguish between the driving out of the devil and the cure of the disease.

The disciples had, of course, kept in the background in presence of their Master. They were upset by their failure. What was the cause of their failure? The answer given by

St. Mark[1] is one that applies to this case alone. It was an exceptionally difficult case, said Jesus, probably because the obstinate and sullen silence of the devil left the exorcist with nothing by which he might, so to say, lay hold of him. In such a case a devil might be present without anyone even suspecting his presence. The disciples should therefore have had recourse to prayer. It is true that Jesus Himself had uttered no prayer ; but then His Father heard Him always.[2] The disciples, however, who had allowed themselves to be drawn too easily into this perilous enterprise, should have been more conscious of their own powerlessness and ought to have appealed to heaven for help.

The symptoms of the child's malady are evident ; St. Mark describes the signs of epilepsy even better than St. Luke who was a physician. In this we find remarkable proof of the exactitude of St. Peter's interpreter who thus records the details which his master's memory so faithfully reproduced. But if the child was an epileptic, we are inclined to think that the fits were not the result of diabolic influence. How many in these days would regard epilepsy as caused by a devil residing in the victim's body? Even at that time the natural character of the disease had been recognized by Hippocrates, though it was still called the sacred disease. There is no question of our returning to the old popular superstition, yet at the same time we have good reasons for admitting that cases of diabolic possession do exist, and no reason for considering that epileptics are exempt from diabolic possession. And it may well be that the physical and moral depression caused by epilepsy may offer fewer obstacles to diabolic influence than does a healthy constitution. The epileptic would not on that account be worse off than a healthy man from the religious point of view, for possession of the body by the devil gives him no control over a man's free will. In the case described by the gospel Jesus recognized the presence of the devil ; that is enough for us, and we take His word for it.

But, it may be asked, why did He not attack the prevailing

[1] The reason given by St. Matthew is the disciples' lack of faith. But that is a common remark of Matthew's (vi, 30 ; viii, 26 ; xiv, 31 ; xvi, 8), and indicates a general condition of mind which is always at the root of any failure. St. Matthew introduces it here to lead up to a saying of Jesus which is placed by Mark and Luke in other circumstances. The reason given here by Mark is found in Matthew xvii, 21, which is not considered authentic.

[2] John xi, 42.

error by which men assigned a preternatural cause to epilepsy? Because it was not part of His mission to teach truths of natural science even in the smallest detail.[1] On the other hand, there is nothing to show that He subscribed to the common error. The father of the epileptic quite clearly shares that error, and the evangelists have faithfully reproduced His words. But they seem to have distinguished carefully between the expulsion of the devil and the cure of the disease. That is clear enough at any rate in St. Luke,[2] and even St. Mark shows that it is after the spirit has gone out of the child that he suffers his last convulsion. It is only then that Jesus as it were restores him to life after he was thought to be dead.[3]

The second prediction of the Passion and Resurrection (128).

Luke ix, 43b–45; Mark ix, 30–32; Matt. xvii, 22–23.

The Transfiguration had provided a splendid lesson for Peter, James, and John: it had been followed by an instruction on the mission fulfilled by Elias. Then had occurred the cure of the epileptic boy which had been such a painful experience for the rest of the disciples, and from it Jesus had drawn a lesson for the benefit of them all. Thus it was His chief purpose to teach them, and St. Mark indeed now tell us how He strove to remain hidden as He passed through Galilee[4] in order that He might be more at liberty to devote His attention to His disciples.

The chief point on which He insisted was the Passion, and He added that it was to be followed by the Resurrection. But the mind of the disciples was so fixed upon the scandal they found in the idea of the Messiah put to death before receiving the homage of Israel and the Gentiles, or rather in the notion of His being delivered over to the Gentiles

[1] We shall return to this point later. Cf. Epilogue, II. [2] ix, 42.

[3] ix, 27. According to the commentary of Huby, S.J. (p. 207) the explanation that the epilepsy was caused by diabolic possession is more in accordance with the gospel text: 'the expulsion of the devil is at the same time the cure of the child.' It should rather be said that Jesus was responsible both for the expulsion and the cure.

[4] Leaving some spot at the foot of the mountain of the Transfiguration, Jesus passes through Galilee. Now Thabor is in Galilee, and that is the chief difficulty against identifying the mountain of the Transfiguration with Thabor. Strictly speaking, however, we could understand the text as meaning 'having left that place, they continued to pass through Galilee.'

by Israel, that they found it impossible to overcome this obstacle and so reach the hope that lay beyond it. Once again therefore they do not understand. They allow themselves to be overcome by sadness and do not even dare to interrogate their Master on this subject which they find so distressing to their feelings. Gradually, however, they dismiss from their minds the unwelcome and gloomy picture and begin once more to occupy themselves with more hopeful and consoling thoughts, to such an extent, indeed, that they begin even now to dispute among themselves about which of them shall have the first place in the kingdom of which they dream.

He that is greatest must become the least of all (129).

Luke ix, 46–48 ; Mark ix, 33–37 ; Matt. xviii, 1–4.

It was natural that they should touch Capharnaum in passing through Galilee.[1] There, in what the gospels call 'the house'—perhaps that of St. Peter or a house put at the service of his Master by St. Matthew—Jesus was sure to find a safe refuge where He would not be disturbed. When they reached the house Jesus, wearied by the journey, sat down, for He desired to gather together the Twelve and teach them a lesson. On the road they had argued hotly. He had not interfered, but now He asks : 'What was the subject of your dispute ?' He knew perfectly well how this question would embarrass them, for they knew their Master well enough to understand that ambition was displeasing to Him. Yet they had not been able to resist the temptation to dispute among themselves about the question of precedence in the kingdom of God, such as they conceived it to be and which they expected soon to appear. But was it not already settled that the first place was promised to Peter ? Perhaps it was precisely Peter's privilege that had aroused the rivalry, nay even the envy, of the others. It was not an easy thing to acknowledge all this to their Master, so the Apostles remained silent. In few words Jesus teaches them what are the conditions necessary for spiritual power. He who has the right to command ought to exercise that right only in the general interest ; he is the servant of all. Do you each desire to be first ? Good ! Then let each one of

[1] See on p. 288 the position assigned to the former No. 129 of the Synopsis.

you strive to be really the least in his heart, for only thus, and only if he be sincere, will he find the secret of ruling others for their good, that is by having the firm will to be the servant of all.

To the spoken lesson He proceeds to add a symbolic one. Taking a child, He sets him in the midst of them all, and embracing him (thus showing, in view of the words He has just spoken, that He is ready to serve the child) declares: 'Whosoever receiveth one such little child in My name receiveth Me; and whosoever receiveth Me, receiveth not Me but Him that sent Me.' Such is the highest dignity of those who exercise authority in the name of Christ: to devote themselves with love and even with tenderness to the care of the least of all. And these little ones, if they are taken care of for Jesus' sake, because they are His or in order that they may be His, stand for Jesus Himself and for the Father who sent Him. In this as in everything else the Master sets the example by taking care of the smallest.[1]

Forbearance is to be shown towards those who use the name of Jesus (130).

Luke ix, 49–50; Mark ix, 38–40.

In these conversations which take place between Jesus and His disciples everything seems spontaneous; they have not the character of some prearranged study of a set subject. Some slight incident will arouse in the minds of the disciples doubts which they immediately expose to their Master; and Jesus does not disdain to follow them in the wanderings

[1] This is one of the most interesting examples for seeing the relation between the Synoptic Gospels, and between the Synoptists and tradition. Mark relies on his readers' powers of penetration and has merely juxtaposed the verbal teaching and the object lesson; the first gives the key to the second, which is a much more moving lesson, in such a way that each completes the other. St. Luke, however, applies the words to the example and shows in explicit terms the moral connection between the two. Yet we need to complete the conclusion he draws: he is great who is the least of the disciples; therefore seek true greatness in littleness. Finally, Matthew does not tell us that the question arose through the conduct of the disciples; he puts the question on their lips. The child is made the type of that humility of heart which is needed if one is to become the servant of all. Fundamentally, however, the lesson is the same: the disciples must have only one concern, to make themselves very small by humility of heart; the least shall be the greatest. Possibly, also, Matthew wished to turn his readers' thoughts towards the kingdom of God which is in heaven.

of their thoughts. John had been struck by the saying 'to receive a child in the name of Jesus'; he and his brother James had been given by their Master the name 'Sons of Thunder.'[1] John understands that to receive a child in the name of Jesus means to act for Jesus, and consequently for God. Then he remembers that only a short time before the disciples had heard someone driving out devils in the name of Jesus; they had forbidden him to do this, perhaps at the suggestion of the zealous John, because the man did not belong to their group. What was his authority for using the patronage of their Master, a thing reserved to His disciples?

Such oversensitiveness does not meet with the approval of Jesus. The man had been successful in his exorcisms; therefore God had not condemned him. If he had used the name of Jesus, then he must have believed in the authority of Jesus, and the fact that he had found his use of that name efficacious could only serve to confirm his newly-born faith. Being in such dispositions it was morally impossible that he should take sides against Jesus. Though he did not yet follow the example of the disciples, surely he would be led to seek that favour. In these circumstances, declares the Master, 'he that is not against us is for us.' To repulse him by forbidding him to perform an act that was good in itself, simply because he was not one of the chosen group, would mean to drive him away for ever; and that was neither charitable nor just.

The Church has never held that this decision of Jesus authorizes anyone to practise exorcism. At that time anyone was free to attempt it, but later it was reserved to competent authority. But the words of Jesus serve as a permanent lesson for the members of the Church not to reject the co-operation of those outside the Church when it is a question of doing good. To do good is to approach Christ, especially when the good is done in His name; and to avail one's self of a good that is imperfect is to enter on the path that leads to something better. Instead of always remembering what separates us, we should think of the things that would unite us.

This lesson was not forgotten by John, the apostle of charity. But neither did he forget his zeal. On one occasion when he found himself in the same place with Cerinthus,

[1] Mark iii, 17.

who was an open enemy of his Master Jesus Christ, he refused to remain under the same roof with such an enemy of the truth.[1]

Charity towards the disciples of Jesus. The danger of scandal (131–132).

Mark ix, 41–49 ; cf. Matt. x, 42 ; xviii, 5–9 ; Luke xvii, 1–3.

After teaching John that the name of Jesus forms a sort of bond between all those who invoke it, the Master returns to His earlier thought about the help to be given to children for His name's sake, having been interrupted for a moment by the question concerning the exorcist. It is chiefly His disciples that He includes under this name of children ; whoever shall give them a cup of water because they are Christ's shall not lose his reward. It is a very ordinary kindness to give a cup of water, or in Palestine to let someone drink from the water-skin filled at the well. To refuse such a favour would be a disgrace, and no one claims merit for granting it. But what is done for Christ[2] takes on a new value in God's sight, and what is done for the disciples is done for Christ. Thus there has sprung up in the Church a new fountain of charity flowing inexhaustibly. Those who are the recipients of that charity, especially such as take upon themselves the obligation of voluntary poverty, ought seriously to ask themselves whether they are really Christ's.

Jesus began by speaking of duties towards a child, and He intended the child to stand for His disciples. His meaning is summed up as follows : the disciples are 'the little ones who believe.' If we have an obligation of helping them, then our first and special obligation is the sacred and formidable duty of not scandalizing them. This is a grave admonition to those who consider themselves to be strong, and who need to be strong seeing that they are commissioned to teach and rule the little ones. Woe unto those whose weakness is an occasion of falling for others ! St. Paul has dealt more fully with this precept. He who is so enlightened

[1] A tradition of St. Polycarp handed down by Irenæus and found in Eusebius, H.E., III, 28, 6.

[2] This expression owes its origin to later Christian ages ; but the thought owes its origin to Jesus. It is recorded by St. Matthew (x, 42) in different terms and another context.

that he can do certain things without going against his conscience, let him refrain from those things if there is a weak brother who will be led to imitate his example without being able to discern that the act is not sinful.[1] St. Mark, who is often said to be Pauline, was certainly not ignorant of the admirable way in which the Apostle thus developed the precept laid down by his Master, but he preferred to set it down as Jesus spoke it, without any comment or addition, in that familiar manner so characteristic of Him; and St. Mark was imitated in this by St. Luke and St. Matthew. If anyone gives scandal to one of these little ones that believe, 'it were better for him that a mill-stone were hanged about his neck and he were cast into the sea.' The disciples were familiar with the mill turned by an ass, *mola asinaria* as it was called in Latin and similarly in Greek. The lower stone was like an inverted hollow cone with a perforation below to allow the flour to escape when the corn had been ground between the upper and nether mill-stones. It may be that they had seen some wretched individual thrown into the water with such a perforated stone about his neck like a collar. A striking illustration of a terrible fate! It is intended to show how earnest we should be to avoid giving scandal.

Still the fact remains that there is scandal all around us, and we have to take measures to keep ourselves from being influenced by it. Jesus therefore proceeds, as St. Mark and St. Matthew relate, to speak of those who might be affected by it. The disciple ought to be as determined to flee from scandal as he is to avoid causing it, even were this to mean sacrificing all that he holds dearest; he is hardly likely to be affected by scandal caused by persons who mean nothing to him. The danger is lest anyone should be led into sin through the affection he feels for some master who has taught him or for someone he loves; their error may be the cause of his own going astray; their bad example may lead to his doing the same thing. In a word there is danger of failing in our duty through even legitimate affection. In such a case it is necessary to keep at a distance from the source of temptation, to part company and discipline our affections. As Bossuet says: 'There is need of all violence in this matter.' And indeed Jesus treats of the subject with a vigour unparalleled in any other circumstances,

[1] Romans xiv, 13 ff.; 1 Corinthians viii, 9 ff.

going straight to the heart of the matter with what would be a ferocious paradox[1] were we to take His words literally. But His words merely typify a firm resolve to sacrifice everything if necessary—a hand, a foot, or even an eye. In all that He here says there is a sort of fixed rhythm; we are left with no choice but the repeated alternative, Life or the Gehenna of unquenchable fire. We need not ask here what is meant by the hand, the foot, or the eye. The elements of this threefold comparison are chosen for the purpose of indicating an increasingly costly sacrifice; and we must cut more completely and more irrevocably in proportion as the danger of sin is more pressing. This danger is all the more to be feared when it touches the soul through the medium of the heart, drawn by the attraction and charm of the objects with which it comes into contact. The temptation enters within us very often through the eyes; hence St. Matthew was able to include this warning in his Sermon on the Mount when he wrote of adultery. The words of Jesus could be interpreted in that sense also, but it is in connection with scandal given by our neighbour that they have all their primitive signification; they are intended in a purely parabolic fashion without any distinct allegorical meaning.

The things that might need to be cut off from ourselves are too varied to be enumerated: the application of the parable must depend on the circumstances. But, at all events, there is no mistake about the manner in which the two terms, Life and Gehenna,[2] are opposed one to the other. They represent two kingdoms to be entered; we shall either live with the life of God or we shall suffer punishment, and there is no escape from one or the other. It might be thought that the fire would soon devour those cast into it. But no; that strange fire both devours and at the same time preserves, as though it were salt. It never dies says St. Mark, 'for everyone (who is cast into it) shall be salted with fire,'[3] that is, they shall not be destroyed but preserved by the fire.

Thus distinctly does Jesus envisage the final destiny that

[1] It is clear that the disciple will find again in the kingdom of God what he has sacrificed in order to get there.

[2] The abode of fire is called Gehenna in memory of the valley near Jerusalem, formerly called *Ge-hinnom*, where children were sacrificed to Moloch by being passed through fire. See the book of Henoch, XXVII, 2.

[3] Mark ix, 49. This seems to us the meaning of the verse, as is easily perceived if v. 49 be separated from what follows.

lies before every single one ; he must either go freely and joyfully to God, or he will be cast whether he likes it or not into the place of torment. He therefore ought to measure everything with relation to this final destiny. These dreadful words dull the edge of many a temptation ; the appeal they contain calls forth many a generous resolve.

Salt (133).

Luke xiv, 34–35 ; Mark ix, 50 ; Matt. v, 13.

It was either on this occasion or during the Sermon on the Mount that Jesus used salt as the symbol of the influence that His disciples ought to exercise over others. Salt both preserves and seasons, the second of these functions being far the more important of the two, and it is of this that there is question here. ' Salt is good,' says the Master ; in Arabic the word ' salted ' is constantly used in the sense of ' good.' If, to suppose an impossibility, salt were to lose its flavour, what else could be used to restore its loss ? This is its peculiar character : it flavours everything, and nothing can flavour salt. Plutarch[1] even says that by the virtue of salt a certain life is given to dead meat which otherwise would be fit for nothing but to be thrown on the dunghill. With such a savour as this must the disciples be penetrated, a savour from which proceeds that lofty moral worth which is the very animating principle of human life. If they were to lose this, who would give it back to them ? There is no one. Let them therefore be animated by this energizing virtue which, though like the flavour of salt it is somewhat sharp, yet nevertheless is a salutary virtue ; all the same, they must remain at peace with one another.[2] That is St. Mark's concluding word to the teaching given here.

[1] Cf. *Quæst. Conv.*, 669a.

[2] This passage appears in Matthew under a more emphatic form : ' You are the salt of the earth.' Under this form it serves as a suitable introduction to the other statement : ' You are the light of the world ' (v, 14). There the passage is in excellent context, but it would not have been so if Matthew had preserved the more impressive form used by Mark : ' Have salt in yourselves ' (ix, 50). There is no appropriate context in Luke. For the introduction of the subject he follows Mark : ' Salt is good ' (xiv, 34), without, however, taking any account of why Mark introduces the subject ; which proves that according to Luke it has a meaning of its own independently of what precedes in Mark. But like St. Matthew he insists on the unhappy fate reserved for salt that has lost its savour. A further idea is introduced in Mark by the thought of peace, for salt cannot be the symbol of peace. He seems therefore to have intended a contrast : not too much salt if you want peace !

Fraternal unity and the power of absolution (134a).

Matt. xviii, 15–20.

In this section of St. Matthew's gospel we find the Master's teaching concerning the duties disciples owe to one another, along with the advantages to be gained from their union in one body. The faithful are all members of the one holy Church ; consequently it is their duty to guard her purity by doing their utmost to keep her far from all sin. It is for this same purpose that she has been provided with the power of absolution. Furthermore, her unity which is so dear to God is a guarantee that her children's prayers will be heard when they pray as one. It is the conception of the Church, then, that is the dominating thought in all this, and it is that which gives unity to the various subjects touched on by Jesus here. This view is peculiar to St. Matthew and is followed out by him in logical order. All that he here relates takes for granted the passage dealing with the foundation of the Church which follows Peter's confession. Here, as before, the terms in which Jesus speaks of the Church are sufficiently general in character to have provided a basis for the ecclesiastical developments with which St. Paul makes us familiar.

The subject of fraternal correction grows quite naturally out of what has been said concerning solicitude for little ones, among whom are included those who are weak and liable to stray like sheep that have wandered far from the fold. If they have sinned, then it is the business of all to strive to lead them back to the right path—not by being quick to denounce their fault, but by speaking to them privately, or as we should say, in a heart to heart talk. If the one in fault refuses to listen, then two or three others ought to lend their charitable aid ; and this will serve as a threat towards the obstinate sinner, since they will perhaps be witnesses against him. The sinner who is accused of a fault about which there is no doubt—and it is assumed that the fault is grave—if he refuses to submit, then the Church must intervene ; and if he will not listen even to the Church, let her exclude him from her bosom. After that he is to be looked on as a Gentile and a publican. Not that he is excluded from the pale of charity ; Jesus was kindness itself even to publicans, who were considered worse than Gentiles. But the Church ceases to take responsibility for conduct which would cause her to be put to shame ; whatever scandal may come from him after this will come from outside the Church. The disciples were familiar with the manner in which the heads of the Synagogue dealt with such cases, though with them there was no thought of any obligation to try gentle means of converting the offender to begin with ; hence it must have been clear to the disciples that by this separation of the sinner from the rest of the community Jesus meant anathema or excommunication. But the Church is slower to use severity, and has a power which the Synagogue allowed to no one but God, the power to absolve from sin. When Jesus here says : 'If thy brother hath sinned,' He is not addressing any and every Christian ; He is speaking to the group of those who are immediately associated with Him, His intimate disciples and the future heads of the Church, men who, as we have seen, are already ambitious to occupy the chief places therein. He gives to all of them power to loose and to bind in such a way that their decision shall be ratified in heaven. In acting thus He was not taking back from Peter the supreme power which He had formerly entrusted to him, but He was making the others share in it. It is in a general way only that He refers to the future, but they must have gathered that He was speaking of His future Church which was to be firmly established on Peter and would be attacked by the powers of evil ; for as long as Jesus was with them all jurisdiction belonged to Him.

But He will not always be with them ; He is to leave them. Nevertheless those who are faithful to Him will remain united, and if two or three of them gather together to pray the Father will grant their prayer, always in virtue of Jesus' name which shall as it were envelope them. And not only will His name be a pledge of His protection ; He Himself will remain in the midst of His own by virtue of a special spiritual presence.[1] It is in prayer in common that we find the most natural fulfilment of this saying of Jesus, and within the Church it has always been held in favour and encouraged. When a group of people pray together, they pray better, especially if they are gathered together in the presence of Christ in the Eucharist ; but not even literal

[1] Matthew xviii, 20 ; xxviii, 20. Parallel in John xiv, 23.

interpretation of the most extravagant kind could deduce from the words of Jesus that none but public prayer is heard by God. What is insisted on as essential is that the followers of Christ should be of one mind about the object of their prayer and that they should pray in the name of Christ who is in the Church ; the Church being therefore, as St. Paul concluded, the body of Christ. Surely all the followers of Christ are at one in having the same general intentions to pray for ! It was doubtless for the purpose of reassuring those who prayed in desert solitudes or alone at home that a saying came to be attributed to Jesus which was conceived in this manner : 'Wherever there are two together, they are not without God ; and wherever there is one only, I say unto you that I am with him.'[1]

The pardoned debtor who becomes a pitiless creditor (134b).

Matt. xviii, 21–35 ; Luke xvii, 3–4.

With his usual promptness Peter understood that if God forgives, and if the Church forgives in His name, then the disciple must be ready to forgive also. Jesus had already said as much and in strong terms, even commanding His disciples to love their enemies.[2] There was no doubt about the principle. But the generous, open-hearted Apostle envisaged a forgiveness that was repeated again and again. Ought one to go on forgiving as often as seven times ? To go beyond that number seemed too much to ask ; for if a man continued to offend again and again after having been forgiven so many times he would seem to be indulging in mere mockery, and it surely was not right to take part in such a farce. But God's mercy is infinite ; He never wearies of forgiving. Therefore Peter must forgive seventy times seven times, that is to say always. Can he who is always in need of mercy refuse it to others ? One might almost say that such a one ought to be more disposed to pardon even than God Himself, since he has so often received pardon for his own offences.

This Jesus explains in a parable suited to the question raised by Peter. It is the parable of the discharged debtor who becomes a pitiless creditor. The conclusion is that he

[1] The first of the Logia of the Oxyrynchus papyrus.
[2] Matthew v, 44.

whom God has forgiven and who refuses to pardon his brother has shown himself unworthy of God's mercy. He has been treated with great indulgence ; had his heart been touched by this, surely he would have been only too ready to forgive his neighbour a trifling debt !

Here Jesus compares the government of God with that of an earthly king. But we are not to see in the king a complete metaphor for God ; God does not need, like this king, to seek information from others. And yet the king certainly does represent God, for no earthly prince would be so merciful as he ; moreover the sum owed is altogether enormous and improbable, and there is something of an infinite character about man's offences against God. The parable is therefore coloured with allegory, as is so often the case with the gospel parables. It has also a certain Semitic character ; the servants of the king are in reality his ministers. The debt is not the result of a private loan ; the king commands a tax-gatherer to render his accounts. The tax-gatherer finds himself with a deficit for a ridiculous sum, equivalent to £2,000,000 in gold ! Surely he must have enriched himself at his master's expense on a tremendous scale. But the royal treasury had the same privileges as the king and could refund itself by seizing all the goods of the debtor ; the man, along with his wife and children, would even be sold into slavery. Such was the law. The guilty man—for certainly he is guilty—begs for mercy and the king pardons him : an act of divine mercy rather than royal clemency, for the debt also is forgiven. As he goes out, just when his heart ought to be overflowing with gratitude and in the mood for pitying others, the wretched man sees one of his colleagues who has the misfortune to be in his debt for about three pounds : a colleague who was probably in a station very inferior to his own, but who nevertheless was a man like himself serving the same master. There was no question of needing such a small sum to make some payment towards the enormous debt he had incurred towards his master ; he no longer owed anything and he had even been left in possession of his ill-gotten property. Churlishly he seizes his fellow-servant by the throat, and it is in vain that the latter entreats him and prostrates himself at his feet : a mark of respect to which the unmerciful servant was not entitled. He throws the poor wretch into prison as though it were a matter of money owing to the treasury. The other servants, courtiers who have access to the king, inform him of their sorrow and indignation. In his anger the master hands over the hard-hearted servant to the torturers until he repays all that he formerly owed. But what chance was there of his paying? It was equivalent to condemning him to lifelong imprisonment.

These acts of the king we may compare with the manner in which God acts, provided we make due allowance for God's infinite perfection; for God does not withdraw pardon that He has once granted. Knowing well that such a sinner's heart has no room for compassion towards others, He would not have granted pardon in the first place. We all stand in need of forgiveness; we must begin, then, by forgiving our neighbours. Such is the practical conclusion to be drawn from the parable.

Jesus pays the Temple dues though there is no obligation on His part (135).

Matt. xvii, 24–27.[1]

The presence of Jesus at Capharnaum could not long remain a secret. In spite of His precautions to prevent recognition, it became known to the collectors of the Temple tax that He was in the town. They knew Him to be the Master, but Peter, as we have said, often took charge of the temporal affairs of the group; they apply therefore to him: 'Doth not your master pay the didrachmas?' Every Israelite was under an obligation to pay a half-shekel a year,[2] two drachmas[3] in Greek coinage, for the upkeep of the Sanctuary. Perhaps the tax-collectors merely wished to draw attention in an indulgent and friendly manner to the fact that the tax had not yet been paid. It may be also that they wondered whether Jesus does not perhaps think Himself exempt from it, both on His own account and as regards His disciples too. Prompt as ever Peter replies: 'Certainly,' either failing to realize that a question of

[1] Matthew places this incident before the dispute about precedence, thus suggesting that the dispute may have been occasioned by it. He alludes vaguely, however, to the stay at Capharnaum, while Mark says explicitly that the dispute took place on the way thither. We feel bound, therefore, to adopt this order. In the Synopsis, No. 129 should follow No. 136.

[2] Exodus xxx, 13; Esdras B, x, 32.

[3] In other words a didrachma.

principle is involved, or else solving the question without any hesitation. He goes into the house—either his own or Matthew's—rather to obtain the money than to ask the advice of his Master. But Jesus has no money, and He determines to make Peter consider the matter, this man who but recently had declared Him to be the Son of God. Does a king ask his own children to pay taxes? The logical conclusion to be drawn from the principle of oriental despotism is that the king alone is the real owner of all the goods of his subjects. He permits them the free use of these goods on condition of their paying him a tax by way of rent. But the goods of his own sons are exempt from this tax.

If God then, the ruler of Israel, demanded money for the upkeep of His worship, His Son was under no obligation of contributing towards it. Nevertheless He observed the Law as if it had been binding on Him so that He might not give occasion of surprise or scandal to others. He would therefore continue to pay the didrachma, but Peter is to understand that this is without detriment to the right as Son of God which the disciple has recognized that He possesses. And since, on the occasion of Peter's confession, Jesus shared with him the government of His Church, He determines now to pay the tax for them both. He does so by a miracle, as if the better to show both that He was completely free from any obligation in the matter, and also that He possessed nothing, He who might have had all the treasures of the world for His own.

Fish greedily swallow whatever comes their way. Peter, the fisherman, goes out and finds in the mouth of the first fish he catches a stater or shekel, enough to pay the tax for two. This sacred tax was collected, according to the Talmud,[1] before one of the three great feasts. Easter and Pentecost were past; it must have been, therefore, before the feast of Tabernacles, and it does indeed seem from the gospel that they were nearing this feast. After the great rebellion and defeat of the Jews in A.D. 70 the tax was still collected and paid to the temple of Jupiter Capitolinus. St. Matthew has not the slightest suspicion of such a thing; he views things just as they were in the time of Jesus. Here again, then, we find another point that tells in favour of Simon Peter, such as could not possibly have been invented at a late date for the glorification of the Church of Rome.

[1] Mishnah, Shekalim, III, 1.

Jesus leaves the cities of the lake-side (136).

Luke x, 13–15 ; Matt. xi, 20–24.[1]

The mission in the north of the Holy Land was now finished. When He first left Nazareth Jesus had devoted Himself specially to the cities of the lake-side, Capharnaum, Corozain, Bethsaida. There he had recruited His best disciples, though of the people as a whole in those cities it might be said that they had eyes not to see with and ears not to hear with. But He desired to make one last appeal to them, an appeal so much the more earnest in that it was more sad, in which He summoned the guilty cities to the judgement seat of God. On the other side of the mountains, standing by the open sea, were Tyre and Sidon, cities of luxury and commercial grandeur, all the more given up to pleasure on account of the sensual and brutal character of their religion. These cities had merited a dreadful punishment. Jesus had merely passed through them without preaching repentance ; He had kept all His energy for His fellow-countrymen of Galilee ; to them He had opened His heart and promised salvation, offering Himself now to them to be their light and life, the beginning of eternal light and the pledge of everlasting life. They refused, and they are in consequence far more guilty than Tyre and Sidon. God's contemned appeal falls back heavily on their rebellious heads, for sin against the light is the gravest of all sins. This is the Master's last lesson and it is in the formidable shape of a curse : 'Woe to thee Corozain ! Woe to thee Bethsaida ! For if in Tyre and Sidon had been wrought the miracles that have been wrought in you, their inhabitants would have long ago done penance, sitting in sackcloth and ashes. And thou Capharnaum, shalt thou be exalted to heaven ? No, thou shalt be cast down to hell.'

Thus Capharnaum has become an accursed city ; nay, it is brought lower than Sodom and Gomorrha, the two cities which, as types of crime, were struck down by God's curse. Despite their abominable vices, they would yet have been more obedient to the word than proud Capharnaum, and consequently Capharnaum shall be judged more

[1] This farewell to the cities is better placed in Matthew than in Luke, who interposes it in the mission of the seventy-two disciples.

severely than they. But not even a threat such as this caused that city to tremble. And to-day there is no sadder place to the follower of Jesus Christ than the shores of the lake of Genesareth, so full of beauty in the springtime. The word that awoke the great hope of salvation on those shores has gone into the whole world, and everywhere it is heard and kept, everywhere it brings salvation. Here by the lake it is no longer heard. In their town of Tiberias the Jews seek to preserve only the memory of their great rabbis ; the Rabbi Meir, at whose grand tomb they keep lighted lamps ; Moses-ben-Maimon, the master whom they compare to Moses.[1] A handful of Franciscans venerate the presence of Jesus at Capharnaum, which, like Corozain, is in complete ruins. As for Bethsaida, nothing is left but a few traces and even of those we are doubtful.

After making this farewell Jesus set His face towards Jerusalem. There His reception will be even less favourable than in Galilee, and He will be obliged there also to predict the judgement that it shall draw down upon the city. The mission in Judæa like the mission in Galilee will end in failure ; in each case there is the same sorrow in the Master's loving heart, the same hardening of the heart among the leaders of the Jews as there has been among the Galilæans : but the former are the more guilty of the two, for they have been the more favoured.

III. AT THE FEAST OF TABERNACLES

The third of the feasts on which the Israelites were commanded to go on pilgrimage to Jerusalem was 'the feast of Tents,' or as we say 'of Tabernacles.' These tents were not like the tents of the Bedouin, 'houses of hair' as they call them because made of camel hair cloth ; they were huts of boughs. In every vineyard there was a tower of uncemented stone on the flat roof of which it was a simple thing to erect one of these huts. It was there that the owner of the vineyard slept at the time when the grapes were ripening in order to protect them against jackals, and against human thieves too. When the grape-harvest was over a few days were spent there in rejoicings. Just as the feast of the

[1] The Hebrew inscription on the tomb of Moses Maimonides sounds like a defiance : 'From Moses to Moses none hath risen like Moses.'

first fruits had grown into a commemoration of the giving of the Law on Sinai, so also the feast of Tents had been consecrated to the memory of the exodus from Egypt;[1] but the latter identification was of much earlier date than the former. It was in this way that God educated His people, transforming the rejoicings of the grape-harvest, which were not infrequently the occasion of licentiousness, by providing them with another and higher motive. Thus gratitude to God for the natural blessings of the earth was by this commemoration directed towards the great supernatural favours which Israel had received. That divine process finds its completion in the Christian religion which has made all feasts serve to recall some mystery of our salvation.

In consequence of its origin the feast of Tabernacles was not considered to be so great as the Pasch; it did not call up such sacred memories of the past, pledges of a still holier time to come. But, on the other hand, the feast of Tabernacles was a more joyful occasion, as vintage feasts are all over the world. Apart from the special sacrifices that were common to all festivals, the special rite of this feast was that worshippers carried during the ceremony a sort of bouquet made of branches and fruit. Originally the Law had prescribed a bunch of palm and willow branches. By the time of Josephus, almost contemporary with Jesus, tradition had interpreted this as meaning branches of myrtle, willow, and palm, along with Persian apples, that is to say lemons. At the time of the celebration, the end of September or beginning of October, the agricultural year was at an end[2] and the land was parched by the sun. The thoughts of all were now turned towards the next sowing, and this would depend on the gift of rain. Doubtless it was to symbolize the hoped-for rain that water was brought from Siloe in a precious vessel during the feast and poured upon the altar. It expressed their desire that the water from the spring might thus go up to heaven and fall upon

[1] Exodus xxiii, 16: 'Thou shalt observe the feast of the harvest of the first fruits of thy work (later become the feast of the Law) . . . (and) the feast also in the end of the year when thou hast gathered in all thy corn out of the field.' Cf. Leviticus xxiii, 43: 'that your posterity may know that I made the children of Israel to dwell in tabernacles when I brought them out of the land of Egypt.'

[2] The agricultural year regulated the civil year. The new year began and still begins on the first day of Tishri; the feast of Tabernacles began on the 15th.

Israel afresh. The rite was performed on each of the seven days of the feast, perhaps on the eighth day also, though this had the character of a distinct feast. We do not learn explicitly from the Jewish writings that the pilgrims were welcomed at Jerusalem with great pomp and ceremony, but it is probable that they were so received. Doubtless also they brought with them their bunches of boughs and fruit so as not to pay the great price that would be demanded at Jerusalem. Entering thus into the city with a company of Galilæans was for Jesus a kind of foretaste of the modest triumph He was to enjoy in a similar manner at the following Pasch.

The refusal of Jesus to manifest Himself at Jerusalem (137).
John vii, 1–13.

We left Jesus after His farewell to Galilee. He had traversed that country almost secretly in order that He might not be disturbed in the attention He was devoting to His disciples. We here pick up again the thread of the fourth gospel, where too we find Jesus in His own country, for He had not returned to Judæa since the last Pentecost. On that occasion, after He had cured the paralytic on the Sabbath day, the Jews had made up their minds to do Him to death. Four months had passed and it was time to go up to the Holy City again for the celebration of the feast of Tabernacles. The brethren of Jesus, His near relations that is to say, knew of His presence in their neighbourhood and were becoming impatient at His evasions of public notice. They had not a belief in Him like that of the Apostles ;[1] but if their kinsman was thinking of playing a great part, and if, as seemed possible, His undeniable miracles gave Him some chance of success, why all this evasion? Let Him make the attempt. As far as Galilee was concerned the cause seemed hopeless ; but Jesus had followers at Jerusalem; that was the right place to manifest Himself to the world, a place where He would find the élite of Israel. A triumphal entry into the Holy City surrounded by a group of resolute Galilæans shouting joyful Hosannas, what an opportunity

[1] None of them, that is with the exception of James, the son of Alphæus ; if this James, indeed, is 'the brother of the Lord,' as we think him to be, and the son of either a sister or a cousin of the Blessed Virgin. Whether Alphæus be the same as Cleophas or not cannot be said with certainty.

that would be for Him to set up as a Liberator ! It almost seems as though His brethren offered to join His supporters.

But Jesus prefers to let them go up without Him : 'Go you up to the feast, but as for Me, I go not up to this feast because My time is not yet accomplished' ; the time of which He speaks is the time appointed by God. There is no question of the evangelist's wishing to accuse his Master of dissimulation ; he simply means that Jesus reserved His liberty to do as He liked. Though it is forbidden to lie even to one that asks indiscreet questions, yet there is no obligation of revealing our intentions to such a one when there is need to keep them secret. And secrecy was precisely what Jesus required, that is to say, He wished to arrive in Jerusalem quietly.[1] It was necessary for Him to take this precaution because the Jews were waiting for Him, and among the crowd people were discussing Him in whispers, some for, others against Him, no one daring to commit himself too openly until the authorities had declared their mind.

Jesus goes up to Jerusalem (138).

Luke ix, 51–56.

Jesus therefore took the road to Jerusalem accompanied by a few disciples only. He was leaving Galilee for the last time. St. Luke has laid emphasis on the decisive character of this moment, this journey which was to end in death after the lapse of a few months. From now on that is the prospect which dominates the whole situation.

The shortest route to Jerusalem was through the land of the Samaritans and it was in Jesus' mind to ask hospitality of them. But at the season of the great pilgrimages feelings were more than usually excited. His little band was going in the direction of Jerusalem evidently with the intention of carrying out the rites which it was forbidden to celebrate in any other place ; that in itself was an insult to the claims of Mount Garizim, and the Samaritans refused to receive Jesus and His followers. James and John, the Sons of Thunder,[2] found it impossible on this occasion to put a charitable construction on such a refusal ; people who scorned the sacred law of hospitality could only be regarded

[1] The meaning is therefore : 'I go not up *yet*,' as very many MSS. have it.
[2] See above, p. 279.

as open enemies. Confident in their ability to imitate the example of Elias,[1] if only their Master would allow it, they appeal to Him : 'Lord, wilt Thou that we command fire to come down from heaven and consume them ?' But He turned and rebuked them,[2] patiently content to go on and look for some other place of shelter.

First conversations and impressions during the feast (139–141). John vii, 14–36.

When they arrived in Jerusalem the feast had already begun ; it was already the middle of the week dedicated to that feast. Jesus went into the Temple. After the ceremonies were over it was the custom of the Jews to stay talking in the great enclosure surrounding the altar and the Holy Place. There the rabbis taught, and Jesus followed their example. By this He caused some surprise, for people held that He had not attended the rabbinical schools long enough to acquire authority in them, to have His opinions quoted with the conventional formula : Rabbi so-and-so has said. This was the honour chiefly coveted by those who devoted themselves day and night to the study of the Law. These Jewish masters put themselves forward merely as repeating the teaching handed down by tradition ; but, despite this affectation of modesty, they not infrequently yielded to the temptation of making some new solution—their own, namely—prevail by dint of subtlety. These solutions had necessarily to be derived from the Law, but they were sometimes drawn at the expense of legitimate exegesis, and not without doing injury to the authority acquired by other teachers. But Jesus, far from making any claim to originality in His doctrine and to the honour which might accrue to Him on that account, declares that His doctrine is not His own ; it comes from the One who

[1] 4 Kings i, 10–12.

[2] The primitive text of St. Luke said no more than this, that He rebuked them ; but certain MSS. have added the words : 'And He said to them : You know not of what spirit you are. The Son of Man came not to destroy men's souls but to save them.' This addition may be derived from Marcion who tried to show the opposition that existed, in his opinion, between the New and the Old Testaments. He would be right in seeing an opposition of some sort here, for the spirit of the New Testament is different in so far as Jesus has come to save mankind. And indeed the Church has never seen anything objectionable in this gloss, for the words appear in the Vulgate to this day.

sent Him, and to Him all the glory should be attributed. By thus renouncing all self-interest, He left no occasion for anyone to suspect Him of perverting the truth out of vainglory.

By the One who has sent Him He means God. But how were they to be sure of that? That was the whole point at issue between His adversaries and Himself. First, He makes appeal to the testimony of an upright conscience. A will that cleaves to God is of more use for judging of divine things than is the search for light by means of study. In saying this Jesus lays down one of the great principles of mystical theology, that God is known by means of the resemblance of the knower to the divine object of His knowledge. A simple and uneducated woman, if she is good, has a truer sense of moral goodness than a theologian who is a bad man. And this is precisely the case with the Jews who are hostile to Jesus. They have the Law of Moses always on their lips, but they do not practise it according to its spirit; that is why they fail to see that Jesus interprets the Law in the spirit of Him who gave it. Most certainly no one ought to claim the right to act contrary to the positive law of God on the ground that he has received private mystical inspirations. But in the matter with which He is reproached, namely the cure of a man on the Sabbath, Jesus shows that there was no real transgression of the positive law of God. Was not the law of the Sabbath set on one side in order to carry out the rite of circumcision on newly-born children? That law then ought not to be made an obstacle to restoring health. Indeed did it not stand aside of itself when there was a question of the law of charity?

Here Jesus was alluding to the cure of the paralytic at the pool of Bezatha during the last feast of Pentecost, and recalling the fact that the Jews had then resolved to put Him to death. Some of the crowd, perhaps people from a distance, thought that He was suffering from persecution mania and said: 'Thou art possessed by the devil. Who seeketh to kill Thee?'[1] Others, however, living at Jerusalem,[2] were better acquainted with the ill-feeling entertained for Jesus by their leaders, and this made them all the more surprised that they allowed Him to speak so freely. Was it possible that their leaders had changed their

[1] John vii, 20. [2] John vii, 25.

minds and were now disposed to acknowledge Him as the Messiah? Surely not, for the Messiah was to appear without anyone's knowing whence He came, in some miraculous fashion; and it was only too well known where Jesus came from. True, He proceeded to say; you know Me and you know whence I have come. But that is not the thing of importance. My earthly origin does not prevent My having come from somewhere higher than this earth, sent by Him who has the right to send; and even if you do not know who He is, nevertheless I know Him—I who am with Him and who have been sent by Him. Thus in His forbearance Jesus solved the difficulty at which these thoughtless people had stumbled. They reckoned on some extraordinary origin for the Messiah; *His* was more divine than they think, though it is not inconsistent with those earthly relationships of which they are well aware. His extraordinary origin is pre-existence with God, who has sent Him and with whom He dwells. At this declaration some of them were violently shocked and wished to lay hands on Him; but others said: 'Why not believe Him, seeing that He has confirmed what He says by miracles? Will the Messiah furnish more splendid proofs than those when He comes?' And they believed in Him.

The Pharisees were alarmed and sought out the chief priests to whom was reserved the authority to employ the police in the Temple. Officers were charged to arrest Jesus formally; but He read their intentions and forewarned them of their powerlessness over Him. He will return to Him who has sent Him at the appointed time, and nothing can hinder that. When that time comes they will seek Him in vain, for they will not be able to come to Him. As they will not consider the idea that Jesus may be sent by God, the Jews do not understand what He means. Does He intend to go and preach to the Children of Israel dispersed among the Gentiles, or even to those Gentile nations themselves? He will not have time for that, for orders have already been issued against Him.

Teaching on the last day of the feast; disagreement even among the Pharisees (142–143).

John vii, 37–52.

In what He had said so far, according to what we learn from St. John's summary of it, Jesus had answered what was in the mind of those around Him, and which they either more or less openly expressed or else pretended they did not think. On the last day of the feast He takes the initiative and teaches them a lesson full of meaning, taking His inspiration from the ceremony of the pouring of water over the altar. It was the most solemn day of all,[1] and to it was given the special name of Hosanna from the psalm[2] that was sung during the procession in which the willow branches were carried. On this day the prayer for rain was more insistent, for the end of this time of supplication was drawing near.

All water, even spring water, comes down from the heavens; that is why Jesus likened this pure and limpid element to a gift of God. In this He was only following the tradition of the prophets who looked on water poured out upon a parched land as an image of the new spirit that was to be characteristic of the time of salvation.[3] As Saviour, therefore, Jesus was the bestower of that water which He would give to those who believed in Him. We find all that in His words: 'If any man thirst, let him come to Me and drink. He that believeth in Me, as the Scripture hath said: Out of him shall flow rivers of living water.'[4] The allusion was enigmatic in character, but it was clear enough for anyone who understood, as did St. Paul,[5] that Christ was typified by the rock from which miraculous water gushed forth in the desert; that miracle was to be renewed in a spiritual fashion in the days of Messianic salvation, as had been foretold by Isaias: 'Say: Jahweh hath redeemed his servant Jacob. . . . He hath caused water to flow from the rock and the waters have been poured out.'[6] The Greek version of this passage adds: 'And my people shall drink.'

[1] It was the seventh day, not the eighth, which had a distinct significance of its own.

[2] Psalm cxvii, 25 (cxviii in Heb.). [3] Isaias xliv, 3 ff., etc.

[4] John vii, 37 ff. [5] 1 Corinthians x, 4. [6] Isaias xlviii, 20 ff.

The evangelist admits, however, that this doctrine was not clear at the time when Jesus uttered it. He understood it better later when Jesus revealed it clearly to His disciples.[1] He therefore here gives us an explanation of it: 'This He said of the Spirit which those should receive who believed in Him; for as yet the Spirit was not given, because Jesus had not yet been glorified.' In the time of the old covenant the Spirit had intervened in the affairs of the world, suddenly, irresistibly, bringing light and strength to those heroes and temporary saviours of Israel such as Othoniel, Gedeon, Jephte, Samson, Saul, men who were sometimes later deprived of the favour of which they proved themselves unworthy. But the source of this favour was not at men's disposal to have recourse to at free-will, nor was there anyone who possessed the plenitude of the Spirit so that he might pass the Spirit on to others at will. Jesus, however, did possess that plenitude, but His bestowal of the Spirit on others was to wait till after His Passion and entrance into glory by His Resurrection. It was well known to all Christians that by the coming down of the Holy Ghost at the first Christian Pentecost there had been inaugurated an era of salvation which was permanent and unchangeable.

As for us, who realize how faith in Christ has been the source of love for God and charity towards men, of noble thoughts and magnificent deeds, we cannot but be struck by the force of this prophecy of Christ which stands there in the Gospel, all the more splendid for its isolation. It may be that Jesus at the time explained it so clearly that these people of Jerusalem, just as much moved as formerly the Galilæans had been by the manner in which He spoke to them the word of God, repeated in their turn: 'This is the prophet indeed,' the great prophet whom they were all looking for. Some went even further and uttered the word Messiah. But if Jesus were the Messiah, what would become of Juda's prerogative as the Messiah's place of origin? The people would have been deceived in attaching their confidence to the word of Scripture. Was not the Messiah to be a descendant of the race of David and consequently to be born at Bethlehem, the cradle of David's family? Thus the thing was left in a state of uncertainty, and meanwhile Jesus was finding more and more partisans, especially from the ranks of the Galilæans, while opposition towards

[1] John xvi, 7.

Him was becoming more timid. The officers of the law sent by the chief priests and the Pharisees did not dare to discharge their mission ; accustomed to deal with a very different type of person, they were affected by Jesus and made no secret of this to those who had commanded them to arrest such a man. But the opinion of common people who had not searched out the texts of the Law had but little influence on the minds of the Pharisees, who held that without this knowledge of the Scriptures there could be no real virtue ; the crowd was therefore of no account before God and was the object of His curses. Hereupon Nicodemus, who was as learned as any of the rabbis, ventured on an objection. Were they going to pass judgement on Jesus without giving Him a hearing ? Surely that was contrary to the Law ! There ought to be a fair enquiry into His doings. An answer had to be found to the objections of such a rabbi as Nicodemus. He was bent upon getting at the facts of the case ; the others replied by appealing to law. What was the good of an enquiry about Jesus seeing that no prophet could arise from Galilee ? Was Nicodemus himself perhaps a Galilæan ? Let him first prove, if he can, that the claim of this fellow-countryman of his was grounded on the Scriptures !

It appears then that the Pharisees did not know that Jesus had in fact been born at Bethlehem. They could always find a way out of a difficulty by exegetical subtleties ; but God found a more natural way of fulfilling the words of the prophets.

The woman taken in adultery (144).

John vii, 53–viii, 11.[1]

After these heated discussions all went their way ; Jesus withdrew to the Mount of Olives where He had friends. We shall find Him there again later.[2] Early each morning He came to the Temple to teach, and the crowd flocked about

[1] There are good grounds for thinking that this incident is not a part of the original fourth gospel ; but the fact remains that it is canonical and inspired Scripture. It may have been inserted here as part of the tradition handed down by St. John's disciples. But it has rather the appearance of belonging to Synoptic narrative. In any case there is no reason for doubt with regard to the truth of the facts narrated.

[2] Luke xxi, 37 ff.

Him. He sat as He taught, for the excitement of the feast had died down. One day He was interrupted by the arrival of a noisy throng of people. A woman had been caught in adultery and had been taken before the Scribes and Pharisees ; it was left to their zeal to see that she should be punished as the Law demanded and by the proper tribunal. The fact that she had been taken in the act seemed to justify summary execution. From every point of view it was a good opportunity for finding out what Jesus would say. He was reputed to be kind in His treatment of sinners ; He was even said to be their friend. Would He presume to pardon in such a serious case as this ? The Pharisees, followed by a violently excited crowd, drag the woman before Him and describe the case. Somewhat naïvely they manifest the motive that lies behind all this : 'In the Law Moses commanded us to stone such as she. But Thou, what sayest Thou ?' They do not quote the Law very exactly : it did indeed condemn a guilty wife to death,[1] but it only prescribed stoning for infidelity on the part of a betrothed woman,[2] and there were some who maintained that the punishment was not the same for either case. However, as there was greater guilt in the case of a wife than in the case of a woman who was merely betrothed, it seemed reasonable that the former also should receive the terrible penalty of stoning. Hence Jesus did not raise any quibble ; but He does not consider that He is called upon to pass judgement at all ; He has not come as an official of a court of justice charged with the duty of giving sentence in accordance with the law, but to invite sinners to ward off God's judgements by repentance. With an appearance of having nothing to do with this distressing scene, He has stooped down and is writing with His finger on the ground, as though merely to pass the time until they go away and leave Him to resume His teaching, or as if He wishes to fix certain thoughts in writing. St. Jerome, having read in Jeremias :[3] 'They that turn away from Thee shall be written on the earth,' considered that Jesus was writing down the sins of the accusers. The comparison was an ingenious one and made good the gap left by the silence of the gospel text ; moreover it satisfied curiosity. It still satisfies some people, but there are no grounds for it, for the zealots do

[1] Leviticus xx, 10. [2] Deuteronomy xxii, 23 ff.
[3] Jeremias xvii, 13 (different in Greek Version).

not show any sign that they feel implicated ; all that they show is annoyance with Jesus for upsetting their calculations by His appearance of indifference. They obstinately insist on an answer. Then He says to them : ‘ Let him that is without sin among you cast the first stone at her.’ In truth it was the duty of the denouncer to strike the first blow.[1]

There are cases in which a judge, with shame in his heart, has the duty as representing the law of condemning a person who is guilty of crimes which he himself commits ; but that is one of the defects of all human justice. These people, however, who were so enthusiastic about the letter of the law, would have done better if they had first examined their own consciences before showing such zeal. The older ones among them are suspicious. Has Jesus read the secrets of their hearts ? Perhaps He was setting a trap for them in thus showing such apparent indifference at first, merely in order that He might later intervene with all the more effect. These are the first to go away, and the rest of the self-constituted judges follow their example. Thus Jesus is left alone with the woman, except doubtless for His disciples and a few curious lookers-on. He sits up and questions the woman who is still terror-stricken. It would be pleasing to think of her begging forgiveness on her knees. But Jesus says to her : ‘ Hath no one condemned thee ? ’ Still frightened she replies simply to the question : ‘ No one, Lord.’ Whereupon Jesus says : ‘ Neither do I condemn thee,’ that is, to the terrible death of stoning. But there is another judge. She must take heed : ‘ Go thy way and sin no more.’ Justice and mercy have met together. Justice could not allow a judicial discharge and take no account of the anti-social character of her crime ; mercy will not agree to condemnation because it sees repentance in that still terror-stricken heart. The existence of such repentance is implied by the fact that He urges a firm purpose of amendment.

[1] Deuteronomy xiii, 9, 10 ; xvii, 7.

The light gives testimony of itself, and that testimony is confirmed by the Father (145).

John viii, 12–20.

The feast was over. From now on the crowd ceases to play an active part in the drama which continues to take place between Jesus and the Jews. On the first evening of the solemnity four great candelabra were lit up in the Court of the Women ; the Talmud speaks in moving terms of the way in which the brightness of the light was shed over Jerusalem and all the surrounding district. But as there is no proof that this rite was performed on the succeeding days, we cannot say that it was the occasion for the discourse in which Jesus proclaimed that He was the light of the world. All that we can suppose is that He may have heard people speaking of the grandeur of the ceremony, and thus took occasion to say : 'I am the light of the world ; he that followeth Me walketh not in darkness, but he shall have the light of life.' That light, then, would not be a knowledge in His disciple that produced no fruits ; it would touch the heart and stir up the will ; it would be a live spark serving as a principle of moral and religious life, a ray from the light by which Jesus was scattering the darkness in which man was striving to find his way.[1]

In speaking after this fashion, Jesus did not lay down clearly that He was God, but surely He was proclaiming Himself as the Messiah. The prophets had foretold that the Messiah should be the light of the Gentiles,[2] as the Scribes well knew. They must have understood, therefore, that Jesus was claiming to have been sent by God. But nobody has the right to bear witness to himself ; Jesus had admitted that of His own accord when He last spoke with them at the feast of Pentecost ; but He had gone on to add that His Father bore witness to Him, as was proved by the fact that the works He did bore the stamp of divine power. He now gives them to understand that this stamp or seal was merely a preliminary guarantee of His mission from God. When a prophet speaks, he speaks in God's name ; but he has to prove by signs that he has been sent by God. Once he has done that, it is only from the prophet himself

[1] Luke i, 79.

[2] Isaias xlii, 6 ; xlix, 6, etc. *Le Messianisme*, p. 47 and *passim*.

that his hearers can find out in what his mission consists. Now Jesus by His miracles had proved His truthfulness, for God does not bestow His divine authority on what is not true. As Jesus was the channel of truth He was the Light, and light has only to shine in order to show itself. Therefore when He speaks of His mission they ought to believe Him; He alone knows whence He comes and whither He is going. Nevertheless, let them bear in mind what He has said to them on another occasion,[1] namely that God has given authority to His words. Since that is so, Jesus is not alone. The old adage—too pessimistic by far—that no notice can be taken of an isolated witness, cannot, therefore, be brought against Jesus. Even if the Law says such a thing, yet He is still in a safe position with regard to the Law; His Father is with Him, so there are two. As His Father has vouched for His word, what Jesus says ought to be believed.

The Jews affect to take no notice of the miracles of which Jesus speaks, the testimony that has accompanied and accredited His word. They pretend to understand Him as offering to show them His Father. Where is He, then? If He is speaking of Joseph, whom everyone regards as His father, then He must be laughing at them. If He is speaking of God, then He blasphemes by making Himself God's Son. Again Jesus avoids too pointed a declaration. They may well say that they know nothing about the Father of whom He speaks. If only they knew His Son Jesus, they would know the Father as well. He left them to understand that the Son was of the same nature as the Father. And if such an idea seemed to them blasphemous, it was their duty at least to acknowledge that He was sent by God and so listen to Him; and in that case they would know His Father better. The first thing to be done was to trust God's interpreter. But the Jews refused to take this first step; foreseeing already that if they did they would then have to admit that He was equal to God, they preferred to put an end to the conversation by arresting Him. His hour was not yet come; the evangelist continually reverts to that. It is like a plaintive refrain that closes sadly all these conversations. But the distinguishing mark of the important teaching given on this occasion is obtained from the place in which it was given: it was near the Temple treasury, in a court where all Israelites were free to enter.

[1] John v, 31 ff.

The danger of refusing to acknowledge God's envoy (146).
John viii, 21–30.

It seems to have been very shortly afterwards that Jesus again pressed upon the Jews the necessity of making up their minds. They argue, they find fault, they shuffle, and the time is going by. But His time is strictly determined, and He will not be long before He goes away. Then they will seek Him (either at the time of the great siege of Jerusalem, or when they run after false Messiahs) and will call in vain for a saviour. But it will then be too late ; they will die in their impenitence with this added to all their other sins, that they despised the Saviour sent them by God.

The Jews are more angered by this mysterious threat than when He had made it before,[1] yet now they understand by His going away He means His death. But if Jesus is going to God, surely they will meet Him again there ! Does He mean to destroy Himself and so cast Himself into Gehenna ? To this dreadful suggestion He simply replies : 'No, if we are never to meet again it is because we are not of the same world. Your inclinations drag you down, and I am from above. It would be your salvation if you believed in Me ; then you would be transported to the sphere to which I belong.' The terms in which Jesus expresses this, though obscure to people not conversant with the Scripture, are clear enough to the Jews. He says to them : 'You must believe "that I am" ' ; and it is in these words that the Greek version of the Scriptures translates the two Hebrew words *Ani Hu* (that is 'I He') by which God refers to Himself,[2] meaning 'I am indeed He, He who is from on high, He who is the Saviour.' The claim Jesus puts forward in these words is so lofty that the Jews answer with the sneering question : 'Thou ; who then art Thou ?'[3]

Was it worth while repeating more clearly that of which they must already have had a presentiment, merely for the sake of replying to an ironical question ? Just as on the former occasion when He was speaking of the epileptic boy,[4] so now Jesus gives vent to a kind of sad discouragement, like a man whose efforts are disregarded : 'Should I even speak

[1] Cf. vii, 31–36, p. 297 above.
[2] Deuteronomy xxxii, 39 ; Isaias xliii, 10–15. [3] Cf. Acts xix, 15.
[4] Mark ix, 18 ; Luke ix, 41, p. 274 above.

to you at all?' Yet He is the mouthpiece of truth; He says once more that He speaks nothing but what He has heard from the one who sent Him. It may not have been a direct answer, but it was at any rate a reassertion of His right to be believed. For the most part, however, the Jews would not understand. Nevertheless amongst them were some who were animated by a sincere desire to follow the way shown by God, and it is doubtless to these that Jesus addresses a final appeal: 'When you shall have lifted up the Son of Man, then you shall know who I am.' These men of good will were not to die in their sin; struck by the noble expression of this Son of Man who followed His Father's will so humbly, they believed in Him. Seeing them gather together in order to make known to Him their dawning conviction, He bids them welcome; but at the same time He reminds them of the conditions He has already laid down in the Sermon on the Mount. His truth is not just a light and nothing more; it is not enough to accept that truth. They must remain in it, that is to say, they must live in it by making their acts correspond to their belief.[1] This done there follows a blessed result: truth that is put into practice grows within the soul and bestows upon it a power that brings real deliverance and freedom.

In Jesus is the salvation announced to Abraham (147).

John viii, 31–59.

These words addressed to the new converts, which seemed so simple, contained the whole plan of salvation: to believe in Him who has been sent by God; to live by His truth and so be delivered from the error which is driven out by the coming of truth—and the error in question is chiefly religious error; and finally to be set free from sin, thanks to the operation within us of that vital principle which is the truth of Christ. We know not how far the new converts profited by this teaching. But there were others who listened to it, the bitter adversaries of Jesus, and they began to dispute.[2] They have well understood the supreme import-

[1] Luke vi, 46–49.

[2] An exaggerated attachment to the literal sense which was badly understood has led some to attribute to these new converts a versatility that is beyond belief. In the language of that day, 'to answer' often meant no more than 'to begin to speak,' and for the first time. The people in question here are new speakers, as St. Augustine has well understood.

ance of the principle He has just laid down and they will have none of it. There followed a lively dialogue in which words pass from one side to the other like the quick flash of swords ; it cannot be treated like a well-prepared thesis which is proved by the analysis of ideas and elaborated with skill. The answers made by the Jews, and even those of Jesus, spring altogether spontaneously from the circumstances of the dispute and are due to the strong convictions felt by either side, convictions which are irreconcilable. It is none the less true that the whole debate turns upon a point of decisive character, and this must be made clear if the significance of the exchange of replies is to be understood.

Jesus offers salvation to those who believe in Him and His mission ; that is the price of deliverance from sin. Those who enter on this path must draw the conclusion that salvation is no longer to be sought from the Law. The Jews refused vehemently to accept such a position. Those who sprang from Abraham have long been furnished with all that was required for salvation. Through Abraham they have God for their Father, and it is for Jesus to be related to God in the same way as other Jews. By what right does He call Himself the Son of God proceeding directly from the bosom of the Father ? To speak thus is to utter a blasphemy that deserves death. In this way the Jews close the way to the truth which Jesus is preaching to them ; they sink deeper still into falsehood as is proved by the hatred they bear Him, for hatred is begotten of falsehood, just as charity is begotten of truth. Therefore they are no longer children of God, nor even children of Abraham ; rather are they the children of him who, at the very commencement of history in the Garden of Eden, was a liar and a murderer, a murderer through his lying. The Jews hotly return this reproach of untruth, and they refuse to admit any alteration in the order of things established since the time of Abraham ; whereupon Jesus immediately allies Himself with Abraham : not that He is dependent on Abraham, but rather on the ground that Abraham had placed his hopes in the Messiah, that is to say in Jesus, for He was before Abraham. With that the discussion comes to an end. There is nothing left now but either to believe in Jesus and worship Him along with the Father, or else to stone Him as a blasphemer.

Abraham's name appears repeatedly in this discussion, or the Messianism of the people of Israel begins with him ;

Jesus admits that as much as the Jews. But to their mind the Messiah is at the most to be only another Abraham, perhaps merely sent to restore the faith of Abraham. The idea of associating the Messiah with the worship they pay to the God of Abraham completely disconcerts them. The fact is that they have no deep sense of the supernatural character of the Messiah's work, or of His mission not merely as a preacher of repentance but as one who comes in order to destroy sin. Thus, in the opposition they raise to the claims of this Saviour who is Jesus, they go straight to this point and begin by saying that things are not so bad. The children of Abraham have never been slaves ; they have therefore no need for anyone to deliver them. It is unnecessary to observe that they are not so impudent as to deny that the nation of Israel was once in a state of subjection to Assyrians, Babylonians, Persians, Macedonians, and now is vassal to the Romans. Nor has Jesus made any promise to free them from earthly slavery. What the Jews mean is that, whatever may be said of their past sad history, at any rate since the tribe of Juda (later called the Jews) returned from captivity in Babylon, they have never bowed before strange gods. Of what sort of liberty, then, does Jesus speak ?

They forgot that salvation is not to be gained merely by orthodoxy in matters of faith. And even if all the descendants of Abraham had been orthodox in faith, which was far from true in a great many cases, the fact remained that religious truth had not been able of itself to root out sin ; sin had even grown more widespread. Why, then, do not the Jews imitate the heart-felt contrition of such a man as Daniel ? There never can be pardon for sin without contrition like that ; it is truth's first step in the way that leads to life. No ; blinded by their hatred and resolutely refusing the help of Jesus, they tell Him bluntly that they do not need Him.

It is in reply to this that He tears the veil from what they hide in their hearts, their desire, namely, to put Him to death. And despite what they say, they are in reality the slaves of sin. This is the very implication of all their Law with its unending rites of purification ; it is indicated by the anguished cries of their prophets. Consequently, they ought to be afraid lest they be driven out of the Father's house if they do not seek the help of the Son who abides in that house for ever. This refusal of Messianic salvation, which was their nation's supreme hope, comes so strangely from those who are descended from Abraham, that it seems necessary to conclude that such a refusal proceeds from an alien spirit. It is as much as to declare that they have a father who is not God.

At first the Jews refuse to understand. 'Our father is Abraham,' they repeat. Then, replies Jesus: 'Do the works of Abraham' and not those of a different father. At this thrust the Jews no longer try to shun the issue. They have been told that they are not children of God. But it is well known that their recent ancestors had not worshipped strange gods, and only a crime of that sort would have constituted an apostasy of the nation of Israel which had been joined to its God by the tender bonds of lawful love. Such an apostasy was equivalent to a veritable spiritual adultery such as would have made the Jews, according to the cutting reproach of the prophet Osee,[1] children of a prostitute. But as this was not the case, these Jews are conscious that they are children of God.

Jesus then replies: 'If God were your Father, you would love Me, for from God I came forth.' He does not accuse them of offering sacrifices to strange gods, like the gods of the Greeks and the Romans. But their own Scriptures tell them of the old adversary of God through whom death came into the world; and whoever harbours murderous desires towards one who is innocent shows himself to be the child of that first murderer, the father of lies. It may be lawful to punish a criminal with death. But what is Jesus' crime? What sin can they reproach Him with? His only crime is that He has told them the truth, the truth which they reject because they are not of God.

The Jews are not willing to admit their murderous intentions. It is, as they have said once before, merely an illusion on the part of Jesus who is possessed by the devil; or perhaps He is a Samaritan. This was to give tit for tat. Jesus merely wards off the thrust. It is of no use to employ the operating knife on those who are dead, and these Jews are spiritually dead; so He offers them once more the gift of life for their souls: 'If anyone keep My word, he shall not see death for ever.' So far every word that had passed between the two parties to the discussion had been

[1] Osee i, 2.

concerned with spiritual realities; deliverance from slavery had stood for freedom from sin; and here preservation from death was also to be understood of eternal death. The Jews, now suddenly changing their point of view and understanding these things in a material fashion, seize on this last word of Jesus and try to put Him in a difficult position. Will He escape bodily death and cause others to escape it, when Abraham is dead and the prophets are dead too? A man who talks in that fashion must think himself greater than Abraham; in truth he is possessed by the devil.

Jesus therefore has to protest against this new attack, and in doing so He must assert His rightful rank. He modestly excuses Himself for so doing, but nevertheless He does it, or rather He leaves it to His Father to do so. Were He not to reveal the truth, were He to leave them to believe that He does not know His Father, would be equivalent to taking a way that leads to falsehood; truth had been given to Him in order that He might manifest it when the time was fitting. Yes, then; He is greater than Abraham. He is the one for whom Abraham their father had longed; the one whom Abraham their father, by the light of prophetic vision, had beheld in the secret future, and seeing Him had thrilled with joy.

So Jesus thought Himself remarkably well-informed indeed concerning Abraham's feelings! Had He then seen Abraham, though He was not yet fifty years old?

To this Jesus replies very simply: 'Before Abraham was born, I am.' This was the signal for the stones. But Jesus saved Himself from the stones by leaving the Temple.

It is impossible not to see a certain analogy between this discussion concerning the true children of Abraham and what St. Paul has to say on the subject.[1] John certainly wrote long after St. Paul. Shall we say that he is here preaching Pauline doctrine, that the teaching which flows from this discussion is consequently a mere product of Christianity which is placed by anticipation on the lips of Jesus? If we do then we shall have failed to understand how the two doctrines, that of St. John and that of St. Paul, are related because they have the same source. St. Paul wants to show that justice does not depend on works, but on faith in Christ. He proves it by the fact that the faith

[1] Romans iv; Galatians iii.

of Christians is the same as that of Abraham, who believed in the promise and was straightway declared to be just. Then, returning from Abraham to the Christian faithful, St. Paul identifies him as their father. They are all sons of God by faith in Christ, and having the same faith as Abraham they are his true posterity, even though they may not be circumcised. Arguing in this fashion, St. Paul has drawn a positive conclusion from what the argument of Jesus teaches only implicitly, and almost merely negatively. Our Lord simply showed, in order to answer the objection the Jews raised from their privilege as sons of Abraham, that they were not even children of Abraham, since they were not really children of God. This is precisely the answer that was called for in the circumstances ; there was no need for anything to be said about the advantages of those who believe in Him. Now St. John had certainly read the epistles of St. Paul ; and it is hardly likely that his critical judgement would have been so great as to preserve him, in writing his gospel, from betraying the influence upon him of the triumphant results of the Apostle's reasoning, or from exceeding the bounds of historical probability in making use of St. Paul's conclusions, if he had not been guided in his writing by a vivid recollection of what Our Lord had revealed during His mission.

Here, then, Jesus affirms His pre-existence plainly and in terms that involve a declaration of divinity. The Jews judge that He has said enough to justify their closing His mouth by stoning Him to death. Later He will express this truth still more plainly.

The man born blind (148).

John ix, 1–41.

On leaving the Temple Jesus was no longer molested ; the plot had failed. No one could be put to death without the leave of the Roman authorities, though in cases where the offender was taken in the very act of his crime the indignation roused by this fact was looked on as an excuse for taking the law into one's own hands. Hence Jesus went about freely and thus one day[1] met a man who had

[1] Nothing in St. John's text shows explicitly the chronological connection of this with the preceding incident ; but it seems that there was no great interval.

been blind from birth. In order to call forth the pity of the passers-by the man was crying out his misfortune. Of what this misfortune really was he could have had only a hazy idea, but he knew that it was the frequent cause of his parents' lamentations. The disciples, who had not dared to intervene during the recent dispute, now that they are once more alone with their Master regain their freedom of speech; and without any hesitation for reflection they declare how perplexed they are in face of a hard case like this. Despite the abundantly clear and wonderful lesson of the book of Job, the people were reluctant to admit that suffering would be inflicted on one who had not merited it. Now as this man had been born blind, he had not brought the punishment upon himself by his own sins. To the disciples this barely expressed supposition seemed patently false. Was the fault, then, on the side of his parents? They do not know what to think.

Jesus knows that suffering is not always in proportion to sin; God has His own designs that are beyond our powers to fathom. But He knows further that in this case it is God's purpose to manifest the goodness of His Son who, being the light of the world, is well able to cure a blind man. Whereupon, in order to test the man's confidence, He puts a little earth moistened with spittle on his eyes and bids him: 'Go and wash in the pool of Siloe.' It was commonly held that spittle put on the eyes early in the morning was a remedy against eye strain, but no one claimed the same virtue for mud.[1] It may be that Jesus applied this curious remedy merely as a symbol to demonstrate in external fashion the man's defect of sight. At that time the waters of Siloe were not regarded as possessing the healing qualities of the pool at Bezatha, but they were the more famous. Isaias had spoken of them,[2] and the Scriptures spoke in several places of the tunnel cut by Ezechias through the rock in order to lead into the lower part of Jerusalem the waters of the spring which supplied the ancient citadel of

[1] Among the texts cited by Fouard, there is one of Suetonius who speaks of spittle (*Vespas.* VII), and another of Pliny (H. N., XXVIII, 4). Mud is only spoken of as a remedy for the special case of tumour on the eyes; it is in a poem attributed, rightly or wrongly, to Serenus Sammonicus (third cent. A.D.). Cf. *Poetæ Latinæ Minores*, by Bährens, III, v, 214 ff.

Si tumor insolitus typho se tollat inani
Turgentes oculos vili circumline cæno.

[2] Isaias viii, 6.

the city. The water was thus brought to a pool named Siloe after the tunnel, ‘ the sender ’ of the water. The evangelist takes the word Siloe as being in the passive voice and interprets it as meaning ‘ sent.’ Symbolism is displayed here, but symbolism without any mystery. That, however, does not give us the right to load the text with symbolism when the author himself makes no suggestion of it. Still less have we the right to treat real incidents as mere symbols when the evangelist's intention, as in the present case, is to emphasize the glaring objectivity of the facts. Jesus has but recently demanded belief in Himself as in one sent by God, who alone is capable of taking away sin ; and now He sees fit to provide by this miracle a type of the pardon granted in the waters of baptism through faith in Him who is sent by God. It was not until later, however, that this lesson was understood.

The man went, washed, and received his sight.[1] Now it was a Sabbath day, a day on which it was not lawful to use remedies. Thus a new complaint was added to Jesus' record. But in the then state of affairs one more offence was of no interest to His enemies except in so far as it was connected with His claim to call Himself the Son of God. The miracle was altogether an extraordinary one, and it came opportunely to give authority to His words, and consequently to win support for Him in people's minds. To them it must have seemed that He who had come forth from the Father and asserted so emphatically that He knew the Father, must be a better interpreter than the Scribes of what were the obligations of the Sabbath. The Pharisees, therefore, will leave no stone unturned to deny the reality of this cure, the like of which had never been heard before ; but, as happens when a fact is well established, their efforts only succeeded in making the truth more plain than ever. The evangelist's purpose in relating all the comings and goings that took place is not so much to prove the truth of the miracle to his Christian readers as to show clearly that the Jews sinned in the full light of knowledge.

At first it is the neighbours who are slow to recognise the blind man. But he says : ‘ It is really I ’—a fact which

[1] It is owing to this miracle that the Christian faithful, and after them the Mohammedans, began to bathe in the pool of Siloe in order to seek health. The Empress Eudoxia built a church there, the ruins of which can still be seen. Cf. Vincent and Abel's *Jerusalem*, II, pp. 860–864.

no one could doubt. But how has it happened? Where is the man who accomplished it with a remedy which was clearly ineffectual? As always, the common people have recourse to their masters, the Pharisees. They lead the man to them, and he persists in repeating what he has said before. Enquiries are made of his parents, who, to tell the truth, are anxious to keep out of the affair. They have seen nothing of the matter. But that their son was born blind and now has received his sight they are unable to deny. Let them ask him for themselves; he is of age. He is old enough to get out of the difficulty for himself, they mean; for the parents are afraid of the Jews. If they show signs of believing in Jesus they will be expelled from the synagogue; that is the penalty determined on by the Jews for any who believe in Jesus, and it will be applied mercilessly.

The blind man who has been healed is therefore summoned again. The Pharisees fully realize their power over the parents and the fear with which they are inspired; perhaps their son will be equally amenable. Provided that he just consents to say with them that Jesus is a sinner, perhaps they will let the matter drop. The man admits with an air of prudence: 'If He be a sinner I know not,' as though to give more emphasis to the fact of which he is absolutely certain, namely that he himself was once blind and now he sees. But that is precisely what the Pharisees refuse to admit. There have been many others since their time who have refused to admit miracles on principle. That is the whole essence of rationalism. At last the man gets tired of this repetition of questions which throw doubt on his truthfulness. Are they really so very anxious to find out what has happened? With a touch of mockery he adds: 'Will you also become His disciples?' They the disciples of Jesus! Let him keep the title for himself! Then in one word they reveal the whole bearing of the recent discussion with Jesus. They do not wish to run the risk of being unfaithful to Moses by listening to a man no one knows. Whereupon the man, now that he is thoroughly exasperated, continues in his former strain: 'When anyone works miracles in Israel, you, the masters, surely ought to know who he is. You want me to declare that He is a sinner. Does His power not prove rather that He is from God?' These masters do not like being lectured and let slip an insult that borders on heresy; for in reproaching him with having been wholly born in sins they certainly seem to charge him with responsibility for his misfortune of blindness. Their final argument is to drive him off.

But this gave him the opportunity of meeting Jesus who was looking for him. He was prepared for faith by his courage and gratitude. He who had cured him asked him to believe in the Son of Man. Let Jesus only point him out! Then Jesus said to him: 'Thou seest Him; He who speaks to thee is He.' The man replied: 'I believe, Lord,' and fell down at His feet. And this faith, being faith in Jesus, was faith in the Son of God.

The miraculous bestowal of bodily sight now passed into the shadow before the supernatural shining of that light which Jesus gave to this poor ignorant man who, according to the Pharisees, was blind to the things of God; and all the while the learned grew more obstinate in their pride. This is what Jesus meant when He said: 'For judgement I am come into this world; that they who see not may see; and they who see may become blind.' These words, in the light of the recent event, express exactly the idea which we find also in the Synoptists: 'I confess to Thee, O Father . . . because Thou hast hid these things from the wise and prudent, and hast revealed them to little ones.'[1]

The Pharisees had given up the thought of violence, but they had not ceased to watch. They are there as though by chance. It is evident that Jesus is referring to them, but they seek to force Him to indicate it more clearly so that they may be seen to have reason for their hatred: 'Are we also blind?' they ask. In His reply Jesus touches them on the tender spot of their vanity as men of learning. It would not be so bad if they were blind, whatever they may think or say about the implications of blindness. The dangerous thing is that they consider themselves discerning and pose as righteous men. How can a sin be forgiven when the sinner refuses to admit it? 'Your sin remaineth.'[2] In these words the Pharisees are to find the stern conclusion of all that has been said since the Feast of Tabernacles.

[1] Matthew xi, 25; Luke x, 21. [2] John ix, 41.

Jesus the door of the sheepfold and the Good Shepherd (149–150).

John x, 1–21.

Later on, while still at Jerusalem, Jesus again taught the crowd which pressed about Him. His words have some connection with what has just been said, though now they are of a much gentler character. So, in the words of the prophets, do the joys of the promised restoration follow close upon the threat of punishment ; mercy follows justice.

We must admit that the foregoing words of Jesus were very severe. He had made the hostile Jews understand that He was well aware of the intention to put Him to death, and He had to give them warning of the consequences the nation would have to suffer afterwards through their churlish ill-will towards the Saviour sent to them by God. The eyes of faith detect in these stern admonitions, in this use of the knife in order to probe and open the wound, a sincere and earnest desire on His part to bring about repentance and healing. But the Jews were blind to these generous intentions. They surmised that He would do all in His power to escape the death which in His sadness He foresaw. Little did they know Him ! It was necessary for Him then to open His heart. Now that He has warned those who are obstinately hostile to Him, He turns to those who are of better dispositions and tells them with what tender love for men He accepts the death He is to suffer for their sakes. Far from being afraid of it, He longs for it, because He knows that the accomplishment of His work is to consist in the sacrifice of the shepherd for the sake of his sheep. When that is done His murderers in their blindness will run after a saviour of their own fancy, but it will then be too late ; in despair they will die in their sin. Others shall take their place ; already He sees in the future the sheepfold thrown open to other sheep, all under one shepherd.

The lesson Jesus thus gave touched all hearts and was not interrupted by a single discordant voice. Not all were won over, but so long as He spoke His audience was doubtless spell-bound, as are our own souls even yet when we read His words.

We do not know the precise place where Jesus uttered the words in which He revealed this great secret concerning His redeeming death. It may have been within sight of the Desert of Judæa, for He begins with a comparison drawn from the life of a shepherd, a real parable with a few allegorical touches relating to persons or circumstances connected with the religious life of Israel. The desert was inhabited, as it is to-day, by nomads dwelling in tents who went from one hill to another in search of the scanty traces of pasture. In the day-time each drives the sheep or goats belonging to him, unless he be rich enough to hire the services of a shepherd. But at night all the flocks of the tribe are shut up in a fold which is sometimes enclosed by a wall. Only one shepherd is required to guard the enclosure. When morning comes he opens the door to the other shepherds, and each one on entering gives a cry that his flock recognizes, and they follow him at once. If one of his sheep should stray, he brings it back to the flock by calling its name, a name which he bestows on it from its colour, agility, obedience, or tendency to stray. A thief who had made up his mind to get into the fold at night would certainly not knock upon the door and so attract the shepherd's attention ; rather would he climb over the low wall or fence. And if he succeeded in carrying off some of the sheep, they certainly would not follow him of their own accord, for they would not be used to the sound of his voice or his peculiar call. Jesus reminds the Jews of all this.

They did not understand what He meant by it, and at first it was hardly possible for them to do so. No parable is clear until we know to what it is to be applied ; but Jesus is about to tell them. We, of course, who have had the benefit of Christian education, cry out : It is Jesus who is the Good Shepherd. But let us wait a little.

The comparison made by Jesus supposes that there are good relations between the sheep and their shepherd, but it also lays emphasis on the contrast between true shepherds who enter by the door, and thieves who climb over the wall. Thus the door of the sheepfold becomes the sign of the good shepherd. Jesus says then : 'I am the door of the sheep.' Before He came no one had passed through that door ; others who had come were thieves, and consequently the sheep had paid no heed to them.

But others shall come and they shall enter through Him, the true door, and shall lead the sheep out to pasture. These last are unmistakably His disciples, those who believe in Him and teach His doctrine. Who, then, were the robbers? It is obvious that Jesus does not intend this to be a description of Moses or the prophets, or even of the good kings of the past. There had always been good shepherds in Israel as well as wicked ones, veritable stealers of the sheep.[1] But the parable has not those long past days in view. Even in Jesus' own time the Pharisees, who thought themselves shepherds even if they were not so in reality, had managed to get themselves accepted by the sheep.

It must be remembered that here Jesus is speaking in His rôle of Messiah; therefore those whom He is blaming are persons who have given themselves out unwarrantably as Messiahs, like for example Judas the Galilæan, Simon one of Herod's slaves, Athronges, and others still.[2] To satisfy their ambition they had tried in vain to arouse the people; or if they had succeeded through their religious fanaticism, the only consequence was that their followers had been massacred. Now Jesus had no mission of this kind; on the contrary He had come that men might have life, and life in abundance.

Hereupon, with the flexibility of this parabolic figure of speech which, like the riddle, loves to baffle the attention in order to cause pleasure by surprise, the parable of Jesus takes a different turn. As He has contrasted Himself with false shepherds, He now goes on to say what we were expecting: 'I am the good shepherd.' But then comes something which goes beyond all that might have been expected or hoped for: 'The good shepherd giveth his life for his sheep.' How different from the hireling who flees at the sight of the wolf! Then again: 'I am the good shepherd . . . and I lay down My life for My sheep.' The sheep are those who know Him and are known by Him. All the knowledge in question comes down from the Father. He knows His Son and His Son knows Him; the Son knows His sheep and His sheep know Him. As already shown in the parable, it is Jesus who first comes to seek His sheep and to make Himself known to them in the sheepfold of Israel. But there are others who have

[1] Zach. xi, 15–17. [2] *Le Messianisme*, p. 18 ff.

never heard of Him ; them, too, He will seek out, and there shall be but one flock and one shepherd.

There was no difficulty in seeing this wonderful prospect of the future, for the prophets had often spoken of it : the Messiah was to be the light of the Gentiles, joining them to Israel in the worship of the one true God. One point, however, still seemed obscure even to the extent of contradiction. How could Jesus do His work as a shepherd once He had laid down His life for His sheep ? This He now reveals. He will lay down His life at His Father's command, but His divine being, derived from the Father who begot Him, eternally guarantees that His sacrifice will attain its purpose. Not only has He power to lay down His life for the salvation of the world, but He also has power to take it up again and bestow upon the world that which His life has bought. And even while He is thus revealing His greatness, the Son emphasizes His submission to the Father, as though He wishes to quieten the scruples of His Jewish hearers by thus subordinating Himself to the pleasure of the God of Israel and to those hopes of Israel which His mission confirms : 'This commandment have I received of My Father.'

All had listened attentively. Many of His hearers are unmoved by His words and say once more that Jesus is possessed by the devil ; thus they confess that they are insensible to love and merit the judgements of justice which they bring down upon themselves. But there are others who are conscious that His words proceed not from the spirit of evil but from the Spirit of God, and that they must be believed, seeing that they have been confirmed by a miracle like the cure of the man born blind.

When the Greek and Roman Gentiles were brought into the one fold which held the revelation granted to Israel, this picture of the Good Shepherd appealed to them greatly ; it is often found drawn on the walls of the catacombs in Rome. Those early artists were full of faith, but they had received their artistic training in the school of the mythological painters ; it is suggested, therefore, that they got their inspiration from the wonderful picture of Hermes carrying the ram. But the meaning of that was very different, for it was the ram, not the shepherd, which was the victim of sacrifice. This pagan imagery had never penetrated into Judæa, moreover, while the Sacred Scriptures were full of allusions to the Good Shepherd that God proved Himself to be of old, and that the Messiah was destined to be in the future. Scholars may, if they please, look in pagan religions for notions that are analogous to the truths of Christianity, though to tell the truth they do not find many such notions that will stand examination ; but they exceed all bounds when they maintain that the author of the fourth gospel drew his inspiration from such notions and then attributed them to Jesus. They would do well to keep in mind that ironical proverb of Attica : Taking owls to Athens ! Israel had often spoken in praise of the Good Shepherd,[1] though she never knew that He was to lay down His life for His sheep. That revelation comes as something new even in the gospel.[2] Jesus will later return to it.

[1] See Psalms (Hebrew numbering), xxiii ; lxxiv, 1 ; lxxviii, 52 ; lxxix, 13 ; lxxx, 2 ; xcv, 7 ; Isaias xl, 11 ; Jeremias xxxi, 10 ; Ezechiel xxxiv, 11–16 ; also the so-called Psalms of Solomon, xvii, 45.

[2] Always excepting John vi, 51 (Vulg. v. 52), but which is not so plain-spoken.

END OF VOL. I

THE GOSPEL OF JESUS CHRIST

VOLUME TWO

NIHIL OBSTAT:

Mauritius Watson, O.P.
Benedictus O'Driscoll, O.P.

IMPRIMI POTEST:

Bernardus Delany, O.P.
Prior Provincialis Provinciæ Angliæ.

NIHIL OBSTAT:

Reginaldus Phillips, S.Th.L.,
Censor Deputatus.

IMPRIMATUR:

Leonellus Can. Evans.
Vic. Gen.

Westmonasterii,
die 5a Octobris, 1938.

CONTENTS

CHAPTER PAGE

IV. Preaching chiefly outside Galilee and the Formation of the Disciples (*continued*) 1

iv. From the Feast of Tabernacles to the going up to Jerusalem for the Feast of the Dedication . 1

Calling of several disciples 2

The mission of the seventy-two disciples . . . 4

The revelation of the Father and the Son 7

Charity towards our neighbour. The parable of the Good Samaritan 9

Mary and Martha 13

The Our Father 14

Prayer always heard 17

The casting out of a devil. The slander of the Pharisees 19

The blessedness of the Mother of Jesus . . . 24

Jesus Himself is a sign 25

Jesus is the light. How we can receive that light . 26

The Pharisees and Doctors of the Law 27

Instructions to the disciples concerning their future preaching 33

Detachment from the goods of this earth 35

God's Providence may be trusted for the needs of life . 36

Be ready for the Master's coming 37

Jesus is a sign of contradiction 40

It is time to be reconciled with God 41

The need of immediate repentance 43

The cure of the deformed woman on the Sabbath . 45

v. From the Feast of the Dedication to Christ's going up for the Last Pasch 46

Jesus goes up to Jerusalem 46

A solemn declaration at the feast of the Dedication . 48

Jesus goes into Peræa 51

The narrow gate and the closed door. Those who enter and those who are shut out 52

The cunning of Herod and God's plan 54

Jesus dines in the house of a leader of the Pharisees . 56

What dispositions are necessary for following Jesus . 61

God's joy in pardoning sinners 62

The use of earthly goods 67

Unprofitable servants 75

CHAPTER PAGE

IV. vi. THE LAST JOURNEY BEFORE GOING UP TO JERUSALEM . 76
The healing of the ten lepers 77
The kingdom of God already come 78
The coming of the Son of Man 79
Persevering prayer in time of persecution . . . 82
The Pharisee and the Publican 83
The indissolubility of the marriage bond . . . 85
Jesus welcomes the little children 92
The rich young man whom Jesus loves has not the courage to follow Him 93
It is very hard for a rich man, and very easy for one who is voluntarily poor, to gain everlasting life . 94
The grace of God and those who murmur against grace 96
The resurrection of Lazarus 99
The definite resolve to put Jesus to death . . . 104
The eve of the great event 106

V. THE LAST PREACHING OF JESUS AT JERUSALEM . . . 108
I. THE LAST JOURNEY TO JERUSALEM 108
The third prediction of the Passion and Resurrection . 108
The sort of ambition to be looked for in those who desire to reign with Jesus 109
Jesus has come to give His life as a ransom 112
In the neighbourhood of Jericho. The cure of Bartimæus and another blind man 113
Jesus in the house of Zachæus 115
The parable of the pounds or talents 116

II. SATURDAY BEFORE PALM SUNDAY 118
The anointing at Bethany 118

III. PALM SUNDAY 121
The Messianic entry of Jesus into Jerusalem . . 121
The death of the Messiah is the way to His glory . . 125

IV. MONDAY IN HOLY WEEK 128
The barren fig tree 128

V. TUESDAY IN HOLY WEEK 130
The withered fig tree and the power of faith . . 130
The source of Jesus' authority 131
The parable of the two sons 133
The parable of the wicked husbandmen 134
The question of the tribute 138
Jesus defends the resurrection of the dead against the Sadducees 142
The Christ is both Son and Lord of David 148
A warning against the Scribes and Pharisees . . . 149
Looking back over the ministry of Jesus 153
The widow's mite 170

CHAPTER PAGE

V. A twofold warning: the destruction of the Temple and the coming of the Son of Man 170
The discourse on the destruction of the Temple . . 176
Discourse on the coming of the Son of Man . . 179
The time of the destruction of the Temple and the time of the coming of the Son of Man 181
Whatever be the time when the Son of Man shall come, we must watch 184
The parable of the wise and foolish virgins . . . 185
The Last Judgement 187

VI. Wednesday of Holy Week 189
The treachery of Judas 189

VII. Maundy Thursday 191
Preparations for the Last Supper 191
The Paschal Supper 196
The prelude to the supper 198
Jesus rebukes the disciples for their ambition and washes their feet 199
Jesus denounces His betrayal. Judas departs . . 202
The institution of the Eucharist 205
Jesus who is about to be glorified gives a new commandment 208
Jesus foretells the scattering of the Apostles and Peter's denials of Him 209
The days of happiness and the time of great trial . . 211
Jesus promises His disciples His presence and that of the Father and the Holy Spirit 211
Jesus is the true vine 217
The world's hatred and the promise of the Holy Ghost . 219
The office of the Holy Spirit. The speedy return of Jesus. The faith of the disciples 221
Christ's prayer for the unity of the Church . . . 226

VI. The Passion 230
I. Gethsemani 230

II. Jesus is Judged by the Jews 233
His arrest 233
Jesus is led to the house of Annas 236
Jesus at the house of Caiaphas. Peter's threefold denial 237
Scenes of outrage 242
The Sanhedrin condemns Jesus to death 243
The despair of Judas 246

III. Jesus before the Judgement Seat of Pilate . . 248
Jesus is taken to Pilate 250
The Jews accuse Jesus before Pilate 251
Jesus is questioned by Pilate 251

CHAPTER PAGE

VI. Jesus before Herod 253
Barabbas 255
The scourging 257
The crowning with thorns 258
Jesus is condemned to death by Pilate 259
The way of the cross 263
The crucifixion. Jesus upon the cross 265
The death of Jesus 273
After the death of Christ 273
The intervention of Joseph of Arimathæa 275
Jesus' side is pierced with a spear 276
Jesus is laid in the tomb 277
The watch over the tomb 279

VII. The Resurrection, Apparitions, and Ascension of Christ . 282
The tomb found empty 283
Apparitions of Christ in Judæa 286
Appearances of Christ in Galilee 298
The last appearance in Jerusalem. The Ascension . 303

Epilogue. The Gospel of Jesus Christ, God and Man . . . 306
I. Jesus of Nazareth, Martyr for Religious Truth . . 306
II. Jesus the Son of God, God like His Father . . . 319
III. The Word of St. John and the Living Gospel . . 335

THE GOSPEL OF JESUS CHRIST

CHAPTER IV

PREACHING CHIEFLY OUTSIDE GALILEE AND THE FORMATION OF THE DISCIPLES (*continued*)

IV. FROM THE FEAST OF TABERNACLES TO THE GOING UP TO JERUSALEM FOR THE FEAST OF THE DEDICATION

WE do not know how long Jesus stayed at Jerusalem after the feast of Tabernacles. The fourth gospel proceeds to speak of the feast of the Dedication immediately after the parable of the Good Shepherd. But it would seem that the two months intervening between these feasts were taken up with preaching the gospel ; the chief features of this teaching have been preserved for us by St. Luke. He spreads them over a period of time which elapses between two journeys of Jesus up to Jerusalem ; the first of these appears to coincide with that which Jesus made for the feast of Tabernacles, hence the other[1] must be His pilgrimage to the Holy City for the feast of the Dedication.

In the whole of this section[2] St. Luke is free of any dependence on St. Mark ; indeed there is scarcely anything in common between them. But several passages of St. Luke's narrative are found in St. Matthew, though not in parallel places. We have no information as to the sources used by St. Luke for this section, but it would seem that he learnt but little from such sources as he had concerning the localities in which Jesus worked and taught. At all events there is much less topographical detail here than in the section dealing with the Galilæan ministry. He gives us much less information too about the people concerned ; we know nothing of their personality, their feelings, their

[1] Luke ix, 51. [2] Luke xiii, 22.

words and behaviour. All we know, from St. Luke's very explicit assurance, is that he used reliable sources ; and it is probable also that he has arranged the events according to their chronological order, at least in a general way. There are certain hints which lead us to conjecture that the scene is laid in Judæa, though neither St. Mark nor St. Matthew have anything to say about a ministry in Judæa until they come to the events which lead up to the final Pasch. We may therefore regard the whole of this section as an exceedingly valuable supplement to the synoptic narrative provided for us by the third gospel.

Calling of several disciples (151).

Luke ix, 57–62 ; Matthew viii, 19–22.

One might conclude that St. Luke has grouped together here these three examples of the calling of disciples in order to throw light on the method Jesus used in inviting men to follow Him ; or else, if the first step was taken by the future disciple, to show how He subjected them to certain tests. But the setting seems to convey the idea that the evangelist is recording things just as they happened, for he is dealing with the period which preceded the great mission of the disciples. Hence it is easily comprehensible that Jesus refused to grant any delay at all to those men of good will who offered themselves to Him.

It is a fact that these little incidents are linked up in Luke's narrative with Jesus' journey up to Jerusalem, but we may easily suppose that the evangelist passed over in silence the stay at the Holy City and resumed the thread of his narrative when the Master departed again after the feast of Tabernacles. Opposition to Him had become more pronounced, though on the other hand He had gained a large number of adherents. He had plainly foretold His approaching death : little time was left for Him before the night came if He was to make one last effort for the sake of the lost sheep of the house of Israel. Is there any improbability in His sending disciples out into Judæa and even Peræa ? To some scholars the mission of the seventy-two disciples placed in Galilee has seemed nothing more than a mere repetition of the mission of the Twelve ; but it can adequately be accounted for if it be assigned to a district other than Galilee. Before proceeding to this step Jesus wishes to gather around Him followers of whom He can be sure, men completely devoted to Him and resolute in their determination to occupy themselves exclusively with the work of the kingdom of God.

First there comes forward a man whom St. Matthew calls a scribe, which does not mean that he was lacking in sincerity or disinterestedness. He offers himself to Jesus unreservedly: 'I will follow Thee whithersoever Thou goest.' Jesus does not repel him, though He takes care to warn him: 'The foxes have holes, and the birds of the air nests; but the Son of Man has not where to lay His head.' By the Son of Man He means Himself, subject as He is to conditions of human life that are sometimes very hard, since He has chosen for Himself the life of a homeless wanderer. It has been alleged against this that at any rate He had the house at Capharnaum. But was that really His? More probably it belonged either to Peter or to Matthew. Driven out of Nazareth, disregarded in Galilee, rejected by Samaria, threatened with death at Jerusalem, what chance had He of resting His head anywhere during His passage through Judæa except on some clod of earth beneath the open sky? The evangelists have omitted to tell us whether the enthusiasm of this would-be disciple was strong enough to keep him to his resolve or whether his courage failed.

To another, as once before to St. Matthew, Jesus said: 'Follow me!' Matthew had followed.[1] This man accepts the call, but asks for delay. 'Lord, suffer me first to go and bury my father.' There seemed nothing unreasonable in such a demand, for it was a sacred duty. Yet it was one of the duties that can be deputed to others in a case of urgent necessity; and perhaps the Master feared lest the man, after having done his duty as a son, might be tempted to fail in his duty as a disciple through attachment to his kinsfolk. It sometimes is the case that a man needs to perform some act of heroism in order to keep himself from failing completely, though more often than not his act of heroism will be misunderstood.[2] The evangelist omits all

[1] Matthew ix, 9.

[2] It was thus in the case of St. Jeanne de Chantal, who fulfilled her vocation so courageously once she had made sure that her children were provided for.

mention of such considerations, for they are not needed by one who is convinced of the wisdom and goodness of Our Lord. His own reply suffices : 'Let the dead bury their dead.' The disciple is called to undertake a work that has to do with spiritual life : the affairs of the present life are a sort of death by comparison, and those engrossed in these affairs should be left by the disciple to render the services which they willingly do for one another. There was no one to take his place in the work of preaching the kingdom of God. The Master therefore gave him a formal command, and doubtless he obeyed it.

There was also a third,[1] though we can hardly say that he received a call, who offered himself half-heartedly : 'I will follow Thee, Lord ; but let me first take leave of them that are at my house.' This, too, may be quite lawful, provided that we do not go back on the resolution once formed. Jesus replies with a short parable. Can a man plough a straight furrow if he looks behind instead of keeping his eyes fixed on the mark before him ? This man of faltering heart doubtless stayed at home.

The mission of the seventy-two disciples (152–153).

Luke x, 1–12 ; 16–20.

Jesus was now confident of the dispositions of those whom He was about to send out and could count on their zeal. He appointed seventy-two,[2] among them perhaps some of the Twelve, and gave them the same instructions as He had already given to the Apostles.[3] There is nothing surprising in this, seeing that the object was the same. This object, however, is now expressed in different terms : He 'sent them two and two before His face into every city and place whither He Himself was to come.' Some have imagined that they served as forerunners to Jesus who followed immediately on their steps in such a way that they all met again at the end of the journey.[4] But we can hardly

[1] Proper to St. Luke.

[2] Possibly the number should be seventy, but we prefer the reading seventy-two.

[3] M. Levesque has even concluded from this that both missions took place at the same time (*Nos quatre evangiles . . .*, p. 119 ff.), but that is altogether contrary to St. Luke's evident meaning.

[4] So Fillion in *Vie de N. S. Jésus-Christ*, III, p. 23.

imagine an advance line formed of thirty-five or thirty-six pairs of disciples with Jesus marching behind them, running to and fro from one end of the line to the other and visiting all the places that they had visited. A considerable time would have been necessary for that; nor would the disciples have returned to their Master: He would have rejoined them after a long time. St. Luke does not even say that they were sent in the same direction. He seems to convey the idea that time pressed. So far only Galilee, including the country on its northern frontier, had received the good news; Jesus was unable to devote as much time to the other districts occupied by the children of Abraham and Jacob as He had given to Galilee. He therefore sent a large number of disciples because they had to go to several districts at the same time. After their return, then He would set out, passing through the various localities where the disciples had visited the towns and villages. So we may imagine one group spread over Judæa, another along the coast passing through Lydda and Jaffa up to Carmel, a third in the land beyond the Jordan.

There is similar disagreement about the place from which they started. Some[1] commentators make Jesus return to Galilee, and suppose that it was either Galilee or Peræa which the disciples evangelized. We prefer to think that the departure for the mission occurred somewhere in Judæa. St. Luke has omitted all mention of Our Lord's presence at Jerusalem for the feast of Tabernacles because he thinks of the Holy City merely as the scene of Christ's Passion and Resurrection. Perhaps Bethany, where we shall find Him

[1] The reason alleged is that the malediction upon the cities of the lakeside (Luke x, 13–15) is comprehensible only if it were uttered before people who had been guilty of despising grace. It is, of course, evident that these gloomy forebodings were expressed on the shores of the lake, as St. Matthew has shown (xi, 20 ff.). But we understood them above (Vol. I, p. 290) in the sense of a farewell spoken by Jesus at the time when He was about to turn to others who would perhaps be more docile to His teaching, and St. Luke intends no more than that. Seeing that his narrative has now conducted us beyond Samaria on the way to Jerusalem, whither all the Gospel preaching leads, it is more simple to suppose that he has put these curses out of their proper order rather than to make the narrative lead Jesus back to the shores of the lake, a supposition that runs counter to St. Luke's plan.

A similar thing must be said of the words in which Jesus apostrophizes Jerusalem in xiii, 34. The evangelist attaches little importance to the effort to visualize what he describes. Moreover, it is easy to see in the present case that the apostrophizing of the lakeside cities breaks into the continuity of the words addressed to the disciples which are taken up again in v. 16.

later, was the place where Jesus arranged to meet the disciples again in ten or fifteen days' time. The time of their return could not be settled exactly, nor could it be the same for all, since there would be different routes and delays of varying length. It was not St. Luke's intention to show all the disciples coming back to the appointed place together like a regiment of soldiers. He has gathered up into one typical moment and one dominant impression what must in reality have been a number of very different impressions in the minds of the seventy-two disciples. The disciples returned full of joy, no doubt because of the good reception they had met with, and also because they felt that their words had borne fruit. More especially were they grateful to the Lord for His protection of them. He had given them power to heal the sick, and behold even the devils had been subject to them in Jesus' name.

In this same abridged narrative of the event, which is merely sketched in its general lines, Jesus says to the disciples : 'I saw Satan falling like lightning from heaven.' It is the vision of Isaias : 'How art thou fallen from heaven, O Lucifer, son of the morning ?' But here there is a more sinister radiance, that of the lightning which cleaves the dark clouds and is blotted out on the ground. Satan then has felt the blow and his dominion is already shaken, for the kingdom of God has begun. But although the disciples had gone before Jesus on this occasion, they will have to carry on His work after Him. Hence the Master bestows on them as a permanent gift the power which they have just used so well. Before sending out His disciples He had already laid the foundations of the hierarchy involving the principle of obedience and discipline by which the Church is governed : 'He that heareth you, heareth Me, and he that despiseth you despiseth Me. And he that despiseth Me despiseth Him that sent Me.' When they set out, what the disciples needed most of all was encouragement. On their return He emphasizes the need of self-sacrifice on the part of superiors : they are not to be intoxicated with joy at their success for they have no cause for pride or even for rejoicing at the powers conferred on them : 'But yet rejoice not in this that spirits are subject unto you ; but rejoice in this that your names are written in heaven.' It is only in heaven that Satan is completely vanquished.

The revelation of the Father and the Son (154–156).

Luke x, 21–24 ; Matthew xi, 25–30 ; xiii, 16–17.

The soul of Jesus was rapt in a transport of joy by the thought of these gifts bestowed on His disciples, by their joyful gratitude, and by this auspicious beginning of the kingdom of God. He was already too closely united to the Godhead to feel anything like an ecstasy, that rapture of the soul by which it is snatched out of its normal course of life in order to be drawn to God ; nevertheless He betrays more than usual the satisfaction and gratitude with which He is filled by the consideration of God's designs. 'He thrilled with joy in the Holy Ghost,' says St. Luke, as though to associate the Holy Spirit with the procession of the Son within the bosom of the Father. Jesus renders homage to the Father, not as to an unknown God whom He is about to reveal for the first time, but to the Lord of heaven and earth adored by Israel, to the one and only God who has created the world as the opening words of the Scripture declare ; and He gives Him thanks for having 'hidden these things from the wise and the prudent and revealed them to little ones.'

Had He not spent Himself in the endeavour to enlighten the wise and the prudent ? But because they thought themselves wise and trusted in their own light, not realizing their blindness, God had abandoned them in order to heal others who indeed were blind but who begged for sight. He had opened their eyes through His Son, to whom everything had been delivered by the Father—all that He knew, all that He could do, all that He was, all that had been committed to His care. And so mysterious is this gift, so exalted is the Person of the Son, that 'no one knoweth who the Son is but the Father,' just as 'no one knoweth who the Father is but the Son, and he to whom the Son will reveal Him' ; and even then, this revelation is only in the measure in which the mind of man is capable of containing such a secret. According to St. John, Jesus had said after the feast of Tabernacles : 'As my Father knoweth Me, so I too know the Father.'[1] But the words, though very similar to those of Luke and Matthew, were not so emphatic. Strictly speaking, they might be under-

[1] John x, 15.

stood as referring to the knowledge the Father has of His chosen instrument the Messiah, distinguished from other men by the fact that He knows God as His Father better than any other knows Him. But Jesus' words in St. Luke and St. Matthew are more explicit in excluding this explanation based merely on the relationship of the Messiah to God; they transport us more distinctly to that transcendent and metaphysical sphere where knowledge is the measure of being, and being is the principle of knowledge. All created beings are shut out from that which is proper to God Himself—the Father's knowledge of the Son and the Son's knowledge of the Father—except in so far as that knowledge is communicated to them by a special gift of the Son revealing the Father.

It has been alleged that these words are 'a meteor fallen from St. John's heaven,' the meaning, of course, being that St. Luke and St. Matthew have drawn the idea from St. John's teaching about the divinity of Jesus. But this overlooks the fact that the fourth gospel was written a considerable time after the other three; consequently we have proof here that St. John's teaching was neither different from that of the others nor new. We may add that it is far too original to be merely a reflection or a development of the teaching found in the Synoptists and St. Paul. No other course was left open, therefore, to the rationalistic critics, disappointed in their attempts to find some commonplace explanation of the words, than to throw doubt on the passage in St. Luke and St. Matthew. But it is so well attested by manuscript tradition and by the versions that not a single editor of the gospels has dared to alter it. It cannot be retouched or forced. It is authentic and it means what it says. That is the essential point. But it will also be observed that it is altogether in keeping with the circumstances: namely, Christ's failure in Galilee and with the Pharisees at Jerusalem, the growing revelation in St. John's gospel, the trustful fidelity and enthusiasm of the disciples, those 'little ones' who have been preferred before the masters in Israel.

To these little ones Jesus now addresses an appeal the like of which never was heard before on the lips of a master teaching his disciples: 'Accept what I teach you, not because I am more learned than you, but because I am meek and humble of heart.' Learned He was—the only one indeed who was learned in the most unfathomable of mysteries. But seeing that God reveals His secrets only to the humble, it was not fitting that He should give them a teacher who was proud of his learning. It is by His meekness and gentleness that Jesus disposes men's minds to receive His teaching. That teaching is nevertheless a yoke and a burden ; it is not a mere matter of idle speculation, but a doctrine to be put into practice by amendment of life, repentance, and self-denial. All this He had already declared most emphatically. But at the same time His yoke is easy and His burden light, and they who are weary of striving in vain to perform the crushing and heavy observances imposed on them by the wise and prudent will find rest with this meek and humble Master.

But the disciples, full of supernatural joy though they were, did they know how to set the true value on such graces ? Jesus bids them to think well on this. The prophets and saintly kings of the past were blessed in the eyes of all, enshrined as they were in the Scriptures and praised by the Holy Ghost. And yet all their greatness really sprang from the desire which filled their hearts to see and hear the things that these little ones were now seeing and hearing.

Charity towards our neighbour. The parable of the Good Samaritan (157–158).

Luke x, 25–37.

All had heard Jesus announcing that the kingdom of God was about to come on earth. They were aware that the purpose of this kingdom was to lead men to eternal life ; on this point the teaching of Jesus was at one with that of the Pharisees. But at the same time He demanded a righteousness greater than that of the Pharisees, while He freed people from the obligation of adopting the observances which they had added to the Law. Would He have the temerity to promulgate new commandments or to abrogate the ancient ones ? A scribe or doctor of the Law came forward ; and although he did not give utterance to so outrageous a suspicion as that, yet he wished to assure himself that Jesus had no such intention. He demands therefore of the young Master with an aspect of docility : ' Master, what must I *do* to possess eternal life ? ' He raises the question of observance. Without any hesitation Jesus refers him to the Law, as much as to ask who could dream of seeking an answer anywhere else. 'What is written in the Law ?' As though discussing a problem of exegesis with a fellow-student, He adds : 'How readest *thou* ?'

The scribe accepts this polite invitation to display his erudition and at once quotes the Scripture with amazing aptness ; for along with the passage concerning the love of God[1] which it was the duty of every Jew to recite twice a day, he quotes the command about loving our neighbour.[2] This combination of texts is not found in the rabbinical writings, and one might be tempted to see in it the hand of St. Luke, attributing to a scribe the doctrine which Our Lord promulgates in the gospels of St. Matthew and St. Mark[3] as a thing conceded by all, and thus providing a foundation on which to build a fuller teaching. The scribe recites as the commandment which lies at the base of all the rest : 'Thou shalt love the Lord thy God with thy whole heart and with thy whole soul, and with all thy strength, and with all thy mind, and thy neighbour as thyself.' That was Christ's own mind, and He therefore replies : 'Thou hast answered right. This do, and thou shalt live.'

Questioned thus with apparent sincerity, Jesus fulfilled His office as teacher authoritatively, not leaving anything for ill-will to lay hold of. But the man was unwilling to be dismissed like a schoolboy who has answered satisfactorily ; after all, his question was not so easily answered as that. It may be that he thought Jesus, in deciding the matter so simply, had failed to see the serious difficulty contained in the solution even though it might be accepted in principle as satisfactory. He therefore asks : 'And who is my neighbour ?' Scripture had taught the Jews in the first place to look on every fellow-Israelite as a neighbour, in so far as he was descended from Abraham. But it was realized that during the centuries that had gone by since the days of Abraham other races had mixed with Israel. Strangers had come to dwell in the land among the children of Abraham, living the same life as they. Were they also to be regarded as neighbours ? Must some modification be made on their behalf in that narrow law common to all

[1] Deuteronomy vi, 5. [2] Leviticus xix, 18.
[3] Matthew xxii, 34–40 ; Mark xii, 28–34.

peoples of the ancient world, that every foreigner is an enemy and not a neighbour? True, owing to the conquests of Alexander the Great, which had caused the decline of the Greek city-states, and owing also to the influence of the Stoic philosophers, there had been a widening of that old narrow idea which regarded each man as a citizen of some one city; the world had come to be regarded as the city of all men. But that had not prevented wars from breaking out again, as cruel as ever before, nor slavery from becoming more harsh. In face of this the philosophers were powerless, nor did they really care. The new principle of solidarity among men, therefore, was nowhere admitted in practice; and it had not even penetrated among the Jews. Try as they may, modern Jewish scholars have failed to discover in all their ancient literature anything that really resembles love for all men irrespective of race and country. If Jesus was not the first to proclaim the solidarity of all men, He was at all events the first to interpret the words of the Law in that sense and so bring it to perfection. Nay, more, He was absolutely the first to give vitality and fruitfulness to a theoretical principle which had remained a dead letter so long as love of one's neighbour had not been linked up with the love of God, which is the true fount of brotherly love.

Jesus answered this question, 'And who is my neighbour?' with a parable, thus following His custom of giving picturesque and concrete answers even to questions dealing with matters of the most sublime character. The theme of the parable was provided for Him by the dangers that beset the road leading to Jericho, along which dwellers at Jerusalem could hardly venture without fear of being robbed. In all probability the dialogue between Jesus and the scribe took place on one of the hills overlooking the Holy City, whence can plainly be seen, at a spot half-way between Jerusalem and Jericho, a mass of rock stained red by oozings of manganese. On this account the Israelites called the place 'Ascent of Redness,' or as the Arabs have interpreted it, 'Ascent of Blood.'[1] It was a regular den of thieves.

Jesus relates that a man was going down to Jericho, which lies at a level nearly four thousand feet lower than Jerusalem. The road crosses the desert, and nothing was easier than for the Bedouin who made their camps in the surrounding

[1] Josue xv, 7, 'Ascent of Adommin.'

valleys to waylay travellers. They did not kill them, they merely stripped and beat them if they showed signs of resistance. This was what had happened to the traveller in the parable, who was robbed of his purse and beast and left half dead on the ground. There came a priest, and then a Levite ; but they passed by very quickly. As they lived on tithes they ought to have shown themselves more charitable than others, for those who fed them were certainly their neighbours. But they do not even look to see whether the wounded man is an Israelite. Then comes a Samaritan, a member of that tiny nation hated by the Jews more than any other, and hating the Jews in return with no less vehemence. He does not stop to consider that the place is none too safe ; he is not afraid of losing time ; he does not grudge the trouble. Travelling far from home, he has wine and oil in his saddle-bag, and these he pours into the wounds, bandaging them as well as he can. He puts the wounded man on his own beast and is content to go slowly, supporting him the while as best he may. When they come to the inn—perhaps one which marked the half-way point on the route to Jericho and still pointed out under the name of the *khan* of the Good Samaritan—he still looks after his patient. He would be unlikely to have much money with him for fear of robbers ; but at any rate he takes two pence from his girdle, which represents the wage for two days' work ; he will pay the rest on his return. And Jesus ends : 'Which of these three, in thy opinion, was neighbour to him that fell among the robbers ?'

The question is not worded as we should have expected. Our neighbour, according to the question raised at the beginning, is he to whom we should show mercy. The application here inverts the rôles ; that is one of the surprises of the Semitic parable. The meaning, however, is perfectly plain. You wish to know who is your neighbour ? Ask each of these three men. The first two are not much concerned about the matter, but the third, the Samaritan, he will tell you. Your neighbour is whosoever is in need of your help, whatsoever be his race or his creed. In case of need everyone is our neighbour, and we are his neighbour too. The scribe made no mistake : he who realized who was his neighbour was the man who showed charity. And Jesus said : 'Go, and do thou also in like manner.' This simple dialogue establishes a date in the history of humanity.

Mary and Martha (159).

Luke x, 38–42.

The parable of the Good Samaritan suggests the neighbourhood of Jerusalem, for the Ascent of Blood is seen from there but not from Jericho. The charming episode of the two sisters, Martha and Mary, is situated in the same locality. St. Luke, the teller of the story, omits to give the name of their village, but Martha and Mary are surely the same as those of whom St. John speaks[1] and who dwelt at Bethany, about two miles east of Jerusalem.

At the time at which this episode took place Jesus was engaged on His apostolic journey. It would seem, according to St. Luke's arrangement, to have been after the return of the seventy-two ; but, on the other hand, it may be that he has narrated their return immediately after their mission in order to be done with the subject, keeping what Jesus had done in the interval to be narrated afterwards.

The Master enters a house where He is already known and loved. It passed as Martha's house, doubtless because she was the elder of the two sisters, perhaps also because her character and capability had made others regard her as the mistress of the house. It is she, therefore, who undertakes the duties which hospitality demands, duties looked on as sacred in the East, and attention to these did not permit of her remaining in the company of her guest. The reason of His coming was to speak the good word to them and He gave Himself wholly to that task, while Mary sat at His feet and listened. Martha was full of energy and would have been able to do all the work required without help. But she wondered whether her sister realized the importance of this duty, seeing that Mary was not offering to help, just as though the work would get done of itself. She manifests a familiarity which proves that she has known Jesus for a long time when she seeks to assure herself that He is more conscious than her sister of all the trouble she is taking : 'Lord, hast Thou no care that my sister hath left me alone to serve ? Speak to her, therefore, that she help me.' In this the worthy Martha went a little too far, for her eagerness was turning into criticism. But Our Lord answered kindly : 'Martha, Martha, thou art careful

[1] John xi, 1. We shall speak of Bethany when we deal with that passage.

and art troubled about many things, whereas few things are necessary or even only one.' Does He mean that bread by itself would be sufficient for the meal she is preparing, or is He speaking of the Word, which is the essential nourishment of the soul? As for making Mary share Martha's work, useful as it is, Our Lord refuses to do that: 'For Mary hath chosen the good part which shall not be taken away from her.' This good part, the best part, was to draw very close to Jesus to hear the words He spoke to her heart.[1] And so great is the authority of Our Saviour's least word that the Church has always considered that a life spent in listening to the word of God by reading, meditation, and prayer is higher than the mere practice of good works. More especially has she understood that union with God in prayer must be the principle of the active life; if that be present then everything is in good order. However, the superiority of a particular form of life does not necessarily imply greater sanctity in those who adopt it: he is most loved who loves most.

The Our Father (160).

Luke xi, 1–4; Matthew vi, 7–15.

Leaving the house of Martha and Mary, Jesus continued His journey in company with the most intimate of His disciples. After a time He stopped in order to pray, and the sight of Him caused His disciples to remark to one another: 'How He prays!' They wondered why He had not taught them to pray as John had taught his disciples. When Jesus had finished, therefore, they complained of this to Him, and He more than granted their request in teaching them the Our Father. Such is the way in which St. Luke introduces the Lord's prayer,[2] and it has every appearance of being a statement of fact. It teaches us that

[1] The text that we follow here, the one guaranteed by the best authorities, gives substantially the same sense as that of the Vulgate: 'But one thing is necessary, Mary hath chosen the best part. . . .' Even if we adopt the wording of the Vulgate, the meaning is not that the contemplative life is the one thing necessary, but that, as salvation is the one thing necessary, we should first of all make sure of it by hearing the word of God. Whatever reading we adopt there is something that must be understood which is not expressed. The best authenticated text is also the one most in keeping with the situation and the most subtle in meaning.

[2] St. Matthew has placed the Lord's prayer in the Sermon on the Mount, but it is easy to see that it forms an addition to the original texture of the discourse.

we must begin with a request if we would learn how to pray. There is no reason why we should not add to this lesson the warning contained in St. Matthew about the unsuitability of vain repetition in prayer.

The Apostles no doubt expected Jesus to teach them a long prayer, at any rate as long as the Jewish daily prayer with its eighteen benedictions.[1] There is no need to speak of the flood of words used by the heathen to inform the gods of their petty interests and to gain them over to their side. Our Father is well aware of our necessities. Therefore a short form of words is enough to give glory to God and beseech Him for such help as all men need. Not only are purely personal desires passed over in silence by the prayer Jesus taught, but even that exceedingly earnest and moving supplication which the Jews made on behalf of Israel is omitted. As charity ought to embrace all men, so the prayer is deemed to be uttered by all the faithful speaking as one to the one true God, who is the Father of them all. Thus they are to say :[2]

'Our Father, who art in heaven' : not our Master, nor our King, but our Father ; whose dwelling-place is higher than our thoughts can reach, or rather it is within our souls where Thou abidest ;

'Hallowed be thy name' : may all men acknowledge Thee to be infinite perfection and the source of every perfection ;

'Thy kingdom come' : that is to say, that bountiful outpouring of Thy grace which we look for from Thee ;

'Thy will be done on earth, as it is in heaven' : for the establishment and extension of Thy kingdom are according to the measure in which we obey Thy will ;

'Give us this day our daily bread' : both the bread that feeds the body and the bread that nourishes the soul ;

'And forgive us our debts as we forgive our debtors' : that is to say, not, forgive us our trespasses *in proportion* as

[1] Composed later than the year A.D. 70, but the elements of it were in existence before that date.

[2] We follow the text according to St. Matthew, which is the one adopted for use by the Church. St. Luke omits the third petition and the latter part of the sixth, perhaps because they are merely complementary to what has preceded. Moreover, as St. Luke's terminology is not so near to a Semitic original as St. Matthew's, we are led to conclude that the former's version is an abridgment rather than that the latter's is an expansion of the original, more especially as St. Matthew's six petitions plus an invocation form the perfect number seven.

we forgive—which would be a piece of insolent and foolish bargaining—but, forgive us *because* we forgive others ;

'And lead us not into temptation' : may Thy Providence, always ready to hear our prayer, never forsake us in the snare of sinful occasions which threaten us in our weakness ;

'But deliver us from evil' : both from physical evil, which saddens and weighs us down unless by Thy help we are led to abandon ourselves wholly to Thee ; and from moral evil save us by Thy light, Thy forgiveness, and Thy protection.

First an uplifting of the heart towards our Father. Then three desires uttered by a soul united to that Father by the bonds of friendship and animated by a desire for His good : the soul's good is the outpouring of the Father's good and returns to Him again in glory. There follow three petitions expressing our need and the weakness which seeks strength in God. Such is this prayer. It takes for granted all the revelation of the Old Testament, a revelation which Jesus has not come to annul but to complete and set free from the restrictions imposed on it by a narrow and scornful spirit of nationalism. Individually, the Jews were far superior to the Gentiles by their faith in God and their sense of the inestimable value of the blessings of religion ; but when the Jews prayed, they prayed as a nation, and after the death of Jesus the nation was to add to its prayer a special so-called blessing which had for its object to call down curses on the followers of Christ.[1]

The prayer thus taught by Our Lord is the prayer of the Church, and the Church knows neither Jew nor Gentile ; she blesses nation and family alike, desiring that all may be the children of one and the same Father.

It may be asked where Jesus taught His disciples this prayer. As early as the fourth century the faithful venerated a site on the Mount of Olives as the spot where He had taught, and a beautiful great basilica, called the Eleona from the name of the hill, was built there to commemorate the fact. But it was chiefly His eschatological discourse that they commemorated in this place, for that discourse was explicitly referred to the Mount of Olives by the synoptic evangelists. It is probable, however, that they

[1] Schürer, *Geschichte des jüdischen Volkes*, 4 ed., II, p. 543 ; the Hebrew text of the prayer will be found in *Le Messianisme* . . . , p. 338 ff.

included the *Pater Noster* in that discourse, as was done by commentators in the ninth century. And now once more that prayer will again be heard in the basilica that is being built there as a votive offering to the Sacred Heart of Jesus, a monument intended to mark the reconciliation of the nations after the Great War.[1]

Prayer always heard (161–162)

Luke xi, 5–13 ; Matthew vii, 7–11.

It is necessary to know how we ought to pray. But in addition to knowing what we ought to ask of God, we must also firmly believe that prayer is efficacious ; and if prayer is what it ought to be, it will always be heard. This further lesson is rightly in place after the first. We are not to imagine that our formula of prayer exercises a sort of compulsion over God, no matter what be the object of our prayer. That would be to look on prayer rather as a magical rite than as an act of religion. St. Luke has therefore arranged this teaching in excellent order, and it is very likely that it is the order Jesus Himself followed in teaching His disciples.[2] In his easy and familiar way He solves the problem which is such a worry to the philosophers : does God pay heed to our prayers ? Is it possible that He, who in His infinite wisdom determined all things with finality, will change His plan at the demand of an insignificant creature ? Is divine omnipotence at our command ? These are questions which Jesus does not answer. All can be reconciled by goodness ; that is the secret. And Jesus knows that we can count on the goodness of God. *Men* sometimes hear even an inopportune request ; how much readier than men is God to hear us ! Jesus throws light on this by a parable.

Night has fallen. The good man has fastened his door. His wife has spread mats and bed-coverings on the floor. They and their children have retired to rest, the children perhaps lying near the door. Someone knocks, and a conversation is held through the chinks of the door. 'Friend,'

[1] The chief promoters of this plan were the Visitandines of Toulouse. The crypt was blessed on September 28, 1927. For the ancient basilica see *Jérusalem*, by Vincent and Abel, Vol. II, p. 375 ff.

[2] A little later the mention of bread and fish may tempt one to think that the scene is laid by the lake of Tiberias. But Galilæans must have found it very natural to use such an example anywhere.

says the visitor, 'lend me three loaves, because a friend of mine is come off his journey to me and I have not what to set before him.' It is a loan that is never refused among poor people. But now the children are asleep, and the good man will have to move the bedding from the bread-bin and the door. That will mean disturbing the sleepers. Really the neighbour is unreasonable, and what does he mean by travelling so late at night? But the neighbour who is begging on behalf of another goes on knocking; the harm is done; everyone is awake already, or soon will be. He had better be given what he wants and sent away.

No moral is drawn, nor is the name of God so much as mentioned. Dare we attribute to God such petty feelings as those of this man who is so slow to oblige his friend, and who finally gives what is asked only in order that he may be left in peace? At such a thing as that, the philosophers complain more loudly than ever. But our heart tells us what is meant: insistent, unwearying prayer is irresistible. We understand, of course, that God does not give way for the sake of peace; we learn from His Son, who knows the Father so well, that when He seems deaf to our entreaties it is only to make us persevere in the prayer that is so beneficial to us. For every prayer is heard. 'Ask, and it shall be given to you; seek, and you shall find; knock, and it shall be opened to you.' Ask, seek, knock; these are indispensable conditions. Prayer, therefore, is necessary. But is it efficacious? In the world of men we often ask without obtaining what we ask, we seek and we do not find, we knock and the door remains firmly closed. It is not so with God. Those who pray are His children; they are speaking to their Father.

'What man is there among you, of whom if his son shall ask bread, will he reach him a stone? Or if he shall ask him a fish, will he reach him a serpent?' Or a scorpion instead of an egg? And yet you could hardly be called good! 'If you then being evil, know how to give good gifts to your children, how much more will your Father who is in heaven give good things to them that ask Him?' That is, as St. Luke explains, He will give the Holy Spirit, who is poured into us in the measure in which we pray so as to make us like our Father. It is goodness which gives itself, the goodness in which we put our trust. Can all that be reconciled with the unchangeableness of God? Certainly

He is unchangeable, but His unchangeable purpose was not settled without the counsel of His divine goodness.

The casting out of a devil. The slander of the Pharisees. (164–167).[1]

Luke xi, 14–26 ; xii, 10 ; Mark iii, 22–30 ; Matthew xii, 22–32 ; 43–45.

The instruction on prayer was interrupted by the arrival of a group of people who brought to Jesus a man who was both dumb and blind. Blindness never seems to have been attributed to demoniacal influence ; thus St. Matthew says that Jesus healed this man, giving him back his sight,[2] and at the same time drove out the devil who, according to St. Luke,[3] was the cause of the man's being dumb. We see here, then, and more clearly than in the case of the epileptic above, an instance of sickness and possession affecting one and the same person. The Scribes who have come down from Jerusalem,[4] far from offering thanks for this great favour bestowed by Jesus, take advantage of it to say again what they have recently so maliciously said at the feast of Tabernacles, namely that Jesus is possessed by the devil. This devil, they now say, is Beelzebul the prince of devils ; it is he who has given Jesus power to cast out devils, these being thus obliged to obey their master.

The insult would have been an abominable one had it been spoken in the heat of dispute ; but put forward thus, in answer to an act of goodness on Jesus' part, it was inspired by a sort of cold venom. They do not even say 'Satan,' the adversary, a name that at any rate possessed a certain grandeur ; but they speak of 'Beelzebul,' in order to express their contempt. It was, in fact, a name they themselves had invented with ingenious malice and subtlety. Baal or Beelzebub,[5] the god worshipped at Accaron, they

[1] No. 163 in the Synopsis contains two miracles related by St. Matthew as taking place in Galilee. They provide two examples of Our Saviour's goodness but need no special comment. Precisely the same characteristics are found here and in No. 225.

[2] Matthew xii, 22.

[3] Luke xi, 14.

[4] A detail added by Mark (iii, 22), which forms a valuable point of agreement with St. John, although Mark seems to have placed this incident much earlier than Matthew and Luke.

[5] Either meaning the god of flies or of some place named Zebub. Probably there was also a play upon words in the choice of the name 'god of flies' for Satan. In Aramaic 'Lord of flies' meant 'Lord of enmity.'

pronounced Beelzebul, which in the Aramaic then spoken means 'the god of dung.' This insulting nickname of the prince of devils was the name they connected with Jesus.

Such a violent attack as this, made as it was by persons credited with such personal authority as that of the Scribes, was of a character to turn even men of good will from Jesus. It was with the Scribes, then, that He would have to deal. He bids them come forward and, calling Satan by his proper name, He asks sharply: 'How can Satan cast out Satan?'[1] Is it thus that things are done in the political or social order? There all division means destruction; when a kingdom becomes a prey to civil war, when the members of a family are divided,[2] it is all over with that kingdom and that house. Do you suppose that Satan is casting out Satan and fighting against himself? That would be equivalent to working for the end of his own sway over men. If we think he is defeated, then he is indeed already defeated, for his empire over men is due to his prestige and the fear he inspires.

Such was the common view of the matter in the minds of the Jews; they attached great importance to exorcisms, and to drive out Beelzebul was considered a triumph. Were the Scribes going to assert that their followers were mistaken in so thinking? Hardly. And yet, whatever they may say to justify themselves will be nothing less than a condemnation of their own slander against Jesus. There are only two powers: the kingdom of God and the tyranny of Satan. Satan cannot be overthrown except by the power of God or in the Spirit of God. Therefore, if Jesus casts out so many devils—and that without the aid of elaborate formulas of exorcism—it means that God is working in Him with greater power, and that the kingdom of God has already begun. For if Satan allows himself to be defeated little by little, so to say, if his conquests are thus wrested from him, if he is driven from the places where he is established, it means that he is already vanquished. Jesus makes that plain by the use of a very simple example, again taken from the ordinary sphere: 'How can anyone enter into the house of a strong man and rifle his goods, unless he first bind the strong man? And then he will

[1] Mark iii, 23.

[2] Luke has turned the two similes into one by using the image of a ruined kingdom in which the houses are falling one upon another.

rifle his house.'[1] Hence Satan is already defeated ; that is God's purpose in sending His Son into the world. What remains to be done is that this defeat should be followed up. The mission of the seventy-two had been an important moment in that campaign, when Satan had fallen from heaven like lightning.[2] The conflict then had begun, and it was necessary to take sides. The Master had ordered His disciples to deal gently with those who took it upon themselves to invoke His name in their exorcisms, even though they had not become His disciples.[3] Very different from these were the Scribes in their attitude. Of them it could truly be said : 'He that is not with Me is against Me.' Those who do not join with Jesus in order to gather along with Him, they scatter instead of gathering.[4]

After giving this warning, which was capable of being applied to other circumstances also, Jesus points out forcibly how serious is the position in which the Scribes have put themselves by their attitude towards Him : 'Amen I say to you, that all sins shall be forgiven unto the sons of men, and the blasphemies wherewith they blaspheme ; but whosoever shall blaspheme against the Holy Ghost shall never have forgiveness, but shall be guilty of an everlasting sin.'[5] These are mysterious words, and they are very difficult to explain.

If Jesus wished to say that all sins are forgivable except the sin against the Holy Spirit, why did He not put it in that very simple way ? We, with our strict logic, would express it in that way. But Jesus' thought has much finer shades of meaning and is considering the soul's attitude towards God. He declares that all sins are forgiven, and even all blasphemies ; hence there is a sort of paradox in afterwards making exception for a single sin, and such a paradox invites His hearers to reflect. All sins are forgiven, on condition, of course, that the sinner asks for forgiveness. No Israelite could have any doubt about the necessity of repentance. If, therefore, there is a sin which is never forgiven, does not this mean that the sin, of its very nature

[1] Matthew xii, 29. His expression is more vivid and probably nearer the original than Mark's, while Luke has thrown the passage into a literary form.

[2] Luke x, 18.

[3] Mark ix, 38–40 ; Luke ix, 49–50.

[4] Matthew xii, 30 ; Luke xi, 23. It is possible that this saying was uttered on some other occasion. It is not in Mark, nor does it flow from the context.

[5] Mark iii, 28 ff.

and so long as it lasts, shuts out repentance? That is how the Church understands the matter, and it is certainly the meaning of the text. Such a sin is the act of one who blasphemes against the Holy Spirit; it is the direct and deliberate sin of open enmity, which bursts all the bonds between the soul and God. The Holy Spirit here does not stand for the third person of the Holy Trinity so much as for God's readiness to forgive. When the Psalmist prays God to forgive him his sin, he says: 'Cast me not away from Thy face, and take not Thy Holy Spirit from me.'[1] So long as he has not blasphemed divine mercy, even though he be a sinner, he has not cast off all contact with the Holy Spirit who cleanses the soul from sin. Thus John the Baptist had pointed to Jesus' baptism, which was really to take away sin, as baptism in the Holy Spirit. Hence he who blasphemes the Holy Ghost does not desire forgiveness and, as St. Mark says, 'is guilty of an everlasting sin'; which means that he is fixed for ever, and for ever answerable for the blasphemy to which he has committed himself. It is this disposition which is the cause of his sin never being forgiven; it cannot be, for once the sinner seeks the help of God's goodness he thereby ceases to blaspheme against the Holy Spirit. Hence it was possible for the Scribes themselves, even after their gross insult, to obtain pardon. Meanwhile, however, Jesus gives them this warning precisely because of their wilful blindness and the peril of final impenitence which threatens them; for as St. Mark says: 'Because they said: He hath an unclean spirit.' To attribute the work of the Holy Ghost, the cause of all purity and the source of pardon and life, to the chief of the devils who is the unclean spirit *par excellence*, was to blaspheme the Holy Ghost and put oneself beyond the scope of pardon. Jesus made a point of telling the Scribes[2] that God was ready to forgive things said against the Son of Man, that is Our Lord Himself, who had been sent by the Father to obtain pardon for men by the sacrifice of His life. It might have been asked whether blasphemies against the Son of Man did not also put a sinner outside the way of salvation and in danger of eternal death. But St. Paul was in such case, and yet he became an apostle. Others can be like

[1] Psalm l, 13 (in Hebrew li).

[2] Only in Matthew and Luke; but there is no reason for questioning the authenticity of the saying. Who would have dared to add it to the Gospel?

him, provided they do not persist in denying and blaspheming the divine prerogative of mercy.

Availing Himself of the sensation aroused by the expulsion of the devils, Jesus referred to the audacity with which the evil spirits behave in order to teach a very useful lesson to His hearers. It cannot be pointed out too often that the chief obstacle to the kingdom of God preached by Our Lord was the pride of the religious leaders of the people, consisting in a feeling of self-satisfaction and contentment with their moral state which ran completely counter to the spirit of repentance, a spirit which He demanded as a necessary preliminary to the kingdom of God. He had come to bring pardon, but men had to ask for it; and in order to ask for it they had first of all to acknowledge their sinfulness. But the Jews considered that they were not sinners like the Gentiles. Were they not established in the very house of God which had now been cleansed from its former wickedness and adorned with divine favours?

They ought to have known that the enemy of mankind never lays aside his arms. Though he may be driven off, he nevertheless returns to the attack, and the ensuing defeat is all the more sad. The Master might have drawn a comparison from what happens in human affairs when a nation, at first beaten, makes energetic preparations and overcomes its enemies who have become enervated and too confident in their own strength. But He chose rather to show them a picture of an evil spirit, who has taken possession of a man and established a dwelling within him. The fact that a man is possessed does not of itself imply that he has been guilty of sin. Hence in this picture we are not given a description of a sinner reconciled first by repentance and enriched by grace, then falling back through his own fault into more serious crimes than before. Our Saviour is rather drawing attention to the indomitable energy of an adversary whom nothing can disconcert. Driven out of a house where he was comfortably settled, he is reduced to taking refuge in places without water, such as the desert of Judæa which the listeners probably have before their eyes. There he finds no pleasant place of shelter. Inspired by longing to recover his former ease, he returns, keeps watch, and sees that the house which he had left in disorder has now been swept and furnished. It is empty. He goes and finds seven villains worse than himself, and there they establish themselves as masters. The poor possessed man, represented by the house, is worse off than before.

So will it be, concludes St. Matthew, with this sinful generation. At that very moment, Satan, angered by the victory which Jesus was gaining over him, was making a last assault upon the house of Israel. Up to the present it had escaped him, at least by comparison with the pagan world over which he exercised dominion. Since Israel would not realize its danger and do penance, its fate would be worse than before. At the voice of the prophets it had been horrified by the thought of the idolatries committed in the past ; but now lulled to a false sense of security by its teachers, not even the thunderclap of punishment would arouse it from its spiritual torpor.

The blessedness of the Mother of Jesus (168).

Luke xi, 27–28.

All that we have just seen is full of sadness and gloom ; now we see the sun breaking through again. Women show more boldness than men in siding with those who have been wronged. They obey the bidding of their hearts and are more outspoken. One of the women present is full of admiration at the calm manifested by Jesus and at the composure of His replies, those words of His which so completely control the situation and which threaten merely in order to lead the hearers to change of heart. With admirable simplicity she thinks how honoured she would be if she were the mother of such a son, who might well be the Messiah. 'Blessed is the womb that bore thee,' she cries, 'and the breasts that gave thee suck.' But Jesus, quick to turn attention from Himself so as to focus it upon the object of His mission, replies : 'Yea, rather blessed are they who hear the word of God and keep it !'

He does not reject the congratulations addressed to His Mother ; rather He makes everyone who is of good will a sharer in those congratulations. The Church has adopted the woman's words for her own use ; when she speaks of the Mother of Jesus she calls her 'the Blessed Virgin Mary.' The Church also judges that Mary was less blessed in having given birth to Jesus in the flesh than in having been so faithful a virgin, endowed with that indescribable holiness which was becoming for one who was to be the Mother of God.

Jesus Himself is a sign (169).

Luke xi, 29–32 ; Matthew xii, 38–42.

Gradually a great crowd of people had gathered round Jesus and His adversaries. The most hostile of His adversaries had been reduced to silence, feeling themselves completely defeated by the intervention of this unknown woman who had so courageously taken the Master's part in face of their calumnies. Nothing delights a crowd so much as a quick, spontaneous retort. It had cleared the air. There were present, however, a number of Scribes who, although less prejudiced than their companions, thought themselves entitled to sit in judgement upon Jesus' mission ; these begin again[1] to ask Him to give proof of His mission by showing some sign in the sky, as Samuel had brought thunder and rain in the season of the wheat harvest,[2] and Elias had made fire fall from the heavens,[3] or later punished the land with a three years' drought which he had brought to an end by his prayer.[4] When asked on a former occasion Jesus had bluntly refused to give a sign from heaven. His determination is still the same, but now it is His desire to explain more clearly to this generation which is never satisfied that His words and miracles are sign enough, and that His hearers are gravely to blame for stubbornly shutting their hearts to the significance of this sign. To pretend to see the work of the devil in these miracles, especially in the driving out of the demons, was to exceed the normal limits of human malice. But when the day of judgement came, they would have to render an account of their failure to recognize a divine sign in that wholly divine life which Jesus led.[5] It was thus that Jonas

[1] See Vol. I, p. 252. [2] 1 Kings xii, 16 ff.
[3] 3 Kings xviii, 38. [4] 3 Kings xvii, 1 ; xviii, 45.
[5] St. Matthew dwells on the following point of resemblance between Jonas and Jesus : as Jonas remained in the belly of the whale three days and three nights, so Jesus will be in the heart of the earth. But it is not that which constitutes the sign of which Jesus is speaking at the moment, for He speaks of a sign that has already been given and ought to be understood. Later on the Resurrection was to be the chief sign of all, and that is doubtless the reason why Matthew speaks of it here.

had served as a sign for the idolatrous Ninivites, who had obeyed his preaching and done penance. Yet He who now spoke in the very midst of Israel was greater than Jonas. The Queen of Sheba had come from the ends of the earth to render homage to the wisdom of Solomon, merely at the rumour of him. And He who was speaking to them was wiser than Solomon. But they remained deaf to the words of life, their eyes were closed to the evidence of His miracles; they wanted signs of their own choosing. That was equivalent to what has been done in our own days: summoning God to work a miracle before the scientific societies. God works miracles out of goodness, in order to enlighten men of good will; He does not allow Himself to be summoned before a bench of experts.

Jesus is the light. How we can receive that light (170).

Luke xi, 33–36; Matthew v, 14–16; vi, 22–23.

The true sign then had been given, but men refused to accept it. When God sent Jesus as a light into the world, it was certainly not in order that the light might be put under a bushel, but on a candlestick so that it might enlighten every man that cometh into the world. Then why did people not see it? Because it is not enough that the light should shine; the eye must be healthy in order to see it. If the eye is sound it gives the whole body the benefit of the light; if it be diseased, a man will think that he is in the dark. Such was the state of the Pharisees, men who were ill-disposed towards the light; Jesus draws attention to the source of their error and thus bids them to think. Persuading themselves that they have light within themselves, they shut their eyes to the veritable light and so remain in darkness. In this way, by the use of homely comparisons which hover on the border line separating the world of sense from the world of spiritual realities and throw light on God's designs, Jesus propounds the mystical doctrine later handed down to us by St. John in a series of more clear-cut formulas. Jesus is the light, but a light that first must be desired, a light that grows in the measure that a man strips himself of false knowledge and exposes himself to its rays, while it is hidden from those who are proud. This is essentially true of Jesus, but it is also true of His disciples ; He is the light of the world, and they too are light.

The first of these declarations made by Jesus is found in St. John,[1] the second in St. Matthew.[2] But how did the disciples receive that light, which is not theirs by any right? As St. Luke explains, they opened their eyes to the light that Jesus is in Himself, while others shut themselves up in their darkness ?[3] These ideas therefore of light and darkness, claimed by some to be peculiar to St. John, have derived from Jesus, but under a variety of forms which it is not difficult to restore to their original unity. In the present instance St. Matthew dwells upon that sad warning which comes from Jesus like a groan : 'If then the light that is in thee be darkness, the darkness itself how great shall it be!'[4] But St. Luke adopts a more joyful view : 'If then thy whole body be lightsome, having no part dark, the whole shall be lightsome as when the lamp with its shining enlightens thee.'[5] St. John, in our opinion speaking in his own name but confidently reproducing the teaching of Jesus, has summed it all up in the following synthesis :[6] 'The light is come into the world and men have loved darkness rather than the light, because their works were evil. For everyone that doth evil hateth the light and cometh not to the light, that his works may not be reproved (known for what they are). But he that doth the truth cometh to the light, that it may be manifested that his works are done in God.' We confess therefore that it is impossible to say in what circumstances, and even in what precise order, Jesus gave this teaching about light ; nevertheless that does not prevent our seeing its shining and reflection.

The Pharisees and Doctors of the Law. (171–172).

Luke xi, 37–48 ; 52–54 ; Matthew xxiii.

The most striking characteristic of the ministry of Jesus, and the one which brought about His condemnation, was the difference between His teaching and that of the Doctors of the Law who belonged to the party of the Pharisees. Already in His opening discourse He had marked out His

[1] John viii, 12.
[2] Matthew v, 14.
[3] Luke xi, 33–36.
[4] Matthew vi, 23.
[5] Luke xi, 36 (from variant Greek reading).
[6] John iii, 19–21 (No. 31 in the Synopsis).

own way along lines altogether different from theirs. He was not one of them, as they realized at once. In order to make sure of Him they kept watch, set traps for Him, endeavoured to compromise Him, to seize Him, to have Him suddenly stoned. They pushed their hatred so far as to accuse Him of being a tool of Satan even while He was working for the kingdom of God, the kingdom of which they looked on themselves as the appointed representatives. When they attacked Him, He was of course on the defensive and justifiably so ; and He certainly had the right to attack them in His turn. Not that we wish to account in this manner for the stern warnings He addressed to the Pharisees. Since He was the light, He had to distinguish Himself from the darkness ; and since the Pharisees claimed that they worshipped the true God who was their Father, Jesus had to show how their piety towards God differed from His own. We might say that He owed this explanation to all those whom His enemies were turning aside from the path that leads to God by love. The religious sentiments of the Pharisees were little better than the attitude of the servant who thinks he has done enough when he has performed his appointed task, a service that is chiefly external and devoid of affection for the master. Instead of showing charity for the ignorant people whom they despised, they claimed to discharge their duty to them by binding them more strictly to this same sort of service. Jesus on the other hand ardently desired to instruct the populace ; but such large-heartedness seemed to the Pharisees out of keeping with that precious knowledge for the acquisition of which they themselves had laboured so indefatigably in studying the sacred text. With what care, also, had they not devoted themselves to the task of gathering from former masters the tradition handed down from generation to generation, a tradition which unceasingly sprang up around the Law like some luxuriant growth ! It was high time that this tradition should be shown up for what it was, a parasitical growth that was exhausting the sap of the tree. The stronger and greener the parasite, the more the tree withers and rots.

Briefly, Jesus had come to heal sinners, and the Pharisees too were sinners, but it was impossible to heal them without the wholesome though painful use of the knife. It would be an error to take His ' Woe unto you ! ' merely as a curse, a calling down of evil. The primitive use of the curse was for the purpose of devoting the object of the curse to the gods of the lower regions. That is not the meaning of the phrase 'Woe to . . .', any more than it is the meaning of the Greek *οὐάι* or the Latin *vae*. It was the fashion to employ the expression 'Woe is me!' to signify 'How unfortunate I am in this!' It is an expression of grief or lamentation uttered from a foreboding of approaching misfortune. If it be a question of another's misfortune, and a misfortune that is deserved, one's sorrow concerning the impending punishment is generally mixed with certain feelings of reproach. But out of friendship we warn the offender betimes that he may be saved while there is still opportunity. It was after this fashion that the prophet Jeremias spoke:[1] 'Woe unto thee, Jerusalem; thou art unclean, how long yet?'

The prophets had always used severe language of this kind. Already at the feast of Tabernacles had Jesus forsaken His customary gentleness. It is the same time and the same situation that is here indicated by St. Luke, for Jesus is still in Judæa where the Scribes plumed themselves on their greater authority and added to the heavy yoke of the external observances with which they had surrounded the Law. He chooses His opportunity during a meal in the house of a Pharisee; but it is hardly likely that He would break out into hostile words at table in a house to which He had gone by invitation. It was during the meal, however, that there first arose expressions of disagreement. St. Luke appears to have strung together a series of six warnings, three addressed to the Pharisees and three to the Doctors of the Law. Two distinct groups are visualized, and they would hardly appear as such round the same table. It is somewhat later that St. Matthew has put these identical words, according to him addressed to Scribes and Pharisees together. But the important thing is that they were uttered and that they dealt with evils that were only too real.

It was therefore immediately after His instruction on the light that is invisible to those who obstinately remain in darkness, and who mistake this darkness that is within them for the true light, that Jesus was invited by a Pharisee to share the morning meal with him. We may well imagine that the man was not altogether wanting in sympathy towards Jesus since the Master accepts the invitation and

[1] Jeremias xiii, 27.

sits down to meat with him. But at the same time he was wedded to the Pharisaic observances and showed surprise that his guest has not washed[1] before eating. Thereupon Jesus begins to speak, and to show that His words were not particularly addressed to His host, He speaks as though addressing people who were not present : 'Now you Pharisees make clean the outside of the cup and the platter, but within you are full of rapine and iniquity. . . .' Then with a subtle turn He sets charity above this observance, declaring that it has the power of meriting forgiveness for injustice and of restoring purity of life : 'Yet give in alms that which is within, and all things are clean unto you.' By this cordial invitation Our Lord shows that He intends to be severe without going so far as to utter a curse against them. It was thus that God spoke by the mouth of Isaias : 'Remember this and be ashamed : return, ye transgressors, to the heart,'[2] or as the Septuagint translates : 'Return to Me with all your hearts.' For what they lack, these men who are so strict about keeping the Law and paying tithes of mint and rue and every kind of herb, is that righteousness which is constituted by inward holiness and the love of God. This grave reproach, which includes everything, had already been addressed to them by Jesus at Jerusalem : 'You have not the love of God in you.'[3] That is what they ought to have begun with, though they were not to neglect other things. Had they that love in their hearts they would never have dreamt of seeking the places of honour in the synagogue or of looking for those salutations in the market-place which they acknowledged with a slight inclination of the head. It was nothing but contemptible vanity, and it was likely to do harm to those who looked on these men as mirrors of holiness. They were more like tombs which betray no sign of their existence ; men walked over hidden tombs unconsciously and by doing so contracted ceremonial defilement. Thus people were guided by the Pharisees, eagerly took their advice and imitated their conduct . . . but God was not any better loved.

[1] The Greek term seems to indicate a bath, which not even the strictest observance prescribed before every meal. Did the Pharisee imagine that Jesus was more nice about ritual cleanliness than was ordinary, particularly as He had just been holding converse with an audience composed of very mixed elements ? Or are we to understand the washing here spoken of as a mere rinsing of the hands ?

[2] Isaias xlvi, 8. [3] John v, 42.

Strong words like these struck at the Scribes just as much as the Pharisees; they belonged to the same group. But such of them as had acquired the reputation of being learned commentators on the Law showed more sensitiveness than the rest. One of these, indisposed to accept the correction, regards it as nothing less than an insult: 'Master, Thou insultest us also.' But it was precisely the Doctors of the Law who were most to be blamed, for they did not stop at merely expounding the Law; under the cloak of exegesis they created Law and imposed it upon others. It was a load which they laid on other men's shoulders but never lent a finger of their own to carry. Did the Scribes indeed merit this reproach? Did they not rather set an example of the most meticulous observance? Doubtless they did when it cost them little; but the cleverest of the Doctors of the Law knew how to make their casuistry serve, when it pleased them, either for dispensing from the obligation of the Law or for adding to that obligation. In after years they were to declare that a man ought to be more severe with himself than he is with others[1] and we are bound to pay due respect to this tardy protestation; but at the same time it must be admitted that their protestation condemns in its turn what Christ had condemned long before, and that it presupposes the contrary practice to have been in vogue. The contrary practice might consist, for example, in applying the indulgent decisions of Hillel in one's own case and reserving the very severe decisions of Shammai for application to other people. Thus there were those who would not allow the sick to be healed on the Sabbath day, though they made no scruple about pulling their cow out of a pit on the same day.[2]

The Scribes of that time, much as they were absorbed in the study of the Law, nevertheless paid more attention to the writings of the prophets than their successors have paid even up to our own day. To the prophets and to those whom they called 'the just,' that is the men who had received

[1] Cf. the Palestinian Talmud (*Sota*, III, 19a, 16). Rabbi Zeriqa, who lived about A.D. 300, cites Rab Houna (died 297) as saying: 'He who decides in a way that lightens the burden where he himself is concerned, and in a way that increases the burden where others are concerned, is a crafty wretch.' (Quoted by Strack and Billerbeck, Vol. I, p. 913.)

[2] The tendency of Christian theologians is surely quite the opposite. Some moralists who are convinced probabiliorists in theory have no hesitation in using the principles of probabilism when hearing confessions.

and handed on Tradition, they rendered homage. Even to this day at Jerusalem a special national festival is set aside when the Jews pay a visit to the tomb of Simeon the Just. With regard to those prophets who had been martyred, as tradition said that Isaias was, the Scribes were loud in condemnation of their executioners, and considered that they themselves made reparation for the crime by building monuments to the martyrs who had borne witness to God.[1] This was a new and very noticeable mark of their zeal, but Jesus turned it against them. For by thus making reparation for the crimes committed by their ancestors they admitted that they were of the same race ; their protestations were nothing but an empty show, for they inherited the spirit as well as the blood of those murderers since they were even now preparing to shed the blood of Jesus : 'Fill ye up, then, the measure of your fathers.'[2]

Last of all there comes a third reproach against the Doctors of the Law : they keep the knowledge of the Law to themselves. The Law of Moses, which is the subject of Israel's legitimate pride, is like a palace of which they have the key. They prevent others from entering, yet they themselves do not penetrate to the very heart of God's word which teaches first of all that we should love God. They stay outside, busy planting round the Law a hedge that preserves the letter but prevents men from grasping the spirit of the Law. We need hardly say that both Scribes and Pharisees were displeased with these sharp words. The consequence was that the former tried all the harder to catch Jesus by insidious questions in order to surprise Him into the utterance of some imprudent word which would put Him in explicit contradiction with the Law.[3]

[1] The gospels, especially that of St. Matthew (xxiii, 29), are our sole source of information here. No trace of these monuments remains.

[2] This final remark is missing in St. Luke, though it has to be understood if we are to solve the enigma proposed. Since burial is the last act in the slaying of the prophets, so the Doctors of the Law complete the murderous work of their ancestors by putting Jesus in the tomb. They would understand Him very well if only they thought of their hatred of Him. Moreover, Luke (xi, 49 ff.) has explained the parable by allusion to the actual events when he speaks of the way in which the Jews persecuted the prophets and apostles ; but it seems to us that St. Matthew has placed this remark in a better context when he reserves it for the last week of Jesus' life.

[3] Luke xi, 53 ff. This is merely the conclusion of the quarrel (cf. Commentary on St. Luke). Too much emphasis is given to it in the Synopsis (No. 172), as though it were a second act in the proceedings.

Instructions to the disciples concerning their future preaching (173–174)

Luke xii, 1–12 ; Matthew x, 24–33 ; x, 19–20.

Jesus did not expose Himself thus openly to the anger of the Doctors of the Law merely for the pleasure of provoking them ; it was necessary for Him to show wherein His spirit differed from theirs. Having thus shown up their methods, He will now tell His disciples[1] what He looks for in those who are called to teach a doctrine that is ancient as far as its principles are concerned, a doctrine, however, which has been completed by Him and taught with a spirit that is new. It is possible that rumour had gone round about His open denunciation of the deceitful practices of the Doctors of the Law, for a great crowd had assembled. Whilst people were wrangling for the foremost places near the Master, He managed to draw to one side along with His disciples. Throughout the whole instruction the dominant idea, suggested by the occasion, is that they must put away from themselves the leaven of the Pharisees, or that method of dissimulation by which they would teach the people only just what they pleased.

In His own case Jesus is still obliged to exercise a certain discretion ; He whispers, so to speak, in the ear and speaks darkly ; and with much more reason the disciples, when they go to preach in the houses, are not to say more than their Master has said. What disciple would venture to flatter himself that he could act in any other way ? Yet the time will come when all will be revealed. Jesus' doctrine has not two meanings, one for the initiated which they are obliged to keep secret, and the other for the general run of people. On the contrary, what Jesus now teaches His disciples will later have to be preached on the house-tops. And if the Master is wrongly judged and exposed to persecution and death His disciples must expect the same. Let them, however, not fear those who can kill only the body

[1] This discourse is placed by Matthew (Ch. x) in a setting that deals with the sending out of the disciples ; but there are several points which are not concerned with the present and envisage a future that is distant. Such is precisely the force of the discourse as St. Luke gives it, though the surprising thing is that he shows Our Lord addressing it to the disciples in the presence of a great crowd ; we conclude therefore that he intends us to understand that the little group was able to withdraw a little from the crowd.

and not the soul, but let them fear Him alone who can cast both body and soul into Gehenna.

Then we are given three wonderful motives for confidence which, without any show of metaphysics, illustrate the attributes of the Father, the Son, and the Spirit : 'Are not two sparrows sold for one farthing? And not one of them falleth to the ground without your Father. Fear not, therefore ; better are you than many sparrows.' And even if it should please the Father, who had numbered the hairs of their head, that they should fall victims to the wickedness of men, like the sparrow that falls to the ground to die, He, the Son of God, would in His turn confess them before His Father in heaven.

And would they be abandoned and left to themselves in the ordeal? These Galilæan disciples belonged to a brave and generous race ; death was not the thing that frightened them most. What put them out of countenance was the idea of appearing before cunning judges, who were so well versed in that book learning of which the teachers in the synagogues had hardly taught them the first words. In all disputes it had been their custom to keep silence, leaving their Master to defend both them and Himself. What will they do when He is no longer there? Then they shall have the help of the Holy Spirit : 'When they shall deliver you up, be not anxious about how or what to speak, for it shall be given to you in that hour what to speak. For it is not you that speak, but the Spirit of your Father that speaketh in you.'[1]

And it is indeed the voice of the Spirit of God that men of good will have recognized in the confession of faith made by the Apostles and martyrs. It was no longer a question of the written word of a book, a book indeed sacred in itself but which was glossed, forced in its interpretation, abused by the subtlety of men in order that it might minister to their prejudices, until finally it became unrecognizable beneath the mass of superfluities which stifled its simplicity and grandeur. This was the sincere speech of men who feared none but God, who followed in the footsteps of God's Son and were ready to brave death itself for love of Him, who used the same language to all men and spoke to all with genuine fellow-feeling in the spirit of charity. It was the Gospel.

[1] We follow Luke's order and the text of Matthew x, 28, 29, 30, 31, 32, 19,

Detachment from the goods of this earth (175).

Luke xii, 13–21.

In the meantime the crowd had gathered round the Master in a more or less orderly manner so that someone managed to come forward in order to ask Him to settle a dispute he had with his brother : 'Master, speak to my brother that he divide the inheritance with me.' Had the man seemed to Jesus capable of perfection, the Master would probably have said to him : 'Give him your share joyfully and follow Me.' He had no intention, however, of doing away with the exercise of the right of property among men. But He wished to make it clear that arrangements about property were not His affair ; He had not been sent for that. His mission was rather to preach detachment from earthly possessions ; and so He replied : 'Man, who hath appointed Me judge or divider over you ?'[1] Then He propounded the following parable.

A man who was already rich had an exceptionally good harvest. But in a country where little is exported and the crop may be more than doubled in a season of good rainfall, too much good fortune is apt to become embarrassing. Perhaps, too, this man had gone to much expense in clearing and improving his land with a view to many years of abundant harvest. So he pulled down the barns in which he stored the grain and built bigger ones. The storehouses for things of greater value, his wine-jars, linen-chests, plate, and money he has nearer at hand. Then, addressing that part of himself which enjoys earthly goods and which he thinks is his soul, he says : 'My soul, eat, drink, and take thy ease ; thou hast enough for a long time.' Night falls ; he cannot so much as see his coffers which are the joy of his eyes ; he is alone. God speaks to his soul, his real soul, that immortal soul to which he has never given a thought and which is going to be demanded again of him, doubtless that it may be judged. And when that happens the possessions of which he had made so sure will perish as far as he is concerned. To whom will they go ? Perhaps, too sure of life to make a will, he has but amassed them for an heir whom he detests. In any case they must now pass to someone else.

[1] Luke xii, 14.

Such is the fate of those who hoard up simply with a view to enjoying the goods of this earth and forget that their soul belongs to God. This is a favourite subject for moralists and satirists—the wealth that slips from the icy fingers of the dead ; but not one of them has been moved by such an emotion as is here represented in this description of a lost soul that has valued itself no more highly than gold. Jesus alone has made us hear that inward voice which comes in the night, God's final warning to a man who is on the way to damnation but who can yet be saved.

God's Providence may be trusted for the needs of life (176–177).

Luke xii, 22–34 ; Matthew vi, 25–34 ; 19–21.

After this interruption, as we may call it, Jesus turns back to His disciples. There is nothing in St. Luke's account to tell us what has brought the group of His intimate friends together again ; the setting in which he places the instructions that now follow is somewhat vague. But perhaps we shall understand them best if we take them to be a continuation of the instruction on the future preaching of the gospel. The ordinary faithful, indeed, who are obliged to obtain their food and clothing by the labour of their hands, could hardly be expected to accept what Jesus says literally in the light of a command. But for those who build their apostolic work on a foundation of poverty and consequently must trust to God for their food and clothing, His words are the exact expression of truth. These in their state of voluntary poverty hear the words at first with trust, then with thankfulness, and always with delight ; moreover, all Christians ought at least to be imbued with the spirit of Christ's words. 'Behold the birds of the air, for they neither sow, nor do they reap, nor gather into barns' like the rich fool, 'and your heavenly Father feedeth them. . . . Consider the lilies of the field, how they grow ; they labour not, neither do they spin. But I say to you that not even Solomon in all his glory was arrayed as one of these.'[1] Was there ever an artist who had a greater appreciation of nature ? But the thing that transports Our Lord with joy is the thought of his Father's Providence.

Then He speaks with gentle irony : 'Be not solicitous,

[1] Matthew vi, 25 ff.

saying : What shall we eat? or : What shall we drink? or : Wherewith shall we be clothed? For after all these things do the heathens seek, but your heavenly Father knoweth that you have need of all these things.' But again He speaks with pity for the sad race of mortal men tormented by anxiety for the future : 'Be not solicitous, therefore, for the morrow, for the morrow will have its own anxieties ; sufficient for the day is the evil thereof.'

You, then, who do not give up earthly possessions, labour for your needs, but leave aside all excessive anxiety, since 'sufficient for the day is the evil thereof.'[1] But you who have agreed to follow Jesus and preach the kingdom of God in imitation of Him, 'sell what you possess and give alms.'[2] And all of you, set your souls free from attachment to perishable goods and store up for yourselves treasure in heaven, 'for where your treasure is, there will your heart also be.'[3]

Be ready for the Master's coming (178–179).

Luke xii, 35–48 ; Mark xiii, 33–37 ; Matthew xxiv, 43–51.

Despite the various ways in which He has applied His teaching, nevertheless all that Jesus has said since He left the Pharisees has had to do with the pre-eminence of the soul, and all that concerns the soul has reference to the question of its eternal salvation. A wise man will risk his life in order to save his soul, but it is folly to debase one's soul in the enjoyment of earthly goods. Not even the most pressing anxieties ought to turn a man from seeking the kingdom of God. Yet no matter how earnest a man has been in this matter, all would be of no avail if he grew slack in his fidelity at the last moment. He is lost unless he has the courage to watch. First, then, Jesus teaches this by showing us a picture of true fidelity and by describing the inestimable reward that is the crown of such fidelity.

Servants are waiting for their master who has been attending a wedding and is consequently kept until a late hour. They watch for him, keeping alight the lamps, and when he knocks at the door they open it immediately, all ready

[1] This appears to be Matthew's meaning, for Our Lord's opening discourse deals with Christian perfection.

[2] These are the express words of Luke (xii, 33), addressed to future apostles.

[3] Common to both evangelists, Matthew beginning with it, Luke putting it at the end of this section.

to bring him in to the light. And he, delighted with their promptitude, makes them sit down at the table, while he girds up his garments in order to wait on them. To judge by common custom, this is an exaggeration ; but it serves as a good illustration of what an infinite condescension there is where God is concerned, for it is easy to understand that it is He who knocks at the door. So shall it be for the whole world at the time of Our Saviour's coming,[1] when the fate of every soul shall be at stake, as it was in the case of the rich fool. The master's coming is the moment awaited by every good servant, and it is the Son of Man who is to come and will make His servant sit down at His feast.

The same illustration, but now reversed so to speak, shows even better how sudden and unexpected His coming may be. The master has been careful to warn his servants that he would be late. But a thief gives no such warning. If the master of the house suspected that a thief was coming, how carefully would he not watch ! And God's coming is oftentimes so unexpected that it can only be compared to the coming of a thief who has laid all his plans with a view to taking people by surprise.

Here Peter interposes. It is the sole occasion on which we find him mentioned during all this journey in Judæa. He wishes to know whether these words of Jesus are meant for the disciples alone or for everyone. Previously it was to the little group alone[2] that Jesus was speaking when He counselled them to detach themselves completely from earthly goods ; that applied merely to His most intimate followers. But this advice to be watchful concerns everyone, though the Master has spoken only of the servants, the guardians of the house. What about others ? It is in fact of servants only that Jesus speaks when He enjoins that vigilance on which the soul's fate depends. But are not all who are in the world in His house ? He is the Lord. Moreover, that which counts in His eyes is not the mere waiting for a Master who is certain to come ; it is fidelity to that Master, such a fidelity as never grows slack, for it is never safe from a surprise. No one can avoid the judgement ; the more complete has been the Master's trust, the greater will

[1] Hence Matthew could place xxiv, 43–50 at the end of a discourse on the second coming of Christ ; the same with regard to Mark xiii, 33–37.

[2] Luke xii, 32.

the reward be on the one hand, but the greater also the punishment on the other.

Here we are shown a servant, or rather a steward, set over all the other servants of the house, invested with such privileges that some have wished to see in him a type of Peter himself, the head of the Church. It is unlikely, however, that Jesus desired to go beyond the limits of parable and make this personal application to Peter. The advice given here applies to anyone who is in authority over others. If such a one is faithful, he will be set over all that belongs to his master. But if that steward, who after all is no more than a servant, begins to say to himself: 'My lord is long a-coming; and shall begin to strike the men-servants and the maid-servants, and to eat and to drink and be drunk: the lord of that servant will come in the day that he hopeth not, and at the hour that he knoweth not, and shall separate him and shall appoint him his portion with the unfaithful.'[1] Other servants, less loved and less honoured, but who likewise have been told what is the will of the master and have paid no attention to it, will be punished and severely beaten. Finally, those to whom the master gave no orders, but who have done ill, will suffer lighter punishment. Peter now knows what he wanted to know: 'Unto whomsoever much is given, of him much shall be required.'[2] Others will settle their account more easily.

We have just seen Peter asking for an explanation in the manner that he used in Galilee. Are we to conclude that the reason why he appears in Judæa only on this occasion was because he had been compelled to absent himself for reasons of which we have no idea? Is it not more probable that, being out of his element in a land that is unfamiliar to him and where he had no landmarks, he did not dwell upon that period of Our Lord's teaching in his catechesis as handed on to us by St. Mark? Luke on the other hand has collected information from reliable witnesses, but it lacks the vividness that Peter could have given to it. We are compelled therefore to draw our own conclusions concerning changes of scene and the various impressions produced on the hearers. We find Luke, after narrating that all-important instruction which has chiefly in view the destiny of the Gospel in the remote future and the eternal fate of the soul, returning again to the burning questions

[1] Luke xii, 45 ff. [2] Luke xii, 48.

of the day—the excitement produced in men's minds by the preaching of Jesus, the signs of the times, the necessity of doing penance immediately. Seeing that the calumnies of the Pharisees occasioned by Jesus' miracle gave rise to His discussions with them, it is safe to surmise that the people were variously stirred up in consequence, and that somewhere in Judæa actual disputes arose between the followers of Jesus and His enemies.

Jesus is a sign of contradiction (180).

Luke xii, 49–53 ; Matthew x, 34–36.

Jesus had won the affection of His disciples, and those who followed Him were conscious of the desire to love God more. He foresaw the coming of that new fire of charity which was to burn within men's hearts, and He cried out : 'I am come to cast fire upon the earth, and how greatly I desire that it be even now enkindled !' But He will not touch the hearts of men until He has given His life for them, and would that the hour for that were past ; for in the sensitive part of His soul He feels a shrinking from all the sufferings He will have to endure, and He knows that only after those sufferings will the flame of that love which He desires so ardently to enkindle be spread amongst men. He likens His Passion to a baptism :[1] 'I have a baptism wherewith I am to be baptized, and how am I straitened until it be accomplished !' Surely then at least there will be peace ! But no, on the contrary ; it is also His lot to kindle another fire, one of hatred and dissension : 'Think ye that I am come to give peace on earth ? No, I tell you, but division. For there shall be from henceforth five in one house divided, three against two, and two against three. The father shall be divided against the son, and the son against the father. . . .'

These words are astonishing, like so many others of His, and it is from their tone rather than from the words themselves that we must gather their meaning. Who could bring himself to credit Jesus with the intention of sowing discord in the family ? St. John makes no mistake about His desire for unity, His supreme desire ;[2] and while He was full of that desire He knew very well that His disciples

[1] Cf. Mark x, 38 [section (224) below]. [2] John xvii, 11.

would be the object of the world's hatred. It is one of the sad aspects of His mission that it not only inspires love ; it is also an occasion for the breaking out of discord.

Such is what He has come to do. The fire is about to be kindled. Has He the right to complain, then ? Though He shudders at the prospect, He goes forward to a Passion that He wills for the salvation of the world ; and even after that there will be a breaking of the tenderest family ties. Was it not believed by all that the Messiah was to be the prince of peace ? Yet see what a travesty the malice of men is already making of His rôle !

Were it legitimate to try to forget the profound impression made by this pathetic disclosure, which everything that we know of Jesus forbids us to take in its literal sense, we might do so by calling to mind that this is only one aspect of His mission, though it is such a distressing aspect that it seems to hide all the rest. He had come also to restore to men inward peace and to reunite them all in a society whose one law is the law of love. It is also to be observed that these sayings of Jesus which are so obviously authentic—for who would have dared to risk such a paradox as they imply ? —disprove in a most decided fashion the contention of certain critics, who see in Jesus merely a prophet proclaiming a kingdom of God which is to come in the immediate future, a kingdom in which perfect innocence will reign and come to pass under the very eyes of the Messiah. Jesus had already foretold the persecution which awaited His messengers, and He now sees it all in one glance. And what He sees is most painful to His loving heart, for it is one long series of quarrels and dissensions. Would that such dissensions and quarrels were to be confined to His disciples and their opponents outside the Church, and were not to exist between His own followers !

It is time to be reconciled with God (181).

Luke xii, 54–59 ; Matthew xvi, 2–3 ; v, 25–26.

In the presence of His disciples Jesus had opened His heart. To the crowd, always eager to hear Him, He still speaks in parables which appeal to the understanding by their simplicity and clarity, and which of themselves call out for application to those who flatter themselves that they alone are the present teachers of the people. They draw near, and Luke labels them hypocrites[1] a title under which we recognize those whom Matthew calls here[2] the Pharisees and Sadducees. The first parable is given under different forms by the two evangelists, and it is probable that it was twice spoken by Jesus. It is time for His adversaries to realize that the fate of Israel is at stake. At no previous period had its history seemed more pregnant with consequences; would Israel do homage to the Messiah, or would it reject Him and so commit a crime beyond repair?

These men who are so wise know, like everyone else, how to foretell the weather. The two comparisons used by Jesus here have, each in its own way, a Palestinian character. The chief question in that country is whether rain may be expected. St. Luke's account says that when clouds come up from the south-west, driven before a strong wind, rain may be looked for; if the wind blows from the south-east, it will be hot.[3] St. Matthew's account is more subtle in its discernment; the sky is red in both instances. If it be evening, a red sky means fine weather, for the very atmosphere is glowing with the sun; if it be morning, then redness in the clouds is a sign of rain. A certain habit of observation is needed to make these forecasts; but would it be possible for any one who could do that to make a mistake about the seriousness of the times, when one saw Jews faithful to the Law living in a state of semi-slavery, self-appointed Messiahs coming forward to summon them to revolt, while Jesus, recognized as the Messiah by the Baptist, was preaching repentance in view of the kingdom of God and working miracles on every side?

Even if people still hesitated to come to a decision as to whether they should follow Jesus or not, surely all at any rate were agreed about the need of divine help and, consequently, about the immediate necessity of being reconciled with God. Do the leaders of the people want to find God in the camp of their opponents during the great crisis of the nation? They are loud in their claims to represent His cause, yet they are just the ones who neglect to do penance and so put themselves right with Him. They show more prudence in the management of their business dealings;

[1] Luke xii, 56. [2] Matthew xvi, 1.
[3] This would be the case at the end of October, the season of scorching sirocco.

they know that it is better to come to any sort of agreement with one's adversary than to risk going to law. Even when it is a case of homicide, the offended relatives will perhaps consent to accept a reasonable pecuniary settlement. Once the case has been put in the hands of the judge, he will have to pass sentence according to the rigour of the law. Try, then, to come to terms with your adversary, even when it is only a question of a debt, lest he hand you over to the judge ; for the judge will force you to pay the last farthing. The appearance of the judge and the threat of condemnation throw light on the situation. There is just time for the Jews to be converted before the hour of divine chastisement begins.[1]

The need of immediate repentance (182).

Luke xiii, 1–9.

It was at this time that someone told Jesus how Pilate had caused certain Galilæans to be massacred whilst they were offering sacrifices in the Temple.[2] It was news that affected Him closely, seeing that He was a Galilæan Himself. The ordinary Galilæans were men of great spirit, quick to take action, and Pilate had shown himself merciless on more than one occasion. It is possible that some popular stir, perhaps of a Messianic character, had happened even though it was not the time of some great feast when such things might be expected. For this reason we see how prudent Jesus had been when He declined to accompany His kinsmen at the last feast of Tabernacles.[3] Had the above-mentioned massacre taken place in Galilee there would no doubt have been plenty ready to take the part of their countrymen. But the Jews argued thus : the victims must have deserved their punishment, since God had decreed that they should suffer in this manner. Now that they had received their punishment there was no reason for any one else to fear God's anger. In reasoning thus, the Doctors of the Law made a twofold mistake. They were interpreting a divine judgement according to the principles of their own religious fatalism when they ought to have accepted it as a

[1] This, at any rate, is Luke's meaning, as we see from the context. Matthew has rather stressed the importance of peace with one's neighbour.
[2] The text of St. Luke is our only evidence for this incident.
[3] John vii, 1–10.

warning to everyone to repent. They had forgotten the lesson of the book of Job. Jesus therefore rebukes them: 'Think you that these Galilæans[1] were sinners above all the men of Galilee, because they suffered such things? No, I say to you: but unless you do penance, you shall all likewise perish.' All the same, the severity of Pilate's action suggests that there had been some fault on the part of the victims, slight though it may have been. But if it was a case of some accidental misfortune it is quite evident that to condemn the victims as guilty was an act of imprudence. For example, the tower of Siloe had recently fallen and crushed eighteen people. Was it to be concluded that they were the most guilty people in Jerusalem, and that divine justice was completely satisfied by their death? 'No, I say to you: but unless you do penance, you shall all likewise perish.'

When Jesus recalled this accident, well-known among His hearers, He could not have been very far from Jerusalem. These were sinister omens: the cruelty of Pilate, agent of the emperor Tiberius, and the destruction of a tower that was in all probability part of the fortifications of the Holy City.[2] But when it is a question of individuals God's justice is secret; it is not always the most guilty who are struck down by sudden calamity. And as His justice is united with mercy, it serves as a warning to others that they should do penance and so escape catastrophe while there is still time. Thus the days of Christ's preaching were a merciful delay of justice, a final manifestation of God's goodness to His chosen people.

This is made sufficiently clear by the parable of the fig-tree, a parable at once homely and menacing. This fig-tree had been planted in a vineyard, as is still the custom in Palestine. We are not told whether or not it yielded fruit at first; but for several years at least—three is a conventional number—it had borne none. The master determined to remove it. The gardener, annoyed by the thought that he has had all his trouble to no purpose, offers to try once more; for a short time he will take all the responsibility for failure. Give it another year! He will dig the earth

[1] An expression that would be surprising were Jesus speaking in Galilee.

[2] The excavations carried out by Captain Weill in 1914 brought to light the lower courses of a tower which had once stood in the lower wall of the city in the valley of the Kedron.

about the tree to give the roots air, and will manure it: 'And if it should bear fruit this next year . . .' Alas! the poor man has so little hope of improvement that he does not finish the sentence; he resigns himself to the inevitable: 'But if not, thou shalt cut it down.'

What a fixed determination to hope for the best is conveyed by this! And when the parable is applied to men, what a strong appeal is manifested in these final marks of devotion which are bestowed so unstintingly!

The cure of the deformed woman on the Sabbath (183).

Luke xiii, 10–17.

The evangelist does not inform us how these most urgent invitations to repentance were received: he goes on immediately to something else. Perhaps he here gives us the Master's last teaching in a synagogue. Or is it possible, after all, that this most careful author has used an apparently isolated incident to explain the secret of Our Lord's lack of success? Has he, in a word, given us the answer of the Synagogue to the offers made by Him who had come in His love to heal? Thus it sometimes happens that when a spiritual counsellor is hoping to see his stern exhortations, listened to with bowed head, produce some salutary effect, he sees by means of some word or some careless movement of the head that he has not been understood or even listened to seriously. This is what happens here.

The leaders were thinking of nothing but the exact observance of the tradition of the rabbis; in their eyes even a miracle of goodness was out of place if it seemed to come into conflict with that. They did not stop to inquire whether the worker of this miracle was not likely to be more conversant with the meaning of the Law than were the Scribes, or whether this healer who was breaking their Sabbath precepts was not sent to heal the nation itself. This woman, this daughter of Abraham who has been deformed and bowed by Satan[1] for eighteen years, is she not the very symbol of the Jewish nation? In any case the lesson is quite obvious without the need of any recourse to allegory. Jesus heals her without a word, but He lays His

[1] There is not the slightest question of possession. It is more like the case of Job, covered with sores by Satan.

hand on her. It was doubtless this action—on a Sabbath day !—that aroused the displeasure of the chief of the synagogue. He has heard from others that Jesus works many miracles ; but that does not concern him, it is not his affair. His duty is to see that the Sabbath rest is observed in his synagogue. The conflict between charity and legality terminates in his mind with a reconciliation of the opposing claims that is almost comic : 'Six days there are in which you ought to work. Come, therefore, on them and be healed, and not on the Sabbath day' ; as though Jesus had a surgery, and ought to have closed it on Saturdays ! Our Lord answered him in the plural, for he represented the whole of his caste : 'Ye hypocrites ! Doth not every one of you on the Sabbath day loose his ox or his ass from the manger and lead it to water ? And ought not this daughter of Abraham whom Satan hath bound, lo, these eighteen years, be loosed from this bond on the Sabbath day ?' And perhaps we are given to understand that deliverance from Satan's bonds—speaking in the moral order, remission of sins—is not only permissible, but most fitting on the day consecrated to God. The time of the Messiah was to be a time of remission and grace.[1]

The adversaries of Jesus had nothing to say : they were baffled but not moved by His words. The crowd rejoiced at these miracles, but they likewise were unable to draw the inference, namely that the season of repentance had come. They did not know that not only are God's graces given in consequence of repentance, but are also granted to move and turn the heart.[2]

V. FROM THE FEAST OF THE DEDICATION TO CHRIST'S GOING UP FOR THE LAST PASCH

Jesus goes up to Jerusalem (184).

Luke xiii, 22.

We have nothing to indicate to us how far westward Jesus went in His journey through Judæa, not a single

[1] Luke iv, 18, 19.

[2] Luke has placed after this the parables of the mustard seed and the leaven, as though to show that the kingdom of God once begun would establish itself in spite of all. We have spoken of these parables above, Vol. I, pp. 187, 189.

landmark in the gospel. But we may fittingly take note of a tradition recorded by the historian Sozomen.[1] Near Emmaus Nicopolis[2] there was a spring credited with power to restore health to mankind and even to animals. This power it was said to have received from the fact that Christ, 'coming with His disciples when travelling hither from a certain place, washed His feet in the spring and the water acquired thereby the property of healing sickness.' This humble detail of Christ's washing His feet after walking deserves to be preserved. If the tradition is authentic, as it seems to be, Jesus must have gone at least as far as Emmaus in the Macchabean country. Did He go as far as Cæsarea? Apart from St. John, who speaks only of Jerusalem, St. Luke is our sole source of information concerning this Judæan period. Now St. Luke certainly went to Cæsarea in company with St. Paul.[3] He may have obtained some of his information concerning the gospel from people living there who had been 'eye-witnesses and ministers of the word,' and we can well imagine that they would have preserved memories of Our Lord's visit to the city. But we must beware of basing one hypothesis on another. When the evangelist tells us that Jesus 'went through the cities and villages, teaching and making His journey to Jerusalem,'[4] we wonder whether his intention is simply to remind us in a general way of Christ's drawing near to the scene of His Passion, a thing that was indicated at the time of His departure from Galilee;[5] or whether he is not rather observing that at this moment there was a fresh and definite turning in the direction of Jerusalem. We are inclined in favour of the latter explanation, and precisely because after a few more verses we find ourselves in the territory of Herod. This cannot be Galilee, for Jesus has left Galilee for good.[6] It must therefore be Peræa. Now St. John tells us that Jesus went to Peræa after the feast of the Dedication. Hence we are of opinion that St. Luke is here giving us the most westerly point which Jesus reached during His Judæan

[1] His history covers the years 324–425. Migne, P.G. XLVII, col. 1281.
[2] It is this Emmaus which is seen on our map. Its site has been ascertained.
[3] Acts xxi, 8. [4] Luke xiii, 22. [5] Luke ix, 51.
[6] Luke ix, 51. For the reasons given above we have modified the order formerly adopted in the Synopsis. No. 186 should follow immediately after Luke xiii, 22. The instruction on the Narrow Gate must have been given in Peræa, where we find ourselves in Luke xiii, 31 (No. 185), and also after No. 187. It is necessary, therefore, to put No 184 (save the first verse) and No. 185 after No. 187.

mission, whence He makes His way straight to Jerusalem where we shall find Him for the feast of the Dedication. The third gospel does not speak of His presence at that feast or at the feast of Tabernacles, for its plan, which is modelled on that of St. Mark, arranged for only one visit to Jerusalem, namely the last paid by Jesus.

A solemn declaration at the feast of the Dedication (185).

John x, 22–39.

It is from St. John that we learn how Jesus went up to Jerusalem on occasion of the Dedication. The Law did not prescribe this as a pilgrimage feast like the Pasch, Pentecost, and Tabernacles. The feast was of recent origin and recalled the rededication of the Temple, after its profanation by Antiochus Epiphanes, along with the erection of a new altar on the 25th day of the month Casleu in the year 165 B.C. The anniversary was celebrated about two months and a half after the termination of the feast of Tabernacles, that is to say towards the end of December.[1] This festival also lasted eight days, during which there were splendid illuminations and a large gathering of people. It remains even to our own day as the great festival of Jewish nationalism.

St. John informs us that it was winter ; therefore, because of the inclemency of the weather, Jesus was in Solomon's porch which lay to the east of the courts within the sacred enclosure. He walked as He taught, for the cold was somewhat bitter. The Jews, determined to make an end of Him, gathered round and put the decisive question : 'If Thou be the Christ, tell us plainly.' It was precisely the question which Jesus had never chosen to answer openly with a simple affirmative, and here St. John is in complete agreement with the other evangelists ; knowledge of the Messianic secret was kept for the disciples. To them alone it was the Master's intention to explain it ; He would insist on the sorrowful nature of His mission which had a character wholly spiritual, and would lead them on to recognize in Him one who was the Son of God. Here again, therefore, since His questioners were not the supreme tribunal of the nation, He refuses to answer yes ; had He

[1] In 1927 it fell on December 19.

done so, He would have risked the exciting of political hopes as well as have given His adversaries a pretext for denouncing Him to the Roman procurator. To admit that He was the Messiah was a dangerous confession to make ; moreover it was only a partial truth, for He was much more than that. He prefers, then, to expose Himself to their rage ; once He has been solemnly charged to say who He is, He will speak without any concealment. But now He reminds them that once before He has appealed to the testimony rendered to Him by the works that He has performed, which give witness to Him in His Father's name. Why have they refused to believe ? They would believe if they were willing to be counted among His sheep.[1] He is calling them, and He will give them eternal life if they will follow Him. Here He returns to the theme of the Good Shepherd which He had expounded at the feast of Tabernacles. Perhaps they had forgotten it, but a mere bald statement of the terms of the comparison was sufficient to make His meaning understood.

If Jesus be the Messiah, it is not that He may show Himself forth as a king in glory, but that He may bring salvation to those who believe in Him. They must trust Him, for no one can do harm to those whom His Father has given Him and who have given themselves to Him. Nothing can be plucked out of His hand, because nothing can be plucked out of the hand of His Father. Finally comes the word which is the revelation of all : 'I and my Father are but one.' He has called Himself God's envoy, God's Son who has the same knowledge and the same power as His Father.[2] Here he still distinguishes Himself from His Father ; They are two distinct persons, but at the same time They are only one, and this can be understood only as meaning some kind of identity. The Jews think they understand what He means ; He is making Himself equal to God : He is blaspheming. They take up stones to cast at Him.

Indeed they were right in seeing in this language something absolutely new. Among the pagans divinity was shared by so many gods and attributed to such a variety of beings

[1] Literally : 'You do not believe because you are not of my sheep' (v. 26), which is equivalent to saying : 'You are not of mine because you will not recognize Me as shepherd.'

[2] John v, 17, 19, 20 ; vii, 29 ; x, 15.

that no one was much surprised at hearing a man style himself god. But for the Jews it was equivalent to a terrible scandal, seeing that for them there was but one God. Jesus, however, had dared to do something more than put Himself on the same level as God ; He had claimed to be the only God, though He regarded that God as His Father whom He worshipped, for whom He showed His love. In what sense, then, was He at once one with God and yet distinct from His Father ? Observing that He was about to speak, probably with the intention of explaining this strange declaration of His, the Jews, though on the point of stoning Him, consent to listen. At first He seems disposed to adapt His meaning in order to make it more acceptable to them ; He refers them to the Scripture : 'Is it not written in your Law'—that is, in your Sacred Scriptures—'I said you are gods ?'[1] The Scripture had called them gods to whom the word of God was spoken, and the Scripture could not be broken. How then can they say of Him whom the Father had consecrated and sent into the world 'Thou blasphemest,' because He has said 'I am the Son of God' ? Jesus does not infer from the words of Scripture that He is the Son of God ; they are too vague and were not addressed to Him in person but to the magistrates of Israel. The title 'Son of God' was given them merely as a name of honour in their quality as representatives of divine authority. The Master's intention is to calm the minds of His hearers by professing His respect for Scripture, and still more for Him who gave the Scriptures, as well as to show them how they were mistaken. Have they any justification in thus making an accusation of blasphemy against a man who assumed a title allowed by Scripture ? In a matter so serious such rash haste was foolish.

Jesus thus gives them time for reflection, but He has not the slightest intention of withdrawing anything whatsoever of His declaration. Let them understand well that He does not mean to detract in the smallest degree from the honour due to His Father, much less to take His place. His works are the works of His Father and they render witness to Him, for the union between the Father and Son is perfect, being not merely a union formed by unity of thought and love, but a union that is due to a real intercommunication, and the result of this communication is that the Father is in the

[1] Psalm lxxxi, 6 (Heb. lxxxii).

Son and the Son in the Father. In saying this He returns to His first declaration in all its essence. Hence the Jews, their first fury now abated, strive to lay hold of Him in order to lead Him before the regular judges. But He escapes out of their hands.

The word of Jesus was beyond the comprehension of the Jews ; indeed it surpasses all human understanding. Nevertheless it pointed out a way that was easy to follow · first to be convinced about the fact that He had certainly done miraculous works, then to believe in Him ; to believe, namely, that He had a mission from His Father to bestow eternal life, and the first step towards that was the knowledge of the truth about the Father and the Son ; to believe that inexpressible truth concerning their unity, a glimpse of which is furnished in these declarations of His.

Jesus goes into Peræa (186a).

John x, 40–42 ; Mark x, 1 ; Matthew xix, 1–2 ; cf. Luke xiii, 31–33.

After the feast of the Dedication Jesus went beyond the Jordan, where He had been when the Baptist first bore witness to Him.[1] This is explicitly said by the fourth gospel, which also indicates that He stayed some time there, though it is possible that He made a few journeys in the meantime in order to preach the kingdom of God. There are no grounds, however, for supposing that Jesus went up to the plateau farther east in the direction of the Greek cities of Philadelphia and Gerasa. St. John clearly indicates the low-lying country in the Jordan valley as the place of His stay, and the same is plainly enough suggested by St. Matthew's 'He departed from Galilee and came into the coasts of Judæa beyond the Jordan'—that is, to the southern part of the land on the other side of the Jordan which everyone regarded as belonging to Judæa, though at the time of which we speak it was part of the territory under the rule of Herod Antipas. It is true that St. Matthew seems to describe Jesus as arriving there immediately on leaving Galilee ; but that is because he has nothing to record between His departing thence and the time of His arrival somewhere near Jericho. St. Mark is more definite still ;

[1] John i, 28.

he makes Jesus leave Galilee at the same time as in St. Matthew and go 'into the coasts of Judæa beyond the Jordan.' There is room in St. Mark's account to allow of a journey into Judæa, the journey, namely, of which St. Luke has recorded a few episodes though he does not actually say that they occurred in Judæa ; yet he gives us a hint that this was the fact, at least by his allusion to the tower of Siloe, and in his story of the Martha and Mary episode, which St. John indicates must have taken place at Bethany near Jerusalem.

It would be natural for the journey beyond the Jordan to take place after that through Judæa. In Peræa we shall meet all four evangelists again, for St. Luke accompanies us there. It is from him we learn during the progress of the journey that we are in the territory of Herod Antipas,[1] and therefore in the land of Peræa, for as we have already observed Luke has quitted Galilee for good. Thus Mark provides a framework into which we may fit the two halves of Luke's great journey, one in Judæa and the other in Peræa, which the evangelist has separated by means of a clearly indicated visit to Jerusalem by Jesus.[2] And thus we find the four evangelists in agreement about the destination where Our Lord's journeys ended when He left Galilee and came into the valley of the Jordan previous to His going up to Jerusalem for the last Pasch : Mark and John agreeing explicitly about an earlier journey in Judæa, Luke and John agreeing implicitly that Jesus passed from Judæa into Peræa. Hence there is no reason to doubt about the main route followed by Him in His preaching, namely from Galilee to Jericho by way of Judæa and Peræa. These last two journeys take each about three months.

The narrow gate and the closed door. Those who enter and those who are shut out (186b).

Luke xiii, 23–30 ; Matthew vii, 13–14 ; 22–23 ; viii, 11–12.

In the course of this journey[3] a question was put to Jesus which still troubles many souls precisely because He refused to reveal His Father's secret. But He has told us all that it

[1] Luke xiii, 31–32. [2] Luke xiii, 22.
[3] He was already in Peræa, for it is immediately after this that the Pharisees come forward (Luke xiii, 31).

is profitable for us to know. Someone who seems to have been not ill-disposed and who had listened with gladness to the Master's words, proposed this question : ' Lord, are they few that are saved ? ' It was a problem which troubled the rabbis a good deal. In their mind the question was chiefly concerned with the eternal salvation of the Israelites ; other people, they thought, had certainly deserved to be lost, and there was a tendency to rejoice over the fact. In principle it was readily admitted that all Israelites who had been faithful in reciting the profession of faith would be saved. But there were some of these who none the less guilty were great sinners, and there were some who had been unfaithful in this duty. The reply of Jesus bears upon three points : salvation requires effort ; it is impossible to be saved without obedience to God ; and there are Gentiles who will be accepted, while there are Jews who will be condemned.

First there is the lesson of the narrow gate, best preserved by St. Matthew who keeps more closely to our Saviour's own words ; or, if we admit that the instruction was delivered on two separate occasions, then we conclude that he has preserved it in its fullest and clearest form. He pictures a man who is trying to find his way. Before him opens a wide and spacious road into which many people are hurrying ; but it leads to perdition. What we must find, and it is no easy thing, is a little gate of the city where a narrow path begins ; that is the road which leads to life. In His love Jesus is going in search of sinners and bringing many of them back ; not all of those who at first took the broad way will in the end be lost. But how important it is to take the difficult road ! It is the way of virtue and leads straight to life.

The second lesson and illustration show the necessity of duly appearing at the gate of heaven laden with good works. This time Jesus pictures a banqueting chamber, amongst the Jews a common symbol of life with God. Those who have obeyed the invitation have come in and the master of the house has risen to shut the door. Others present themselves and beg to be admitted, but the master says : ' I know you not.' They are astonished : ' We have eaten and drunk in thy presence : and thou hast taught in our streets.' These people, therefore, are Jesus' compatriots and have listened to the Messiah who opens the door of the kingdom of God. Nay, more ; according to St. Matthew they add : 'Lord, Lord ! Have we not prophesied in Thy name, and cast out devils in Thy name, and done many miracles in Thy name ?' It is vain to place hope in such things as these. The essential thing was to do the will of God, and they have followed only their own. The conclusion is the same in both evangelists : 'Depart from Me, you that work iniquity !'

Will, then, this privilege of being Jews and brethren of the Messiah according to the flesh, to which they appealed in the first place, avail them nothing ? No ; and this is the third lesson. The door is opened, but not to admit *them*. Within they catch sight of their great ancestors, the forefathers in whom they took such pride, Abraham, Isaac, and Jacob, sitting at meat in the kingdom of God. And even while they are being shut out and driven back so as to leave the entrance clear, others come from the East and West and sit down with the patriarchs. The guilty ones are cast into the outer darkness where there shall be weeping and gnashing of teeth.[1]

How strange a contradiction that they should boast before Jesus of having heard His word, when they have refused to put it into practice ! Had he not often said that good works were the thing of chief importance ? That sort of righteousness, in truth, is not the man-made righteousness on which the Jews prided themselves ; it is the righteousness which is bestowed by grace working through charity. The explanation of this was reserved for St. Paul. The evangelists knew it, but they have not recorded it in the gospels.

The cunning of Herod and God's plan (187).
Luke xiii, 31–33.

Jesus had ended His reply to the question with these words : 'And behold, they that are last shall be first : and they that are first shall be last.' There was no difficulty in

[1] Thus we find exactly the same teaching and same illustrations in both Matthew and Luke, but it is difficult to say whether the three illustrations were arranged in this order by Our Lord. There is a certain abruptness in the transition from the narrow gate to the closed door, and they have a decided appearance of being two completely distinct comparisons. As for the rest, it is well knit together in St. Luke, and it seems probable that the discourse was delivered in this form as a warning to the Jews not to reckon on their privilege of being compatriots of Christ.

understanding that those called first were the Jewish teachers, who were in danger of coming too late through their refusal to listen to the true Teacher sent by God; whilst others, who had at first gone astray, would be admitted when they had done penance even if they came from the Gentile world.

Such an allusion could hardly be pleasing to the Pharisees; but they dissembled, as usual, and feigning a friendly anxiety for His safety, told Jesus with a bluntness that betrayed their real motive: 'Depart, and get Thee hence, for Herod hath a mind to kill Thee.' It is easy to understand that Herod found in them accomplices who were eager to fall in with his wishes. He was more inclined to use cunning than violence, and he did not wish to stir up any more trouble. Jesus' return to the territory under his control meant a further outbreak of the agitation that had shaken Galilee, and it would be still more dangerous on the Nabatæan frontier, for since he had divorced their king's daughter the Nabatæans were his foes. To do away with Jesus and repeat once more the tragedy of John the Baptist's murder appeared to Herod a very extreme and unsatisfactory solution of the difficulty. It seemed best to get rid of this undesirable individual by means of a discreet and benevolent piece of advice, given in such a way that Jesus would be left to think that in departing He was defeating a plot against Himself. But Our Lord was ruled solely by His Father's will; His mission was not yet ended. 'Go and tell that fox'—his trick was well worthy of the cunning beast that is ever ready with some ruse—'behold, I cast out devils and do cures to-day and to-morrow, and the third day I shall be consummated.' Not until then will He go to Jerusalem, where a prophet's words reach further and are more charged with consequences than anywhere else, whether he be listened to, as in the case of Isaias, or scorned and ill-treated, as was the fate of Jeremias; for it is not fitting that a prophet, and especially such a one as He, should perish outside Jerusalem. So He has nothing to fear from Herod, and Herod need only have patience for a little while: 'I must walk to-day and to-morrow and the day following.' Twice, then, does Jesus speak of this three days' delay, obviously with prophetic meaning; that they are not ordinary days is clear from what follows. Nor are they years, for the Passion is nigh; therefore, it is more likely that they stand for months. Now if these words were spoken after the feast of the Dedication, towards the end of January, as seems very likely, there still remained to Jesus two and a half months before His death at Jerusalem.

Nothing is said of the way in which the tetrarch received this answer, which the Pharisees doubtless did not fail to envenom rather than soften in their report. But it only the more excited his curiosity, at present restrained through political prudence, and which he was forced by Jesus to moderate respectfully at the time of the Passion.[1]

Jesus dines in the house of a leader of the Pharisees (188–191).

Luke xiv, 1–24 ; Matthew xxii, 1–14.

The Pharisees come from Herod had now gone away, and Jesus was met by another group. These show much less sign of the prejudice found in the Pharisees of Jerusalem, or even those of Judæa,[2] and they have not yet had the time to form as hostile an opinion of Jesus as the Pharisees of Galilee had done. Everything points to the fact that this is their first contact with Him. It seems as if He is entering new territory ; the Pharisees here have the same prepossessions as their colleagues in other places, but they have not yet reached a final decision about Him. On His side, He treats them with less severity than He has shown to their colleagues. He is invited to the table of one of the most influential members of the party—a chief of the Pharisees, says St. Luke—and He takes advantage of the opportunity to give advice which seems to have no great religious significance ; it is concerned with the way to behave on such occasions. But if we follow the direction of His thought we shall see that it rises to God, using the ways of human etiquette as a stepping-stone to the soul's interests. Now Jesus understood these interests in a manner far different from that of the Pharisees. Consequently, although the meeting came to an end without an open breach, yet the first uneasiness of the latter was not dispelled, but rather turned into distrust.

[1] Luke xxiii, 8 ff. Luke has here inserted (xiii, 34–35) Our Lord's appeal to Jerusalem, a thing that seems natural enough after the recent reference to the death of the prophets at Jerusalem ; but it is in better place in Matthew, where Christ is looking down on the city.

[2] Luke xi, 53.

The Pharisees chose a Sabbath day to invite Jesus. Though the food would have to be served cold, yet by preparing the dishes on the day before the Sabbath a good meal could be provided, and indeed good living was customary on the Sabbath day. Jesus had therefore no grounds for suspecting an ulterior motive. All the same, the Pharisees lost no opportunity of keeping watch on Him. On this occasion their attention was not attracted by His neglecting to wash His hands; but hardly had the guests taken their places on the couches set for the meal when a man with dropsy presented himself. Is it possible that he had been surreptitiously introduced into the room in order that a case of conscience might be raised? Our Saviour would not have countenanced such a manœuvre. His interest was aroused in the man because his hopes for a cure were quite genuine. To indicate that He is not blind to the expectant attitude of the Doctors of the Law who are present—some were always to be found where there were Pharisees—Jesus puts a question to them: 'Is it lawful to heal on the Sabbath day or not?' As a matter of fact they refuse to commit themselves and hold their peace, as their Galilæan colleagues had done.[1] Jesus heals the man of his dropsy and sends him away. Then, without emphasizing the implied rebuke, for their hostility was not so violent as that of their colleagues elsewhere, He suggests the right answer to His own question by asking another dealing with what they themselves would do in given circumstances: 'Which of you shall have a son[2] or an ox fall into a pit and will not immediately draw him out on the Sabbath day?' We can easily imagine a young boy careless enough to fall into a well, but hardly an ox. Yet in Palestine the surprising thing is that the cattle do not oftener fall into the wells, which lie open and unprotected alongside the roads through the desert and even at the very gates of the town. Even the most scrupulous Jew of those days would not hesitate to pull them out on the Sabbath day if they did fall in. The Pharisees are silenced, but they show no great evidence of annoyance. At the moment they were more preoccupied with one of those questions which most touched their vanity, the matter of precedence.

When invited to some house, they would steal into the

[1] Mark iii, 4.
[2] Luke xiv, 5. Variant reading in the Greek.

best places at table as near the master of the house as possible. It was one of their weaknesses, and Jesus decided to give them a lesson. He gives it in the transparent guise of a parable, addressing Himself out of delicacy not to any person present but to that imaginary character who so often figures in the moralizings of the ancient philosophers. He advises such a one, supposing he be invited to a wedding, not to choose the foremost place ; for if a more important guest were to come in he will have to make way for him. Whereas he who modestly takes a place very low down the table will be urged to go up higher. But what would be the good of this petty advantage unless it were true that a humble estimation of oneself were pleasing in God's sight? The implication is that the misfortune and the good fortune mentioned in the parable are merely symbolic of what takes place in the moral sphere, and even on that great day when God shall assign us our places at His banquet : 'Everyone that exalteth himself shall be humbled, and he that humbleth himself shall be exalted.'[1] The warning was very pointed, but at the same time very much more kindly than those former rebukes which Jesus had addressed bluntly to the Pharisees who sought the places of honour.[2]

Then turning to the host himself, the Master gives him a lesson that would seem very misplaced according to our western ideas of what is fitting, even among the humbler classes. But in the East hospitality is considered so sacred a duty that there is a place for the poor man even at the tables of the rich. More especially, when a feast is given in honour of some distinguished guest, no one is excluded. Jesus commends this custom, and pleasantly adds, with a light touch of paradox which is easily understood : 'When thou makest a dinner or a supper, call not thy friends nor thy brethren nor thy kinsmen nor thy neighbours who are rich lest perhaps they also invite thee again and a recompense be made to thee.' To be invited to a rich man's table is not usually looked on as undesirable : it is just what many people most eagerly desire. Jesus dismisses these foibles of vanity and dwells only on what is of importance, namely that we should act with a view to an eternal reward. The poor, the lame, the blind, those who eat their crust at the street-corner, are not likely to return the

[1] The same maxim has an explicitly religious bearing in Luke xviii, 14.
[2] Luke xi, 43.

compliment when we invite them to a feast. God will charge Himself with that at the resurrection of the just.

Struck by these words one of the guests cried out: 'Blessed is he that shall eat bread in the kingdom of God!' Thus was Our Lord's purpose achieved. In this company, where there was such a readiness to discuss spiritual matters—not so frequently perhaps at table—He had gradually raised their thoughts to that consideration of the kingdom of God which was the principal subject of His teaching. But did not these men, who knew what a supreme happiness it was to be admitted to the kingdom of God, regard themselves as entitled to enter it? Their devotion to the study of the Law, their upbringing, and the fact that they belonged to the same party as their host, had gained for them their welcome to the house of this distinguished Pharisee. The Pharisees, the *élite* of Israel, counted on entering the kingdom of God as though it were their own home. But alas! they were in a fair way to lose their places there through the contemptuous way in which they received the summons of God's ambassador. He therefore tells them the following parable.

A man gave a feast and invited many guests of his own rank in society, as we should say nowadays. Following ancient custom, he sent a servant immediately before the feast to remind them that they had promised to come and to warn them that all was prepared. Everyone makes some excuse. One has bought a field, probably through the instrumentality of an agent so as not to appear in the transaction himself, and is anxious to go and see it. Another has bought five yoke of oxen, and wishes to try them at once in order to see whether he has been cheated. A third has just been married, which is sufficient explanation of his not coming. Not one of those invited comes to the feast. Thereupon the master of the house sends his servant into the streets to summon the poor, the lame, the blind, all those, in fact, whom no one usually troubles about. These need no persuading. But there is still room, and the servant goes outside the city, along the highways and hedges, where he finds others who are more wretched than the poor, the lame and the blind. Perhaps they object that it is too far, or make some other excuse; but the servant must insist and bring them all in. All the seats must be filled, and none of those who treated the invitation so contemptuously will be allowed to enter.[1]

We are not to look for positive allegory in all these details. The servant is not Jesus, with the mission of inviting men to repentance. In reply to those who say that, at any rate, the first to be invited are Jews, it may be pointed out that the first group of people called in to take their place are also from the city and therefore Jews also; hence it would have to be said that the guests first invited ought to be the Pharisees. Yet none of the excuses offered in the parable are characteristic of the opposition offered to Jesus by the Pharisees. Nor have the chance guests given any proofs of goodwill before they were invited, and this is especially true of those who come last. The meaning is, therefore, that the master of the house will carry out his plan whatever happens; that they who have treated him with contempt will be excluded and replaced by others, even should those be such as people are not usually proud to have at their table. Obviously it must be applied to the kingdom of God, hence it necessarily follows that the master of the house represents God. Those whom He has invited must beware of being absorbed by the cares of this present world to such an extent as not to answer His summons when the time comes. Blessed, said Our Lord's fellow-guest, is he who shall eat bread in the kingdom of God! Blessed, answers Jesus, are they who do not forget that they have been invited and are not shut out at the critical moment. That moment does not refer to the coming of the kingdom of God upon earth, since the matter in question was the kingdom of the world to come. There is, then, no question of Messianism here. As the summons comes to all at the same time, what Jesus is contemplating is the last judgement rather than the death of each individual. But it comes to the same thing. Thus He does not leave His hosts without uttering a very serious warning which they may take to themselves with advantage. But no dispute was started. Decidedly the atmosphere in Peræa was not so charged as in Judæa.

[1] This is an analysis of St. Luke's text. That of St. Matthew is substantially the same. It is possible that the parable was spoken only once, and that each of the evangelists arranged it to suit his own purpose. Such, at any rate, is the opinion of certain eminent Catholic exegetes. Hence we shall not dwell upon St. Matthew's arrangement, which brings out the Messianic theme in greater relief.

What dispositions are necessary for following Jesus (192–193).

Luke xiv, 25–33.

Jesus had not hitherto appeared in these parts, though He had sent His disciples there to prepare the way for Him. For this reason, and also because of the miracles He worked, the crowd accompanied Him in order to listen to Him when He taught. It is probable also that some regarded Him as the Messiah ; hence there were those who followed Him in the expectation of some sensational event, and some among these were prepared to fight for Him. But people like these were not true disciples ; what Jesus wanted was disciples ready to leave all and suffer all with Him. The difficulties a disciple must encounter are enumerated in three strophes, the ending of each one, 'He cannot be My disciple,' showing that they all have the same object in view.[1] It is cause for surprise that the obstacles are not put in order of increasing difficulty, as the rules of simple rhetoric would have prescribed. It would seem that Jesus first of all makes greater demands on the devotion of certain individuals in extreme cases, and then proceeds to propose a less degree of renunciation for the generality of people.

He who would follow Jesus, then, must first realize that he may find himself at variance with his nearest relations ; he will in that case have to sacrifice his affections even though they be most legitimate in character. This is expressed in the rugged antithetical fashion of the Semites as hating father and mother, wife and children. It might be necessary for a man to sacrifice even his own life. And finally he must reckon with the necessity of having to sacrifice temporal possessions, though to generous souls this loss is not so formidable : it is taken as part of the bargain, to speak colloquially. But why this prospect of death ? Because it was present to Jesus' mind, and in the then very common form of crucifixion. A man condemned to crucifixion had first to carry the cross to the place of execution ; the disciple therefore must be prepared to walk, not in a triumphal procession, but in a grim file of condemned criminals with his cross upon his shoulder. If a man does not feel that he has courage to go to such lengths it would be better that

[1] Luke xiv, 26, 27, 33.

he should not come to follow Jesus than that he should follow Him first only to desert Him afterwards.

The enthusiasm of a crowd is easily aroused, but their ardour flags at the least check. Presumption is more dangerous still, for it not only makes us more liable to fail through lack of reflection, but it also exposes us to ridicule.

This lesson the Master teaches by the aid of two parables. When a man has a mind to build a house he should make certain before beginning that he has enough money to finish it. Before going to war, even for a just cause, we must first estimate our own forces and those of our enemy ; if we find that we are the weaker it would be wiser to come to terms and so avoid disaster. Does this mean that Jesus wishes to dissuade those from following Him who are timid and not inspired by heroic sentiments ? No, for His purpose is rather to counsel prudence to those who are over-daring ; their thoughtless impulse is very different from a serious determination. The good disciple will ensure success by using the proper means. In the affairs of the present world the requisite means for accomplishing our purpose is money ; it is necessary if one wishes to build, and it has been called the sinews of war. But in the spiritual order values are reversed, hence the paradoxical appearance of the conclusion to the two parables. The first of the resources with which a true disciple must be provided is renunciation of all earthly possessions. Once freed from their weight he will be able to follow Jesus joyfully and with a light step. As we have said above regarding family relationship, this is to be understood in the measure that circumstances and God's call demand ; we may be called either to detachment only from affection for all earthly goods, or else to the renunciation of all possessions in actual fact.

God's joy in pardoning sinners (194–197).

Luke xv, 1–32 ; Matthew xviii, 12–14.

The whole of this fifteenth chapter of St. Luke is a revelation of divine mercy towards sinners, a mercy that even anticipates the repentance of the sinner and pursues him in order to render him worthy of pardon. And even that is not all ; for with mercy the Israelites were already familiar, and they glorified it in the Psalms as well as in all the history of their past. What is here revealed by the Son is the joy that overflows from the Father's heart when He wins back one of His children by repentance. Who would have presumed to believe such a thing unless it had first been affirmed by Him who alone has entered into this secret, who Himself shares that infinite clemency with His Father, who is the instrument of it, and who has made it known to us in words which have drawn tears from the eyes of so many?

No doubt one of the reasons why the publicans and sinners in Peræa, as in Galilee, drew near to hear Jesus was because He received them kindly and encouraged them to return to God. But the Master went a step further—in the eyes of some a step too far in the wrong direction: He ate with these sinners and so risked being contaminated, if not by their example at any rate by their touch. The Pharisees and Scribes, everywhere the same, showed themselves scandalized; but Jesus refused to begin a formal debate with them on the subject. That would have been to meet them on their own ground and would not have left Him the last word. He therefore drew them into His own sphere in order to teach them, and still more these despised sinners, what takes place in heaven amongst the angels—nay, even in the very heart of God—when a straying sinner returns to the fold, is restored to God's treasure, receives from his Father the kiss of peace. These three things are shown by three parables whose meaning touches even the hardest of hearts.

What are the feelings of the Creator when one of these insignificant creatures of His forsakes Him or dares to offend Him? His one thought, if we may speak in such a way, is to bring that creature back to Himself. God is like a man who owns a hundred sheep, one of which has strayed. The sheep are in the desert, whither the flocks are led in the winter season in order to feed on the scanty covering of grass which then tinges the tawny hills of Palestine with green. One of the flock, more avid than the rest, has strayed in search of better grass and has thus been lost to sight. What will the owner do? He will leave the other ninety-nine where they are, no doubt entrusting them to the other shepherds; but the chief thing to observe here is that he goes himself to seek the sheep that has disappeared. And when he has found it all tired out he brings it back on his shoulders—a thing that is never done except in the case of the tiny lambs—because he is full of joy ; so full indeed that he wishes his friends and neighbours to share his joy. That is what happens amongst men ; and Jesus concludes : 'I say to you'—and what follows is hardly conceivable—'there shall be joy in heaven upon one sinner that doth penance more than upon ninety-nine just who need not penance.' The just, no doubt, are loved more ; but they have not given cause in heaven for so much solicitude, a solicitude which has borne fruit in so much joy.[1]

And now see a woman, a good housewife, who had ten drachmas (about eight shillings) for household expenses. She discovers that one is missing, but it is impossible to find it in the poorly lighted room amongst all the things with which the floor is littered. She lights a lamp, sweeps the room, and searches unwearyingly until she finds her drachma again. Assuredly she had told her neighbours about her loss, and she also gives them the good news when she finds it, calling them in to share her joy. That is how God's angels rejoice over a repentant sinner ; there is joy in heaven amongst the angels, and joy in God too, for is not divine life all happiness and joy ? But how can we attribute to God anything resembling anxiety, for we learn from the philosophers that God is impassible ? There is no doubt about that truth of philosophy, but expressed in such a manner it does not help us very much spiritually. What does help us is to know that in the fulness of the divine perfections there is something that takes the place of, while infinitely surpassing, the most tender human solicitude. It is knowledge of this which gives the sinner courage to love God. Those feelings of His Father have been revealed to us by Jesus in the parable of the prodigal son.

A father had two sons. The younger, tired of his regular and monotonous life at home, attracted by the mirage of the blue hills in the distance, comes to his father and bluntly asks him to give him now the inheritance that is one day to be his. That means stripping the father of his property even before his death. But, without any remonstrance, the

[1] The parable in Matthew xviii, 12–14 is evidently the same though it gives only the main points. Told in connection with the care of little ones, it calls upon superiors, who should be the shepherds, not to let the weak members of the community be lost. This is the desire of the Father who is in heaven, and it is precisely these sentiments of the Father that are the essence of the parable.

father at once divides all his property between his two sons, caring nothing about his fortune since he is to lose his child. The prodigal—such is the name preserved for him—sells the very land on which he has grown up from childhood, and soon dissipates the money by foolish extravagance in a far city. Now his position is wretched enough, but it becomes more wretched still because of a famine ; everyone's thoughts are concerned with how to keep himself alive : there is no allowance or alms to spare for strangers. Being thus without resources of any kind, the prodigal enters the service of a rich man and is sent to live in the country, where living is cheaper, to tend pigs. His food is cut down to a mere pittance, more carefully measured out than that of the animals being fattened for sale, so that he is reduced to the desire of filling his empty stomach with the carob pods or locust beans thrown to the swine—no great feast ! Then he begins to reflect. Superficial allurements had dazzled his eyes, but now his wretchedness opens his eyes to the truth within his soul. His first cry is that of a suffering animal : I am dying of hunger. But recollections of the past bring back the memory of his father and of his goodness, while at the same time he realizes how great has been his own ingratitude. Though fainting at first from weakness, he now rises confidently : ' I will arise and go to my father and say to him : Father, I have sinned against heaven and before thee. I am not worthy to be called thy son ; make me as one of thy hired servants.' Thus we see him already haunted by the thought of God, the sense of his own unworthiness, and the determination to make amends for the wrong he has done. He returns home.

He is still a long way off when his father, standing in the noonday heat and once more scanning the paths which lead down from the dusty hills, catches sight of his son. He is walking along weary and ashamed. The father runs and, throwing his arms about his child's neck, covers him with kisses. He listens to the confession whispered brokenly in his ear : ' Father, I have sinned against heaven and before thee. I am not now worthy to be called thy son.' The son says nothing, however, about becoming ' a hireling,' for he knows that his father would not even listen to the word ; and to utter it in the midst of this tender welcome would sound like an insult offered to a kindness so great. Moreover, there was no time to utter it, for the father breaks in upon him—and what human father has ever carried forgetfulness of an injury so far as thus to blot out the past completely ?—' Bring forth quickly the best robe and put it on him ; and put a ring on his hand and shoes on his feet. And bring hither the fatted calf, kill it, and let us eat and make merry. For this my son was dead and is come to life again, he was lost and is found again.' We are carried to such heights that it is heaven we see, and there is nothing higher. But Jesus goes on to say that mercy does justice no wrong, and it is necessary for the just to understand this well.

The elder son had behaved as a good son when the younger went away ; his share of the property he had left at his father's disposal. But to-day, as he returns from the fields where he has been working as usual, he hears the sounds of music and dancing, which means that some occasion has arisen for rejoicing out of the ordinary. Why has his father said nothing about it to him ? In order to find out what is happening he is obliged to ask a servant—a low fellow with no delicacy of feeling, inclined to treat the matter as a subject for jesting, and caring only for the good cheer which it has occasioned : ' Thy brother is come, and thy father hath killed the fatted calf because he hath received him safe.' Safe, that is to say, in good health ! The elder brother enquires no further. He has not seen the rags, the bare feet, the wasted body, the wan features, the failing knees, the tears. So then, after devouring his property with harlots, his brother, still in good health despite so many excesses, has come back quite pleased with himself and unashamed, doubtless with no further idea than to wring from his father's weakness the means of pursuing the same course all over again. It is in this way that we may often find an explanation of the severity of good people ; they know nothing of what the sinner has suffered, nor whether, in his contrition, he may not have accepted the sufferings in expiation of his sins. Under the influence of this picture which he has drawn for himself, the elder son grows angry and refuses to join in the rejoicings ; and when his father comes to meet him his ill-humour breaks forth without restraint : ' Behold for so many years do I serve thee and I have never transgressed thy commandment, and yet thou hast never given me a kid to make merry with my friends. But as soon as this thy son is come, who hath devoured his substance with harlots, thou hast killed for him the fatted calf.'

Unconsciously, he betrays how imperfect are his own dispositions. He does not say ' my brother,' but ' thy son ' ; and that, perhaps, is not inexcusable. But why does he not say ' my father ' ? The truth is that though he has done his duty, he has done it more like a servant than a son. He has not been guilty of disobedience, and that is very much ; but it was not a smile or a loving word that he looked for as a reward for his obedience : he would have been content with the presents that are given to servants. All the same his father loved him, and loved him more than he thought. And if this father had not heaped marks of affection on him, perhaps it was because he had been kept at a distance by the coldness of his son. Therefore, he gently reminds his son that he has failed to appreciate his happiness, the happiness of being with his father and sharing all his possessions. Let him now be content to share also his father's joy at having found his lost son once more.

Jesus gives no explanation of the parable : it does not need it. The prodigal son is the sinner ; his father is God, the Father of mercies. The elder son is a little like the Pharisees who murmured at Our Saviour's indulgence towards publicans and sinners ; but his intimacy with his father, though he fails to realize its value, makes him rather the type of the just who serve the Lord faithfully, but emphasize too much the notion of service. God invites them to be more open-hearted with Him and more indulgent towards others. Divine mercy, like all the attributes of God, infinitely surpasses our understanding ; but our holding it so dear dates from the day when Jesus uttered the parable of the prodigal son.

The use of earthly goods (198–202).

Luke xvi, 1–31.

With this glimpse of the friendship between the just man and his Lord ends the parables about God's joy over the return of the sinner. These parables do not alter in any way the fundamental principle that men must resolve to serve Him at all costs, and it would seem that Jesus returns now to the subject of renunciation in order to show that there is a positive aspect of renunciation which is very encouraging. He had said before : 'He that doth not renounce all that he possesseth cannot be my disciple.'[1] But was it necessary for a man to strip himself of everything ? And what was to be done with the things a man gave up in order to follow Jesus ? Here we learn that Jesus does not teach a doctrine of destructive nihilism, but makes an appeal for charity towards our neighbour. It is to the poor we must give the wealth of which we rid ourselves ; and if we keep it for ourselves we must consider that we are merely acting as God's stewards in its administration. This lesson begins with the parable of the unfaithful steward, generally regarded as a very difficult parable though indeed its meaning is very clear.

A rich man had a steward or farm bailiff, who was in a position to enter into what bargains he chose with such as traded with his master. Nothing was easier than to put into his own pocket part of the money he received ; but by doing so he ran the risk of information being carried to his master by discontented purchasers who suspected that they might have fared better with the master than with the steward. That is what happened. The master did not deal with him severely, however, for profits or commissions of that kind are common enough ; but he did at any rate call for an account, which was to be the last, for he refused to have such an unscrupulous servant in his employment any longer. The steward, unused to any sort of work but that of superintending and accustomed to deference at the hands of his master's workmen and customers, does not know what to do. He is not made for manual labour, and it would cover him with shame to beg. An idea comes to him : he knows what he will do. Far from feeling repentance under the blow of his disgrace, the unfaithful steward turns to theft and forgery, but he manages it so cleverly that he succeeds in making others commit the actual forgery. There were several of the traders dealing with his master who owed him large amounts. He gives them back their notes of hand : 'Quick now ! Instead of the hundred barrels of oil that you owe, write that you have had fifty, and instead of the hundred measures of wheat, put eighty.' They will not go now and inform against him ! No ; on the contrary he will have them at his mercy.

[1] Luke xiv, 33.

When he is dismissed by his master he will go and ask hospitality, now of one, now of another, and if they do not receive him willingly they will have to put up with him. And how they will laugh together, he and they, over the manner in which they have got the better of his master !

The master, however, got to know of it, though he had been cheated so skilfully that it was difficult for him to get evidence against the man who had robbed him. He decided to treat it as a joke and made the same comment as anyone else would under the circumstances : A rascal, but a clever rascal !

All the same there was a distinct lack of zeal for any ideal of justice in all this, and Jesus blames both the guilty connivance of those who stood to gain and the amused indulgence of the master. Conduct of that kind is characteristic of the children of this world who think only of temporal things and of gain ; they are quick to understand one another and show greater shrewdness in their business dealings than the children of light. The children of light ! This is the first time the expression appears in the gospels, for the light in question is the light which now shines forth from this parable and casts its rays upon the faces of those whose eyes are fixed on God. What is it that the children of light are to do ?

These temporal goods, which only too often are acquired, handed on, accumulated, or gained, by none too scrupulous means, stand for money. Injustice has left its defiling touch on money. Those who have control of it must be merely the administrators of it, like the steward in the parable. They should then use as much astuteness as he employed, not like him in order to cheat their Master, but by setting aside a portion of their wealth for the poor who are the friends of their Master, if they desire to be received into an everlasting home by those poor who will one day be reigning with God in heaven. And those who wish to be disciples must examine the matter still more closely. Their Lord has already charged them with the administration of the things necessary for the life of the body, that is to say the goods of this world—a very small matter. But if they are not faithful in using these things as He intends them to be used, how will they be faithful when they are given charge of more important affairs, namely the interests of the soul ? If the things that are external to themselves lead them astray they will be incapable of guarding the treasure that is part of themselves; hence that treasure, which is their only true good, God's destiny for them, their real possession, will not be entrusted to their care. For in that case it will be money which rules them, the money which they turn into an instrument of pleasure or power. In so far as they are unwilling to strip themselves of it in order to strive after a more noble end they become slaves to money. Now no one can serve two masters, one that makes him labour outside, and one that bids him to work within: 'You cannot serve God and *Mamôna*.'[1]

To serve money means to be so desirous of possessing it that all means of winning it are considered good. But it also means to give one's heart to it, to be really in love with it. These and other distinctions were to be made by the theologians; but the chief point that emerges from Our Lord's teaching is that we cannot rise towards God until we have freed our hearts from the love of money. Those who do not possess great wealth find the renunciation less difficult, although there are poor men who are consumed with covetousness and rich men who are poor in spirit. But taking everything into account wealth is by no means a divine blessing: it is easier for the poor than for the rich to be saints and friends of God.

Now that moral truth, already hinted at in many of the Psalms, was not taught by the Old Law in which the Scribes were masters. A nation as such has no eternal destiny, and the Law was a covenant made with the whole nation of Israel; it promised the people earthly possessions if they would observe the precepts of the Lord. It is still true, indeed, that the keeping of God's commandments is the best way to prosperity, even to material prosperity, for a nation. But this was a social morality, and the Pharisees made it apply to individuals. Like Job's friends, they were persuaded that God always rewards virtue upon earth, and particularly with wealth. A servant of God could not long be condemned to suffering, and above all it was not to be thought of that he should die in suffering. That is to this day the great objection of Islam against Christianity: one sent by God could not have been rejected and put to death, for God is always right, and God's rightness means victory. The Pharisees, therefore, regarded wealth as a sign of

[1] Luke xvi, 13; cf. Matthew vi, 24. *Mamôna* is Aramaic for 'money.'

divine favour, a reward of virtue, and these specious theories made a fine cloak for their avarice. It was very well for Jesus, who was penniless, to preach liberality! They snapped their fingers at Him. But He dealt them a direct blow which went straight home. They wished to appear righteous in men's eyes, and did they put forward their wealth as a proof that God held them as righteous? God, however, judges very differently from that, for he who is exalted amongst men, especially anyone that proudly exalts himself, is an abomination in the eyes of God. All that exterior parade of virtue, the pretence that God's approval is shown by prosperity and honour, cannot deceive the Lord. He knows that when a man's heart is preoccupied with these outward shows it is empty of all true good.

Perhaps the Pharisees sought to defend themselves precisely by appealing to the Law and the explicit promises it contained of temporal blessings.[1] If so, that would explain the position occupied by certain verses in the narrative of St. Luke[2] which seem to stand on their own, unconnected with one another or with the general tenor of this instruction on the right use of riches; and these verses would contain Jesus' reply, namely that now a new order of things had begun. The Law had been upheld by the prophets, of whom John the Baptist was the last, but from now onwards the kingdom of God was to be preached, and the people were rushing into that kingdom with a sort of violence, especially the poor whom the Pharisees despised. Whether this be the true explanation or not, it was the Master's pleasure to show these Pharisees that the teaching of the Old Law sufficiently condemned the proud contempt they showed for poverty. Hence He framed the parable of Dives and Lazarus having their ideas in view, using imagery that was familiar to them, with the result that they could not but see His meaning.

Is it parable or history? Some of the early Fathers took it to be the story of actual events on account of the name of Lazarus; and, as a matter of fact, proper names are not generally found in parables. But if we admit the reality of this person we ought also to admit that all the other details of the story are historical; and if we were to do

[1] Leviticus xxvi, 3–13.
[2] Luke xvi, 16–17. It seems impossible to connect verse 18 with the context.

this, under the pretext of making Our Lord's teaching more historical, we should find ourselves involved in a number of theological difficulties. For instance, the rich man in hell speaks as if he had his body, and that before the general resurrection; he manifests feelings of charity for his brethren, which would be incompatible with the state of a soul in hell; and Abraham's bosom, as the place of rest for the poor man, certainly seems to be a metaphor. If we cannot therefore reasonably rely on every detail in order to learn what are the conditions in the world to come, as Fr. Knabenbauer has pointed out, then we must conclude that Jesus has here given us a genuine parable, which He has composed as He chooses with the aid of such images in common use as are calculated to bring out the lesson He intends. That lesson is easily gathered from the little story, especially when we consider the place it occupies, following on the parable of the unjust steward and the counsel that we should give alms to the poor in view of eternal life. A man who is devoid of sympathy for the poor, even though his hard-heartedness be due only to indifference, who has no thought but that of enjoying his wealth and neglects the care of his soul, such a heartless lover of pleasure runs the risk of meeting in the next world with terrible punishments which nothing can mitigate. There is no excuse, for Moses and the prophets have taught him what is God's will.

On the other hand, the poor man had shown himself deserving of happiness, but how we do not know; the parable was not meant to tell us that, for there was no immediate intention of teaching a lesson to the poor. We must suppose that he had borne his miserable lot patiently, like the many humble people we meet with in the psalms who have neither wealth nor honour from men. In these passages of the psalms the word which stands for the poor is used also to signify those who are meek in bearing their lot, meek also towards God. The name of Lazarus, given to the poor man in the parable, was quite a common name; it was also the name of one of Our Lord's friends.[1] Owing to the ever-itching desire of multiplying historical details, early writers have bestowed on the rich man sometimes the name Nineve, sometimes that of Phineas. Jesus pictures him

[1] Renan has concluded from this coincidence that the resurrection of Lazarus was drawn by St. John from this parable which he had wrongly understood.

clothed in a fine linen tunic with a purple cloak, and giving sumptuous banquets daily. Wastefulness went along with his prodigality, for no care was taken of what remained over ; instead of putting it aside for the poor it was thrown away, and Lazarus, lying at the main entrance, was too weak to struggle for it with the dogs which collected there for this free meal and even licked his sores.

At last the poor man died and was carried by angels to Abraham's bosom, a place chosen for him near that friend of God. The rich man, too, was buried, with honour, of course ; but that was the last advantage he gained from his riches. It goes without saying that in the abode of the dead he was in torment. Above that place, according to the Jews,[1] was a region of light where a clear fountain sprang up. Lifting up his eyes, the rich man beheld Abraham with Lazarus in his bosom : 'Father Abraham, have mercy on me and send Lazarus, that he may dip the tip of his finger in the water to cool my tongue, for I am tormented in this flame.' Abraham in replying still calls him his child, but he can do nothing for him. The change in condition is irrevocable, and no one is empowered to cross the gulf that divides the righteous from the wicked. Whereupon the rich man, less as a lost soul breathing only hatred than as a man who now understands what suffering is and what God's justice requires—such a man, in fine, as suits the arrangement of the parable—feels pity for his five brethren who are living as he had lived, and who consequently are threatened with similar punishments. If Lazarus cannot come down to where he is, let him at least go back to earth where his brethren, warned of what happens in the world to come, will not fail to be converted. Abraham refuses even that : 'They have Moses and the Prophets. Let them hear them.' But the man replies : 'No, father Abraham : but if one went to them from the dead, they will do penance.' Abraham does not think so : nothing would bend their obstinate will : 'If they hear not Moses and the prophets, neither will they believe if one rise again from the dead.' The reason given is surprising. What man would not heed a word from beyond the grave ? Yet in one of the masterpieces of human ingenuity we find Hamlet talking with his father's ghost and then beginning to doubt about his own immortality. Doubtless the impression produced by an

[1] Book of Henoch xxii, 9.

apparition would be more vivid and more disturbing than that produced by the teaching of faith. But the shock to the imagination would pass away and would not penetrate the soul as surely as does repeated meditation on the word of God. Moreover the Jews had no doubts about the world to come or the justice administered there by God.

The object of the parable was to teach the rich the duty of assisting the poor. The notion, however, of a despised poor man coming to remind the rich of their duty ran some risk of being made fun of by gay companions as though it were a fantastic scruple. Moreover, a man is, after all, the master of his own actions ; if, believing in Revelation, he refuses to obey it, he will not be made more docile to its teaching by the apparition of a dead man. The Law and the Prophets did indeed counsel, and peremptorily counsel, charity. The owner of a field was not to gather every stalk of his corn, every single olive, or every bunch of grapes ; a creditor was to return before sunset a garment he had received in pledge.[1] And even though it was not within the scope of the Law's intention to deal in detail with the individual's obligation of giving alms, yet how forcibly had men like the prophet Amos scourged the senseless luxury of the rich who lay on beds of ivory while they were so hard towards the poor ![2] How emphatically had Isaias stigmatized the blindness of those who thought to please God by fasting while they neglected to show charity towards their neighbour ! These Pharisees who sneered at their Saviour might have recognized themselves in the picture of their forefathers :

'To bow the head like a reed,
  to lie upon sackcloth and ashes—
Is that what you call a fast,
  a day acceptable to Jahweh ?
Know you not the fast that pleases Me ?
To share thy bread with the hungry,
  to shelter the harbourless poor ;
Whosoever is naked to clothe him,
  not to shun thy brother.
Then shall thy light break forth as the morning. . . .'[3]

A voice from beyond the grave would have aroused a fear of hell springing from selfishness. But the Law and the

[1] Deuteronomy xxiv, 13, 19–22. [2] Amos vi, 4 ff. ; viii, 4.
[3] Isaias lviii, 5–8 (following Condamin's translation).

Prophets, and Jesus above all, teach the lesson of humanity towards one another, inspiring men with the love of their neighbour and the desire to please God ; it is there that true persuasion is to be found, or there is no means of truly persuading men. The parable as it stands, terrifying as it is, carries also a message of peace and calm, in that it reminds us of a duty easy to perform. With such a lesson we may well be content.

According to certain over-wise critics, St. Luke here meant to explain why the Jews of his day refused to believe in the resurrection of Jesus. Is it surprising, he is made to argue, that they will not accept the risen Christ, seeing that they do not believe in Moses either? But as a matter of fact the Jews did not refuse to believe in Moses, and an argument of this kind would have completely missed the mark ; whereas it was a fact—and this is really Luke's meaning—that the Pharisees, who had only listened to Jesus in order to find Him in the wrong, had been obliged to admit that His doctrine concerning wealth, which had hit them so hard, was precisely what was taught by the authorities they professed to follow.

It was in this fashion, then, that Jesus taught in Israel, now warning His would-be disciples of the necessity of detachment, but a detachment that He could make easy for them, now replying to the ill-humoured attacks of the Pharisees. At other times He would take to one side the disciples who were already devoted to Him, more especially the Apostles, and would instruct them on their relations to each other and to God.[1] In this connection a short parable deals with humility.

Unprofitable servants (203).

Luke xvii, 7–10.

In this world masters do not usually express gratitude to their servants when they do their duty. This was particularly true in ancient times. The slave of a master who lived quietly in the country would be expected to get dinner ready after having worked in the fields all day. Who would

[1] It is here that St. Luke places the teachings concerning giving scandal to the weak, forgiving our neighbour, and the virtue of faith. We have already met with these instructions (Vol. I, pp. 281, 286) or we shall find them later.

think of suggesting that it was then the master's turn to take a hand in the work and serve at table, for example? No, the slave, wearied as he is by the day's labour, will have to make himself tidy, fill his master's cup, and serve him attentively ; and only after his master has finished will he be able to satisfy his own hunger. All that is so sanctioned by custom that no master would consider himself under any obligation of gratitude. It seems strange that Jesus recalls such an attitude to our minds without uttering a word of condemnation. Does He wish us to draw the conclusion that God, the Master of us all, will be in no wise grateful to those who have carried out all His commandments? Surely that is not the meaning of the parable. He intends only to urge His Apostles to adopt the attitude of the poor slave who knows quite well that he has no right to anything but his mere pittance, and that only after his master has been served. It does not enter his head to pride himself on all the work that he has done ; it is his humble daily task. And Jesus invites His disciples also to say : 'We are unprofitable servants ; we have done that which we ought to do.' When the Apostles have converted souls by their preaching and, as they think, furthered God's glory, the temptation may arise to ascribe some of that glory to themselves. This would mean that they have misunderstood what their part in the work of salvation really is. Even the good they do comes from God. Hence it is simple truth when they say : 'We are unprofitable servants.'

VI. THE LAST JOURNEY BEFORE GOING UP TO JERUSALEM (204).

Luke xvii, 11.

Jesus had apparently delivered His instruction concerning riches while on His way northward in the country east of the Jordan. He either followed the road that runs along the slopes arising immediately out of the valley, or more probably He made His way through the Jordan valley itself. But the time came for Him to resume His journey to Jerusalem and He then crossed the Jordan, for St. Luke speaks of Him going to the Holy City by a way that passed between

Samaria and Galilee.[1] Taking this expression literally, it would mean that Jesus traversed the plain of Esdrælon which lies between those two districts; but in that case, when He struck the road from Nazareth to Jerusalem, He ought to have gone up to the Holy City through Samaria. Luke, however, says nothing of that. It would seem, then, that He went only so far as a point on the frontier separating Galilee from Samaria, perhaps Scythopolis (formerly named Beth-Shan by the Hebrews and now given the same name under the form of Beîsan by the Arabs), and then came down the right bank of the Jordan towards Jericho. To this journey Luke assigns a few episodes and discourses peculiar to himself, but he very soon rejoins the narrative of St. Mark and St. Matthew. It was about this time that the Master crossed over again to the other side of the Jordan, as we learn from St. John, supposing that it was there He learnt of the illness of Lazarus which was the occasion of a hurried visit He paid to Bethany near Jerusalem. From there He went down again into the Jordan valley by way of Ephraim, entered Jericho, then went up to Bethany and made His entrance into Jerusalem where He was to die. All four evangelists will be found in unison for that entry into Jerusalem on Palm Sunday.

The healing of the ten lepers (205).
Luke xvii, 12–19.

Jesus was then making for Jerusalem. On His way He was about to enter a small village when ten lepers came to meet Him with the evident intention of asking Him to heal them. But, obedient to what the Law prescribed, they stood at some distance away and cried aloud: 'Jesus, Master, have mercy on us.' This is the sixth time in the gospel of St. Luke that Jesus receives the title of Master, having the meaning of teacher; He was therefore regarded as one eminent in sacred learning, even though He was not a disciple of the Pharisees and taught after another fashion than that of the Scribes. And here, indeed, He gives the lepers an answer which is in accordance with the precept of the Law: 'Go, show yourselves to the priests.' They obey without resistance, and their obedience is

[1] Luke xvii, 11.

rewarded. They are healed as they go, and before they have gone very far; for one of them at once retraces his steps to find Him who has healed him, casts himself at Jesus' feet, and gives thanks glorifying God. And this man was a Samaritan.

In confirming the favour of the cure which the man's faith has won, the Master shows something like surprise at the ingratitude of the other nine. The evangelist is silent about the nationality of these others, but as they were not foreigners they must have been Jews. The Samaritan is grateful because he had no claim to the cure, especially from the hands of the Jew. The others probably told themselves that this was a great prophet who had been sent to their race, and that miracles were their due.

The kingdom of God already come (206).

Luke xvii, 20–21.

There were Pharisees everywhere. Even during this journey which Jesus made over new ground they learnt that He was preaching the kingdom of God, which His disciples had first announced. But when, after all, would it come? That was what the Pharisees very much wished to know. They, no doubt, like the author of the Assumption of Moses, were expecting to see the kingdom of God manifested in a striking fashion:

> 'Then shall His kingdom appear over all His creation. . . .
> For the Heavenly One shall arise from the throne of His kingdom,
> And shall go forth from His holy dwelling-place. . . .'[1]

But Jesus tells them that the coming of the kingdom of God is not a phenomenon that can be watched like the appearance of a comet in the sky or the arrival of a conquering general; one cannot say: 'Here it is!' or 'There it is!' for 'Lo, the kingdom of God is in the midst of you.'

What does this mean? It is certainly most true that God dwells in the hearts of those that love Him, where He reigns as king; but the Pharisees were not people of that kind. Moreover, Jesus nowhere teaches that the kingdom of God

[1] Cf. *Messianisme chez les Juifs*, p. 85.

is invisible : just the opposite, indeed, since He begins by organizing that kingdom and providing it with a head. Therefore in these words He merely intends to answer the question proposed : When will the kingdom of God come ? It is there already, He says, growing up in the midst of them and they cannot see it because it does not appear with a brilliance that strikes the bodily eye. What they need is the eye of faith.

The coming of the Son of Man (207–211).

Luke xvii, 22–37 ; Matthew xxiv, 26–27 ; 37–41 ; 28.

This reply caused some surprise even to the disciples. He was the Son of Man, founding the kingdom of God by His deeds, His teaching, and His miracles ; but He lived nevertheless very humbly, going from town to town, depending on a hospitality that was very precarious, and not always finding shelter. Would He not one day manifest Himself in glory, like Daniel's 'son of man' coming on the clouds ? With what impatience did those who loved Him best long for that moment to come ! By what signs would its approach be announced ?

Jesus resolved to put an end to these dreams, for they gave rise to barren expectations which would only paralyse the energies of His followers. His disciples must be like neither the worldlings, whose minds are preoccupied with their own temporal interests and pleasures, nor those visionaries who go no further than looking out for the signs of salvation ; they must live like men whose hopes are set on eternity. But at the same time, knowing that the Son of Man will not come till His hour arrives, and then He will come suddenly, they must work in constant readiness for the time when He will call them to rejoin Him. This provides the subject of an instruction concerning the Son of Man's coming at the last day which St. Luke gives in a form peculiar to himself, though the original terms in which the instruction was given seem to have been better preserved by St. Matthew.[1]

[1] In St. Mark and St. Matthew this subject is treated along with that of the destruction of Jerusalem, as we shall see later. In his last great discourse Matthew has collected details which we here find in St. Luke, whilst Luke has placed in his last discourse details which seem more natural in the different places where they are found in Matthew and Mark.

The Master, therefore, reminds His disciples that the Son of Man must first suffer much and be rejected by the generation in which He lives. The disciples will be left alone. They will know well that He is in glory and will long for Him to manifest Himself to them were it but for a single day. But no, He will not show Himself. 'If therefore they shall say to you : Behold He is in the desert ! go ye not out : Behold He is in the inner-chambers ! believe it not.'[1] For when the Son of Man comes 'in His day,' that is to say for judgement, He will come with the flash and suddenness of lightning which 'cometh out of the east and appeareth even unto the west.'[2] But if the disciples are to avoid wasting their energies in vain endeavours, much more must they be on their guard against that indifference which takes no account of the judgements of God ; and despite the establishment of the kingdom of God with so many miracles, despite the fulfilment of the prophecies He has uttered, Jesus foresees with sorrow that at the last hour it will be as it was in the days of Noe : 'For as in the days before the flood they were eating and drinking, marrying and giving in marriage, even till that day in which Noe entered into the ark : and they knew not till the flood came and took them all away : so also shall the coming of the Son of Man be.'[3] There was the same blind heedlessness in the time of Lot : 'They did eat and drink, they bought and sold, they planted and built. And in the day that Lot went out of Sodom it rained fire and brimstone from heaven and destroyed them all. Even thus shall it be in the day when the Son of Man shall be revealed.'[4]

What are they to answer to this who make Jesus out to be a visionary, dreaming of a kingdom of God established on earth in holiness and innocence ? Is not His prophecy being now fulfilled, though it is being fulfilled, we may say, contrary to His own heart's desire ?

What, then, are His disciples to do ? Remember Lot's wife, whose heart stayed behind in Sodom with her goods, who desired to see her burning house again for the last time because in her heart she had the wish to save something from it. Therefore it is always the same advice : be detached from everything, and sacrifice life itself if necessary. Instead of being carried away by the stream of daily

[1] Matthew xxiv, 26. [2] Matthew xxiv, 27.
[3] Matthew xxiv, 37 ff. [4] Luke xvii, 28–30.

occupations, live in the conviction that it is better to lose the life of the body than to risk the salvation of the soul. That is the way to make sure of a favourable judgement, for God judges according to the heart of men which He alone can read. It is lawful to be busied with the necessities of life, and even obligatory ; but it is not that which distinguishes man from man in God's sight. Two shall be in the fields ; one shall be accepted, the other left. Two women shall be grinding at the same mill ; one shall be accepted, the other left. Two shall be in one bed ; one shall be accepted, the other left. And yet God is infinitely just ; He will accept those who set their soul's worth above all other things : He will reject those who have thought only of the life here below which, after all, has been given only as a preparation for the life of eternity. But those who are taken, where will they go to when the Son of Man comes ? The disciples ask this question, bewildered at hearing these words which are so simple and yet so much more forcible than the terrifying images presented by the apocalyptic writings : 'Where, Lord ?' Jesus answers : 'Wheresoever the corpse shall be, there shall the vultures also be gathered together.'[1] Are we to understand the corpse as representing Jesus Himself? No, for such direct parallelism would be altogether contrary to the proper character of these parabolic comparisons which are quite different from allegories. Yet it is indeed to Himself that the elect will flock, though it is merely to show the swiftness and sureness of their movement towards Him that He compares them with vultures, flying straight to their prey with so sure an instinct that we need only to see them wheeling in the air to know where the corpse is.[2]

[1] Matthew xxiv, 28.

[2] Many commentators, shrinking from comparing the Son of Man with a corpse, have taken these last words as referring to God's sentence concerning the damned which the devils carry out. But that is certainly not Matthew's meaning in the parallel passage. They would not have proposed such an interpretation had they understood that a parable is a comparison of one set of circumstances with another : it is not a succession of metaphors. We are about to see the picture of a wicked judge whose behaviour enables us to understand God's way of acting ; yet the wicked judge does not stand for God. I once watched one of the Bedouin near Petra follow the flight of the vultures in order to discover the body of Père Vincent, my companion, who was thought to be dead. Happily, however, he reappeared safe and sound soon after.

Persevering prayer in time of persecution (212).

Luke xviii, 1–8.

The glimpse just given by the Master of how His work was to fare in the future was of a forbidding character, despite the certainty that nothing could hinder the development of the kingdom of God. His disciples were told that occasions would arise when they must be ready to sacrifice their lives, for example in times of persecution such as had already been foretold by Jesus.[1] In that case, what were they to think of the loving care of the Father watching over the little flock?[2] They would certainly call upon Him in their distress. How could He be deaf to their prayers when they invoked His aid at the moment of danger?

There was a constant and formidable occasion of stumbling here, and Jesus desired to prepare them for this temptation. Since God was all powerful, they might ask, could He not save them without so much as lifting a finger? He therefore propounded to them a parable. There was in a certain city a judge who feared not God nor regarded man. In the same city was a widow who asked him for justice against her adversary. Since she plays the part of plaintiff in the case, the poor woman cannot have been the aggressor. Deprived both of the support of her parents whom she had left and of her husband whom she had lost, she was threatened with loss in her property, or perhaps in something that concerned the interests of her children, by enemies of whom the judge was afraid; for, despite the command of the Law, which earnestly recommended the cause of the widow and the orphan to the protection of mercy and justice, this wicked judge refused to grant her request. But the widow persisted in her demand, with the tenacity of those who have nothing more to lose and who will not give up hope; and although the judge cared little about the judgements of God or the esteem of men, provided they were not influential persons, he at last found the widow's importunity a burden. Realizing that the stubborn woman would give him no peace, he decided to do her justice.

You see, then, says the Master, what even an unrighteous judge will do in the end. And do you think that God, who

[1] Luke vi, 22; xii, 11. [2] Luke xii, 22–32.

is infinitely just, would not do justice to those whom He has chosen to do His work, who cry to Him day and night, and who will not give up hope despite the patience He shows towards their adversaries? 'I say to you that He will quickly revenge them.'

These are the words of Him who alone knew the Father, words of consolation and support for us all. But in what way are we to understand them? When peace was restored to the Church under Constantine, Lactantius wrote a book on the death of persecutors. But persecution began again, nevertheless, and many persecutors have died a peaceful death long after the martyrs, their victims, had succumbed to apparent defeat. Therefore the promise here made by Jesus must be taken in connection with His constant teaching, that death in the service of truth means deliverance and victory. There are times when the earnest prayer of the faithful obtains the deliverance of the Church: thus Pius VII returned to Rome with universal acclamation, having quietly vanquished a power which had never hitherto met defeat. But St. Gregory VII died in exile. The one thing certain is that the assaults of evil will not finally prevail. Whatever lot God may have in store for His friends in this world, He is watching over them and hears their prayers. Therefore, let them not weary of praying; they will be delivered, but in the way that seems good to God in His infinite Wisdom. This does not necessarily mean a series of miraculous victories that will convert the world, as we gather from the closing words of Jesus to His disciples which leave them with a sense of anxiety and sadness: 'But yet the Son of Man, when He cometh, shall He find, think you, faith on earth?' He will find some faith, as He has just told us, seeing that so many souls will be saved. But those last days, with their indifference to divine justice, will be times of trial, and it is then that prayer will have to redouble its efforts.

The Pharisee and the Publican (213).

Luke xviii, 9–14.

Not all the Pharisees were quarrelsome, but there were few that were not self-satisfied and did not think themselves more pious and learned than other people. This, at any rate, is the description Josephus gives of them.[1] Some of them made no effort to hide this disagreeable attitude. The persuasion of their own righteousness led them to despise their neighbours, the common people, whose ignorance of the Law exposed them to constant transgression of its precepts. To the Pharisees Jesus gave a lesson under the form of a little story with a touch of satire, but one that stirs our emotions by the manner in which it contrasts pride with genuine humility.

As every Jew was aware, the Temple of Jerusalem was built on the ancient mount of Sion. Thither the people went up for the solemn celebration of the liturgy. There also in the Temple the faithful approached God present in His sanctuary and addressed their prayers to Him. On a certain day there chanced to be two men, a Pharisee and a publican, together in one of the Temple courts. The Pharisee was praying, standing, as was the custom, and he condescended to thank God that he was not a sinner like the rest of men, so many of whom are thieves, unjust, adulterers, after the fashion of this publican whom he saw bowed down very low under the weight of his sins. Having paid this tribute to the favour which God had shown towards him, it pleased him to run over the chief points of the righteousness which he had accomplished, a righteousness which considerably exceeded the standard prescribed by the Law for those who desired to be correct in the eyes of God. The Law, for instance, prescribed one fast day a year, the Day of Atonement ; this Pharisee fasted twice every week, as did the most fervent of the Jews.[2] The Law commanded the husbandman to pay tithes of all the produce of his fields ;[3] the Pharisee, scrupling lest the produce sold in the market had not discharged this debt due to the priests and levites, set aside a tithe of all that he bought, and even perhaps of what he earned by his own labour.

Even the Lord Himself could hardly have demanded more than this, though He might very well have desired a little less vain complacency ; for Jesus goes on to say that the publican, standing farther away from the sanctuary

[1] *Jewish War*, I, V, 2 : 'A sect of Jews who thought themselves more pious than others and considered their way of explaining the laws more exact.'

[2] On Monday and Thursday. Thus we read in the *Didache of the Apostles* (VIII, 1) : 'Fast not on the same days as the hypocrites, on Monday and Thursday, but on Wednesday and Friday.'

[3] Deuteronomy xiv, 22 ff.

where the just God dwelt, did not even presume to raise his eyes to heaven, but stood and beat his breast. His very attitude was sufficient to manifest to all what he was saying in his heart : 'O God, be merciful to me a sinner!' The doctors of the Law would not have denied the value of these feelings of repentance, but, all the same, the man was a publican, a receiver of customs, and as such was in constant danger of wronging his neighbour ; and that was assuredly where he had sinned. And in their opinion God owed it to Himself not to pardon until reparation had been made for the injustice committed.[1] But Jesus had a better understanding of His Father's mercy and knew that He was satisfied with the genuine repentance which includes the intention to make restitution. Hence, without entirely condemning the proud righteous Pharisee, He declares that the repentant sinner is more pleasing in God's sight than the man who has so generously awarded himself a certificate of righteousness: 'Because every one that exalteth himself shall be humbled, and he that humbleth himself shall be exalted.' The parable is another and more concrete expression of the lesson already given to the Pharisees: 'You are they who justify yourselves before men, but God knoweth your hearts. For that which is high to man is an abomination before God.'[2]

The indissolubility of the marriage bond (214)

Matthew xix, 3–12 ; Mark x, 2–12 ; Luke xvi, 18.

Jesus had now definitely turned His face towards Jerusalem. Mark and Matthew, who indicate His journey into Judæa and Peræa with a single remark,[3] rejoin one another in their narrative just before the entry of Jesus into Jericho. As He draws near to the Holy City, the Pharisees once more come forward promptly to attack Him, conscious that they are now in a more favourable position for bringing up difficult questions in which the young Master will perhaps stumble.[4] Thus they ask on what grounds a husband might

[1] Strack & Billerbeck, II, p. 248.
[2] Luke xvi, 15. [3] Cf. p. 51, above.
[4] In Matthew and Mark the question of divorce is immediately followed by the bringing of the children to Jesus. It is with this latter incident that the three synoptists rejoin one another in their narrative. Luke places it after the parable of the Pharisee and Publican (xviii, 15), and the question of divorce a little earlier (xvi, 18), but with no context. We may therefore conclude that he has put it in its chronological situation.

lawfully repudiate his wife. It seemed a harmless sort of question, seeing that it was a subject of disagreement even between the two great schools of Hillel and Shammai ; but the danger lay in the fact that the questioners assumed there was no doubt about the husband's right to dissolve the marriage bond, given the lawful circumstances. That is precisely what Jesus will not allow to be taken for granted. The discussion once begun, He resolves to throw full light upon this point, a vital matter, as we may say, in the moral life of every people.

Substantially, there is no ambiguity about His reply. The Catholic Church takes it as a prohibition of remarriage so long as both parties to the first marriage are alive, and this is certainly the sense of the texts in question. They are as follows :

St. Luke :—'Every one that putteth away his wife and marrieth another committeth adultery : and he that marrieth her that is put away from her husband committeth adultery.'[1]

St. Mark :—'Whosoever shall put away his wife and marry another committeth adultery against her. And if the wife shall put away her husband and be married to another, she committeth adultery.'[2]

St. Paul to the Corinthians :—'But to them that are married, not I but the Lord commandeth that the wife depart not from her husband ; and if she depart, that she remain unmarried or be reconciled to her husband. And let not the husband put away his wife.'[3]

There was agreement, then, in the primitive Church about what was the command of Christ : husband and wife are not to separate ; and if they do separate because they cannot live together, the bond of marriage still remains intact, so that a second marriage would be unlawful for the husband as for the wife. This being so, on what grounds do Protestants, and even the Greek Orthodox Church, abandon this command of the Master and permit one of the parties to re-marry if the other has been guilty of infidelity and is convicted of adultery ? They base their practice on the interpretation given to St. Matthew's text in this

[1] Luke xvi, 18.

[2] Mark x, 11, 12. There is a variant reading of no importance regarding the question of the indissolubility of marriage.

[3] 1 Corinthians vii, 10–11.

place, although in doing so, according to many modern critics of the radical school, they neglect a perfectly authentic declaration of Jesus for the sake of what is merely an addition to His words originating with St. Matthew. This addition, they maintain, is only a provision added later for the benefit of Jewish converts who were unwilling to yield their pretended right of repudiation in case of adultery. These critics, however, agree with the Orthodox and Protestant theologians in interpreting the text of St. Matthew as permitting repudiation in such a case, even though they do not admit that it is an authentic utterance of Our Lord. It is the text of St. Matthew, then, that we must examine.

Let it be said, first of all, that far from accepting the hypothesis that the evangelist has altered the teaching of his Master, we hold on the contrary that it is St. Matthew who has best reproduced for us, at least towards the beginning of the dispute, the flow of the dialogue and the actual expressions used by Jesus. St. Mark is usually the one who does that best, but in this place he has neglected to record that interchange of remarks in the debate which tends to destroy the logical sequence, in order to draw up the argument in order. In telling us that it is to the disciples when by themselves that Jesus spoke when He made application of the principle He had just laid down in answer to the Pharisees, St. Mark lays emphasis on the fact that Jesus was promulgating a decision for His followers, and consequently for His Church ; and the evangelist pays no further attention to the reply given to the Pharisees' question, which, indeed, he has failed to record with perfect accuracy. The final answer of Jesus to the Pharisees recorded by St. Matthew groups together both the special solution of the difficulty they had proposed and the practical conclusion to be drawn from the principle He had laid down. It will be seen that all the difficulty about his text springs from the fact that he has not sufficiently distinguished these two points.

The question arose because some of the Pharisees asked Jesus : 'Is it lawful for a man to put away his wife for every cause ? ' They do not ask if divorce is lawful, as do modern people who grant the same rights to wife as to husband. It is true that this latter view was already current in Rome, but among the Jews, as among orthodox Moslems even to this day, the husband alone was given the right to take the first step in the matter of separation. It was plain enough in the Mosaic Law that the husband could repudiate his wife ; no more was required than that he should give her a certificate of divorce expressive of the fact that he repudiated her irrevocably. Without this certificate, if she married again, her second husband might have been exposed to the annoyance of claims made by the former husband. Once the woman had been put away in due form she was free to marry again and had a chance of securing a husband. All the same, her position was a precarious one. Even when she had public opinion on her side, a divorced woman was not well regarded. Hence a husband was bound not to exercise his right except for serious reasons. The reason given by the Law was 'something unseemly (some uncleanness).'[1] This was interpreted by the school of Shammai as signifying some very grave cause ; the followers of the school of Hillel, on the other hand, explained it in such a way as to give free rein to every whim on the part of the husband. According to the latter school, it was sufficient that a wife should have burnt her husband's dinner. Later, it was permitted by the great Rabbi Aqiba that a husband should send away his wife merely in order that he might marry a prettier one. The Jews had given up their ancient polygamy, but even in the days of polygamous marriage a cast-off wife had not been treated so unjustly as this.

It was not the character of Jesus to enter into such controversies as these of the different rabbinical schools. He cuts straight to the root of the matter ; to His mind the question of repudiation does not even arise. He questions these masters in Sacred Scripture with a kind of impatience : 'Have ye not read that He who made man from the beginning made them male and female ? And He[2] has said : *For this cause shall a man leave father and mother and shall cleave to his wife, and they two shall be in one flesh.* Therefore now they are not two but one flesh. What therefore God hath joined together let no man put asunder.'

It may be asked how Jesus could have more forcibly expressed the indissolubility of marriage, or at the same time have better shown that God's purpose in creating the sexes different was to bring them into unity and thereby ensure the continuance of the human race. Yet it is not

[1] Deuteronomy xxiv, 1.
[2] I.e. God, speaking through the words of the sacred writer.

merely by the union of husband and wife in conjugal relationship that they are made but one 'flesh'; the word 'flesh' in Hebrew usage denotes also the bond which unites those who are very closely related to one another. This bond of family relationship, which among nomads and communities of a primitive character is held in the most sacred esteem, is therefore that which unites married people; the union of man and woman in marriage creates a new family. By the power of the divine will they become inseparable, and no human rights can prevail which are contrary to the will of God.

But if that be the case, what did Moses mean? For a moment, hopes may have risen in the hearts of the Pharisees that Jesus had ruined Himself by this imprudent answer, in which He had opposed His interpretation of Genesis to an explicit text of the Law. Either from indignation or else out of an intention to lead Him astray, they seek to emphasize this opposition by confusing together the *permission* to repudiate which is implied by the words of the Mosaic Law, and the *command* of that Law not to repudiate a wife without giving her a certificate of divorce: 'Why then did Moses command to give a bill of divorce and to put away?' Jesus replies calmly and puts the matter in its true light: 'Because Moses by reason of the hardness of your heart permitted you to put away your wives; but in the beginning it was not so.'

It would be an impertinence to praise Our Lord for His critical sense; it ought rather to be said that here He has indicated the manner in which the Mosaic Law ought to be understood. That Law is not to be taken as a series of commandments promulgated from heaven as they stand in order to reveal God's purposes, and binding the people of Israel to a perfection which was ideal. The Israelites had their customs; some of them were good, and these were approved; others were altogether bad, such as the practice of idolatry or sorcery, and these were condemned; others again, like polygamy and repudiation, were signs of a low ideal of morality, and these God condescended to tolerate for the time being. But the Lawgiver now sent by God, one greater than Moses, had authority to bring the Law to its perfection in accordance with what was God's primary intention; and in the present case He did not hesitate to use that authority. The question therefore was settled.

Nevertheless, it would be very hard for a husband to be compelled to keep an unfaithful wife under his roof if she proved so incorrigible that further indulgence on his part might seem nothing less than complicity in her sin. In case, therefore, of adultery on his wife's part, a husband was still permitted to repudiate her ; and repudiation, be it noted, was the only point about which there was dispute amongst the Jews and the only point that was in question here. But repudiation is man's doing and cannot change the law of God ; hence he who repudiates his wife and marries another woman is guilty of adultery. Had St. Matthew expressed himself with this precision his text would never have given rise to any controversy. The employment of some typographical sign such as a bracket or a hyphen—had these been in use—would have been sufficient to remove every shadow of contradiction between his later words and the principle he had just laid down. But he has chosen to put everything into a single sentence, making even his direct reply to the Pharisees' question a mere incidental phrase of that sentence, and men with their sensual inclinations have managed to find in this somewhat awkward construction a pretext for evading Christ's formal command : 'And I say to you that whosoever shall put away his wife—except it be for fornication[1]—and shall marry another, committeth adultery.'[2]

Again, neither does it seem that St. Matthew, in thus grouping together in one phrase the solutions to two different questions, distinguishes the two different sets of circumstances in which these solutions were given. According to St. Mark it was to the disciples alone, and in a house, that Jesus gave the final and decisive explanation of the question proposed to Him ; and in reality St. Matthew leaves us with the same impression, for in his narrative the discussion continues between Jesus and the disciples who have been surprised by the answer of their Master to the Pharisees.

If, therefore, by the aid of the two different accounts we reconstruct the situation in a critical manner the result will

[1] Repudiation for such a cause is still lawful.

[2] Matthew xix, 9. Remarriage is then never lawful (while the former spouse is living). The same solution applies to Matthew's passage in the Sermon on the Mount (v, 32), and with even greater ease than here. 'But I say to you, that whosoever shall put away his wife, excepting for the cause of fornication, maketh her to commit adultery : and he that shall marry her that is put away committeth adultery.'

be as follows. Having first laid down his declaration of principle regarding the indissolubility of marriage, Jesus intends to answer the precise question proposed by the Pharisees regarding the legitimate grounds for repudiation. He concedes that a wife guilty of infidelity may be repudiated, but denies that by repudiating her the bond of kinship (one flesh) is dissolved. Afterwards, speaking to the disciples alone, He explains more clearly what is the consequence of this doctrine, namely, that remarriage after repudiation is unlawful. It is perfectly evident that to St. Matthew's mind this decision appeared absolutely opposed to the opinion of the day, for he alone of the evangelists records the surprise and almost the dissatisfaction of the disciples : 'If the case of a man with his wife be so, it is not expedient to marry.' It was a shock to the disciples, who realized that it completely transcended the limits of the controversy on the subject carried on by the different rabbinical schools, who all agreed in leaving the question of repudiation to the arbitrary will of the husband, even if one school was stricter than the other in the conditions for repudiation. Jesus was well aware that He was demanding from His disciples a high ideal, though not one that was too high for mankind, even if it was an ideal that went far beyond the limits which it is claimed may be set by the private interest of the individuals concerned. The private good of individuals may sometimes demand great consideration, but here there is question of the good of society, and of a good which is so essential that its safeguarding demands sacrifice on the part of individuals. The man to whom remarriage is forbidden is not in a worse case than the unfortunate eunuch, who is incapable of marriage either through natural defect or because he is rendered so by the cruelty or selfishness of others ;[1] and by voluntarily accepting this sacrifice such a man may gain great merit.

The prohibition of complete divorce, in the modern acceptation of the term, forms part of a religious economy in which such self-denial is not only understood, but also carried so far as the renunciation of marriage altogether in view of the kingdom of God. Mere human wisdom is not capable of rising to such heights as that ; faith is needed, and faith is a gift of God's grace. Even at the time of which

[1] The Jews classified two kinds of eunuchs, those born so and those made so by operation ; but they gave them all the same name.

we are speaking there were holy men and women who put themselves in this position by forming a resolution of observing perpetual continence. Our Lord referred to them in drawing the attention of His disciples to something that was already in existence : 'There are eunuchs who have made themselves eunuchs for the kingdom of heaven.' Perhaps He meant John the Baptist, or one or other of His disciples, such as John the son of Zebedee. At the same time He was even then inviting those to whom the inspiration would be given to imitate them ; and if continence ever becomes a necessity in a particular case it is always made possible by prayer.

Jesus welcomes the little children (215).

Luke xviii, 15–17 ; Mark x, 13–16 ; Matt. xix, 13–15.

Jesus was in some house where He and His disciples were being entertained when children were brought to Him that He might touch them.[1] We may be sure that they were brought, perhaps carried in arms, by their mothers who in their faith expected some wonderful effect as a result of the contact of their beloved little ones with Jesus. The disciples grumbled at His being pestered in this fashion. Had the children been ill, at least, it would have been a different matter. And what did they mean by coming into the house like that ? It is true that in the East a house is open to everyone ; yet when such a thing happens it puts an end to intimate conversation such as had just been begun.

But the disciples were in the wrong, and the Master showed His great displeasure, says St. Mark, by saying to them : 'Suffer the little children to come unto Me and forbid them not ; for of such is the kingdom of heaven.' The kingdom is the kingdom of the Father, and the best condition for entering it is to come with the simplicity, the trust, and the self-surrender of children. We have to strive, therefore, to be like them, and God will reign within us—that is to say, we shall receive an invitation into His kingdom—if we cast ourselves into our Father's arms like children who are sure of being welcomed by Him. Hence there is good reason for fear that those who rely upon their

[1] According to St. Mark, whose narrative is more detailed than that of the others.

own merits in order to gain a good place within the kingdom will never be admitted.

Then Jesus, to the great joy of the mothers who had not asked for such a favour, embraces the children, lays His hands on them and blesses them.

The rich young man whom Jesus loves has not the courage to follow Him (216).

Luke xviii, 18–23 ; Mark x, 17–22 ; Matt. xix, 16–22.[1]

The time came to resume His journey and Jesus departed from the house. Just then, it was seen that someone who had nearly missed Him was running up. The man knelt before Jesus, both to compel Him to listen and in order to show the great reverence he felt. It was not the custom to make prostrations before the Doctors of the Law, nor did people usually address them in words so deferential as these : 'Good Master, what shall I do that I may inherit life everlasting ?' It was rare that Jesus met with anyone so docile, or whose attention was so completely absorbed in that which He recommended above all things, the eternal good of the soul. Nevertheless there was a touch of exaggeration about this enthusiasm, sincere as it was. Jesus moved among men as a real man, and as man was always on the alert to raise their thoughts to God. He answered, therefore : 'Why callest thou Me good ? None is good but God alone.'[2] The stranger made no reply. Had he answered : 'Art Thou not the Son of God ?' perhaps he would have been admitted further into the mystery. But his intention had only been to address Jesus in a flattering way, and the good Master does no more than give him this kindly lesson ! Besides, did not every Jew know well that eternal life is to be obtained by keeping the commandments ? Jesus reminds him of them, but omits to mention the chief of them all, which is to love God, either because it is more difficult to be sure that it has been properly kept, or else, more probably, because it cannot fail to be kept if

[1] As usual, Mark's account is more natural, and Luke has followed him. We shall add a few touches from Matthew's account.

[2] In Matthew : 'Master, what good shall I do that I may have life everlasting ? Who said to him : Why askest thou Me concerning good ? One is good, God.'

we do not infringe those other commandments which concern our neighbour, and which are merely different manifestations of the first and only commandment : 'Thou shalt not kill ; thou shalt not commit adultery . . . do no fraud. . . .' This last precept was not written in the Law, but it flowed from the spirit of it which Jesus understood better than anyone, for it was His mission to bring the Law to perfection.

The man replied : 'Master, all these things I have observed from my youth.'[1] This was said with youthful daring, but yet with candour. Jesus reads his look, and sees there good will and an upright character ; He loves him, and because He loves him He proposes to him that he should sell all his goods and give alms to the poor and so enter on the way of perfection. Matthew expresses this more fully. Jesus had already taught that this was the way to acquire treasure in heaven, where eternal life is to be found. As for this present life, He invites the young man : 'Come, follow Me.'

In the case of Peter and Andrew, James and John, and of Matthew and the other Apostles, the Master's call had been effective ; but it does not work like a magic charm which forces the will. The will remains free. It possesses the formidable power of resisting. The young man's face, a moment ago radiant with enthusiasm, clouded over. He was sorry not to follow Jesus and went away sad at heart. But he did go away, after all, and the reason was that he had great possessions. 'For he had great possessions !' How right, then, Jesus had been in teaching men to beware of riches !

It is very hard for a rich man, and very easy for one who is voluntarily poor, to gain everlasting life (217–218).

Luke xviii, 24–30 ; Mark x, 23–31 ; Matt. xix, 23–30.

The rich man went away sorrowful, and his sadness lay heavy on Jesus and on His disciples too. Twice the Master said with a sigh : 'How hardly shall they that have riches enter into the kingdom of God !' Twice the disciples were stupified with amazement ; His words were so stern :

[1] According to Matthew it is a young man. But young folks often speak of the past as though they were already old.

'For it is easier for a camel to pass through the eye of a needle than for a rich man to enter into the kingdom of God.' Might He not just as well have said that the thing was absolutely impossible? What is bulkier than a camel or smaller than the eye of a needle, which only those with good sight can thread? Looking at one another without daring to question their Master, they say among themselves: 'Who then can be saved?' They were overwhelmed by the thought that it was possible for a rich man to keep all the commandments and yet be kept from salvation by his great possessions. It looked, then, as if the rich were condemned to perdition because of this fatal tendency to love wealth. Still it was not impossible to overcome this love of wealth, and just as Jesus had before fixed His eyes on the rich young man, so He now fixes them on His disciples in order to engrave this truth on their minds: 'With men it is impossible, but not with God; for all things are possible with God.' Therefore, there will be rich men saved by His grace, those, namely, who are obedient to His call. Already there were men who had voluntarily accepted poverty.

The gloom which overshadowed them was now lit up through the intervention of Peter who, as usual, is the one to take the initiative. He makes profession of his fidelity to his Master with the idea of consoling Him for the sadness He feels at the failure of this young man, whom Jesus would have preferred to love for ever: 'Behold, we have left all things and have followed Thee.'[1] Immediately the grave words, heavy with grim foreboding, which the Master had just spoken, are exchanged for words of encouragement, words which reveal to our eyes a happy prospect: 'Amen, I say to you, there is no man who hath left house or brethren or sisters or father or mother or children or lands for My sake and for the Gospel, who shall not receive an hundred times as much, now in this time; houses and brethren and sisters and mothers and children and lands.' Yet there is a shadow even here, for to mention the Gospel is to foretell opposition. Hence persecution must be reckoned with in this world; the unspoilt reward is to be found in the world to come, that is to say, in everlasting life.

In making this promise to His friends Jesus is speaking as God, disposing of the future according to His will. It is

[1] Matthew inserts here the special reward promised to the twelve Apostles; but it is better placed by Luke in the discourse after the Last Supper.

within His power to bestow eternal life, and to give help and consolation even in this life to those who have left all to follow Him in the religious life. How faithfully He has kept His word will be testified by so many of those who live a life of voluntary poverty, full of gratitude for the life of peace they owe to Him ; and it is but rarely that their peace is destroyed by persecution. All the same, provided that they practise genuine poverty, the world will hold them in the lowest esteem ; yet one day they will be not the last but the first, and along with them will be ranked all those who have been just as much detached from riches, even though they have gone on using their wealth, for they have used it in the way that God wills it to be used. Hence the final remark with which St. Mark closes this episode : ' Many that are first shall be last : and the last (shall be) first.'

The grace of God and those who murmur against grace (219).

Matthew xx, 1–16.

God, therefore, does not judge like men. He gives eternal life to those who are reckoned of no account in this world. Further, we are assured that He rewards those who have left all things for His sake. In all this there appears clearly enough what part is played by the human will in the work of salvation. But there is another element in the work of salvation which man tends to disregard, that is, the gratuitous character of God's gift and that divine freedom of action for which He is accountable to none. According to St. Luke, Our Lord had uttered these words : ' Behold, they that are last shall be first, and they that are first shall be last,'[1] when He declared that Gentiles should be admitted with the patriarchs into the kingdom of God while Jews should be excluded. St. Matthew establishes this verdict on a wider basis ; he brings all men before God in the parable of the labourers invited to work in the vineyard, a parable which closes with the above words. The object of the parable is twofold. Its chief purpose is to show that God has the right to bestow the favour of eternal life even on those who have done but little work for Him, provided always that they have in the end responded to His call. This principle laid down, the parable proceeds to

[1] Luke xiii, 30.

draw the conclusion that there is no justification for murmuring at divine mercy; and those who do murmur run the risk of sacrificing the merit of all the good deeds they may have performed during a long life.

The owner of a vineyard goes out at daybreak to hire labourers, doubtless for the work of weeding, though this is the sort of work not much attended to in Palestine. But, as we shall see, the master in the parable is one who supervises the work himself, and that very thoroughly. Skilled workmen and the casual labourers that are ready for any sort of work were generally to be found gathered about the gates of the town, where they waited to make bargains about conditions of work and wages. In this case the wage is fixed at a penny a day, and the labourers set off for the vineyard. Three hours later, that is about nine o'clock, the owner of the vineyard, anxious to get the work completed, returns to the gate where he finds there are men still waiting for employment. Glad to get work, they are satisfied with a vague promise of a fair wage. The same thing happens at midday and three o'clock. Finally, an hour before sunset, the master finds other labourers, gathered there by chance and standing idle. At his invitation, and without being promised anything, they too go off to the vineyard.

When sunset comes, the steward is charged to pay the wages, commencing from the last comers. This is a device of the parable to arrange that the first comers shall see in what way the master understands justice and favour; for each labourer, as soon as he is paid, shoulders his hoe and goes home. Seated at a table on which is a pile of pennies, the steward begins to pay the wages in sight of all the labourers. Those who have worked only an hour, and that in the cool of the evening, receive a penny. Those who have toiled since early morning expect to receive more, therefore; for it seems to them altogether becoming to the master's generosity that it should be extended to them also in like proportion. But they too receive a penny. They express their dissatisfaction, and so loudly that they are overheard: 'These last have worked one hour, and thou hast made them equal to us that have borne the burden of the day and the heats.' If only they had been content to beg for a little more! But they give vent to their jealousy, and even let it turn into reproaching the master for what they consider his misplaced goodness. The latter takes the most dissatisfied of them to task for this : ' Friend, I do thee no wrong. . . . Take what is thine and go thy way. Is it not lawful for me to do what I will with my own ? Or is thy eye evil because I am good ? ' Thus ' the last shall be first, and the first last.'

As this is a parable of the kingdom of God, the master must be no other than the Lord Himself, and the reward given is eternal life. There is only one wage, the same for all, for the question of different degrees of glory does not arise here. God is more intent on procuring the salvation of men than on increasing His own good ; thus He does not cease to invite them to come. Those who respond to His call receive the reward which He wills to grant them gratuitously, even though they may not have had time to do much in the way of good works, or to do anything that costs them very much. The Lord, in His infinite goodness, is satisfied with this little and looks only at their resolute good will. The righteous, that is they who have toiled long, ought to be moved by this spectacle of divine goodness and give glory to the mercy of God. If, on the contrary, they begin to murmur, they put themselves in the way of losing that which they regard as their due, for they commit the serious fault of not realizing that they, like everyone else, owe all to the gratuitous call of their Master.

It is a very profitable lesson, and it is surely unnecessary to raise the question of how the righteous, who are already endowed with everlasting life, could murmur against their Master. The warning of the parable is rather addressed to the righteous who are still on earth, bidding them not to oppose themselves to God's free giving of grace if they desire not to be deprived of their own righteousness. Nor ought we to treat the parable in an historical fashion, and regard this series of invitations to the labourers as representing the call of Adam, Noe, Moses, and the Prophets, finding the last call in the preaching of Jesus to the Jews. All the same it is true that Jesus was addressing this very grave warning to His own generation, to those who were surprised to see Him welcoming publicans and sinners. These others had been called long before, and considered themselves loaded with merits. Their reward, they thought, was certain. But it was certain only on condition that they did not criticize Our Saviour's kindness to these eleventh-hour labourers, and did not make His goodness an occasion of stumbling for themselves. The evil eye means envy, and an evil eye, in spite of what superstitious people generally thought about it, harms none but those who regard their neighbour with ill-will.

The resurrection of Lazarus (220).

John xi, 1–44.

In the course of these encounters Jesus had approached Jerusalem. He was following the course of the Jordan, the left bank of which was in the territory of Herod Antipas, the right being dependent on the Roman procurator of Judæa. According to St. John's account, Jesus was apparently on the farther side of the river when He received the news of His friend Lazarus' illness, in consequence of which He set off for Judæa. It may be, however, that He was already in the neighbourhood of Jericho, having finished His journey in Peræa and now making preparations for going up to Jerusalem. But, to tell the truth, either bank of the river might well be considered as part of Judæa, and, on the other hand, sometimes the title Judæa was reserved merely for the hill country west of the Jordan. Whatever may have been the case, Jesus was a good day's journey from Bethany, which was situated fifteen stades (a little more than a mile and a half) from the Holy City. Bethany was the village of Martha and Mary, and it was the two sisters who had sent Jesus word of their brother's illness. They had not asked Him to come in so many words, but knowing how He loved Lazarus they had simply said : 'Lord, he whom Thou lovest is sick.'

This introduction of St. John's provides a striking example of that unapparent harmony which we have insisted on. We already are familiar with Martha and Mary from the gospel of St. Luke,[1] and here they appear again with the same distinct characters. But it is only here we learn that the name of their village is Bethany, the position of which St. John describes, and that they have a brother. St. John completes his information by telling us that this Mary is the same as she whom all Christians knew had anointed the Lord with oil, as he will tell later in the gospel.[2]

Jesus loved Lazarus, as He loved Martha and Mary ; yet

[1] Luke x, 38 ff.
[2] John xii, 1–11 ; cf. Mark xiv, 9 ; Matthew xxvi, 13.

He did not set out at once, but waited two days where He was. He already knew that a wonderful design of God was about to be fulfilled which had for its object to glorify the Son of God, who Himself was seeking the glory of His Father. When the two days were over He said to His disciples: 'Let us go into Judæa again.' This was to run into danger of death, for to the mind of the disciples Judæa meant Jerusalem and plots against the life of their Master. But He, knowing that His hour had not yet come, though it was very near at hand, assured His friends that there was nothing to fear so long as God made His light to shine. The hour of His enemies He described as the hour of darkness, and it was still day. The disciples either do not or will not understand His meaning. They remain silent. Then Jesus says: 'Lazarus our friend'—he who has given us all hospitality—'hath fallen asleep'; and since you do not seem willing to come with Me: 'I am going to awake him.' They all know that Lazarus has been ill; the meaning of these words, then, is quite plain. It is evident that Jesus does not intend to make a whole day's journey merely to go and wake a sick man. Lazarus was dead.

But these other friends of Jesus must decidedly have been deaf to His words. A sick man asleep! That was a very good sign![1] The Master, therefore, has to speak openly and emphatically: 'Lazarus is dead.' You knew that I could heal him, but I have not done so, in order that you may witness a greater miracle. 'Let us go to him!' It was of no use holding back any longer. Thomas, called Didymus in Greek, has the merit of being the one who gave the lead to the rest: 'Let us also go, that we may die with Him.' Full of courage as he was, he saw nothing but the prospect of death in that dreaded approach to Jerusalem.

Lazarus had already been in the tomb four days when Jesus arrived near Bethany.[2] News of His approach was immediately carried to Martha, she being the more active of the sisters as well as the one in charge of the household. She came out to meet Him. Ah! if only Jesus had been there, He who had the power—as she still believes—of

[1] Père Jaussen has met with the proverb: 'He who sleeps is cured.' Cf. his *Naplouse*, p. 153.

[2] That is, it was the fourth day since his death. The messenger would have left a little before Lazarus' death and would have taken a day for the journey to Jesus, who had waited two days before going to Bethany on what was thus the fourth day.

obtaining anything from God ! It is her faith in the resurrection that she expresses rather than a mere vague hope of Lazarus' resurrection from the dead. Hence, when Jesus comforts her with the words : 'Thy brother shall rise again,' she takes His words as referring to the resurrection on the last day, an object of faith for those Jews who had not been won over to the scepticism of the Sadducees. Jesus replies to her : 'I am the resurrection and the life : he that believeth in Me, although he were dead, shall live ; and everyone that liveth and believeth in Me shall not die for ever. Believest thou this ?' She answers : 'Yea, Lord, I believe that Thou art the Christ, the Son of God, who art come into the world' ; and since she believes the declaration which He has just made, she also believes that He will raise the dead, seeing that He is Life. Nevertheless, her thoughts remain fixed upon those lofty truths of faith, and she keeps in view that general judgement of mankind when all graves shall be opened together. She does not comfort herself with the thought that He who will raise all the dead at the general resurrection is able to restore to her brother the few days of life that he has lost. She goes away.

Mary had stayed at home along with the Jews who had come from Jerusalem to mourn with the two sisters. Such visits of condolence were always accompanied by tears and lamentations. Martha comes and says privately to her sister : 'The Master is come and calleth for thee.' Up to the present it is their relatives who have come one after the other to condole with them, some affectionately, others more or less indifferently ; but now it is a friend who is here, and a word or two with a friend would be sweet. Mary rises to go at once. Coming, she falls at the Master's feet and says like Martha : 'Lord, if Thou hadst been here, my brother had not died.' She says no more except by her tears. Meanwhile, true to their role as comforters and thinking that Mary has gone to mourn at the tomb, the Jews arrive and begin to lament in order to show their sympathy. Jesus moans to Himself and asks with repressed emotion : 'Where have you laid him ?' He was asking for the tomb, but His thoughts were with His friend. They reply : 'Come and see.' Jesus wept. They were not tears of sympathy ; He was weeping because of His love, and the Jews understood. Some of them, however, were unable to refrain from criticism : 'Could not He that opened the eyes of the man born blind have caused that this man should not die?' But Jesus seemed not to hear them. Absorbed in His grief He again groaned, moved this time perhaps by the thought of the mighty act He was about to perform.

The tomb was hollowed out of the rock, as was the custom, and a flight of steps led down to the vault.[1] A stone was placed over the place of burial. 'Take away the stone!' Jesus ordered. Martha was disturbed; it was sacrilege to violate a dead man's repose. Doubtless Jesus wished to see His friend for the last time, but in what sort of state would He find him? 'Lord, by this time he stinketh, for he is (now dead) four days.' Among families of some social standing it was the custom to embalm their dead speedily, but that was not able to arrest the rapid decomposition of the corpse, as Jesus knew well enough. But He upheld what He had commanded: 'Did I not say to thee that if thou believe thou shalt see the glory of God?' Thereupon He raised his eyes to heaven and prayed aloud: not that His voice might be heard by His Father, who had granted His prayer even before it was made, but to testify before the bystanders that in the name of God He was about to give a sign of His mission. Then, with a loud voice, He cried out: 'Lazarus, come forth!' And the dead man came out of the tomb clothed in the garments of his burial, his feet and hands bound with bands of linen, his body wrapped in a shroud. 'Loose him,' said Jesus, 'and let him go.' The man restored to life stood in need of their help, indeed, but it was equally important that they, by touching with their hands the risen body in thus unfastening the burial cloths, should be convinced of the reality of the miracle. That done, Lazarus needed their help no further, for he had been restored to normal life.

It is with very exact detail that the fourth evangelist has narrated for us the resurrection of Lazarus and with an evident emotion that he communicates to his readers. He describes with great solemnity the majestic act by which life is made to triumph over death, a personal triumph of Jesus, a symbol and an anticipation of that final victory which He is to gain in the time to come. But along with the light darkness appears, spreading itself over the enemies of the Son of God, who are more than ever determined to

[1] The modern name for Bethany, *El-Azarieh*, recalls Lazarus.

put to death Him who is Life itself. To the mind of St. John this is the summit of Our Lord's teaching, the introduction to His death and the pledge of His resurrection. It is from this summit that the Son of Man is to be cast down. We are not alone in saying this, for the modern critics are of the same opinion, emulating the ancient commentators in the emphasis they lay on the importance of this miracle for the gospel of St. John ; but they emphasize only in order that they may deny the miracle more securely. How, they ask, could the other evangelists have remained in ignorance of a fact of such importance as this ? They have passed it over in silence, and therefore it can be nothing else than a myth intended to show how Jesus is the resurrection and the life.

But St. John, no more than any one else before our day, never entertained the impossible hope of founding something on nothing. He puts forward this fact as an objective reality with circumstantial details. If he invented the miracle, then it is not lawful to call it a symbol ; it is a lie. We shall be told that it is a poetical fiction, invented by one who is the divinely inspired poet of friendship, grief, and tears, of the irrepressible hopes of mankind. That is all very beautiful, but it is not what St. John wanted to show. It was his desire to render testimony to the truth : to the truth of religion certainly, but first of all to the truth of actual facts.[1]

But there remains the fact of the silence of the Synoptists. What Catholic in these days would dream of writing a life of Jesus without mentioning that miracle which furnished such a wonderful manifestation of Him, though it was a manifestation so soon to be overshadowed ? Certainly no one, if he had ever read the fourth gospel. But the first three evangelists had never done so. We may be sure that they were well acquainted with the fact of the miracle. It was an extraordinary miracle, to be sure, but had they not already described similar resurrections from the dead ? What writer or reader of French history would concern himself with Henrietta of France or Henrietta of England were it not for Bossuet's funeral orations ? What should we know of Ctesiphon, the follower of Demosthenes, were it not for the latter's *Oration on the Crown ?*

Now the first catechesis of the Gospel drawn up by the

[1] John xx, 30 f.

Apostles followed a definite itinerary, and with relation to that itinerary this visit of Jesus to Bethany was merely a digression, a departure from plan such as upset the general arrangement of the catechesis. It could be left out without the loss of anything essential to the Gospel. We will venture to suggest an hypothesis. Why should the right to do so be denied to us when it is conceded to so many others?

It is probable that Peter was not present during any part of this section of the Gospel history. Had he been there, he whose courage was not always distinguishable from presumption, he who was always ready to take the lead, would he have stood back while Thomas led the others on to face death? Now Peter was the author of the primitive catechesis, and if he was not present at this miracle, he would not have included it in his catechesis. But here, as in other instances, it is John, the friend of Peter, who has supplied the things passed over in silence by Peter. It is not without probability also that the first evangelists wished to avoid narrating anything which might compromise the family at Bethany who were at the mercy of the Sanhedrin. When St. Luke speaks of Martha and Mary he omits the name of their village; St. Matthew and St. Mark relate the story of the anointing at Bethany but without giving the names of Jesus' hosts. St. John's intention to fill up these omissions is evident. As we say, he dots the i's and crosses the t's in thus supplying the smallest details, and he does this with complete assurance though with no show of affectation. Thus, either he meant to present the resurrection of Lazarus in the full light of an historical fact, or else he obligingly furnished means to all those who wished to accuse him of deliberate invention. The miracles that he has related are but few in number, but he has given those in so detailed a manner that we can only conclude that it was his deliberate intention to furnish a solid foundation for his declaration that Jesus was the Son of God.

The definite resolve to put Jesus to death (221).

John xi, 45–53.

The raising of Lazarus brought conviction to such of the Jews as witnessed it, and they believed in Jesus in so far, at least, as to accept His solemn declaration that He had been sent by God. The mere narration of the miracle did not have an equal effect upon other Jews, who refused to abandon their hatred of Him. These informed the Pharisees of what had happened, but the Pharisees did not dare to undertake any course of action on that account without the consent of the chief priests. A council was therefore held, similar to a meeting of the Sanhedrin, and although it enjoyed no official character, its decisions nevertheless were certain to prevail.[1] The president of such a meeting was obviously the high priest. The whole gathering was unanimous in its hostility towards Jesus, but hesitated about what course to pursue. His miracles were patent and undeniable facts, the common people were stirred by them, and the Prophet could easily, did He so wish, gather a group of supporters about Him. The Romans were already masters in Palestine, though they respected the Temple and granted to the Jewish nation a certain measure of self-government. But, it was argued, were they not merely waiting for a favourable opportunity of taking the decisive step which would take back even those concessions? If occasion were given for them to use armed force and spill Roman blood, would not that mean the end of all Jewish independence and perhaps the suppression of the Temple worship also? The council had to admit that so far Jesus had refrained from all agitation of a revolutionary character; but perhaps that was merely part of His plan. Would He be capable of restraining His partisans once they were stirred to action? He would rather be compelled to fall in with them.

When a group of men gathered together for deliberation is under the influence of fear, there will always arise someone with a base proposal. So it was here, and the man was Caiaphas, the high priest that year. He had held the office for a dozen years, and his authority was increased by the fact that his father-in-law, Annas, was the former high priest. Some of his colleagues in the council were still hesitating about condemning an Israelite who was manifestly innocent, but whose life it was proposed to sacrifice in order to ward off the displeasure of heathen foreigners. To overweigh their scruples Caiaphas throws into the scales the safety of the country. At the time of the French Revolution

[1] As happens in the case of private meetings of parliamentary groups who can count on commanding a majority in the House.

the question was asked: Which is the more important, the nation or the king? To a question proposed in such a way there was but one answer. Caiaphas does not bring up the question of whether Jesus is guilty or not; that will be the business of the tribunal officially summoned to judge Him. The question they have to decide is whether His life is of more value, politically speaking, than the existence of the whole nation. As far as Caiaphas is concerned, there is no question; it is better 'that one man should die for the people and that the whole nation perish not.' The words 'should die for the people' were well chosen. What Israelite would refuse to die for his own people? At the same time these words expressed a profound hidden meaning, namely, that the death of Jesus was destined to be the salvation not only of the Jews, if they were willing, but also of all the children of God called together by Him into a single nation.

But of this meaning Caiaphas had no suspicion. Still it was not unheard of that the high priest should utter words of prophecy; it was said that even John Hyrcanus had done so,[1] and about this time Philo was saying that every high priest had the gift of prophecy.[2] St. John expresses no opinion about the matter, but he observes that Caiaphas, who was high priest for that year—the last year of the priesthood of the Old Covenant—and was shortly to forfeit his office in God's eyes for having exercised his power against God's own Son, Caiaphas had unconsciously paid homage to Him who was the victim of his injustice. The various groups within the council also, they saw no more in all this than the very opportune sacrifice of an innocent man, a thing which they found agreeable. There was now nothing more to be done but to lay hold of Jesus, find accusations against Him, and do Him to death.

The eve of the great event (222).

John xi, 54–57.

Jesus avoided showing Himself in Jerusalem, warned, perhaps, of these threatening intentions by some of the highly connected kinsmen of John, the son of Zebedee. He

[1] Josephus, *Antiquities*, XIII, x, 3.
[2] Philo, *De Spec. Leg.*, IV, 192; II, 367 f.

withdrew to a city named Ephraim near to the wilderness, placed by ancient tradition[1] at a spot twenty miles north of Jerusalem. The modern village of *Taiybeh* occupies precisely that position, lying a little to the north-east and overlooking the desert and the Jordan valley. From there an easy way lies open to Jericho by way of *Ain-Duk*. In that place Jesus spent a few days in a final close intercourse with His disciples ; it was like a period of recollection preparatory to the forming of some supreme resolution.

The feast of the Pasch was approaching, and it was expected that He would come up to Jerusalem. His enemies were prepared and ordered that those who knew where He was were to give information, so that He might be seized. The Jews who had come up from the country to the Holy City some days before, in order to purify themselves in preparation for the feast, felt a presentiment of some approaching tragedy. But the question was whether the principal actor would be tempted to escape instead of coming up to the feast.

[1] Eusebius and St. Jerome.

CHAPTER V

THE LAST PREACHING OF JESUS AT JERUSALEM

JESUS left Ephraim before the feast of the Pasch. St. John does not say explicity that He went down from there to Jericho, but that is suggested. He makes Jesus come to Bethany six days before the feast; but to travel from *Taiybeh* to Bethany it is necessary to pass either very close to Jerusalem or else through Jericho. The first route is shorter. But we learn, also from St. John, that Jesus did not make His entry into Jerusalem until after His visit to Bethany; and as a close watch was kept on Him, it would not have been possible for Him to reach the Mount of Olives so surreptitiously as not to be seen. In this case again, we find a real harmony between St. John and the Synoptists, concealed beneath what looks like disagreement to those who follow the itinerary of the Gospel journeys without taking the lie of the land into account. The only road from Ephraim to Jericho descends through *Ain-Duk*, and as Jesus went down that way the shadow of the Passion was already beginning to envelop Him. Soon after His arrival in the plain of Jericho He began the ascent to Jerusalem, one of the episodes of which was the triumph of Palm Sunday.

I. THE LAST JOURNEY TO JERUSALEM

The third prediction of the Passion and Resurrection (223).

Luke xviii, 31–34; Mark x, 32–34; Matthew xx, 17–19.[1]

We see Jesus, therefore, making His way through the Jordan valley which is wide enough to form a great plain. Westward arise precipitously the lofty hills forming the lowest of the three stages on the way up to Jerusalem, which

[1] The three Synoptists are in perfect agreement. Luke merely adds that the Apostles fail to understand. We follow Mark, whose account is the most detailed.

dominates them all. He has just seemed to run away from the threats of the Jews, but now He is making for the road which climbs from Jericho up the first slopes of these hills. He walks in front like a resolute leader. Those nearest to Him, His Apostles, are amazed ; there are others who still follow Him, but they are beginning to be afraid. Then the Master, counting only on His most faithful disciples, calls the Twelve to Him in order to encourage them beforehand with words they are to remember afterwards, showing them that glory will follow trial. He foretells that He is to be delivered up to the chief priests and doctors of the Law, to be ill-treated by them, condemned to death, handed over to the Gentiles who will mock Him, spit upon Him, scourge Him, and put Him to death. But afterwards comes the certain promise of the Resurrection, in preparation for which it was necessary to endure these sufferings described in detail and to pass through these hours of darkness ; for the Resurrection was a shining goal only to be reached after three grievous days of waiting. The Apostles do not understand Him. Why did not God manifest the Messiah in His glory from the very first?

The sort of ambition to be looked for in those who desire to reign with Jesus (224).

Mark x, 35–41 ; Matthew xx, 20–24.

Among those now following Jesus were certain courageous women of Galilee, who supplied by their attentions for the indifference with which He regarded His own material comfort. There is less pessimism in women, especially if they be mothers, than in men. The light of promise they see in the faces of their sons makes mothers ready to brave any danger. The mother of the sons of Zebedee, probably the woman named Salome, took a bold step when she saw Jesus walking ahead so resolutely. She decided to ask Him now to promise that He would give her sons the two chief places in His kingdom. She knows that this is what they desire, and she is only too glad to be their mouthpiece. She[1]

[1] This is Matthew's account. According to Mark it is the sons themselves who make the request. The wish was certainly their own, but that they should have got their mother to voice it for them is a very natural circumstance that Matthew had no reason for inventing.

approaches Jesus, therefore, and imagining Him already on His messianic throne she falls down at His feet, thus clearly showing that she has a favour to ask. 'What wilt thou?' Jesus asks. She has her answer ready: 'Say that these my two sons may sit, the one on Thy right hand, and the other on Thy left, in Thy kingdom.' But Jesus sees through the clever subterfuge of the two brothers, and His answer is addressed to them: 'You know not what you ask.'

Had they not heard, or had they not understood what He had just told them, namely, that He Himself would enter into His glory only after He had suffered? Was it fitting that they should ask for places at His side in glory if they were not ready to share His lot, even in death? He compares His sufferings and death to a cup of bitterness that He must drink,[1] as well as to deep water into which He must be plunged.[2] The two brothers, whom He had previously named the Sons of Thunder,[3] are attentive only to the voice of their heart, and reply: 'We can.' Jesus accepts this assurance of their fidelity: 'You shall indeed drink of the chalice that I drink of, and with the baptism wherewith I am baptized you shall be baptized.' Assuredly, they will be rewarded for this suffering; but it is not for the Son of God, in His role of Messiah, to allot places at His right hand and His left: that belongs to the Father. Doubtless the two brothers drew no clear distinction between the kingdom the Messiah was to found on earth, which was in a special way His kingdom,[4] and the kingdom of the elect which belonged to the Father. Their minds ran on the thought of glory. Now glory meant a state of beatitude with God, where Jesus too would reign; but the degrees of blessedness in God's kingdom were determined by His eternal decree.

Thus did Jesus turn aside the request of the two brothers without either admitting or rejecting it, for the intentions of His Father were not to be disclosed. Their earthly destiny, however, He unfolded to them: they were to be admitted to a share in their Master's sufferings. In what degree was this to be fulfilled? The answer to this was made clear in

[1] Psalm lxxiv, 9; Isaias li, 17–22; Lamentations iv, 21; Ezechiel xxiii, 31.

[2] To be baptized, i.e. plunged, in misfortune, is a common expression in profane writers. Mark alone adds this, but it is certainly authentic.

[3] Mark iii, 17.

[4] Matthew xiii, 41.

the case of James, the elder of the brothers, who was beheaded by Herod Agrippa[1] a few years after the death of Jesus, in the year 44. But ancient tradition held it for certain that John had ended his life by a natural death. Nevertheless, his banishment to Patmos was a very severe hardship for his Master's sake. Tertullian believed also that he had been plunged into a cauldron of boiling oil by order of Domitian. Others again declared that he had drunk of a poisoned cup without any evil result.[2] But these traditions apart, it may still be said that the metaphor of the cup and baptism is vague enough to be understood of a long life spent in the apostolate, a life, therefore, of labour, suffering, and persecution. Some modern writers, however, are so exacting that they insist on reading into Mark's text the conviction that the two brothers had suffered death by martyrdom at the time when the evangelist wrote. This is an ingenious way of depriving John, the son of Zebedee, of the authorship of the fourth gospel; but it will not stand against the constant tradition. And is it only in this case that we are to interpret the figurative expressions of the gospel with such rigour?[3]

The other ten Apostles certainly did not understand the prediction of Jesus in so tragic a manner. They were much less struck by the courageous fidelity of the two sons of Zebedee than by their ambition. Far from pitying them, they were indignant;[4] so much more ready were they to turn their imagination to the glory of the Messiah than to His sufferings. The mother of the two sons had wanted to speak to Jesus confidentially, but the others had heard everything from a distance. The Master now makes them come near that He may give them all the lesson which is called for by the leaning they all have towards ambition, a lesson which was rendered all the more opportune by their persistent misunderstanding of the part He was to play as the Messiah.

[1] Acts xii, 2. [2] Leucius Charinus in the *Acta Johannis*, 9.

[3] An article by the Rev. J. H. Bernard in the *Journal of Theological Studies*, 1927, April, pp. 262 ff., shows that the first of the two metaphors *may* refer to death, but not the second; also that the idea of baptism by blood is a later and derived notion within the Church, dating only from the time of Origen.

[4] This only too human feature is in St. Matthew's account also: hence it cannot be said that he has put the mother forward in order to spare the Apostles.

Jesus has come to give His life as a ransom (257).

Mark x, 42–45 ; Matthew xx, 25–28 ; Luke xxii, 25–26, 30b.[1]

Then Jesus said to the Twelve gathered around Him : 'They that are in positions of command over the Gentiles lord it over them, and the great ones exercise authority over the people. But it is not so among you.'[2] They ought not to desire to be amongst the great and the foremost, and even if they have to perform functions of authority for the common good, they must act in reality as the servants of all. Amongst Christians, indeed, he who is called to rule must act boldly as leader ; but he will only be accepted as leader if it is realized that he does in truth humble himself beneath everyone. Hence the title chosen for the Roman Pontiff, who is the chief pastor, is 'Servant of the servants of God.' And the motive in all this must be the desire to imitate the Son of Man, who came not to be served but to serve. Before He came the word 'serve' had an ill repute, but it has taken on a noble signification on account of His example. Then He proceeds to show them what is the inward motive of His own loving self-abasement, the hour for which has now arrived : the Son of Man was come to serve and to give His soul, that is to say, His life, as a ransom on behalf of many. This is what the Good Shepherd had already said of the laying down of His life for His sheep.[3]

What did Jesus mean here ? His words are obscure if we try to apply each one of them directly to Him. The 'many' in question seem to stand for the human race which is delivered by one man. But was humanity held captive ? By whom ? To whom was the ransom to be paid, and in what sense can the death of Jesus be regarded as the payment of a ransom ? Early commentators occupied themselves with the solution of such questions as these, sometimes going beyond the bounds of what is strictly legitimate in the application of this parabolic saying to the Redemption.[4]

[1] These texts of St. Luke are to be found in No. 257 of the Synopsis amongst the discourses delivered at the Last Supper. But it seems to us now preferable to regard them as an instruction given to the disciples after the inopportune request of the mother of James and John. As Luke, however, had not mentioned this incident he put this instruction along with that given at the Last Supper. There is good reason, then, for transferring Luke xxii, 25–26, 30b, to this place.

[2] Mark x, 42 f. [3] John x, 15.

[4] Some have imagined that the ransom was paid to the devil, and so on. . . .

Those to whom Jesus spoke gathered this much, at least: that He was comparing Himself to a servant intensely devoted to his master who was condemned to die if no one was found willing to die for him, and the servant gladly offers his own life as a ransom. He, the Son of Man, who had condescended to live among them like one of themselves in the guise of a servant, was offering His life not for a single person, however, but for all mankind. He was willing to die for them, and in a certain sense instead of them. God accepted that sacrifice for the salvation of men, offered out of the greatest love that could possibly be conceived. Such a thing was enough to inspire souls to love One who has loved us so much, to love other men too and devote our energies to the service of our neighbour in imitation of Him, serving them out of charity.

St. Paul, as we know, devoted much attention to the development of this dogma of the redeeming death of Christ. We see here how he drew his inspiration from the teaching of Jesus. It would be idle to object that this teaching is merely a trace of the Paulinism that has crept into the gospels. On the contrary, it is another example of the manner in which it was Jesus' custom to teach, taking a doctrine of salvation and hiding it, like a fertile seed, beneath that parabolic form of instruction which He adopted for His use. In the gospel of St. John we find that doctrine in the allegory of the Good Shepherd giving His life for His sheep; in St. Matthew and St. Mark it is contained in the parable of the servant who gives his life for his master. The figures are different, but the revelation is the same. In the fourth gospel, as in the two Synoptists, Jesus holds back this revelation until He is near His Passion. He has often declared that He must suffer and die; now, at last, He explains that He accepts death for the salvation of mankind.

In the neighbourhood of Jericho. The cure of Bartimæus and another blind man (225).

Luke xviii, 35–43; Mark x, 46–52; Matthew xx, 29–34.

Words such as these were well calculated to reconcile the Apostles with one another; uncontrolled and disappointed ambition was put to shame by the living example of their Master; fraternal charity came to life again when brought into contact with such a great love as this. They continue their journey, and from now on they think more of the fate which threatens Him, a fate they also must share, and they are content to leave to God the care of assigning to each of them his place in the glory of the kingdom.

Traversing the foot of the hills they passed the beautiful spring at Douka (*Ain Duk*) and came to the even larger fountain (*Ain Sultan*) which supplied ancient Jericho with water. At this time the Canaanite fortress conquered by Josue had scarcely any inhabitants, but its site, which has[1] been discovered, was then well known. The way that led to the new Jericho, built in ornate fashion by Herod the Great, passed through the ancient city. The new city had been built near the entrance to the precipitous valley of the brook Kelt, and in that valley Herod had collected the mountain streams in order to water his pleasure city. As Jesus was entering there, about half an hour after passing through ancient Jericho,[2] a large crowd collected behind Him, telling each other His name and enthusiastically applauding Him. In the midst of all this a blind man began to cry out : ' Son of David, Jesus, have mercy on me ! ' St. Mark, who had probably been acquainted with him among the Christian brethren, tells us that his name was Bartimæus. No doubt he was sitting by the roadside along with another blind man, for it was the practice of these unfortunates to go about in pairs. This other man was also cured, but he remains unidentified.[3] Bartimæus, eager and impulsive by character, cried out so loudly that he was ordered to be silent. But he only cried out still more loudly : ' Son of David, have mercy on me ! '

Jesus had already gone by ; but touched by the misfortune and also by the great confidence of the man, He stopped and

[1] Cf. *Revue Biblique*, 1909, pp. 270 ff. ; 1910, pp. 405 ff.

[2] There is a temptation to make use of the two Jerichos in order to bring Luke, who places the miracle before, into harmony with Matthew and Mark, who place it after the entry into Jericho. But the miracle must have been performed near the Jericho of Herod. Mark and Matthew, however, may have been thinking of the ancient Jericho when they wrote ' after.' Luke, who laid emphasis on the enthusiasm stirred up in the Jericho where Jesus stayed, could only place the miracle ' before ' His entry. However, in this case as in so many others, it is the miracle that is of chief importance, not its chronological position.

[3] Matthew is alone in speaking of two blind men. Whilst fully admitting the cure of two, we must recognize that the second is a mere supernumerary who is deemed to have said the same thing as Bartimæus because he shared his sentiments.

said : ' Call him ! ' The crowd, fickle as ever, now becomes interested in the blind man. ' Courage ! ' they say ; ' Arise ! He calleth thee.' Then, far from groping his way forward so as to make his blindness noticeable and thus inspire pity, the man throws off his cloak so as to be freer, leaps forward, and with the surest of instincts finds himself at the feet of Jesus. In order to give him an opportunity of voicing his faith publicly, our Saviour asks him : ' What wilt thou that I should do to thee ? ' But what could a blind man desire ? ' Master, that I may see.' Jesus says to him : ' Go ; thy faith hath saved thee.' Immediately he was cured and followed Jesus, his gratitude breaking out into praise of God, so that the curiosity of the crowd changed into religious awe.

Jesus in the house of Zachæus (226).

Luke xix, 1–10.

Then Jesus entered Jericho. Along the streets and in the open places there were trees, planted in that haphazard fashion which is a not unpleasing feature of oriental cities, ancient and modern alike. To this day beautiful dark green sycamores grow at Jericho and the roots of these trees, rising out of the ground and supporting the trunk like flying buttresses, almost touch the lower branches!

Now the head of the publicans' office at Jericho, a Jew named Zachæus, was desirous of seeing the face of this Jesus whose name flew from mouth to mouth in the crowd. He was a small man, and so, stirred by the common enthusiasm which makes all things permissible, he clambered up a sycamore at the risk of being made the butt of joking comments. A publican up a sycamore tree ! Jesus also raised His eyes to look at him, but it was only to say kindly : ' Zachæus, come down quickly, for this day I must abide in thy house.' An incorrigible prophet was this Jesus ! Behold Him now choosing a sinner's house for His lodging even while He is in the act of being saluted as Son of David, or in other words as Messiah. There was a sign of murmuring and we can guess from whom it came.

Zachæus, the publican, was deeply touched by this kindness and showed himself to be a man of feeling. Even before our Saviour had sat down at his table, Zachæus stood at the entrance of his house and showed unwillingness to receive Him into the dwelling of a rich sinner. Confident of understanding the wishes of his guest, for Jesus had made no secret about what He desired, the publican declared that he gave half of his possessions to the poor. There were plenty of opportunities for defrauding others in his work ; and even without actually committing fraud, how easy it was to demand a little more than the fixed sum under the pretext of covering oneself against risks ! Therefore, if he had done wrong to any one, he would make good the injustice, and he condemned himself to the penalty assigned to theft ; he would restore fourfold.[1] The Master approves this action. He was indeed bringing salvation into that house. A son of Israel, who has compromised himself by his dealings with Gentiles, becomes a genuine son of Abraham once more. In reply to the murmurings, perhaps being uttered by those who were just coming in, Jesus now declares, as He had formerly declared about that other publican, Levi-Matthew[2] : 'The Son of Man is come to seek and save that which was lost.'

The Semi-Pelagians appealed to this incident of Zachæus to support their contention that the first movement in the work of salvation must proceed from the human soul. But would Zachæus have climbed up the sycamore unless his heart had first been touched by the presence of Jesus, who had come to Jericho in order to convert him ? It is God, then, who begins the good work, but it is for us to follow His call as Zachæus did. This friend of Our Saviour is honoured in France as a saint at the sanctuary of Rocamadour.

The parable of the pounds or talents (227).

Luke xix, 11–28 ; Matthew xxv, 14–30.[3]

People came in freely after the meal, and probably during the course of the meal also ; this was the custom then, and it is still observed in the East. Moreover, the curiosity aroused by Jesus would have excused breaches of custom even had they taken place. There was a feeling of great

[1] This was the Roman law for open theft. Hebrew law imposed this penalty for cattle thieving (Exod. xxii, 1).

[2] Luke v, 32.

[3] Matthew speaks of talents, Luke of *minæ* (pounds). As usual, Matthew has preserved only what is essential in the teaching of Jesus. Luke, whom we follow, has kept its historical setting which suits the circumstances and brings the teaching out in relief.

agitation. He whom men were already saluting as the Messiah would not go up to Jerusalem like an ordinary pilgrim. Doubtless there was to occur some spectacular manifestation of divine intervention ; the kingdom of God would be proclaimed. But Jesus was determined to say once more that it was not His intention to set Himself up as a political Messiah, to start a revolution in order to seat Himself on the throne of Israel. King He was indeed by right of birth, but He was to disappear before receiving the crown from His Father ; those who professed to be His disciples would have to show loyalty to Him during an absence that was to last long. In order to impress this truth upon His hearers, who were so slow to understand it, He made use of a parable addressed to people of the higher classes who mixed in politics and public affairs.

In these circles it was remembered that the first Herod had been to Rome to ask the Senate to grant him the title of King of Judæa. His son Archelaus, whom he had nominated in his will as his successor, had not dared to assume the crown without first receiving permission at Rome from the emperor Augustus. When he went thither he was followed by some of the Jews who were resolved to oppose his claim.[1] Jesus could, therefore, without causing any surprise to people who knew what had happened, propose the case of a man of noble birth setting out for a distant country in the hope of being there invested with the royal dignity and returning as king. This heir to the throne was Himself. What were his servants to do in the meantime? Had they nothing to do but await his speedy return? No ; for perhaps his return might be delayed. They were therefore to look after their master's interests, and even work to increase his goods. Ten of them had received a *mina* each with instructions to turn it to good account. Not that Jesus is thinking of recommending letting out money at interest—He who had said that we should lend looking for nothing thereby ;[2] but He speaks to publicans in a language they can well understand. What was more suitable in the circumstances was a hard-working fidelity to their master, in view of the fact that the enemies of the prince were working against him in his absence. Everyone knew that Jesus also had adversaries who were determined to do all in their power to thwart Him. But a parable is not an allegory, and

[1] Josephus, *Antiquities*, XVII, ix, 3–6. [2] Luke vi, 35.

the Master does not lay emphasis on this passionate opposition of His enemies ; He leaves it in the secrecy where it works. On his return with royal power, the new sovereign's first care is concerned with his servants! The first says simply : 'Lord, thy *mina* hath gained ten.' The king expresses his thanks and, being now at liberty to dispose of all the offices of state, entrusts the government of ten cities to his servant. Another has gained five *minæ*, and is set over five cities. We are left to form for ourselves an idea of what happened to the rest by comparison with the first two. Finally, the last of them comes forward, and the suggestion here is that he has not dared to make up his mind between his prince and the party of opposition. He has not wasted his *mina ;* he has taken no risks and has tied it up in his handkerchief. He has done nothing for his master, but neither has he endangered his interests! All the same he is fully aware that he is not blameless, but instead of modestly excusing himself, he throws the blame on the king : 'I feared thee, because thou art a stern man. Thou takest up what thou didst not lay down, and thou reapest that which thou didst not sow.' In truth he goes beyond all limits. On what are his complaints founded ? He makes it look as though nothing had been given him. The king, therefore, has the right to be stern, but he merely orders the *mina* to be taken away from the servant and, disdaining to take it back, he gives it to the most deserving of the others.

The punishment of his enemies is harsher : he orders them to be put to death before him. With that sentence the parable comes to a close, a sentence which terminates the period of opposition and inaugurates his kingship. The stage is now set ; the enemy is duly warned, and the disciples are encouraged to do their duty in their Lord's absence, assured of His return and of their reward. Then Jesus turns His steps towards Jerusalem.

II. SATURDAY BEFORE PALM SUNDAY

The anointing at Bethany (228).

Mark xiv, 3–9 ; Matthew xxvi, 6–13 ; John xii, 1–11.

Had we only the first three gospels we might conclude that Jesus went straight from Jericho to Jerusalem without interruption. We have already seen how their summary record of His journey from Galilee is restricted to one main route (save for the occasional departures from that route which in our opinion are to be found in the gospel of St. Luke), and how they mention no stopping-place except Jericho, whence Jesus departs for Jerusalem. St. John, however, has informed us of another halt between Jericho and the Holy City. Jesus had to pass through Bethany, and He stayed there on the sixth day before the Pasch when a feast was held in His honour. This sixth day before the Pasch was a Saturday, the Pasch falling on Friday that year, as we shall see later. Now Jesus would not have walked for five or six hours on a Sabbath day ; it is therefore probable that He left Jericho on Friday and spent the night in the open, as caravans often do before entering cities, so as to arrive at Bethany on Saturday morning without exceeding the distance allowed on the Sabbath, that is, about six furlongs.[1] The fact that it was the day of rest did not stand in the way of people having a somewhat carefully prepared meal on the evening of the Sabbath, as we have said before.[2]

According to Mark and Matthew, this repast took place on the evening of the Sabbath day in the house of Simon the leper : doubtless a leper cured by Jesus, but still known by the title his former disease had conferred on him. St. John omits all mention of him, but tells us that Lazarus, the man raised from the dead, was one of those who sat down at table. He makes Martha also appear as the housewife attending to the arrangements of the feast, while Mary later enters on the scene with the perfume. Judas, too, is mentioned. It looks very much as though the fourth evangelist had the intention here of revealing the names of persons hitherto unknown outside Palestine, while he refrains from repeating the name of Simon already mentioned by other evangelists.[3] The presence of these three friends of Jesus at the feast leads us to think that it was their house at which He was staying while at Bethany, and that Simon had

[1] Acts i, 12.

[2] Cf. p. 57, above. Matthew and Mark have recorded this meal later. In their narrative it partly explains Judas' betrayal ; hence they have interposed it between the perplexity of the priests concerning the means of laying hold of Jesus and their bargain with Judas.

[3] We follow, therefore, the narrative of John, supplementing it with that of Mark. There are no special details furnished by Matthew.

invited them to his house along with Jesus, either out of politeness, or perhaps because they were friends of his.

The meal had already begun when Mary, the sister of Lazarus, took a pound of scented spikenard of the purest quality, and, following the customary usage, anointed the head of Jesus. Then, as there was still much left, she poured it profusely over His feet, breaking the alabaster vessel so as to pour out every drop of the perfume. So copiously did she anoint His feet that she felt it incumbent on her to wipe them, and this she did with her hair. The odour of the scented oil filled all the house.

Amongst the disciples present was Judas Iscariot, the one to whom the Master had given charge of the scanty common purse. Avaricious by disposition and uneasy about the future, Judas was laying money aside. Such a piece of extravagance as this was shocking to him. A perfume that might have been sold for three hundred pence! But he hides his inward feelings and appeals to what he considers Jesus's weak point in saying that this perfume ought to have been sold and the money given to the poor. For once the Master seems less concerned to help the poor than to defend this noble woman against such a hypocrite. 'Let her alone,' He said. 'You wonder why she has not sold this perfume? It was so that she could keep it for the day of My burial.' Her mindful heart had indeed been touched by a foreboding to which the others had been insensible, and she had anointed her beloved Master's body before the time. It was a gesture so full of beauty, for it was inspired by light from above, that Jesus declared in solemn fashion: 'Wheresoever this gospel shall be preached in the whole world, that also which she hath done shall be told for a memorial of her.' The prophecy is fulfilled in every pulpit from which the Passion is preached.

As for the poor, Jesus who is about to die can do nothing more for them Himself, but He leaves the care of them to His disciples. At present, however, He would like to move their hearts with the tender and sad feelings which have touched the heart of Mary: 'The poor you have always with you; but Me you have not always.' Never before had Jesus so strongly declared the imminence of His death. Already He saw Himself lying embalmed by the loving hands of women. . . .

Judas says to himself that it is useless to count any further on Jesus ; He is lost, and the only thing to do is to get what benefit one can from the situation. Stirred to resentment by the rebuke he has received, the idea of betraying his Master enters his mind. It was only very gently that Jesus had reproved him, but the idea of *his* sober judgement being set on one side because of the feelings of a woman ! His base soul measures everything by its worth in cash. No longer does he believe in his Master, whom, it may be, he has never really loved : a leader who has let Himself be carried away by vain dreams, but who is now a prey to discouragement. This is where Judas begins to play his part : it is he who will be the traitor.

III. PALM SUNDAY

The Messianic entry of Jesus into Jerusalem (229).

Luke xix, 29–44 ; Mark xi, 1–11a ; Matthew xxi, 1–11, 14–16 ; John xii, 12–19.

The next day Jesus prepared for His entry into Jerusalem. Knowing that He was at Bethany, a considerable crowd of people had come out to meet Him, too impatient to await the arrival of this famous rabbi in the Holy City. They also wanted to see Lazarus whom He had raised from the dead. On seeing Lazarus, their enthusiasm increased, to the exasperation of the chief priests. These had already made up their minds to do Jesus to death, but now they resolved to make away with Lazarus also ; he would not rise again, once Jesus was dead.

In spite of the chief priests, the number of those who wished to applaud the Master by thus accompanying Him into Jerusalem increased. On the occasion of the bringing of the first-fruits[1] up to the Temple, it was the custom of the people of the city to go out to meet the pilgrims and to return with them in a joyful and clamorous procession. Musical instruments were played and hymns chanted. On this occasion the leaders of the priesthood kept sullenly aloof. The Galilæans who accompanied Jesus and the inhabitants of the city shared views with one another, and on the spur of the moment an escort was formed for Jesus. It was perhaps because He was unwilling to compromise His

[1] Mishnah, *Bikkurim*, III, 3.

friends in any way that He had not asked at Bethany for the lowly beast on which it was His purpose to make His entry into the city. The village of Bethphage lay on His road, somewhere on the slopes of the Mount of Olives between Bethany and Jerusalem. Thither He sent two of His disciples with the rather strange mission to bring Him an ass's colt, which they would find tied up at the entrance to the village, and they were to bring it without asking any one's leave. It is probable that, in His thoughtfulness for others, He thus provided the owner with the opportunity of disclaiming all responsibility before the authorities, though He knew that He could count on the owner's consent, for He said to His disciples : 'If any man shall ask you : Why do you loose him ? You shall say : Because the Lord hath need of him and will send him back at once.' Everything happened as Jesus had foretold. They found an ass's colt tied up at a door in the street and loosed it. When surprise was shown at this, the disciples related what their Master had bidden them to say and were allowed to depart with the colt.

It was the object of Jesus to fulfil a well-known prophecy of the prophet Zacharias,[1] introduced here by St. Matthew with a few words from Isaias which are intended to diminish the note of triumph which is conveyed in the passage from Zacharias. Instead of that prophet's : 'Rejoice greatly, O daughter of Sion, shout for gladness, O daughter of Jerusalem !' St. Matthew, realizing that the chief value of the imposing imagery used by the prophets is to bring out the spiritual lesson they teach,[2] thinking also of the secret hostility which filled the hearts of the princes of the daughter of Sion, omits the invitation to rejoice and writes merely : 'Tell ye the daughter of Sion,' in the more modest fashion of Isaias.[3] Further, Zacharias had said : 'Behold thy king cometh to thee, just and victorious, humble and riding upon an ass, and on a colt, the foal of asses.' Here again St. Matthew suppresses what gives too glorious an aspect ; all that he leaves is that the king is meek and riding upon an ass. Therefore, Jesus who up to this always declined the title of Messiah, except secretly and from His most faithful followers, was here giving His approval to what was in effect a

[1] Zachary ix, 9.
[2] See *Pascal et les prophéties messianiques,* Rev. Biblique, 1906, pp. 533–560.
[3] Isaias lxii, 11.

Messianic entry into the Holy City. But the time had come when He was about to declare before the Sanhedrin that He was indeed the Messiah, and He now allows the multitude to hail Him by that title.

It was also His desire that the pomp of His entry should be so unassuming as to give no cause of offence to the Roman authorities, and that it should have nothing of a riotous or revolutionary character. A good deal has been written about the way in which Orientals are said to regard the ass as a noble animal. But a Roman passing by on a well-trained horse, helmet on head and lance in hand, would have been more likely to smile at what would seem to him a ludicrous procession or masquerade, a caricature of the triumphant ascent to the Capitol. Jesus, however, accepted this humble homage, humble and meek King as He was; these good folk were doing the best that lay in their power. Those who were nearest laid their garments upon the ass's colt[1] to do duty for a saddle, others spread their cloaks upon the ground along with green branches cut from the fields, while they carried branches of palm in their hands. Then surrounding Jesus, some running ahead, others following behind, and all crying: 'Hosanna! Blessed be He that cometh in the name of the Lord! Blessed be the kingdom that cometh, the kingdom of our father David! Hosanna in the highest!'[2] Hosanna, meaning 'Save, then!' was an acclamation devoted by custom for use in processions. Thus they were hailing the Son of David, the King of Israel, the Messiah whom they so ardently desired.

The Pharisees, though they were powerless to forestall and to check this popular outburst, at any rate found this advantage in it, that they could make Jesus responsible for the disorder: 'Master, rebuke Thy disciples.' But the Master is unwilling to give the lie to those who thus believe in Him; they are only carrying out God's design: 'If these shall hold their peace, the very stones will cry out.'[3] Amid this general enthusiasm His enemies are discouraged and admit with bad grace: 'Do you see that we prevail nothing? Behold the whole world is gone after Him.'

Nevertheless Jesus was very far removed from the

[1] St. Matthew says that there was a she-ass also, the mother of the foal, which would not have come without her.

[2] Mark xi, 9 f.

[3] Luke xix, 39 ff.; John xii, 19. See also Matthew xxi, 15 ff.

triumphant sentiments of the victorious generals of antiquity. After mounting to the Capitol, these generals would descend to see the slaughter of the kings they had conquered. But in this case it was Jesus Himself who was to be the victim, and the city of Jerusalem that He had come to save was to suffer with Him. As He saw spread out before Him, still fresh with the brilliance of their great white stones, the palaces, the ramparts, the Temple of the Lord shining with gold, and all that holy Sion where hatred and treachery awaited Him, He burst into tears. Many a saint has wept with Him in reading this lament :[1] 'Ah ! if thou also hadst known on this day that which was necessary for thy peace ! But now it is hidden from thy eyes. For the days shall come upon thee when thy enemies shall cast a rampart about thee, and compass thee round about, and straiten thee on every side, and dash thee to the ground and thy children who are in thee, and shall not leave in thee a stone upon a stone, because thou hast not known the time of thy visitation.' It is the ever repeated refrain of unrequited love. Thou, thou, ever thou ! It is not that Jesus is looking over Jerusalem to see the place where He is to die. His eyes are not fixed upon the site of Golgotha. What weighs upon His mind is the vision of a people delivered over to madness, factions on every side, divisions healed for a time by a despairing rage against a determined enemy who is tightening his toils about the city and advancing to attack ; it is the wailing of children crushed under the falling stones, the burning torch thrown into the Temple, God's worship coming to an end in those sacred courts. As we pause to-day for a moment at the place where Jesus wept, our hearts turn straight to Calvary, but our eyes are irresistibly drawn towards the shining splendour of the Mosque of Omar, lying peacefully within the ancient enclosure walls of the Temple as though confident in its beauty. It bears witness to the end of the old covenant even more than did the old altar lying in its ruins on the site now occupied by the Mosque. And even if, by some impossibility, it were delivered up to the destroying hammers of the Jews, who now mourn against its walls, so that they might build once more their Temple, they would not dare to shed again the blood of victims so near to Calvary, where flowed the blood of Him whom they caused to be sacrificed. Oxen and

[1] Luke xix, 41 ff.

lambs have nothing to fear from them. Mankind will no longer call for any sacrifice of blood except that of the cross.

The death of the Messiah is the way to His glory (230).
John xii, 20–36.

At length Jesus reached Jerusalem and entered the Temple enclosure whither the multitude followed Him. Gentiles might enter the outer courts, but they were forbidden under pain of death to enter the inner courts.[1] Gradually the enthusiasm of the morning waned. All departed to seek food. In the evening Jesus was probably in the Temple once more, and again, as the hero of the day, He was surrounded by eager listeners ; but there was little or no excitement. Perhaps He would now give some watch-word, explain His plans, or show what sort of mission He thought Himself called to perform. Some Gentiles were present, men sympathetic towards Judaism and already attached to the worship of the one God, proselytes who had come to adore the Lord during the feast, sharing in the prayers if not in the rites of the Jews. Through the instrumentality of Philip and Andrew—both hailing from Bethsaida of Galilee which was bordering on the Gentile countries, and both bearing Greek names—they were able to satisfy their desire to see Jesus. In this way they were privileged to be present at a veritable revelation of the manner in which Jesus understood the part He was to play.

His opening words were of a character to encourage them : 'The hour is come that the Son of Man should be glorified.' It pleased Him to assume that little-known title of Son of Man, but it was indeed as Messiah that He was going to glory. Then, immediately, He compares Himself to a grain of wheat : if it be not sown, if it die not in the soil, it cannot bring forth fruit. Is it necessary, then, that He should die ? Must all anticipate the same fate who resolve to follow Him ? Yes, for we must hate our lives, that is, we must accept death, if we would gain eternal life. Thus He shows that He has no idea of reigning now, but is thinking only of life in the world to come. Here He summons those who are willing to follow Him, for the true way

[1] Recently one of the tablets containing a Greek inscription prohibiting their entry was discovered.

of serving Him is to imitate Him. It is not He who will reward His followers but His Father; the reward also, then, will be in that mysterious world which is to come. But the near approach of death makes nature tremble, and Jesus confesses that His soul is troubled. Will He therefore cry out for mercy and say: 'Father, save Me from this hour?' No, for it is by His own free choice that He has come to this painful moment, in the knowledge that by doing so He gives glory to His Father. Hence, He prays: 'O Father, glorify Thy name!'

The miracles Jesus had worked had already displayed the glory of that divine name; accordingly a voice from Heaven now declared: 'I have both glorified it and will glorify it again.' Not that the voice came for the sake of Jesus; He already knew His Father's will and command. The Father had spoken that others might give credit to His Son. But God's word is differently understood by men according to the different dispositions in which it finds them. The Jews were already familiar with this 'daughter of the voice,' as they called it, which resounded from heaven. The best disposed among them said to one another: 'An angel spoke to Him.' Others merely thought it was the sound of thunder, for it was the springtime when thunder is sometimes heard,[1] and for the Hebrews thunder was the voice of God. But on this occasion there was some astonishment at the way in which the sound of the thunder came as a response to the Messiah's appeal to His Father. Jesus proceeded to explain to them what was the meaning of this voice.

God was about to judge the world, not in thunder and lightning as on Sinai, but up in heaven, and His judgement would consist in casting out Satan, whom the Jews themselves called the ruler of the world. The defeat of Satan had already begun;[2] it would be complete when Jesus, lifted up from the earth, would be in a position to draw all men to Himself.[3] But in what way was He to be lifted up? The

[1] Thunder is also heard in Palestine during the autumn, but never in summer or winter.

[2] Luke x, 18; xi, 20.

[3] St. Augustine has seen the objection to this, based on the fact that human nature is in a perpetual state of conflict with evil. But although, before our redemption, Satan was master within us, yet now, though he still attacks, his attack comes from without. We can now meet his darts with the armour of the Apostle. And if we are wounded our Healer is nigh.

phrase was not so obscure for the Jews as it is for us ; it could refer to being raised on a cross as well as being lifted up in dignity. And after all that Jesus had said about His death, they must have concluded that He was speaking of His being lifted up for execution. The crowd, at any rate, was under no misapprehension ; but the saying caused the listeners further surprise and doubt : 'We have heard,' they said, 'from the Law (meaning here the Sacred Scriptures, including the Prophets and the Psalms) that the Christ abideth for ever ; and how sayest Thou that the Son of Man must be lifted up ?' They are aware that Jesus is referring to Himself under this title of Son of Man, but what does He really mean by it ? They are not accustomed to regard it as a synonym for the Messiah. Not all of them have read Daniel. And even in Daniel the Son of Man comes down from the clouds, and that is not true of Jesus. They do not know what to think.

Here, as formerly, this presentiment of ignominious suffering brings stupefaction to the minds of the hearers. The crowd can hardly credit its own enthusiasm of that very morning, for now it begins to doubt Him whom it had applauded as the Messiah. Thus was Israel always, as in the days of Osee, 'like the cloud at daybreak, and like the morning dew that passeth away.'[1]

Night was now falling.[2] The last rays of the setting sun were shining on the summit of the Mount of Olives and lighting up the mountains of Moab in the distance. This provided Jesus with His text : 'Yet a little while the Light is among you' ; the Light was He Himself, for had not Isaias said that the Messiah was to be the Light of the Nations ?[3] To believe in that Light was to become the children of light, with power to discern God's mysterious purpose in the Messiah's death. Those who did not believe would be shrouded in the ever-growing darkness, and would consequently walk without knowing whither they were going. As a result of these grave words, no one ventured to offer Jesus hospitality in Jerusalem ; He therefore withdrew to Bethany[4] with His disciples, sure of being welcomed there by the children of light.

[1] Osee xiii, 3.
[2] A conjecture based on Mark xi, 11.
[3] Isaias xlii, 6 ; xlix, 6.
[4] Mark xi, 11 ; Matthew xxi, 17.

IV. MONDAY IN HOLY WEEK[1]

Jesus had still left four days in which to bring light to men of good will and to show the others that He was fully aware of their plots, which were to have such disastrous consequences for the whole nation. Would that we knew how those precious days were spent ! St. Luke gives us merely a general idea when he tells us that 'in the daytime, He was teaching in the Temple ; but at night He went out and abode on the mount that is called Olivet.'[2] We must understand by this that Jesus either spent the night in the garden of Gethsemani or else in the place of hospitality offered Him at Bethany ; Bethany is mentioned by St. Matthew and St. Mark, and it does actually crown the eastern slope of the Mount of Olives. St. Matthew says nothing which enables us to distribute the events over the different days, but a careful reading of St. Mark's text enables us to distinguish the sequence of the days. We find, however, that all the discussions and discourses are assigned to Tuesday in Holy Week, perhaps by a slightly artificial arrangement. Had we been writing the gospel, should we have carefully preserved all that was said on that day and neglected everything said on the other days ? This may be the reason why St. Luke has refrained from entering into precise details about this period. Apart, then, from the above reservation, we shall here follow the order suggested by St. Mark.

The barren fig tree (232–234).

Mark xi, 12–19 ; Matt. xxi, 18–19a ; Luke xix, 47–48.

On the day after His entry into Jerusalem Jesus left Bethany in the early morning. The incident that follows is very strange, especially with the details given by St. Mark. The story contains features that appear most unlikely, but it seems quite clear that they are told with deliberate intention for the purpose of emphasizing the strangeness of the story. We do not insinuate that the story was invented ; the incident took place exactly as it is related. But at the same time it would be an error to regard it as an event which contains its own explanation, to be estimated according to

[1] We follow Mark's chronology, which is more precise.
[2] Luke xxi, 37.

the natural order of things ; it is rather a symbolic action, after the fashion of those employed by the prophets,[1] who did things which appeared to be meaningless but which were done with the intention of attracting attention.

To begin with, we are surprised to find Jesus hungry immediately after leaving the house of His friends. He approaches a fig tree in order to find means of satisfying His hunger. On the sunny slopes of Bethany there could have been leaves on the tree at the beginning of April, but certainly not fruit. St. Mark puts the exegetes at their ease by making the precise observation : 'For it was not the time for figs.' Then we behold Our Lord, so to speak, cursing the fig tree : 'May no man hereafter eat fruit of thee any more for ever!' If ever it were possible for a tree to be guilty, that one at any rate seems to have been free from blame. But the disciples who were listening with great attention ought to have realized that Jesus was alluding to the time of His visit to Jerusalem. On His coming thither, He had been offered the show of a deceptive welcome, a welcome that bore no fruit in the shape of a sincere attachment to Jesus, even after God had paid such great attentions to the tree of His election. Israel was that tree, and Israel was guilty ; the measure was full to overflowing ; henceforth God would look for no good from the people He had loved.

What happened to the fig tree in consequence of the curse ? Curiosity prefers St. Matthew's order, which tells us everything immediately. But the historical sequence followed by St. Mark compels us to wait.

Crossing the shoulder of the Mount of Olives, Jesus arrives once more in Jerusalem. It is at this moment that St. Mark places the expulsion of the traders from the Temple, assigned by St. Luke and St. Matthew to the previous day, and related by St. John at the time of Jesus' first pilgrimage to the Temple at the date of His commencement of the public ministry. If we admit that the expulsion of the traders took place on two different occasions, it will be preferable to put the second on the Monday rather than the Sunday ; it would have been singularly surprising on that day in the midst of all the joyous acclamations. The modest triumph which Jesus enjoyed on the Sunday gives sufficient explanation of the displeasure shown by the leaders of the Jews.

[1] D. Buzy, *Les symboles de l'Ancien Testament ;* and A. Régnier, *Le réalisme dans les symboles des Prophètes* (*Revue Biblique*, 1923, pp. 383–408).

The chief priests, the doctors of the Law, and the principal men of the country—the Sanhedrin, in other words—were from this time forward possessed by their determination to get rid of Jesus. They feared lest His favour with the people might once more revive and defeat their plan. Hence they held a succession of meetings ; indeed it seemed almost as though the Sanhedrin was in permanent session until their plan was accomplished. Meanwhile Jesus was left undisturbed to carry on His teaching until evening, when He left the city and returned to His retreat at Bethany.

V. TUESDAY IN HOLY WEEK

The withered fig tree and the power of faith (235).

Mark xi, 20–25 ; Matthew xxi, 19b–22.

Early on the next day Jesus returned to Jerusalem, and as He naturally went by the same way, His disciples observed that the fig tree was withered down to the roots. Peter provides the occasion for an explanation : 'Rabbi, behold the fig tree which Thou didst curse is withered away !' Surely they had grasped the symbolism of their Master's act ! Were they thinking with terror of the fate which threatened Jerusalem ? It was the sole instance of a miracle worked by Him that did not proceed from His goodness of heart. At present it is not His desire to dwell upon this sinister omen, the realization of which is left to be seen later. He wishes them now to learn from it the lesson of the power that they themselves can exercise by means of faith and prayer. Pointing to the summit of the Mount of Olives, its enormous mass overlooking the Dead Sea, He says to them : 'Have faith in God. Amen I say to you that whosoever shall say to this mountain : Be thou moved and be cast into the sea ; and shall not stagger in his heart, but believe that what he saith shall be done, it shall be done for him.'[1] There is hardly any need for us to draw attention to the speculative character of these words, or to say how scrupulous the true disciples of the crucified Master have always been to avoid even the appearance of ostentation. And those who have not been His disciples have striven in vain to work striking marvels. What the disciples chiefly stood in need of was

[1] Mark xi, 22 f.

encouragement. Their faith was about to be subjected to a severe trial, and Jesus seeks to strengthen it by promising them that they shall have the power of working miracles. In St. John's discourses after the Last Supper we find a similar assurance of miracles even greater than those which Jesus Himself had worked, along with an urgent exhortation to prayer.[1] The watchword, therefore, of these last days is confidence in prayer.

The source of Jesus' authority (236).

Luke xx, 1–8 ; Mark xi, 27–33 ; Matt. xxi, 23–27 ;[2] *cf.* John ii, 18–22.

The leaders, at the meeting of the Sanhedrin on the previous day, had failed in their efforts to prepare a well-founded accusation against Jesus ; therefore they must try to destroy His reputation among the populace. This they seek to bring about by taxing Him with embarrassing questions. For two days He had held triumphant sway in the Temple. At this very moment, He was walking there surrounded by a crowd, preaching His doctrine and, it might be, stirring them up to some boldness or other. Some of the chief priests, scribes, and elders asked Him point-blank : 'By what authority dost Thou these things ? And who hath given Thee this authority that Thou shouldst do these things ?' It might have been said that they behaved as though they already had Him at the bar, He the accused and they the judges, with the president of the Sanhedrin commencing the formal interrogation of the prisoner. But Jesus was still at liberty and could rely upon the loyalty of His friends, and He now chose to associate the people with His cause by indicating that He shared their admiration for John the Baptist. Therefore, adopting the custom that was common among the rabbis, He replied by putting a question Himself, as though to establish some common ground of discussion between Him and His questioners. Once agreed on this first point, it would be possible by comparison to throw its light on the point that as yet remained obscure : 'I will also ask you one word. Answer you Me, and I will

[1] John xiv, 12 f.
[2] The three Synoptists have the same general plan ; Mark's narrative is the most natural of the three, composed in a superbly unstudied manner.

tell you by what authority I do these things. The baptism of John, was it from heaven or from men ? '

His adversaries were silent, manifestly put out of countenance ; but Jesus insists : 'Answer Me ! ' What could they answer ? That John's baptism came from heaven ? If they did, then they would lay themselves open to the rejoinder : 'Why, then, did you not believe in him ? ' It was well, indeed, for *them* to hold an enquiry about the mission of prophets, if they refused to believe the prophets when they spoke in God's name ! Had they answered what they really felt, they would have said: 'From men.' But John, especially since his martyrdom, was put on a level with the great prophets of the past who, like Elias, had stood up against unbelieving kings ; the people devoutly revered his memory, and it would have been imprudent, especially just then, to incur their anger. So, affecting an air of unconcern, as though the question were not to the point, they answered : 'We know not.' But Jesus had warned them, and He kept His word : 'Neither do I tell you by what authority I do these things.'

By this manœuvre He not only escaped their trap, but also gave a lead to the good sense of the people ; for He had welded His cause with John's, and the people looked on John as a prophet. Yet their leaders were obstinate in refusing to recognize Jesus. How could they justify their efforts to go on preventing people from joining Him, particularly if He was the one whose coming John had announced ?[1]

[1] Nevertheless the efforts of the Sanhedrin were not completely wasted on that day. After the driving out of the traders from the Temple narrated by the fourth gospel, we read (John ii, 18) that the Jews proposed this question to Jesus : 'What miracle dost Thou show us, seeing that Thou dost these things ? ' Jesus replied : 'Destroy this temple, and in three days I will raise it up.' What He was referring to was the temple of His body which was restored to life in three days by means of the Resurrection ; but the Jews understood His words as an allusion to their Temple, and, neglecting the fact that Jesus spoke only of restoring and left to them the work of destroying, some of them took Him to mean that He was taking it upon Himself to overthrow the house of God. Whether the expulsion of the traders from the Temple is to be assigned to the last week of Jesus' life, or whether St. John took these words out of their chronological situation in order to connect them with the Pasch Jesus spent at Jerusalem two years before, it seems certain that they were not uttered until a few days before His death, for this answer of His was the chief accusation brought against Him when He appeared before the Sanhedrin. We may easily suppose that during this preliminary enquiry made by the members of the Sanhedrin, with which we have just dealt in the text, they asked both these questions : first demanding a sign ; then, to finish with, whether they took the sign as proof or not, asking in whose name Jesus claimed to do as He did.

The parable of the two sons (237).

Matt. xxi, 28–32 ; cf. Luke vii, 29–30.[1]

These officials of the Sanhedrin, having been thus put to confusion and thinking it beneath their dignity to stand round with those who were being taught by Jesus, would have very much liked to slip away. No doubt some of them succeeded in doing so ; but Jesus now turned to the Pharisees and doctors[2] of the Law, always the foremost when there was a dispute, and bade them reflect on their lack of docility towards God which had led them astray with regard to John and was still blinding their eyes—they, the teachers of the Law ; while others, even sinners, showed themselves more obedient to God. By the aid of a parable He provides them with the means of judging the case for themselves ; when they have done so He will apply to them the judgement they have passed.

A man had two sons.[3] To one of them he said : 'Son, go work to-day in my vineyard.' He answered : 'I will not,' then repented and went. Either knowing nothing of this sudden change of mind, or else simply because he needed two workers in the vineyard, the father bade his other son to go to work also. In the case of this son there is an affected deference to his father as great as was the rudeness of the other : 'I go, sir.' But he did not go. 'Which of the two,' asks Jesus, 'did his father's will ?' There was only one answer : 'The first.'

Now what was the state of things at that very moment ? The publicans and harlots, though at first disobedient to the law of God, were doing penance and entering the kingdom of God, the foundations of which kingdom Jesus was now laying. The Pharisees, on the other hand, had always been vociferous about their determination to do the will of the Lord and live righteously according to all the righteousness of the Law. But now that God had revealed His will, what did they do ? Jesus leaves out all reference to Himself at first, for they might have objected that He was preaching a righteousness higher than that prescribed by the Law, and

[1] The parable appears to be in its proper place in St. Matthew. The fragment which Luke has preserved (vii, 29 ff.) must refer to this occasion.

[2] So in St. Luke.

[3] The order in which the two sons should come is a very difficult problem of textual criticism. But whatever be the order the lesson remains the same.

in doing so running the risk of upsetting the balance which all legislation should maintain. But no one could raise this objection against John the Baptist. He, although they refused to acknowledge the heavenly origin of his mission, had come in the way of strict legal righteousness, living with the austerity of an Elias and dying for one of the commandments of the Law of Moses. Yet the Pharisees had despised him, while the publicans and harlots had believed in him ; not even such a sight as that could persuade the Pharisees to follow in the way of repentance. And now, once more, in despising Jesus they refuse to follow the lead of John the Baptist, so fixed are they in their prejudice, so hardened are their hearts to the signs given by their Lord. Moreover, John was but a prophet sent by God, even though the last and greatest of the prophets : he was not the Son of God.

The parable of the wicked husbandmen (238–239).

Luke xx, 9–19 ; Mark xii, 1–12 ; Matt. xxi, 33–46.[1]

Having thus dealt with John and put to shame these obstinately hostile members of the Sanhedrin, Jesus now boldly draws their attention to Himself, for on their attitude to Himself hangs the salvation or the ruin of the whole nation. Once more He uses a parable as a means of leading their minds to the desired point; a parable which accomplishes its purpose all the more easily in that it has certain allegorical features. The owner of the vineyard is God Himself ; the vineyard is the land of Israel ; the servants are the prophets ; the wicked husbandmen are the stubborn and unfaithful leaders of the people ; the son is none other than Jesus the Son of God. The characters of the story move in a Palestinian setting, with sentiments that have the flavour of the land, and it would be a mistake to press every single detail in order to extract some symbolic meaning. The parable begins by conducting us to those rock-strewn hills on which the vine thrives so well in the Holy Land. The vineyard is enclosed with a wall of uncemented stones, and the owner has hollowed out a basin in the rock to receive the grape juice, squeezed from the fruit by a rude press fixed upon two beams

[1] Mark and Luke send the servants singly, Matthew in groups. Luke and Matthew apply the lesson completely, Mark only in part, leaving the rest to be understood.

of wood. In the vineyard there is a roughly built round tower with a flat terraced roof, on which the owner spends the night under a tent made of boughs during the season when the grapes are ripening, in order to protect them against thieves and jackals.

Here, whether we are learned or unlearned in the Scriptures, there will come to our minds the memory of that celebrated passage in Isaias :

> 'My beloved had a vineyard
>   on a fertile hill-side.
> He digged it, he weeded it,
>   he planted it with choicest vines.
> He built a tower in the midst of it,
>   he also digged a wine-press in it. . . .
> The vineyard of Jahweh of hosts
>   is the house of Israel.'[1]

In the parable of Jesus it is the husbandmen who stand for Israel, and consequently there is no allusion, as in the parable of Isaias, to the quality of the grapes, for that depends on the soil of the vineyard.

The master of the vineyard, who is absent—we must here picture God far above in heaven—sends a servant to receive the share of the harvest that is due ; but the husbandmen beat him and send him back empty-handed. A second messenger is wounded in the head and shamefully treated. A third is put to death, and others too are beaten and killed. It seems as if the husbandmen were doing their best to exasperate the lord of the vineyard. Nevertheless he still has hopes of touching their hearts. There remains one that he can send, namely his own beloved son, which is as much as to say that he is an only son. Him he sends last of all, saying to Himself : 'They will reverence my son.' But little does he know them ! Such an act of kindness merely excites their covetousness ; they have robbed their master of the rent which was his due : now, if they kill the son and heir, the land itself will become theirs. They lay hands on him, put him to death, and cast his body out of the vineyard. They imagine that their master, now deprived of all support, will be unable to do anything of any avail for the regaining of his rights, so completely blind have they become. Not that we are to imagine that the leaders of the Jews

[1] Isaias v, 2–7, following Condamin's translation.

thought they could deprive God of His rights, nor are we to suppose that God is ignorant of the secret thoughts of His creatures. Such details in the parable are merely necessary for the development of the story; they have no allegorical character. At the most, the only allegorical feature we can find consists in the fact that possibly St. Luke and St. Matthew, regarding the vineyard as Jerusalem, have been led to write that the only son was put to death outside the vineyard; St. Mark says that he was killed before being cast out.

The lord of the vineyard is far from being reduced to helplessness: 'He will come and destroy those husbandmen and will give the vineyard to others.' The parable was plain enough, so plain indeed to the more discerning that, instead of commending the justice of this sentence of condemnation, they betrayed their apprehensions by the 'God forbid!'[1] which escaped from their lips. Were they, to whom had been committed the care of the vineyard, whose forefathers had ill-treated and slaughtered those whom God had sent, they who at that very moment were resolved to put to death this latest messenger who claimed to be God's own Son, were they then threatened with death in some future disturbance which would end in their country's being delivered over to the complete domination of the Romans? Or was it that God would choose other more faithful workers for His vineyard who would render Him its fruits? Their conjectures were cut short by Jesus with words which change the symbolism. The new metaphor is also drawn from Isaias,[2] though the words quoted are taken from the Psalmist's[3] application of the prophet's imagery, and the words are brought to mind by the beautiful sight of the Temple roofs: 'Have you not read in the Scripture? The stone which the builders rejected, the same is become the head of the corner.' In rejecting that corner-stone with contempt, the wretched builders had prepared their own ruin: 'Whoever shall fall upon that stone shall be bruised; and upon whomsoever it shall fall, it shall grind him to powder.'

This unforgettable warning Jesus now gave to these men who were so obstinate in denying His mission and His rights. Its details are so Palestinian in character and the lesson is taught in that parabolic fashion so favoured by the

[1] Luke xx, 16. [2] Isaias xxviii, 16.
[3] Psalm cxvii, 22 (Heb. cxviii).

Master, the parable being so well attested by the agreement of all the Synoptists, moreover the teaching it contains is so close in its resemblance to the doctrine of the fourth gospel that all attacks on the authenticity of this unpleasant passage are in vain. These attacks have generally been based on the allegorical character of the similitude attributed to Jesus, as though we had the right to deny Him—and, we may add, His fellow Semites also—the liberty to use the parable except within the limits prescribed by Aristotle for the demonstrative parable! Again and again we see in the parables certain symbolic features appearing among other details which have no other purpose than to complete the natural description of the scene used by the speaker. Those who bring forward this groundless objection prove, at any rate, that the meaning of these symbolic features is very plain.

In the present parable the servants were evidently all those whom God had sent to His people; we are quite at liberty to put Moses at the head of them. That long series of divine ambassadors having come to an end, there then comes God's last hope in the person of His beloved Son, clearly His only Son; and that Son is Jesus, who is as superior to Moses as a son is to a servant, as the Epistle to the Hebrews was afterwards to declare.[1] It is the killing of that Son which was to be the final crime, and after the final crime comes the final punishment. Jesus does not here explicitly say, as He says in St. John, that He is one with the Father,[2] but He claims that He possesses the title of Son of God in a unique sense. His enemies understood that the wicked husbandmen were they themselves, and far from disclaiming their criminal intentions they only wished that they could lay hold of Jesus and destroy Him there and then; it even looks as though they showed threatening signs of such a procedure.[3] But the attitude of the crowd forced them back to the policy they had already decided upon, namely, to seek some plausible pretext for accomplishing their plan. Jesus had just provided them with such a pretext by saying that He was the Son of God, and so plainly that they thought themselves justified in taking immediate steps for His execution, just as formerly when He had called

[1] Hebrews iii, 3. [2] John x, 30.

[3] The three Synoptists say 'they sought.' This does not mean that a council was held, as the Synopsis wrongly says.

Himself Son of God at the feast of the Dedication.[1] But their attempt had come to nothing ; there was nothing left but to bring the law into play by putting Jesus into opposition with the Roman authorities.

The question of the tribute (240).

Luke xx, 20–26 ; Mark xii, 13–17 ; Matt. xxii, 15–22.

Losing no time the members of the Sanhedrim choose certain of their followers to keep an eye on Jesus, for they do not wish to appear themselves in the affair. These followers pose as men resolved to act only as their conscience dictates whatever be the consequences, and as though they have certain doubts which they wish to settle about some very important point. They were, as a matter of fact, Pharisees in company with some partisans or friends of Herod Antipas. The latter had come up to Jerusalem for the feast of the Pasch. His personal relations with the procurator, Pontius Pilate, were strained ; and although Herod and the Pharisees had not much in common, some of Herod's subjects had bowed to expediency and entered into union with the Pharisaic party, making their common religious worship and national sentiments serve as a basis for this union. To tell the truth, neither the Pharisees nor the party of Herod offered open opposition to Roman domination. Thus, being at once both Jewish and Roman, their divided allegiance would serve as a recommendation to Pilate if they went of their own accord to denounce a man of their own race, on the ground that he was in open revolt against the procurator's authority. Such was the attitude they adopted at the Passion, when they succeeded in remedying the failure of their former attempt.

They now beg Jesus to solve an anxious case of conscience. They make no attempt at clumsy flattery by praising His ability ; the trap they lay for Him takes the form of a question that might have been put by an honourable man. They appeal to His sincerity, to His well-known candour, to that integrity of His which will not allow Him to humour the powerful in things that are dishonest, and finally to His zeal for teaching the way of God in accordance with the truth. How will He be able to escape a snare so delicately set that

[1] John x, 31–36.

it entraps its victim without his perceiving it? Suddenly the spring is loosed and the victim is caught. 'Is it lawful to pay tribute to Cæsar or not?' Twenty or thirty years ago this had been a burning question, just after the death of Archelaus, at the time of the annexation of Judæa to the Empire. The question had been settled by Judas the Galilæan in favour of the rights of God: to obey foreigners meant surrendering the obedience due to God, who was the only true ruler in Israel. Gathering around him those who were most zealous in support of this contention he started a revolt. It came to nothing and a most harsh punishment was exacted. What would Jesus say? If He said that tribute should not be paid, it would be almost equivalent to a revolt; it would at least constitute grave insubordination, the foreshadowing of revolution. If, on the other hand, He said that tribute should be paid, He would be false to Israel's most cherished hopes; and as far as He Himself was concerned, such a reply would constitute a public renunciation of the Messianic character which so excited the enthusiasm of the people. After that it would be an easy thing to put an end to His career.

Either answer, then, would be fatal. But He sees through their artifice—for He knew that they had no scruples of conscience when, either as peaceful students or friends of the government, they paid the tax—and willingly enters into their manœuvre: 'Bring Me a penny that I may see it.' Does this mean that He had never had one of these silver coins in His possession? It may be so, for Rome still allowed the Jewish princes to coin money of bronze, but ever since the time of Herod the Great she had reserved to herself the issue of coins of precious metal. By accepting these coins Judæa confessed that she had lost her independence. The penny is brought and Jesus asks: 'Whose image and inscription is this?' The head on the coin was probably that of Tiberius, and the inscription would give the usual titles to this 'son of the divine Augustus.' But whichever of these emperors it was whose head was stamped on the penny, he was at any rate a Cæsar; hence they answered: 'Cæsar's.' Whereupon Jesus replied: 'Render then to Cæsar the things that are Cæsar's, and to God the things that are God's.' They marvelled at His answer.

Their admiration has been echoed by men of great genius. To characterize Jesus' answer as a flash of wit would be nothing less than to show lack of appreciation for this profound remark which, in two or three words solved, and solved for ever, a problem generally considered to be very involved. In the eyes of the Jews the question came to this : was it possible, without disloyalty to God, to recognize a *de facto* authority by paying the taxes it demanded for the maintenance of public order ? Jesus answered yes. It is much easier to answer that question when the authority in question is recognized as lawful by the majority of upright men. But if it is lawful to show that respect to a human authority, how much graver is our obligation to pay what we owe to God, the sovereign ruler ! When Jesus bade the Jews to render to Cæsar the things that are Cæsar's, He did much more than give a permission ; He laid down a rule to be followed, the rule that His disciples must submit to established order. Later St. Paul was to give the basic reason for this, which is that all authority is derived from God. But it was not Our Lord's intention to distinguish two separate spheres of authority, as though every nation had two heads, God and some Cæsar or other, both on the same footing, with the consequence that we could never claim to resist the wicked and tyrannical commands of the latter in the name of God. But who is to speak in God's name ? Without any doubt the Son of God had the right to do so, and He had appointed His disciple Peter to be the foundation of His Church. The Church has acknowledged that this sovereign right persists in Peter's successors. Like Jesus, therefore, the Pope continues to say to the faithful : Render to Cæsar the things that are Cæsar's. He counsels obedience ; he has nothing to do with the temporal government of states. Yet, in order that the things that are God's may be rendered to God, it is necessary that political power should at times be warned by a higher authority not to go beyond its own limits.

After this even those who were most deaf to His words could no longer remain in ignorance of the fact that Jesus was not a political or bellicose Messiah. But if love of one's native land is a lawful passion, if it is a noble and generous sentiment, which has the power to raise a man even to the sacrifice of his life ; if Jesus was animated by such a feeling, as the tenderness He showed for Galilee and Jerusalem showed that He was, then why did He not at least deliver His country from the Roman yoke ? Before answering this question let us observe that Roman domination left the Jews a certain measure of autonomy which allowed them to govern themselves by their own civil laws and to practise their own religious worship. What was due to God was left untouched, and the priesthood was very content to submit to this kind of protectorate. It was an effective defence for a small nation against aggression from without as well as from the peril of civil war from within. Even the Pharisees, when Herod the Great died, had begged Augustus to deliver them from the rule of kings and similar authorities and to join Palestine to Syria under the rule of that country's Roman governors.[1] But all this had to do with politics, and Jesus would have no concern with political affairs, in which He refused to take sides precisely because He was charged with a mission which was for the whole of humanity. His concern was with mankind's spiritual welfare, and that, as Pascal has said, belongs to another sphere ; the sphere of the political and the temporal must not be confused.

Moreover, we are unable to say what Providence would have done if only the Jews had not rejected the gift of God who is faithful to His promises. Even after the Jewish rebellion against Rome, Israel managed to create for herself a privileged position within the Empire. When Christianity finally won the day, Israel often became the object of reproach because she refused ever to acknowledge her error in putting Jesus to death, a thing which, to say the least, was the murder of an innocent and harmless man. But if only she had believed in Jesus ! The new law would have come forth from a renovated Sion, and what glory would not that have been for the children of Abraham, made by their faith in Christ the firstborn of the children of God ! We should have seen a literal and splendid fulfilment of the ancient prophecies when, by the triumph of Christianity, the Jews had been raised to a position of pre-eminence, which would have secured for them not merely independence but spiritual supremacy. It was only necessary for them to show patience, to enter on the path marked out for them by the Messiah, that is, to suffer the torments of the martyrs if called upon instead of lending their aid to His executioners. . . . But God's ways are unfathomable. The unbelief of the Jews, an unbelief that was so deliberately wilful, was to be the means which God was to use in order to glorify His Christ.

[1] *Antiquities of Josephus*, XVII, xi, 2.

Jesus defends the resurrection of the dead against the Sadducees (241).

Luke xx, 27–40 ; Mark xii, 18–27 ; Matt. xxii, 23–33.

Though the religious leaders of the Jews were united in league against Jesus, they were nevertheless hopelessly divided amongst themselves. The Pharisees and Sadducees could not meet without quarrelling. Now for the first time the Sadducees appear before us as exponents of one of their most distinctive teachings, the denial of the resurrection of the body which was taught as a dogma by the Pharisees. Josephus chooses to represent these two parties as philosophical sects in order to raise them in the estimation of the Greeks. The Pharisees he compares to the Stoics,[1] though he does not dare to say that the Sadducees remind him of the disciples of Epicurus, for these were in too ill a repute amongst the Jews, especially on account of their denial of Providence. Modern writers insist that the division of Pharisees and Sadducees represents parties rather than schools of thought, the former being the party of the popular leaders who manifested an attachment to the ancient traditions, the latter being the party of the priesthood. The Sadducees are said to have derived their name from the Sadocites, the members of that line of high-priests who were descendants of the high-priest Sadoc.[2] It is to be observed, however, that we must not lose sight of the fact that the points of difference between the two parties were chiefly religious. There were, it is true, differences between them in the political sphere also, but these were only slight, for the Pharisees, unlike the Zealots, accepted the Roman occupation as a *fait accompli*, even though they still continued to nurse hopes of a Messianic character regarding the race of David ; whereas the Sadducees gave unreserved adherence to the authority of the Empire. The latter were by that very fact more liable to be attracted to that materialistic philosophy which was professed by so many in the upper classes of Roman society.

As long ago as the time of the conquest of Palestine by the Hellenistic kings of Syria, two centuries before this date, the priesthood had shown itself very lukewarm in the defence of the religious traditions of the nation. There were times when priests even lent their aid to those who had

[1] *Life of Josephus*, II. [2] Ezechiel xl, 46, etc.

sworn to destroy these traditions. They were not like that in the days of Jesus, but all the same it might easily have been said that their motto was that of Talleyrand : Not too much zeal ! They were willing to hold firmly to the teaching of Moses provided nothing was added to it. Josephus reproaches them with not admitting the immortality of the soul.[1] But this expression, immortality of the soul, though very familiar to the Greeks since the days of Plato, was not in use among Jewish scholars. Hence the Acts of the Apostles is much more correct in saying that the Sadducees admitted neither the resurrection nor the existence of angels and spirits.[2] Conservative as they were in religious matters and at the same time on good terms with the manners and men of the world—two things which go very well together—they are hardly likely to have given up the ancient belief of the Semites, and particularly of the Israelites, regarding man's survival after death in the underworld of Sheol, where he led the life of a shade, an attenuated and wretched existence. About the time of the Macchabees, however, or even earlier still, such an expression of the dogma of survival after death was found insufficient to satisfy the growing religious sense of Israel. Religion was becoming less of a national and more of an individual concern, and in that degree religious feeling became more interior and more heartfelt. Consequently holy people could not accept the idea that they were to be separated from their God for ever among the shades in Sheol ; it was their ardent desire to live with Him, to be united with Him for ever. And such a desire was not based on the notion of a purely spiritual soul which was to be freed from the body after death ; it rested rather on the belief that there was to be a new life altogether for the mortal body in which the Israelite had worshipped God in His Temple, and which he would one day inhabit in a better world where he would enter into closer communion with God. The religious wars stirred up by the brutal intolerance of the Syrian Hellenists had made that hope grow stronger. Surely God would bring back to life the bodies of those who had been executed for obedience to His Law !

Such an expression of the dogma of survival after death was relatively new, and it was in this that the Sadducees refused to believe. They were strengthened in their opposition to it by the opinion common to the Greek philosophers,

[1] *Antiquities*, XVIII, i, 4. [2] Acts xxiii, 8.

whether they were Epicureans, Stoics,[1] or Platonists, who were all hostile to the notion of individual resurrection. It was this point that was chiefly debated in the daily controversies that took place between Sadducees and Pharisees, whether there was to be a resurrection of the body. The former, after they had heard Jesus solving the great problem of relations with the Romans in the way that they themselves solved it—at least they might think so—flattered themselves perhaps that their favourite argument against the resurrection might appeal to the young Master. If they succeeded they would score a point over the Pharisees. They could have hoped for no more than that, for the matter under dispute was not likely to be the cause of any alarm to the Roman authorities. We conclude, therefore, that those who come forward on this occasion are not members of the higher ranks of the priesthood who have already determined to get rid of Jesus as a measure of political expediency, but rather professional controversialists, ready to enter into discussion with all comers. It is they who propose the case very simply, without any introduction which suggests a trap.

Mosaic legislation, though quite free from all traces of ancestor worship, preserved a relic of the care shown by peoples of the ancient world to leave a male heir who should perpetuate the rites of the domestic hearth. To this day the people of the East attach supreme importance to having a son. Moses therefore had prescribed—despite the normal prohibition of incest—that if there were a number of brothers living together, one of them should marry his deceased brother's wife when that brother had died without leaving male issue. In such a case the first son of this marriage would be counted as the son of the deceased brother.[2] That was the principle; now for the case proposed by the Sadducees.

The supposition is that there are seven brothers. The first dies without leaving any children, and one of the others marries the widow and dies in his turn without having a son. So on with all the rest. Last of all the woman herself dies, having had seven husbands all under the same conditions, for not one of them had given her a son. The question is,

[1] It is true that the Stoics granted that the same individuals did, after an immense lapse of time, return to earth; but the Jews meant something very different from that when they spoke of resurrection.

[2] Deuteronomy xxv, 5–10. It went by the name of the law of the Levirate.

when the great day of resurrection arrives, to which of the seven brethren will the woman belong? No doubt the argument had been stated in this way before, and possibly to the embarrassment of the Pharisees; for if we are to judge by the writings of the Mishnah and the Talmud which, though of later date, are representative of the position adopted by the Pharisees, the latter spoke of resurrection to life in the world to come as though it were the same as a resurrection brought about here below by a prophet. Everyone would return to earth under the usual conditions, complete down to his hat and walking stick, so to say.[1] But although life after the resurrection was thought to be ordinary in that sense, there was another sense in which it was to have extraordinary characteristics. For example, women were to enjoy an abnormal fecundity. Thus Rabbi Gamaliel II, who flourished in the time of Titus, said: 'A time will come when a woman will bring forth daily.'[2] If that was to be the case the seven times widowed woman in the case proposed by the Sadducees would have been compensated in the next world.

In answer to this rather clumsy ruse of these material-minded individuals, who are incapable of conceiving the notion of a spiritual resurrection seeing that they have no idea of what is a spirit, Jesus replies first of all from His own knowledge of the matter, and thus wonderfully completes what had been taught by the ancient revelation: 'In the resurrection they shall neither marry nor be married, but shall be as the angels of God in heaven.' But, having thus thrown light on the manner of the resurrection, it was still necessary for Him to furnish an argument for the fact of the resurrection. St. Jerome long ago observed that Jesus might very well have quoted the prophets Isaias[3] and Daniel.[4] But the Sadducees refused to accept any authority but the

[1] 'Rabbi Jeremias enjoined them to clothe him in shining white clothes and in his richest garments, to put sandals on his feet and his staff in his hand, and to lay him on his side and not on his back, that he might be all ready to follow the Messiah on the day of his coming.' Talmud of Jerusalem, *Kilaïm*, after translation by Schwab, II, p. 315 f.

[2] Talmud of Babylon, Shabbath, 30 b.

[3] Isaias xxvi, 19: 'The dead shall live, (their) bodies shall rise again. Awake, sing, you that lie in the dust! For thy dew is a dew of light, and from the womb of the earth the shades shall be born again.' (After Condamin's translation.)

[4] Daniel xii, 2: 'And many of those that sleep in the dust of the earth shall awake: some unto life everlasting, and others unto reproach. . . .'

Law of Moses, that is to say, the Pentateuch. This was inconvenient for the Pharisees ; but they came forward boldly and, assuming the dogma of the resurrection to be beyond dispute, asserted without hesitation that ' whenever a commandment of the Torah makes mention of a reward, it is to be understood as alluding to the resurrection of the dead.'[1] For example, there is a precept which promises long life to all who shall observe it. Long life on this earth, assuredly, says the literalist interpreter. But, replies the Pharisee, suppose that he breaks his neck while observing the commandment, where then will he enjoy long life if it be not after the resurrection ? His opponent might have retorted that the law does not concern itself with exceptional cases. There was, however, some ground for such begging of the question on the part of the Pharisees, and it was this : since the Platonic idea of the soul's immortality did not form part of the religious notions of Israel, we must conclude that when the Scripture spoke of survival after death such a survival could only be understood as referring to resurrection.

And indeed Jesus adopts that manner of argumentation : ' Have you not read in the book of Moses, in the place of the bush '—that is, the burning bush at Sinai—' how God spoke to him saying : I am the God of Abraham, and the God of Isaac, and the God of Jacob ? He is not the God of the dead but of the living. You therefore do greatly err.' Those great ancestors of the Jews are still living, in God's sight. Could the miserable existence of the shades in Sheol be really called life ? Is that the reward God gives to His friends ? They have longed to be in His presence, and He too has desired to have them near to Him. And even if they have not yet received back their bodies by resurrection, nevertheless they now live with a life that will enable them to do so one day ; they will not be defrauded of eternal life.

Some sixty years later Rabbi Gamaliel the second also used a very apt quotation to illustrate the same point : ' And you that adhere to Jahweh your God are all alive until this present day.'[2] But it lacked the force of Jesus' argument, for in His text God was speaking to living men, not concerning dead men whom He considers still His friends. Moreover,

[1] Cf. *Le Messianisme chez les Juifs*, p. 179.
[2] Deuteronomy iv, 4. Cf. *Messianisme*, p. 179.

Gamaliel only found a convincing text after many unavailing attempts. Accordingly, it is not surprising to learn from St. Mark that a certain doctor of the Law, surely one of the Pharisees who had been present during the conversation, betrayed great satisfaction at the way in which Jesus had answered the objection raised by the Sadducees.[1] It might be surmised too that other Pharisees would gather round this new speaker, expecting him to put a question to the Master. This he did, asking which was the most important of the commandments. Jesus answered him, in accordance with His now well-known teaching,[2] that the first of the commandments was to love God with the whole heart, and the next, to love our neighbour as we love ourselves. On these two commandments depend the Law and the Prophets,[3] like a chain hung from a golden nail. The rabbi was struck by this answer, uttered no doubt with an earnestness that expressed Jesus' love for His Father. The man had studied the Law assiduously and with a right intention, as the gospel indicates. The evangelists make a point of remarking on the good will manifested by some of these doctors of the Law, who generally were attached to the Pharisaic party. What invaluable recruits for the gospel would they have proved, had they only been humble enough to accept the young Master's teaching ! On hearing His reply the man cried out : ' Master, Thou hast said with truth that there is one God and that there is no other besides Him ; and that He should be loved with our whole heart and with our whole understanding and with our whole strength ; and that to love our neighbour as ourselves is far better than all holocausts and sacrifices.'[4] It showed that the man already had the spirit of Jesus, and therefore he received the reply : ' Thou art not far from the kingdom of God.' We are curious to know what subsequently became of him, but the evangelists have not told us.[5] St. Mark, however, leaves us with a very favourable impression.

[1] Mark xii, 28.

[2] Luke x, 25 ff. It is natural enough that the question should have been asked several times ; the answer could only be the same.

[3] Matthew xxii, 40.

[4] Mark xii, 32 f.

[5] When Matthew writes that the scribe wanted to tempt Jesus (xxii, 35), that is to try Him, he does not necessarily mean that the question was a trap. The expression is rather strong because the scribe is considered to be animated with the ordinary dispositions of the Pharisees. Mark has insisted more on the individual character of the questioner.

The Christ is both Son and Lord of David (242).

Luke xx, 41–44 ; Mark xii, 35–37 ; Matt. xxii, 41–46.

Leaving the doctor of the Law to his own reflections, Jesus takes advantage of this gathering of the Pharisees[1] to put them a question about which there was no dispute. His purpose was to have the answer from their own mouths publicly. He therefore asks them what they think of the Messiah, and in particular whose son He is supposed to be. They reply without hesitation : 'David's.' Then why, Jesus desires to know, should David, when speaking in a divinely inspired psalm as the mouthpiece of the Holy Ghost, call the Messiah his Lord ? For do we not read in the psalm ? :

> 'The Lord said to my Lord : Sit thou on my right hand
> Till I make thy enemies thy footstool.'

How did David come to give the name of Lord to one who was to be his own son ? Even if the future Messiah, whom he foresaw as one of his descendants, appeared to him merely as a king greater than he was himself, even though he saw Him as ruler of the whole earth, was that any reason for David to salute Him as his Lord ? It was necessary to conclude, then, that the Messiah belonged to a sphere that was not of the earth but divine, more especially as He had been invited by the Lord God to sit at His right hand.

The Pharisees could not deny that the psalm was David's ; they were therefore embarrassed by the argument. And even if the psalm had been written by someone other than David, there was no doubt that it was written with a view to the Messiah whom it invited to sit at God's right hand ; but it was placed among the other psalms which were put in David's mouth and attributed to divine inspiration. Once more, then, under another form and with a basis in the Scriptures, Jesus renews His declaration that He ranks above all the servants of God. He does not say, as He has said in the parable of the wicked husbandmen, that He is the Son of God ; but what else could He mean if He is the one who is to sit in triumph on God's right hand ? Nor does He deny that He is the Son of David ; rather does He imply it by thus accepting the traditional view concerning the

[1] Here we follow Matthew, whose order seems the more probable. According to Mark, whom Luke follows, Jesus assumes the answer of the Pharisees and shows the crowd the difficulties which it involves.

Messiah, without which this appeal to David would be meaningless. He merely declares His knowledge that He is much more than a son of David, whatever that son of David might be. This is the problem that St. Paul was to face later on, namely, to harmonize Christ's dignity as Son of God with His human origin as Son of David.[1] The evangelists adhere soberly to the words of Our Lord. But the Pharisees, who set up as teachers, are thus convicted of inconsistency, for they sacrifice a perfectly clear text of Scripture rather than acknowledge a Messiah who goes beyond what *they* look for in the Messiah. And rather than submit to being questioned by Jesus, they cease to question Him.

A warning against the Scribes and Pharisees (243).

Luke xx, 45–47 ; xiii, 34–35 ; Mark xii, 37–40 ; Matt. xxiii.[2]

After His enemies have withdrawn, determined to have His blood in revenge, Jesus has no thought of stirring up partisans of His own to defend Him ; He does not even say a word in support of His own right. But He thinks well to caution the people against leaders whom they will follow only to their own ruin. He is severe, but that is because He has a very clear perception of the catastrophe that threatens, a feeling of compassion for His fellow-countrymen, and a duty to liberate them from a yoke which, far from being a wholesome discipline, is nothing more than a deceitful show of exactitude in God's service, which is a very poor substitute for the love of God.

Yet that service was an obligation so long as the Old Law remained in force, and Jesus did not wish to abrogate the Law. Its national and ceremonial character was to pass away, but only when He had offered the sacrifice of His life. The hour of that sacrifice is nigh, it is true, but He does not choose to be accused of driving men to disobedience, nor even of having opposed the doctors of the Law in so far as they duly fulfilled their duties. What He does here, therefore, is to determine the principle which regulates His attitude both towards the Law and its interpreters, at

[1] Romans i, 1 ff., etc.

[2] The three Synoptists are in agreement about the fact that a warning was given on this occasion. But Mark records it very shortly, as also does Luke, who has already given (cf. No. 171) a large part of what occurs in Matthew xxiii. We shall therefore comment here only on what is not included by Luke.

least when these confine themselves to its legitimate explanation. He has already, on more than one occasion, drawn a distinction between the sacred text and the glosses with which they have overloaded it on the one hand and the traditions they have added to it on the other.[1] The sacred text alone has full authority, and He is careful to state precisely: 'The scribes and the Pharisees have sitten on the chair of Moses. All things therefore whatsoever they shall say to you, observe and do.' The chair of Moses was the authority of the Pharisees and doctors of the Law when they performed their office as readers of God's word from the pulpit in the synagogue, but this gave no authority to the particular teachings they mingled with that word.

Having made that reservation, Jesus warns the people and His disciples against the chief characteristic of the Pharisees, very zealous as they were in preaching to other people, but not so eager when it came to practising themselves what they preached, though it was necessary for them to make it seem that they did. Here lay the root of their principal failing, that desire to be honoured as men of piety. Hence they walked along slowly in their long robes, on the look-out for opportunities of offering their hands to be kissed respectfully as they passed through the public streets. They seated themselves in the front row of the stone benches in the synagogues, and claimed the places of honour on the banquet couches. They would take up a position in some conspicuous place and stand with their eyes half-closed as if engaged in long prayers, while at that very moment they were perhaps wondering how they might rob the widows with whose interests they were charged. And these were the teachers, the spiritual fathers of the people, their masters in doctrine! Turning to His disciples, Jesus says: 'One is your Father, He who is in heaven; and one is your Master, Christ.'

Have not we ourselves forgotten this admonition, be it precept or counsel? It might be thought so, judging by appearances, for we address men as father or master. But it is always the things of the spirit that Jesus wishes to arrive at. It matters little what words men use. The thing condemned is that seeking after titles which is equivalent to a claim to the reality which those titles represent. But is there any spiritual father, be he merely a humble teacher of the

[1] Cf. Mark vii, 1–23; Matthew v, 20; and the questions about the Sabbath, etc.

catechism or renowned preacher, who does not realize that he is only speaking in Christ's name and that he has no spiritual fatherhood but what he derives from God? The Pharisees were wrong because they took pleasure in these tokens of reverence; and after this charitable warning given by Christ, any of His disciples who entertains such feelings would be even more to be condemned than they.

There was self-seeking even in the zeal of the Pharisees. They traversed land and sea and thought themselves well repaid for their labour if they converted a single proselyte. That seems admirable. But when their motive was to bind him to their own party and make him like themselves, the result was that they made him more a child of Gehenna than they themselves; such a one would have all the neophyte's lack of moderation, as well as the pride of having by his own free choice become affiliated to the Chosen People with all its privileges. These proselytes were taught that truth which is Israel's chief glory from an intellectual point of view, the doctrine, namely, concerning the unity of God. But then the Pharisees immediately proceeded to confuse everything with a mass of subtle casuistry. For example, instead of dissuading men from swearing, telling them that a vow made to God is a serious matter and that He is not to be deceived by quibbling, they taught that if any one swore by the holy place of the Temple the promise was not binding; but if he swore by the gold of the sanctuary he was bound by his promise. If he swore by the altar, the oath was invalid; but if by the offering placed upon the altar, it was valid. It is true that these precise instances have never been found in the rabbinical books, yet problems of exactly the same kind are settled there. He who swears by the Torah is not bound; but he who swears by the contents of the Torah is under obligation to fulfil his word. Thus it would seem that they considered the part of more importance than the whole, perhaps on the ground that a man might have a little gold or an offering at his disposition, but who could hold the Temple or the altar as his own? But a contrary solution was sometimes given; thus some rabbis were of opinion, in the matter of swearing by the Torah, that the Torah might stand for the mere parchment as opposed to the sacred text written upon it.[1]

[1] Strack and Billerbeck, *Kommentar zum neuen Testament aus Talmud und Midrash*, I, p. 931.

Even the most ingenious of the rabbis ended by getting entangled in such casuistry ; and all of them together were unconsciously making a mockery of the Sovereign Lord of all things whose witness is invoked every time an oath is taken. This Jesus recalls to their minds in energetic terms : ' Whosoever shall swear by the sanctuary sweareth by it and by Him that dwelleth in it ; and he that sweareth by heaven sweareth by the throne of God and by Him that sitteth thereon. . . . Blind guides that you are, who strain out a gnat and swallow a camel. . . . You serpents, brood of vipers, how will you escape from the judgement of Gehenna ? '[1]

We must not forget that, in addressing the Pharisees, Jesus does more than merely speak to men who are endangering their own eternal salvation. The Pharisees formed a party, almost a corporation, much more unified by their common ideas than was the priesthood by the performance of common sacerdotal functions. It was they and not the priests who were the spiritual guides of the people ; on them lay the moral responsibility for the nation's spiritual welfare. The Master therefore addresses to them a final warning in view of the evils which threaten the whole nation, before proceeding to speak of this matter to His own disciples. Speaking in His own name but at the same time in the name of God,[2] He reveals to them what is to happen in the near future : ' Behold I send to you prophets and wise men and scribes ' ;—by these ancient names He designates His disciples, apostles, teachers and writers—' some of them you will put to death and crucify : and some you will scourge in your synagogues and persecute from city to city, that upon you may come all the innocent blood that hath been shed upon the earth, from the blood of Abel the just even unto the blood of Zacharias the son of Barachias,[3] whom you killed between the sanctuary and the altar. In truth I say to you, all these things shall come upon this generation.'[4]

The justice of God, long hanging over their heads, is about

[1] Matthew xxiii, 19 f., 24, 33.

[2] In Luke xi, 49, Jesus makes reference to the Wisdom of God, whose purpose He knows and whose oracle He proclaims.

[3] This is a celebrated difficulty, for the high priest Zacharias who was killed in the Temple was the son of Joiada (II Paralipomenon, xxiv, 20). The prophet Zacharias was the son of Barachias (Zacharias, i, 7). Perhaps a tradition described him as a martyr. Or was Barachias regarded as an equivalent of Joiada ?

[4] Matthew xxiii, 35 f.

to smite them. Jesus shows how the Chosen People, whose election was typified by Abel, have fallen into the dispositions of Cain in their attitude towards the Messiah, their brother, sprung from their own race, sent to them by God. Indeed they will go further still and pursue with their hatred the bearers of pardon who are to come after Him. A man is only punished for his own sins, but now the nation is about to burden itself with a crime that sums up all the sins that have been heaped up since the beginning of the world; its punishment, though long deferred, will be final: 'Jerusalem, Jerusalem! Thou that killest the prophets and stonest them that are sent to thee, how often would I have gathered together thy children, as the hen doth gather her chickens under her wings, and thou wouldest not? Behold your house shall be left to you desolate.' And yet, why should we speak of a punishment that is final? Ruin is certain, but it does not preclude hope and certain repentance: 'For I say to you, you shall not see me henceforth till you say: Blessed is He that cometh in the name of the Lord.'

It is doubtless on these words that St. Paul founds his prophecy of the return of the Jews to their Messiah.[1] Of that the Church has never despaired; she waits for it still.

Looking back over the ministry of Jesus (244).

John xii, 37–50.

With the denunciation of the Pharisees the public ministry of Jesus comes to an end; the remainder of His life is devoted to His most intimate disciples. Here St. John pauses for a moment to revert to the causes which kept the Jews from believing in Him, and he points out that the chief reason, apart from the divine decree, was the opposition of the Pharisees. No one can seriously dispute this. But many historians—including, we may say, all those who belong to Israel or are under Jewish influence, however well-disposed they sometimes may be towards Jesus—have no hesitation in laying the blame upon Him, reproaching Him sharply for having been not merely harsh, but even unjust towards the Pharisees, to whom the Jewish nation assuredly owes its

[1] Romans ix, ff.

preservation to this day. We must therefore consider briefly these two points :

1. Why did Jesus judge the Pharisees so severely ?
2. Why did the Pharisees condemn Jesus ?

In doing this it will be necessary to repeat many observations made above, but only a comprehensive survey can provide a convincing answer to these questions.

(1) Jesus characterized the spirit of the Pharisees as a deviation from genuine religion, an obstacle to any reformation which had for its object to lead men back to the love of God. The underlying reason of this was the fact that the Pharisee—and here we speak of the best of them—gave his attention first of all to the works of the Law ; he delighted in them, and put all his trust in them. He sought righteousness resolutely, but imagined that he could acquire it by his own efforts. This righteousness included love for God—that was plain from the Law itself—and also petition for mercy, especially on behalf of others ; but very rarely—hardly ever, we may say—did it include petition for grace to avoid sin. Fortified by his good works—his own property, so to say—the Pharisee was perfectly content with himself and approached the judgement seat of God with confidence. This account of the matter coincides with that of St. Paul. His account takes the form of argumentation, but the whole of his reasoning is contained potentially in the situation reproduced by the parable of the Pharisee and the publican.[1]

From that evil root of self-sufficiency in the performance of works arose the other characteristic of the Pharisee : his religion tended to become a mere matter of externals. The Law, Deuteronomy especially, insisted in the most persuasive language on Israel's duties of gratitude and love towards her God. But if He was to be paid for His blessings by the fidelity with which one observed His commands, then religion seemed to consist in a scrupulous care not to transgress any of these commands. Again, since God attached so much importance to external acts or abstention from such acts, the Pharisees were prompted to multiply them. In the matter of the Sabbath especially had the Pharisaic traditions made a very heavy burden of that commandment, in its aspect as a negative precept obliging men to refrain from action. Such was their preoccupation not to fail at all in

[1] Luke xviii, 9–14.

these observances that their thoughts had no leisure to turn to God, their hearts no care for Him ; men do not feel affection for a master who keeps them in so strict a bondage.

Nevertheless, it was their duty to avoid multiplying sins. Since the legal precepts concerned external acts that were easily verifiable, and since transgression was frequent on account of the great mass of regulations, hence, in cases where some breach of the rules had become almost inevitable, what means was there of saving these human actions from the stigma of moral fault ? The Pharisees sought such an escape by means of a subtle exegesis of the Law which engendered interminable disputes between the rabbinical doctors, instead of candidly admitting that the Law ceased to bind when there was question of a greater good, or that a purely formal decision of the Law ought to yield before the supreme command of charity. It was because they were alarmed by their own work that the rabbis spent as much time in extracting lenient solutions from the text of the Law as in adding to its obligations.

Again there were two ways in which they monopolized the keys of knowledge. It was made impossible for anyone to form his conscience about right and wrong except under the direction of their decisions, and we know with what energetic expressions Jesus had stigmatized their decisions as mere formalism. It might have been said that the Pharisees had the monopoly of a secret process for the interpretation of the Mosaic Law, just as the old Roman aristocracy possessed the exclusive secret of what was correct in the forms of law, no plebeian person having any hope of winning his case without the employment of the terms and gestures consecrated by tradition. The Roman patricians had the prestige of birth and landed property ; the Pharisees had gradually gained their influence over the people on account of the fidelity they had shown to the Law ever since the time of the Macchabees, as well as by the fact that they were the recognized authorities concerning what was of obligation and liberty in matters of conscience. Unlike the priesthood, they had no official rank in the social order. It appears, then, that their influence sprang from a very laudable origin ; but it was a consequence of this origin that their authority depended entirely on their personal reputation. Thus it was a matter of absolute necessity that their reputation should be maintained undimmed. At all costs they had not merely to preserve their repute as learned men, but also to win for themselves the veneration paid by the common people to holy men. Moreover, their religion being so much concerned with externals, it could not fail to render them conspicuous. Here we see the ground of Our Lord's comments on the Pharisees who stood to pray in public, whose emaciated features were a token of their frequent fasts. Such apparently manifest sanctity inspired widows with a confidence such as the Pharisee did not always merit.

Nevertheless, it is not impossible for men to be perfectly sincere in this quest for authority, esteem, and veneration ; it is in this sense that we speak kindly of 'sincere hypocrites.'[1] But a religion of externals, one that is full of ostentatious display, easily becomes a merely superficial religion. What we term hypocrisy is the last stage arrived at in this decay of true religious feeling ; it consists in an affectation of a religion which is not real, serving as a cloak for behaviour which that religion condemns. Is there anyone who would venture to maintain that none of the Pharisees were in that state ? We should not be able to maintain it of all our own co-religionists. And Jesus did not say this extreme case was that of the majority of the Pharisees ; the term 'hypocrite' which He applied to the sect as a whole, or rather to the more zealous members who pursued Him, does not mean that they had lost all belief in the God whom they aspired to serve, but simply that their religion was not a religion of the spirit. It was a religion of the lips,[2] an affair of mere legalism, wholly external and lacking in sincerity. The Pharisee sought to display his righteousness instead of considering his own wretchedness ; the praise he uttered with his lips tended to his own glory rather than to the glory of God. 'My God, I thank Thee that I am not as the rest of men.' It was rare that a Pharisee turned his eyes within in order to say with Isaias : 'All our righteousness is like an unclean rag.'[3]

As the love of God was not the ruling principle of their religious observance, it was but natural that charity towards their neighbour, even to their fellow-Israelite, had grown cold. To their mind, all were sinners who did not observe the Law of Moses with all the additions which they considered indispensable ; and a sinner who did not hesitate to

[1] See Lucien Gautier, *Études sur la religion d'Israel*, p. 151.
[2] Mark vii, 6. [3] Isaias lxiv, 6.

break the laws of ceremonial purity was not merely an object of scandal ; he gave rise to a perpetual danger of contamination for others, and hence was to be avoided. In addition there was the common workman or husbandman, completely ignorant of the intricacies of the Law, and consequently bound to fall into the like transgressions. The Pharisee therefore thought it his duty to avoid contact with these 'people of the land,' who lived without any care for the Pharisaic observances and thus were worthy only of contempt. Finally, as there was nothing for God to forgive on the part of the Pharisees, so they told themselves, they missed that strong motive for seeking mercy and feeling gratitude which is based on sin repented of and forgiven ; consequently they were the less disposed to take pity on the wretchedness of their neighbour and to help him to escape from it. The Stoic banned pity on the ground that it was a disturbing passion ; the Pharisee feared it as a danger to his own righteousness.

Such, in a general way, is the judgement passed by Jesus on Pharisaism. Is it exaggerated or unjust ?—if we may be allowed to ask such a question when there is no doubt about the answer, in view of the wisdom, and more especially the goodness, of Our Lord. He came as a physician to heal, and He would have dealt more tenderly with that dangerous moral infirmity of the Pharisees had He not been conscious that, in the interest both of these wilfully blind men and of others also, the best remedy was to denounce it fearlessly. It would be easy to find grave charges against them in the writings of their adversaries, for example in the Assumption of Moses[1] or in the recently discovered work composed by the Damascene refugees.[2] Even in the Talmud it is possible to discover pungent remarks about the Pharisees.[3] But, it might be answered, what religious body is there which has never been slandered ? What we require for our purpose here is a broad and undisputed historical survey.

Now it is common knowledge that after the capture of Jerusalem by Titus the Jews submitted completely to the influence of the Pharisees. Once the Temple had been

[1] *Revue Biblique*, 1905, p. 483.

[2] *Revue Biblique*, 1912, pp. 213 ff. and 321 ff.

[3] Both the Talmuds give a list of seven kinds of Pharisees, and find words of praise for only one. Cf. Commentary on St. Mark xii, 40. The predominating characteristic they give of them all is precisely the showing off of their good works.

destroyed the priesthood had no reason of existence; the Sadducees became merely a sect, still zealous, but flatly rejected as heretical by the majority of the Jews. Thus the Judaism that has survived is the work of the Pharisees. That fact is to their credit, for it is no ordinary thing for a religion to persist unconquered through the centuries, and Judaism persisted owing to their efforts. Now the date of the fall of Jerusalem was not very long after the preaching of Jesus, and it may be assumed that the Pharisees of that date were inspired by the same sentiments as their predecessors, although in truth they had reason enough to be more moderate. But what course did they follow after the nation had been thus punished? What commands did they give to the people? We do indeed now hear the lamentations of contrite hearts confessing their sins, imploring mercy, recognizing that the judgements of God have been deserved. So we read in the fourth book of Esdras, but it is a book that was completely ignored by Judaism. The Apocalypse of Baruch comes nearest to it in spirit; its author was conscious that there were sinners in Israel, but considered that, when all was said and done, Israel was of far greater worth than those who were responsible for her ruin. Her religion, her morality, her behaviour were all of a higher order than theirs. And if she had been punished, it was chiefly because she was not yet as faithful as she ought to have been to the observance of the Law. The pseudo-Baruch arrives at this plain conclusion: 'Now the righteous are dead, the prophets sleep their last sleep, we ourselves have departed from our land, Sion has been taken from us, and there is nothing left to us but the Mighty One and His Law.'[1] Thus, Israel proceeded to raise higher than ever the barrier of protection by which the Law was hedged in.[2]

In the second century came the cruel failure of the Messianic war stirred up by Bar-Cochebas, after which all hope completely collapsed. About 200 A.D. the ancient Pharisaic traditions were consigned to writing in the form known as the Mishnah. To it were added the rabbinical commentaries which make up the twofold Gemara, that of Jerusalem and that of Babylon. The Mishnah and the Gemara united together have furnished us with the Talmud of Babylon and the Talmud of Jerusalem, composed during

[1] Apocalypse of Baruch, lxxxv, 2.
[2] *Messianisme* . . . , pp. 137 ff.

the fifth and sixth centuries A.D. From that time Israel shut herself up, as it were, in the Talmud. The Talmud being the work of Pharisaism, we may judge the Pharisees by the Talmud ; and the resulting picture is not very different from that drawn by Jesus. We find the religion and the morality of the Old Testament preserved, but all efforts are concentrated on uniformity and exactness of observance.

But we must meet one objection. ' Where,' asks M. Israel Levi,[1] ' do we find a religious society's ideal manifested, in its *corpus juris* or in its sermon collections, in its canon law or in its works of edification ? Is it in the Gospels or in the laws of the Visigoths that the spirit of Christianity dwells ? ' It is in the Gospels certainly, and in works of edification. But where are works comparable to these to be found in Judaism ? The strict party of the Pharisees disowned such bold works as the Psalms of Solomon, the fourth book of Esdras, and other apocalyptic writings, and their successors have always regarded them as dangerous dreamings. We are told to read the *Haggadah*, which is the name given to those stories of edifying character composed after the style of sermons. And where is the *Haggadah* to be discovered ? Very little of it is to be found in the Talmuds or in that supplement to the Talmud called the *Tosephtah*. It is found scattered through the great *Midrashim*, which are chiefly commentaries on the Law. Lastly we find it in those works of especially *Haggadic* character which were composed in Palestine towards the end of the fifth century, mostly in the form of commentaries, like that on the book of Genesis. But with regard to these writings, a scholar very favourable to Judaism has recently told us in a very erudite work[2] that there is little originality of ideas in them. Their authors, he says, manifest great ingenuity by the way in which they read homely lessons and morals into, and then proceed to draw them out of, biblical texts where no one would dream of looking for them. They use a similar ingenuity in illustrating these lessons and morals by means of examples, both biblical and legendary, and new-found parables. Instead of ' ingenuity ' we ought to read ' puerility.' Whatever is

[1] *Revue des études juives*, XLI, p. 28.

[2] *Judaism in the first centuries of the Christian era. The age of the Tannaim*, by George Foot Moore, professor of the History of Religions in the University of Harvard ; Cambridge, 1927 ; Vol. I, p. 133.

most characteristic in the *Haggadah* is stamped with greater unreality even than that which characterizes the Talmudic jurisprudence which goes by the name of the *Halakah*.

The religious foundation on which the rabbinical doctors built is solid enough, since it is no other than that on which the Old Testament itself rests ; and it is that which has produced in Judaism those admirable moral virtues which are so worthy of respect. But was any advantage secured by the fact that this religious foundation developed under the guiding hands of a group of biblical exegetes whose ruling passion was a prejudice in favour of external observances? The ancient scribes were very familiar with the works of the prophets and frequently quoted them, but merely in order to confirm the Law. There exists no *Midrash* on the prophets apart from that on Lamentations ; and we cannot doubt that the discredit into which the prophets gradually sank was due to the small esteem they had shown for the religion of external observance. It is only recently that certain Jews of our own day, after the example of J. Darmsteter, have shown signs of appreciating what a glory for their nation were those men of the Spirit, those preachers of the religion of the heart.

Another, and even more characteristic defect, is the complete absence of mysticism from the religion of Judaism. By mysticism we mean the knowledge of God by contact with Him in prayer. It is to be found in the Old Testament, but the Jews disregarded it, substituting for it an esoteric cabbala, a doctrine only for the initiated few, which was nothing but a confused excrescence and counterfeit of the real thing.

The Talmud was not yet written in the time of Jesus, but the minds of the rabbinical doctors were already animated with its spirit. Israel had not yet gone into voluntary isolation, for she was still living in hopes of converting the Gentiles to the Law—or rather it was to the yoke of the Law and to the yoke of Israel also that she sought to bring them into subjection. The Pharisees, however, as their very name implies, were already fixed in a place apart by their preoccupation with legal purity and the minute fulfilment of their endless precepts. The Book of Jubilees, certain parts of Henoch, and the Psalms of Solomon, works that can safely be dated anterior to Jesus, already breathe a spirit of

Pharisaism which is akin to those characteristics of the Pharisees condemned by Him.[1]

(2) It is plain, therefore, that Jesus fathomed the mind of the Pharisees and expressed it fairly. They did not reduce religion altogether to mere legalism, but they stifled it by the misuse of legalism, and an arbitrary legalism which was their own creation.

Did they in their turn understand Jesus? We ought rather to ask, why did they reject Him? And we must answer that it was precisely because He revived religion by shaking it free from legalism and thus presented it in its pure essence, in a way more worthy of Him who is the common Father of all mankind. This preaching of His, so different from their own, a preaching that conducted men straight to God intuitively, leading their hearts immediately to God, dispensing with the authority and methods of the Pharisees and even refusing to be controlled by them, was a source of astonishment to them; it put them immediately on their guard against such novelties and against the author of them. That attitude of theirs lasted right to the end.

What did Jesus claim, and first of all who did He claim to be? At the time of His appearance they had already been stirred by the preaching of John the Baptist and must have joined the common folk in asking whether He was not putting Himself forward as the Messiah. Before they could acknowledge Him as such they had to inquire into the rights He claimed to that title. Jesus was working miracles; but the prophets also had worked miracles. If He was to be received as the expected Messiah, He would have to work such miracles as manifested this beyond doubt. Messianic expectations at that date were of a complex character. Ordinary people were looking for a Messiah who should lead them in war. The Pharisees, however, had no revolutionary tendencies of that kind, considering that the established political order was due to the will of God. They had no responsibility for the war with Titus. It is true that Aqiba, the greatest of the rabbis, hailed Bar-Cochebas, 'the Son of the Star,' as the Messiah; but that was a departure from Pharisaic tradition. As doctors of the Law, they would have been pleased to find the Messiah a doctor also.

[1] Ryle and James, in their edition of the Psalms of Solomon (Cambridge, 1891), observe that the righteousness of these psalms is manifestly 'the righteousness of the Pharisees' (p. xlix).

But by definition the Messiah was a king whose royal character God would make manifest. Hence things must be allowed to take their course without any effort to precipitate them. God's wisdom would take action when the appointed time came. Once He, who was the Ruler of the world, had entered on the scene, there was no question of His being defeated. No matter what might be the special character of the Messiah, one thing was certain: His reign would be glorious, all would joyfully acclaim His dominion over Israel, and that dominion would be extended over all the other nations. He would make the Law to reign along with righteousness, and would suppress sin by force; Israel would reign with him.

Now there were no signs of all this in Jesus. On the contrary, it was public knowledge that He invited His disciples, and with them all who showed inclination to join Him, to share His lot of suffering and to die with Him. The conception of God's suffering servant, who was to expiate Israel's sins by His wounds, was found described with great poignancy in Isaias. It shocked the rabbis. When describing the Messiah, they replaced every outrage, every wound, by such honourable qualities as they considered worthy of Him. Jesus, the poor man without repute or fame, who refused to call down from heaven some manifestation of power that would work a transformation in the world, might perhaps be a descendant of David; He certainly was not to their mind the long-expected Son of David. He was not the Messiah, and they refused to hail Him as such. But, to tell the truth, He never asked them to do so. Surprising as this may seem to some people, it is true. It was not until Palm Sunday that they were invited to do so. After His death and resurrection the first step to be taken by faith was belief in Jesus Christ, that is to say, to believe first of all that Jesus was the Messiah because He was the Son of God become incarnate as a descendant of David. But the biblical critics are perfectly aware how careful Jesus was not to broadcast His Messianic character. St. Mark's gospel is the gospel of the Messianic secret.[1] We have often noted the reason for this: the dispositions of the Jews being what they were, to have allowed Himself to be acclaimed as Messiah would have been to unloose revolution on the part

[1] W. Wrede, *Das Messiasgeheimnis in den Evangelien*, 1901; *Revue Biblique*, 1903, p. 625 ff.

of the people ; and more than that, on His own part, it would have meant exposing His real mission and His teaching to misunderstanding. St. John, who wrote in order that people in his own day might believe that Jesus was the Christ, the Son of God,[1] does not speak of the Messianic secret ; he always takes it for granted. In his gospel Jesus does not present Himself as the Messiah, but as God's ambassador, who preaches God's word and speaks in His name. Others had come before Him ; the prophets had performed that office. But for a long time prophecy had not been heard, yet the people were in hopes that the spirit of God would once again inspire holy men. Why ; then—leaving aside the problem of Messianism, as Jesus did—did not the Pharisees acknowledge Him as a prophet ?

We have already shown to what degree there was opposition between His doctrine and theirs, but we must now examine more closely why their opposition to Him filled them with such apprehension and repugnance. Unfortunately, they do not give us the key to this in their ancient writings, and that is thoroughly in conformity with their character. But we may find some light on the matter amongst those who would be flattered to be told that they inherit the spirit of the Pharisees, or who at least defend them and associate themselves with the choice they made regarding Jesus. Such is the position adopted by Dr. Klausner in his Life of Jesus.[2] We choose him for quotation because he seems to us to provide an exact example of the complaints made by those whom St. John calls the Jews, who are in reality Pharisees, but called Jews because they echoed the sentiments of official Judaism. The point at issue between Dr. Klausner and ourselves is whether these complaints were well-founded or not.

During the ministry of Jesus the question of the abrogation of the Mosaic Law was not presented so clearly as in the time of St. Paul. Nevertheless the Pharisees perfectly understood that Jesus did not stand by their acceptation of the Law. Not merely did He show no consideration for their customs regarding the frequent washing of the hands, He also did not hesitate to heal on the Sabbath day any sick

[1] John xx, 31.
[2] *Jesus of Nazareth, His Life, Times and Teaching*, by Joseph Klausner, Ph.D. (Heidelberg) ; Jerusalem ; translated from the original Hebrew by Herbert Danby, D.D. (Oxford), Residentiary Canon, St. George's Cathedral Church, Jerusalem.

who were waiting. He had no fear of being defiled by contact with sinners; He even spoke of His doctrine as a new garment and of His refusal to put a new piece on to an old garment, going so far in that direction as altogether to forbid husbands to repudiate their wives. In all this, says Dr. Klausner, Jesus 'so discredits the value of the ceremonial laws as to recognize in them only a secondary importance compared with the moral laws, and *almost* to annul them.'[1] The author honestly underlines the word 'almost,' for Jesus Himself did not cease to observe the Law. The term Dr. Klausner arrives at in order to express the attitude of Jesus is the somewhat exquisite word 'super-Judaism.' He rose above Judaism; that is what the Jews could not stand: the mother feared her daughter's fatal kiss and turned away.[2]

But what had Judaism to fear in thus surpassing herself by becoming a religion that was higher and purer? To the mind of the Pharisees the mistake of Jesus was that all His preoccupations were concerned with God, the worship due to Him, the perfection all men should seek, and that He had no care about what was to happen to Judaism. He was sacrificing the very existence of His nation, for the national life was closely bound up with the Law. The Law was its moral and religious life, its social life, its civil and criminal legislation, its family life—in a word, the whole life of the nation. Now it was from the Pharisees that the nation received its life, for as Dr. Klausner declares, the Pharisee was lawyer, judge, notary, lawmaker, naturalist, botanist, agriculturist. Religious literature embraced algebra, medicine, astronomy, history, and geography. The whole of this would collapse were Jesus to evolve a religion and a morality that were universal in character from the ancient Law of the Jews. As a matter of fact the moral law, as Dr. Klausner perceives very clearly, is one and the same for all men; there is nothing national about that. But in sacrificing that which was special to Judaism, and thus threatening the existence of the national religion, Jesus was sacrificing the nation itself at a time when it was about to be uprooted from its native soil. But it resisted Him and refused to accept the kiss of death; nay, it was the nation which delivered the death blow.

According to this view of the situation, the antagonism shown by the Pharisees for Jesus would appear to have had

[1] *Jesus of Nazareth, His Life, Times and Teaching*, p. 370. [2] Ibid., p. 375.

the same motive as the charges made against Socrates by his accusers, the motive that is everywhere found in the ancient world when action was taken against one accused of impiety. The national worship was simply defending itself against innovations which disturbed the established order of the city or the nation. This brings up once more the question of the future of the Jewish nation. Will the Jews remain strictly faithful to the Talmud and the Talmudic party that has ensured the survival of the nation down the centuries, or will they break free from such restraining fetters and develop into a nation that will settle its social and political life, after the fashion of other nations, according to what is most advantageous for human beings, and under the protection of a religious faith that is inviolable ? That question has now been raised more clearly than ever before by the modern Sionist movement, and it remains to be settled.[1]

But whatever be the destinies of the Jewish nation, the fact remains that thinking men have long ago decided in favour of Jesus by comparison with Judaism. There is no need for us to emphasize such things as the poor quality of the astronomy presented to us in the Book of Henoch, which makes such a pitiable show when compared even with the Greek learning of its own time. All that pseudo-scientific rubbish no longer deceives educated Jews. Jesus may have taught no truths of natural science, but at any rate He rendered great service to science by raising religion to an altogether higher sphere, and thus giving back to science its liberty. Once we have adopted belief in one only God, the Creator of the world, it follows as a natural consequence that religion must be the same for all men, and morality likewise. All nations have adapted themselves to

[1] To go to the real root of the matter, it is not merely a question now of whether or not the yoke of the Talmud is to be shaken off ; it is the Law of Moses itself that is at stake. For if the Jews were allowed to rebuild their Temple they would, of course, be obliged by that Law to recommence the sacrifices of blood, and, quite reasonably, they will not hear of that. But once again rabbinical casuistry comes forward to help out the Law. According to some of the modern rabbinical masters, the Law allows sacrifice only if the priests are in a state of ceremonial purity ; but they are no longer in such a state, for the red heifer has not been sacrificed in order to purify them ; and in order to sacrifice the red heifer, the sacrificing priest would have to be in a state of ceremonial purity, and so on. . . . By this subterfuge they cover up the obvious fact that they count the law of bloody sacrifice—which occupies so predominant a place in the Pentateuch—as abrogated. What could be more characteristic than that ?

that idea without thereby losing their special character, their independence, and all that goes to make up their individual national life. The Jews might have followed the same path. To go on asserting that the 'super-Judaism' of Jesus was merely fanciful is simply to close one's eyes to the facts of history. The Pharisees ought to have understood, as did Christians, the distinction between precepts and counsels, the letter and the spirit. The counsels, accepted as such, have been put into practice just as much as the precepts, and they have been no less fruitful in results.

If the Pharisees indeed rejected the doctrine of Jesus because they were unwilling to endanger the existence of their own nation, then their national pride misled them. Their error consisted precisely in this, that they turned what was purely a matter of religious teaching into a question touching the life of the nation. The most sacred of their traditions was that which concerned divine intervention through the intermediary of God's ambassadors, or interpreters as we may call them, for that was precisely the function of the prophets. The Pharisees had only to find out whether the prophet's teaching about God was the same as that contained in the Law, and whether he who claimed to be God's ambassador gave convincing proofs of his mission. Now no prophet had given more signs than Jesus: He ought therefore to have been believed when He declared that He spoke in God's name. Doubtless many Jews would have embraced His 'super-Judaism' during His lifetime had it not seemed to them, apart from the danger to the nation, to attack the very foundation of revealed religion, namely, the doctrine of the unity of the Lord God. Jesus had indeed declared Himself to be not merely the only ambassador of God who knew His secret thought, but also the Son of God, and He had not hesitated to place Himself on a level with His Father.

The Jews might have allowed, provided some explanation was added to tone it down, that the Messiah in the splendour of His glory should take the title of Son of God. They would not even have found any great difficulty in justifying that privilege. Already in the past the king had been regarded as in some special way the adopted son of God, who was the Father of Israel. But that Jesus, a poor individual, should usurp divine rank, and that in the strict sense, was intolerable. That has been the complaint of Jews of all time. The homage paid to Jesus Christ by the world might be considered as compensation for the glory that was denied Him in His lifetime ; but no man has the right to make himself equal with God. With the strength of its deep conviction concerning the unity of God and His infinite greatness, the Jewish mind rebels against the dogma of the Incarnation. The protests of the Pharisees, the sense of outrage they showed at hearing what seemed to them a blasphemy, and the action they took to punish such a blasphemy, are to this day their chief title to honour in the eyes of modern Jews. It was they who saved their nation from the crime for which there is no atonement, the crime of apostasy.

But supposing that the murderous intentions of the Pharisees towards Jesus can be fully accounted for in this way, and in this way only, that is not to say they are thereby justified or even excused. In His teaching Jesus had transported the question of Messianism into a different sphere from that of this world, in fact into the sphere of divine things. The triumph of the Messiah was made God's victory over sin and Satan. The question once raised to such heights as that, all the temporal prerogatives that were thought of necessity to belong to the Messiah become singularly unimportant. Indeed we may go so far as to say that they were incompatible with the dignity of one who was God. It may be said that this is because we have been taught to believe in the mystery of the Cross ever since the days of our childhood. But to aspire to a crown seems to us unworthy of an incarnate God ; diamonds and pearls would be merely sham ornaments on His brow. Since He had come to redeem mankind from sin, the Son of God could claim only a crown of thorns ; but once that mission was accomplished, the ancient prophecies would regain their true force, yet in the spiritual sphere. It ought not to have been beyond the capacity of the Jewish doctors of the Law to discover such a transformed interpretation of the Scriptures, seeing that the Apostles managed this so easily under the inspiration of their faith. Is not that what Pascal has said ? 'Jesus Christ was slain, they say ; He succumbed ; He did not subdue the pagans by force ; He did not bestow on us their spoils ; He does not give us wealth. Is that all they have to say ? But that is what I find lovable in Him. I should not want the sort of man they imagine for themselves. . . . Jesus Christ, poor and without any outward show of learning, exemplified the holiness which He required of others. He gave us no new invention, He did not reign as king ; but He was humble, patient, holy, holy in the eyes even of God, terrible to the devils, free from all sin. With what grand pomp, therefore, and unspeakable magnificence has He come, when He is beheld with those eyes of our heart which look upon Wisdom.'[1]

It was not the business, then, of the Pharisees to examine whether Jesus had the characteristics which they expected in their Messiah, but whether He was justified in calling Himself the only Son of God. In face of so many wonderful miracles obtained from His goodness by those who believed in Him, so many easy victories over demons who gave such trouble to the Jewish exorcists, and so holy a life, the Pharisees ought to have been induced to listen to Him with docility and to trust Him. Then they might have gone back to their study of the Scriptures and there learnt to recognize that He was the one in whom the two converging lines of prophecies met : one foretelling the coming of God in person to establish His kingdom, the other promising the same work to the Son of David, the Emmanuel of Isaias, who was to be called the Mighty God, that Son of David who was also David's Lord seated at God's right hand.

It is no paradox, therefore, to say that the unheard-of greatness that belonged to Him as Son of God dispensed Jesus altogether from the duty of manifesting Himself during His mortal life as the glorious king that popular imagination had pictured. His mission of offering Himself as a sacrifice precluded this ; it would have been a premature triumph. It was for this reason that He did not claim the title of Messiah ; He only accepted it at the hour of His death. The Pharisees would have made no difficulty about giving Him that title once they had admitted what He really was, if only they had been sufficiently docile to accept His testimony which was confirmed by the Father's testimony. But docility was not in their nature. They refused to surrender by one act both their conviction that they alone were competent to judge, and the reputation they had as masters in Israel. This is what St. John remarks, viewing things from the higher standpoint of God's designs. God had blinded them and hardened their hearts, which means—for those

[1] *Pensées de Pascal*, Brunschwig's edition, pp. 686, 696. *Pascal et les prophéties messianiques*, *Revue Biblique*, 1906, pp. 533–560.

who, like St. John, believe in human liberty and responsibility—that they had blinded themselves and grown obdurate. This is seen all the more clearly from what he says of those who did believe in Jesus, but ' because of the Pharisees they did not confess it, for they *preferred* '—hence it was a free act—' the glory of men more than the glory of God.'[1] In His eternal designs God permitted this blindness and obduracy which, though unintentionally on the part of the Pharisees, carried out His divine plan.

St. John proceeds to put on the lips of Jesus a few words which sum up all that He has just said and answer the chief complaint of the Pharisees. They are about to put Him to death as an innovator, because He sets Himself up as a judge, because He attacks the majesty of God by proposing Himself as an object of their faith. It was true indeed that He had set Himself so high, in demanding faith in Himself and a love of Himself greater than the love they bore to all else, that no justification of His would have been of any avail unless He had carried His claims right to their conclusion and declared Himself on an equality with God. But if that was only His right, then faith in Him was nothing new, since it was nothing else but faith in God ; to hear His word was to hear the word of God, to reject it was equivalent to self-condemnation. But He was the light, and He spoke the truth ; He had come to be the Saviour of the world, to help men to practise the commandment of eternal life.

This is what the Pharisees refused to hear. They refused to believe that God had united Himself to Man in human flesh : at the same time they refused to believe that man could unite himself to God in the spirit. Thus the old religion which God had revealed was split into two distinct forms of religion : the religion of legalism, which excluded everything of a mystical character and fulfilled its duties by the observance of commandments, the first of these being the obligation to love God ; on the other hand, there is that other form of religion which understands all the precepts as being summed up in the one precept of charity, the aim of which is to bring the soul into union with God by a love of friendship, that union taking place in Jesus, who is both God and Man. The first has remained the national religion of a race that is fettered by the letter of the law even in its merely

[1] John xii, 43.

human development, whose only progress can be accomplished by straining at the letter ; the other forms a bond of union for all mankind, and being based on a foundation of dogmatic truth that is immutable, it makes continual progress by means of the operation of the Holy Spirit in the souls of men, an operation which is daily more extensive and ever reaches more profoundly into the soul. This division was brought into being by the refusal of the Pharisees to accept the kingdom of God announced by Jesus Christ.

The widow's mite (245).

Luke xxi, 1–14 ; Mark xii, 41–44.

This incident comes like a spell of clear sky between two storms. Jesus has just foretold in the hearing of the Pharisees what sort of punishment is hanging over Jerusalem ; before resuming this terrifying subject He sits down over by the Treasury of the Temple. Through the openings in the walls of the Treasury, intended for the gifts of the faithful to the Temple, the rich were throwing their liberal gifts of money. Then came a poor widow woman who slipped in two coins worth a quarter of an *as*, a coin of very small value. This provided Jesus with a final opportunity for teaching His disciples that the only gift that matters is the gift of the heart to God. It matters little what may be the quality of the external observance paid to Him ; all its religious value lies in the intention. Hence He says : 'Verily, I say to you that this poor widow hath cast in more than they all who have cast into the Treasury. For all they did cast in of their abundance ; but she of her want cast in all she had, even her whole living.'

A twofold warning : the destruction of the Temple and the coming of the Son of Man (246–249).

Luke xxi, 5–33 ; Mark xiii, 1–32 ; Matthew xxiv, 1–36 ; x, 17–18, 21–23.

Several of His most intimate disciples had been present when Jesus uttered the threat : 'Behold your house shall be left to you desolate.' These words are more fearful in their simplicity than all the calamities and terrors heaped up by the apocalyptic writings. Any ruin can be built up again; but to be left abandoned by God is to be deprived of all hope—unless there be repentance sincere enough to send up the cry: 'Blessed be He that cometh in the name of the Lord.'[1] But the disciples may have thought to themselves that a house is still left standing even though it be deserted, and consequently did not understand that here Jesus prophesied the destruction of the Temple. Accordingly, when they were going out with their Master from that splendid enclosure which formed a court of honour for the Sanctuary, putting aside all anxiety about the future, they expressed their admiration like strangers amazed at the sight of the immense blocks of stone in the walls. These stones were still in their original whiteness, their roughly hewn surface bringing out the light and shade, and were fitted together so perfectly that the joints could scarcely be perceived. In his simplicity one of the disciples tells Jesus what his impressions are: 'Master, behold what manner of stones and buildings!' But the Master even now sees them as they will be in the future: 'There shall not be left a stone upon a stone that shall not be thrown down.' This was a clear prediction of the destruction of the Temple, and principally of the Holy Place. The surrounding walls were also demolished, and it makes little difference to the fulfilment of the prophecy if a few bits of these walls are still standing as witnesses to the ancient splendour that has vanished. Artists come to admire them now as they were once admired by the simple Galilæans.

This was a shock to the disciples and they were seized with fear. The little group descended the slope of the Temple hill, crossed the Cedron, and in silence slowly climbed the hill opposite. Having reached the summit of Olivet facing the Temple, which from there could be seen in all its glory, Peter could no longer restrain his anxiety and began to question his Master. Along with him are his brother Andrew, with James and John. After what Jesus has said, there can be no doubt about the fact of the catastrophe to come, but Peter is burning to know when this stupendous event shall take place and what signs will herald its coming. His curiosity was not destined to be satisfied. Even to His own disciples Jesus would never give precise dates. It was enough for them to know how they ought to shape their

[1] Matthew xxiii, 38 f.

conduct. The discourse that now follows is, like all its predecessors, chiefly an admonition concerning the dispositions required by all if they are to be ready for the hour when the judgements of God shall fall. The answer given by Jesus certainly comprises two things: the overthrow of the Temple and the coming of the Son of Man. This fact is so plain that no one questions it. But are these two incidents so connected in the mind of Jesus that they are merely two views of the same picture, in the sense that He understood the destruction of the Temple to be the signal for the end of the world, as was first strongly maintained by Reimarus, a German scholar of the end of the eighteenth century? In his opinion, Jesus expressed this in terms so precise that, as the prophecy was not fulfilled in that manner, this one text was enough to prove for him that the Founder of Christianity was convicted of error and Christianity of being false. In our own time the difficulty has been raised again and expressed with much force by a certain school of exegesis, which makes all the teaching of Jesus lead up to this prediction of a catastrophe which failed to be realized at the appointed time. It is a question with which minds have been preoccupied since the days of St. Augustine. Seeing that the coming of the Son of Man was in fact included in the prospect of the Temple's destruction, St. Augustine proposed that it should be understood of a spiritual coming of Jesus Christ. This was fulfilled in the visible protection which Jesus showed for His Church at the time of the destruction of Jerusalem, an event which spelt deliverance for the Church and was the signal for her advance, since the ancient worship which His death had abrogated was now made impossible even for the Jews through the ruin of the Temple. It is a very attractive solution of the difficulty, and one that we should be tempted to apply to the text of St. Luke, were it not that the evangelist has indicated a period of interval, 'the times of the nations,'[1] between the laying waste of Jerusalem and the coming of the Son of Man. Moreover, it conflicts with the texts of St. Mark and St. Matthew where they allude to the end of all things.

The inclination nowadays is to meet the critics with a purely critical method of our own,[2] and it would ill become recent critics to blame us for any boldness we showed in doing so. Our explanation would consist in maintaining

[1] Luke xxi, 24. [2] See commentary on St. Luke, p. 53.

that it was not in one and the same discourse that Jesus spoke of these two different events. Generally St. Matthew composes his long sermons from things said by Jesus on different occasions, and such would be the case here. In his text we find sayings that St. Luke has placed in the discourses on the sudden advent of the Son of Man which we have seen in following his narrative.[1] There are other phrases too which might very well belong to a subject different from that of the destruction of the Temple. The same would be true equally of St. Mark, though here we could not say that he is following his usual custom, seeing that this is the only discourse of any length that his gospel contains ; but he may easily have followed the example of St. Matthew in this case. As for St. Luke, who had already related a discourse on the coming of the Son of Man, he would have returned to that here merely in order to follow St. Mark. It would be an example of a literary doublet in Luke's gospel and would be no proof that Jesus had treated of both points, the destruction of Jerusalem and the Second Coming, in the sermon in question. Thus we should be left simply with a discourse on the destruction of the Temple.

Such an analysis would serve as an answer to critics who are in the habit of indulging in literary dissections of a much more reckless character. However, we have no intention of adopting it for our own, because the agreement of the Synoptists is too weighty to be ignored. What then must be said ? Simply this, and it furnishes a very solid reply to the difficulty : even if Jesus dealt with both questions in the one discourse, He at any rate did not say that both events were to be contemporaneous.[2] Nay, He signalized two points in which they differ in this respect, points that are of first-rate importance for the solution of the problem here

[1] Luke xvii, 22–37. See p. 79 above.

[2] Joseph de Maistre puts the matter admirably in his *Soirées de St. Pétersbourg*, Entretien XI : 'The prophet enjoyed the privilege of being outside time ; his ideas, being no longer distributed according to time, are joined one with another simply by virtue of their likeness and are mixed up, which is the reason why there is great confusion in his discourses. Our Saviour Himself submitted to that condition of things when, allowing Himself to be caught up by the prophetic spirit, He was led to mingle the destruction of Jerusalem with the destruction of the world by the thought of these two great catastrophes, which were of an analogous character though separated from one another by time.' This explanation by the use of analogy is a happy thought. The theory may be applied to the prophecies of the Old Testament, but in the present case Jesus rather disentangled what was confused than caused the confusion.

involved. The first event was a catastrophe which the disciples might and should escape by flight, and that is precisely the reason why Jesus indicated the signs which were to precede its coming. The other event was to be a universal catastrophe which would strike all men at once. That is the first difference. The second is this : the first event is spoken of as relatively near, to take place before the generation of men then living should be dead. Regarding the time of the second event Jesus refuses to say anything at all ; it is the Father's secret.

But it may still be asked why did He treat of both subjects at the same time ? Was not that as good as to suggest to His disciples that both were to form one and the same divine judgement ? To this we must bluntly answer that there was no question of the *danger* of leading the disciples into such a confusion, seeing that the confusion certainly existed in their minds already. This is plain from their question as expressed in the text of St. Matthew : 'Tell us when shall these things be (that is the destruction of the Temple), and what shall be the sign of Thy coming and of the consummation of the world.'[1] In fact Jesus had just said before them all that Jerusalem would be left desolate until she saluted His return, and they now understood that by this abandonment He meant the complete destruction of the Temple. But, on the other hand, being good Israelites, they were unable to imagine the Temple ruined for ever, and the consequent bringing to an end of Jewish worship. The Temple had been destroyed by Nabuchodonosor, but it was built up again by the Jews returned from Babylon ; Herod had demolished the second Temple, but only to replace it by a more splendid building. Therefore the return of the Messiah—since it was necessary that He should go away, and they had difficulty enough in getting that idea into their minds—could only be looked upon as the salvation of the nation and the restoration of the Temple. What were they to do when the menacing signs of the catastrophe appeared ? Wait for deliverance, they thought ; wait for the miracle of the return of the Messiah, that is, Jesus Himself come back once more to reign. The rapid succession of the two events must have been firmly fixed in their minds, and it exposed them to the danger of being involved in the coming ruin, and, what was still worse, of

[1] Matthew xxiv, 3.

sharing the hopes of the rebels to overthrow the domination of Rome, of making common cause with them, and of losing sight of the mission which their Master had given them to carry out. Hence they had to be forewarned. It was on their account that Jesus found it necessary to deal with both events at the same time, and in doing so there was no risk of His confusing them ; on the contrary, His purpose was to dispel this unfortunate confusion. Nevertheless He would not lift the veil which hid His second coming ; He goes so far as to say that He had no authority to do so. He gives a clear command as to what they are to do when the first event arrives : they must take to flight. And this command was so well understood that at the first signs of the siege of Jerusalem the Christian faithful fled to Pella.[1] In case of the second event there was only one thing to be done, to stand fast in the faith ; that is why Jesus puts them on their guard, and along with them all who will come after, against the seductions of error and the appearance of false Christs and false prophets.

Once this principal consideration has been stated, it is not difficult to allot what belongs to each subject. If the distinction is not now apparent, that is because the first two evangelists have not emphasized it, though they faithfully recorded the mind of Jesus. The fact that they were still, at one time or another, dominated by the unfailing hope of the speedy coming of their Master, would rather have inclined them to leave the question vague. Perhaps the reason why they abstained from more precise definition regarding the two events was their desire to conform to the will of their Master, who had refused to say anything on the matter ; in that case, the perplexity in which they left succeeding generations of Christian faithful is a decisive proof that they wrote their gospels before the fall of Jerusalem.

St. Luke, who understood the signs of the times, has expressed in clearer terms what was left obscure in the gospels of Matthew and Mark.[2] Consequently, if we wish to find the oldest tradition of the discourse we must seek it chiefly in the latter, and preferably in St. Mark, who has

[1] See p. 178, below.

[2] This is what St. Augustine says in a very important passage (Epist. CXCIX) : 'Tamen Lucas evangelista et hanc dierum breviationem et abominationem desolationis, quæ duo ipse non dicit sed Matthæus Marcusque dixerunt, ad eversionem Jerusalem docuit pertinere, alia cum eis dicens apertius de hac eadem re, quæ illi posuerunt obscurius.'

given us the discourse free from the admixture of elements not concerned with its principal subject. The picture he presents to us has the appearance of being formed by the juxtaposition of a double theme which might be arranged in parallel columns.[1] On the one side would be the subject of the ruin of the Temple, concerning which Jesus speaks successively of the coming time of distress, the way in which His disciples must conduct themselves, and finally the catastrophe itself. On the other side the same points are followed again in the instruction concerning His second coming, and it is only here that the contrast in regard to the time of these two events is indicated.

The discourse on the destruction of the Temple.

First of all Jesus desires to forewarn His disciples against any premature expectation of His coming. It will be said to them : 'Behold He is here,' and that will be an evident sign that the great event is at hand. Some, when they hear of the Messiah, will let themselves be led astray into error. There will be wars—nay more, a general conflict between the nations—earthquakes, and famines. . . . But these calamities will be only the premonitory signs of what is to come ; the disciples are not to be disturbed by them.

The picture is a gloomy one, but all the elements of it belong to the natural order of this world and are familiar to all minds. It would not be difficult to point them out in the period that elapsed between A.D. 30 and A.D. 70. The civil war that followed Nero's death in A.D. 68, so short a time before the fall of Jerusalem, in which there perished three claimants to the imperial throne, Galba, Otho, and Vitellius, must have appealed very forcibly to the imagination of their contemporaries. But it does not seem that Jesus was thinking particularly of such events : He is speaking like the prophets of old.[2] The ills that afflict humanity and cause mankind to cry out with pain are likened to the pangs of childbirth, which are succeeded by great joy once the crisis is over. What are the disciples to do during that time? Wait in terror for some miraculous deliverance? No, they are to preach the good news of the salvation wrought by Jesus, with such energy and zeal that it may

[1] See *Revue Biblique*, 1906, *L'Avènement du Fils de l'homme*, pp. 382–411.
[2] Isaias viii, 22 ; xiii, 13 ; xix, 2 ; Ezechiel, v, 12, etc.

be carried to all nations—to all those peoples, pre-eminent in mental culture, dwelling on the shores of the Mediterranean, the sea which unites them rather than divides them from one another. St. Paul was of opinion that this miracle had been accomplished by his own time.[1] The good news they are to preach will be the Gospel of Jesus, so called not only because it will record His words, but also because it will announce salvation in Him. The disciples will be persecuted for His name's sake, because they will bear witness to Jesus. When that happens there will be no need for them to prepare their defence, like scribes pondering over decisions they have extracted from the Scriptures. What they say will not even be according to their own spirit, for the Holy Spirit will speak for them. But persecution there will be, for opposition will not be lacking: relations, brethren, and parents, will deliver up their own kindred to their enemies, disciples will be dragged before tribunals and beaten with rods in the synagogues, and will appear before governors and kings. But he that shall persevere unto the end shall be saved; that is, he that shall hold fast to the end shall obtain the salvation of his soul, that salvation of which Jesus has said so often that it was worth more than the treasures of the whole world.[2]

After this rapid glance at eternity, Jesus passes to the distressing subject of the last days of the Temple worship. The expressions He used would have been obscure to people dwelling outside the Holy Land, hence St. Luke omits them. But a Jew who was at all regular in the worship of the synagogue, even though he had never studied the actual text of the prophets, could not be ignorant of the celebrated passages in Daniel[3] concerning the abomination of desolation which was to defile the Temple. When Antiochus Epiphanes profaned the Sanctuary by erecting there a statue of Jupiter Olympus, the Jews had regarded it as the fulfilment of Daniel's prophecy.[4] But although the symbolic expression of the prophet was worth retaining because it was traditional and striking, Jesus knew that history never repeats itself in exactly the same way. He suggests that the abomination of desolation in this case will be not an inanimate thing but an intelligent being, and He does not mention the Temple by name but leaves things vague. Some person—

[1] Romans x, 18.
[2] Mark viii, 35; x, 26 ff.
[3] Daniel ix, 27; xi, 31.
[4] 1 Macchabees, i, 57.

or is it a body of people ?—' will stand where he ought not to be,' and to emphasize the mysterious aspect of the expression Mark adds : ' He that readeth let him understand ! ' There is nothing here, however, to indicate that a conflict between the powers of heaven is in question ; the theme is still the destruction of the Temple. St. Luke hesitates to refer his Gentile readers to Daniel, and thinks he may set the matter down in plain language thus : ' Now when you shall see Jerusalem compassed about with an army, then know that the desolation thereof is at hand.'[1] The care with which he preserves the word ' desolation ' clearly proves that his idea is to reproduce the meaning and not to change it, and his interpretation of the meaning was surely that made by all the Christians when the Jewish rebellion arose. To remain in Jerusalem then would have meant running the risk of being involved whether one liked it or not in the insurrection and its repression. Jesus had foretold the destruction of the Temple, and therefore the disciples were to look neither to men nor to God for its preservation. There was no time to be lost, for once the city was surrounded escape would be impossible, as the story of the siege in Josephus shows. There was the same danger in the whole of Judæa : ' Then let those who are in Judæa flee to the mountains.' But whither were they to flee, for Judæa proper is all mountains ? People on the Mount of Olives could not say : ' Let us go to the mountains ' when they meant to go to the region of Hebron. But on the other side of the Jordan and the Dead Sea lies the steep mountain range of Moab and Ammon, with that of Edom farther south : that was where shelter lay, far from the spot in which war was raging. As a matter of fact we learn from Eusebius[2] that the Christians of Jerusalem, warned by a revelation before the siege, took refuge among these mountains at Pella.[3] This revelation was none other than the one here given by our Saviour, which they understood better at the time in question.

They are bidden to flee without encumbering themselves with baggage, to flee for their lives. It was much to be able to save one's life in that bloody war which brought death to so many Jews. The wording is urgent and startling in its

[1] Luke xxi, 20. [2] Eccles. Hist., III, v, 3.
[3] *Revue Biblique*, 1911, p. 418 ff. ; the place is a little too far to the north-east of Jerusalem to be seen from the Mount of Olives.

realism. We can picture the Roman soldier, exasperated by the savage resistance he met, more eager to kill even than to pillage : ' Let him that is on the housetop not go down into the house nor enter therein to take anything out of the house.[1] And let him that shall be in the field '—where men work with little more clothing than a tunic—' not turn back to take up his garment '—which yet would be his only protection against the cold of the night on his journey. ' And woe to them that are with child and give suck in those days ! But pray that it happen not in the winter '—when it is so difficult to make one's way through the mud and across the streams swollen by the rain, when an icy downpour soaks the wayfarer to the skin. It was to be a cruel deluge of misfortunes, especially for poor mothers. Jesus sees all these things beforehand, and they cause Him to suffer on account of those who will be faithful to Him. His compassion here springs from the sight of what they will endure as the normal, even though distressing, consequence of the circumstances in which they will be placed. They are human miseries, and it is in His human nature that He feels them.

Discourse on the coming of the Son of Man.

Now the scene changes,[2] but neither St. Mark nor St. Matthew warns us of the fact, any more than Daniel warns his readers that he has now finished with the enemy of Israel and is about to speak of a time of distress ' such as never was from the time that nations began even until that time.'[3] St. Mark and St. Matthew use the same expressions, except that the terms are stronger in their gospels than in Daniel. In the gospels as in the prophet a new period is indicated : in Daniel it is the era of the resurrection of the dead, a time bordering on eternity. We ought, therefore, to understand that the gospels also have reference to that era, the consummation of all things, introduced by the evangelists without any mark of transition.

Here again St. Luke has taken pity on his Hellenistic readers who are not accustomed to such sudden leaps from earth to heaven. In the historic style of his narrative he

[1] The stairway from the housetop is often outside the house.

[2] That is the conclusion at which we have arrived in our Commentaries. We wish to correct the arrangement we made in the original Synopsis, and join Mark xiii, 19–23, along with Matthew xxiv, 21–25, to the second discourse.

[3] Daniel xii, 1.

indicates a pause in the story: 'And they shall fall by the edge of the sword and shall be led away captives into all nations. And Jerusalem shall be trodden down by the Gentiles till the times of the nations be fulfilled.'[1] Thereupon he rejoins St. Mark and St. Matthew in the imposing description of the last days. When those days come no one must think of taking flight: it is no longer a case of war waged by soldiers from whom escape is possible, but by the superhuman powers of evil. And such is their fury, such the sway they have been granted over the whole world, that no living person could withstand them, no soul be saved, were it permitted to them to prolong their assault. But God, in the interests of His chosen ones, has shortened those days. The worst danger will spring from the fact that evil suggestions will not always be offered in a direct and open manner; false Christs and false prophets will arise and will be permitted to manifest such signs and prodigies that even the elect would be astonished and led astray, were it possible for God's chosen ones to perish. This war is altogether different from the one which will end in the fall of Jerusalem; it may be far distant, but on the other hand it may be not far off. Let the disciples accept this warning, and all men with them.

When that distress is over, consisting chiefly in the outpouring of the powers of evil in the religious and moral sphere, the very forces of nature will begin to totter. The sun will be darkened, the moon will cease to give its light, the stars will fall from the sky, the powers of the heavens will be shaken. Such is the traditional grandiose imagery found in the prophets, revived later by the apocalyptic writers; what is said here is not to be interpreted as a strict prediction, any more than we are to accept the abomination of desolation in that fashion. How can we take an instance in which Jesus has used the traditional expressions of antiquity and suppose that in this case alone He abandons His usual practice of referring to the elements of the world in the language of His time, in order to begin speaking as a

[1] Luke xxi, 24. Many are tempted to suppose that Luke's narrative has been composed in the light of events already witnessed. But since we are compelled by strong reasons to date the composition of the evangelist's two works, the Gospel and the Acts, before the year 70, we may say with a great deal of probability that these events were already beginning to be perceptible, and that Christian tradition was by that time settled with regard to the manner in which the discourse was to be interpreted.

man of science ? All that He adds to the signs He has just given is this : 'Then shall appear the sign of the Son of Man in heaven,'[1] where we may recognize His cross, at first the symbol of punishment, but afterwards the trophy of His victory. Last of all will be seen the Son of Man Himself—and here again appears a description that had become traditional ever since the time of Daniel[2]—'coming in the clouds with great power and glory. And then shall He send His angels and shall gather together His elect from the four winds, from the uttermost part of the earth to the uttermost part of heaven.' The Son of Man, as every disciple knew, was Jesus Himself coming to inaugurate the kingdom of God at the end of the world.

The time of the destruction of the Temple and the time of the coming of the Son of Man.

It seems therefore quite clear enough, even from the text of St. Mark, who seems best to have preserved the original style of the discourse and to have excluded other matter which had to do with the subject, that Jesus here deals with two different subjects. The first of these, the destruction of the Temple, is left wrapped up in symbolism, but only as regards the main occurrence. The whole event is accomplished in earthly conditions, with an action that is natural, and men are able to seek safety in flight. The second event also takes place upon earth, but accompanied by incidents that have a marvellous character performed by false Christs, and the close of the event is the end of the world.

So far no interval has been spoken of between the two events. Perhaps they were to be contemporaneous, the second being but the continuation and completion of the first. But that was not the opinion held at the time when St. Luke wrote. After giving what is a sufficient indication of an interval between the two events, namely, 'the times of the nations,' the evangelist does not make any further explicit reference to their relative positions in time. He merely shows that the first signs of the coming trouble will be a promise of deliverance for the Christian faithful. The menace that casts down the Jews is an uplifting hope for the faithful : 'Look up and lift up your heads, because your redemption is at hand.' Thus suffering gives place to joy ;

[1] Matthew xxiv, 30. [2] Daniel vii, 13.

the Church is truly born on the ruins of the Synagogue. There follows in St. Luke the parable of the fig tree ; hence he must have understood that parable of the dawn of God's kingdom upon earth. The fig tree has its first leaves in the springtime—a season that hardly exists in the Palestinian round of seasons, since summer succeeds winter almost immediately. For St. Luke summer stands for the kingdom of God. The generation then alive will not have disappeared completely before the kingdom of God and the deliverance of the faithful shall have come to pass : ' Heaven and earth shall pass away,' said Jesus, ' but My words shall not pass away ' ; words in which He announced the kingdom of God, words which are still living and effectual, and ever shall be.

Now there is no reason why we should interpret this parable differently in the gospels of St. Mark and St. Matthew ; the terms are similar, with the sole exception that these two evangelists have added the mysterious remark: ' Know that it is nigh at the doors,' whereas St. Luke says plainly : ' Know that the kingdom of God is at hand.' Mark and Matthew, however, have emphasized the coming of the Son of Man much more than Luke, and have seemed to identify it with the destruction of Jerusalem. But they draw a distinction between the two events, without however throwing light on the time of the second coming of Christ, by adding : ' *But,* of that day or hour no one knoweth, neither the angels in heaven nor the Son, but the Father only.'[1]

It has been maintained by some that in these words Jesus declared that He was in a position to describe, by means of the two pictures contained in this discourse, what were to be the premonitory signs of this one event, at the same time confessing that He was ignorant of the precise moment when it would take place, namely, the exact day and hour. But that would have been equivalent to attaching an importance that was excessive to a precise determination of time, a thing that was quite immaterial compared with the essential point of the discourse, namely, that men should prepare for God's judgement of which they would be forewarned by signs. What leads to the conclusion that the gospels indicate two different times for the two events is the fact that the first

[1] Mark xiii, 32 ; cf. Matthew xxiv, 36, which omits ' neither the Son ' from the Vulgate version.

event does not spell the end of all things ; no matter how sudden its coming might be, it was still possible to escape the catastrophe. But flight from it would be senseless if there was nothing to follow. The first event, then, was to be of some duration, in its consequences at least ; there was nothing of an instantaneous character about it. That, on the contrary, is precisely the characteristic note of the coming of the Son of Man, on which St. Matthew lays such stress in this discourse.[1]

Therefore the clearly marked contrast indicated in the above text from St. Mark by its initial *but* is not a contrast between an approximate time and an exact time, but between the two pictures drawn by Jesus of the events to come, pictures which differed so much in their features. There are two different pictures ; that is obvious to all. We are aware now that it was possible for the disciples to be taught about the proximity of the first event—' before this generation has passed away '—without being informed concerning the moment when the second was to take place ; and that is quite natural, seeing that the two pictures drawn by Jesus relate to two different events.

That the words above quoted from St. Mark were uttered by Jesus, that the distinction between the times of the two events really did originate with Him, is proved by the interpretation placed upon the discourse by St. Luke ; it is proved still more clearly by the astonishing declaration that the time of the end of the world was a secret not communicated even to the Son. Which of His disciples would have had the hardihood to impose such a limitation upon Him ? Even now it seems strange to us, though it is possible for us to understand its meaning. The knowledge of the Son of God is equal to that of His Father, or rather it is the same as the Father's. Nevertheless the Son became incarnate and when He acted in His character as Son of Man and Messiah He regulated His knowledge by what that role required. The work of creation is attributed to the Father, and if we judge according to such attribution it would seem that it is only the Creator of the world who knows at what moment the world will come to an end. At that moment the Son will return as Judge, and it is not His business to say when that will be ; it is not His secret ; He is considered as not knowing it. In His character as Messiah He

[1] Matthew xxiv, 27.

is a prophet, and as such He predicts with as much precision as is expedient the destruction of the Temple. He also warns His disciples to be ever on the watch, for no one but the Father knows when the end of time will come. Moreover, for each one of them the end of time is the end of his life.

Whatever be the time when the Son of Man shall come, we must watch (250).

Luke xxi, 34–35 ; Mark xiii, 33–37 ; Matt. xxiv, 42.[1]

The Father had willed not to reveal the time of the coming of the Son of Man, and that was a decisive reason why the disciples should always be ready so as not to be taken by surprise. Jesus laid stress on the duty of vigilance, and here again He points out repeatedly that the moment of His coming remains a secret : 'Take heed, watch, for ye know not when the time is. It is like as when a man has gone on a journey and left his house and given authority to his servants, to each one his work, and charged the porter to watch.' The porter is mentioned separately because his special duty is to watch in order to open the door immediately so as not to keep the master waiting. But in the application of the parable the command to watch is given to everyone : 'Watch ye therefore, for ye know not when the lord of the house cometh, at even, or at midnight, or at cockcrow or in the morning.' If he did not come then, the servants had to suppose that their master had received hospitality somewhere else, and that he would not return that night. These are expressive words, very characteristic of Jesus, and they say metaphorically, but plainly all the same, that the Son of Man will perhaps be a long time coming. Why, then, did He give His disciples this warning ? It may be that they will be a long time asleep with the sleep of death. That is why Jesus concludes with : 'What I say to you I say to all,' a solemn warning to be handed on, a password to be handed down from one generation to another : 'Watch !'[2]

St. Luke shows in his usual manner that the warning is

[1] The explicit counsel about the necessity of watching in Mark and Matthew is stated more generally in Luke, who has already recommended vigilance (Luke xii, 35–40, in Section 178, parallel to Matthew xxiv, 43–44).

[2] Mark xiii, 33–37.

given not so much to the Apostles as to the generations to come. They, not the Apostles, were in danger of letting their hearts grow heavy with drunkenness and the anxieties of life. He concludes by recalling 'that day,' which Mark and Matthew had distinguished from the time of destruction of the Temple, and by calling special attention to its suddenness; it will burst upon them unexpectedly. He notes also that the blow will fall on all without exception, for it will smite all who are on the face of the whole earth; there will be no longer any question of flight. None can therefore hope to escape its formidable onslaught. The chief thing is to watch and pray so that we may not be found with the guilty, but rather standing ready for the Son of Man.

The parable of the wise and foolish virgins (251).

Matt. xxv. 1–13.

Now that, at this solemn moment, He has broached the subject of vigilance, Jesus strives to engrave deep on the minds of His disciples the necessity of being prepared. All His teaching concerning the value of the soul was at stake. Hence he fixes His gaze on the last hour and devotes His final parables to this subject. We may say that the parable of the ten virgins is framed within two warnings about the necessity of vigilance, on which our salvation hangs: 'Watch ye therefore, because you know not at what hour your Lord will come.[1] . . . Watch ye therefore, because you know neither the day nor the hour.'[2] The real point of the parable on which especial insistence is laid is that we must be ready even though the Son of Man be long in coming.

We are given a picture of ten young maidens invited to the wedding of one of their friends; they have gone to her home to congratulate her, help her to dress, and entertain her until the arrival of the bridegroom for the marriage feast.[3] As night has already fallen, the girls have gone with their little clay lamps alight. These lamps hold very little oil, so five of the girls, the wise virgins, have brought with them small flasks full of oil; the rest are not so prudent—they are called foolish virgins—and have supposed that the

[1] Matthew xxiv, 42, followed by the parable of the servants.
[2] Matthew xxv, 13.
[3] Cf. *Naplouse* by Jaussen, O.P., p. 72 ff.

bridegroom would not be long coming. But he does not come, and gradually silence reigns, for these young people are drowsy ; and finally they all fall asleep. In the middle of the night a cry goes up : ' Behold the bridegroom cometh ! Go ye forth to meet him.' Straightway the wise virgins fill their lamps which are nearly out. They are besought by their friends, the foolish virgins, to give them oil, but they refuse : ' Lest perhaps there be not enough for us and for you, go ye rather to them that sell and buy for yourselves.' But how could they get oil at such an hour ? And in any case it takes time even if someone could be persuaded to open his shop. Hence, when the foolish virgins return the bridegroom has already gone into the chamber of the wedding feast with the others, and the door is shut. They knock, saying : ' Lord, Lord, open unto us ! ' But He answers : ' I know you not.'

This parable has been justly admired as a picture of Oriental life. We see the girls asleep, their lamps lit but already beginning to smoke. We hear the cry ringing through the night. Then all hurry, some with confidence, the rest grievously embarrassed. The procession with its lights forms up while the foolish virgins are wandering about in the dark ; and when they come back they find the door shut, and no entreaties will open it. There is nothing to indicate that the bridegroom did this on purpose to punish them for their lack of foresight ; the door was not shut until everybody in the procession was inside. The fact is that the bridegroom does not want to open it for people whom he does not know ; once open, it will be impossible to prevent anyone from coming in. Poor girls ! We pity their fate, we are tempted to find fault with the selfishness of their too prudent companions and with the bridegroom's severity. But we must not be led astray by these appearances. It may be that the wise virgins were wanting in charity, but what does that matter ? Perhaps the others were not seriously to blame. Be it so ! But the parable is not an allegory. The bridegroom does not judge like the Son of Man, for he does not directly represent Him ; he is not able to read the heart. The comparison in the parable is intended to bring out this one point—and how wonderfully it succeeds !—that nothing is of any avail if we are not ready at the moment when the Son of Man appears in order to lead the guests to His banquet.

It is a lesson for the whole Christian community. When we find that Christ has not come, we begin to stop looking for Him, to disbelieve any longer in His coming, to have doubts even about the judgement for the performance of which He was to come ; finally we begin to doubt His word. This, we may say, is the state of many Christians in our own day, who are baptized but who have given up their faith because God allows things to take their course and does not execute His judgements upon earth often enough to please them. But it is also a lesson for each one of us. At first we eagerly prepare ourselves, as though we were immediately to appear before God. But time goes by, we get used to living in this world, and when death comes, perhaps after a long life, we are not ready and all our store of fervour is exhausted.

The conclusion is that we must leave God to choose His comings and to fix the time of them ; our business is to be always ready. As for the dispositions with which we must appear before the judgement seat, Jesus has made them known to us both in the parable of the talents,[1] which deals with the question of fidelity in working for Him whilst we await His coming, and especially in the picture of the Last Judgement.

The Last Judgement (252).

Matt. xxv, 31–46.

The Son of Man seemed inflexible in the parable of the ten virgins ; but if He is now inflexible as judge, at all events the motives which lead Him to form His decisions enable us to see that His heart is full of mercy. Jesus announces that He will come to judge all mankind. Ever since the ancient days of the prophets, and especially since Amos, the thought of judgement had haunted the anxious mind of Israel. At first she regarded it as being merely intended for the punishment of *her* enemies. But the prophets had taught her that God would judge according to justice, would judge His own people also if they were guilty. Then, when the nation was converted from its wickedness and when the holy remnant had returned from

[1] We have already said that we look on this parable of the talents as substantially identical with the parable of the pounds in Luke. Cf. p. 116, above.

captivity in Babylon, the righteous—that is, the Pharisees—fully persuaded that there was nothing in their conduct which could be criticized from the standpoint of legal observance, longed for the judgement to come, as we read in the Book of Henoch ; but the judgement they desired meant the revenge of the righteous in Israel on the Gentiles, and still more revenge on the sinners of the Jewish faction opposed to the Pharisaic party, indifferent as these sinners were to religion and even tainted with heterodox opinions.

Jesus views the judgement only in its religious and moral aspect, therefore as reaching all men without distinction, though His discourse is intended first of all for His disciples. Among the Jews no one would have dared to make the Messiah assume the function of supreme judge which belonged to the Lord God alone ; but Jesus shows Himself at His last coming seated on God's throne of glory, which now becomes His own throne. In this He makes a declaration almost as solemn as that He will make concerning His rank as Son of God before the Sanhedrin. Here we behold Him surrounded by all His angels, separating the elect from the rest as a shepherd separates his white docile sheep from the black and stubborn goats. The elect are at His right hand, the place of His friends ; the goats on His left hand represent the reprobate. Then the King says to those on His right hand : 'Come, ye blessed of My Father. Possess the kingdom prepared for you from the creation of the world.' God had prepared it for them, and He had therefore called them to it. How have they merited to enter it ? By all that they have done for their Lord Jesus. He was hungry, and they gave Him to eat ; He was thirsty, and they gave Him to drink ; they sheltered and clothed Him ; He was sick and in prison, and they visited Him. Although the just rely little on their own merits, nevertheless they cannot have forgotten that they have had pity on the poor and unfortunate, and their natural feelings of compassion had found a motive for action in their habitual determination to serve God. But when had they ever seen Jesus suffering hunger and thirst, or homeless, naked, sick, or in prison ? They are amazed. Then the King answers them, addressing them as His brethren who have lived among other brethren of His : 'Inasmuch as you did it to one of these my brethren, to one of the least, you did it to Me.'

These simple words raised to the divine sphere the most

delicate acts of human kindness. Compassion was branded as a weakness by the Stoic philosophers, but it is in reality the sign of nobility of heart, especially if the objects of our compassion be the sick or poor. But how many there are who undertake these works of charity moved merely by human feeling, when they are duties which demand the sacrifice of oneself? Altruism, as we call it nowadays, is not a very powerful incentive to such things. Jesus has taught us that the question of eternal salvation is involved for each one of us in this matter, and those who are filled with love for Him realize that whatever they do for the poor and the afflicted is done for Him. Thus was Christian charity born, and in its turn it brings forth miracles. We do not, of course, imagine that Jesus here gave licence to commit whatever evil we like provided only we are charitable. The fact is that when we act charitably for His sake we are fulfilling the command to love God, for the second commandment is the same as the first.

Nevertheless we are led by this parable to hope for mercy even for sinners if they have shown themselves charitable to their neighbour. By God's grace their evil dispositions will have changed for the better and they will pass over to the right hand of Christ. But other sinners, who have had no compassion for the unfortunate, have for that reason neglected to do anything for Christ and are therefore condemned to the fire prepared for the devil, where they are sent by the King to punish them for their hardness of heart.

Eternal punishment or eternal life: the Judge has given sentence.

VI. WEDNESDAY OF HOLY WEEK

The treachery of Judas (254).

Luke xxii, 1–6; Mark xiv, 1–2, 10–11; Matt. xxvi, 1–5, 14–16.

With this glance at the last end of the world Jesus puts the seal to His Gospel. From the Mount of Olives He descends to Bethany. The feast of the Pasch was drawing near and the leaders of the Sanhedrin felt some anxiety, for they knew that during the eight days of the feast Pilate would be on the watch. If the Galilæan conceived the idea of arousing the populace, the governor would not lose the opportunity of striking hard. They must hurry, for if they arrested Jesus during the ceremonies of the feast they would be provoking the very tumult they feared.[1] But secrecy was of no less importance than speed, and there were now only two days before the feast. Eventually the action of Judas Iscariot extricated the chief priests and the group of Pharisaic rabbis from their difficulty.

Judas, one of the Twelve, is a special favourite of anti-Christian critics of the Gospel, particularly of several Jewish scholars who have devoted themselves to a study of the history of Jesus.[2] He originated from Qarioth in the south of Judæa, and was of colder disposition than the enthusiastic Gaililæans ; but he was, so we are assured by the critics, more intelligent and better educated than they, and well worthy of the confidence that Jesus showed by sending him to preach the kingdom of God. Gradually, they tell us, he discovered how extravagant were the claims of his Master, who was calling Himself the Messiah and Son of God, though he saw that Jesus knew how to slip out of danger in time of need. Consequently He must be a seducer, and the Law commanded that such a one be denounced to the authorities. Judas did his duty, and would such an honest fellow as he was ever have been willing to accept money as the price of his obedience to the laws of his country? We must confess, indeed, that the other disciples were not at hand to witness the bargain made between Judas and the leaders of the Sanhedrin, but at all events the fact became notorious enough. Besides, had they not witnessed Judas betray his Master with a kiss? And that kiss is sufficient indication of the sort of man he was.

There is this much truth in the conjecture of the critics, that Judas had in fact begun with good dispositions. Had that not been so, Jesus would never have admitted him among the Twelve. But He saw no reason for not admitting him in His foreknowledge of the future, which resembled the foreknowledge of His Father, who gives very great graces even to those who will fall away in the future. Moreover, it is quite possible that Judas, as he came from Judæa, was more imbued than other disciples with the doctrines

[1] But Rabbi Aqiba counselled that dangerous teachers should be put to death on the occasion of the pilgrimage feasts (Sanhedrin xi, 4). His object in this, to create a stronger impression on a larger number of people, was achieved in this case by anticipating the feast by one day.

[2] See, for example, the work of Dr. Klausner quoted above.

of the Pharisees and thus more disposed to forsake his Master whom the Pharisees pursued with such fury. No doubt he had hopes—and some of the other disciples were at first in almost the same case; but his ambition was meaner than theirs and he was moved by love of money—that the kingdom of God would turn to his own personal advantage. When his calculations miscarried, he broke away. It is also possible that when St. Matthew makes him take the initiative in asking for money, he may have only interpreted the greedy desire of Judas' heart. According to St. Mark and St. Luke, it was the chief priests, delighted at this piece of good fortune, who made the offer of a reward. But the main point is that Judas had taken the initiative in the act of betrayal and that he agreed to accept the price of the betrayal. The sum agreed on was thirty pieces of silver.[1]

All that remained for the miserable man to do now was to find a suitable opportunity; in other words, to arrange some means of entrapping Jesus in such a way that the populace might know nothing of the matter until the thing was accomplished. These chief priests and Pharisees, princes of the nation by birth and by intelligence, despised the people but also feared them. As if already oppressed by the mournful realization of the betrayal, the narrative of St. Matthew and St. Mark relates nothing further for that day save the anointing at Bethany,[2] which seems to have been the determining cause of Judas' action and which was, as it were, an act of loving reparation anticipating the crime. According to these two evangelists the traitor's interview with those who paid him the money took place at night.

VII. MAUNDY THURSDAY

Preparations for the Last Supper (255).

Luke xxii, 7–13; Mark xiv, 12–16; Matt. xxvi, 17–19.

The next morning Jesus bade His disciples to make preparations for the Pasch on that very day. The day was unquestionably a Thursday, for all four evangelists agree in saying that Jesus died on the eve of the Sabbath, that is to

[1] Matthew xxvi, 15.
[2] Following the explicit witness of St. John we have assigned it to the previous Saturday.

say, on a Friday. Now His arrest took place after the evening meal on the day before His death, that is, the day of which the first three evangelists here speak. It is also certain that the latter give to the meal of Thursday evening the character of a Paschal feast. It has been maintained, it is true, that the Last Supper was only symbolically a Paschal meal, in that it commenced a new covenant between God and His faithful, a covenant that was no longer made in the blood of a lamb as in the days of the Exodus, but in the blood of Jesus. That is indeed the true meaning of the Last Supper, but if the Last Supper is merely a figure, where is the reality on which it is based? The evangelists have said very little concerning the Jewish Paschal ritual during the meal; but if the Last Supper *may* be the Paschal meal, then that is what is *was* in their minds, for it was the meal which followed the preparations that had been made in view of the Pasch, and these preparations are expressly called preparations for the Pasch in the gospel narrative.

How, then, has it come about that even Catholic commentators have felt themselves bound to maintain that there were no Jewish Paschal rites observed on that evening? It is because, as we shall read in St. John,[1] the enemies of Jesus refused to enter the Prætorium on the Friday lest they might be defiled and so rendered unable to eat the Pasch that same evening. Did Jesus therefore eat the Pasch a day earlier than the priests? Or did St. John put it a day later? In other words, on what day of the week fell the day of the Pasch, the day following the Paschal meal of the evening before? It was a very solemn feast; rest from work was of strict obligation. All the busy comings and goings of the chief priests and the leaders of the Pharisees, the appearance of Jesus before the Sanhedrin, His prosecution before Pilate, everything in fact that all the four evangelists by common consent assign to the Friday, could not possibly have taken place on the most solemn feast of the year. In particular the Synoptists state that the Jews wished to have the matter finished before the feast began. It must therefore be regarded as certain that the feast of the Pasch did not fall on Friday that year, but on Saturday. It remains for us to explain why Jesus celebrated the Paschal meal a day earlier than the leaders of the people.

We might allege His sovereign right to do as He wished;

[1] John xviii, 28.

but against that we have to say that the disciples showed no surprise at His choice of day, and the earlier evangelists suggest that it was the day prescribed by the Law. As we must provide some explanation, we shall give the one which seems to us the most probable in view of the customs obtaining among the Jews at that time. According to the Law the Paschal meal was to be celebrated in the evening of the 14th day of Nisan. The Jews did not begin their day at midnight as we do, but reckoned from sunset to sunset. They counted the days, nevertheless, just as we do; thus the evening of the 14th Nisan was reckoned as part of the 15th day, but it was described as the evening of the 14th day. Therefore it could be said that the Paschal meal took place on the 14th day of Nisan. In the morning the house was swept and all traces of leavened bread were removed, for unleavened bread was of obligation at the Paschal meal on the eight days during which the feast lasted. The 15th day of Nisan was more especially the day of unleavened bread, receiving the name of the feast of the Pasch or the feast of Unleavened Bread indiscriminately. The Paschal lamb was a sacred victim, the practice being to sacrifice it in the Temple and to sprinkle the altar with its blood. That done, he who had offered it took it and had it roasted at home. Night having fallen, the meal was begun, and it had to be finished by two o'clock in the morning at the latest.

Now at what time did the sacrifice of the lamb take place? This is the point on which the whole question turns. The words of the Law, 'between the two evenings,' certainly pointed to the dusk, and the Sadducees held firmly to the opinion that the right time was between six and half-past seven in the evening. But we learn from Josephus that the Pharisees allowed the sacrifice to be begun as early as half-past three, and if the Pasch fell on a Sabbath day, even an hour earlier. Occasionally it happened that the 15th Nisan was a Saturday, and as all work was forbidden as soon as that day began—that is to say, from sunset on the evening before—how could a lamb be sacrificed about sunset? Ought the Sabbath obligation to give way before the Pasch? Hillel, about 25 B.C., was of opinion that it ought to do so, and his opinion prevailed among the Pharisees. It is given validity by the *Mishnah*. But even in the *Mishnah* only the sacrifice of the lamb was permitted, on the ground that it was an act of public worship, and not the cooking of it. Hence, no doubt, it was to ensure that everything should be done according to the Law that the hour of the sacrifice had been put earlier, so that there might still be time to roast the lamb before sunset. But after all it was possible to give a broader interpretation of Hillel's principle, that the Pasch was above the Sabbath, than the *Mishnah* allowed. But we are not sure that this principle was at first admitted by the Sadducees, or even by all the Pharisees. After the Temple had been destroyed, the Pharisees of Hillel's school had the supremacy. Forty years earlier the Sadducees had the deciding voice concerning all that took place in the Temple. If they refused to give up either of their two principles, the immolation of the lamb at dusk and the strict observance of the Sabbath rest, there was only one thing that was left for them to do, namely, to immolate the lamb a day earlier. This was not to put the feast a day earlier, but merely to put themselves right with regard to the law of the Sabbath. They ate the lamb at the proper time on the appointed evening. But there were some who thought that once the lamb was slaughtered in this fashion, they were bound to eat it on the same day. It may be that the Galilæans, being of provincial origin and therefore more attached to the old customs, kept to this practice; hence the disciples would have felt no surprise when Jesus proposed to keep the Pasch on the 13th day of Nisan, as the Sabbath fell on the 15th that year.

And if anyone ate the Paschal lamb on the evening of the 13th, then it is evident that they must have eaten it with unleavened bread; otherwise they would have ended by changing completely the character of the Paschal ritual.[1] Thus what actually would happen was merely that certain groups among the Israelites hastened the feast by one day. The diversity thus created was not of such consequence as we might be led to think. A similar case is found in Palestine to this day, where the Moslem feast of Beïram, which follows the fast of the Ramadan, is not kept on the same day by the Mohammedans of Jerusalem and those of Nablus. Again, until the time of Pope St. Victor, the churches of Asia did not keep Easter on the same date as the church at Rome. True, in the case of which we are speaking, the feast

[1] Cf. Exodus xii, 8. Chevolson, in *Das letzte Passamahl Christi*, thinks the contrary.

was celebrated on different days in the same city, but at the same time there was an artificial grouping of the pilgrims gathered in the city for the feast. They came there in separate companies, each of which followed the local customs of the district from which it came. There were not enough priests to sacrifice all the lambs required for the Pasch,[1] and in any case they would have made no objection against sacrificing lambs for Galilæans who were keeping the feast a day earlier, on the ground that they had seen the new moon a day sooner than it was seen in Judæa (it was thus that the date of the Pasch was fixed), or if they wished to have the lambs sacrificed a day earlier, as was thought lawful by people at Jerusalem, in order to avoid working on the Sabbath. For the inhabitants of Jerusalem, guided as they were by their religious leaders, the feast did not begin that year until Friday evening. Jesus and His disciples celebrated the Paschal supper on the Thursday evening.

So sure are the disciples of doing what they have a right to do, that it is they who take the initiative on the morning of the day which St. Mark calls ‘ the first day of the Unleavened Bread, when the Pasch (that is, the Paschal lamb) was sacrificed.’[2] They ask : ‘ Whither wilt Thou that we go and prepare for Thee to eat the Pasch ? ’ It could not be done at Bethany, for the rite had to be performed at Jerusalem. It was necessary to secure a large room, for Jesus desired to have the Twelve with Him that evening. But He had friends at Jerusalem, and knew that He could count on one of them to provide for Him ; perhaps He had even let them know of His intention. Nevertheless He wished to test the faith of the disciples and to show them that there was no such thing as chance where He was concerned. They were still on the Mount of Olives. He therefore sends two of them to the city—Luke names Peter and John, disciples who were united in special friendship—and gives them instructions to follow blindly a man whom they would meet near the gate carrying a pitcher of water. Such a sight was rare, for it is usually the women who go to the spring and bring back the large pitcher of water balanced on their heads. Following this man without drawing his

[1] Josephus (*Jewish War*, VI, ix, 3) speaks of 256,500 lambs, an exaggeration, but significant all the same.

[2] Matthew merely says the day of the Unleavened Bread. Luke emphasizes the obligation of sacrificing the Pasch on that day.

notice, the disciples are to enter a house after him and there say to the owner : 'The Master saith : Where is My guest-chamber where I am to eat the Pasch with My disciples?' Jesus goes on to say : 'He will show you a large upper room spread with mats, ready. And there prepare ye for us.'

All took place as Jesus had foretold. In the homes of people in easy circumstances, above the rooms reserved for the family where strangers were not received, there would be a large and well-lit upper chamber, used for the reception of guests. It is still the custom to this day in Palestine. This room could be entered by an outside staircase without disturbing the inhabitants of the house, and the owner of the house had already spread the mats on which the guests could recline round the dishes placed in the centre ; there might be cushions also to support the body and the elbow on which the diners leaned during the meal. The Law had commanded that the first Pasch in Egypt was to be eaten 'with the loins girt, shoes on the feet, and a staff in the hand,'[1] and consequently standing. This custom was long maintained. But the rabbis had seen the Greeks taking their meals lying down, as was the prerogative of men that were free, and it was as free men that Jews should keep the Pasch. Hence they had adopted this practice. They used couches instead of mats, but these couches were very low and covered with rugs. The disciples found the room arranged so ; and as the servant had even brought the water they would need, they had nothing to do but procure the usual provisions for the meal. Perhaps the friend of Jesus had even taken it upon himself to provide these. But the disciples would have to see that the lamb was sacrificed in the Temple and bring it back to the house, and this was probably the duty that Peter and John fulfilled.

The Paschal Supper.

The order followed by the Jews in the celebration of the Paschal Supper is described in a special treatise of the *Mishnah* devoted to the Pasch, named *Pesahim.*[2] It may be that a few details had been changed between the time of Jesus and the date of the composition of the *Mishnah*, about

[1] Exodus xii, 11.

[2] See the introduction and notes to this treatise by George Beer, Töpelmann edition, Giessen, 1912.

a hundred and fifty years later, but the ritual as a whole had certainly not changed. It was a development of the ancient and very simple ritual of Exodus. The feast was the most joyful one of the year, though a strict fast was enjoined from the morning meal until the Paschal Supper. Hence the latter had gradually become abundant, resembling perhaps those feasts in use among the Greeks which had nothing in them contrary to religion and the stricter morality observed among the Jews. Wine had always played a large part in the banquets of the Israelites, for their country, Judæa especially, is a land of vineyards. Four cups at least of wine was the amount determined by the Paschal ritual, and these were to be drunk together by all those at table, though a further quantity was not prohibited, each one being left to his own choice in the matter. Among the Greeks it was customary for the guests to mix a little water with the wine according to their individual taste. Further, they made no difficulty about using the same cup, and in this they were sometimes followed by the Jews, though it seems that each had his own cup at the Paschal supper. There is no rule laid down, however, on the subject, and no one could deny the right of the master of the house to pass his own cup round the table so that all the others might wet their lips.

The ceremony began with the blessing of the first cup, a prayer which called down a blessing on the wine and on the day according to the opinion of Hillel, but on the day first and then on the wine according to Shammai. Then herbs were brought in with a dishful of sauce.[1] The Jews were acquainted with the use of forks, but on this occasion they used their fingers, dipping the herbs into the sauce. When this course was finished the Paschal lamb was placed on the table, and a commemoration was made of the mercies of God. The head of the family explained the reason for which they were performing this rite, recalling the deliverance of Israel. No strict formula was prescribed, though the *Mishnah* suggests the subjects to be spoken of, after the manner of our own homiletical works. The second cup was drunk and the lamb eaten along with bitter herbs. But after the destruction of the Temple the Paschal supper was celebrated without the sacrificial lamb, since without the Temple there could be no sacrifice. In our own time we

[1] Called *haroseth*, made of pounded nuts and fruit with vinegar. *Pesahim*, X, 3.

have seen its place taken in the homes of the Jews at Jerusalem by turkey or roast meat. It was not forbidden, however, to introduce other foods into this Paschal meal, such as eggs, or even other meats which had been offered in sacrifice in the Temple.

After the eating of the lamb the third cup was poured out and an act of thanksgiving was offered. The fourth cup is mentioned immediately afterwards, being followed by the hymn *Hallel*, which was composed of Psalms cxv to cxviii.[1] The last of these psalms with 'Blessed be he that cometh in the name of Jahweh' gave occasion for the expression of Messianic hopes. To this Jesus Himself had alluded in His farewell words to Jerusalem.[2] Conversation was carried on by those gathered at table, and usually went on so far into the night that the provisions of the *Mishnah* command that those who have fallen asleep should be wakened.

Of such a character as this was the meal that Jesus took with His disciples on the eve of His death, though the evangelists make no mention of the Paschal lamb, referring only to the bread and wine because of the Eucharist. They attach no importance to the exact observance of this ancient rite precisely because they are aware that it has been replaced by a new rite. This is what Jesus gave His disciples to understand right from the beginning of the meal, making it clear that it was indeed the traditional Pasch which they were observing, but at the same time the inauguration of a new covenant.

The prelude to the supper (256).

Luke xxii, 14–18 ; Mark xiv, 17–25 ; Matt. xxvi, 20–29.

It is in St. Luke's gospel especially that the Last Supper appears primarily as a Paschal rite. There Jesus says in fact : 'I have ardently desired to eat this Pasch with you before I suffer.' The Passion is to be a necessary preliminary of the institution of a new Pasch in which the ancient Pasch finds its fulfilment, in the sense that the new Pasch is the essential reality growing out of another reality which was its type : 'For I say to you that I will not eat it henceforth until it be fulfilled in the kingdom of God.' We here see in how pre-eminent a manner Jesus had come to 'perfect' the

[1] In the Vulgate numbering Psalms cxiii, 8–18 cxiv–cxvii.
[2] Matthew xxiii, 39.

Old Law in the kingdom of God which was about to be spread throughout the earth.

Then, following the Jewish custom, He begins the meal by blessing the first cup of wine. We said above that the Jewish authors themselves are not at one about the use of the cup, but it appears from the *Mishnah* that each had his own for the Paschal supper ; and this is what Jesus seems to assume for this first cup. He blesses a sort of bowl, from which the disciples are to fill their cups : 'Take this and divide it among you.'[1] Then He says : 'For I say to you that I will drink no more of the fruit of the vine till that day when I shall drink it new in the kingdom of God.'[2] In this He alludes to His approaching death which will enable Him to ascend to God, and at that moment the kingdom of God will be established on earth. It was another way of telling them that this would be the last Pasch of His mortal life.[3]

Jesus rebukes the disciples for their ambition and washes their feet (257).

Luke xxii, 24, 27, 28, 29, 30a ; John xiii, 1–20.

At this moment a sort of rivalry sprang up between the disciples.[4] Notwithstanding the solemnity of the sacred ritual they began to quarrel, not being satisfied perhaps with the places allotted to them, each wanting to be nearest the Master. It was a strange time for the display of petty vanity, and Jesus reduced it to its due insignificance by His wonderful example of humility. He, who alone should have sat down to be waited on by them, becomes the servant of them all. Let them raise their minds to the thought of the

[1] Luke xxii, 17.

[2] Mark xiv, 25 ; cf. Matthew xxvi, 29. A stricter parallelism with the words relating to the Pasch is obtained by Luke's words 'till the kingdom of God come.'

[3] Luke places the institution of the Eucharist immediately afterwards, following his usual custom of completing an incident he has begun, without troubling about the intervening events (cf. iii, 19). But he makes us understand that the institution occurred later, since the eucharistic cup is placed at the end of the meal.

[4] What follows is from St. Luke. He has placed here things which come better after the request of the sons of Zebedee, where Mark and Matthew have placed them (cf. Luke xxii, 25, 26, 30 b) ; perhaps he considered the words used by Jesus at that time suit the occasion here. Certainly the words here related by Luke correspond perfectly with the lesson given by Jesus in washing the feet of His disciples, as related by St. John.

place where the reward is eternal. He loves them all because they have remained steadfastly loyal to Him in His trials. Instead of quarrelling over the places at that poor table just before His death, let them look into the future and see the places of honour they will occupy when they eat and drink at His table in the kingdom which His Father has given Him. Then Jesus adds example to precept and, taking quite seriously the part of a servant which He has just said was His, outstripping the humility of His words by abasing Himself to the task of a slave, He prepares to wash His disciples' feet. This we learn from the fourth gospel.

St. John, by relating the warning to the traitor and the prediction of Peter's denial, has obviously implied that Jesus celebrated the Paschal meal, the Last Supper. He says nothing about the Eucharist, probably because he does not wish to describe this Paschal meal which introduced and typified the Eucharist. He could not have mentioned the Paschal rite without long and difficult explanations, seeing that he is about to remark further on[1] that the Jews ate the Pasch on the following day. Moreover, he has already, earlier in his gospel, dealt with the subject of Christ's Flesh and Blood as the food and drink of the faithful.[2] He therefore contents himself with confirming the narrative of the Synoptists on certain points and completing it on certain others. Thus he has placed the washing of the feet at a time when the supper had hardly commenced, and when it was still the proper time for such ablutions.[3]

The chief purpose which Jesus had in view was to give His disciples an example of humility such as should provide an everlasting lesson to His Church. What raises this servile act even to the heights of heroism is the fact that He, who had come from God and was going to God, knew perfectly well that Judas Iscariot, one of the Twelve, was at that very moment intending to betray Him. Yet He would wash his feet as He washed the feet of the rest. And Judas was not the one who protested ! It was Peter, full of astonishment at seeing Jesus rise from the table, put off His upper garments, gird Himself with a towel, pour water into the

[1] John xviii, 28. [2] John vi, 51 ff.

[3] The reading γινομένου, 'having begun' (xiii, 2) is better supported by the MSS, though more difficult, than γενομένου, 'having been finished'; it is more in harmony with what the Synoptists relate and is absolutely demanded by verse 12.

basin, and kneel down—for how else could He have done what He wished to do?—to wash the feet of His own disciple.[1] Peter seemed as if he would refuse, though with a gentleness that must have caused a great effort to a man of his disposition: 'Lord, *Thou* washest my feet!' Jesus replies in the same tone: 'What I am doing thou knowest not now, but thou shalt understand hereafter.' But Peter wants an explanation of this incomprehensible thing now. He is unable to contain himself and bursts out with: 'No, Thou shalt never wash my feet.' In his emotion he was entering on the way to disobedience. Jesus therefore adopts a sterner tone: 'If I wash thee not, thou shalt have no part with Me.' Peter's loving heart takes alarm; he is softened, he yields, he becomes hot with emotion; and now he is excessive in his submission: 'Lord, not only my feet, but also my hands and my head!' The good Simon Peter!

As for Judas, he does not stir; he says nothing, fearing lest he may perhaps denounce himself. Moreover, he feels very contemptuous of what is being done. It is of him that Jesus is thinking when He says to Peter: 'He that is bathed needeth not to wash,[2] for he is clean wholly. And you are clean, but not all.' This was as much as to declare plainly that Peter had, after all, no need of the extra purification which he demanded; both he and the others were clean except Judas, whose heart no washing could cleanse. What Jesus had done was therefore done simply to bring down for ever these upliftings of pride and vanity in His friends; this He says openly, without alluding to any inferior condition of purity that He has thus rendered more perfect: 'Know you what I have done to you? You call Me Master and Lord, and you say well, for so I am. If then I, being Lord and Master, have washed your feet, you ought also to wash one another's feet.' The faithful know perfectly well that they ought to imitate Christ in all their actions, all their thoughts, and in their whole life; there is no special obligation attached to this particular example which He shows us here. Nevertheless it was the custom of kings to wash the feet of the poor on Maundy Thursday in honourable memory of Christ, and the prelates of the Church observe the custom still. There is no longer any room to

[1] It seems most probable that Jesus began with Peter.

[2] We prefer to follow authoritative MSS. in omitting the words 'except his feet.'

plead that it is unseemly to demean oneself before a brother who at heart may be an apostate. Jesus acted thus before Judas, although He knew that His disciple was prefigured in the Scripture which says: 'He that eateth my bread hath lifted up his heel against me.'[1] Jesus uttered these words of the psalmist after He had retaken His place at the table.

Jesus denounces His betrayal. Judas departs (258).

Luke xxii, 21–23; Mark xiv, 18–21; Matthew xxvi, 21–25; John xiii, 21–30.[2]

After recovering from their emotion the disciples had begun to eat. The herbs had been placed on the table along with the dish of sauce into which they were dipped. We find complete identity with the Paschal ritual here, since all helped themselves from the same dish and we see Jesus holding out a dipped morsel to Judas. They were therefore at the first course of the meal. The Master's earlier allusions to His betrayal had not been understood, or at all events the disciples seem not to have been upset by them. He Himself was troubled in spirit, saddened by the unfaithfulness of this man whom He had admitted to His friendship and who was now hastening to his own ruin. Perhaps a final warning might stop him yet. Not that Jesus would thwart the designs of His Father, but He had come to save men, and He truly wills to save them if only their own wills consent to let themselves be influenced. He owes it to His mission, He owes it above all to His love, disregarded though it be, to warn the traitor without denouncing him by name, so that he may have one last chance to repent. All the same it was not in accordance with His dignity to pretend that He was deceived. He therefore denounces the betrayal rather than the traitor in the hearing of them all: 'Verily I say to you that one of you will betray Me, one that eateth with Me.' In their grief the disciples made their protest in the form of a question: 'Is it I Thou meanest?' thus showing that they harboured no such thought. Jesus did not answer. Had He done so, that would finally have led to the denunciation of the traitor. But when Judas in his

[1] Psalm xl, 10 (Hebrew xli).

[2] The Synoptists are more detailed for the earlier part. John continues their account.

turn, and perhaps among the first, said : 'Master, is it I ?' He answered him very softly : 'Thou hast said it.'[1]

No one heard, and the disciples in their uneasiness exchanged comments on this painful incident[2] whilst Jesus tried once more to make the traitor reflect on what he was intending to do : 'The Son of Man goeth away, as it is written of Him, but woe to that man by whom the Son of Man is betrayed ! It were better for that man if he had not been born.'[3]

To understand the scene that is about to follow we should need to know the place occupied by each of those at table. They were reclining on their left side with their elbow on the mat, their right hand thus remaining free for taking food. There was then no strict rule of precedence,[4] nor do we know whether a rule of any sort was observed. During their meals in the open, which they took wherever they found a convenient place on some rock or under a tree, the disciples no doubt had sat as they wished. Probably the same thing happened on this evening and some of them complained of it, thinking that the solemnity of the occasion required some allocation of places according to rank, perhaps according to seniority ; and the dispute must have been all the keener, because in that company of very simple men there was not much certainty about the rules of etiquette. However, it seems beyond question that Jesus occupied a place almost in the middle of the group, facing the gap left in the circle of diners so that the meal might be served. On His right hand He had the disciple whom He loved, since this disciple was able to rest on Jesus' breast ; that is to say, he was lying alongside his Master and a little in front of Him with relation to the table, his head opposite the Master's left elbow which was resting on a cushion. Judas Iscariot was very near to Jesus, since the Master was able to pass him a morsel that He had dipped, but on the other side from the beloved disciple. He also would be resting on his left elbow, his feet turned out away from the table, and not near enough to have the head of Jesus on his breast ; he was thus able to rise and go out without disturbing any of the others. Peter could not have been near

[1] Matthew xxvi, 25 ; but it is possible that here Matthew means that Jesus revealed the traitor's name to one of the others, just as John has described.

[2] Luke xxii, 23.

[3] Mark xiv, 21.

[4] Cf. Prat, S.J., in *Recherches de science religieuse*, 1925, pp. 512 ff.

to Jesus, otherwise he could have questioned Him directly. But he was near to John, and able to lean on his breast. As to the place of the other disciples, we are ignorant and it would be idle to make conjectures.

After this denunciation of the betrayal, the protests of the Apostles, the anxious questions exchanged between them, and the menacing words addressed to the traitor who refused to declare himself, an atmosphere heavy with suspicion weighed upon the faithful ones. Peter cannot support this state of uncertainty. Beckoning to John to draw his attention to what he wants to whisper, under the impression that the Master has confided in His beloved disciple, or at least that the latter has overheard something, Peter asks him : 'Who is it of whom He speaketh ?' But John knows nothing. Lying with his head against the heart of Jesus he dares to search its secret : 'Lord, who is it ?' Confident that John is moved by an affection that makes him want to know in order that he may help if possible, Jesus replies : 'He it is to whom I shall give the morsel I have dipped.' Thus they were still at that part of the supper when the master of the house and those at table with him ate the herbs dipped in sauce.[1] When the Greeks spoke of a morsel, ψωμίον, they meant bread or meat, but the word can evidently be understood of anything eatable. It was an honour for a guest when the host handed him with his fingers a morsel dipped in this fashion, and the custom is preserved among the Bedouin to this day. As Jesus was near Judas, He could easily put a dipped morsel to the traitor's mouth. It was a last mark of intimate familiarity ; but Judas was obdurate, and this callousness at such a time made Satan the master of his soul.[2] Judas was to follow that master's suggestions right to the end.

It was he who still had charge of the material needs of the little community, which perhaps explains his position near the Master so that he might be at hand to receive and carry out His commands. At this juncture Jesus, as though after receiving such a blow He could no longer endure the traitor's presence, just when He was about to pour out His soul to those who loved Him, said to Judas : 'That which

[1] *Mishnah, Pesahim*, x, 3.

[2] The Arabs still excuse themselves from fault by alleging the interference of Satan. A young man whom we caught stealing in our priory at Jerusalem gave as his excuse to the police : 'It was Satan who entered into me.'

thou dost, do quickly.' It was better to have it over and done with than to continue thus under false pretences. None of the others understood, save perhaps the one who had received his Master's confidence[1] and his friend Peter, if indeed he had already communicated the secret to Peter. The shrewder ones among them thought that Jesus was whispering instructions to Judas in his capacity as keeper of the purse : as, for instance, to buy what was necessary in order that they might take part in the official observance of the feast on the morrow, or else to distribute a little money to the poor on occasion of the feast. 'And it was night !' observes St. John. Indeed the powers of darkness were unloosed.[2]

After this first part of the supper, or rather these preliminaries, the Paschal lamb was brought to the table and the second cup of wine served. The Synoptists do not mention this, for their attention is all focused on that solemn act which was to render the ancient rite needless.

The institution of the Eucharist (259).

Luke xxii, 19–20 ; Mark xiv, 22–24 ; Matt. xxvi, 26–28.

The supper was drawing to a close when Jesus took bread and, following the sacred custom, blessed it, broke it, and gave it to His disciples with the words : 'Take ye ; this is My Body.' This was the last act of the supper, for it seems most probable that immediately afterwards He took a cup of wine, the one that was appointed to be drunk in thanksgiving for the Paschal supper,[3] the third according to Jewish ritual. This He gave to them so that they all might drink, saying : 'This is My Blood of the covenant, shed for many.' At the end of the Paschal rite it may have been the custom among some of the Jews to pass the same cup round to all. If so, then Jesus would not have been departing from custom. At all events He intended to make this cup serve as a token of union among His friends ; they all drank from the same

[1] The positive expression 'none' must be understood according to the mind of the author of the fourth gospel, who relies on the intelligence of the reader.

[2] Judging from the order of events, it seems clear that Judas did not receive Holy Communion with the rest ; this is the opinion of most modern writers.

[3] Luke xxii, 20 ; 1 Corinthians xi, 25.

vessel the Blood shed for them and for that multitude of people which comprises the whole of humanity.

The words of consecration we have quoted are those of St. Mark, who gives the shortest form. St. Matthew wrote : 'Take ye and eat ; this is My Body.' Then for the chalice : 'Drink ye all of this, for this is My Blood of the new covenant, shed for many unto the remission of sins.' In St. Luke we find : 'This is My Body which is given for you ; do this in remembrance of Me' ; and : 'This chalice is the new covenant in My Blood, shed for you.' St. Paul has : 'This is My Body, (delivered) for you ; do this in remembrance of Me.' . . . 'This chalice is the new covenant in My Blood ; do this, as often as you shall drink (it), in remembrance of Me.'[1]

The words differ slightly in the four accounts, but there is no disagreement over the essential points. That which had been bread became the Body of Jesus ; the wine became His Blood. That Blood serves like the blood that was used in the ritual of making a covenant, according to which those entering into the covenant were sprinkled with the blood of a sacrificial victim ;[2] in this case the victim was Jesus, whose Blood was in the cup. Thus He was inaugurating a new covenant.[3] His disciples were to feed on that Body and drink that Blood. Although there is nothing in Mark or Matthew commanding that the sacred rite just performed by Jesus is to be repeated by the disciples, yet St. Paul bears witness to the fact that the practice of the Church in this respect was in obedience to a command given by Our Lord. That command is mentioned by St. Luke also. And certainly no one would have dared, without the authority of some positive command, to repeat what Jesus had done on the eve of His death, what at first sight it would have seemed could not be done except with Jesus present. Yet St. Paul declares that it is the very Body and Blood of Jesus that is consumed by the faithful.[4] It follows that they thought—let us say rather that they were certain—that Christ had transmitted to His own followers the power to work this incomprehensible change of bread and wine into

[1] I Corinthians xi, 24 f.

[2] Exodus xxiv, 8.

[3] The word 'new' is omitted by St. Mark alone.

[4] I Corinthians xi, 27 : 'Therefore, whosoever shall eat this bread or drink the chalice of the Lord unworthily shall be guilty of the Body and Blood of the Lord.'

His own Body and Blood by virtue of the words which He had been the first to utter. When, therefore, He instituted the Eucharist, He at the same time appointed priests invested with the right and power to perpetuate it.

We have outlived the days when it was the common practice, outside the Catholic Church and the several sects of the Orthodox Church, to understand these words of Christ in a figurative sense, as though He said : 'When you gather together to pray, celebrate the supper in remembrance of Me by eating bread and drinking wine in the spirit of My disciples as though I were still in the midst of you, as though the bread you bless in My name were My Body, and the wine My Blood which was shed for you.' Even if there still remain a few belated Protestant exegetes who exchange the realistic interpretation of the primitive Church for one which makes of the Eucharist no more than a tender remembrance, nevertheless there are many learned scholars of to-day—and they are men with no leaning at all towards the teachings of the Catholic Church—who admit that every sincere student of the Scriptures is bound to take the words of Jesus regarding the Eucharist in the literal sense, which is the sense they obviously bear. It must be said that while admitting this they refuse to see in those words anything but a survival of an old barbaric rite, in which the believers sacrificed the animal they worshipped and ate its flesh, perhaps even cutting the beast up while still living, under the persuasion that in this way they were made sharers in a divine energy. It was, according to these scholars, a rite which expressed in a brutal and savage fashion that which is the noblest and boldest aspiration in religion, the desire of union with God.

But as God has come down to our level in His Incarnate Son, it follows that our union with the Father must be in and through Him ; and why should it not be by means of His Flesh and His Blood that was shed for us, so that we may find strength in Him after we have obtained pardon ? The masterpiece of the Eucharist, that which showed its divine character, was this : that, by the fullness of the gift it bestows, it far surpassed the unreasoning ambition of man's desires, but at the same time fulfilled that ambition in such a delicate and spiritual fashion as to exclude every gross idea and leave us to understand that the true union which it accomplishes in us is something beyond the eating of

Christ's Body. The external act of eating will always have for its object the real Body of Christ, but unless love brings the spirit of man and the spirit of Christ into union the faithful will not truly feed on Him. We may leave evil-minded critics to give vent to their sarcasm with the word 'Magic!' Certainly the Eucharist is a charm, full of divine power and able to bring joy to the hearts of all those who believe, and on it depends the whole spiritual life of the Church, our love for God and for our neighbour.

Jesus, who is about to be glorified, gives a new commandment (260).

John xiii, 31–35.

After thus instituting the sacrament of love, Jesus now opens His heart to His disciples more unreservedly than ever. Judas has gone to seek the aid of the authorities, and therefore the Passion has already begun. By His Passion Jesus performs an act of obedience which is at once His own glory and also the glory of His Father, to whom He refers all that He does. His Father does not consent to keep that glory hidden in the mystery of His eternity; He will cause it to flow out upon His Son, and that before very long, namely, by His resurrection and exaltation. But in order that this may come to pass Jesus must leave His friends. He is moved to emotion at the thought, calling them His little children, a title He gives them on no other occasion, and telling them, as He has already told the Jews, that where He goes they cannot follow. Therefore He bequeaths to them a final word, a new commandment: that they love one another as He has loved them. This is to be a sign for the world that they are truly His disciples. It is a new commandment recalling to mind the new covenant which He has only just promulgated. The commandment, like the covenant, was already in existence: it becomes new because Jesus is the pattern of it, its inspirer, the very reason of it, as St. Matthew has already shown in the picture of the last judgement. His friends must love one another because they are His, and that mutual love of theirs will demonstrate the fact that they are His. If that is so, then their charity will flow out towards all men, just like the charity of Christ Himself who has given His Blood to save the world.

Jesus foretells the scattering of the Apostles and Peter's denials of Him (261).

Luke xxii, 31–34 ; Mark xiv, 27–31 ; Matt. xxvi, 31–35 ; John xvi, 31–32 ; xiii, 36–38.

His betrayal by Judas was but the first of several blows which Jesus was to receive ; others were now to follow. The sorrow weighing upon His heart breaks forth. First, His disciples are to be scattered ; they will all desert Him just when He is stricken by His enemies. But that had been foretold by an ancient prophecy of Zacharias : 'I will strike the shepherd, and the sheep shall be scattered.'[1] Yet here again, as is the case of the predictions in the prophets, hope comes after threatening, and Jesus comforts His timid sheep : 'After I am risen again I will go before you into Galilee.'[2]

What was the reason why the Lord God permitted this fall of the Apostles ? His purpose is unfathomable, but nothing happens without His will ; although He allowed Satan to sift the Apostles like wheat, which is shaken and somewhat bruised in the process of sifting, yet He set a limit to his power. It was Peter, the head of the Apostles, whom Satan desired most of all to bring down. Jesus was well aware of the danger that threatened His disciple, nor did He wish to preserve him from it entirely ; but He protected his faith by His own prayer, so that it might not fail ; and when Peter had repented of his fall, it was to be his duty to strengthen his brethren. There is no question here of the other Apostles losing their faith, since Peter is only bidden to strengthen them ; but the privilege of a faith that never fails is guaranteed only to Peter. The Protestant commentator Bengel has remarked on this, in his usual concise manner : 'In preserving Peter, whose fall would have dragged down all the others, Jesus preserved them all. The whole of this discourse of Our Lord presupposes that Peter was the chief of the Apostles, and that on his resistance

[1] Zacharias xiii, 7 : 'O sword. . . . Strike the shepherd, and the sheep shall be scattered.' God who gives the sword the order to strike is He who strikes the blow.

[2] Luke, who does not mention the later appearances in Galilee, omits likewise all mention of the scattering of the Apostles and the appointment of the meeting place.

or fall would depend more or less the fate of the rest.'[1]

This prediction of Christ in the text of St. Luke, were we to consider it by itself, might be taken as referring merely to the approaching occasion when the Apostles were to be scandalized. But, on the other hand, it contains no restriction as to time and circumstances, and this authorizes us to connect it with the promise already made to St. Peter, that he was the unshakable rock on which the Church was to be built.[2] The new declaration here made by Christ thus reveals to us that the solidity belonging to Peter as the rock is the solidity of a faith that nothing can shake because it is founded on the prayer of Christ. This prerogative of Peter will enable him to strengthen even his fellow Apostles in their faith, not to speak of the rest of the faithful ; and as long as the Church endures, that Church against which the gates of Hell shall never prevail, so long will he continue to strengthen the faith of his fellow-believers.

As might be expected from Peter's character and deep affection for Jesus, he refuses to entertain the idea that he will forsake his Master ; he would rather face imprisonment and death. In his rashness he sets himself even higher above his companions than Jesus has given him authority for : 'Even though all shall be scandalized in Thee, yet not I.'[3] A little before, he had not been willing to admit, as far as he was concerned, that Jesus might be going where he could not follow Him : 'I will lay down my life for Thee.'[4] He was quite sincere, but it was necessary that his resolution should find a more solid foundation on his future repentance than it had at present on his eager and presumptuous devotion. Accordingly Jesus warns him : 'Amen, I say to thee, to-day, even in this night, before the cock crow twice, thou shalt deny Me thrice.' Peter only repeats the more earnestly: 'Although I should die together with Thee, I will not deny Thee.' Such a contradiction could only be excused by affection so strong that it was driven to declare itself still stronger. Peter's Master, however, was entitled to have His word more fully respected. The others added their protests to Peter's. Jesus had spoken, and He made no reply ; but He warned His friends, for they did not realize sufficiently the imminence of the danger.

[1] The Latin text of Bengel will be found in our Commentary on St. Luke.
[2] Matthew xvi, 17 ff. [3] Mark xiv, 29. [4] John xiii, 37.

The days of happiness and the time of great trial (262).

Luke xxii, 35–38.

All was now so different from what it was before. In former times it had been so pleasant when they had been able to rely upon the general sympathy shown to them, or at all events on the traditional hospitality of the country. In those days Jesus had sent His disciples out to preach without money or wallet, even without shoes. But now, if a man was not well provided with the necessities of life, the only thing to do was to sell his cloak and buy a sword so as to obtain food by violence. Here was an evil and extreme state of things to which Jesus most certainly never advised His disciples to have recourse ; but it well describes the accusations which will be levelled against them ; for in their Master is about to be fulfilled that word of Isaias relating to the suffering servant of God : 'He hath been reckoned with the wicked.'[1] His office among men was soon to come to an end.

The mention of the sword arouses the attention of these Galilæans, ever quick to come to blows. They have two swords, probably brought in case of emergency. But Jesus has no wish to be defended by the sword, and when later on it leaves its scabbard He will say so plainly. Therefore, when they now tell Him : 'Lord, behold here are two swords,' He answers smilingly :[2] 'It is enough.' He has yet to speak on a more important subject.

Jesus promises His disciples His presence and that of the Father and the Holy Spirit (263).

John xiv, 1–31.

We have already remarked that it was the custom amongst the Jews to join in conversation when the Paschal supper was over. With the Greeks and Romans drinking continued after the banquet was done, and it was then that flute-players, both men and women, were brought into the banqueting chamber, not infrequently providing an occasion

[1] Isaias liii, 12.
[2] As St. Cyril of Alexandria has remarked.

for scenes of extreme licence; and even those who were above such exhibitions of viciousness were not above indulging in vile conversation. To avoid everything of this character the Jewish doctors of the Law forbade all further drinking at the Paschal supper between the third cup of wine and the last, that is to say, the one appointed to be drunk before the *Hallel*; there was less need for drinking then, they said, because no one could offer the excuse that he wished to drink while taking food.[1] The conversation enjoyed at this stage of the celebration was not of a religious character like the explanation of the Pasch given by the head of the family at the moment when the Paschal lamb was brought in; they may even have mixed singing with their talk.

At the Last Supper it was Jesus who opened the conversation, as though He wished to explain the institution of the new covenant by revealing the mysteries it contained. We owe to St. John the preservation of this sublime and fruitful discourse in which Jesus opens to us the very secrets of His heart. It contains instructions that He had already given before,[2] but on this occasion they are, so to say, steeped in the mournful tenderness with which He spoke His departing words; hence they will be always remembered under that aspect, lit up, as it were, amidst the shadows of that last night.

The first part of the discourse forms a complete whole by itself: its subject deals with His departure from His disciples and their hope of seeing Him once more. Separation from Him is a necessary condition of the work they are to do, but the separation is only apparent, not real, for the Father, Son and Holy Ghost will always be present in spirit in the souls of those who have faith and charity. Therefore there is no need for any uneasiness; rather should they rejoice.

The beloved disciple has entered his Master's thought more deeply than the other evangelists. He saw the promises of Jesus fulfilled, and there would be matter for surprise if the sight of that fulfilment had not coloured somewhat the manner in which he expressed the prediction made

[1] Nevertheless the Jews gave the name ἐπικώμιον (revelling), under the form *Apikomin*, to this part of the Paschal celebration. Cf. op. cit. of Beer, *Pesahim*, p. 74.

[2] This is dealt with in detail in the Commentary on St. John.

by his Master. Yet the reason why so strong an impression was left upon him was because the things of which he was the witness had not only been foretold, but were at the same time revealed in their supernatural character by Him who alone had the power to promise the gift of the Holy Ghost.

The initial idea is that Master and disciples will meet again in the presence of the Father, thanks to Jesus who is one with the Father.[1] It is true that Jesus will appear to His disciples after the Resurrection, but that will be for a few days only. What He has in mind here is the situation in which the Apostles will find themselves when deprived of His visible presence. Faith must make up for that presence. They believe in the Father, the Creator of all things : they must also believe in Him. This faith is to be the foundation of their whole life. Just as a man charged by his friends to find lodging for them at the end of the day's journey sets out ahead of them, so Jesus is going to His Father's house where there are many places of residence ; He knows that, for He goes to make ready a place for them. When He has done that, He will return and take them back with Him so that He may be with them. Nevertheless, it is necessary that they should know the way. Thomas is in doubt, for he has understood all this as referring to some departure of Jesus in an ordinary fashion. Where then exactly is Jesus going ? Unless they know, how can they know the way thither ? The way, as He has just told them, is faith in Him, for He is the Way, since it is by Him that the Father is known. And as that way is in the order of understanding, it is followed by means of the apprehension of truth, and Jesus is the Truth. That truth, moreover, is the life of the soul, and that life is in Him too, for He is the Life. But His disciples have seen Him ; therefore, they have already seen the Father.

Their vision of the Father is the obscure vision of faith, and faith tells them that the Son is the same as the Father. Philip would like to know more still : 'Lord, show us the Father, and it is enough for us.' But that cannot be, for perfect vision is reserved for eternity. Philip must be content to believe what Jesus has already revealed to the Jews in His last conversation with them at the feast of the Dedication,[2] and which He now declares more plainly : 'Dost thou not believe that I am in the Father and the Father in

[1] John xiv, 1–11. [2] John x, 30.

Me ?' That astounding statement, 'I and the Father are one,' which the Jews had condemned as blasphemous, was also a declaration that the Father abides in Jesus. His word provides the strongest motive for belief ; but at any rate no one can reject the witness of His works, the miracles which His Father has worked in Him.

The faith of the disciples ought not to be idle. Those who believe should not be troubled, first of all ; but, more than that, they have work to do, and their Master will give them the help they need. This is His second exhortation. Their best resource will be prayer. It will always be heard because the disciples will pray to the Father in the name of Jesus ; and such is the unity of Father and Son that the Son will do what they ask, for the order henceforth is that the Father should be glorified in the Son. He who has faith and is armed with this prayer will do the works that Jesus has done, and even greater. Jesus, in fact, had not gone outside the borders of Israel, but He sends them to convert the Gentiles. For that task it is also necessary that they should be filled with the love of God, the love that keeps the commandments. Faith alone would not be enough to bring down the gift that Jesus by His prayer will obtain from the Father, the gift of the Paraclete, who is their defender, their protector, their mighty friend, none other than the Spirit of truth Himself. He will assist the disciples on their way as their light, dispelling the darkness that paralyses activity, restoring confidence so that they may go forward to their work. But that light is to be within them ; the world will not have the benefit of it, for the world's eyes are fixed on that which is external, and the light cannot be seen there. The disciples will have it as their own, for they will find it within themselves.

Jesus Himself will come to them. The world will not perceive Him, for His life is a spiritual life ; but the disciples who live by that same life will see Him and will know the secret of that union which binds them to the Father : Jesus in them, they in Him, and He in His Father. It is not only faith which effects that union, for if the believer truly loves the Son—he does indeed love Him if he keeps the commandments of Jesus, and here timid souls find great encouragement—then he will be loved by the Father and the Son, and the Son will manifest Himself to him. In these words Jesus describes that almost intuitive vision of God which results from the intimate contact of the mind with Infinite Truth, giving a knowledge that is clearer and more fruitful than any knowledge acquired by the use of the reason, though it does not completely dispel the darkness that belongs to our life here below.

But the minds of the disciples were still occupied with the grandiose ideas cherished in Jewish Messianic dreams. When Jesus speaks of ' manifesting ' Himself, the word calls up to their minds the glorious apparition of the Messiah by which all doubts were to be ended and the world subjected beneath His feet. Judas—not the Iscariot, but Jude the Apostle—had always cherished hopes regarding this dramatic appearance which was part of the programme assigned to the Jewish notion of the Messiah : ' Lord,' he says, ' how is it that Thou wilt manifest Thyself to us and not to the world ? ' Jesus replies that it is to be an inward manifestation which demands love, and a great love : it will consist in the coming of the Father and the Son into the soul where charity dwells, a visit which will be prolonged into an abiding presence. Once more the Master declares that He is only delivering to them the teaching of His Father. It was ordained that He should instruct His disciples during His lifetime, and St. John is here the witness of the truth of this declaration ; but Jesus knew that it was only by the operation of the Paraclete within them that they would be enabled to understand what He taught them. The Paraclete was to be sent to them by the Father in order to recall to their minds all that they had been taught, to set it in a clearer light with all necessary developments and emphasis, so that the doctrine might be firmly fixed in the minds of those who were its guardians, charged with the duty of spreading it abroad.

Jesus ends as He has begun : ' Let not your heart be troubled ! ' He leaves them peace : not in the way in which their fellow-Jews are wont to wish each other ' Peace !'[1] when they meet and part, but by really leaving them His friendship. And if they were truly His friends they would not merely be free from all trouble, they would rejoice because He is going to the Father who is greater than He. The Father is greater, for He who is departing from them is not just the Eternal Son, for *He* has never left the bosom of

[1] To this day they salute each other with ' Shalom ! '. Hebrew for peace.

the Father ; but it is that Eternal Son in His human condition, united to God even so, but at the same time inferior to God in that human nature which He has assumed and will bear with Him into glory. His departure will not long be delayed, for the prince of the world cometh, Satan who reigns through sin ; and although Satan has no hold on Him, nevertheless Jesus consents to bear what the prince of the world has contrived against Him, for He loves His Father and obeys Him out of that love. Then, as if there is no more that He wishes to say, He adds : 'Arise, let us go hence.' Yet He continues His conversation with His disciples.

There is a serious difficulty here. He might have said what follows on the roads of Galilee, or while they were in the desert, or again while seated under some terebinth tree ; but it would be very difficult to imagine that this discourse continued as they walked through the streets or suburbs of a city. The solemn prayer for unity can only have been uttered in private. But to tell the truth, that is not the main difficulty. We can well believe that Jesus may have risen and drunk the fourth cup of wine at the supper with the disciples, and then before going out said that prayer standing, after the *Hallel* or perhaps instead of the *Hallel*. But is it likely that the two discourses contained in chapters xv and xvi, which precede the prayer, were uttered while He was standing thus after He had given the signal for their departure ? We are disposed therefore to think that the interruption signified by the signal for departure indicates the last act of this gathering of Christ and His disciples for the Paschal rite ; that act was the thanksgiving called the *Hallel*, which in the Jewish rite was distinct from the act of thanksgiving with which the supper was concluded. The *Hallel* was made up of acts of praise offered to God for the feast of the Pasch and for His deliverance of Israel, both past and to come. Having already completed the arrangement of his gospel, it is possible that St. John later may have wished to add what are the contents of chapters xv and xvi, and have inserted them or caused someone else to insert them here without making any alteration in the existing narrative. It is not impossible that thus he ingeniously indicated that the contents of these two chapters are of a supplementary character.

Jesus is the true vine (264).
John xv, 1–17.

At the beginning of this supplementary discourse we find a distinct and separate instruction dealing with the union between Christ and His disciples, which He compares to the junction of the branches with the stem of the vine. It is a union accomplished by the charity that exists between Jesus and His followers, whom it would almost appear that He is just choosing for the first time, for He dilates on the dignity of the honour of being chosen and on the nobility of the bond that is formed between Him and them. It may be that the first time the subject of this discourse was treated of by Jesus was after His choosing of the Twelve ; but the emphasis He now lays on the union of charity is more easily understood after the revelation He has just made to them concerning His spiritual presence in their souls. Such emphasis seems more natural now that He is filled with sorrowful tenderness at the thought of the imminent separation. In His words we find evidences of those sweet impressions first received when friends perceive their mutual love for one another, along with that more virile note which conveys the impression of devotion even unto death.

The comparison with the vine is presented in the form of an allegory ; it is Jesus who is the vine, and His Father is the husbandman. Hence the disciples are the branches, which live by the sap of the stem and through it are enabled to bear fruit ; they are shoots that wither if they are cut off, and then are good for nothing but to be thrown into the fire. A good husbandman does not neglect his vine ; he prunes it and removes parasitical growths in order that it may bear fruit in greater abundance. These things represent the trials sent by God. And the husbandman also cuts off shoots from the vine, but this point has no application in the moral lesson to be conveyed. Jesus is careful to save free will : 'You cannot bear fruit unless you abide in Me.' If they abide in Him, it is because they will to do so, and abiding in Him they bring forth much fruit ; but that is due to Him, for without Him they can do nothing. If they do not abide in Him, it is through their own fault ; and they will be thrown out like useless wood, cast on the fire so that the ground may be rid of them. A dismal prospect ! But Our

Saviour does not dwell upon it. What have His disciples to be afraid of? All that they ask for will come to them, for it is the Father's will and the Father's glory that they should bear much fruit. Then, indeed, they will be truly His disciples.

Thus was the allegory of the vine ended. Jesus had told them whom it represented, but there remained still to be explained what application to human beings had that 'abiding' in another, that comparison of branches joined to a trunk and drawing sap from the parent stem; it was necessary that His friends should know what was expected of them by their Master. All is made clear by the word charity, that affection which here means friendship. God the Father loved His Son, and an especial manifestation of that eternal love was shown when He willed that the Son should become man. In becoming man the Son had to carry out the Father's commands as a means of manifesting to Him the love He bore Him. Jesus has loved His disciples in the same manner as the Father has loved Him, and it is for them, too, to show their love for Jesus by keeping His commandments. He *loves* them! Their hearts leap for joy at these sublime words. Here is the great joy of Christianity, a joy that nothing can mar. Christianity preaches discipline, self-denial, resignation to suffering; but all that is merely the self-surrender of one who is conscious that he is loved by Christ, and sorrow is swallowed up by joy at that thought.

The love that comes down from the Father does not stop short at each individual disciple; it must be communicated from one to the other; and it is to be no fictitious love, but a self-giving like that of Jesus which extends even to the sacrifice of life itself, as He gently reminds them. Love can go no further than that! To obey is the office of a servant, and yet Jesus tells His disciples: 'You are My friends if you do the things that I command you.' And confident of their obedience He adds: 'I will not now call you servants . . . but I have called you friends, because all things whatsoever I have heard from My Father I have made known to you': the eternal language of love! It will be their duty to call themselves always His servants, for they must know that it is He who has chosen them, and not they who first had the confidence to join Him. But His choice of them is their best encouragement to go wherever He will send them, in order that they may bring forth the fruit which, as they well know, means to lead men into the kingdom of God. Servants, yes, that they will always remain ; but servants who are certain of obtaining everything they ask because they are also His friends. Yet the condition of this is that they love one another.

There are but few words here, yet they hold the secret of the spiritual life and the principle of all apostolic work. From now on, the friends of Jesus are to live by His life and carry out His work. They abide in God by charity, which is a love consisting of friendship, that charity which is the first of the commandments. Here we have the whole theology of grace, which, though it has been developed by theologians in so wonderful a manner, has so plain and so beautiful a beginning as this.

The world's hatred and the promise of the Holy Ghost (265).

John xv, 18–xvi, 4.

The Father, the Incarnate Son, and their friends who have love for one another : a world of light and joy because it is the reign of charity. But it is not what *we* name the world. To-day, as in the days of Christ, the world stands for the great mass of humanity who are only too often the slaves of their lower appetites, unwilling to submit their reason to faith or to govern their hearts by the law of supernatural charity.

After having inflamed His disciples with these tender words which spring from His heart and which hardly refer to the difficulty of the work that lies before them, Jesus suddenly brings them face to face with the stern reality : they must suffer the hatred of the world whose evil ways it will be their duty to oppose. Jesus has chosen disciples for Himself and therefore has brought them out of the world, but only in order that He may send them into the world, for He wishes to convert it. As a general rule they will be hated by the world, as He has been hated by the Jews. Nevertheless they will always have reason for joy, for they may console themselves with the thought that they are ill-treated for His sake. He has already told them that ' the servant is not above his master ' ;[1] but the servant will

[1] John xiii, 16 and Matthew x, 24.

collaborate with his Master for the good cause, and will be as innocent as is his Master. Hatred is always painful to him who is its object ; yet, if it be undeserved, it is no more than a trial for his virtue. And who is more innocent than Jesus ? Yet in His goodness He does not fail to appreciate that the Jews might have been able to plead some excuse for their hatred, had He proclaimed Himself as God's ambassador without assuring them on what grounds He did so or giving them proofs of His mission. But He has talked with them in order to instruct them concerning that divine life which He understands so much better than they ; He has done the works of His Father, which are justice, mercy, charity, and has performed miracles such as only one sent by God could have performed, deeds that surpassed even the most wonderful things known in ancient times. But the Jews have refused to open their eyes or their ears ; they have hated the Son of God, and in hating Him they have hated His Father also, whose work of mercy they have scornfully rejected. He may say with the persecuted just man who typifies the suffering Messiah : 'They have hated Me without cause.'[1]

But will Christ's faithful Apostles be left to suffer this trouble alone, to bear on their own shoulders the burden of hatred which clever men will heap up against Him whose name the faithful invoke ? And although they are His witnesses, and undeniable witnesses, since they have been with Jesus from the time He began the ministry that drew the hatred of the Jews upon Him, yet will they be more successful than He proved to be ? They will, for the Master will not forget them. He will send them a helper and a defender, the mysterious Paraclete who is the Spirit of truth, who also proceeds from the Father, though not as His Son ; who proceeds from the Son also, because it is the Son who will send the Paraclete. He will bear witness to Jesus as do the disciples, and a witness that will be conclusive. Nothing is said to show the character of this testimony rendered by the Holy Spirit ;[2] we may think, however, of the ancient prophecies dictated by Him concerning the person and the work of the Messiah, or of the sanctity which will be diffused from the Church later and which provides the strongest proof of her divine origin. But we learn without any doubt

[1] Psalms xxxiv, 19 ; lxviii, 5 (Hebrew xxxv and lxix).
[2] Jesus returns to it later ; John xvi, 8–10.

from the earlier evangelists that the witness of the Spirit will be one with that of the Apostles, since it is He who will speak in them.[1]

But no matter what happens, the world will refuse to give up its hatred ; nay, on the contrary it will rage the more against them. Convinced that the disciples commit blasphemy by believing that Jesus is God, the Jews will excommunicate them from the synagogue and even imagine that they will be doing a service to God by putting them to death, in this way denying the Father as well as the Son. It was only too necessary to return to this melancholy subject again,[2] for the disciples would suffer the risk of demoralization once they saw the religious authority of the priests and doctors against them. But when they remembered that all this had been foretold by their Master, such persecution would have no power to shake their resolution. In those early days they had spent by the shores of the lake, there had been no one to disturb their confidence which Jesus maintained by His words and deeds. Henceforth their confidence must lean solely on their memory of the past, and their memory must therefore be exact and convincing.

The office of the Holy Spirit. The speedy return of Jesus. The faith of the disciples (266).

John xvi, 5–33.

In reminding His disciples that He has chosen them and made them His friends, in predicting also the world's hatred of them and the persecutions they will have to endure, Jesus returns to a subject which He has enlarged on long before, for it appears much earlier in the other gospels and in almost the same form. Thus He is recalling memories of the past and looking forward into the future. But now He returns once more to the actual situation, and there follows what may be described as a supplement to the discourse which occupies the fourteenth chapter of St. John. Jesus has already promised that the Holy Spirit would come, but has not said what His function was to be ; this He now proceeds

[1] Matthew x, 20 ; Mark xiii, 11 ; Luke xii, 12.
[2] Persecution was often foretold : Matthew v, 11 ; x, 16–21 ; xxiii, 34; xxiv, 9 ; Luke vi, 22 ; xii, 4 ; xxi, 12–19 ; Mark xiii, 9–13.

to do. His approaching departure far from His disciples, who do not understand whither He is going, He has described as a return to the eternal mansions, going back to His Father, making scarcely any allusion to His resurrection ;[1] but now He speaks once more of that joyful event so soon to come. Finally, the discourse ends with the thought of the faith begotten in the minds of the Apostles, while the sad prospect of their being scattered before the enemy is laid clearly before them. Again the Apostles, perceiving how much this teaching of their Master relates to their present situation, join in conversation with Him, although on this occasion the evangelist names none of the speakers.

The discourse begins, then, with further information about the coming of the Holy Ghost. The Apostles have asked Jesus whither He is going. He tells them, and they are satisfied ; but although their minds are set at rest, their hearts are full of sorrow. How, they ask themselves, can the Christ go away, even before He has come to His kingdom ? Jesus answers with a certain air of mystery : 'It is expedient for you that I go away, for if I go not the Paraclete will not come to you ; but if I go, I will send Him to you.' After the Resurrection the humble and suffering period of His life would be passed. Once He has entered into His glory He will not stay long with His friends, for they have to learn how to live in the spirit of faith. His bodily presence will be absent and its place taken by a spiritual presence brought about by the operation of the Paraclete, the Holy Spirit. After His departure, Jesus will no longer have to defend Himself against the world ; it will be the Paraclete who will accomplish that too, for He will be able to justify Jesus before the tribunal of man's judgement, a tribunal which will always be in session owing to the restlessness of the human mind. The Paraclete will convince the world that it is at fault 'concerning sin, and justice, and judgement.' The sin in question is the sin of the Jews who have refused to recognize One who has been sent by God, as well as the still graver crime of having put Him to death, as they are at present preparing to do. And that sin will be shown up in all its heinousness by contrast with the gifts of the Holy Ghost that will be poured out upon the baptized Gentiles, by contrast also with the manifesta-

[1] John xiv, 18–20.

tions of extraordinary grace granted to the early Church, and with all the heroic desires that have been born within the Church all down the ages. When they made away with Jesus, the Jewish people, with Rome's representative as their partner in the crime, must have had some idea that they were condemning a just man. But the Holy Ghost will proclaim the justice of Jesus by means of the witness borne by the Apostles who have been allowed to share His life, and who will continually declare His innocence, made all the more clear to them by His return to the Father. Finally the Holy Ghost will convince the world that it has made a false judgement in its condemnation of Christ; or rather, it will be seen how this judgement will recoil on the head of him who, by means of his instruments, caused it to be made: that is to say on the head of Satan, now condemned for the most terrible of all his crimes, Satan whom his followers acknowledge as lord of the world. But the worship of Satan will be superseded by the worship of Jesus, now to be consecrated king by means of this very Passion, from which Satan had anticipated that he himself would emerge victorious.

As regards the disciples, the Paraclete, just shown to be the defender of Christ, is to perform a function of a more intimate character; He is the Spirit of truth who will enlighten their understanding. At present, when they are on the eve of showing moral weakness, before they have received the light of the Resurrection, they are unable to comprehend all that Jesus has to say to them. But the Holy Spirit will lead them to the full truth. Not, however, that He is to be understood as an independent source of truth, for there is but one source. Just as Jesus has said nothing but what He has learnt from His father, so the Holy Spirit will say nothing of Himself but only what has been given to Him to repeat. It would be wrong to think that truth flows from the Father into the Son and the Holy Ghost in the same manner. No; the Holy Ghost receives the truth from the Son, since all that the Father has belongs to the Son. It is therefore impossible to conceive that the Holy Ghost's teaching should be contrary to that of the Son, or even different in any degree. It is one and the same teaching. What the Holy Ghost has to say is already known by the Son, and would have been spoken by the Son had the circumstances called for it. There are two ways of understanding the promise here made by Jesus: either the Holy Ghost will bestow clearer light on what the Son has already said, or else He will add new ideas perfectly in harmony with the teaching of the Son. If we understand it in the latter sense, then we must take it to be a privilege bestowed only on the Apostles, for the Church teaches quite plainly that revelation closed with the death of the Apostles. But progress towards a better comprehension of the truth ought, in the very nature of things, to continue as long as man endures. When Jesus speaks to His Apostles, whom He charges to defend Him with the help of the Holy Ghost and to preach the truth to the world, He speaks to all those who will believe through the preaching of the Apostles and their successors. The help of the Holy Spirit is consequently promised for all time to the successors of the Apostles and to all who shall, under their guidance, believe in Jesus. In particular, the Holy Spirit will bestow the gift of knowing the future, along with that gift of prophecy which the Church has always enjoyed.

The Spirit of God had already been revealed in the Old Testament, which showed Him in His function of teaching truth and inspiring men to heroic deeds. Here Jesus adds the knowledge of the relation of the Spirit to the Father and the Son. He had not spoken of this to the Jews, for no one could understand this doctrine unless they first believed in the Son. As the Son is God like the Father, it follows that the Spirit of God is also the Spirit of the Son. The Apostles understand this now; they will comprehend it better later on.

As Jesus promised the Holy Spirit in order to help the Apostles and to console them at His departure, the Church understood the name Paraclete, literally 'Helper' or 'Defender,' in the sense of 'Comforter.' As a helper the Paraclete comes to the aid especially of the teaching Church; as a comforter He is the welcome and beloved guest of every soul.[1]

All that Jesus has just said, had in view the indefinite period that was to elapse between the time of His departure from His disciples and the moment of their reunion in heaven. But there was a more speedy happiness in store for them, and on this He wished to dwell for a little in order

1 Cf. *Consolator optime, dulcis hospes animæ,* in the beautiful Sequence for Pentecost.

to strengthen them for the trial they had shortly to bear: 'A little while and you shall not see Me, and again a little while and you shall see Me.' There was nothing new in this announcement of His resurrection, nevertheless it was not understood by the Apostles who did not know how to reconcile 'a little while' with the end in which that journey to the Father was to terminate, an end which appeared so far off. Hence they asked: 'What is this that He saith: A little while? We know not what He speaketh.'

First of all, He desired to strengthen their faith. They were to be plunged into sadness by the betrayal, the trial of their Master, the crucifixion, the satisfaction and sarcasms of the Jews. But these sorrows of theirs will be like the pains of a woman in childbirth: they will be succeeded by a great joy. Jesus will come back to His disciples. They will see Him and their hearts will rejoice. He will speak to them openly of the Father.

Here again a limitless period of time stretches out before Him; the day of joy is prolonged and is turned into a day in which they shall pray in the name of Jesus who is with the Father, without there being any need for Him to intercede with the Father for them, because the Father loves those who have believed in His Son. Here at last they must face the fact that Jesus is to be separated from them, at least while they are on earth. He sums up the whole of His human life in the words: 'I came forth from the Father and am come into the world: again I leave the world and I go to the Father.' This saying was so plain—even the mysterious background against which Jesus had placed it seemed as though illuminated by the clearness of His words—that the disciples thought they understood His meaning. Forgetting that their Master had warned them that fuller understanding was only to come later, and seeing that the declaration He had just made had no admixture of parabolic comparison, they sought to prove that they really understood by repeating with an air of certainty: 'We believe that Thou camest forth from God.' Their good will was perfect, nevertheless their courage would fail, and Jesus gives them warning of it: 'You shall be scattered every man to his own and shall leave Me alone.'[1] Yet He is

[1] We have already met these words in the Synoptists (p. 209). John appears to have transferred them to this place in order to provide a conclusion for the conversation.

never alone, for He is always with His Father, and so is certain of victory. Victory is already His. His concluding words are that they should have trust in Him whatever may happen.

Christ's prayer for the unity of the Church (267).

John xvii, 1–26.

After these conversations were ended, Jesus began a prayer. It is commonly imagined by the pilgrims who to-day, in solitude and silence, follow the steep road leading down from the Upper Room to Gethsemani on the evening of Maundy Thursday, that this prayer was uttered while Jesus stood on the bank of the Cedron looking up to the sky, with His disciples gathered around Him. But, as we have already said, it is difficult to suppose that the discourses we have just seen were spoken while the little band was traversing an inhabited locality (as the way from the Upper Room to Gethsemani then was), and passing through streets which would be fuller than usual owing to the Paschal season. The quiet of the Upper Room would be more suitable. Moreover, St. John says quite definitely that after uttering the prayer Jesus went out.[1] This prayer was consequently the final act of praise offered at the conclusion of the Paschal supper. It was the custom of the Jews to recite the *Hallel* then, that is to say, Psalms cxv to cxviii,[2] and Jesus probably observed the custom with His disciples. But there was an incomparable dignity in that gathering which took place on this last evening of Christ's life, for on that occasion the type was followed by the reality. In Psalm cxviii they sang of one who was blessed because he came in the name of the Lord. He had now come, His task was completed, His Father was glorified by the work He had done. Since that work was to be continued and widespread through the instrumentality of the Apostles, it was Jesus' desire to pray for them and for all who should believe through them, all in fact who were to form what we now call the Church. And for that Church He desired unity. He asked it of His Father, He recommended it to His disciples—a unity not only in imitation of the mutual love of the Father and the

[1] John xviii, 1.
[2] Hebrew numbering. In Vulgate cxiii, 8–18 ; cxiv–cxvii.

Son, but a unity obtained by making themselves one with the Father and the Son by faith and charity.

To begin with, Jesus asks for glory. He has come that He may give men eternal life,[1] and eternal life is glory. It is only right that He should enter as man into the glory which from all eternity He had with the Father as His Son.

Then He brings forward His Apostles. The Father already knows them, seeing that He has given them to Jesus, having in His own counsel chosen them out long before. But it is for the Son to bear witness that they have heard and received the words which He has delivered to them by believing that He was the one sent by the Father. Hence they are really the Son's, and by that fact they belong to the Father, for Father and Son hold everything in common. Jesus prays for them because they have much reason to fear the world. No one is excluded from His prayer ; but since it is a question of preparing workers precisely for the purpose of converting the world, they must first of all be put on their guard against the allurements of the world and preserved from all its evil. Such was the mission of Jesus in the land of Israel. Now that He is about to leave His disciples He confides them to the care of His Father. He does not ask Him to take them out of the world —otherwise, how could they perform their mission there ?— but He prays that they may be sanctified in truth, that is, that they may be strengthened in their will to believe the word of God. The pattern of their sanctification is Jesus Himself. True, He is already holy, but it is His will nevertheless to offer Himself to the Father and to consecrate Himself for their sake in order that He may serve as an example, so that they may share in the infinite merits of His offering ; as Bossuet says, ' in order that, by sharing in the grace of His priesthood through their ministry, they may at the same time take upon themselves His condition as a victim, and that they may find in Him that which they do not possess of themselves, namely, the sanctity required for such as are ambassadors and ministers of Jesus Christ.'

The Apostles must realize, then, that they have to sanctify themselves before they preach to others : a formidable task ! But they must realize, too, that the holiness required of them

[1] In the phrase : ' This is eternal life, that they may know Thee the one true God and Him whom Thou hast sent, Jesus Christ,' the words ' Jesus Christ ' are rather the author's than the speaker's.

is the holiness of Jesus Christ who desires to communicate it to them : and in that they find a sweet encouragement.

Finally the Master casts a confident glance beyond the confines of the Upper Room. He beholds His disciples spread throughout the whole world preaching faith in Him. Other men in the past who put themselves forward as the lovers of truth had gathered disciples around them, and at first these disciples had collected partisans for their masters. But as time went by each had gone his own way and numerous sects had been formed. Jesus knew that a like danger threatened the society He was about to found, as it threatens all human societies. Accordingly He prays for unity, and He desires a unity so complete that He includes in His desire not only the Apostles, but also the least of the faithful ; nay more, it is the supreme appeal of His heart that all the faithful scattered throughout the whole world should be sharers in that essential and infinitely simple unity, which is the one and unique unity of God, embracing the Father and the Son. All who long for the unity of Christians ought to feel the fire of this desire within them when they read these words of Christ praying 'that they all may be one, as Thou Father in Me and I in Thee, that they also may be one in Us.' This unity is the divine mark of the religion of Jesus Christ : 'So that the world may believe that Thou hast sent Me.' He repeats once more with increasing energy : 'That they may be one, as We also are one.' This unity is not to be obtained simply by the imitation of a model. It is union with the Father through Jesus that will make perfect unity : 'I in them and Thou in Me, that they may be made perfect in unity.'[1]

As for wounded vanity or rebellious pride—common causes of schism—hereditary prejudice, or even those objections arising from spurious nationalism which perpetuate such prejudice, what weight ought such things to have against this desire of Jesus ? And who does not see that the union He desires surpasses all vague sentiments of solidarity, whether human or Christian, and that it is a unity of faith? Lord Jesus, may Thy prayer be heard !

It is to such as have kept unity that Jesus finally promises that they shall be again united to Him in the glory which the eternal decrees of His Father have bestowed upon Him.

[1] The whole of this doctrine has been beautifully developed in the encyclical *Mortalium Animos* of our Holy Father, Pius XI.

Sure of having accomplished His mission, Jesus now appeals to the Father's justice. That mission He will continue in a more hidden manner in order, as He says to His Father, 'that the love wherewith Thou hast loved Me may be in them, and I in them.'

CHAPTER VI

THE PASSION

I. GETHSEMANI (268–269).

Luke xxii, 39–46 ; Mark xiv, 26, 32–42 ; Matt. xxvi, 30, 36–46 ; John xviii, 1.

AFTER reciting the *Hallel*[1] with the Eleven and praying to His Father, Jesus left[2] the Upper Room and made His way to the Mount of Olives ; crossing the brook Cedron, He went to a place called Gethsemani where there was a garden. St. John mentions neither Gethsemani nor the Mount of Olives, but it may be said that he is careful to show that the place to which Jesus went was at the foot of the hill and that a garden was there. David had crossed the *Qidron*, or 'black torrent,' amidst the tears of the people, after Achitophel's treachery.[3] The brook is always dry except after the heavy rains, but there were doubtless bridges for crossing then as there are now. It is possible that Jesus and His disciples made the steep descent from the upper city into the valley by the street of steps which has been recently discovered.[4] The little group would not have dreamed of traversing the Temple enclosure so late at night ; they went round, passing under the pinnacle formed by the south-eastern angle of the Temple walls on which the light of the full moon shone. Then they entered the narrow valley which would be shrouded in darkness, passing the tombs

[1] According to Mark and Matthew, ὑμνήσαντες. The singing of a hymn (that is, a psalm) might have occurred at the close of an ordinary meal, but as the two evangelists have mentioned the Pasch, the hymn here can only be the *Hallel*. Before this time the book of Jubilees (xlix, 6) had already made mention of the thanksgiving after the Pasch.

[2] All four evangelists use ἐξέρχομαι, which St. Luke expressly understands of the departure from the Upper Room, and this is the natural meaning in the other gospels.

[3] 2 Kings xv, 23.

[4] Discovered by the Assumptionist Fathers in their grounds. The steps are shown in our plan of Jerusalem.

which line its eastern side, finally arriving at a walled enclosure whither Jesus had often resorted with His disciples. It was there that they spent the night when there was no time to get as far as Bethany. The name Gethsemani, 'oil-press,' shows that there must have been a rustic apparatus among the olive trees which were in sufficient numbers to give the place the appearance of an Oriental garden. At the beginning of April, if the sirocco blows, the nights are already warm enough to make it possible to sleep on the ground wrapped in a cloak. If, on the other hand, it was cold, as it appears to have been that night,[1] the Apostles would seek the shelter of some sort of barn and lie on mats.

Accustomed to this casual manner of spending the night, the Eleven were ready to settle down without ceremony; but Jesus said to them: 'Sit you here while I pray.' Then, full of sadness, He took with Him Peter, James and John, as on the day of the Transfiguration, wishing to have the support of their sympathy: 'My soul is sorrowful even unto death. Stay you here and watch.' Then, as it were tearing Himself from the comfort of their presence, He went forward about a stone's throw. There, beset by fear and despondency, He sank to the ground and prayed.[2] St. Luke has given His anguish the name *agonia*, which does not mean the pangs of death, as 'agony' does with us, but the anxiety caused by some undefined apprehension of impending evil. It was of such a nature that our Saviour's sweat became like drops of blood trickling to the ground.

Prostrate on the ground Jesus prayed that, if it were possible, the approaching hour might pass by Him, as a flood might spare some little nook from destruction. He prayed: 'Abba, Father, all things are possible to Thee. Remove this chalice from Me. But not what I will, only what Thou wilt.' The despondency, the bloody sweat, the fear shown in the presence of torment of soul and body, the prayer to avert the chalice which He had so greatly desired to drink, that poor humanity so like to our own: these things have not been able to scandalize the worshippers of Jesus. On the contrary, they find in them only a strong

[1] Mark xiv, 54.

[2] Where this prayer was uttered a memorial church was built at the end of the fourth century, since discovered by the Franciscans. (Cf. *Jérusalem*, by Vincent and Abel, II, pp. 1007 ff.) They have rebuilt the basilica, where liturgical prayer is offered to God day and night in union with the agonizing heart of Jesus.

appeal to their love. Nowhere was the Son of God brought lower for our sakes. Even those who do not believe are unable, if they have any feeling at all, to remain insensible to so deep an expression of human affliction. Yet there are some who show surprise that Jesus, but lately so confident of His triumph over death, should so soon afterwards allow Himself to be thus overwhelmed by His forebodings. But they forget that this is characteristic of our nature, a characteristic which is found more emphatically in the noblest specimens of human nature and renders them more responsive and more sensitive to adverse impressions. When a general launches his troops to victory he fires them with his own enthusiasm ; when he has a foreboding that he will die in the battle his soul is troubled. So it was with Wolfe on the eve of the battle of Quebec against Montcalm. We are not ashamed to use such examples, for they are not profane merely because they are human ; and it is the humanity of Jesus that is here revealed to us, a humanity altogether like to our own save for sin, even with a completely human will that abhors suffering—and what suffering ! That suffering was all the greater in that the will of Jesus did not hesitate for a moment. The only thing He willed was His Father's will : 'Not what I will, but what Thou wilt.'

He who descended by His human nature 'a little lower than the angels,'[1] was aided by an angel from heaven. But He specially needed the comfort of His friends. He returns, therefore, to His disciples, but finds them sleeping—even Peter who had so vehemently protested his friendship. Jesus says to him : 'Simon, sleepest thou ? Couldst thou not watch one hour ? Watch and pray that you enter not into temptation. The spirit is willing '—Simon knew that —' but the flesh is weak '—and he was about to prove that once more. To add example to precept, as Jesus always did, and especially because His burdened soul felt eased only in His Father's presence, He again withdraws to pray. Again He returns to the disciples and finds the same disheartening apathy : they are again sleeping, that first deep and overpowering sleep of which they are ashamed and for which they know not how to excuse themselves. Jesus prays a third time and again returns ; but on this occasion He turns no more to seek the sympathy of His friends. He

[1] Psalm viii, 6 (LXX Version).

faces the danger that is fast approaching by His Father's order. Hence He says to the stupefied sleepers : ' Sleep on now and take your rest. The time for prayer is gone. The hour is come ; behold the Son of Man is to be betrayed into the hands of sinners.' Then, no doubt seeing that they feel this friendly irony more than His reproaches, He says : ' Rise up : let us go. Behold he that betrayeth Me is at hand.' The time had come to gather together. Perhaps the other eight Apostles ran up at hearing the noise, or more probably Jesus with Peter, James and John came and rejoined them in some sheltered place where, as we may well suppose, they were still asleep.

II. JESUS IS JUDGED BY THE JEWS

His arrest (270).

Luke xxii, 47–53 ; Mark xiv, 43–52 ; Matt. xxvi, 47–56 ; John xviii, 2–11.

Judas drew near. He knew the way, for he too had often been to that place along with the other disciples. He was well aware that Jesus would not go as far as Bethany that night, for the night of the Pasch had to be spent at Jerusalem; the Mount of Olives counted as part of Jerusalem.

The lost disciple was acting merely as guide for the police, for the chief priests who had planned Jesus' arrest had provided their own men for the purpose, armed with swords and cudgels. But to make doubly sure they had demanded from the Roman tribune responsible for the guard of the Temple a detachment of the cohort assigned to that task. The tribune, either after consulting Pilate or else acting on his own authority, came in person, ordering his soldiers to follow with arms and torches. He brought them merely to keep order, ready to intervene in case the Galilæans showed signs of resistance ; but they took no part in the arrest, as even the fourth gospel declares, the only one of the four to make mention of their presence. There the Roman soldiery are naturally put in the place of honour, the priests and Jewish captains of the Temple bringing up the rear. Judas had given the leaders of the band the following sign : ' Whomsoever I shall kiss, that is He. Lay hold on Him and lead Him away securely.' Coming up to Jesus, who from a distance was still indistinguishable from His disciples in the dim light, he courteously saluted Him as Rabbi and kissed Him. Thereupon Jesus for the last time called him 'Friend,' and then, as though sickened by the thought of that kiss, added : '(A kiss) for what thou art come (to do)!'[1]

But the Son of God refused to permit such a base betrayal to overshadow the dignity of His attitude and His resolution. Therefore He went forward and said : 'Whom seek ye?' and received the answer : 'Jesus of Nazareth.' He replied simply : 'I am He.' At this, those who had spoken started back and fell to the ground. This incident is preserved for us by St. John alone, who saw in it a sign of the supernatural power of Jesus manifested by His accent, His look, and by the authority which emanated from His person. Doubtless it would be an exaggerated view were we to picture all the bystanders falling down like tin soldiers. Those who had pushed forward to speak fell back overwhelmed by His majesty[2] and fell over the others ; but they picked themselves up quickly enough. Jesus again asked them whom they were seeking so that He might secure the release of His disciples, like a leader who shoulders all the responsibility and refuses to implicate anyone : 'If therefore you seek Me, let these go their way.'[3] His aggressors at once laid hands on Him.

A proof that these were not Roman soldiers but the Jewish Temple guard is the fact that the first to come forward, desirous of showing his zeal, though without incurring much danger seeing that Jesus had excluded His followers from the affair, was a servant of the high priest named Malchos.[4] But he had failed to reckon with the impulsive courage of Peter who drew his sword and cut off the man's right ear. All four evangelists agree in describing him as a

[1] Matthew xxvi, 50. Cf. the note on these words in the author's commentary on St. Matthew : "ἐφ' ὃ πάρει has the appearance of a sudden exclamation, but it is difficult to explain. It cannot be a question, *ad quod* or *ad quid venisti?*, for the relative is never used as an interrogative. It is not an exclamation like : 'That is what you have come for, then!', for ὅ is never used as a synonym for οἷον. Some have understood the addition of a word, as : 'Do what you have come for,' or : 'What you have come here for I know not' (Schanz). Perhaps the best solution is to understand the words as referring to the kiss just given : 'A kiss, friend, for what you have come to do!' (Wellhausen). This would be exactly what St. Luke has said more plainly (xxii, 48)."

[2] Cf. John vii, 44 ff.

[3] St. John here applies to this occasion of temporal danger what Jesus had formerly (xvii, 12) said of the danger threatening His Apostles from the religious and moral point of view.

[4] The name Malchos is a Semitic name with a Greek termination.

servant of the high priest and ascribing the deed to one of the disciples ; but St. John alone names Malchos and Simon Peter, the others probably omitting the names out of caution, at least as regards the name of Peter. St. John's positive designation of Peter, however, is completely in accord with the character of the gallant friend of Jesus who had so sincerely declared himself ready to die with Him. Then Jesus intervened and, as St. John records, said to Peter : 'Put up thy sword into the scabbard. The chalice which My Father hath given Me, shall I not drink it ?'[1] These words form a sort of echo to His agony in the garden, which thus begins and ends with the acceptance of the chalice. St. John has passed over the scene of the agony in silence, as he does with many other incidents which are sufficiently recorded by the earlier gospels, though he here makes reference to it. Before His Father Jesus had lain prostrate. Before the band sent against Him by the Sanhedrin He stands erect. Is there not a noble human touch in that also ? It reminds us of St. Thomas More who conscientiously strove to escape death, but went to it with heroic fortitude.

St. Matthew records that Jesus added : 'All that take the sword shall perish by the sword.' Without doubt the cause was a just one, but resistance was bound to fail. The violence done was perpetrated by the authority which had the power of the sword and would have had no hesitation in using it. Peter is not blamed, but his example might have been contagious. Jesus has no desire that a fight should begin on His account. That was not in accordance with His part as Messiah. Moreover, He adds with certainty of His supernatural power : 'Or thinkest thou that I cannot ask My Father, who would immediately send Me more than twelve legions of angels ?' But, so to say, He denied Himself this resource in consenting to drink the chalice. Had he not resolved to suffer, then how would the Scriptures be fulfilled which spoke of the sufferings of the just one, especially that passage which showed to all nations the servant of Jahweh expiating by His death the sins of all that were His ?[2]

Then turning to address all the disciples Jesus said : 'Suffer things to go thus far,' and He healed the wound inflicted by the sword. This we gather from St. Luke alone ; but had He not performed that act of kindness, would not

[1] John xviii, 11. [2] Isaias liii.

Jesus have been reproached at His trial for the rash deed done by Peter? He healed Malchos, for the man was but the instrument in the abominable work of his masters. In the darkness Jesus could discern the ringleaders: priests, captains of the Temple guard, and elders of the people, who had come to seize their victim and, now that the deed had been done without much difficulty, were bold enough to show their faces. To them He said: 'Are ye come out as it were against a robber, with swords and staves? When I was daily with you in the Temple you did not stretch forth your hands against Me; but this is your hour and the power of darkness.'[1]

Now came the catastrophe. The presence of such important personages completely undermined the disciples' courage; they all deserted their Master and fled. There was someone, however, who tried to follow Him, a young man who had been sleeping near at hand clad only in a light cloth. Attracted by the commotion, he had come upon the scene wearing nothing but that simple garment. He must have been devoted to Jesus, seeing that he sought to follow Him at that hour, despite the cold and his scanty clothing. He also was seized by the rabble, but leaving his linen cloth in their hands, he fled away naked. We learn this strange incident only from St. Mark, and we may ask who was this young man. Certainly not one of the Apostles; rather was it someone who had become attached to Jesus on occasion of His visits to that place with His friends. Probably it was St. Mark himself. If so, then this incident which had remained graven on his heart was the sign manual of his book. That night he had deserted Jesus with the rest; but he had understood better how much He deserved to be loved.

Jesus is led to the house of Annas (271).

John xviii, 12–13, 24.[2]

After Jesus had been arrested and His hands manacled, the tribune who retained command of the armed force led

[1] These words are recorded by St. Luke, but they are quite in the style of St. John.

[2] In our commentary on St. John we give the reasons for placing in the house of Caiaphas what, according to John, would have to be reserved for the house of Annas, did we not follow the Syriac Sinaitic MS. and St. Cyril of Alexandria in transposing v. 24 to follow v. 13.

Him to the house of Annas,[1] the father-in-law of Caiaphas who was high priest that year. That done, the soldiers fulfilled their office and probably returned to barracks. It may be wondered at that Jesus should be led to the house of Annas if Caiaphas was high priest. Annas also had been high priest, and after he had been deposed by the procurator Valerius Gratus in A.D. 15 he saw five of his sons raised to the same dignity during his long life. His influence among the Jews had always been great, and no doubt Caiaphas his son-in-law wished to show him deference. It is no slander against this somewhat unscrupulous politician to judge, too, that he was in no way sorry to have the support of his father-in-law in this business, which had such bad beginnings and was to end in the delivery of an innocent fellow-Jew to the Romans. As we understand the sequence of events, it seems that Annas, once his curiosity had been satisfied, refused to take any responsibility. He had learned discretion and if, as Josephus tells us, he was regarded as an example of the fortunate man,[2] this was probably due to the fact that he had had as little as possible to do with public affairs. Without so much as ordering the removal of the bonds from the hands of Jesus, he sent Him off to Caiaphas.

Jesus at the house of Caiaphas. Peter's threefold denial (272).

Luke xxii, 54–62 ; Mark xiv, 53–54, 66–72 ; Matt. xxvi, 57–58, 69–75 ; John xviii, 14–27.[3]

It was Caiaphas, as St. John recalls, who had recommended that one man should be put to death in order to save the whole nation. Almost at the same time as Jesus there arrived at his house some of the influential members of the priesthood, along with doctors of the Law and elders

[1] It is not known where the house of Annas stood. It is only since the thirteenth century that topographical tradition has concerned itself with the question (cf. *Jérusalem*, by Vincent and Abel, II, p. 492). In order to bring Peter's denials into harmony, according to the evidence of the Synoptists and St. John, Annas and Caiaphas have been supposed to have had separate apartments in the same house.

[2] *Antiquities*, XX, ix, 1 : 'This eldest Annas proved a most fortunate man, for he had five sons who had all performed the office of high priest.'

[3] We follow Luke's order, which puts the decisive meeting of the Sanhedrin in the morning—the meeting which Mark and Matthew place at night. This first session at the house of Caiaphas is from John's narrative. Peter's denial is taken from all four gospels, with the slight differences which we indicate in the notes.

of the people, these having been sent for in order to conduct a preliminary examination of the prisoner. According to the traditional usage which was codified in the oral teaching of the rabbis, it was forbidden to hold trials during the night when these trials were such as might lead up to a death sentence. Hence this meeting at the house of Caiaphas was of an unofficial character ; it was a sort of commission, composed of those members of the Sanhedrin who were known to be sympathetic towards the plot, for the purpose of having everything in readiness for the morrow. The high priest saw clearly in his own mind that the matter was likely to prove another incident in his relations with the Roman authorities, relations that were already difficult enough with a man like Pilate. It was impossible for him, however, simply to rest content with pointing out before this tribunal of the Jewish nation, and in the hearing of the prisoner, the political advantages that would ensue from the execution of Jesus. He must find charges that were calculated to move the most influential section of the assembly, the Pharisees namely ; that is to say, charges of a doctrinal character must be found. He therefore began to question Jesus about what He had taught His disciples. The dreamings of a mere individual visionary would have been counted of little importance ; but it was known that Jesus had taught His doctrine to certain Galilæans who followed Him wherever He went, and the whole group were suspected of holding novel opinions. What, then, was Jesus' teaching ? Many visionaries are glad enough of an opportunity of setting forth their revelations and opinions before an important audience. If Jesus was of that character and made some admission that could immediately be taken up by the Scribes, the plot would be greatly advanced.

But Jesus, though so eager to preach the kingdom of God to men of good will, had nothing to say before this assembly. His position was not that of a preacher ; He stood in the place of the accused. It was therefore the business of His accusers to find out His crime. As far as He Himself was concerned—and the point was of greatest importance—He was no conspirator, and He had no secret doctrine : 'I have spoken openly to the world ; I have always taught in the synagogue and in the Temple, whither all the Jews resort ; and in secret I have spoken nothing. Why askest thou Me ? Ask them who have heard what I have spoken unto them.'

The high priest saw at once that his end was not to be gained so easily as he had imagined ; Jesus was on His guard. Doubtless he betrayed his annoyance by some gesture of irritation, for one of his underlings interpreted it by an act of brutality. The man stationed by the side of the prisoner as His guard gave Jesus a blow with the words : 'Answerest Thou the high priest so ?' With complete self-control, Jesus reminded His judges, in the person of this menial, of the respect due to the Law : 'If I have spoken ill, show where is the evil ; but if well, why strikest thou Me ?' The defendant at the bar still stood awaiting the charges against Him with perfect self-composure. It was evident that Jesus had no intention of confessing. They would therefore have to call witnesses, and the witnesses would have to be allowed to make their depositions in public and before a regular court. The high priest decided not to continue the proceedings and adjourned till the morning in order to hold a trial in due form.

That night it was not only people hostile or indifferent towards Jesus that were to be found in the palace of Caiaphas.[1] Two friends had crept in. Peter, after delivering the blow with his sword, had been compelled by His Master to remain quiet ; but he had not abandoned Jesus. He followed Him at some distance so as not to be arrested, as had nearly befallen the young stranger. The four evangelists agree on this point ; the fourth gospel adds that Peter was in the company of another disciple. The discreet way in which St. John refers to himself and his friends allows us to suppose that he himself was that disciple, and this conjecture can also be based upon his friendship for Peter, even though we leave out of count St. John's love for Jesus that later took him to the foot of the cross. This disciple, whoever he was, was known to the high priest. It may seem astonishing that this should be said of a man like John, who was merely a fisherman from the shores of the lake of Galilee. But, on the other hand, it is to be remembered that we know nothing of where his mother, probably Salome, came from. She may have had relations at Jerusalem. And we need see no reason for criticism in the fact that one of Jesus' friends should enter the company of Caiaphas at a time when the latter was acting so odious a part, seeing that

[1] Regarding the site of this place, cf. *Jérusalem*, II, pp. 482 ff.

the disciple's motive may have been to try to make himself useful to his Master. Moreover, the relations between the high priest and the friend of Jesus were doubtless of very slight a character ; it was not necessary to be a familiar acquaintance in order to have free entry into the palace, for the place was usually open to all and sundry. That night, however, those in the palace were on the watch for suspected persons. The disciple known to the high priest went in first without any difficulty and spoke to the portress, who thereupon admitted Peter. All the same she questioned him, as was not altogether unnatural : 'Art thou also one of this man's disciples ?' But as she let him pass, this clearly meant : 'At all events, you are not one of that lot, are you ?' Peter answered : 'I am not.' Critics who claim to have seen in St. John's gospel a consistent effort to disparage Peter must allow that in this passage, at any rate, St. John has rather excused the latter's fault ; for the 'subterfuge' practised here might very well be termed a trivial officious lie, told for the purpose of gaining admittance to the courtyard.

All three Synoptists agree with St. John on this point, that the first 'denial' occurred through a maidservant. All are in agreement too about the fact that Peter, once he had entered the courtyard, approached the servants who had lighted a fire to warm themselves. Doubtless the night air was fresh ; moreover, in the hills of Judæa it is a common practice to sit round a fire at night during all seasons of the year. According to the Synoptists, it was there by the fire that the maidservant stared at Peter's face, lit up by the flame as St. Luke explains. She addressed him with more assurance than the woman mentioned by St. John : 'Thou also wast with the Nazarene, Jesus.'[1] Peter, as a Galilæan, could excuse himself as not understanding what she said : 'I do not know, I do not understand what thou sayest.' It is not difficult for a stranger to get rid of embarrassing questioners by pretending not to understand. But an evasion such as that could not succeed for long, and Peter thought it wise to creep away towards the entrance porch. St. Mark notes that at this time a cock crowed. According to his account Our Saviour's prediction ran as follows : 'Before the cock crow twice, thou shalt deny Me thrice.'

[1] Mark xiv, 67.

Therefore the crowing of the cock was a warning; but Peter in his confusion did not heed it.

Then the same maidservant (according to St. Mark), another (according to St. Matthew), someone (according to St. Luke), several people (according to St. John), denounced Peter as a disciple or denounced him afresh. It is only those who are completely ignorant of the inevitable law that governs all historical narrative who will take scandal at these different ways of relating the same incident. At all events the four evangelists are in agreement regarding Peter's unequivocal reply: 'I am not one of His disciples'; and Peter was the head of the Apostles!

About an hour went by.[1] Peter had been foolhardy enough to enter into conversation with others, perhaps in order to show a bold front, fearing lest his silence might seem suspicious. They knew that he was a Galilæan by his accent, his way of pronouncing certain consonants, perhaps too by the manner in which he used certain words. Suddenly there was a general outburst,[2] someone expressing what was thought by all:[3] 'Of a truth thou art one of them, for thou art a Galilæan; thy way of speaking betrayeth thee.' The danger became still more pressing when one of the priest's servants, a relation of the man whose ear Peter had cut off, came out with a definite accusation: 'Did I not see thee in the garden with Him?'[4] Now Peter thought he was lost and 'began to curse and swear: I know not the man of whom you speak.'[5] Just then the crowing of the cock was heard for the second time,[6] and Peter remembered what the Master had said. One look from Jesus stirred him to the very depths of his soul. Exhausted by the struggle against the danger that had threatened, and still more by the struggle against his own heart, when his eyes met those sad eyes of Him whom he loved and in whom he still believed he burst into sobs, and going out he wept bitterly.[7] This sorrowful incident occurred while Jesus

[1] Luke xxii, 59. [2] In Matthew, Mark, and John.
[3] In Luke. [4] John xviii, 26. [5] Mark xiv, 71.

[6] The writer has often in Jerusalem listened to the first cock crow at the beginning of April. The time varies much, but 2.30 a.m. appears to be the earliest.

[7] Tradition at Jerusalem venerated the place of Peter's repentance at the eastern side of the upper city. A church built in the fifth or sixth century bore the title of St. Peter *in Gallicantu*. The Assumptionist Fathers have restored it.

was being questioned, and as the examination took place behind closed doors, Peter was not present at it. Therefore it was probably when Jesus came out from the room that He looked upon Peter.[1]

Scenes of outrage (273).

Luke xxii, 63–65 ; Mark xiv, 65 ; Matt. xxvi, 67–68.

When the members of the Sanhedrin withdrew, some of them so far degraded themselves as to heap insults on their innocent victim. But it was far worse when He was left in the hands of their servants, enraged on account of the wearisome night they had been compelled to spend, or perhaps simply led on by their baseness of soul and cruelty. They had their own fashion of showing that they shared their masters' feelings. What ! A prophet who had not foreseen his own ill-fortune ! A Christ who had none to defend Him ! Heartlessly they spat in His face and, covering His head with a cloth, they struck Him saying : 'Prophesy ! Tell us, O Christ, who hath struck Thee ?' Becoming weary and ceasing to find amusement in this horrible scene, they doubtless locked up Jesus in some dark corner till daybreak.

[1] We see that if it be admitted that the interrogation of Jesus took place in the house of Caiaphas, or in a part of the same house occupied by Annas, the supposed contradictions of the evangelists regarding the circumstances of Peter's denials amount to very little. It would be both very ill-advised and altogether uncritical to multiply those denials in order to justify every detail of the gospel narratives. The number three is affirmed by all four evangelists both in the prediction and in the event. As for the denials in themselves, John gives them as simple, straightforward denials. In Luke they seem to become less categoric as they proceed. In Matthew the second is with an oath, the third accompanied by cursing. The progression seems most natural in Mark, and we have preferred his precise information regarding the cock crows.

M. Fillion (*Vie de Jésus Christ*, III, p. 428) declares that St. Peter denied his Master perhaps seven or eight times, but maintains the essential point that it was on three occasions. The prediction of Jesus, however, speaks of three denials, and as that prediction is found in all four gospels its authority is as strong as the authority of the details of each separate narrative. If M. Fillion is satisfied with a less strict fulfilment of Christ's words it is because, as he says, 'prophecy admits of a wider meaning.' But this is to fail to understand that history is an approximate account of the past, just as prophecy is an approximation to the future.

The Sanhedrin condemns Jesus to death (274).

Luke xxii, 66–71 ; Mark xv, 1a ; xiv, 55–64 ; Matt. xxvii, 1 ; xxvi, 59–66.[1]

Very early in the morning the whole Sanhedrin was called together. The high priest, at the head of the priesthood, presided over the assembly ;[2] the elders represented the aristocracy and wealthy landowners ; the party of the Pharisees was there with its learned followers bearing their traditional title of Scribes. These Scribes were indispensable in all matters that appertained to the political, civil or criminal sphere, for all had to be done in accordance with the Law of which they alone possessed the secret. All three classes had answered the high priest's summons, the object of which had been made known to them. There was not one of them but knew that they had no right to pass an effective sentence of death. The Roman governor alone had the power of life and death. But to tell the truth, this was a time of transition, and it is difficult to judge precisely concerning the situation. The Roman principle was that provinces of the Empire, and this applied especially to the Jews who had long been treated as allies, should be allowed a certain autonomy in their internal, and particularly their religious, affairs. Had a Jew been condemned to death by his own people for some notorious crime of impiety, Pilate would doubtless have made no difficulty about signing the death warrant. But the Sanhedrin was by no means anxious to assume the whole responsibility in this case, particularly since it was a question of Messianic affairs and precisely because Messianism was involved, for to the Romans the word Messianic spelt political. As Caiaphas in the beginning of this business had proposed to put it forward as a display

[1] The morning session of the Sanhedrin, passed over in silence by John like so many other facts which he considered sufficiently described by the Synoptists, is related by the latter, though Mark and Matthew seem to have transferred the proceedings of this session to the one that took place during the night ; consequently they have nothing to add here. The sequence of events in Luke, who assigns to the morning the interrogatory and condemnation of Jesus (as do Mark and Matthew), is much more probable. It seems impossible to admit that the incidents of each session were very much the same.

[2] Later the rabbis imagined that the president of the Sanhedrin had been one belonging to their own group, and their false claim has thrown matters into some confusion. But modern critics prefer the evidence of the New Testament to that of the Talmud.

of loyalty to the existing authorities, it was necessary that Pilate should give sentence. But, on the other hand, no Jew ought to be handed over to the governor until the national tribunal had found him guilty.

Thus the matter assumed a double aspect. To the Jews it was a religious trial ; but they were careful to give it the appearance of a political case in order to win an understanding approval from the Roman procurator. The first necessity, therefore, was to discover some religious charge involving the death sentence ; and since Jesus had referred the high priest to the testimony of those who had heard what He taught, witnesses had been sought out. But as He had always been strict about the observance of the Law and moreover, even up to the last, had taught that people ought to follow the literal interpretation of it given by the Scribes, there was some difficulty in finding witnesses for the prosecution. Eventually some came forward, and the evangelists call them false witnesses because they perverted a harmless utterance into the accusation of an attack on the Temple, which was so reckless as to be senseless. Jesus had in fact spoken words like those attributed to Him, mysterious it is true, but words that ought to have been explained rather than cited as blasphemy : 'Destroy this Temple, and in three days I will raise it up.'[1] It was a veiled allusion to His resurrection, the miracle which He awaited with certainty, one which gave Him even during His lifetime the right to act as Master in that Temple. But He was made to say : 'I will destroy this Temple made with hands, and within three days I will build another not made with hands.' Destroy the Lord's Temple? What wicked audacity ! And He had offered to build another with the aid of divine power ! What a blasphemous delusion ! Was God then at the service of a mere visionary? However it was taken, the accusation was certainly a dangerous one, bearing an obviously subversive character at such a time as that, when so many charlatans had already abused the credulity of the people by promising them all sorts of prodigies.

But as the so-called witnesses were not repeating a genuine utterance, they could not agree, and embarrassment was caused to the formalistic minds of the doctors of the Law who were more accustomed to examine words than facts.

[1] John ii, 19.

The trial was threatening to drag out to great lengths, and it was necessary that everything should be finished by evening. What the high priest desired was that Jesus should protest, explain, and so compromise Himself. Hence he bade Him to answer the witnesses and give the lie to them ; but Jesus remained silent. Then Caiaphas took the short cut to the end he desired. During the night session Jesus had refused to set forth His doctrine before that casual assembly ; but it might be that He would consent to answer a definite question on the subject proposed to Him in the presence of these His judges, such a question as would decide His fate. Therefore with some solemnity he asked : 'If Thou be the Christ, tell us.' Jesus replied : 'If I tell you, you will not believe ; and if I ask you, you will not answer.' If the point was to be settled clearly, it was indeed necessary for Him to question them about the way they understood the terms. What, for instance, did they understand by the word Messiah or Christ ? Was it a crime to believe oneself to be the Christ provided that there was no exciting of the people to disturbance ? Where did the crime begin ? But, questioned by the high priest, Jesus did not take refuge in that manner. He confessed that He was the Christ, and added that He would soon be acknowledged as the sort of Christ He was, the Son of Man, seated at the right hand of the power of God and coming with the clouds of heaven. They knew the Psalms,[1] they knew Daniel.[2] In the past Jesus had reminded the Pharisees[3] that the Messiah would be more than a son of David, since the Lord would invite Him to sit on His right hand ; yet, because He was man, He had loved to call Himself the Son of Man. Now He made allusion to that vision of Daniel's in which a heavenly being like to a man came with the clouds. A heavenly being, yet a human being, destined to be glorified at the right hand of God ! Such was the Messiah that He was.

In the eyes of His judges it was a piece of undreamed-of audacity that He should speak so : He a man deceived by the treachery of His own friends, incapable of doing anything to defend Himself against the insulting mockery shown to Him by the servants, completely at their mercy. It was merely the act of a pitiable visionary. But if that

[1] Psalm cx, 1 (Hebrew). [2] Daniel vii, 9.
[3] Cf. page 157 ff., above.

was the case, was not hallucination a reason for excusing a man from fault? A person ought not to be condemned to death for being subject to hallucinations. Anyone might, if he liked, lay claim to being the Messiah, so long as he did not mind being taken for a madman.

But this self-styled Messiah had already given the doctors of the Law much trouble. Here He was even now seeing Himself at the right hand of God. In what capacity did He imagine that He was to occupy such a position? More than once He had given Himself the name Son of God in a sense which far surpassed what belonged to their ideal of the Messiah, adding insinuations, and even declarations concerning Himself which had the appearance of blasphemy. There burst forth from the assembly a general cry[1] of: 'Art Thou then the Son of God?' Jesus replied: 'I am,' probably in the form: 'You say that I am,'[2] as though He wished to take note of their involuntary confession. In the eyes of the Sanhedrin it was blasphemy. Then, so as to leave upon Jesus the full responsibility for the blasphemy and to express his horror and reprobation of it according to the ritual form, the high priest rent his garments. 'What further need of witnesses have we?' he cried, more content with the outcome of his question than might have been judged from his external gesture of grief. 'You have heard the blasphemy,' he said to his colleagues; 'what think you?' It only remained to take the vote. Sentence of death was already pronounced as far as the Law was concerned,[3] and Jesus was condemned to death.

The despair of Judas (275).

Matthew xxvii, 3–10.

The soul of Judas was shaken to its very depths by the condemnation of his Master. His was one of those strange minds which fail to realize the gravity of a crime until after it is committed. He could hardly have been ignorant of the fact that it was the intention of the chief priests to do Jesus to death, and he must from the start have taken for

[1] Luke xxii, 70, where the distinction between the two questions put to Jesus is made.

[2] The high priest, the mouthpiece of them all, must have said 'Son of the Blessed,' according to the narrative of St. Mark.

[3] Deuteronomy xiii, 2–6.

granted that consequence of his own action in betraying Him. But he recoiled in horror when he realized that the death of the Master who had loved him was now inevitable and as good as accomplished. The price of the betrayal weighed so heavily on his soul that he took the thirty pieces of silver back to the priests and elders with whom he had made the bargain. Indeed he came very nigh to repentance when he admitted his crime: 'I have sinned in betraying innocent blood.' But now that their spite was gratified, the members of the Sanhedrin would have nothing more to do with the traitor. They answered coldly: 'What is that to us? Look thou to it.' That money had been too well spent to be taken back, and as Judas had fulfilled his part of the contract these scrupulous consciences did not wish to deprive him of his gain. Desperate with shame, Judas threw down the thirty pieces of silver in the Temple, as though there were still some vestiges of honour within him which made him indignant with such hypocrisy. So that was the sort of men to whom he had sold his Master! But his remorse went no further. To be forgiven he ought to have asked forgiveness. And there was still time; Jesus would have granted it with a look as He had granted it to Peter, if only He had seen such a prayer in the beseeching eyes of Judas. But Judas doubted His mercy, shutting himself out far from God in sullen despair, and hanged himself.[1]

The high priests, who behaved like true Pharisees throughout the affair, did not at first show any fastidiousness concerning the money; they picked it up, though it had been, so to speak, flung in their faces. Then their scruples again got the upper hand. The Law forbade the profanation of the Temple Treasury by gifts coming from an unclean source.[2] Judas, the trafficker in blood, was not an honourable donor. All the same, those thirty pieces of silver were worth taking; they could be used to buy the Potter's Field, a well-known plot of land probably situated near the Pottery Gate[3] which led from the city into the valley of

[1] Until lately people pointed out a fig tree near Jerusalem on which Judas was supposed to have hanged himself with a rope made of his girdle. In the course of the centuries trees in different places near the city have been indicated, but as early as the fourth century the tradition was attached to a fig tree. Cf. *Jérusalem*, II, p. 865, where the authors quote Juvencus concerning the question.

[2] Cf. Deuteronomy xxiii, 18.

[3] The Pottery or Ceramic Gate, probably identical with the Dung Gate shown on the plan of Jerusalem. Cf. *Jérusalem*, I, pp. 128 ff.

Gê-Hinnom, a place with sinister associations. At the seasons when great numbers of Jews both from Palestine and from all parts of the known world gathered at Jerusalem for the feasts, it sometimes happened that pilgrims died, and provision had to be made for their burial. This field seemed suitable for the purpose. After deliberation by the council it was bought with Judas' money, and thus received the name of *Hakeldama*, or 'the field of blood.'[1] St. Matthew joins two Scriptural texts, one from Jeremias and the other from Zacharias, under the name of the more illustrious of those prophets and fits them on to this incident: 'And they took the thirty pieces of silver, the price of him that was priced, whom they priced of the children of Israel, and they gave them for the potter's field, as the Lord appointed to me.'[2] The place was altogether becoming to the memory of Judas, for it was close to the ancient Topheth where children had been sacrificed to Moloch down in the valley of Gehenna (*Gê-Hinnom*), the name now given to the place of eternal punishment.

III. JESUS BEFORE THE JUDGEMENT SEAT OF PILATE[3]

Pontius Pilate, mentioned under the same name by Tacitus,[4] did not owe his position to membership of one of those great aristocratic families of Rome whose power the emperor Tiberius had overthrown, though he had only ventured to do so by the use of crafty ingenuity. Nor had Pilate forced his way into a senatorial career either by intrigue or by talent. He belonged to the equestrian rank from which the emperor selected his procurators, whom he could recall at will. Were we to give credit to the Jewish writers of the time, Philo[5] and Josephus,[6] we should see in Pilate a bad man, much worse than the proconsul Verres,

[1] For this field see *Jérusalem*, II, p. 863. According to Jer. xix, 2 (Septuagint) there was already a πολυάνδριον or common burying ground in that place. They may have added to it by the use of Judas' money. Christian tradition has consistently connected the memory of Judas with that place. Cf. Acts i, 19.

[2] Zacharias xi, 13 and Jeremias xviii, 3; xxxii, 7–9.

[3] The four gospels are in harmony here, but we follow John, whose account is the most complete.

[4] *Annals*, XV, 44.

[5] *Legatio ad Caium*, Mangey, II, pp. 589 ff.; ed. of Reiter, Vol. VI, pp. 210 ff.

[6] *Passim*.

whose name was a byword for venality. But when they come to positive charges against him, we discover that their adverse estimate of his character is merely a reflection of their exasperated national sentiment. Pilate indeed had no love for the Jews, but his behaviour towards them was that of a severe governor, not that of a cruel man or a plunderer. When rebellion arose he put it down with a heavy hand. Hence Jewish critics of the gospels have concluded that the evangelists have drawn an altogether false picture of the man in his attitude towards Jesus: he would not have cared two straws about the blood of a Galilæan. They forget that Jesus had not been arrested in open rebellion, and that when a legal trial had begun, every Roman was bound to observe the rules of the law. Pilate despised the leaders of the Jews and distrusted them even more. The Sanhedrin was asking for Jesus' death, while other Jews, especially those who were of royal blood, might seize the opportunity of denouncing the procurator to Tiberius for having caused innocent blood to be shed. It would not be the first time they had intervened, for they had got the better of him over the golden shields which he had caused to be hung up in the royal palace at Jerusalem, but had been obliged to remove to Cæsarea.[1] And speaking of the members of the royal family, at that very moment Herod Antipas was present in Jerusalem. Moreover, to what ridicule was not Pilate exposing himself by making a tragedy out of this affair of a miserable visionary! These Jews—both priests and Pharisees—saw sacrilege at every turn.[2] All the same, when they threatened him formally with a denunciation to Rome, after Herod had ceased to take any interest in the matter, Pilate took refuge in the safest course. It was criminal, of course. Nevertheless the early Christians judged him less harshly than modern Catholic scholars, who suffer too much from the influence of the Jewish writers.[3] If we take into account the character of the man and the

[1] *Leg. ad Caium*, loc. cit. M. Fillion (*Vie de J.C.*, I, 132) speaks of 'idolatrous inscriptions or symbols' on these shields. But Philo expressly says that they had no images on them nor anything of a character forbidden by the Law, but merely the maker's name and that of the one to whom they were dedicated.

[2] As happened in the case of the shields, and again when the Roman soldiers under arms marched into the city with their standards, or when Pilate took money from the Temple Treasury in order to build an aqueduct for Jerusalem (Josephus, *Bellum*, II, ix, 2 ff.).

[3] See the excellent account of Pilate by Von Dobschütz in *Realencyklopädie für protestantische Theologie und Kirche*.

difficulties of his position, then his attitude at the trial of Jesus has every appearance of historical probability. The authority of the gospel account stands unshaken.

Jesus is taken to Pilate (276).

Luke xxiii, 1 ; Mark xv, 1 ; Matt. xxvii, 2 ; John xviii, 28.

The prisoner had been released from His chains during His examination, but He was bound again when they took Him before Pilate very early in the morning. The procurators of Judæa generally resided at Cæsarea. During their visits to Jerusalem they usually established themselves in the former palace of Herod, which stood on the highest position in the upper city.[1] But ever since the fourth century Christian tradition has placed the Prætorium near the Temple, at the other side of the city, and has never varied on this point. The tradition is well-founded if we suppose that at the great feasts, particularly during the Pasch, Pilate took up his residence in the fortress of the Antonia overlooking the Temple, so as to keep an eye on the doings of the pilgrims. We have already seen how he had caused a number of Galilæans to be massacred in the Temple.[2] Now the Prætorium was wherever the procurator held his residence, for he was a military leader like a prætor and his Prætorium was where he established his camp. In every palace there was a large courtyard where the Roman commander could muster his men, give audience to such as desired it, and administer justice. Thus the courtyard became the Prætorium, and round about there would be chambers in which the military standards adorned with religious emblems could be kept. But since the Jews had won their case against Pilate in the dispute about these standards, there would be nothing in his Prætorium itself that might offend their religious susceptibilities. Yet as the palace itself was inhabited by pagans and used for the administration of their authority, it was none the less to the minds of the Jews ritually unclean in the highest degree. Thus St. John tells us what we might have conjectured for ourselves, that the priests and their followers would not

[1] On the site where the building called the Tower of David is to-day. There are Herodian foundations of this tower, which owes its construction to Pisan and Turkish builders. It is now a museum. See *Jérusalem*, II, pp. 562 ff.

[2] Luke xiii, 1–2.

enter it for fear of contracting defilement and so be prevented from eating the Pasch, which can be nothing else but the Paschal supper of the Jewish ritual appointed for that same evening by the hierarchy at Jerusalem.

The Jews accuse Jesus before Pilate (277).

Luke xxiii, 2 ; John xviii, 29–32.

Pilate, having been informed that Jesus had been brought before him and most probably already fully acquainted with the matter by his police, appeared at some balcony of the palace overlooking the street, or perhaps at the head of a flight of steps. After the exchange of polite greetings between himself and the Jews, the procurator came to the point : ‘ What accusation bring you against this man ? ’ The emissaries of the Sanhedrin thought well to pave the way for the sensational denunciation they were about to make. The charge in question was a very serious matter ! Unfavourably impressed by their circumlocutions, Pilate, who no doubt had already learnt that the matter was of a religious character, preferred to have nothing to do with it : ‘ Take Him yourselves, and judge Him according to your Law.’ Did that involve a formal permission to put Jesus to death ? The word death had not been so much as mentioned. Then the Jews showed their hand. ‘ We are not allowed to put any man to death.’ And to prove to Pilate that the matter was really serious and more than a little to do with the sphere of his authority, they said : ‘ We have found this man perverting our nation, forbidding men to pay tribute to Cæsar, and saying that He is the Messiah, that is to say, a king.’[1] They showed their craftiness in thus giving the matter a political complexion, adding touches which were well calculated to over-excite the irascible temper of Pilate.

Jesus is questioned by Pilate (278–279).

Luke xxiii, 3 ; Mark xv, 2–5 ; Matt. xxvii, 11–14 ; John xviii, 33–38.

The procurator therefore went into the Prætorium and, sending for Jesus, questioned Him himself : ‘ Art Thou the

[1] Luke xxiii, 2.

king of the Jews?'[1] In the mouth of the Roman official this was to accuse Jesus of rebellion. Jesus could not give an affirmative answer in that sense. There is an Arab proverb which says that the question is the mother of the answer. Therefore, in order to learn what was the charge against Him, Jesus asked Pilate whether he was speaking on his own initiative or merely repeating something the Jews have alleged. This was not exceeding the rights of defence in any way, but we may well imagine that such a question was in no way palatable to Pilate, obliged to admit that he accepted a charge which he did not even understand. He evades the difficulty by a scornful question: 'Am I a Jew? Thy own nation and the chief priests have delivered Thee up to me. What hast Thou done?' This is exactly the method of a magistrate investigating a case in which the charges are overwhelming. In order to elicit a definite confession it is taken for granted that there is undoubtedly guilt of some sort.

But Jesus refused to go beyond the charge formulated against Him. He has never put Himself forward as king in a political sense; had He done so He could surely have relied on His adherents drawing the sword in His defence. Pilate can see for himself that this is not the case. Therefore His kingdom is not a kingdom of this world. Pilate, surprised and embarrassed by this distinction of kingdoms and having little familiarity with spiritual ideas, adheres to his own point of view: 'Thou art a king then, all the same?' Jesus admitted that, in the sense He has just indicated: 'Thou hast said it. I am a king,'[2] and He proceeded to make His meaning clear. He had come into the world to bear witness to the truth; that is to say, His first object was to reign over men's minds, and all those who looked for the truth listened to Him. Pilate was a man of somewhat limited mental capacity and, like many better men than himself, had seen no reason why he should give his name to some philosophical sect or other; he professed contempt for lofty speculations, a contempt shared by many practical men who none the less make excellent officials. 'What is truth?' he asked. Whatever it might be, it was something

[1] Cf. John xviii, 33, where nothing has been said to give rise to Pilate's question. But John bases himself on the accusations given in the narrative of Luke.

[2] All three Synoptists relate this admission of Jesus: 'Art Thou the king of the Jews? Thou hast said it.'

which he thought did not concern him. From that moment, however, his common sense told him that there was nothing to be afraid of in what Jesus had done, so far as the interests of Rome were concerned. He might very well have upset the public order, but it was merely one of those religious squabbles that excited Jewish passions so strongly. And indeed the clamour outside the palace was even now growing louder and could be heard within. After His admission Jesus remained silent. Pilate would have liked, if only out of curiosity, to hear what He had to say in reply. He suspected that behind the matter there lay a Jewish intrigue, meant for the purpose of leading him into some trap so that he might be denounced to Rome. He wondered whether they were all of one mind about Jesus. What did Herod Antipas, and the other Jewish princes who had denounced him to Rome over the golden shields, think of all this?[1]

Jesus before Herod (280).

Luke xxiii, 4–12.

Pilate was therefore left in a state of indecision. The first thing he ought to have done, now that he had the evidence, was to declare in the name of Rome that he did not find Jesus guilty; His claim to royal dignity was of serious consequence to no one but Himself, absorbed as He was in His phantasy of truth; there was no law which forbade philosophers from looking on themselves as kings over the minds of men. He again went out to the Jews and said: 'There is no case against this man for me to try.'[2] Being thus compelled to make some accusation that should not be too evidently remote from the truth, the Jews vigorously insisted: 'He stirreth up the people, teaching throughout Judæa, from Galilee where He began even as far as this place.' This accusation concerning His teaching sounded plausible. Jesus was setting up then as a teacher of truth! But was He indeed a Galilæan? This was the first Pilate had heard

[1] Schürer is of opinion that this affair of the shields did not occur until after the death of Sejanus (A.D. 34), who was hostile to the Jews; but this reason is not decisive. If it was not the opening move in the contest between Pilate and the Jews it may have been the latter's reply to the check he had given them in the affair of the standards, which took place at the beginning of his administration.

[2] According to both John and Luke.

about that. He therefore ascertained that it was true, and learning that Jesus was under the jurisdiction of Herod who was himself at Jerusalem for the Pasch, decided to refer the whole matter to him.

This episode, related by Luke alone, has been the object of much attack by the critics. They point out that Luke himself relates that Pilate had worried little about slaughtering Galilæans in the very Temple. But we may well argue that this was doubtless a case in which the culprits were caught red-handed in a riot which he wished to suppress on the spot. And was that not the very reason why Pilate and Herod had become enemies? Luke here relates the fact of their enmity without giving the cause: his readers were in a position to guess it without much difficulty.[1] We can imagine that Herod did not fail to complain to Rome after the massacre. Pilate, therefore, was not sorry to have an opportunity of showing that he did not disregard Herod's authority when there was occasion for its exercise; at the same time he was ridding himself of a business in which he felt somewhat lost. There is a certain amount of guesswork in the above reasoning, but it is at any rate based on passages of weight, either in Luke or in Philo,[2] who shows what influence the Herodian princes possessed at the court of Tiberius. Before laying himself open to a denunciation for showing too much leniency, Pilate desired to forestall a denunciation against his severity.

Herod was exceedingly gratified by this mark of attention. He had heard about Jesus for a long time. After his violent treatment of the Baptist he no longer dared to brave discontent on the part of public opinion, and had thought it best to remove Jesus by cunning instead of putting Him in prison. Now Pilate was giving him the opportunity of meeting Jesus and of getting Him to work a miracle as a means of escape. Accordingly he questioned Him about the charges urged against Him by His accusers who were so ruthlessly set upon bringing Him to ruin. Jesus regarded Herod as a fox,[3] a cunning but vile animal. He refused to answer him. Knowing Pilate's opinion of Jesus, Herod could but share it: the prisoner was simply suffering from

[1] Similarly he mentions the mission of Jesus in Judæa, giving many episodes of it without saying explicitly where they occurred.

[2] *Legatio ad Caium* quoted above.

[3] Luke xiii, 32; p. 55, above.

hallucinations and well-nigh mad. The guards who had brought Him from Pilate echoed this opinion or even expressed it in stronger terms. They made a joke of pretending to humour what they considered the illusion of a poor wretch, clothing Him in a brilliantly coloured garment. It was in this garb that He was sent back by Herod to Pilate. Herod cared little about such foolish proceedings; but he was too shrewd to make enemies of the leaders of the Jews. Moreover Rome might have let him know that he had come to Jerusalem as a pilgrim, not to act as judge. All the same he felt obliged to Pilate for the attention he had showed him, and the old quarrel was made up. Coming after the massacre of the Galilæans, the incident served as a kind of apology.

Barabbas (281–282).

Luke xxiii, 13–23; Mark xv, 6–14; Matt. xxvii, 15–23; John xviii, 39–40.

Pilate was left just where he was before. Obstinacy was a dominant trait of his character, such as it is depicted for us by the story of his relations with the Jews; and that is why critics protest against the hesitancy which the gospel narrative attributes to him. Actually, however, Pilate did not at first show lack of decision. The life of an individual Jew mattered little to him, and he had still less regard for their prejudices. In proportion as the Jews persist in trying to force his hand, he persists in showing leniency. He is determined to tell them exactly what he thinks of them: 'You have brought me this man as a revolutionary. I have examined Him in your presence and find Him guilty of none of the deeds of which you accuse Him. Nor has Herod come to any other conclusion, for he has just sent Him back to me. On what ground, then, can He be said to deserve death?'

A strange incident now ensued. During the time that Jesus had been with Herod, the city had been busy over the preparations for the Paschal feast. Word had gone round that negotiations were in process between the governor and the leaders of the people. This provided a good opportunity for reminding Pilate of an old custom which had the force of law, namely, that on the feast day it was usual for the governor to set a prisoner free. The choice in the matter belonged to the people themselves. They therefore set about the work of petitioning for this favour. In this they were acting as unconscious agents. Whose pardon were they to ask for? At present they did not know; they would see when they were on the spot. The main object in question was to secure the exercise of their right and make Pilate's severity bend to their will. Efforts have been made to stamp this account as yet another popular legend which has found place in the gospels. It is, however, certain that among the Greeks and Romans it was the custom to release prisoners at certain festivals.[1] An Egyptian papyrus dating from A.D. 86 to 88 shows us the prefect of Egypt, a greater personage than Pilate, on the point of condemning a certain Phibion to be scourged; but instead he says: 'I grant your pardon to the multitude.'[2] The Jerusalem crowd also was about to ask for a pardon, and they grouped themselves before the governor's palace. At the first shout of 'Pardon! Liberty!' Pilate seized the opportunity of bringing this painful business to an end in accordance with his own desires. He therefore called out to them: 'Will you that I release to you the king of the Jews?'[3] It was a clumsy way of wording his question; once again he showed himself more tactless than cruel in his dealings with the Jews. He imagined that the people would be glad to free a man who had sacrificed himself for the cause of independence, and his reasoning was sound; but he made the mistake of calling Jesus the king of the Jews, as though the people had already acknowledged Him as such and consequently had suffered defeat in His person, thus being brought to disgrace by His pitiful failure.

Moreover, the high priests and the doctors of the Law were present to parry this stroke of Pilate with another suggestion. Barabbas, a man taken in the very act of sedition, there was the hero of national independence. According to the indictment brought against him, he was a murderer; but had not the murder been done in a good cause? He was the man for the people, a resolute fellow, rather than that dreamer. The people cried out the name of their man: 'Barabbas!' It was clear to Pilate that the hand of the chief

[1] Cf. Livy, v, 13; Athenæus, xiv, 45.
[2] Cf. *Papiri Greco-egizii*, No. 61.
[3] Both Mark xv, 9 and John xviii, 39.

priests was in this, moved by their jealousy of Jesus' influence. With insistence, therefore, he demanded of the people : 'Do you really want Barabbas[1] or Jesus, who is called the Messiah ?' The crowd, more determined than ever when they saw him ill-disposed towards their choice, cried again : 'Barabbas !' And once again Pilate unconsciously exasperates them : 'Then what is to be done with Him whom you say is king of the Jews ?' No, He is not their king and never has been, and they will not have Him. If He has made claim to be king, then Pilate knows very well what to do with Him. Had not Varus, the governor of Syria, a few years before crucified two thousand Jews for rebellion ?[2] Let Jesus be crucified !

The scourging (283).

Mark xv, 15 ; Matt. xxvii, 26 ; John xix, 1.

But Pilate refused to change his mind : Jesus had not deserved death. However He was causing enough trouble, thought the governor, to merit being scourged with rods. If he granted this concession to Jesus' accusers, perhaps they would rest content with that. This was as far as his feelings of humanity would carry him, and he therefore handed Jesus over to the soldiers to be scourged.

No one seeks to deny the fact of this scourging. It was the normal procedure after death sentence had been delivered, and preceded the crucifixion of the condemned man. That is the order followed by St. Mark and St. Matthew in relating the fact of the scourging ; but St. John puts it earlier, and he is supported in this by the words of St. Luke : 'I will chastise Him therefore and release Him.'[3] Moreover, it is certain also that scourging was sometimes inflicted under the Romans by way of a punishment less severe than the death penalty, as a good means also of persuading fanatics to hold their tongues. This was the case with the individual who had predicted disaster at Jerusalem, whom the procurator Albinus had beaten with rods until his bones were exposed, though the man could not be persuaded even

[1] According to an ancient reading of Matthew xxvii, 16–17, the first name of Barabbas was Jesus : he was Jesus, the son of Abbas. If this be true it provides a coincidence which gives more emphasis to the choice laid before the crowd by Pilate : Jesus the son of Abbas or Jesus called the Messiah.

[2] Josephus, *Antiquities* XVII, x, 10.

[3] Luke xxiii, 16.

then to say anything about himself and what was his purpose. He was at last released as being completely mad.[1] Pilate may have thought that if Jesus still remained firm after this cruel punishment, it would be generally agreed that He should be released as a man of feeble mind. Perhaps, however, He would beg for pardon, and then Pilate would consider what was to be done.

The administration of the scourging was part of the soldiers' duty. It was a cruel and degrading punishment.[2] The whip, usually made of small iron chains ending in metal balls or points, tore out strips of flesh. The scourge made of thongs, to which were attached small bones, was hardly less terrible. The victim was tied to a post, and his blood would stream down to the ground as the scourge cut the skin. We mentioned above the case of the man who was scourged to the very bone. In the punishment of Jesus the soldiers would amuse themselves to their hearts' content in beating this Jew who posed as a king, and our adorable Saviour thus expiated our sins without complaint, particularly our sins of the flesh, as many of the saints have thought. When it was judged that the prisoner could bear no more, the soldiers indulged in a game of mockery.

The crowning with thorns (284).

Mark xv, 16–19 ; Matt. xxvii, 27–30 ; John xix, 2–3.

Jesus had been stripped of His garments and now, since He thought Himself a king, He was wrapped in a soldier's red chlamys or short mantle, which was made to serve as a purple robe. From a bundle of thorns gathered there to make the fire blaze they wove Him a crown. In His hand was placed a reed by way of sceptre. Kneeling before Him with ribald laughter the soldiers hailed Him as king of the Jews, while they struck Him on the head with the reed. The nature of the homage they paid Him was clearly demonstrated by the blows and spittle with which it was accompanied.

Some years later, when King Agrippa had gained favour with the emperor Caligula, who had made him king in place of Antipas, the populace of Alexandria laid hold of a poor madman named Carabas who was in the habit of running

[1] Josephus, *War*, VI, v, 3. [2] Acts xxii, 24–25.

naked through the streets of the city, and forced him to play the part of a Jewish king. He was taken to the gymnasium and set on a sort of throne, where he was crowned with an old basket full of holes, robed in a dirty mat, and given a roll of papyrus picked up in the street to hold in his hand as a sceptre. Then they held a comedy, treating Carabas as though he were king, calling him by the Syriac title of *Marin*, which means Lord, in order to deride Agrippa.[1] But the crowd does not seem to have handled the poor wretch very roughly; after all he was merely a sort of effigy of Agrippa. Jesus, however, claimed to be the real king of the Jews. What a stroke of good luck to have Him at their mercy, the mercy of these Roman soldiers who scorned all kings and held the Jews in contempt!

Jesus is condemned to death by Pilate (285–286).

Luke xxiii, 24–25; Mark xv, 15, 20; Matt. xxvii, 19, 24–26; John xix, 4–16.

Pilate had given orders that Jesus should be scourged. He did not concern himself about his soldiers' amusements; there were other things for him to attend to. But when he beheld the deplorable spectacle of this mock king in the courtyard of the Prætorium, it occurred to him that now the Jews might be led to the same conclusion as himself, namely, that whatever disturbance had been caused by this wretched man, it had been sufficiently punished. Therefore he went out to tell them: 'Behold I am bringing Him forth unto you that you may see for yourselves that there is no reason to condemn Him to death.' Then he ordered that Jesus should be brought out to him, wearing the crown of thorns and the purple cloak. 'Behold the man!' he said. It would have been very simple-minded on his part to have expected the Jews to feel sincere compassion for Jesus. But at any rate he wished them to see that there was nothing to be feared from a man in that condition. Could they even dream of letting their fury still vent itself on these poor tatters of humanity? Could they ask such a thing of him, a magistrate of Rome? He forgot that the chief priests saw but one thing in this sight: that Jesus had just been made mockery of as king of their own nation, and their anger

[1] Philo, *In Flaccum*, edition of Cohn and Reiter, vi, p. 127; Mangey II, 522.

increased at the sight of a spectacle which wounded their national pride. Therefore, as Jesus had already suffered the scourging which was a preliminary to execution, it only remained, as far as they were concerned, to crucify Him. Hence they raised the cry : ' Crucify ! Crucify ! '

Do what he might, Pilate came up against the unfeeling heart of this people. Let them then undertake the odious work of crucifying their king themselves. He would get some satisfaction out of reporting the matter to Rome if they dared to take his proposal seriously. But the Jews had no intention of doing such a thing. Pilate alone had authority to condemn to death, and in the conflict sprung up between them and the procurator, they were determined to keep on the right side of the law. They had no right to execute their victim, but it was Pilate's duty to see that their religion was not treated with contempt by a rebel. Seeing that he was unmoved by their charge against Jesus of being a revolutionary agitator, they at last disclosed their real complaint against Him. In matters concerning their religion, they alone were competent to judge right and wrong ; it was Pilate's duty merely to record their decision. ' We have a law '—the Mosaic Law which the Romans professed to regard with all respect—' and according to that law He ought to die because He made Himself the Son of God.'

We are obliged to interrupt this painful dialogue in order to remark upon the concealed but complete harmony that here exists between St. John and the Synoptists. The former has omitted to relate the appearance of Jesus before the Sanhedrin in the morning, and the delivery of the death sentence which followed that session. But all that is implied in his narrative at this point, where he gives the expression ' Son of God ' the full meaning it bears in his gospel : Jesus had made Himself the equal of God. More than once St. John narrates how the leaders of the Jews had tried to have Jesus apprehended and stoned on the spot, under the excitement of popular religious fanaticism such as would have provided an excuse for the murder. All their efforts had failed because it was appointed that He should die upon the cross. But now they had Him in their power under a charge of blasphemy, and this time they would not let Him escape.

Yet the situation produced was a complicated one ; Pilate, a representative of a religion which detested the

Jewish religion without understanding it, was rather frightened than persuaded against his former opinion by the name Son of God. A Son of God, was He? There were many such in the pagan religions: Bacchus, for example, whom Pentheus king of Thebes refused to acknowledge as such, in consequence of which the divine son took a cunning and cruel revenge in bringing about the death of Pentheus by the hand of his own mother. And so little was known about these Oriental divinities who were said to be more ferocious than those of Greece or Rome. Jesus had been brought into the palace again and Pilate went to Him once more. The Roman governor had shown no interest in the disputes of philosophers, but it by no means follows that he was free from superstition. Ashamed to disclose his secret uneasiness, he put an apparently insignificant question; one, however, which he ought to have put from the beginning; the question now assumed the nature of an enquiry about the world of the gods: 'Whence art Thou?' Jesus gave him no reply. The magistrate of Rome was roused by this and began to speak the language of the law: 'Speakest Thou not to me? Knowest Thou not that I have power to release Thee and I have power to crucify Thee?' But Jesus knew not only that but also what was the source of this power. In a word, Pilate held it, not from the Emperor as representative of the people of Rome, an august authority indeed, but he held it from a far higher power, namely, from heaven. Although he is invested with this delegated power and led on by others to exercise it, yet he is not so guilty as the man who had betrayed Jesus after all the confidence and friendship Jesus had shown him.

That was the last word Jesus gave to Pilate, and by it He proved that He was full of pity for the man's weakness of character. But this heavenly power of which Jesus had spoken, and which corresponded with the heavenly kingship He had claimed as His own; this remarkable resolution on the part of a prisoner to speak only of supernatural things; this calmness with which He rose superior to persons and circumstances, insults and sufferings, as a man quite certain of his hour; all this alarmed the mind of Pilate and made him desirous of releasing a prisoner of so rare a character. The Jews became aware of this and they shot their last bolt, one certain to have effect at a time like this when Tiberius gave every encouragement to informers:

'If thou release this man, thou art not Cæsar's friend: for whosoever maketh himself king declareth himself against Cæsar.' There may have been something divine about Jesus to Pilate's way of thinking; but he was more certain of the divinity of Cæsar, who was a god still more to be feared, and to be satisfied at whatever the cost. He gave way, therefore, and gave orders for his judgement seat to be brought out that he might pronounce sentence of death. This judgement seat was in the form of a platform on which was placed the *sella curulis* or magistrate's chair, the token of Roman majesty giving its decisions. It was set up on the pavement of one of the outer courts, called the Paved Court or *Lithostrotos* in Greek, on account of the great slabs of stone with which the pavement was made.[1] In the native language of Jerusalem it went by the name of *Gabbatha*, which probably signifies a level place.

Hardly was Pilate seated when one of his household slaves approached and whispered in his ear; it was a message from his wife, whom Christian tradition knows by the name of Procula, bidding him: 'Have thou nothing to do with that just man, for I have suffered many things this day in a dream because of Him.' It was a piece of advice not to be despised by a Roman. Had Cæsar listened to Calpurnia on the morning of the Ides of March, he would not have exposed himself to the daggers of the conspirators. Consequently, here on the very point of condemning the just man Pilate hesitated and looked for a way of escape; and when Jesus was brought in Pilate said to the Jews, again without suspicion that he was offering them an affront: 'Behold your king!' The only reply is an uproar: 'Away with Him! Take Him away! Crucify Him!' Unconsciously, or out of defiance, he made the matter worse by asking: 'Shall I crucify your king?' The answer was: 'We have no king but Cæsar'; and Cæsar was a king who made himself feared. Pilate realized that there was nothing more to be said. As St. Matthew observes, the man was doing no good; rather the tumult was growing worse and assuming the formidable character of a riot. Ordering water to be brought, the governor washed his hands before the crowd

[1] Josephus (*War*, VI, i, 8) uses the same word for the pavement of great flagstones in the Temple court near the Antonia. We do not go so far as to say that he intends it as a proper name, but at any rate we have here evidence of the fact that the entrances to the Antonia are described in a similar way by both Josephus and the Gospels (cf. *Jérusalem*, II, p. 563).

in a gesture that was well understood by the Jews,[1] signifying : 'I am innocent of this blood. Look you to it.' But an act of cowardice does not remove responsibility already incurred ; moreover, it appeases nobody. It made no difference whether he took the condemnation on his own shoulders or not. The crowd shouted out, however : 'His blood be upon us and upon our children.' Thus Israel had not only rejected her Messiah and betrayed Him, but, proud as she was of the claim that she obeyed none but God, she now made preference of Cæsar's yoke. In these words she pronounced the sentence of her own condemnation. The day was the day of the preparation of the Pasch. It was about six hours after sunrise, twelve o'clock noon.

Pilate finally commanded Barabbas to be set free and abandoned Jesus to the hatred of the Jews, by which we mean that he judicially condemned Him to death, leaving the work of His execution to be carried out by the Roman soldiery.

The way of the cross (287).

Luke xxiii, 26–33 ; Mark xv, 20–21 ; Matt. xxvii, 31–32 ; John xix, 16–17.

Jesus had already put on His own garments before hearing His death sentence. The manner of death for a person of low degree, classed on the same level as slaves, was the lingering death of the cross, and the condemned man had to carry the instrument of his execution. Such was the rule, and it is in fact what St. John tells us. We learn, however, from the Synoptists that the soldiers pressed a certain Simon of Cyrene into service to carry the cross for Jesus, very soon perceiving that His extreme weakness made Him incapable of bearing the weight of so heavy a burden. Simon was returning from the fields, for it was possible to work up to midday on that day. He was a man well known among the early Christians, for his two sons, Alexander and Rufus, who are mentioned by St. Mark, later joined the number of the faithful.

Now that they were appeased by Pilate's surrender, the bulk of the people had gone to attend to the chief work of that day, the preparation of the Pasch. But Jesus was

[1] Cf. Deuteronomy xxi, 6 f.

accompanied by a number of the Jews who were animated with hostility towards Him—we shall find them later at the foot of the cross—and who gratified their spite by sarcasms such as the crowd usually poured out upon those who were about to die. There were women, too, though these beat their breasts and mourned. They numbered not only the devoted women of Galilee, but also women of Jerusalem who were moved by that compassion which does so much credit to their sex, or perhaps by some vague sense of the enormity of the crime that was being committed. There seems, to be some evidence that there existed among the Jews a sort of confraternity of women, who made it their work to ease the last moments of condemned criminals,[1] especially as at that time so many of these were men who had been victims of their national zeal. Touched by their praiseworthy emotion, Jesus reveals to these daughters of Jerusalem the disasters that threaten their city, themselves, and their children. In this we have a revelation of His tenderness of heart, which renders compassion for compassion. Thus warned, these mothers who now manifest their goodness of heart would be able to guide their children in the way that would enable them to escape the divine punishments which were certain to overtake the guilty: 'Then shall they begin to say to the mountains: Fall upon us! and to the hills: Hide us!' If the justice of God is let loose upon a victim that is innocent—as though one should use green wood for making up the fire—what shall it be with the guilty—the dry wood that is the natural fuel for the flames?

Not Jesus alone, but two evil-doers also were dragged to execution by the soldiers. The procession made its way slowly, retarded by the weight of the crosses, the obstacles met with in the streets, the eager little children who slipped into the ranks so as to get first, and the hustling of the crowd. There was not far to go. As soon as the gate of the city was passed, they found themselves in a place which went by the name of Golgotha or the Skull. An old Christian tradition, not taken very seriously by St. Jerome, saw in this name an allusion to the belief that Adam's skull was buried there, thus making the blood of our Redeemer flow upon our first parent, the one guilty of the first sin. The name has come down to our own days under the Arabic

[1] Cf. Talmud of Babylon, *Sanhedrin*, 43a.

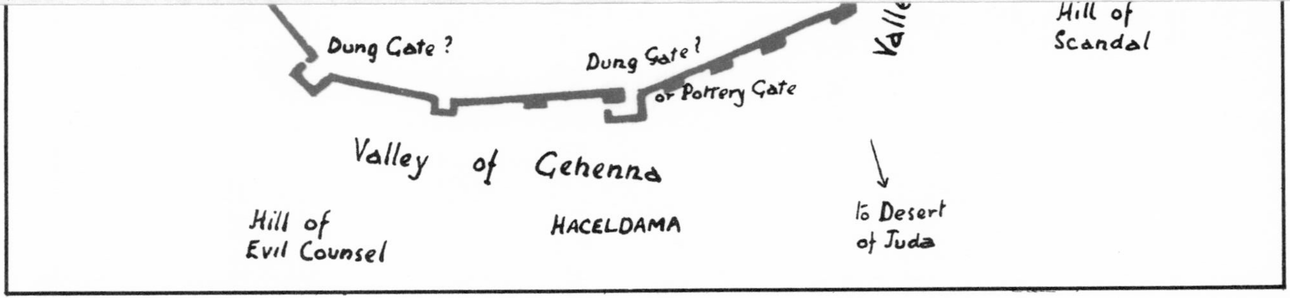
Dung Gate ?
Dung Gate ?
or Pottery Gate
Hill of
Scandal
Valley of Gehenna
Hill of
Evil Counsel
HACELDAMA
To Desert
of Juda

word *ras*, a 'head.'[1] The place indicated is a slight eminence which was levelled somewhat in order to build the church of the Holy Sepulchre. At the time of the crucifixion, however, it stood out more prominently, being separated from the city by the wall and ditch.

The crucifixion. Jesus upon the cross (288–299).

Luke xxiii, 33–46a ; Mark xv, 22–36 ; Matt. xxvii, 33–49 ; John xix, 17–30a.

It was the Roman custom to erect the crosses of execution at the city gates, so that the horrible spectacle of the dying victim might be displayed before the eyes of all who went in and out, or who walked by that way. Hence it was in such a place that the procession of the three condemned men was halted.

The sight of a crucifix is always a pitiful one. But Christian artists have clothed it with a kind of dignity : Christ stands upright on a solid ledge ; His arms extended, but quite symmetrically ; the thorns of His crown are woven with regularity ; His head remains straight against the background of a perfectly made cross. In early days, however, the faithful had a horror of seeing the image of Christ on the cross, for they had seen with their own eyes the sight of poor bodies, stark naked, fastened to a rough stake surmounted by a crossbar in the shape of a T ; their hands and feet nailed to the wood, the body sinking under its own weight, the head swinging from side to side ; dogs drawn by the scent of the blood devouring the feet, while vultures circled overhead above the field of slaughter ;[2] the victims exhausted by torment, burning with thirst, and calling for death with inarticulate cries. It was the mode of execution for slaves and bandits. It was the death that Jesus had suffered. In accordance with a practice that was intended as a mark of compassion, one last touch of humanity in the midst of this barbarity, He was offered wine spiced with myrrh or frankincense. The mixture was believed to

[1] Père Vincent has drawn attention to this. Cf. *Jérusalem*, II, pp. 93 ff., where he establishes the authenticity of Calvary and the Holy Sepulchre. Concerning the fanciful Gordon's Tomb see the same author's article in the *Revue Biblique*, 1925, pp. 401–431.

[2] 2 Kings xxi, 10 ff.

intoxicate and produce unconsciousness.[1] Jesus moistened His lips but refused to drink: it was not that chalice which He had promised His Father to drink. They crucified Him, therefore, first nailing His hands to the cross-bar which was then erected on the upright stake, without any scruples about roughly handling His pain-stricken body. The Fathers of the Church do not appear to have been shocked by the thought of Christ's being crucified in complete nudity. But as the Jews spared even executed criminals from such a disgrace, it may be presumed that the Romans in Palestine respected Jewish custom in this regard.

When the soldiers began to crucify Jesus it was not much later than midday.[2] After Him the two robbers were crucified as well, one on His right hand, the other on the left. It was a final jeer at the King of the Jews: highway robbers in the places of honour beside Him! Isaias had foretold that He was to be numbered among the wicked,[3] but no one could have dreamed that his prophecy would have been fulfilled so literally. Nothing shows better than this the contempt in which Jesus was held. On his side Pilate was planning a piece of irony, but against the Jews rather than against the just man whom he had condemned. He had asked them very soberly whether they desired their king to be crucified. They had no king but Cæsar. But for all that they sought the death of their fellow-countryman. Therefore, when Pilate was asked what crime should be assigned as the reason for the punishment inflicted on Jesus, he ordered that this should be written: 'This is Jesus of Nazareth, the King of the Jews.' A placard was made bearing this inscription and fastened above Christ's head. It was written in three languages: in Hebrew, the language of the country; in Latin, the language of the government; in Greek, the language of the educated classes. The Jews had more interest than others in reading the notice which attracted all eyes, the place being so near to the city. The high priests felt the thrust and carried their complaint about the insult before Pilate: he should not have written 'the King of the Jews,' but that the wretched man had said

[1] Cf. Talmud of Babylon, *Sanhedrin*, 43a.

[2] According to John xix, 14, which gives about the sixth hour for the condemnation. Mark gives the third hour—9 o'clock in the morning—for the crucifixion. But this indication is approximate, for Mark appears to have divided the time on a three-hourly system (cf. Mark xv, 1, 25, 33).

[3] Isaias liii, 12 quoted by Luke xxiii, 37, but not by Mark xv, 28.

that He was King of the Jews. There was still time to correct the mistake. But the mistake was a deliberate one and Pilate, glad to see that he had touched them on a sensitive spot, replied coldly : 'What I have written, I have written,' as though to say : 'That is my doing.'

The first word Jesus spoke on the cross was a word of forgiveness : 'Father, forgive them, for they know not what they do.' The Jews thought they knew, but they were blinded by pride which lay at the root of their hatred ; therefore, as that blindness was wilful in its cause, they had great need of forgiveness. Jesus grants them His and beseeches for them the forgiveness of His Father as He is raised on the cross, for He came precisely for that cause, namely, to suffer and so win pardon for sinners. Apart from the Jews, the others were more ignorant of what they were doing : for example, the soldiers on duty, who even now were busily engaged in dividing the garments of the condemned, assigned to them by custom. These garments were allowed them for their pains, the only pains that they cared anything about in this affair, for they had to do the work of crucifying the victim. There were four soldiers in the party, and they divided the spoils into four. But the tunic of Jesus was woven from top to bottom without a seam. It seemed a pity to cut it up and therefore they drew lots for it, thus without knowing it fulfilling another prophecy : 'They have parted my garments among them, and for my vesture they have cast lots.'[1] A seamless robe was of some value ; the high priest himself wore one like it. The one worn by Jesus had most probably been woven by the hands of some woman who believed in Jesus, perhaps one of the wealthy Galilæan women who had followed Him ; or it may have been made for Him by His Mother. Ever since the time of St. Cyprian it has been regarded by the faithful as the symbol of the Church, which must remain undivided. Woe to those who stir up schism and rend her apart !

The chalice of redemption was a bitter one for Jesus. His sufferings on the cross were excruciating ; His heart was bruised by the desertion of His disciples, the contempt of the Jewish leaders, and the dull indifference of the people in general. Up to this time, even during this sorrowful mystery, the Father had continued to pour great joy into

[1] Psalm xxi, 19 (in LXX).

the soul of Jesus through the love His Mother showed Him. She was there now, suffering along with Him and so adding to His torture, yet consoling Him in His state of desertion. With her was her 'sister,' perhaps her cousin, who was the mother of James and Joses; also Mary the wife of Cleophas, Mary of Magdala, and finally the beloved disciple.[1] No law forbade the relatives approaching men who were being crucified. Soldiers stood by to guard against a surprise attack or else to prevent too great an uproar, but they drove away neither sightseers, nor enemies, nor friends. Jesus, therefore, seeing His Mother and the disciple whom He loved standing by the foot of the cross, said to His Mother: 'Woman, behold thy son!' The term 'woman' has a gentler sound in the ears of an Oriental than in ours, as we have already remarked;[2] and now that Jesus is parting from His Mother He refrains from calling her by that most sweet name any longer. It is another part of His sacrifice. His design is to confide her to the care of him whom He loves best, and by whom she will be best understood when she speaks of her real Son. Since St. John is still very young, his affection for her will be more full of respect and tenderness than would be the case with a man who was older. He must therefore really regard her as his mother: 'Behold thy mother!' From that hour the disciple took her to his home. What a union was created between them by these words and by the memory of this moment! In the same way all Christians who have become the brethren of Jesus by baptism are Mary's children too. They also have drawn near the cross and have heard that word spoken to themselves: Behold thy mother! They know and find by experience that Mary indeed treats them as her children.

While Jesus was uttering these most touching words in a dying voice, so that they were heard only by the little group of His faithful friends, the soldiers were laughing at the jests thrown at Him by the passers-by; honest folks, perhaps,

[1] Many commentators take John xix, 25 to mean that there were only two women besides the Mother of Jesus. We are of the opinion that there were three, as we expressed in the commentary on St. John. But contrary to what we said there, we here return to the opinion we expressed in the commentary on St. Mark, that is to say, we do not regard the sister of the Mother of Jesus as Salome, but rather as another Mary, the mother of James and Joses (cf. Mark xv, 40). Hegesippus does not give the same father to James, the bishop of Jerusalem, called the brother of the Lord, as to Simeon his successor, who is the son of Cleophas, brother of Joseph, the foster father of Jesus.

[2] Cf. Vol. I, p. 92.

but overawed by the fact that here was someone who had been condemned by the Sanhedrin. Hence they cried, wagging their heads to emphasize the rebuke: 'Ho, there, Thou that destroyest the Temple and in three days buildest it up again, save Thyself by descending from the cross!' Then they continued about their business, callous at the sight of a punishment so well deserved, as they thought, and to which they added their ironical taunts. The chief priests and scribes had more reason to feast their eyes on the spectacle. They came to make sure that their work had been done thoroughly and that Jesus would not undo it. He had worked so many miracles! But no, there He was nailed to the cross, and they joked with one another about this would-be Messiah who had saved others but could not save Himself. That would be the great miracle, if He were to save Himself. Come, then, let the Messiah, the King of Israel, come down from the cross and they would believe in Him! They disliked Pilate calling Him the king of the Jews because he meant it seriously, and also because it might create a false impression; but they knew how to take the expression among themselves. As a last and supreme insult, they jeered at the love of Jesus for His Father: 'He trusted in God. Let Him now deliver Him, if He will have Him! For He said: I am the Son of God.' But of course they knew that God too had forsaken Him, or rather was punishing Him for His blasphemy through their instrumentality and thanks to their zeal; and they were satisfied, nay, self-satisfied. They could go and eat the Pasch with a tranquil conscience, and above all with their minds set at ease; their spiritual ascendancy over the people had nothing more to fear from this innovator.

From a distance, the voices of the two thieves seemed audible, blending with the voices of the Jewish leaders, though less wounding than these, for the thieves were ignorant and merely took their share in the chorus of insults out of an ingrained habit of cursing and blaspheming.[1] One of the poor wretches jested up to his last breath: 'Art Thou not the Messiah?' He had just heard the 'Save Thyself!' and on the lips of the Jewish leaders, too; and

[1] Mark and Matthew say that both thieves blasphemed. Luke gives details collected from a trustworthy source, perhaps the Blessed Virgin's account of the scene, or that of Joanna the wife of Chusa, whom he alone mentions (xxiv, 10).

he adds to it on his own account : 'And save us also with Thee.' But the other thief, less hardened, was reflecting within himself at this moment when he was about to appear before God. He passed judgement on himself : his punishment was well deserved. The same sure instinct of grace made him also see that Jesus was innocent. It may be that in the past he had heard this fellow-victim of his, surrounded by the crowd, speaking of the kingdom of God that it was His work as Messiah to establish. The priests, moreover, had only just acknowledged the miracles of Jesus, who nevertheless all this time kept silent. He must be awaiting His hour which would surely come after the sufferings of which He had also spoken in His teaching. Trying therefore to turn his head, the thief gently murmured : 'Jesus ! Remember me when thou shalt come in the glory of Thy kingdom.' It was a wonderful act of faith that Jesus deigned to enlighten further by turning all the repentant sinner's thoughts to his near approach to God : 'In truth I say to thee, this day thou shalt be with Me in Paradise.' The good thief was a Jew and had surely heard of Paradise. The learned men of the Law used to describe the next world in the terms of an earthly paradise, making it a pleasant place in which souls awaited the final judgement. Jesus was indeed to be with the pardoned thief amongst the just men of the Old Testament in the place called Limbo by Christians. According to the Psalms of Solomon, the saints themselves are the Paradise of God and the trees of life.[1] The good thief, Christ's companion on the cross, was henceforth to be in His safe keeping in the presence of God. Thus in very deed did our Saviour serve others even while He was on the cross.

For three hours thick darkness spread over the land ; the sun was hidden and the air was stifling. Jesus remained silent until the ninth hour, full of suffering. Rejected by the leaders of the people as a blasphemer and handed over to strangers, treated by the Romans as a criminal, spurned by the people, jeered at by a thief, and forsaken by His own friends, there was only one more affliction for His soul to bear, but that was the most cruel of all : abandonment by His Father. We have no choice but to believe that this really took place, for it is related by two evangelists. The fact that they have related it is certainly the strongest

[1] Psalms of Solomon, xix, 3.

proof of their honesty. The enemies of Jesus have just insulted Him concerning His trust in God ; let Him not deceive Himself any longer : God has abandoned Him.

In the ears of the Christian faithful such an insult could not but sound as a blasphemy against Him who was the object of their worship, Jesus Christ, the Son of God. Then why do they admit that the insult was true ? Why make Jesus Himself admit it by His distressful cry : 'My God, My God, why has Thou forsaken Me ?' Was not that as good as to invite readers in all ages to shake their heads with the leaders of Israel as a sign of incredulity ? But they have had the courage to record it without attenuation or explanation of any kind. In this, as in other things, they simply narrated that which they knew. Not only is it a proof of their truthfulness, but it is also the most striking manifestation of the soundness of their motives for believing in Jesus. Although they knew of His cry, yet it had not the power to shake their firmly grounded conviction. There was mystery in it, but they did not allow that to be a reason for rejecting the evidence of His miracles and of the Resurrection.

It remains a mystery for us, too, for we may not assume a kind of double personality in Him even at the moment when His soul was on the point of leaving His body. It is still the Son of God who speaks. Nevertheless, the human voice was uttering the feelings of His humanity, the desolation of His soul which felt as though God was withdrawing His presence. It is a more complete desolation than that He had suffered in Gethsemani, as is proved by the fact that Jesus no longer says 'My Father,' but only 'My God,' '*Eloi, Eloi.*' Like all His other sufferings, this also was to be accepted for our sakes, and the thought of it provides a comfort for great souls in those final trials by which God purifies them. If these words of Jesus could be understood by anyone, it would surely be by them ; but even if they could understand them, they would not always be able to explain them. To St. Paul alone has been given the authority to say something about Jesus that seems even stronger still, and what he says partly explains the cry uttered on the cross. Loaded on His gibbet with all the sins of the world, Jesus became a curse.[1] But in submitting to this He delivered us from the curse by taking it upon

[1] Galatians iii, 13.

Himself; and we see how desolation breaks forth into joy in the concluding verses of the psalm of which the cry upon the cross forms the opening words.[1] The afflictions of the just man, the true Messiah, all find an end in the glory of God. The psalm had spoken the ironical challenge of the Jewish rabbis centuries before they uttered it: 'Let him abandon himself to Jahweh! Let Jahweh deliver Him!'[2] He who was abandoned indeed abandoned Himself; He knew that this was the price He had to pay in order that all the ends of the earth might turn to God and all the families of the nations fall down before His face.[3]

Amongst those present only the doctors of the Law realized that Jesus was quoting a psalm; the rest, more simple folk, hardly heard more than the first words and thought that Jesus was calling on Elias. They regarded it as the final delusion of a mind deranged by torments. Elias, as they and every Jew were aware, would return in order to manifest the Messiah; but he would not look for the Messiah on a cross.

Meanwhile Jesus breathed forth the sigh: 'I thirst.' The soldiers, always more or less thirsty themselves, usually had a vessel containing a mixture of water and vinegar with which they satisfied themselves when they had nothing better to drink. One of them took a sponge, possibly that which served as a stopper for the jar, steeped it in the liquid and held it up to the mouth of Jesus on the end of a javelin. His motive was one of compassion—he could only give what he had to give—and when the bystanders, amused by this apparent appeal to the prophet Elias, tried to stop him, he replied to them: 'Stay! Let us see whether Elias comes to take Him down.'[4] The good fellow dared not show even this kindness without joining in the raillery of the others.

In crying 'I thirst,' Jesus had fulfilled the words of one of the psalms concerning the sufferings of the just man.[5]

[1] Psalm xxi (Hebrew, xxii). The psalm is in Hebrew like all the rest, but Jesus spoke it in Aramaic.

[2] v. 9.

[3] Cf. verse 28. Perhaps Luke and John who were writing for Gentile converts especially, left out the cry of dereliction precisely because it was a quotation from a psalm and had to be understood as such.

[4] This follows the account of St. Mark. St. Matthew has put the matter more clearly but less picturesquely.

[5] Psalm lxviii (in Hebrew lxix), 22.

Now He had drunk the chalice even to the last drop, and He cried: 'All is consummated,' like a good workman who has finished his task. Then He called out in a loud voice: 'Father, into Thy hands I commend My spirit.'

The death of Jesus (300).

Luke xxiii, 46b; Mark xv, 37; Matt. xxvii, 50; John xix, 30b.

When He had shown by this great cry that He freely surrendered His spirit to His Father, Jesus died.

Have mercy upon us, sweetest Jesus, who in Thy mercy hast suffered for our sakes!

After the death of Christ (301).

Luke xxiii, 45, 47–49; Mark xv, 38–41; Matt. xxvii, 51–56.

At Christ's death[1] the veil of the Temple was rent in twain from the top to bottom. According to St. Jerome, this was the curtain veiling the entrance to the sanctuary[2] when the doors of the Temple were open. It was not a door-curtain made of two hangings joining in the middle so as to leave the way open, but a single piece hanging from above. It could be seen torn down the middle, as if to signify that the approach to the Temple was now open to everyone and in consequence that holy things were becoming common. It might have been thought that the rent was caused by one of the violent gusts of wind that scatter the dark siroccos of spring in an instant, had not St. Matthew added that an earthquake split the rocks and thus rent open the tombs hewn out of the cliffs. And in the city itself, after the resurrection of Jesus, many people saw holy persons returned to life from the dead, though they appeared after the manner of ghosts, returning to their tombs again, for nothing more is said of them. The whole incident indeed is left in obscurity.

[1] Luke gives the fact immediately before Christ's death, Mark and Matthew after.

[2] Not the second curtain between the Holy Place and the Holy of Holies (Hebrew ix, 3).

By the cross stood a centurion who had been charged with supervising the execution. The victims usually died slowly, executed as they were in the prime of life, consumed gradually by pain, hunger and thirst, now cursing, now lamenting, then gasping for breath, and so on until the end came. Jesus, however, had died at a moment when, by His words, He proved that He still had complete control of Himself, as though He Himself had chosen the precise moment for yielding up His spirit to God. Amazed at what he had heard whispered round about him concerning this crucified man's claims to be Son of God, the centurion saw in the manner of Jesus' death a proof that these claims had been justified; nor did he hesitate to say: 'Indeed the man was Son of God.'[1] Even amongst the crowd a sudden and complete change had set in, as not infrequently happens with simple folk. It seemed to them now that they were burdened by crime, and they beat their breasts. No longer afraid of being involved in the proceedings against their Master, seeing that the high priests were quite content with the result, the friends of Jesus now drew near, though they still stood at some distance. The holy women had stood with their eyes fixed on Him, pushed into the background no doubt when the jeering leaders of the Jews came to the cross. Perhaps His Mother Mary had been allowed to stand near her Son along with St. John, for she is not included among the women named by St. Mark and St. Matthew, and described as looking on from a distance after our Saviour's death; they are probably the same as the women placed by St. John at the foot of the cross: Mary of Magdala, Mary mother of James the Less and Joses or Joseph, Mary of Cleophas, and finally she whom St. Mark calls Salome, who is doubtless the mother of the sons of Zebedee mentioned by St. Matthew.[2] Along with these women who had followed Jesus and ministered to His wants whilst He was preaching in Galilee were other Galilæan women who had come up to Jerusalem for the Pasch in the same pilgrimage as the Master.[3]

[1] St. Luke relates this as 'Truly this was a just man,' a reflection which appeared to him more natural in a pagan.

[2] We identify Mary mother of James and Joses with the sister of the Blessed Virgin. In addition to Mary of Magdala, a third Mary was known who was the wife of Cleophas. According to Hegesippus (quoted by Eusebius, *Hist. Eccl.*, II, xxiii, 4) she was the mother of Simeon (Simon) and Jude.

[3] Mark xv, 41. Matthew expresses all this in a single phrase.

The intervention of Joseph of Arimathea (302).[1]

Luke xxiii, 50–52 ; Mark xv, 42–45 ; Matt. xxvii, 57–58 ; John xix, 38a.

Jesus died about three o'clock in the afternoon, His friends watching Him die as they mourned. Their affection for Him now led them to take very speedy action, for their love made it of supreme importance that His body should not be left to be thrown into a common grave along with the two thieves. He must at least receive decent burial, and that without delay, for everything had to be finished by sunset. The bodies of those who had been executed were rarely refused to their families, but the governor's permission had still to be obtained. Who would dare to appear before him ? Those who felt courageous enough had little chance of being allowed to do so. The influential people who had sympathised with Jesus had not dared to show their sentiments publicly, even at a time when there was some hope of saving Him. Would they now be willing to brave the resentment of the Jews ? As for Pilate, he was known to be indifferent. However, duties to the dead are so sacred that those who perform them, even for criminals, are not molested. Joseph of Arimathea[2] had been touched by Jesus' words about the Kingdom of God.[3] Entreated, no doubt, by the holy women, he made the attempt. He was a senator, that is, a member of the Sanhedrin, rich and respected, like the other 'elders' of the landed gentry admitted to the great council ; he therefore had access to Pilate and took advantage of it to ask him for Jesus' body. The governor did not inquire whether he was appearing as a relative or as a friend ; it was all the same to him. But so speedy a death surprised him, for it was not usually the case. He sent for the centurion who was just returning from Calvary after witnessing a death that had made so strong an impression on him. Permission was given at once, and the body left at Joseph's disposal. The

[1] The four evangelists, as is very natural, speak of this intervention of Joseph of Arimathea at the point where they speak of the laying of Jesus in the tomb. Here we must anticipate their account and put it before the intervention of the Jews, for Pilate would not have sent to verify the death of Jesus had he already given orders for the victims to be killed. Such a command left no doubt about their death.

[2] Rentis near Lydda.

[3] Luke says he was 'a good and just man.'

favour was given as a courtesy, for Pilate was unwilling to extort money from so important a personage.[1] Having thus secured authority, Joseph hastened to make the necessary arrangements for the burial and began by buying a shroud.

Jesus' side is pierced with a spear (303).

John xix, 31–37

In the meantime the Jews, who in their efforts to bring about the death of Jesus had pretended that their only desire was to make Pilate respect their Law, felt compelled on their side to attend to the observance of one of its commands. Deuteronomy expressly prescribed that the body of a man who had been hanged should be buried the same day[2] so that the holy land of Israel might not be defiled by such a repulsive sight. The Jews made the regulation apply even to the crucified,[3] and were consequently obliged to hasten their death. On that day especially it was necessary to hurry : it was the preparation for the Sabbath, and a Sabbath of great importance, for the Pasch was to be celebrated that very evening and the feast of Unleavened Bread would be on the next day, a Saturday. The practice of breaking the victim's legs to hasten death, known to the Romans but not used by them for the crucified, had probably become the normal practice at Jerusalem. When the Jews appeared before Pilate to ask that it might be done, he had no objection to raise. He knew that Jesus was dead, but there remained the two robbers. Accordingly he gave the order and soldiers made their way to Golgotha furnished with the necessary weapons. There they broke the legs of the first of the robbers, perhaps using other means also to despatch him, then proceeded to the second without paying any attention to Jesus whom they saw to be dead. One of the soldiers, however, in order to make assurance doubly sure and guard against any mistake, pierced the side of Jesus with a thrust of his spear—the left side in order that the test might be the more certain ; and immediately there gushed forth blood and water. If the thrust

[1] Common opinion condemned the demand for money made in such a case as a grave abuse of power (Cicero, *In Verrem*, v, 45 and 51), or as a very severe penalty against the vanquished (Justin, ix, 14, 6).

[2] Deuteronomy xxi, 23.

[3] Josephus, *War*, IV, v, 2.

pierced the heart, this result was apparently not contrary to the laws of nature seeing that Jesus had only just died. It is St. John, present at this incident, who declares it, and he takes to witness Him who knows all truth. The reason why he records it is because he saw two prophecies fulfilled by it. The first is written in the Law concerning the paschal lamb, the type of the Deliverer, and runs as follows: 'You shall not break one bone of it.'[1] The second: 'They shall look on him whom they pierced,' is from the prophet Zacharias,[2] who was present in spirit at some fearful scene of the future: he saw Israel in mourning, acknowledging herself guilty of some great crime and lamenting over one who had been pierced, weeping in the way that men weep over an only son. That prophecy, which the evangelist repeats, is fulfilled anew by long generations of the Christian faithful. Contemplative souls run through the mysteries of Christ's life, but they stop before that wound in His side and, entering it, they penetrate to His very heart. The blood that flowed from it is the symbol of redemption; the water, the symbol of baptism, which derives its power from the blood with which it mingles. In addition, the Fathers of the Church have seen in that wound the opening whence the Church came forth. It is the most sacred of the stigmata that Jesus has kept in His glorified body.

Jesus is laid in the tomb (304).

Luke xxiii, 53–56; Mark xv, 46–47; Matt. xxvii, 59–61; John xix, 38b–42.[3]

Joseph of Arimathea lost no time. As he left Pilate's house he may have met the Jews coming to ask permission to have the executed men killed so that they might be buried anywhere. He had to reach the cross before the soldiers started to carry out their orders, which Pilate had doubtless issued without thought of modifying them so far as Jesus was concerned. Joseph did not want merely to receive the body from the soldiers; he meant to take it away himself,[4]

[1] Exodus xii, 46; Numbers ix, 12. [2] Zacharias xii, 10.

[3] John introduces the subject vaguely by 'after these things,' which applies chiefly to the act of burial rather than Joseph's action. Moreover the four gospels relate in the same way how Jesus was buried. John adds special details regarding Nicodemus.

[4] As John xix, 38–40 also shows.

that is, to take it reverently from the cross. We cannot doubt that the holy women helped him in that duty, Mary yielding to no one the privilege of receiving in her loving arms the body of her Son bruised by the unyielding hardness of the arms of the cross. This is the scene represented by the *Pieta*, which has softened so many hearts. Courage, like fear, is contagious. Nicodemus, the timid inquirer but man of upright heart, had joined Joseph. While Joseph was buying the shroud he had procured a great quantity of myrrh and aloes.[1] After the sacred body stained with the precious blood had been washed clean, it was wrapped in linen bands sprinkled with the mixed spices, which were also scattered freely in the tomb where the body was to be laid.

Joseph of Arimathea gave proofs of great generosity. In the past he had caused a tomb to be hewn out for himself from the rock in his garden which lay very near the outer wall of the city, just below the hill on which the cross of Jesus had been raised. It may be assumed that he set a great value upon this tomb, nor would he have chosen it for his resting-place without first ensuring that his body should never be disturbed and that no one else should be laid near him. But he gave it up to his Master.[2] This tomb hewn out for him was doubtless like those Jewish tombs that are still found in the neighbourhood of Jerusalem: a square chamber in the solid rock, leading into a similar chamber containing a shelf on one side in the rock for the corpse. The two chambers are connected by a low doorway, and the entrance into the outer chamber is another low opening which would be closed by a heavy disc of stone, rolling back in a groove cut along the front of the sepulchre, to permit of entrance.[3] The close proximity of the tomb to Calvary may have caused Joseph to offer it for the burial of his Master, for it was now becoming late. If they took the body farther, there was the risk of being stopped by the Jews and being compelled to bury Jesus hurriedly in any quickly dug grave. But as the tomb was so near at hand and all ready for burial, two hours would be quite enough for taking the body of Jesus down from the cross, embalming it quickly, laying it upon its stone bed wrapped in a

[1] John speaks of 100 pounds weight.
[2] See Matthew and the Gospel of Peter.
[3] Cf. *Jérusalem*, IX, p. 96.

shroud, and rolling the stone before the entrance to the tomb.

At sunset, about six o'clock in the evening, all was finished. As the garden was Joseph's own property he had been left undisturbed. Meanwhile, the holy women had watched all that was done. Mary Magdalen and the other Mary had been sitting facing the sepulchre for some time, whilst the others, taking advantage of the closing light of day, had prepared the spices and perfumed oil. Although so great a quantity of myrrh and aloes had been provided, nevertheless the burial had been but a hasty, and to the minds of the women, a provisional one. They had been unable to go and bring their own contribution to the burial and had the intention of coming back to make up for their lack. All day on the Sabbath, however, they stayed at home so as not to break the Law.

All the evangelists pass over Mary the Mother of Jesus in silence, although she was surely more tenderly concerned than them all for the preservation of her Son's body. But for the faithful this silence is amply filled by the unanimous belief of the Church that she hoped for and expected His resurrection ; nay, she was confident of it. Afflicted in heart like Jesus, she also united herself with Him in the certainty of His hope, though she none the less suffered at being deprived of Him. But now John took her as his mother to the shelter he had at Jerusalem.

The watch over the tomb (305).

Matt. xxvii, 62–66.

On Friday evening the chief enemies of Jesus amongst the priests and the Pharisees had piously eaten the Pasch. They were rid of a dangerous innovator whose blood had really saved the people, like the paschal lamb in the days of old. The suspicions of the Roman authorities had been allayed, God's honour had been satisfied. They slept in peace. But in the morning, when they met one another and exchanged views, they were not quite so easy in their minds on the subject.

Jesus had declared that He would rise again. So far as that went they were quite at ease. They were not the people to be imposed on. But the populace was credulous.

Jesus had followers who were firmly convinced of His miracles and confident in His promises, and recently the resurrection of Lazarus had caused general excitement. People thought they had noticed His disciples assembling again. In their own ranks, Joseph of Arimathea and Nicodemus had gone over to the enemy. The body had been laid in a tomb where it would have been possible for Jesus to keep alive if He had not actually breathed His last. They themselves were quite sure of His death ; but what about the public ? As the tomb was in the garden belonging to Joseph it was outside their supervision. The disciples might get in during the night, steal the body, make away with it, and declare that Jesus was alive, hidden away somewhere, and about to reappear as the Messiah victorious over death as He had foretold. These things must be attended to, but a meeting of the Sanhedrin on the feast day would have made them ridiculous. Some of them went to Pilate, the only man who could get them out of their difficulty by taking the matter on his own shoulders : ' Sir, we have remembered how that impostor said, while he was yet alive : After three days I will rise again. Command therefore that the sepulchre be securely guarded until the third day, lest his disciples steal him away and say to the people : He is risen from the dead. And the last deception would be worse than the first.' For who could refuse to believe in a Messiah risen from the dead ?

Pilate, however, had already had enough of them : after bringing him vague accusations against Jesus, here they were again pestering him with childish tales ! Let them attend to the matter for themselves. He allowed them the few soldiers they demanded in case of need, as before when Jesus was arrested. He therefore answered them coldly : ' You have a guard. Go, take what precautions you think fit.' After the fury they had shown on the day before, he knew that this could be left to them without any doubt. They undertook then to take charge of the matter, posted a guard over the tomb and set seals on the stone which closed the entrance. But the presence of the guard and the seals adds little to our faith in the Resurrection. The supposition proposed by the Jews was puerile, like so many others found in the Talmud, for the disciples would very soon have been called on to produce Him whom they claimed to have risen again. St. Matthew did not regret the opportunity of reminding them of all the precautions they had taken; that is why he has preserved this incident for us. Like many other incidents in his gospel, it was well calculated to keep the Christian faithful on their guard against their former spiritual leaders.

CHAPTER VII

THE RESURRECTION, APPARITIONS, AND ASCENSION OF CHRIST

None of the evangelists has told us a single word of the actual resurrection of Jesus. A great artist, François Rude, has carved Napoleon in stone rising from the bed of his tomb and awakening to glory ; but the gospels have made no attempt to picture how Christ's bruised and wounded body thrilled once more at the touch of His soul. That human body of His, by which the Son of God had subjected Himself to the law of suffering, was now transfigured by glorious beatitude, while the Father's voice declared in His eternal day : 'Thou art My Son, this day have I begotten Thee,' and the Son gave thanks to His Father for having given Him the nations for an inheritance. All these things transcend the power of human words to describe and remain hidden in the secret counsels of God.

This discretion manifested by the evangelists is certainly a strong recommendation of the value of their testimony. They bore witness to what was seen upon earth : first that the tomb was found empty, then that Christ was seen alive with a body that shared the glory of His soul, but truly His own body. They do not tell us where His soul had been in the meantime, while it was separated from that most sacred body. But the first epistle of St. Peter gives us an indication—and Christ's words to the good thief already gave us an inkling of it—when it says that Jesus had gone to preach 'to those spirits that were in prison'.[1] Tradition expresses this as the descent of Christ into hell, meaning by hell the abode of the dead where the just men of old awaited the blessing of redemption. Afterwards His soul rejoined His body, and that body, now animated by a more perfect life than before, was enabled to come forth from the tomb without breaking the seals fixed there by His now powerless enemies, after the manner in which,

[1] 1 Peter iii, 19.

as a child, He had come forth from His Mother's womb.[1] Yet it was only fitting that the empty tomb should not remain closed, and St. Matthew tells us that an angel of the Lord shook the earth and rolled away the stone on which he sat in triumph: 'His countenance was as lightning and his raiment white as snow.' At that sound the guards awoke; at that sight they trembled with terror and, though motionless at first with astonishment, took to flight.

The tomb found empty (306–310).

Luke xxiv, 1–12; Mark xvi, 1–8; Matt. xxviii, 1–8; John xx, 1–10.

The four evangelists relate, each in his own way, how the tomb of Jesus was found empty, to the great astonishment of Christ's friends. St. Matthew and St. Mark are the most alike. St. Luke is usually closer to St. Mark. As for St. John, he goes his own way, but is in agreement with St. Luke concerning the search made by St. Peter. The difficulty of harmonizing the four accounts has been greatly exaggerated. Nothing is more simple provided we do not stick at unimportant details, provided also we pay attention to the way in which each gospel was composed.

The Sabbath had ended at sunset on Saturday evening, and with it the prescribed rest of the day of the Pasch. The feast lasted eight days, but only the first and last were days of rest.[2] However the women devoted to Jesus did not leave the house where they were probably together until the next morning, but they went out very early. According to St. Mark, they were Mary of Magdala, Mary the mother of James, and Salome. Instead of Salome St. Luke names Joanna, of whom he alone has told us;[3] whilst St. Matthew only mentions Mary of Magdala and the other Mary. None of the evangelists intended to mention all the women there; each followed his own information without seeking to be in harmony with the others. But it will be observed that Mary of Magdala always heads the list. St. John speaks only of her.

To restore the harmony of events we need only suppose that Mary Magdalen, the most eager of all the group, went

[1] This comparison is often drawn by the Fathers.
[2] Deuteronomy xvi, 8. [3] Luke viii, 3.

straight to the tomb. The other women, according to St. Luke, would appear to have already had spices and perfumed oil ready since Friday evening. But is it likely that they would have had a store of these in their temporary lodging? Probably St. Luke has, in accordance with his method,[1] dealt at once with all that concerned the burial and thus anticipated what St. Mark has placed after the Sabbath, that is, the purchase of the spices. We may well imagine that the women, who had gone out very early when it was still dark, would have lost a great deal of time in getting the shops opened to buy these spices; and so, according to St. Mark, they did not arrive within sight of the sepulchre until after sunrise. Magdalen must have preceded them, since it was still nearly dark when she discovered that the stone had been taken away, in other words, rolled back so that the tomb was open. The guards had disappeared, but she was not surprised at that, for she did not know they had been posted there. By peeping within she saw that the body had disappeared, but she saw no angel, for Jesus intended to tell her Himself. In her extreme anxiety, dreading the thought of some profanation of the adorable body of Jesus, she immediately set off to run back, going straight to Simon Peter and the disciple whom Jesus loved. Quite beside herself, she did not hesitate to declare: 'They have taken away the Lord out of the sepulchre, and we know not where they have laid Him.' She says 'we,' ascribing her conviction also to the women who had started out with her, but who only at that moment were arriving at the tomb.

These women had gone to the tomb at the bidding of their generous hearts, only realizing the difficulty that lay before them as they went along. They knew nothing about the guards. How were they to get into the tomb to anoint the body of Jesus? The heavy mill-stone which closed the entrance would be an insuperable obstacle, for they were not strong enough to roll it back; even a man would need a crow-bar, but they had no hopes of finding a willing helper at that early hour. Such were the anxious thoughts they exchanged when they arrived and found the stone already rolled away. Their joy was great, for the stone 'was very large.' They therefore entered the tomb and found the body was gone. Deep was their astonishment.

[1] Cf. iii, 20; xxii, 19 f.

So it was not the disciples who had rolled back the stone, for they would not have profaned the body by disturbing the sacred rest of the dead. Then they saw a young man seated on their right upon the stone ledge,[1] clothed in a white garment. They cast their eyes to the ground in fear. The young man said : ' Be not affrighted. You seek Jesus of Nazareth, who was crucified ; He is risen, He is not here. Behold the place where they laid Him. But go and tell His disciples and Peter that He goeth before you into Galilee ; there you shall see Him, as He told you.'[2] According to St. Mark, the holy women fled and said nothing to anybody, so frightened were they. After all, that is quite natural : and they must have feared they would not be believed. No doubt they thought better of it, for St. Luke and St. Matthew relate very briefly that they gave their message to the Apostles ; all that must have taken some time and have been accompanied by certain incidents.

St. Mark, who excels in relating the unexpected, would have given us information about this, had not the thread of his discourse been broken at that very point. When his gospel was finished, whether by him or someone else,[3] the gap was not filled up.

The Apostles might have thought they would be demeaning themselves if they gave credence to women's gossip. However, St. Luke tells us how Peter, who had to be informed first for he was still the leader, ran to the tomb which he found empty : he saw nothing but the linen cloths, a fact which made him think.[4]

This incident St. John has related in detail, for he himself took part in that anxious search, describing himself as the ' other disciple whom Jesus loved.' Peter and he were probably together when Mary of Magdala brought them the disastrous news of the removal of the body. They set out at once, and in their great excitement, they both ran.

[1] According to Matthew, whose account is very brief, it might be thought that the angel who had rolled back the stone was still sitting upon it. In Luke the distinction between the discovery that the tomb was empty and the apparition of the angel is made clearer than in Mark. Luke mentions two men clothed in shining raiment who both speak, which can only mean that one spoke for both.

[2] Mark xvi, 6 f. Luke does not mention this meeting-place, having decided to relate only appearances in Judæa.

[3] Fillion (III, p. 515) says of the end of St. Mark : ' Whoever may have been the author of it.'

[4] Luke does not say that the women spoke to all the Apostles immediately ; that would moreover be against all probability.

John, the younger, ran faster than Peter and therefore reached the sepulchre first. But he did not enter, surely out of respect for his companion. He merely stooped and, looking beyond the little antechamber, saw the linen cloths lying there. Peter, who followed him, entered boldly into the tomb itself. He, too, saw the cloths and saw them more plainly; their presence was proof that the body had not been removed, for it would have been taken clothed as it was. And a still more surprising thing was this: the linen that had been put round the head was not lying untidily among the cloths, but folded up and laid aside by itself. The other disciple entered and saw the same thing. Both of them, startled and thoughtful, were silent and said nothing to one another of what they thought. St. John only says that from this time he believed that Jesus had risen again, and this was surely St. Peter's conviction too. Up to that moment they had not understood from the Scriptures that Christ was to rise again, though He Himself had foretold it to all His Apostles. But the occurrence seemed to them so improbable that only the obvious fact had the power to convince them, and then it dawned upon them that this was the predicted fulfilment of the Messiah's final consecration.[1]

Apparitions of Christ in Judæa (311–316).

Luke xxiv, 13–43; Mark xvi, 9–14; Matt. xxviii, 9–15; John xx, 11–29.

Pious children of the Church entertain no doubt that the newly risen Saviour appeared first of all to His most holy Mother. She had fed Him at her breast, she had guided Him in His childhood's years, she had, so to say, introduced Him to the world at the marriage feast of Cana, and beyond that she hardly appears again in the gospel until she stands at the foot of the cross. But to her alone with Joseph Jesus had devoted the thirty years of His hidden life, and would He not have reserved for her alone also the first moments of His new life that was hidden in God? That was no concern of the gospel's spread through the world, for Mary belongs to an order that transcends this world, an order where as the Mother of Jesus she is associated

[1] Isaiah liii, 11.

with the Father in His paternity of Jesus. Let us therefore submit ourselves to that disposition of things which has been willed by the Holy Ghost, and leave this first appearance of the risen Christ to be meditated on by contemplative souls. We may be sure that it had none of those features, which appeal so much to our emotions, found in Christ's manifestation of Himself to Mary of Magdala.

The two disciples most beloved of the Lord had now returned home, as one of them informs us ; but Mary Magdalen did not go away. She had been the last to leave the cross and the sepulchre ; she was the first to come back to the tomb which she had found empty. Now she could not tear herself away from it, but stayed outside and wept. After a while she determined to look again and, entering the antechamber of the tomb, she stooped and peered into the burial chamber as though she might have gathered some information from this fresh glance. It was then that she saw two angels clothed in white, seated one at the head and the other at the foot of the rock shelf on which the body of Jesus had been laid.[1] They said to her : 'Woman, why weepest thou ?' She failed to recognize that they were angels, for would not angels have known why she was weeping ? She replied, therefore : 'Because they have taken away my Lord, and I know not where they have laid Him.' She does not catch sight of the burial garments, nor does she feel alarm at seeing these strangers ; at present, all is emptiness and nothingness for her. She stoops again, this time in order to leave the tomb and go elsewhere to seek Jesus. Then she perceives Him, but without recognizing Him or even paying attention to Him, for she is thinking only of that beloved body which she desires to anoint with precious oil, and which she fears is now in profane hands. Jesus says to her : 'Woman, why weepest thou ? Whom seekest thou ?' Under the impression that He is the guardian of the place, someone she does not know, perhaps one who does not believe in Jesus, and that He must know what has happened to the body of her Lord and consequently ought to understand her distress, she says to Him : 'If thou hast taken Him hence, tell me where thou hast laid Him and I will take Him away.'

[1] Jewish rock tombs discovered near the Dominican Priory of St. Stephen at Jerusalem have a stone rest for the head on the shelf made to receive the corpse.

It is hardly surprising that she set out to come to the sepulchre without giving a thought to the stone which closed it, for all her thoughts and desires are concentrated on Jesus and on Him alone. She is determined to find Him. Then she hears the voice that goes straight to her heart and takes the veil from her eyes, addressing her by her familiar name in her own mother tongue : 'Miriam !' Straightway she returns the cry : 'Rabbouni ! My Master !' and Magdalen is at the feet of Jesus, still weeping, but now for very joy. Now she is in the place of her desire, where she desires to remain so that she may continue to pour out her love. But this was not the time for the sinner to shed tears on the Saviour's feet. Jesus now belonged to the world above, and although He had not yet ascended to His Father, that would take place before long and it was necessary that He should warn His disciples of the fact. This is apparently the meaning of the words : 'Do not touch Me, for I am not yet ascended to My Father, but go to My brethren and say to them : I ascend to My Father and your Father, to My God and your God.' At that moment Mary Magdalen was consecrated to the office of Apostle of the Apostles. She obeys, like those who tear themselves from converse with their Master in order to go and announce the good tidings, and tells the Apostles : 'I have seen the Lord.' But they would not believe her.[1] We do not even learn that any of the disciples, apart from Peter and John, showed any eagerness to verify what the women had said.

Other witnesses of the empty tomb were the guards, who fled when the stone was rolled away. There were not many of them, three or four at the most, and they were not a little bewildered by their experience. When day broke and the city had resumed its daily life the unfortunate men could no longer escape the duty of reporting the event. It was the priests from whom they had received their commission, and it was to the priests that they went to report. The position was embarrassing. Even if the guards had been lacking in vigilance, there was no question of their sincerity ; it could

[1] John's narrative is summed up in one sentence by Mark (xvi, 9–11), who expressly says that Jesus appeared first to Magdalen from whom He had cast seven devils. We are of opinion that Matthew (xxviii, 9–10) is alluding to the same apparition when he speaks of the women. He uses the same method here as he used in speaking of the demoniacs at Gerasa and the blind men at Jericho, i.e. the Magdalen was one of the group of women, and he summarily applies to them all what was applicable to her.

not be supposed that these Roman soldiers had been spirited out of the way. To punish them would be to provoke protests on their part. What could they have done in face of supernatural intervention? In protesting thus the soldiers would merely have spread abroad the rumour that the Jewish leaders precisely wished to prevent, and such a rumour as would be considered no mere conjecture since it was based on evidence provided by the guards. Therefore it seemed the most prudent course to persuade them to say that they had seen nothing, for the only plausible hypothesis open to adoption by the enemies of Jesus was that His disciples had removed the body. A number of the members of the Sanhedrin came to the decision that money should be given to the guards in order to induce them to spread this story in their own name. If Pilate showed any inclination to hold an enquiry and punish the offenders, it would be possible to pacify him, since he had left the matter in the hands of the priests. But it was obvious that the guards could not affirm that they had seen the disciples taking away the body while they themselves were asleep. They would have to admit that they had fallen asleep and that the disciples had taken advantage of their neglect, for none but the disciples could have done the deed. Such was doubtless the solution adopted by many of the Jews when hard pressed about the disappearance of the body of Christ.

At Jerusalem the second day of the Paschal festival was spent in general rejoicing; in the midst of this the disciples alone remained sorrowful, for they did not dare to believe what they looked on as idle tales of the holy women. Two of them made up their minds to return home to their native village; all their hopes were dashed, for although one or two disciples had tried to verify the women's report and had indeed found the tomb empty, yet the Master Himself they had not seen at all. And what sort of state would the body be in after three days? We know from St. Luke that one of these two was named Cleophas, and that they were making for the village of Emmaus which was about sixty stades (or furlongs) from Jerusalem.[1] Whilst they were

[1] There is nothing new, regarding the problem of Emmaus, to be added to what we wrote in our commentary on St. Luke, where we preferred the reading '160 stades.' In the *Revue Biblique*, 1925, pp. 347 ff., Père Abel has satisfactorily shown the probability that, in the itinerary of the Pilgrim of Bordeaux (written in 333), it is assumed that Jerusalem is 160 stades from Emmaus of the Machabean country. The geographer Ptolemy (second

talking sadly together, discussing the terrible incidents of the past few days, suddenly Jesus appeared alongside them as though He were a traveller wishing to join them since He was walking in the same direction. They did not recognize Him ; even His voice seemed that of a stranger, the more especially as He enquired what was the matter they were discussing. Surely, thought they, He must be the only pilgrim at Jerusalem who had failed to hear of the great event : how Jesus of Nazareth had gained the reputation of a prophet mighty in word and deed, and how the chief priests and magistrates had delivered Him up to be condemned to death, and thus had caused Him to be crucified. It was already the third day since these things had taken place. Moreover, certain women belonging to the group of those who believed in Jesus had found His tomb empty and declared that they had seen a vision of angels who told them that He was alive. But the disciples, who alone could be accepted as serious witnesses, had not seen Him. The two pilgrims apparently know nothing of Christ's appearance to Magdalen, or else they refuse to give any credit to her story.

Jesus allowed them to talk on without saying to them : 'It is I,' preferring to teach them once more that lesson in face of which His friends had always been reluctant to believe. Was it not necessary—and the Scriptures bore witness to it—that the Christ should suffer before entering into His glory? That truth followed especially from the prophecy of Isaias concerning the suffering servant of Jahweh,[1] but the risen Christ deigned to explain to them

century A.D.) makes the distance 150 stades ; but he is relying on a small map, and its editor declares that the stations marked upon it are *parum apte dispositæ*. As a matter of fact, the map gives 18 miles from Lydda to Emmaus, and 20 from Emmaus to Jerusalem ! But in showing that the number of 160 stades is arrived at by going from Jerusalem to Emmaus by Beth-horon, Père Abel has done no more than explain how it is possible that the 60 stades of Luke xxiv, 13 were corrected to 160 at the time when the road through Beth-horon was made, probably during the time of Trajan. He points out that the direct route, which is the ancient route, measures 144 stades. Even before that route was made into a carriage road, no pedestrian would ever have dreamed of going to Emmaus by way of Beth-horon. In St. Luke's time, therefore, the road to Emmaus was not 160 stades but 144. Moreover, the evangelist, who gives the name πόλις even to the smallest villages, would never have used κώμη to describe Emmaus-Nicopolis, one of the fortified cities of Judæa. Our map shows this Emmaus, the Emmaus of the Machabees, to-day called *Amwas* by the Palestinian Arabs. As to the position of the gospel Emmaus, we can make no suggestion that has any appearance of certitude.

[1] Isaias liii.

all the Scriptures which spoke of Him, both in the Law of Moses and in the Prophets. By this time they had approached the village to which the two disciples were directing their steps. Jesus kept straight ahead without seeming to observe that they were preparing to take a path leading off the high road. But the charitable pair, enraptured by this explanation of the Scriptures which had opened up a new world for them, were unwilling so soon to lose such a companion. They must have been walking for more than three hours and the day was drawing in. Why should He not spend the night with them? Naturally they make the most of the lateness of the hour, but at any rate it must have been at least three o'clock in the afternoon. They brought their guest in and the evening meal was prepared, whereupon He reclined with them at the table. Then Jesus, whose striking air of authority they had already perceived, took bread into His hands, uttered a blessing, broke the bread, and gave it to them. Their eyes were opened and they recognized Him; but immediately He vanished. Then they said to one another: 'Was not our heart burning within us whilst He spoke in the way and opened to us the Scripture?'

Many have thought that their hearts were burning most of all because they had eaten bread that had been changed into the Body of the Lord; but there is nothing to show that Christ spoke on this occasion the words of consecration. He was only taking ordinary food with His disciples. Why should such a privilege have been granted to these two who, not being of the Twelve, had not been initiated with them into the deed performed by Jesus during the Last Supper? Had their eyes been opened while they were eating, St. Luke would not have told us that they recognized Jesus at the breaking of bread, and consequently before they began to eat. Hence we are not to take this expression to mean the Eucharist.

It would seem that the two disciples, at first startled and then carried away by joy, did not even stop to finish their meal. They must spread the good news as quickly as possible. It was the beginning of a new gospel. Returning to Jerusalem, they found the eleven Apostles reunited along with a few companions, these also under the influence of strong emotion. Before the two new arrivals had time to speak the apostles explained why they were gathered together at so late an hour: 'The Lord is risen indeed and hath appeared to Simon.' It was right that the chief of the Apostles, Simon Peter, should be the first of the disciples to behold Him who was the Master of them all. St. Paul, too, remarked on this.[1] The fact provided proof that Peter's denials of his Master had been pardoned, his position of pre-eminence maintained and thus consecrated. Cleophas and his companion narrated their experience and told how they had recognized the Lord in the breaking of bread.

The great day of the Resurrection was now drawing to a close, but before it ended Jesus manifested Himself to that faithful group, now all impatience to feast their eyes on Him. Yet when they suddenly saw Him in the midst of them before they had heard any knocking on the doors, which were shut fast for fear of the Jews, their first movement was an emotion of holy fear. They recognized Jesus, but thought that they were seeing a spirit. Then He said to them: 'Why are you troubled? Peace be to you!' at the same time showing them His hands and feet which had been nailed to the cross, and His side pierced with the lance.[2] St. Luke, a physician and a good psychologist, who knew the value of material details, adds that excess of joy disturbed their powers of judgement, doubtless because they were afraid lest they might be deceiving themselves into believing that they were actually seeing what they so much desired to see. But Our Lord knew that better than St. Luke, and He now used the most familiar of the ordinary realities of daily life in order to calm and enlighten their minds. He asked them if they had anything they could give Him to eat, and before their eyes He ate a little broiled fish; not that He was restored to the normal life of growth and decline, but solely in order to prove to them the reality of His resurrection.

Having thus been fully convinced and restored to themselves, they stood awaiting some fresh word from their Master. Then they heard Him say again: 'Peace be to you,' and this time peace was already regained. Following that came the mission, the majestic command that threw

[1] 1 Corinthians xv, 5: 'He appeared to Cephas and then to the Twelve'—the latter being the usual word for the Apostolic council. Luke, who was a historian, wrote 'eleven' because of Judas who had been struck off the list of Apostles, and did not concern himself about the fact that Thomas also was not present.

[2] Luke and John complete each other without any forced harmonization.

the world open to them : 'As the Father hath sent Me, I also send you,' and He breathed upon them, saying : 'Receive ye the Holy Ghost. Whose sins you shall forgive, they are forgiven ; and whose sins you shall retain, they are retained.' This is not the great manifestation of the Spirit that He had promised them on the evening of the Last Supper[1]—that will come in due time ; but now, immediately after His resurrection, He is forming them into a spiritual government. From henceforth they have authority over the souls of men, an authority that will be especially exercised in forgiving their sins, in God's name, of course, or else in refusing to forgive owing to the bad dispositions of the sinner ; for where there is sincere repentance God always forgives. Those who are to be the dispensers of this divine pardon must be the judges of the cases proposed ; hence they must be informed of these cases. Therefore the Church has rightly seen in this action of Christ, and in these memorable words, the institution of the Sacrament of Penance.

Now that He was risen Jesus was no longer to live with His disciples as in former days ; His appearances were to be merely exceptional. Neither St. John, nor on this occasion St. Luke, found any need to say that He vanished after His manifestation on the Sunday of the Resurrection. That great day has become the real Paschal festival for the Christian faithful.

Thomas, one of the Apostles, was not present with the rest that evening. In all probability he had been summoned like the others after Christ's appearance to Peter, but it seems that he thought fit not to come because he did not believe Peter any more than the others had believed the women. He even refused to give credence to the witness of all his brethren.

Our own age is not much disposed to believe in miracles ; not that it is any the less credulous for that, particularly when things are put forward in the name of 'Science.' Renan showed his cleverness in asserting, as though it were a fact, that he had seen for himself in the East that Orientals are always on the watch for the intervention of the super-

[1] This is not said merely because Luke gives another account of the descent of the Holy Ghost at Pentecost, but also because John himself regards that solemn sending of the Spirit as a gift sent by the Son after He has ascended to His Father, sent both to console His friends in His absence and to strengthen them (xiv, 16–26 ; xvi, 7–13).

natural and ready to believe it with eagerness. But the fact is that the Jews were no more of that disposition in the time of Our Lord than they are in our own day. From the sublime heights to which they had relegated God, transcendent in all His majesty, they did not allow Him to interfere with things mundane except to keep the world in its regular course. Thus during the whole life of Jesus the Apostles seemed little susceptible to things of the supernatural order. They had expected, of course, the great manifestation of the Messiah, and it had not come. The Passion, the very notion of which they rejected, had unsettled their confidence ; and as they had failed to understand the words of Jesus on this point, the glorious triumph of the Resurrection had not been looked for. After they had been convinced by the event itself Thomas still refused to yield. The disciples, he thought, had surely been the victims of an hallucination ; all they had seen was a ghost. And when they objected that they had seen the wounds of the Crucified, he replied that in a matter like that it was not enough to see : you must touch. And for that he would trust nobody but himself : 'Except I shall see in His hands the print of the nails, and put my finger into the place of the nails, and put my hand into His side, I will not believe.'

Let us learn to be as gentle with doubters as Christ was. First He left Thomas to his obstinate denials for seven days. The Apostles had seen Christ in Jerusalem and were in no hurry to return to Galilee. They met together again on the eighth day, perhaps for a last prayer together, perhaps to arrange for the journey to Galilee. The doors were shut, when suddenly Jesus stood again in their midst : 'Peace be to you !' Then He said to Thomas : 'Put in thy finger here and see my hands, and bring hither thy hand and put it into my side ; and be not faithless, but believing.' Did Thomas allow Christ to take his hand and guide it to the wound in His side, or did he abandon his logic and surrender to the evidence of his senses ? From him, the unbeliever, came the first explicit act of faith in the divinity of the risen Christ when he cried out : 'My Lord and my God !' To that Jesus replied with a smile of forgiveness : 'Thou believest now that thou hast seen ?' That was not very surprising or praiseworthy. 'Blessed are they that have not seen and have believed !'

This was precisely where Thomas had been at fault. He had gone too far in refusing to believe in his Master's resurrection on the evidence of his brethren whose sincerity he already knew. Jesus pointed this out. Thomas had wanted to see the body of his risen Lord with his own eyes; when once he had seen it, there was no longer any need for him to rely upon others for the truth of the Resurrection. But, as St. Gregory has so well pointed out, when he saw the glorified Humanity he believed in the Divinity of Christ, and that is the real act of faith. That act required then, as it requires now, an assent of the mind to a truth revealed by Christ Himself, and consequently by God. Such an assent was easier for the Apostles, because what Jesus had affirmed was confirmed by His resurrection. Nevertheless, they were more blessed in believing in His Divinity than in enjoying the visible presence of His Humanity. That happy blessedness, which is a foretaste of eternal beatitude, is also the portion of those who believe without having experienced the consolation enjoyed by the Apostles. Moreover, that promise of Christ must never be forgotten, in which He assured us that we shall never lack His presence within us, where He is joined by the Father and the Holy Ghost,[1] a presence which makes faith easier and sweeter.

Before leaving Jerusalem with the Apostles, let us first observe that the gospel accounts of the Resurrection present no difficulty except for those reluctant to accept the very fact of the Resurrection, a reluctance already manifested by Thomas. The testimonies to that fact are in an excellent position: not only do they agree about the fact, but also about all the important points concerning it, though each of the different testimonies shows appreciable differences which prove that the authors of the different accounts each followed his own plan, without any preoccupation about not deviating from the other accounts, and still more without any dependence on them. Here even St. Luke, who is usually so faithful to St. Mark, shows complete independence. The comings and goings during the visits to the empty tomb, the appearances of the risen Christ, all fit easily into a consecutive narrative, given the sole condition that, when St. Matthew mentions the holy women, he attributes to the whole group that which belongs to Mary of Magdala alone. It is unnecessary to point out

[1] John xiv, 23, 17.

that it is not unusual to interpret statements in this way in all histories that are composed from various sources. Nor does such a procedure on the part of the evangelists call for any objection to be raised on the score of the dogma of inspiration ; and, in any case, those who do not accept that dogma have no right to raise such an objection, in order to provide a basis for their doubts concerning the truth of a fact that is thoroughly well attested.

No ; the only real difficulty—and in truth it is one that is plain enough—is this : when the angels appeared to the holy women they appointed a meeting-place in the name of Jesus, where He was to be seen by the disciples. The place was in Galilee ; but He had the intention all the time of meeting them in Jerusalem. Even if we learned this from one and the same author, we still could not absolutely say that he had contradicted himself, for there is no contradiction in the idea that Jesus was to appear in both places ; but we should have to say that the author had composed his narrative in a very clumsy fashion, as though he were ignorant of what he was leading up to. But it is not the case that this apparent contradiction is found in one and the same author, although it would be the case if the whole of St. Mark's last chapter had been written all in one piece. But here the critics render us a signal service by the way in which, with a rational comprehension of the literary problem, they have proved that St. Mark's original work ended at the eighth verse of his last chapter. The remaining verses of that sixteenth chapter were written later by another hand, or by St. Mark's own hand if we prefer that opinion, and contain only a summary of what is related by other evangelists. The summary is connected more or less skilfully with what precedes it and must be accepted as strictly true, since it was written under the inspiration of the Holy Ghost in order to complete a book that is of sacred character ; but, this being the case, it ought not to be judged according to the strict laws that are applied to a work written by a single author, or composed by him as a single whole. Hence, if there be literary inconsistency between the conclusion and the rest of the gospel of St. Mark, that ought not to be used as an argument against the consistency of the facts there narrated.

St. Mark, then, gives Galilee as the place where the disciples are to meet Christ ; and, indeed, the last apparition narrated in his gospel ought to be put on a parallel with the last one mentioned by St. Matthew, which was certainly in Galilee. St. Matthew's narrative is altogether coherent: the meeting-place is appointed for Galilee and the appointment is there kept. St. Luke makes no mention of any appearances in Galilee, and this is quite in conformity with his plan which gives much more importance to Judæa than the accounts of St. Matthew and St. Mark; moreover, he had the intention of making his narrative of the preaching of the Apostles begin from Jerusalem in the second volume he was to write, the Acts of the Apostles. It would have been a remarkable want of literary skill to have related an account of the meeting in Galilee; he therefore abstained from doing so. Will it be maintained by anyone that such an example of literary method is tantamount to a denial that there took place any apparitions in Galilee? St. John mentions apparitions first in Jerusalem and then in Galilee; consequently he also makes no mention of the appointment of a meeting place in Galilee.

The much-repeated objection of the critics, then, comes to this: does it not seem that St. Matthew and St. Mark invent this meeting-place in Galilee appointed by the angels in order to prepare for Christ's appearance there, which is the only appearance they could mention? It was as much as to say: 'You will see Jesus again, do not doubt, in Galilee, where you followed Him and lived with Him.' We will go so far as to ask whether the most scrupulous of historians would be led to call the historicity of a fact into question if he actually met with such a literary manipulation of sources, supposing that Matthew and Mark really did act in the manner described by the objection. It would have been a completely harmless proceeding. All the same, the evangelists had no need of it; it was perfectly natural for the Apostles to go back to Galilee.

Only one other difficulty remains to be solved. Why did not St. Matthew make any mention of the apparitions at Jerusalem? Was it because he knew nothing about them? That is as good as to demand why he said nothing about the long mission of Jesus in Judæa narrated by St. Luke, about Martha and Mary, about Zachæus the publican, and so on. The fact is that as he had put practically the whole of Christ's preaching by the shores of the lake of Galilee, he felt it necessary to put the supernatural termination of his gospel there also. Forming a link between St. Matthew the Galilæan and St. Luke, who was preparing to take the gospel from Jerusalem to Rome, comes St. John, who is fuller than either ; he relates the apparitions at Jerusalem, those which were chiefly necessary to convince and reassure the Apostles, along with one of the apparitions in Galilee, which were intended to link their minds to the memories of the past.

Appearances of Christ in Galilee (317–318).

John xxi, 1–23 ; Matt. xxviii, 16–20 ; Mark xvi, 15–18.

St. John is said to have been totally absorbed by the splendour of the Incarnate Word during the mortal life of Jesus ; yet he is the one who succeeds in bestowing a human charm even to the risen Lord who moves in an atmosphere of glory. Never had the shores of the lake of Galilee seen so pure a light as that. Jesus now possesses His supreme liberty as a being of the heavenly sphere, but at the same time He shows Himself as a father who finds his children once again, a kind master who remembers the fault only to forgive it, a friend who renews the old fishing expeditions on the lake, who reopens the former familiar converse with the assurance that now there is a mutual affection which nothing can henceforth mar. John, whom some have turned into a rival of Peter, crowns him with a halo made of a ray of glory taken from the glory of the risen Christ. The gospel ends as it began, with Simon going fishing, Simon who becomes, as Jesus has foretold, the great fisher of men, the master of preaching, and in addition the supreme shepherd on earth of the sheep whose eternal Shepherd is Christ.

They were on the shores of the lake of Tiberias : Simon, Peter, Thomas, Nathanael, and the two sons of Zebedee.[1] After days of anguish and days of joy they had to resume their ordinary occupations. Christ had given His Apostles power over the souls of men, but He had not yet given them the signal they awaited. They knew that they were to see Him again in Galilee and would not begin until

[1] The ' two others of His disciples,' unnamed in the original gospel text, were John and James, thus indicated by the evangelist in his own obscure fashion ; a gloss, naming them, later crept into the text.

they had seen Him. Simon Peter, therefore, said to the others : 'I go a fishing.' Understanding that the words contained an implied invitation, the others, who were obviously gathered around him, replied : 'We also come with thee.' They set out at night as was customary ; but that night they caught nothing. When morning broke they saw someone on shore standing there as though to buy fish when they reached him, but they did not recognize who it was. He cried out to them : 'Young men, have you any fish to eat ?' All they could reply was a 'No' which betrayed their disappointment. In a confident tone the stranger called out : 'Cast the net on the right side of the boat and you shall find.' Weary as they were, the words seemed a good omen to the unlucky fishermen. They therefore let their net slowly down into the water while they pushed their boat off shore, and when they rowed it back dragging in the long net, the weight of the fish twisting in the meshes was so great that they could not pull the net up. At this, a flood of memories burst upon the mind of the disciple whom Jesus loved ; it was after this fashion that the Master had manifested His power in those early days, before He had called them to follow Him once and for all. It could be none but He that was again working this miracle, and turning, John said to Peter : 'It is the Lord !'

Although Peter had been slower to understand, he was quicker to act. Being naked, that is, clothed merely in a sort of shirt for the work of fishing, he quickly tied his girdle round his waist so as to prevent the garment floating on the water, and then cast himself into the water as on the former occasion ; but this time his action was dictated less by natural impetuosity than by his desire to show Christ his eagerness. The other disciples, who were only about a hundred yards from the shore, did not try to haul the net up, but dragged it behind them. Near the water's edge they leapt ashore without now troubling any more about the net, and saw with surprise a charcoal fire on which fish was being cooked, along with some bread. So their Lord had already prepared a meal for them. What was He going to do ? With the simplicity of former days, without the majesty that might have been expected, without a word about the heavenly glory that now was His, Jesus said pleasantly : 'Bring hither of the fishes which you have now caught.' This was not so easy. Peter had to board the boat again to see to the hauling up of the net, and drew it up full of a hundred and fifty-three large fishes which they had the curiosity to count, so little solemnity was there about the scene. And in spite of the great number the net was not broken, a symbol of the great number of souls that the Church can hold without loss of her unity, for she expands to receive them.

But this spiritual lesson is not what Jesus first of all had at heart. With a kindly gesture He said : 'Come and dine.' The disciples well knew that it was He and therefore did not think of questioning Him. And since He seemed to show no desire for their homage, the very respect they felt for Him constrained them to behave just as they had done with Him in the old days by the lake. Above all Jesus wanted them really to understand that He was just the same. As of old, He took bread and distributed it to them, then the fish. But after thus lavishing marks of His care upon these friends of His and seeing their strength was restored—'after they had dined' as the divine simplicity of the gospel text has it—Jesus meant to put a final consecration upon His work, the Church that He had founded, by what He was to do with him who was its head. Simon Peter had denied Him, yet it was to him that He had appeared before them all. He was not therefore thinking of reproaching Peter, but rather He was deigning to show that His disciple's momentary weakness was more than forgotten ; the sorrowful recollection of that fall would intensify the disciple's love for his Master, a love already surpassing that of all the others. His remembrance of the denial was to be transfigured by a supreme testimony that he was to pay to the goodness of Christ.

Jesus now begins to speak with a solemn air : 'Simon, son of John, lovest thou Me more than these ?' There is a clear indication in the concluding words that, on His side, Jesus will grant to Peter more than to the others if he knows that he loves his Master more than they. But now Simon no longer dares to say anything that would lift him up above the rest, and he humbly appeals to the Master's heart : 'Yea, Lord, Thou knowest that I love Thee.' Jesus replies : 'Feed My lambs.' His lambs are those whom He knows and who know Him, the flock whose Shepherd He is and on whose behalf He has laid down His life, for that is why

He has come, as He told the Jews at Jerusalem.[1] Then He says a second time : 'Simon, son of John, lovest thou Me ?' There is the same answer : 'Yea, Lord, Thou knowest that I love Thee' ; and there is the same reward : 'Be the shepherd of My sheep.' Finally, for the third time, He asks : 'Simon, son of John, lovest thou Me ?' ; and certainly three protestations of affection were not too much to ask from the man who had thrice denied. But was Jesus alluding to the past sin ? Did He then still remember it ? Sadness fills Peter's heart, as at that fatal hour when his eyes had met those sorrowful eyes. He finds support in his faith, he appeals to his Master's divine knowledge : 'Lord, Thou knowest all things ; Thou knowest that I love Thee.' This time was really the last. Jesus replies : 'Feed My sheep.' And now, knowing His disciple's love and accepting it, knowing that it will lead him to give his life for the Master he adores, Jesus reveals to him in advance by what death he is to die, a death like His own : 'When thou wast young, thou didst gird thyself and didst walk where thou wouldst. But when thou shalt be old, thou shalt stretch forth thy hands, and another shall gird thee and lead thee whither thou wouldst not.' They were veiled words, pointing to a torture that would be terrible to nature, but accepted out of love : they were better understood when St. John the evangelist wrote, after St. Peter had been crucified, one with his Master in death as in life. Then Jesus said to Peter alone : 'Follow Me.' Peter knew what that meant : 'If anyone will serve Me, let him follow Me ; and where I am, there also shall My servant be.'[2]

Thus was Peter consecrated by Jesus as universal shepherd. To establish his authority, even over those who will also be shepherds of souls,[3] there is no need to look for the faithful in the lambs, and bishops and priests in the sheep. Lambs and sheep are almost synonymous here : both categories form part of Christ's flock. It is this whole flock that is subject to Peter's pastoral care. This investiture by our Saviour is more explicit as regards Peter's universal authority, but does not show its perpetuity so plainly as the words already spoken to him : 'Thou art Peter, and upon this Rock I will build my Church, and the gates of hell shall not prevail against it.'[4] But universality and perpetuity, two

[1] John x, 15.
[2] John xii, 26.
[3] 1 Peter v, 2.
[4] Matthew xvi, 17 ff.

divine attributes, are easily reconciled. They are expressed by two symbols : Peter is the unshakable rock ; he is the shepherd of the whole flock. So long as he is a rock he remains a shepherd. Now this shepherd could not always be Peter himself, just as the Church cannot always be composed of the same people. The Church continually changes yet remains the same, always governed by the same shepherd ; and he too is represented by fresh individuals. Perpetuity is succession through a line of rulers. So long as they are the rock, each in his turn will be the universal shepherd of all the sheep.

When Peter began to follow his Master, the disciple whom Jesus loved, himself a very close friend of Peter's, thought he was not doing anything indiscreet in starting to follow them. Would he, then, be called to the same fate ? Peter asks this out of affection, perhaps thinking that John himself would like to know, just as John had questioned the Master at the Last Supper to satisfy Peter's own curiosity. Jesus means to keep that secret : 'If I would have him remain till I come, what is that to thee ?' In a society like that of the early Christians, all anxiously awaiting the second coming of Christ, this question was interpreted as a declaration of fact. People had grown used to the idea that John would not die before the great advent of Christ, and they spoke of their conviction even in his presence. John himself, when he wrote or dictated his gospel, did not wish to make any alteration in Christ's words which he set down as they were uttered ; he merely noted that they must be taken in their right sense, and not made to represent as certain what Jesus had deliberately left obscure.

The narrative ends with Jesus' departure, not by a sudden mysterious disappearance, but as if He withdraws, followed by His two friends, along those delightful shores of the lake.

St. John has the gift of rising to the loftiest thoughts without the tone of the conversation ceasing to be intimate and cordial. St. Matthew is more solemn. He, too, takes for granted the appearances at Jerusalem, since he says that the Apostles had doubted at first.[1] It was after they had been convinced of their Master's resurrection that they came into Galilee, to a place that He had appointed, on what occasion we do not know. Just as He had gathered them together on a mountain to hear His opening sermon,

[1] xxviii, 17.

so on a mountain again, perhaps the same one, He gave them their mission. At the sight of Him the Eleven fell down before Him : He came as a king. When He had drawn near, He said to them : 'All power hath been given to Me in heaven and on earth. Go therefore, teach all nations, baptizing them in the name of the Father and of the Son and of the Holy Ghost, teaching them to observe all things whatsoever I have commanded you. And behold I am with you all days, even to the end of the world.' The programme for the future was contained in a few lines : Preach, so as to bring forth faith in God, Father, Son, and Holy Ghost, and mark those who believe with the seal of baptism ; then train them in the moral life as the Master taught it.[1]

It was easy to say all that. But who would have ventured to promise that it should be carried out, except He who had been invested with sovereign power, which He would condescend to use for the help of His disciples? That promise is assuredly the most extraordinary prophecy, and its fulfilment the easiest to verify ; for every one of the faithful is conscious that the whole strength of the Church comes to her from the supernatural help of Christ. Her only support is in Him.

The last appearance in Jerusalem. The Ascension (319–320).

Luke xxiv, 44–53 ; Mark xvi, 19–20.

St. Paul mentions an appearance of the risen Christ to more than five hundred brethren at once, some of whom were still alive in his time.[2] Of this the evangelists have said nothing at all, so true is it that they have left out events of the first importance. No doubt it happened in Galilee, for only there could so considerable a number of disciples have assembled at call. And at the same time we realize the suitability of Galilee for these manifestations of Christ. There Jesus had first and longest preached the kingdom of God, declaring that it would not be long in coming ; and there He wished to show this prediction fulfilled in His own Person.

[1] It seems that Mark's gospel puts another appearance to the Eleven in place of the mission here referred to. He adds details concerning the miracles that the disciples will be enabled to perform.

[2] 1 Corinthians xv, 6.

But the word of God was to proceed from Sion and Jerusalem.[1] The old centre of the worship of God had become the first Church of the Christian worship by the institution of the Eucharist. It was from there that the gospel was to spread. Jesus must therefore have given His Apostles the command to return thither. It was surely at Jerusalem that Christ manifested Himself to James,[2] whom St. Paul calls the Lord's brother, and who is most probably the Apostle who was the son of Alphæus, the undisputed head of the Church of Jerusalem. The evangelists have not mentioned this appearance either ; it is preserved by the Gospel according to the Hebrews.[3] As for the last appearance of which St. Paul speaks, which was granted to all the Apostles, it can only be the one that closes the gospel according to St. Luke. If we had not yet understood that the evangelists sometimes group events without troubling to indicate intervals of time, we should have to remark it here. The author of the Acts of the Apostles, in which the interval between the Resurrection and the Ascension is given as forty days, is St. Luke ; and the same St. Luke here seems to put the Ascension on the evening of Easter Sunday. Without any break in continuity, immediately after the first appearance of the Apostles, he places the final instructions of Jesus to them. It is not, therefore, to harmonize two evangelists arbitrarily, it is to comply with the indications of one and the same writer that we must place an interval of time between two scenes appearing in a narrative which seems to refer to only one event.

After eating in the presence of His disciples on the evening of His resurrection, Jesus left them ; and it was at another, and a last, meeting that He reminded them of His former instructions. He had indeed told them that Christ must suffer before rising from the dead : that had been foretold by Moses, the Prophets, and the Psalms. At the same time He gave them understanding of the Scriptures, in order to enable these Galilæan fishermen to explain them from the beginning of their preaching with more insight than the Jewish doctors of the Law. Indeed those very Scriptures had predicted that penance and the remission of sins would be preached to all nations in Christ's name, beginning with Jerusalem. Once they were enlightened with His light it

[1] Isaias ii, 3 ; Micheas iv, 1–5. [2] 1 Corinthians xv, 7.
[3] *Revue biblique*, 1922, p. 323.

would be their duty to solve the questions arising from their preaching. We know how serious those questions were, particularly that of the obligations of Christians in regard to the Law. Nothing was so effective as that example to show that, deprived of the presence of Jesus but helped by His Holy Spirit, the Church had the power to settle the most difficult questions of doctrine.

The time for beginning to preach had not yet come: 'As for you, stay in the city till you be endued with power from on high.' These are Christ's last words in the gospel.

Then He led His disciples in the direction of Bethany. According to ancient tradition, He stopped at the place where He had taught them about the destruction of Jerusalem and His return in glory; there, on the site of the ancient basilica of the Eleona,[1] a church in honour of the Sacred Heart is now being built with the co-operation of all nations as a prayer for peace. On that spot Christ lifted His hands and blessed His followers. Then He withdrew and they saw Him taken up to heaven. Prostrate on the ground they understood that this appearance was the last. And instead of being overwhelmed by sorrow they experienced the great joy He had promised them at the Last Supper.[2]

Where is Jesus Christ? He is seated at the right hand of God, says St. Mark's gospel; that is, He is associated with His Father's power. This contains a mystery for our minds; it is one of the unfathomable features of the mystery of the Incarnation. But in being invited to rejoin our Saviour, the certainty of our hope is in no way lessened by the veil of faith, which indeed will one day be drawn aside from our eyes.

[1] *Jérusalem*, II, ch. xiv. [2] John xvi, 22.

EPILOGUE

THE GOSPEL OF JESUS CHRIST, GOD AND MAN

To begin with, the Gospel was the 'good news' preached by Jesus Christ about the coming of the kingdom or reign of God. But the word gospel, as St. Paul used it and as we understand it to-day, came to mean the preaching by the Apostles of the good news that the Son of God had become incarnate, had taught the way of salvation, had died and rose again, in order to open the gates of heaven to mankind.

According to an opinion of the liberal Protestant scholars, we are not to look for anything in the gospels but the *doctrine* preached by Jesus. But we have only to read those gospels to discover that it was also, and even more, their intention to make known the *Person* of Jesus Christ. The Christian faithful worshipped Him as they worshipped His Father, without ceasing to regard Jesus as man ; and that is how the Gospel represents Him.

In order to give a rapid summary of the impression we have gained, let us recall the characteristics of His humanity, along with what He and His disciples affirmed concerning His divinity, and finally St. John's synthesis in his dogmatic declarations about the Incarnate Word.

I. JESUS OF NAZARETH, MARTYR FOR RELIGIOUS TRUTH

Before the time of Jesus, other men had gained great renown in the field of politics, literature, or war. Philosophy, poetry, and the arts, fell to the lot of Athens. Alexandria had cultivated scholarship and the natural sciences, which owed their beginning to Aristotle. Rome had conquered the Mediterranean world and was already showing her ability to govern it ; while, thanks to Greek philosophy, she had laid the foundations of universal law. All that is foreign to Jesus. Was the reason of this that He might remain faithful to the ideal of the prophets? Certainly the prophets presented themselves to Israel as God's ambassadors, who bore His message and were concerned solely with His interests. Nevertheless this mission of the prophets generally compelled them to mix in wars or alliances, in rivalries between the two kingdoms of Israel, and in political intrigue. But Jesus was concerned solely with the religious ideal: He preached it, and His preaching led Him to His death. None the less the story of His life, as we have read it in the four gospels, has every appearance of truth, on condition we understand how to draw that story from the documents, each of which goes its own way to the goal that is common to them all, documents which are in harmony more by the reality of facts than by any obvious desire for agreement.

At once, however, we are confronted with the objection that this story contains miracles, and the miraculous is impossible. We shall say a few words about this later on; for the moment we merely observe that supposed miracles do not prevent anyone from writing a biography. Phenomena generally taken for miracles are not infrequent occurrences in history, and those who are deemed to have performed them are not on that account blotted out of existence. Ought we, for instance, to be content to remain in ignorance of the history of Rome because Livy has related a few prodigies?

There is presented to us, therefore, a young Israelite not much over thirty who offers Himself to John the Baptist for the reception of that baptism instituted by him. The date of that institution is the autumn of the year A.D. 27, a date established by an unquestionable synchronism of certain events. Some of John's disciples came over to Jesus, but Jesus kept in the background so long as the Baptist was exercising his ministry. Then, when John had been thrown into prison, Jesus too began to preach the kingdom of God. Yet it is not long before we realize that this phrase, the kingdom of God, took on a wider significance on His lips. John had thrown the people into terror by his declarations of a terrible judgement of God to come; Jesus insisted on the reformation of the heart, even exhorting men to a purer religious attitude of mind than that professed—we ought rather to say neglected—by the Jewish doctors of the

Law, who were too much taken up with external observances and preoccupied with subtle disputations. Nevertheless Jesus Himself observed that Law as a faithful Israelite and usually went up to Jerusalem for the pilgrimage feasts, where He was met with scorn by the Pharisees whose stronghold it was. Consequently He devoted Himself entirely to His ministry in Galilee, where the multitudes came to Him, begging from His kindness the miracles which they believed they obtained from Him. Within a year the simple but ardent souls of Galilee were on fire with enthusiasm, eager to hear Him and longing to receive from Him the signal for the liberation of their country. After He had fed a whole multitude with a few loaves and fishes they wanted to proclaim Him Messiah, that is, the king who was to deliver Israel. He would not allow it. From the beginning He had always been careful to avoid every gesture of a revolutionary character; He had even urged that His miracles should not be broadcast. He was certain that He was the Messiah promised by God to His people, but the function of the Messiah as confided to Him by God was to teach men their religious duties, to call them to repentance, to preach the love of God, surrender to His Providence, submission to His will, and love of our neighbour. That was what the kingdom of God consisted in, and of that kingdom, which was to be inaugurated by His death, Jesus would be king for ever when He was risen from the dead and glorified.

But the Jews of that day regarded the Messiah chiefly as a leader in war and as a king whose victories would establish a kingdom of Israel that was to have dominion over all the nations of the world. Even had He not been divinely enlightened, Jesus must very soon have realized that such an opposition of view would spell discouragement and desertion for the bulk of His followers. *He* was not the man they were looking for. They had not the courage to be His disciples in the way of self-denial. Consequently they forsook Him. A mere handful kept their trust in Him, and thenceforward He occupied Himself more with them, leading them into comparative solitude on the frontiers of the land of Israel. He accepted their homage when their leader, Simon Peter, confessed that Jesus was the Messiah. But at the same time He showed—what indeed the attitude of the Jewish leaders made inevitable—that His preaching would lead Him to His death, and that this was precisely the manner in which He was to fulfil His mission.

Then, about the month of September, He left Galilee, to which He had addressed so many appeals, in order to visit Judæa and the country beyond the Jordan. The journey lasted five or six months, in the course of which He went up to Jerusalem for the feasts of Tabernacles and the Dedication, where His debates with the Jews put the finishing touch to their hostility. This time His hour had come. In order to make it quite clear that He came as Messiah, He consented to be led in triumph into the Holy City ; a modest sort of triumph it is true, but one which took on a Messianic character from the acclamations of His disciples.

The chief men of the nation, with the high priest at their head, resolved to get rid of Him before the feast of the Pasch. Through the treachery of Judas, one of the twelve Apostles He had chosen, they succeeded ; and Jesus, first condemned to death by the supreme court of the Jews, then delivered over to the Romans, was by the latter crucified. He died because He was determined to carry out to the end the mission entrusted to Him by God.

This history has the stamp of truth, and there is really nothing to be said against the tradition that has preserved its incidents. Just as there have always been men who had the reputation for working miracles, so there have always been some who thought they were entrusted with a divine mission. Such a man in Israel was given the title of *nabi*, which we translate ' prophet,' and among the pagans there were the soothsayers of every kind. We make this remark merely in order to show to what degree the gospel has all the characteristics of an historical narrative. But a fictitious narrative may have all the appearance of complete likelihood ; that does not guarantee the existence of the hero. And even if the hero never existed, men can still become impassioned for his doctrine ; but in that case it will be really the doctrine of the author of the story. Modern critics know all about that ; and they claim also, and rightly enough, that imagination can be distinguished from fact. Now the disciples of Jesus Christ saw with their own eyes that He existed ; it is they who have told us so, and they were as incapable of inventing His doctrine as they were incapable of inventing the facts of His life. It was on those facts that they based the belief which, as they said, men ought to have in the doctrine He taught. Before many years elapsed they expressed all this in writing.

Therefore Jesus was a man. It has not always been unnecessary to insist on this. So luminous were the traces He left that many of the ancient Fathers of the Church—it has even been thought that the fourth evangelist was amongst them—found themselves compelled vigorously to deny the assertion of the heretics that He was merely a supernatural being who had appeared with a semblance of humanity. To-day no one disputes the fact that He was a man—except those who deny His existence—either amongst the children of the Church or amongst critics who study Him merely as historians. But many who refuse Him miracles and any divine mission, still more any supernatural personality, cannot think of Him as man without human weaknesses, positive imperfections and sins. For our part we say : He was perfectly man, save for sin, and by this limitation we do not surrender the reality of His human nature. If Jesus had had the defects with which He is reproached He would really have been *less* human, in the full sense of the word. What does Renan say ? We apologize for giving his odious words : 'Soon we shall see him, in his bold rebellion against nature . . . crushing under foot everything pertaining to man, race, love, and fatherland, and having no heart or soul but for the idea that presented itself to him as the absolute form of the good and true.'[1] We will pass what regards love, which is only a tribute to Our Saviour's purity. It is enough that He showed all men the greatest of all loves, the love that gives its life. By race Renan means family : 'His family seems to have had no love for him, and at times he is found to be harsh towards it.'[2] He simply showed by His example that attachment to family and clan, though a sacred duty, is not the only, or the supreme duty. He could not enter upon His ministry without leaving His own people, and He chose to declare that He preferred before all others those who were docile to the word of God. But He had devoted Himself for thirty years to His Mother and adoptive father. Those young men who during the war tore themselves from their weeping mothers to go to their duty, who at their death had none but that name on their lips, had they no love for their mothers ? So Jesus, separated from His Mother for

[1] *Vie de Jésus*, 52nd ed., p. 45. [2] *Vie de Jésus*, p. 44.

the service of souls, found her again at the foot of His cross. And as for His country, He joins in all His people's customs, their feasts and their prayers. All His journeys, labours, and weariness He endures for their sakes. He does not leave their borders : it is with the lost sheep of Israel that He has to do. If only Jerusalem would consent to be saved from punishment ! Jerusalem is obdurate, and when He weeps it is not over His own death, but over the Holy City that is to be laid waste.

Will it be said that the obsession of a fixed idea, the religious idea, paralysed the intellectual faculty in Him ? But though He has the warmth, even the vehemence, of the prophets, He has the tranquil clarity of a philosopher. What He says about God and the kingdom of God is often expressed in parables such as all ages have acknowledged to be masterpieces of good sense, in which He has adapted ideas of the loftiest character to the capacity of a race of fishermen, farmers, and shepherds. Jewish scholars strain every nerve to find parables like these in the Talmud. We do not deny that Jesus spoke the language of His day ; but no one used it with the same charm, emotion, almost careless ease, yet with a penetration that reaches the heart. He was severe with Himself without any display of austerity, but gentle with others ; no one could reproach Him with sin, and He was merciful towards sinners. He had friends because He knew how to love them, and He was nobly loyal to them, even to the point of taking upon Himself alone the responsibility for the crime with which He was charged. Amongst a people who observed extreme reserve with regard to women, He allowed women to come near Him and even to supply His needs ; He spoke to them of the approaching salvation just as He did to men.

This much is true in Renan's Galilæan idyll : that the good people were charmed and captivated by Jesus, which is all the more astonishing when we consider that this remarkable Messiah spoke only of repentance and self-abnegation, things left unmentioned by Renan. But although the critic was at heart a sceptic, he himself did not escape the charm of that figure which appeared to him in the transparent atmosphere of the lake. An artist of his stamp, however, could not resign himself to the task—such a task as would make any painter hesitate—of bringing out the lights on his subject without the aid of shadows. Enough of these captious criticisms ! The shadows were near to the light ; they did not comprehend it. At all events, Renan really did understand very well—and this is still the common opinion—that Jesus was dominated by His mission in a way that would be described, were we speaking of anyone else, as being obsessed by His errand ; He completely consecrated His whole self to the mission bestowed on Him by God, that urgent duty of making known to men what God had charged Him to say. Under that aspect we may say that He was already the active word of God. It was to fulfil this errand that He willed to die, and He was the first to accept death at the hands of His own people for the moral and religious truth He was commissioned to proclaim.

Some, however, maintain that He was not the first even in that respect ; there was Socrates before Him. Now the name of Socrates is a very great name, for he was really the first to found a rational science of morality for the Greeks, and through the Greeks for the whole human race. But are we familiar with the sort of man Socrates was ? Those who are the most qualified to answer have never been able to choose between Xenophon's portrait of him, which some consider the best likeness,[1] and the figure that emerges from the *Apologia* and the dialogues of Plato, which is more or less an idealized picture. Let us consider the latter for a moment, the noblest type of intelligent and conscientious humanity that human genius has been able to conceive. Even if there be thinkers more penetrating in analysis than Plato and more solid in their conclusions, at any rate no one in antiquity surpassed him in his enthusiasm for beauty and his art of making it live in the most expressive form with exquisite simplicity. To contrast this idealized picture of Plato's Socrates with Jesus is certainly being very generous to the Greek sage, for it assuredly has less historical truth than the portrait of Jesus found in the gospels.

We are bound to admit the attractiveness of Plato's Socrates, with his power over youth. The youth of Athens was far too much taken up with the charms of beauty of form, carried away too by an ambitious pursuit of a public career which was open to all who wished to follow it, and in which everything could be accomplished by the skilful use of words. Socrates captivated them by the example of his virtue and by that sole passion which men were able to

[1] Renan's opinion.

discover in him, his zeal for truth and justice. During a life of thirty years he renounced not only wealth but even all remuneration for his work, lived sparingly, dressed like the poor, never wearying of inviting his fellow-citizens to set the good of their soul above every advantage, and resolutely to follow justice even should it cost them their lives. He traced the origin of this justice to the divinity which impressed it upon the souls to which its voice was audible.

This teaching of the philosopher was put forward after the manner of an interrogation which led up to discussion between the two persons concerned; as may well be imagined, it did not fail to result in hot disputes in which Socrates generally won, thanks to the keenness of his intellect, his long reflection on the hackneyed answers with which so many intelligent and worthy men were content, and owing especially to his biting irony which he dissimulated under a show of courtesy, and which brought to his side all those who found it entertaining. It would be surprising had he not thus made enemies among those whose vanity was wounded or those who were all for the old-fashioned methods, or if he had not aroused the suspicions of the common people of Athens who held to their national gods. Was not this new style of morality invented in order to satisfy some divinity, and was it not merely the introduction of a new form of worship paid to new gods? Such was the question people asked, and Socrates was accused of denying the divinity of the Athenian gods, of introducing new deities, and also of corrupting youth. There can be no question here of vicious conduct; we know with what precision of unpleasant detail Plato has cleared his master from every suspicion of infamy in this respect. Were this not the case, we should never do Socrates the honour of mentioning him in the same breath with Jesus Christ. The reference to youth was put into the accusation merely to add to it the threat of danger to the public. It would not have been possible for his accusers, Anytos, Meletos, and Lycon, to secure his death merely as a visionary. And Socrates did not deny his influence over the young: it was his pride and his joy, and in the eyes of the republic it ought to have had the same value as his teaching. But it was doubtless with set design that his accusers refrained from attacking him in the sphere of morality, where his chief victories had been gained; instead they ensnared him with an accusation of impiety. It was evident that his views about divinity differed from those of the common people, and once he revealed these views he would be lost. Hence an eminent scholar has written as follows:[1] 'Had (Socrates) revealed to his judges what he really thought, he would have had to tell them that he did not believe in the passions, the loves, and the mutual rivalries of the gods. . . . In doing this, would he not have justified, in the common opinion, those who were accusing him of atheism and contempt for the national gods?' He did not tell them what he thought; he defended himself against the charge of having introduced new gods by declaring that his dæmon, or rather the divinity which manifested itself in him, required worship from no one. He protested that he believed in the dæmons who were the bastard offspring of the gods and nymphs; and consequently that he believed in the gods. In a word he gave no suspicion that there was the least difference in religious matters between his judges and himself.

Was it was because he was afraid of death? No, for he certainly provoked his own condemnation by declaring that he intended to go on as before in spite of everything, and by daring to say, when called upon to give his opinion as to the sort of penalty he should suffer, that as he was innocent there was no need to choose one at all; that, on the contrary, he rather deserved to be supported at the expense of the State among the senators of the Prytaneum. His courage, therefore, is beyond all question. His last moments were passed in calm serenity, like a man who is going towards the light. Even Plato himself wrote nothing more sublime than his description of the philosopher's death.

But it follows that Socrates had no intention of dying for the sake of religious truth. Indeed he had arrived at no certain conclusion regarding God, nor about the immortality of the soul, though he was certain of the superiority of his own views regarding religious ideas, and realized the lamentable character of the errors of popular mythology and the way in which they endangered morality. It was a strange attitude of mind. What is the good of striving to inculcate the practice of a justice measured according to a divine norm, without first seeking to convey an exact idea of what is meant by the divine, or at any rate without

[1] Cf. *Platon*, by M. Maurice Croiset; Budé series, Vol. I, p. 125.

trying to remove gross errors? Yet, at the crucial moment Socrates was silent. When, through the falseness of his accusers, he was confronted with that very point for which he might have died most honourably, he was clever enough to perceive their manœuvre and evaded the point. And, seeing that he doubted about the immortality of the soul,[1] when he called upon his friends to set the care of their souls before all else, what he meant by the good of the soul was its perfection in this world, a perfection that consisted in the practice of justice. Moreover, even if the soul be immortal, he conceives its future life to consist merely in converse with illustrious men whom we shall be able to question without any fear. Thus he is ignorant of the true worth of the soul: and the proof of it lies in a fact which we ought not to hesitate to point out: Socrates never seems to have given a thought to these questions in so far as women were concerned. It was enough for him to have to endure the ill-natured disposition of his own wife. But women have souls as well as men, though at that time it was held that women were of no value to the city except merely to provide it with children, especially boys, whose education was looked on as the business of the State.

We may say, therefore, that Socrates is the hero of justice, especially of justice considered as safeguarding the interests of the State; hence he may be called the martyr of civic justice. It was in the performance of that task right to the end, and for the sake of his own dignity too, that he chose to die. He certainly gave a splendid example of Kant's categorical imperative, that command which issues from the autonomous reason; but it is an example that is powerless to lead men to the practice of a moral life, nor does it even point out the way that leads to God. Thus the ideal conceived by Plato, the most idealistic of all the Greeks, proves to be far inferior to that which the evangelists have drawn of Jesus Christ, who came to preach the truth and who died for that truth. And since Plato's natural genius is without doubt far superior to that of the evangelists, we must conclude that their portrait of Christ is representative of a real person, who not only surpassed all men that ever preceded Him, but who excelled even the most noble of ideals.

[1] In his *Apologia*, where he makes Socrates speak for himself, Plato has not dared to ascribe to him the assurance which he has given him in the Phædo, where Socrates is simply the mouthpiece of Plato.

We have dwelt at some length, perhaps at too great length, on the attractive figure of Plato's Socrates, because in him the cause of religious truth outside Judaism was lost. Plato, who was more religious-minded than Socrates, ascended, in our opinion, to the idea of God the Creator, a Father who was led by His goodness to produce the world. But, content with having attained to this truth, he made no effort to lead others to pay homage to it, but joined with his contemporaries in the city cult, which he justified by his doctrine of the divinity of the celestial bodies. Then there was Aristotle with his incomparable description of the *Primum Movens* and *Actus Purus*, the deity who enjoys infinite beatitude in self-contemplation ; and after writing that, Aristotle faithfully fulfilled his duties to gods whose worship he stigmatized as immoral.

The cynics are perhaps the best representatives of the teaching of Socrates. They based their morality on common sense, in a haphazard sort of fashion, without any foundation of religion ; it was what we should nowadays call a lay morality. The coarseness which characterized their teaching, along with certain deviations from conventional morality in their own moral code, have left them with an unsavoury reputation. They went to extremes in their doctrine, and hence failed to exercise an influence equal to that of the two great schools of Zeno and Epicurus. The only reason, however, why Epicurus admitted the existence of the gods was to satisfy the artistic tradition of the Greek philosophers representing the gods as members of a superior kind of humanity, if that can be called a superior kind of humanity which lives in a state of perpetual joy devoid of every kind of activity. His gods took no interest in human affairs and were of no use during man's life ; of still less advantage were they after death, since the human soul was not immortal.

On the other hand there were the Stoic philosophers, who along with their opponents shared influence over men's minds ; they were the religious party, and they taught the doctrine of the providence of the gods. These gods might equally well be called the Divine World or even God, for, according to the Stoics, the gods and the world were not really distinct one from the other ; the existence, therefore, of the former was as certain as that of the latter, but the existence of the gods was commensurate with the existence of the world. By man's immortality they meant the soul's reabsorption into the one great Totality, where the soul lost its individual existence.

Thus that gleam of spiritual truth which enlightened Attica in the fourth century before our era had become well-nigh extinguished by the time of Jesus Christ. Less than a century before His death, the cause of religious truth appeared before the bar of a far more competent judge than Pilate, namely Cicero. To tell the truth, Cicero was by no means of a genuinely philosophical turn of mind; but as an orator and a statesman, acquainted with all the intellectual movements of Greece, and as a Roman appreciating their moral value for the good of city and citizens, he was in a better position than another, who had a purely speculative mind, for passing judgement on so complex a question as that of religious and moral truth. To his prætorian tribunal he summons Stoics, Epicureans, and the Sceptics of the Academy,[1] and after examining them he gives judgement in favour of traditional religion and the immortality of the soul. His own personal convictions, however, are hardly apparent, and once again the cause of God is lost; indeed His cause is not so much as pleaded. There is no question of God, but only of gods. Cicero pays honour to the gods of Rome. It was not that religion was finally on the decline, though it is true that for a time it had given way before the attacks of the Greek rationalists; but it revived under Augustus. It was to become more than ever the passionate concern of men, for those who believed in the immortality of the soul were now far more concerned about their salvation than was the case with men in the days when the great masterpieces of Attic art appeared. The mystery religions flourished, and to the old national mysteries were added new rites that were open to all nations; and what is more surprising still, Oriental rites penetrated even among the Romans and the Greeks, who were thus subjected to the religious domination of the barbarian East. But although in all this a pre-eminence may have been accorded to one particular deity, as was already the case in the city cults of the Greeks, yet other deities were not excluded. There was only one Deity who refused to share His privilege with other gods, and that was the God of the

[1] In his *De Natura Deorum*, written in 45 B.C.

Jews. It was in His name alone that conscience raised a strong protest against the worship of so many gods.

Political Hellenism, when it came into contact with Judaism at a time of broad toleration, during which people showed more interest in comparing the different deities with one another than in setting them in opposition, was at violent conflict with this worship of one only God and resolved to extirpate such a belief. It was upon this that Antiochus Epiphanes was so obstinately bent. Thus were provided martyrs for religious truth, martyrs commemorated by the Catholic Church. All honour to them! But we must not forget that in this struggle they were supported by national sentiment. They were fighting for hearth as well as altar in a noble war such as was so often waged in ancient times. Their particular claim to superiority lay in the fact that they confessed one only God; but their religious laws, laws of the ancestors and of their race, were precisely similar to the national heritage of other nations which had crushed the religious belief in one God in the cities of antiquity. In Israel, however, the two forces were united, religious belief and national sentiment. The wonderful courage of the faithful Jews triumphed over persecution and war, and the worship of the one only God continued to be the privilege of the Jewish race. That tiny people, carried away by indomitable enthusiasm, for a time even had hopes of being able to dominate the world, if not by force, at any rate by its religious ideal. The God of the Jews inspired respect by His unity, and even the ancient philosophers had seen tha tthe mind was compelledto as sent to this truth. But as God had conquered by means of the Jews, the latter thought that He was in some fashion theirs. Hence, in order to become His worshipper they made it essential to become a Jew, a thing that was by no means to everybody's liking. Very few would consent to accept circumcision.

Then it was that the testimony of Jesus was heard. At first He too seems to be bound up with Judaism; but a closer examination shows that all He says of the Father who is God is said for the sake of all men; that the way to serve Him and to be one with Him is open to all, and that the value of all men's souls is the same. We have already said that the Jews were under no misapprehension about His teaching. He declares the truth simply and without alloy: He has God alone in view and He relies on

God alone, for His fellow-Israelites reject and condemn Him. He is the first witness, but He is followed by an innumerable company of other martyrs who attest the truth of what He taught. This fact must be admitted as one of supreme importance ; it divides the religious history of humanity into two periods : before Jesus Christ, and after Jesus Christ.

II. JESUS THE SON OF GOD, GOD LIKE HIS FATHER

What, then, is the religious truth for which Jesus died, opposed by those who were His own people ? It is clear that He did not die for affirming the unity of God and rejecting the multiplicity of gods, along with the more or less idolatrous worship paid to them. On such a point as that no difference of opinion could arise between true children of Israel. But we have seen, and a number of Jewish scholars agree, that Jesus was at variance with the religious leaders of His race in laying down principles that were to set the worship of God free from the trammels of Jewish nationalism. To the mind of those who are not Jews that is His chief claim to honour. If God is the Father of all mankind, why should He not call all men to the same salvation and by the same road ? There may be differences of opinion about what that road to God is ; some are inclined to take a very broad view about what are its positive obligations. But at any rate we may say that this truth is unanimously accepted in the way that it was formulated by St. Paul : that in the sight of God there is no difference between Gentiles and Jews. Indeed the thing that the modern mind finds so astonishing is that God should have shown so many favours to a race which He called His own people. God's choice of that race is to be understood merely as a temporary measure, intended to safeguard the cultivation of truth in a specially chosen soil where the seed would have a better opportunity of developing. It was a pedagogical process, but such a process must have a limit ; now it was the mission of Jesus Christ to preach, though in Israel alone, a truth which, through the instrumentality of His Church, was to be preached to all mankind.

If we are to gauge more accurately, as it is the historian's office to do, the special character of this idea and its power of penetration, we must remember this: that since Alexander's conquest of the East and owing to his amazing genius, there had arisen a modification of the ancient distinction between Greek and Barbarian. Subsequently, under the influence of Stoic philosophy, thinking men had come to regard all men as citizens of one and the same city, namely the world. But we must also insist on the fact that this new equality between man and man was devoid of religious significance. Men were not regarded as brothers because they were all children of the same God, for it was held that such a God either did not exist, or if He existed He was indistinguishable from the world itself, or else did not concern Himself with the world. Now it was precisely the work of Jesus to establish the unity of the human race, and to base it not merely upon the fact of Creation, after the fashion of the Jews who drew no practical conclusion of the brotherhood of men from that truth, but upon faith in one and the same Father. Had He advanced no further than that, there would still be a mark of genius in the way He had fused together those two ideas about which we are equally certain, but whose connection was not then understood: the unity of God the Creator, and the duty of all His creatures to pay Him the same worship.[1]

Such is the view many religious minds take of the rôle and person of Jesus Christ. His Gospel gave to the world the notion of God the Father of all men, who desires the salvation of all; consequently all men ought to love Him and love one another as brothers. That is supposed by some to be the entire Gospel, the good news announced by one who is possessed of the most astounding religious genius, who has no equal in the religious sphere, who is a sage, a prophet, a man aided or inspired by God, one most fitted to act as guide, whose teaching set down in the gospels ought to be listened to and obeyed. But according to this view the Gospel He preached contains nothing at all about His person; it has but one subject, God the Father, and we are told that there is no reason for making Jesus also the subject of the Gospel. Were such the fact He would be less worthy of our respect, for in so far as He made a place for Himself beside His Father He would be so much the less religious. At the very most will these people grant Him forgiveness for having assumed the title of Messiah in order

[1] John iv, 23.

to render His work acceptable ; but, they tell us, He is neither Son of God nor God Himself. That would be unthinkable. Such is the language of liberal Protestantism and of those who, without being aware of it, are in communion with that school of thought.

Human reason very loudly proclaims that a man who should make himself a place beside God would be a blasphemer. The subject of the Gospel, therefore, must not be divided ; the Gospel has but one subject, and that is God. But Jesus is no other than the Son of God and God like His Father ; this He has made known to us because it is our way to salvation. And that is plainly what the Gospel teaches, as may be seen from the four gospels if we take them just as they are. Here we do not merely mean that we must simply trust their testimony, but that we must understand the manner and significance of that testimony. The Gospel contains a doctrine indeed, but not a doctrine that is expressed in philosophical formulas which abstract from time and place. Above, when we picked out the idea of God as the Father of all men, we used the method of rational analysis. But the Gospel does not use that method ; the Gospel is the representation of something that has taken place, of something that consists of the deeds and words of Jesus, of a fact that is of its nature complex, a fact that has to do with life and is therefore coloured by the customs, the manners of thinking and feeling which were current among the Jews of the time of Tiberius. It is not as though Jesus wrote a treatise about God or gave theological lessons ; what He spoke of was the kingdom of God which was at hand and even then beginning. He let it be seen that He was the Messiah, though He never gave any definition of the meaning of that term which His contemporaries already thought they all understood ; but He showed in what His own mission as Messiah was to consist. In addition to that He frequently spoke in parables concerning both the kingdom of God and Himself, at the same time admitting that this was not the plainest possible style of teaching regarding so lofty a subject.

The method of the evangelists is not that of logical argumentation ; they have not translated this teaching life of Jesus into scholastic formulas which would be easier to understand. But neither have they changed the primitive character of that life nor transformed it in the interests of the doctrine they desired to propagate. When St. John adopted a method somewhat of this kind in his doctrine of the Word, he did not put his teaching in that form on the lips of Jesus. The catechetical style of teaching which we find in the gospels, although it is not so systematic in character or, as we have just admitted, so clear, has nevertheless certain advantages: it has the immediate evidence of contact between the speaker and his audience, the stability of truths that have been heard and are here set down in the gospels along with the particular circumstances in which they were first uttered. There are, of course, variations in expression and slight differences in detail between the various gospels, but only such as must be expected between authors who have made no concerted effort to avoid dissimilarities of this kind. The testimony of the evangelists, such as it is, is in a word very clear; it leads us by way of the divine sonship of Jesus to the truth of His equality with the Father. To say the least, we are bound to admit that the evangelists fully believed this truth, just as did St. Paul and the Apostles, who were at one with him, just as did the Christians who were converted and instructed by them. This is what they called the Gospel of Jesus Christ.

Why not believe the evangelists when they relate the deeds and claims of Jesus? Have we not read the recently published true history of the Persian *Bâby* who gave himself out to be an incarnation of God, who gathered followers, several of whom laid down their lives in support of his assertion which they took as their rule of faith?[1] Many hesitate to accept the story, rather on account of the consequences of accepting it than on account of unjustifiable scruples concerning the history of the matter. The *Bâby* is left to his dreams. But men do not wish to leave Jesus in this manner. It is precisely because He is so great, because He has such a wonderful knowledge of God, because He has taught a moral doctrine that is so truly divine, and because He showed no hesitation in laying down His life for religious truth, that men refuse to admit that He declared Himself to be God incarnate. For if it were proved that such a declaration did emanate from Him, they would be forced to accept it as true, and they refuse to consider it as anything but impossible and unthinkable. Hence He cannot have said such a thing. They are ready to grant that the

[1] Cf. De Gobineau, *Les religions et les philosophies dans l'Asie Centrale.*

evangelists had no intention of lying; they are supposed to have altered their Master's teaching under the inspiration of their own belief. Their faith cannot be the same as the faith of Jesus. But the fact remains that it is easy to see that their faith is bound up with deeds and words which did not originate with them. We are therefore left with the conclusion that the whole Gospel is a falsification, but not a deliberate one, produced for the purpose of buttressing up a faith of which no one can explain the origin.

Certain people have felt so embarrassed at finding themselves in this impossible situation created by the critics that, in their desire for a more honest solution of the difficulty, they have been driven to maintain that the man Jesus never existed. Not all of these, certainly, have gone to such lengths as that merely for the sake of making an entertaining paradox. They find themselves faced with the evident belief of the disciples in the divinity of Jesus, a belief which they are not prepared to share; but they realize that some explanation must be found for it, and they admit that they can find no explanation. Consequently they have imagined that those who adored a God Jesus, never heard of previously, fashioned a history for Him and clothed Him with our humanity, a fact which did not hinder them from still worshipping Him as God.

To tell the truth, there are but three possible courses to take: either the disciples have made up a human history for a God; or they have made a God of a man; or else they have been personally convinced by Jesus Himself that He was divine: and in the latter case, we must choose either to imitate their belief or else attack Jesus openly. A man such as He was cannot be simply dismissed as a a dreamer or a victim of hallucination; and no one in these days any longer voices the odious, nay puerile, accusation of deception and charlatanism with which He was formerly charged. The only thing left to say—Lord, forgive us!—would be that He was mad. That indeed has been said, but it is an accusation really not worth consideration. Madness is sterile. We show our pity for it and pass on our way.

On the other hand the supposition that a God Jesus preceded Jesus of Nazareth has not even the merit of being a conjecture that has interest for anyone. And it is of no use to argue against it, for what sort of reasoning could we possibly use against people who refuse to admit historical evidence? There is nothing to do but shrug our shoulders at such a supposition.

But these are mere diversions, and they must not make us lose sight of the oldest, and still most formidable, attack on the divinity of Jesus, according to which He is regarded as a man whom faith makes divine. What sort of answer can we make to this army of critics who seem ever ready to repair the breach and return to the assault?[1] It is impossible here to recapitulate the different phases of that struggle; we will only indicate in a few words what was the basis on which the belief of the Apostles was grounded. The miracles of Jesus would not have been sufficient by themselves. The prophets also had worked miracles and had even raised the dead. But they were only the servants of God; none of them was the Son of God. As to the prophecies, they were not altogether definite on the point that the Messiah was to be God Himself; in fact the Jews did not so understand them, at all events not those Jewish doctors who were of the highest authority. And in any case it still remained necessary that the one should be pointed out to whom the prophecies were to be applied. Ought Jesus to be believed simply on His own word? His sanctity was indeed a complete guarantee of His trustworthiness. Still the first disciples did not think differently from the masters in Israel on the point of the infinite distance between God and man, and consequently agreed with them about the inconceivable folly of any man who should dare to make himself equal to God. They came from Galilee which had absorbed, whether freely or under compulsion, inhabitants that were foreign to Judaism; but once the Machabees had won that country back and had gained it over to the ardent Judaism which inspired themselves, Galilee fell little short of Judæa in the matter of religious susceptibility. Where lay the evidence strong enough to force upon such stubborn minds a conviction which was so much opposed to the faith they professed, a faith that had stood firm against the alluring charms of Greece, had endured without flinching the bloody persecutions of its enemies, had even

[1] We must not be taken in merely by appearances. It is not the same battalions of the enemy who continue to attack; on the contrary, one battalion follows another, and the ones in front are often crushed by those behind before the attack succeeds.

compelled the respect of Rome whose contempt of conquered barbarians is notorious? It lay in nothing else but Christ's own declarations, which left no room for doubt, compelling the disciples (even as they compel us) to leave Him unless they believed in the words of eternal life—declarations which His miracles prepared the way for and confirmed by endowing them with the authority of God Himself; declarations, finally, which were recognized to be in harmony with the Scriptures. All this formed a triple cord which it was impossible to break. But had there been wanting a single one of these motives for belief, it would be impossible to explain the faith of the Apostles or the origin of Christianity.

Of these three motives the word of Jesus Himself is the clearest. Anyone who says that the Gospel contains nothing about His Person must either not have read the gospels at all or else have explained them away until nothing remains. If Jesus really lived, preached, was condemned to death, then it was as Messiah, and He acknowledged that He was the Messiah. Certainly the kingdom of God was the chief subject of His preaching, yet that was in no way an abstract, but a traditional theme. The kingdom announced by the prophets was to be established in the land of Israel, but at some future indefinite date. The kingdom announced by Jesus was an imminent event, about to come to pass in conditions that seemed easy for everyone to determine, and the dominating feature of that kingdom was the Messiah. The chief mistake of the critics of the eschatological school, who see in Jesus no more than a preacher of a kingdom of God that is at hand, consists not in the fact that they stress the note of imminence, but in their imagining that the kingdom announced by Him was to come without warning, completely revolutionizing the established order of things, and introducing an ideal kingdom in place of the old world which was condemned to disappear altogether. But what Jesus had in mind was a gradual moral reformation, as is proved by His parables, and of that reformation He laid the foundations, knowing that it would be possible only through Him since He was the head appointed by God of the new order of things. He never approved in the slightest degree of the dream of a political Messiah, and the Gospel is evidence enough of that. His Messianism consisted in saving the world from sin by His death, although in teaching

His disciples that, He never failed to add to it an assurance of His Resurrection, which was to serve as the inauguration of His reign.

Let us note that His being the Messiah was not the source of all that belonged to Him in His personal character ; it was, on the contrary, a rôle assumed by one who was a higher personality. Jesus was not merely a descendant of David ; He had a higher origin which bestowed on Him the right to sit at the right hand of God[1] ; in comparison with the prophets He occupied the position held by the only son of the master of the house in relation to the servants.[2] We may content ourselves here with the reference to these two significant passages from St. Mark, whom the critics claim to be a complete stranger to the idea of Jesus described above.

Had Jesus said : 'I am Jahweh," He would have been maintaining Israel in its privileged position. To say : 'I am God,' would have been to put Himself in the place of His Father. He proceeded in a different fashion. By calling Himself the Son of God in the strict and full sense of the word, He claimed for Himself the same nature as His Father, the nature that was transmitted to Him by sonship. In this way the Father's honour remained unimpaired, and it was to that glory of the Father, which was also His own, that the Son devoted Himself. It was this declaration of Jesus which the disciples felt themselves compelled to accept, a declaration so strange to them that it only succeeded in winning over their minds very slowly ; nor would they have completely accepted it without the evidence of His miracles and of the Resurrection, which set God's seal on the entire work of one who dared to call Himself God's own Son.

The adversaries of Jesus bear witness no less clearly to what He affirmed. It was for this blasphemous audacity, as they considered it, that they had Him condemned. Always loath to shed Israelite blood, they would not have been willing to hand over to the Romans one who was merely an imaginary Messiah. Even Pilate himself refused at first to crucify a wretched man for a charge that seemed ridiculous in view of his innocuous character. The high priests made Jesus the victim of political expediency, the Pharisees desired His death out of spite and a hatred that made them see in the future the religious universalism which would be

[1] Mark xii, 35 ff. [2] Mark xii, 1–11.

the result of His doctrine ; but both priests and Pharisees needed a pretext for their action. It was no crime to call oneself the Messiah, but it was blasphemy to make oneself equal to God, and the confession of His equality with God was torn from Him when the high priests called the blessed God to witness. Without the aid of that admission the leaders of Israel would have found themselves in a position of complete inconsistency. But He who laid down His life for religious truth died for *that* particular truth.

The Jews told themselves that the matter was settled to the satisfaction of them all. Yet the Apostles, though overwhelmed by the prospect of the proceedings taken against their Master and still more by the result, nevertheless raised their heads again in hope. To what could this have been due except to the fact of the Resurrection, the last and most significant of Jesus' miracles, the most effective proof of the truth of what He had affirmed.

The Gospel indeed is full of miracles which He performed out of goodness, but with the further intention also of producing faith and confirming His teaching. His numerous miracles are not, we must admit, what commends Him most to the people of our own age. But do these people ever ask whether their prejudice against miracles is justifiable? If miracles can be ascertained, then everyone must admit that miracles were never more opportune than when performed to establish this unprecedented truth, that God had become man in the person of His Son. But in the matter of miracles, unbelief brings forward a question of principle and absolutely refuses to admit them at the judicial bar : it refuses even to discuss the credibility of the witness given. Indeed, the position is reduced to this : far from miracles proving the truth of facts stated in a book, the very mention of miracles proves that the book is not worthy of credence, because its author shows himself convicted of childish credulity and unable to distinguish the true from the false. Such is Renan's thesis. The Gospel is condemned in advance, and there is no appeal.

What, then, is a miracle? I shall not pretend to give a philosophical definition : a mere historian has no need to do that. By miracles the evangelists meant certain events which came to pass without the instrumentality of any appreciable natural cause, but by the sole will of Jesus, through which the power of God was brought directly into action. The immediate objection made to this is that such divine interference would involve self-contradiction on the part of God ; He is the author of nature, He has established invariable laws, and it would be unfitting for Him to introduce disorder by substituting Himself arbitrarily for the secondary causes which He sets in motion according to their various natures and properties. But it is possible that in our own day there is not so much tendency to look on the material universe as a great clock which moves with invariable regularity. However that may be, there are but two ways of explaining the world. Some close their eyes to everything but the material world and its evolution. We abandon that province to them and leave them to it. To these Pascal has already said : 'As for those who think that man's happiness lies in the things of the body, everything being evil which deprives him of the pleasure of the senses, let them satiate themselves with these pleasures and die in them.'[1] But there are others—thank God the greater majority, indeed almost the whole of mankind—who rise to the notion of a moral world, and for them the material world merely serves as the necessary basis of action for spiritual beings united to a material body, a world essentially subordinate to the moral world. It is unnecessary to say that this subordination follows set rules ; the domination exercised by the moral over the material world does not upset the order of the latter, an order which is the consequence of the interplay of the various elements composing the material world. All the same, it is impossible to see why God may not interfere with this order from time to time, should He wish to do so on behalf of the spiritual side of man which is always in danger of allowing itself to be submerged in what is material ; by such intervention He lifts the minds of men to higher things. Such interventions must not be too frequent, otherwise they would fail in their purpose. But they can in no way be called a disorder ; on the contrary, order is rather re-established by their means, we mean the order that consists in the superiority of the moral and religious destinies of the world over its merely material end.

The second objection to the miraculous is that miracles can never be verified because we do not know what is the full extent of the power of natural causes ; there was once

[1] Cf. *Pascal et les prophéties messianiques*, *Revue Biblique*, 1906, p. 560.

a time when men regarded perfectly natural phenomena, like lightning, as miracles. But this objection does not go far enough, for if there is truth in the system of animism, then we must say that uncivilized races ascribed to the deity not merely some, but all the phenomena of nature. However, we ourselves agree with them in this respect, since we admit that without the action of God nothing at all would happen in the world ; the world, in fact, would cease to be. The error of the animists consisted in breaking up this divine action, which in reality is simple and unique, into a number of separate determinations of will, or even in assigning this action to various forces which they considered as separate gods. Moreover, they flattered themselves that they were able to divine the intentions of these gods, imagining, for example, that such and such a god cast the thunderbolt with flashes of lightning just in the way that the savage shakes his assegai in order to cast down his foe. But the result of such a view of the world was that miracles were multiplied to such an extent that the miraculous ceased to exist, these people failing to distinguish ordinary natural causes from supernatural interventions on the part of God. As a matter of fact, without true monotheism there can be no true idea of the miraculous ; this truth is manifested in the case of the evangelists. So far our adversaries are in agreement with us ; but they add that even when men have believed in one only God, people of education have made the mistake of attributing certain effects to the work of demons which in reality are due to perfectly natural causes.

There is no doubt that this is true ; but it is also true that, as a general rule, the evangelists go into details about each miracle which they record. Hence it is easy for those who are learned in such matters to ascertain whether the things described are such as can now be explained by natural agency. So far science has failed to provide an explanation, and there is nothing to make us suppose that it will ever be able to do so. We see Jesus working miracles just when He willed ; His will did not bring occult forces into operation, it made up for the deficiency of ordinary natural means. But it is impossible for the human reason to conclude that such a thing could have taken place without a special act of God's will, His purpose being, as we have said above, to secure the moral and religious welfare of mankind. That ought not to be difficult to accept if we regard God as a Father, and there is no reason to raise any difficulty if the facts of the miraculous event are attested by witnesses worthy of credence. It is true that owing to human curiosity, which is ever on the alert, as well as to our aspirations and passionate longings for the divine, miracles have been plentifully multiplied in the past. Where is the hero around whom men have not woven a legend? But we make bold to say that Jesus never had the reputation of a hero, except in the sphere of holiness and heroic patience; and those are not the things which impress themselves on the human imagination. He occupied a very humble situation in life, although Littré has been stupid enough to put it on a par with the glorious position held by the great emperor Charlemagne.[1] His miracles apart, He was merely a rabbi like many of His contemporaries, and His fellow-rabbis even refused to admit His holiness. He had none of the external signs which were looked for in the expected Messiah; He was rejected by all who were in authority among His people, the priesthood, the teaching authority, and the aristocracy; finally, He was hanged on a gibbet.

His disciples believed in Him on account of His miracles and Resurrection, and it is to these disciples that we owe the recollections of Him preserved by the evangelists. But here Renan comes forward with, as he thinks, the clever suggestion that the evangelists may be compared to three or four old soldiers of the Napoleonic Empire who set to work to write the life of the Emperor from their personal recollections, each one from his own point of view.[2] Let us suppose that by some extraordinary chance the Emperor spoke to each one of them once. Of what value would be their souvenirs of him for the purpose of creating a halo for their hero? Do we imagine that they would have succeeded in drawing a life-like portrait of him?

But it is a far different matter when we come to the Apostles. If Renan wanted a realistic picture of Jesus he had only to turn to that fifth gospel of his which he thought could be obtained by coming into close contact with the East. We ought rather to say that it would have been quite sufficient if he had read again the four canonical

[1] We venture to refer the reader to our conferences on *Le sens du Christianisme*, pp. 147 ff.

[2] Cf. *Vie de Jésus*, p. lxxxix f.

gospels. Let us repeat what we have said elsewhere :[1] ' The sort of intimacy we have with one another in these countries of ours, where the climate is so severe, where the custom of modern life tends so much to create privacy and reserve, can give no idea of the common life lived by Jesus and His disciples, spent beneath the open sky, their bed made in the light of the stars, their food eaten together in some boat or in the fields, their bread baked at some improvised hearth around which they were all collected. Conversation went on without interruption, except when the Master went apart to pray. . . .' Often also the conversation was broken into by the importunity of those who wearied the disciples with their demand for miracles.

The evidence of witnesses like these cannot be set aside. Hence Strauss decided to reject it *en bloc* : ' This argument,' he says, ' would certainly be decisive if it could be shown that biblical history was written by eye-witnesses, or at any rate by men who were near to the events narrated.'[2] Critics have not forgotten this warning, and since his time all their efforts have been directed to prove that the gospels were written later ; and the principal argument used to prove that they were written a long time after the events is precisely the gospel miracles. There is no need for us to point out the vicious circle ; it is enough to observe how inconclusive is the reasoning. The saintly Curé of Ars was not yet dead when people were already writing about his miracles ; and if he had not possessed the reputation of working them during his lifetime, would the crowds have gone to that remote corner of France to beg for them ? Moreover, we may add that apart from the decisive fact of the Resurrection, miracles were not given such importance in the preaching of the Apostles and early apologists of Christianity as we might be led to imagine. The preachers were much more interested in the prophecies. And we know that it was not without a wrench that the Apostles resolved to cut themselves adrift from the Law of their ancestors, as they did by freeing new converts from the law of circumcision. Paul urged this step with all the vehemence of his dialectical reasoning ; yet even he never dreamt for a moment of breaking the chain of divine revelations. The Law had served its purpose because it led up to Christ,

[1] *La vie de Jésus d'après Renan*, p. 64.
[2] *Life of Jesus*, p. 75 f. in Littré's French translation.

who had already come ; but the Law remained, along with the Prophets, as a revelation of the purposes of God. It was from the ancient Scriptures that men sought proof that Jesus was the Christ, and it was owing to its allusions to Christ that the Old Testament was preserved, now with Christ as its support, since it bore testimony to Him. The fact that He had taken His place at the side of God was altogether in conformity with the Scriptures, just as His Passion and Resurrection were in conformity with the same Scriptures.

It is here that we meet with the insurmountable opposition of the Jews, for they have never understood the Bible in that manner. Yet, leaving aside the question of the detailed prophecies concerning the Messiah—as we must here—let us recall the fact that the God of Israel had always claimed it as His office to bring back the lost tribes to Himself. He had accomplished this through the prophets ; but those very prophets had foretold a great manifestation to come, the manifestation of God Himself coming in person to inaugurate His kingdom, and it was towards such a coming of God that their most ardent desires were directed : 'O that Thou wouldst rend the heavens and wouldst come down?'[1] Similar passages are very numerous and very clear. It is true that this coming down of God appeared more glorious in their eyes than His descent upon Sinai, to be accompanied by convulsions of nature, the hills leaping with transports of joy, accompanied also by triumph for Israel ; but it is necessary to understand all these things in a figurative manner. Yet in truth, this imagery, grandiose as it was, was after all but a feeble expression of the unspeakable honour promised to human nature. The spiritual, but for this very reason all the more real, manner of that coming of God had been shown by Isaias. He had foretold the birth of a child named Emmanuel, that is, God with us ; the child was also named 'God-hero,'[2] and Isaias had predicted in so many words that a remnant of Jacob should return to the 'God-hero.'[3] Now there never was any question of Israel being converted to any other than God. It was God, therefore, who was in question in that litany of Isaias where there is an alternation of human properties and divine attributes : 'His name shall be called Wonderful,

[1] Isaias lxiii, 19 (Vulgate lxiv, 1).
[2] Isaias ix, 5. [3] Isaias x, 21.

Counsellor, God Hero, Everlasting Father, Prince of Peace.'[1]

The Alexandrine Jews had recoiled at the thought of the divinity of the Messiah ; hence they had rendered all this as 'Angel of great counsel.' But the Apostles understood that these terms were to be taken literally, and more than one independent exegete is of that opinion to-day. Daniel, foretelling the passing of empires and indicating each of these empires by the symbol of a terrible beast which principally typified their sovereign, had denoted the kingdom of God by a supernatural being like unto a son of man ; yet it was Jesus that he had had in mind, as the latter declared when He stood before His judges. That heavenly being advanced to the Ancient of Days, the symbol of the Father, and received from Him an everlasting dominion. He was not proclaimed to be God, but since He had come from heaven He would return thither in order to be near God, where a throne was prepared for Him.

The prophecies seemed to be divergent. Some spoke of a man, others used the name of God ; some enumerated the sufferings of the Servant of God in the work of expiating sin, others promised to the Messiah an universal dominion. But although the prophecies seemed like lines running parallel to infinity, nevertheless they all converged on the person of Jesus. He was the God whom men awaited, who alone had the power to save His people ; He was also the man who was to be the son of David, subject to suffering and death. In a word He was the Man-God that He claimed to be, in whom the Scriptures were fulfilled.

Enamoured as it is of the positive sciences, our age dislikes being referred to miracles and prophecies ; it would rather put its faith in a scholar than in a wonder-worker. Jesus did nothing for the advance of science. If only He had prophesied one of the discoveries of which we are now so proud, if only He had foretold that we should one day traverse marvellous distances in the air at a speed of which they had no conception in former days, then we should no longer refuse to believe in Him ! But He did no such thing, He 'made no inventions,' as Pascal said long ago, and at first perhaps Pascal's scientific mind was surprised at it. The reason of this was because Jesus kept Himself to His own sphere, that of holiness, and it was better so.

[1] Isaias ix, 5.

Do we not see that, if He had made the prophecy of which we have spoken, it would have been an obstacle to men of good will? It would have led those who were well disposed towards Him to treat Him as a charlatan right up to the beginning of the twentieth century. By that way He would have converted no one, and He would have remained unknown. And supposing that our contemporaries were to discover such a prophecy as that in some old document, what conclusion would they draw except that it was merely a presentiment of genius? Further, such a prophecy, suitable though it might be to the requirements of the time in which we live, would it not exhaust the chances of progress that are reserved for the future? A revelation in the scientific sphere would hold good for people of all ages only on condition that it contained absolute and complete truth. But God alone is such truth as that.

We repeat, therefore, that Jesus Christ revealed none of the scientific knowledge that it is possible for man to acquire by the use of his own reason. He confirmed the truth of that which reason can attain concerning God and the human soul, besides enlightening us regarding that sphere of truth which is inaccessible to reason, that is to say, the life of God Himself. He unfolded to mankind the secret of the love that God bears for men, a great love which makes God desire to be loved in return. Thenceforward those unfathomable depths of divinity, the object of man's restless desire here below, were sufficiently revealed to him to serve as a guide for moral conduct. In consequence, the way was thrown open for the best representatives of human culture to reshape the conditions of family and social life, to base philosophy on solid foundations, and in the course of time to carry on the work of the ancient Greek thinkers so far as to bring the sciences to the wonderful state in which we now find them, with a promise of still further progress in the future. The danger is that our own generation allows itself to be so captivated by these fascinating conquests, already won or else promised as a result of efforts to come, that it turns away its eyes from the eternal truth, the Gospel of Jesus Christ. The essential point of the message of that Gospel is that Jesus Christ is both man and God. The fourth evangelist was not responsible for the beginning of that doctrine; he merely urged it with greater insistence and gave it fresh expression.

III. THE WORD OF ST. JOHN AND THE LIVING GOSPEL

To the Jewish mind, as to the mind of those who still believe in one only God who is an infinitely perfect and purely spiritual being, the notion of a divine sonship suggests no incongruous idea. Christianity, however, very soon found itself no longer in contact merely with Jews, or even with Gentile proselytes already attached to the Jewish faith, but with absolute pagans, accustomed to the idea of a world peopled with children of the gods, on earth as well as on Olympus. In such circumstances it was clearly expedient to point out what was the meaning of the expression Son of God in a nature that was purely spiritual.[1] It was revealed to St. John that the most fitting expression to use was ' Word ' in order to designate an individual—let us use the language long ago fixed by the Church and say ' person ' —who was distinct from God considered as the source of all and thus named the Father, yet who possessed divine nature as completely as the Father.

This could only be expressed in terms of the intelligence, seeing that God is a pure spirit. Under that aspect one could think of His divine Wisdom. Scripture had already indicated in a veiled manner that in God there was a Wisdom in some manner distinguishable from Him, His collaborator in the work of creation, a Wisdom which He complacently beheld as the model and maker of the things that were made.[2] St. Paul followed the same path in describing Christ as the Power, the Wisdom,[3] the Image of God.[4] These are expressions to be retained, since they clearly show that Christ is one with God in the attributes that belong to the divine nature ; but they do not so clearly indicate the distinction between the Son and the Father. St. John has not expressed himself in the precise and technical terminology later used by St. Thomas Aquinas in his

[1] Even to this day Moslems consider that they raise an unanswerable objection to the divinity of Jesus Christ by saying that, as God has no wife, He can have no son.

[2] ' Jahweh possessed me in the beginning of His ways,
Before the most ancient of His works. . . .
When He prepared the heavens I was present,
When He traced a circle on the surface of the abyss . . .
I was at work with Him. . . .'
(Proverbs viii, 22, 27, 30, after Crampon's translation.)

[3] 1 Corinthians i, 24.

[4] Colossians i, 15.

speculations concerning the Word, but he surely intended to say, what everyone could understand, that the Word was an emanation of the divine mind: in other words, the Word spoken within God Himself. Of that inward utterance of God the evangelist had already learnt on the very first page of Scripture, where he had read that God created the world by 'saying.' As the Psalmist had rendered it: 'By the word of the Lord were the heavens established.'[1]

But since God is infinitely simple, being a single and undivided act as the philosophers say, the Word which proceeded from His mind did not go forth out of the divine mind, but remained within Him; consequently, that divine utterance was as eternal as Himself, was God like Himself: 'In the beginning was the Word, and the Word was with God, and the Word was God.'[2] As this Word was God, it was not a mere enunciation which expires when it leaves the lips; it was a living utterance, living with the life of God. Considered under the aspect of intelligence, God is symbolized by light. It is He who is the true light that enlightens the world from the moment of its creation. Consequently the Word is light, and an Israelite ought to have no difficulty in understanding this, seeing that the word of God was so often addressed to His prophets for the purpose of teaching men. In reality truth and light have this in common, that by means of light the eye is enabled to distinguish the forms of objects which remain indistinguishable in the darkness, while truth enables us to discern precisely wherein ideas do not correspond with reality.

After St. John has begun with such an irradiation of divine light, one might be led to think that the Word was about to shed floods of light upon the world. But no; the evangelist well knew that the Word had appeared under a veil, and he had reason to know also that the rays of the Word had not pierced the darkness of unbelief which filled the minds of the Jewish leaders. Nevertheless, so that they might have no excuse, so that future generations might gauge how far the new message was different from the old, God had sent to the world a man who stood for and summed up in himself the whole of ancient prophecy. This man was not the light, but he came to bear witness to the light.

[1] Psalm xxxii, 6 (Hebrew xxxiii).
[2] John i, 1.

His name was John. So great was he, that some contented themselves with his words concerning the baptism of repentance, altogether neglecting the fact that he also foretold a baptism by the Spirit and pointed to one who was the true envoy of God, He who was the Light come into the world, whom His own people, those of His race and blood, refused to receive or hear despite the Baptist's witness. He was the Son of God, and as such He gave those who received Him, and will continue to give those who receive Him, the power to become children of God, a childhood which is after the manner of His own eternal generation, having nothing in common with what men intend, desire, or realize here upon earth. In order that He might unite them to Himself as His brethren, the Word was made flesh, dwelling amongst us in a form more visible and tangible than the cloud which came down upon the tabernacle in the desert, abiding amongst us with a presence that is communicative of grace and truth.

This doctrine of the Word, therefore, had its roots in the Old Testament. But the sure touch with which St. John points out Jesus Christ, the Son of God, as that Word is incomprehensible unless we suppose a special revelation, perhaps the last revelation granted to the Apostles by virtue of the operation of the Holy Ghost promised to them by Jesus at the Last Supper.[1] It may be asked whether the beloved disciple was not set upon the path of this explanation by the philosophical speculations of his time, for it is clear enough that the term Λόγος which he used was current among the philosophers. This is a very difficult point to decide. In the Greek world there was a great deal of discussion about the *Logos* which was considered as both word and reason, although the philosophers preferred to consider it rather under the aspect of reason. The notion originated with Heraclitus, and had been taken up by the Stoic philosophers, whose principal religious dogma, by which they were opposed to the Epicureans and which is their chief claim to honour, was the recognition that there was a Providence, and therefore a divine reason, in the organization of the world. They saw that the world was in order, that it was therefore the work of an active power which pursued a definite end according to a plan. But whereas in Israel it was God who created and organized the world

[1] John xvi, 13.

according to His Wisdom, the Stoics were absolutely determined not to admit the existence of any spirit separate from matter, and consequently refused to make any separation between the world and the principle of intelligence with which it was informed. According to their explanation, reason produced order in the matter with which it was joined, after the fashion of the development of a seed. Reason was conceived both as the law governing the world and as the indwelling active principle which animated the world. Such a doctrine, diametrically opposed as it was to the transcendence of God the Creator, could inspire nothing but horror in the minds of faithful Israelites.

There were certain Jews, however, drawn by the charms of Greek philosophy, yet at the same time determined not to give up monotheism in exchange for these attractive, varied, but unfounded notions, who strove to prove the superiority of their faith by showing how it could be expressed in terms borrowed from the different philosophical systems. Philo of Alexandria, who was a contemporary of Jesus and died some forty years before St. John, conceived a bold theory. Remaining staunchly loyal to the transcendant God of the Jewish faith, he at the same time defended Aristotle's notion of God against the attacks of the Stoics. From the Stoics, however, he borrowed the idea of the *Logos*, though he set the *Logos* free from the conditions of matter, and used it to serve as an intermediary between God and the material world. It is difficult for us to comprehend his motive in this, for it seemed to him that all contact with matter would be a degradation for a God who was the first cause, and whom he considered almost as inactive in His solitude as the God whom Aristotle conceived under the name of *Actus Purus*. Hence he made the *Logos* intervene as creator of the material world, as the light of men's minds, and as the channel of graces bestowed on them. He was by no means a *Logos* as great as the Word of St. John, for he was merely a divinity of inferior rank to the one God ; but on the other hand he did not demean himself so far as to assume the conditions of human nature.

In all these speculations we find that the thinkers rested content with mere vague outlines, with ambiguous statements in which there was a constant fear lest one might say too much, and which were therefore contradicted almost as soon as uttered. Such were the precautions they took that they found themselves reduced to false positions. The intermediary *Logos* they conceived for themselves seemed ever ready to return immediately to the bosom of God if any attempt was made to pay him worship, while on the other hand he was always ready to be distinguished from God if there was any danger of divinity being brought into contact with what was considered unbecoming. If St. John was acquainted with such theories, if he took the trouble to fathom such a chaos of ideas, he would certainly have needed greater genius to disentangle such a maze, than to produce his own conception of the matter straight from the Bible and from Him whom his ravished eyes had contemplated, the object of his loving contemplation. Thus he did not start from the theories of the philosophers but from the reality which was Jesus, truly man and Son of God, God even as was His Father. Christians paid the Son the same worship as the Father Himself received, but they worshipped them as one only God, not as two Gods. It was legitimate to use the term ' Word,' current in the philosophical schools, to describe the eternal generation of the Son by which He received His divine being from the Father, and to describe the distinction between Father and Son who are both spirits. The wonderful thing is that St. John was able in a single phrase to make this idea rise far above all the inventions of the human mind, while at the same time his expression of the truth was well adapted to the Son's descent to the conditions of human nature. As the Word was God's thought, He was the light that enlighteneth man. As He was God's utterance, He was both messenger and message : the messenger that spoke in the flesh, the message which called men to God. As He was life, the Word also became our life. By faith and baptism we are united to Jesus Christ, and through Him to God. Not merely has He promised us divine life in the world to come, He gives it to us already in this world, and the life that He gives is His own. He is the vine, His disciples are the branches. He has departed and gone back to His Father, but He has promised to return to take up His abode in the souls of them that love Him, along with His Father and the Holy Spirit.

This dogma of the Word, therefore, forms the final word of the Gospel concerning Jesus Christ ; but, in the way that it is understood by St. John, it recalls yet another meaning of the Gospel. The Gospel is not only a book, for if it were it would be the perquisite of scholars; it was given to all men. It is not only a doctrine, for doctrine likewise implies the studies and privileges of the literate classes; it was given to the simple and to little ones. We must therefore look upon the Gospel as St. Paul defined it: 'It is the power of God unto salvation for everyone that believeth.'[1] Taken in this way the Gospel is no longer something that happened in the past; it is something that is present to all generations and to all men in each generation. It is the Word, the divine utterance, using His privilege of eternity to make His appeal to all ages. Everyone is enabled to hear that Word in his own heart, by means of the inward perception of the perfect harmony that exists between his most noble aspirations and that which the Church offers to him and brings to pass before his eyes. He beholds Jesus Christ working in the Eucharist, the very source of the virtues; he sees self-denial accompanied by joy, heroic charity practised as something ordinary, bodily virginity abounding in spiritual fruitfulness yet marriage none the less honoured, men equal as brethren yet submitting to the authority of the hierarchy that is essential to the Church, and finally he sees the pardon of sin. There are many other marvels that would have to be recounted—and the most beautiful of them all are hidden—before we could conclude in the words of Pascal: 'All that is brought about by the power which foretold it.'[2]

The Gospel is ever living because Jesus Christ promised His Apostles that He would be with them unto the end of all time, that He would send the Holy Spirit, that He would make His abode in the souls of the faithful along with the Father and the Holy Spirit who proceeds from Father and Son. Such an invasion of the divine into things that are human astonishes the reason. It is nothing less than an implanting of divinity in humanity, grace making human nature a sharer in divine nature. Such a prodigality of gifts and such lofty demands seem to crush rather than allure our very limited reason. We feel tempted to say that it is all too wonderful to be true.

But what is there, apart from this, that is of any value to us, that bears the stamp of the infinite? If we turn away from this, we are confronted with nothingness. Whither

[1] Romans i, 16.
[2] *Pensées*, Brunschwig edition, p. 693.

should we go, O Lord? Shall we shut ourselves up in a state of supercilious or despairing doubt; or shall we not rather gather round Peter, who is still saying: 'Thou hast the words of eternal life,' and surrender ourselves to the embrace of God in Jesus Christ.

INDEX[1]

ABIATHAR, I, 143
ABILENE, I, 60
Abomination of desolation, II, 177 f.
ABRAHAM—and the Messiah, I, 307 ff.; his children, I, 69, 307 ff.; his bosom, II, 72 f.
Adulterous woman, I, 300 ff.
Adultery and the marriage bond, II, 86 ff.
Agony at Gethsemani, II, 231 ff.
AGRIPPA, I, 213 ff.; II, 111, 258 f.
AIN KARIM, I, 22.
AINON (ENNON), I, 105
Allegory and parable, I, 177; II, 137, 217
Almsgiving, I, 156 ff.; II, 30, 69
ALPHÆUS—father of Matthew, I, 138; father of James the Less, I, 148, 293
ANDREW the Apostle—his first call, I, 88; final call, I, 131 f.; intervention at feeding of the five thousand, I, 220; introduces Greeks to Jesus, II, 125
Angels—appearance to Joseph, I, 29, 46; to the shepherds, I, 38; at the Resurrection, II, 283 ff.; ministering to Jesus, I, 82, 90; II, 232; accompanying Jesus at the judgement, I, 187; II, 181, 188; their knowledge of the second coming of Christ, II, 182
ANNA—the mother of Samuel, I, 23; the prophetess, I, 41
ANNAS the high priest, I, 59 f.; II, 236 f.
Annunciation, I, 15 ff.
Anointing: of Jesus—by the sinner, I, 169 f.; by Mary of Bethany, II, 120; of sick, I, 208
ANTIPAS (Herod). His character, I, 212; his rule, I, 212 ff.; relations with John the Baptist, I, 209 f., 215 ff.; with Jesus, II, 54 ff., 253 ff.
Apostles. Office, I, 147; vocation, I, 147; formation, I, 253 ff.; attitude towards Jesus, I, 254, 258; mission, I, 205 ff.; powers conferred on them, I, 206, 284; flight at Gethsemani, II, 236
APULEIUS, I, 103
AQIBA, I, 244; II, 88, 161, 190
Aramaic spoken by Jesus, I, 54, 260
ARCHELAUS, I, 48, 212; II, 117
ARETAS, king of Nabateans, I, 214
ARIMATHEA, II, 275 ff.
ARISTOTLE. Teaching on the parable, I, 177 ff.; on religious truth, II, 316 ff.
Arrest of Jesus, II, 233 ff.
Ascension of Jesus, II, 303 ff.
ASKAR, I, 110 f.
Assumption of Moses, II, 78, 157
AUGUSTUS the emperor, I, 12, 47
Authority, in teaching of Jesus, I, 126 ff.; in His deeds, II, 131 f.
Azymes, feast of Unleavened Bread II, 193

BALAAM, I, 43
Baptism of John, I, 63; in the Spirit, I, 73, 106; John baptizes Jesus, I, 74 ff.; Christian baptism, I, 106; baptism of suffering, II, 40, 110 f.
BARABBAS, II, 255 ff.
BAR-COCHEBAS, II, 158, 161
BARTHOLOMEW, I, 90
BARTIMÆUS, II, 114
BARUCH (pseudo), II, 158
Beatitudes, I, 150 ff.
BEELZEBUL or BEELZEBUB, II, 19 f.
Benedictus, I, 26
BETHANY, beyond the Jordan, I, 84; near Jerusalem, II, 99, 119, 130
BETHLEHEM, I, 33
BETHPHAGE, II, 122

[1] The page references are not to be taken as complete. Moreover, names which reappear very frequently, such as Jesus, Jerusalem, etc., are not included in the Index.

BETHSAIDA, I, 219, 225, 290
Betrothal among the Jews, I, 28
BEZATHA (pool of), I, 238, 296
Birth, of John the Baptist, I, 25 ; of Jesus, I, 33 ; second birth, cf. Regeneration
Blasphemy against the Holy Ghost, II, 21 ff.
Blood of Jesus. Drinking of His blood, I, 232 ff. ; Last Supper, II, 205 ff. ; sweat of blood, II, 231 ; the scourging, II, 258
BOANERGES, I, 149, 279, 294 ; II, 110
Bread. Breaking of bread, I, 221 ; II, 205, 291 ; bread from heaven, I, 229 ff.
Brethren of Jesus, I, 203 ff., 293
Bridegroom, I, 140 ; Jesus the mystical bridegroom, ibid. and I, 107
Burial of Jesus, II, 277 ff.

CÆSAREA, on the coast, II, 47 ; C. PHILIPPI, I, 257
CAIAPHAS, I, 60 ; II, 105, 237 ff.
CALLIRRHOE, I, 47
Calumnies of Pharisees against Jesus, II, 19 ff.
Calvary, II, 264
CANA of Galilee, I, 91 ff.
Canaanite or Syrophenician woman, I, 248
Canticle in use among the Semites, I, 23
CAPHARNAUM, I, 94, 118, 124, 223, 227, 228, 277, 288, 290
Carpenter (Jesus the), I, 54, 202
Catechesis, I, 3, 237
Cave at Bethlehem, I, 37 ; cave-dwellings at Nazareth, I, 16 f.
CEDRON, II, 230
Cenacle, or Upper Room, II, 196, 226 ff.
Centurion, of Capharnaum, I, 161 ; of Jerusalem, II, 274
CEPHAS, I, 260
Chalice of suffering, II, 110
Charity. Cf. Love of God
Childhood (spiritual), II, 7 ff.
Children welcomed by Jesus, II, 92 ff.
CHRIST. Cf. Messiah
Chronology of Gospels, I, 6, 48, 59, 97, 217 ; II, 128, 129, 192 (the Pasch)
Church of Jesus Christ, I, 260 ff., 284 ff. ; II, 277
Circumcision of John the Baptist, I, 25 ; of Jesus, I, 39 ; on the Sabbath, I, 296
CLEOPHAS, I, 293, II, 268, 289
Cloud (miraculous) at the Transfiguration, I, 270
Cockle (parable of), I, 186
Coming (second) of Christ, II, 79 ff., 170 ff. ; coming of Kingdom of God, I, 182 ff., 267 ; II, 181 ff.
Condemnation of Jesus : by the Jews, II, 246 ; by Pilate, II, 262.
Confession : of faith is necessary, II, 34 ; Peter's confession, I, 257, ff. ; confession of sins, II, 293
Conflicts with the Pharisees, I, 134 ff.
Corban, I, 245
Corner-stone (Christ the), II, 136
COROZAIN, I, 290
Correction of our brethren, I, 284 ff.
Counsels (evangelical) of poverty, II, 36 f., 94 f. ; of chastity, II, 91 ; of obedience, II, 6
Credibility of the Gospels, II, 330 ff.
Cross : as form of punishment, II, 265 ; in metaphorical sense, I, 265 ; II, 61, 127 ; as sign of the Son of Man, II, 181
Crowning with thorns, II, 258
Crucifixion of Christ, II, 265 ff.
Crurifragium, II, 276 f.
Cynics, II, 316
Cyrinus (Quirinius), I, 34

DALMANUTHA, I, 251
DANIEL, I, 137 ; II, 177 ff., 245, 333
Darkness at the Crucifixion, II, 270
DAVID : ancestor of Messiah, II, 148 ; prophet of Messiah, II, 148
Death of Christ : on the cross, II, 273 ; as our redemption, II, 112 ff., 125 ff., 273
DECAPOLIS, I, 195, 250
Dedication of Temple by Macchabees, I, 61 ; feast of D., II, 48 ff.
Demoniacs : at Capharnaum, I, 129 ; in country of Gerasenes, I, 193 ff. ; the epileptic boy, I, 273 ff.
Denarium (Roman penny), II, 139
Denials of Peter, II, 237, ff.
Descent of Christ into Hell, II, 282
Didrachma, I, 288 f.
DIDYMUS (Thomas), II, 100, 213, 294 f.
Disciples of Christ : their mission, I, 72 ; II, 4 ff ; conditions of discipleship, II, 61 ff.
Divorce. Cf. Repudiation
Doctors, I, 139 ; Jesus as doctor and healer, I, 139 ; doctors of the Law or Scribes (cf. Pharisees).

Drachma, II, 288 f.
Dualism of Persians, I, 78

Eagle. Cf. Vulture
Ebal (Mount), I, 110
Ecce Homo, II, 259 f.
EGYPT, I, 46
El-Azarieh (Bethany), II, 99 ff.
ELIAS. Type of Precursor, I, 60, 86, 166, 258 ; II, 272 ; at the Transfiguration, I, 269 f. ; his role fulfilled by John the Baptist, I, 271 f.
ELIEZER (rabbi), I, 245
ELISEUS, I, 203
ELIZABETH, mother of John the Baptist, I, 13 f.
EMMANUEL, I, 31 ; II, 332
Emmaus : in St. Luke, II, 289 ff. ; Nicopolis or Emmaus of the Macchabees, II, 47
End of the world, II, 172 ff.
Enemies, love of, I, 156
EPHRAIM, II, 77, 107
Epicureans, II, 142, 316 f.
Epileptic, I, 273 ff.
Epiphany, I, 56, 77
ESDRAS (fourth book of), II, 158
Essenes, I, 27, 64
Eucharist : sermon on, I, 225 ff. ; institution, II, 205 ff. ; eucharistic cup at the Jewish Pasch, II, 205
Eunuchs, II, 91
Exorcists, Jewish, II, 20
Eye : the simple eye, II, 26 f. ; remedy for disease of eyes, I, 312

Faith, I, 192, 199 f., 274 ; II, 83, 115, 130 f.
Falsehood (slavery to), I, 306 ff.
Farewell of Jesus to cities of the lake, I, 290
Fasting : question of, I, 139 ff. ; II, 84 ; fast of Jesus, I, 80
Fever, I, 130
Field of blood, Haceldama, II, 247 f.
Fig tree, parable of, II, 44, 129
Finding in the Temple, I, 50 ff.
Fire : of charity, II, 40 ; of dissension, II, 40 ; of punishment, I, 73, 187 ; II, 73, 189 ; of purification, I, 73
Fishing (miraculous catches), I, 131 ; II, 299
Food and ritual purity, I, 244 ff.
Friend of the Bridegroom, I, 107, 140 ; friends of Jesus, II ,218

GABBATHA, II, 262
GABRIEL : and Zachary, I, 13 ; and Mary, I, 17
GADARA and the Gadarenes, I, 195 ff.
Galilæans : character, I, 125 f. ; massacred by Pilate, II, 43, 254
GAMALA, I, 196
GAMALIEL, II, 145 f.
GARIZIM (Mount), I, 110
Gazophylacium or Temple treasury, II, 170
Gehenna (*Ge-Hinnom*), I, 282, 305 ; II, 248
Genealogy of Christ, I, 31 f.
GENNESARETH, plain of, I, 219 f.
GERASA, Gerasenes, I, 195 ff.
Gergesenes, I, 195 ff.
GETHSEMANI, II, 230 ff.
Glory of Jesus, II, 208, 222 f.
GOLGOTHA, II, 264
GOMORRHA, I, 290
Gospels, date of, I, 6 ; gospel preached by Jesus and about Jesus, II, 306 ff. ; Roman imperial gospel, I, 9
Grace of God, II, 96 ff, 219
Guards at the sepulchre of Jesus, II, 280 f., 288 f.

HACELDAMA, II, 248
Hæmorrhage (woman with issue of blood), I, 198
Haggadah, I, 121 ; II, 159 ff.
Halakah, I, 121 ; II, 160
Hallel, II, 198, 212, 216, 230
Harvest, I, 117, 183 ff.
HASMONEANS, I, 11
Hattin, I, 142, 149
Heaven, Heavens : use of word to designate God, I, 65
Hem or fringe of Jewish garment, I, 198
HENOCH, I, 185
HERACLITUS, II, 337
HERMON (Mount), I, 58, 269
HEROD : the Great—I, 12 ff., 43 ff. ; II, 114 ; Antipas—I, 210 ff. ; Philip—I, 210 ff. ; Agrippa—I, 213 ff. ; II, 111, 258 f.
Herodians, I, 147, 253
HERODIAS, I, 213 ff.
HILLEL, II, 31, 88
HIPPOCRATES on epilepsy, I, 275
HOLY GHOST, I, 100 ff., 299 ; blasphemy against, II, 21 ff. ; help of, II, 34 ; II, 212, 215, 219 ff., 221 ff., 293
Holy Week, II, 128 ff.

Holy Women, I, 172 f. ; II, 274 ; of Jerusalem, II, 264
Hosannah, II, 123
Hypocrites, II, 156 f.

Incarnation of the Word, II, 335 ff.
Innocents (holy), I, 47
Inscription : on coins, II, 139 ; on the cross, II, 266
Insults offered to Christ : during the Passion, II, 242 ; on the cross, II, 269
Iota and the Law, I, 152
ISAIAS, I, 62, 86, 123, 126, 165, 312 ; II, 74, 135, 136, 211, 235, 266, 290, 333.
Iscariot. Cf. Judas

JACOB, the patriarch, I, 43, 110 ; well of Jacob, I, 111.
JAIRUS, I, 198 ff.
JAMES : son of Zebedee, I, 131, 200, 276 ; II, 109 ; son of Alphæus, apostle and probably identical with James the son of Mary and cousin of Jesus (brother of the Lord), I, 102, 293 ; II, 274
JEREMIAS the prophet, I, 202, 258 ; II, 248 ; the rabbi, II, 145
JERICHO, I, 61 ; II, 114
JOANNA the wife of Chusa, I, 173 ; II, 283
John : the Baptist, I, 14, 58 ff., 105 ff., 163 ff., 208 ff., 241 f. ; II, 92, 134 ; the son of Zebedee and brother of James, I, 5, 131, 200, 276 ; II, 92, 111, 192, 195 f., 200, 203 f., 239 f., 268, 285 f., 298, 302
JONAS, II, 25
JORDAN, I, 59
JOSEPH : husband of Mary, I, 28 f., 32 f., 46, 48 f., 55 ; of Arimathea, II, 275 f. ; the historian, I, 47, 52, 64, 70, 92, 97, 110, 212, 292 ; II, 161, 195, 237, 257 f.
JOSES (or Joseph) one of the brethren of the Lord, I, 202, 204 f. ; II, 274
Joy in heaven, II, 62 ff.
JUDA (the tribe), I, 22, 44
JUDÆA, I, 59
JUDAS Iscariot, I, 235 ; II, 120, 190, 233 f., 246 f.
JUDE the apostle, I, 148 ; II, 215
Judgement (the last), II, 187 ff.

Jus gladii denied to the Jews by Romans, II, 243, 260
Justice of Pharisees, II, 150 ff.

Keys, symbol of power, I, 261
Khirbet et-Tawil, I, 84
Kingdom of God (or Heaven), I, 65, 175 ff. ; II, 78 f., 181 ff. ; feast of Kingdom of God, II, 53, 59 f.
Knowledge in Christ, I, 54 ; II, 183
Kursi, I, 197

Lake of Tiberias or Galilee, I, 124
Lament of Jesus over Jerusalem, II, 124
Law among the Jews, I, 126 ff.
LAZARUS : of Bethany, brother of Martha and Mary, II, 99 ff ; of the parable, II, 71 ff.
Leaven, parable of, I, 189
Legion (Roman), I, 194
Leprosy, I, 132 ff. ; ten lepers, II, 77 f.
LEVI or Matthew, I, 3–6, 138 f.
Levirate, law of, II, 144
Levite, I, 86 ; II, 12
Life of the Spirit, I, 104, 241
Light, I, 189, 303 f. ; II, 26 f.
Limbo, II, 270, 282
Lithostrotos, II, 262
Loaning of money, II, 117
LOT, II, 80
Love : of God for man, II, 218 f. ; for God, II, 10 ff, 147 ; for our neighbour, I, 155, 157, 280 ; II, 9 ff., 147, 188 f., 208 ; for our enemies, I, 156
LUKE and his gospel, I, 1 ff.
LYSANIAS, I, 58 ff.

MACCHABEES, I, 11
MACHÆRUS, I, 214–218
MAGDALA, I, 171 f.
Magdalene (cf. Mary)
MAGEDAN, I, 252
Magi, I, 42 ff.
Magnificat, I, 23 f.
MALACHIAS, I, 14; 39, 98, 166
MALCHOS, II, 234
Mamona (Mammon), II, 70
Mandeans, I, 64
Manna, I, 229 ff.
MARCION, I, 167, 295
MARK the evangelist, I, 3 ff ; II, 236
Marriage : among the Jews, I, 28 ; indissolubility of Christian marriage, II, 85 ff.

MARTHA, II, 13 f., 99 ff.
MARY : Mother of Jesus, her name, I, 17 ; origin, I, 18 ; married to Joseph, I, 30 ; her vow of virginity, I, 19 ; her perpetual virginity, I, 204 ; her obedience, I, 21 ; faith, I, 22 ; charity, I, 22 ; sorrow foretold, I, 40 f. ; loss of her Son, I, 52 ; power of intercession, I 92 f. ; mother of all Christians, II, 268 ; at foot of the cross, II, 278 ; at the Resurrection, II, 286 ; chief witness of the Gospel of Infancy, I, 10 ; teacher of Jesus, I, 55 ; her blessedness, II, 24
MARY, wife of Cleophas, II, 268, 274 ; mother of James and Joses, I, 293 ; II, 268, 274 ; of Bethany, I, 170 ff. ; II, 13 f., 99 ff., 119 f. ; of Magdala, I, 170 ff. ; II, 268, 274, 283 f., 287 f.
MATTHEW the evangelist, I, 3–6, 138 f.
MEIR (rabbi), I, 291
Mekawer : arabic name for Machærus, q.v.
Messiah : meaning of word, I, 44 ; his origin, I, 44, 297 ; II, 148, 162 ; expectation of Him, I, 67 f., 115 ; popular ideas concerning Him, I, 226 ; works of Messiah, I, 123, 164 f. ; the spiritual Messiah, I, 226 ; His entry into Jerusalem, II, 122 ff.
Midrash, II, 159 ff.
Miracles : in general, II, 307, 327 ff. ; miracles not dependent on presence of Christ, I, 118 f. ; miracle worked gradually, I, 256
Mishnah, I, 85 ; II, 158, 196 ff., 204
Mite (widow's), II, 170
Moqa Edlo site of cure of Gerasen demoniac, I, 196 f.
MOSES : the prophet and law-giver, I, 72, 242, 268 ff. ; II, 73 ff., 89 ff. ; chair of Moses, II, 150
MOSES ben Maimon, I, 291
Mosque of Omar, site of altar of holocausts, II, 124
Mount : of Beatitudes, I, 149 ; of Transfiguration, I, 269 f. ; of Olives, II, 122, 171
Multiplication of bread : first, I, 220 ff. ; second, I, 251
Mustard seed, parable of, I, 187 ff.
Myrrh : at adoration of Magi, I, 46 ; at burial of Christ, II, 279
Mystery cults, I, 102 ff. ; II, 317
Mystery of the Kingdom, I, 180
Mysticism, II, 160

NAAMAN, the Syrian, I, 203
Nabatæans, I, 212 ff.
NABLUS, I, 110 f.
NAIM, I, 163
Naming : of Jesus, I, 39 ; of John, I, 25 f.
Naos or sanctuary of Temple, I, 95
NATHANIEL, I, 89 f.
NAZARETH, I, 15 ff., 123 f., 201 ff.
Nets (fishing), I, 131 ; II, 299 ff.
NICODEMUS, I, 99 f., 300 ; II, 278
NOE, II, 80
Nunc Dimittis, I, 40

Oaths and swearing among the Jews, II, 151
Observances of Law for newly born, I, 39
Orders (holy), II, 207, 293
Origin (divine) of kings, I, 8 ff.
Origin of Christ, II, 148

Palm Sunday, II, 121 ff.
Parables : nature and purpose, I, 175 ff. ; II, 311 ; parables of the kingdom of God, I, 182–191
Paraclete, II, 220, 222 ff.
Paradise, II, 270
Paralytic, I, 136
Pardon of sin : conditions, I, 286 ff.
PASCAL (Blaise), II, 167 f., 328, 333, 340
Pascal : lamb, II, 193 ff. ; supper, II, 196 ff.
Pasch : first, I, 94 ff. ; second, I, 220 ; third, II, 191 ff.
Passion, prediction of : first, I, 263 f. ; second, I, 276 : third, II, 108 f.
Pater Noster, II, 14 ff. ; sanctuary of *Pater,* II, 16 f.
PAUL (saint) and the teaching of the Gospel, I, 101, 167 f., 243, 298, 310 ; II, 113, 149, 153, 177
PELLA, II, 178
Penance (sacrament), II, 293 ; cf. Repentance
Pentecost, I, 238
PERÆA, I, 59 ; II, 47, 51 f.
Persecution, II, 82
PETER the apostle : his call, I, 88, 131 f. ; his fidelity to Jesus, I, 235 ; confession, I, 258 ; at Last Supper, II, 200 ff. ; his denial of Christ,

II, 239 ff. ; at the sepulchre, II, 284 ff. ; after the resurrection, II, 298 ff. ; promise of the primacy, I, 260 f. ; promise of infallibility, II, 209 ff. ; his authorship of primitive catechesis of the Gospel, I, 3
Pharisees, II, 27 ff., 83 ff., 85 ff. ; their attitude towards Jesus, II, 161 ff. ; attitude of Jesus towards them, II, 154 ff.
PHILIP : the apostle, I, 89, 220 ; II, 213 ; the tetrarch, I, 59, 215 ff. ; Herod Philip, I, 213, 216
PHILO the Jew, I, 99 ; II, 248 ff., 254, 338
PILATE, I, 58 f. ; II, 43 f., 248 ff.
PLATO, I, 67 ; II, 312 f., 316
Plots against Jesus, I, 147 ; II, 104 f., 130
POLYBIUS, I, 1
Pool of Bezatha, I, 238 f., 296 ; of Siloe, I, 312 f.
Porch of Solomon, II, 48
Possession by evil spirits, I, 129, 192 ff., 273 ff. ; II, 19 ff.
Poverty of Apostles, I, 206
Prætorium, II, 250
Prayer : *Pater*, cf. above ; always heard, II, 17 ff. ; persevering prayer, II, 82 ff. ; of Pharisee and Publican, II, 83 ff. ; eucharistic prayer, I, 221 ; prayer in common, I, 285
Preaching : instructions to disciples, II, 33 f.
Precedence, question of, II, 57 ff. (Pharisees), 203 (disciples)
Presence (mystic) of Christ in the faithful, II, 214 ff. ; of Holy Trinity, II, 212 ; of Holy Spirit, II, 221 ff.
Presentation in the Temple, I, 39 f.
Priests (Jewish), cf. Sadducees
Primacy of Peter, cf. Peter
Probatica or Sheep Gate, I, 238
PROCULA, wife of Pilate, II, 262
Prodigal son, parable of, II, 64 ff.
Programme of Jesus' teaching, I, 149 f.
Prophecies. Cf. quotations from the Old Testament
Prophet (the awaited), I, 86, 222, 299
Prophets, I, 60, 152 ff. ; II, 73 ff.
Proselytes, I, 63 ; II, 151
Providence of God, II, 36
Psalms : regarding the Messiah, II, 136, 148 ; *Hallel* psalms, II, 198, 212, 216, 230 ; Psalms of Solomon, II, 160 f., 270
Publicans, I, 70 f., 138 ; II, 63, 83 ff.
Purification : of Mary, I, 39 f. ; of Jews, I, 106, 244
Pythagoreanism, I, 27

Qarantal (mountain of forty days' fast), I, 82
Quirinius or Cyrinus, I, 34 f.
Quotations of Old Testament in the New. Emmanuel, I, 30 ; Son called out of Egypt, I, 46 ; Rachel's sorrow, I, 47 ; the despised Nazorean, I, 49 ; the voice in the desert, I, 86 ; at the Temptation, I, 81 f. ; zeal for the house of God, I, 96 ; the preaching of salvation, I, 123 ; light shines in Galilee, I, 126 ; David and the loaves of proposition, I, 143 ; the old legislation, I, 155 ff. ; God's hardening of the heart of Israel, I, 176 ff. ; favour shown to non-Jews, I, 202 ff ; manna from heaven, I, 229 ; honouring of parents, I, 245 ; the great commandment, II, 10 ; signs from heaven, II, 25 ; men called gods, II, 50 ; marriage in the beginning, II, 88 ; appearance of the Messiah, II, 122 ; the cornerstone, II, 136 ; the burning bush, II, 146 ; David's lord, II, 148 ; blindness of the Jews, II, 169 ; the traitor, II, 202 ; the scattering of the flock, II, 209 ; the Son of Man, II, 245 ; the thirty pieces of silver, II, 248 ; the company of the wicked, II, 266 ; the parting of the garments, II, 267 ; Eloi, Eloi, etc., II, 271 ; the piercing with the lance, II, 277
Qurn Hattin, mountain of the Beatitudes, I, 142, 149

RACHEL, I, 47 f.
Raising of the dead : at Naim, I, 163 ; daughter of Jairus, I, 200 f. ; Lazarus, II, 99 ff.
Ras, Golgotha, II, 264
Reconciliation with God, II, 41 ff.
Redeeming of first-born, I, 39 f.
Redemptive work of Christ, II, 112 ff.
Regeneration, I, 99 ff.
Reign of God. Cf. Kingdom of God.
Relatives of Jesus, I, 172 ff., 203 ff., 293

RENAN, I, 70, 111, 205 ; II, 310 ff., 330 f.
Repentance (messianic), I, 61 f. ; II, 43 f.
Reprobation of Jews, I, 180 ; II, 154 ff.
Repudiation or Divorce, II, 85 ff.
Resurrection——of Christ. Its prediction : first, I, 263 f. ; second, I, 276 ; third, II, 108 f. ;——general resurrection, I, 230, 241 ; II, 142 ff.
Return from the dead, II, 74, 273
Revelation by the Holy Ghost, II, 223 f.
Riches, II, 35, 67 ff., 94 ff.
Roof of Galilæan house, I, 136
RUFUS, II, 263
Ruin of Temple and Jerusalem, II, 124, 170 ff.

Sabbath, I, 139 f., 142 ff., 296, 313 ; II, 57
Sacrifices (legal), I, 61 f., 65
Sadducees, II, 142 ff.
SALEM (*Tell Sarem*), I, 105
SALOME : daughter of Herodias, I, 210, 214; mother of sons of Zebedee, James and John, II, 109, 268
Salt, I, 283
Salvation, I, 264 ff. ; II, 52 ff.
SAMARIA (Sebaste), I, 109
Samaritan : race, I, 109 f ; relations with Jews, I, 109 f. ; woman at Jacob's well, I, 109 ff. ; parable of good Samaritan, II, 9 ff. ; the leper, II, 77
Sanhedrin, I, 43, 84 ff. ; II, 105, 130 ff., 138, 243 ff., 280
SAREPHTA, I, 203
Satan, I, 77 ff. ; II, 6, 19 ff., 46, 204 209
Saviour, I, 10, 38, 117
Scandal, I, 280 f.
Scourging of Jesus, II, 257
Scribes, II, 31. Cf. Pharisees
SCYTHOPOLIS (*Beisan*), II, 77
Sea of Galilee. Cf. Lake of Tiberias
SEBASTE. Cf. Samaria
Secret, the messianic, II, 33, 48, 162
Seleucids, I, 111
Self renunciation, I, 264
Sermon on the Mount, I, 149 ff.
Serpent, the brazen, I, 101
Service of others by superiors, I, 277 f.
SHAMMAI (rabbi), II, 31, 88
Sheba, queen of, II, 26
Sheep, representing the faithful, I, 316 ; II, 49. Cf. Good Shepherd
Shekel, I, 288
Shepherd ; shepherds at Bethlehem, I, 37 ; the hireling, I, 317 f. ; the Good Shepherd, I, 317 ff. ; II, 49, 63 ; origin of symbol of Good Shepherd, I, 319 f.
SICHEM, I, 110 f.
SIDON, I, 249, 290
Signs : of the times, II, 42 ; messianic signs refused by Jesus, I, 252 ; Jesus Himself a sign, II, 25 ff. ; the sign of the resurrection, II, 25 ff.
SILOE : the pool of, I, 312 f. ; the tower of, II, 44
SIMEON (Holy), I, 40
SIMEON the Just, II, 32
SIMON : the Apostle. Cf. Peter ; the Zealot, I, 148 ; the leper, II, 119 ; the Pharisee, I, 168 ff. ; of Cyrene, II, 263 ; cousin of Jesus, I, 205
Sin : the pardon of, I, 136 f. ; the sinful woman, I, 168 f.
Sionism, II, 165
Sleep of Jesus, I, 192
SOCRATES, I, 100 ; II, 165, 312 ff.
SODOM, I, 290 ; II, 80
Soldiers : and John the Baptist, I, 71 ; at the Passion, II, 233 ff. ; at the Resurrection, II, 271, 288 ff.
SOLOMON, II, 26, 36
Son : parable of the two sons, II, 133 ; Son of God, I, 130, 257, 269 ff. ; II, 7 ff., 49 ff., 246, 260 f. ; Son of Man, I, 136 ff., 144 f. ; II, 79 ff., 125 ff., 179 ff., 245
Soul and its value, I, 265 ; II, 35 f.
Sower, parable of, I, 182 ff.
Star of Magi, I, 42 ff.
Stater, I, 289
Stoics, II, 142, 144, 157, 316 ff., 338
Stoning : penalty of, I, 301 ; attempts to stone Jesus, I, 311 ; II, 49.
STRAUSS, II, 331
Superjudaism of Klausner, II, 164 ff.
Supper (Paschal), II, 196 ff.
Susanna, I, 173
Sweat of blood, II, 231
Sword : purchase of II, 211 ; Peter's sword at Gethsemani, II, 234.
SYCHAR (Sichora), I, 110 f.
Symbolism of withered fig tree, II, 129 ff.
Synagogue : origin of I, 120 ; at Capharnaum, I, 162 ; cure of man with withered hand in the synagogue, I, 145 f. ; cure of deformed woman in the synagogue, II, 45 f.
Syrophenician woman, I, 248

Tabernacles, feast of, I, 291
TAIYBEH, II, 107
Talents, parable of, II, 116 ff.
Talionis (*lex*), I, 155
Talmud, I, 156, 289 ; II, 145, 157 ff., 264–266
Taxation in Palestine : Temple tax, I, 288 f. ; Roman tribute, II, 138 ff., 251
Tempests on the lake, I, 192, 223
Temple : description of, I, 95 ; ruin of, II, 170 ff.
Temptation of Christ, I, 77 ff.
Testament of Twelve Patriarchs, I, 186
Testimony. Cf. Witness
Tetrarch, I, 59
THABOR, I, 269
THADDÆUS, name of Jude the Apostle q.v.
THEOPHILUS, I, 1
Thieves crucified with Christ, II, 264, 266, 269
THOMAS (Didymus) the Apostle, II, 100, 293 f.
TIBERIAS (town), I, 291
TIBERIUS (emperor), I, 58, 213
Title : of father and master, II, 150 f. ; on the cross (cf. Inscription)
Tolerance, I, 186 f., 278 ff.
Tomb : of Jesus, II, 278 ff. ; tombs of prophets, II, 32
TOPHETH, II, 248
Tosephtah, II, 159
TRACHONITIS, I, 58
Traders in Temple, I, 95 ff.
Tradition of Pharisees, I, 243 ff. Cf. Pharisees
Transfiguration, I, 266 ff.
TRANSJORDANIA. Cf. Peræa
Treason of Judas, II, 190 f., 202 ff.
Trial of Jesus : before Sanhedrin, II, 243 ff. ; before Pilate, II, 250 ff.
Tribunal of Pilate, II, 262
Tribute. Cf. Taxation
Trinity, II, 34 f., 212, 223 f., 303
Truth, its development and progress, I, 154
Twelve, the. Cf. Disciples
TYRE, I, 248, 290

Unbelief of Jews, I, 180 ; II, 161 ff.
Unity of the Church, I, 284 ff. ; II, 226 ff.
Unjust steward, parable of, II, 67 ff.
Veil of Temple, II, 273
Vigilance required, II, 37 ff., 184 ff.
Vine, symbol of Jesus, II, 217 ff.
Vineyard, labourers in, II, 96 ff. ; parable of wicked husbandmen in the vineyard, II, 134 ff.
Vipers (reproach to Pharisees), I, 68 ; II, 152
Virgil's messianic prediction, I, 9
Virgins, the parable of the ten, II, 185 ff.
Visitation of Mary to Elizabeth, I, 21 ff.
Vocation of disciples, I, 83 ff., 131 f., 138, 147 ; II, 2 ff., 94.
Voice from heaven, I, 75, 269 ; II, 126
Vows and rabbinic casuistry, I, 245
Vultures, II, 81

Washing : of hands among the Jews, I, 244 ; by Pilate, II, 262 ; washing of disciples' feet by Jesus, II, 200 ff.
Water (mystic), I, 112 f., 298 f.
Way of the cross, II, 263 ff.
Weeping of Jesus, II, 101, 124
Well of Jacob, I, 111
Widow : of Naim, I, 163 ; widow's mite, II, 170
Will (human) in Jesus, II, 232
Withered : man with withered hand, I, 145 f. ; withered fig tree, II, 129, 130
Witness : of Jesus, I, 303 f. ; II, 324 ff. ; of the Father, I, 240 ff., 303 f. ; of John the Baptist, I, 241 f. ; of Moses, I, 242 ; of the Apostles, II, 329 f. ; the false witnesses at the trial of Jesus, II, 244
Woes addressed to the Pharisees, II, 28 ff.
Word of God, II, 335

ZACHÆUS, II, 115 ff.
ZACHARIAS : the prophet, II, 209, 248 ; 277 ; the son of Barachias, II, 152
ZACHARY the father of John the Baptist, I, 13 ff.
Zealots, I, 148 ; II, 142
ZEBEDEE, sons of II, 109 ff. (cf. Boanerges)